THE STOIC AND EPICUREAN PHILOSOPHERS

Jane Phillips

THE STOIC AND EPICUREAN PHILOSOPHERS

The complete extant writings of

EPICURUS
EPICTETUS
LUCRETIUS
MARCUS AURELIUS

Edited, and with an Introduction by WHITNEY J. OATES
Professor of Classics, Princeton University

THE MODERN LIBRARY · NEW YORK

By arrangement with the Oxford University Press

Library of Congress Catalog Card Number: 57-6494

THE MODERN LIBRARY
is published by RANDOM HOUSE, INC.

Manufactured in the United States of America by H. Wolff

PREFACE

No acquaintance with the tradition of Greek philosophy can be regarded as adequate without a thorough grasp of the two great systems of Epicureanism and Stoicism, for these two, along with the schools of Plato and Aristotle, constitute the real body of ancient classical thought. The present volume has been prepared in order that there may be readily available to the reader the complete extant writings of Epicurus and Lucretius, the great exponents of the system founded by the former, as well as those of Epictetus and Marcus Aurelius, the major sources for our knowledge of Stoicism. The four authors have all been brilliantly translated, and it is most fortunate that the particular versions of Cyril Bailey, H. A. J. Munro, P. E. Matheson, and George Long can herewith be republished. In order to make more complete the documents on Stoicism, Cleanthes' famous *Hymn to Zeus,* in the version appearing in James Adam's *The Vitality of Platonism,* has been included in the Appendix. Likewise, Matthew Arnold's *Essay on Marcus Aurelius* has been added as an indispensable aid to the interpretation and understanding of that author.

The task of editing the text was rendered somewhat difficult because of the numerous manuscript problems to be found, particularly in Lucretius and Marcus Aurelius. The general policy followed has been to remove in most instances the brackets, asterisks, etc., which serve to mark lacunae and the like in the original editions of the translations, since these are in general of interest only to the scholar. However, the most important imperfections in the Greek or Latin texts have been indicated in the Notes.

Explanatory notes have been given wherever comment or interpretation seemed necessary. Many of these derive from the translators themselves, and in these instances the indebtedness has been duly acknowledged. A Glossary, mainly of proper names, has been added, in order to facilitate the understanding of the more obscure allusions to mythological or historical persons and places. The items in the Glossary cover the writings of all four authors. Particular attention should be called to the fact that the material on many of the names appearing in the *Discourses of Epictetus* has been taken from an index of names in the Oxford edition of Matheson's translation. In the Appendix also is to be found Long's subject index to the *Meditations of Marcus Aurelius,* as well as Matheson's subject index to the *Discourses of Epictetus.* Every effort has been exerted to make the present volume as useful and as complete as possible. On this ground all the extant fragments of Epicurus have been included, though some of them, as they stand alone and out of context, appear to be insignificant. Also for purposes of greater clarity Bailey's admirable analyses of the letters of Epicurus have been reproduced.

Grateful acknowledgement is hereby rendered to the Oxford University Press for permission to reprint Bailey's translation of Epicurus and Matheson's translation of Epictetus. Further thanks are due to Mr. Denys L. Page of Christ Church, Oxford, and Professor D. R. Stuart of Princeton University for their generous assistance and searching criticism in the preparation of the General Introduction. Finally, appreciation must be expressed to Random House and its editor, Mr. Saxe Commins, for the support and care which they have devoted to the publication of these master works of ancient philosophy.

Whitney J. Oates

Princeton, New Jersey
July, 1940

TABLE OF CONTENTS

GENERAL INTRODUCTION

WESTERN EUROPEAN civilization owes to its Greek ancestors one of its greatest debts, because from them sprang philosophy, the speculative spirit of inquiry into the mysteries of life and the universe. In its earlier stages the orientation of philosophy was to the external world. Thales, the traditional founder of this type of speculation, and his immediate successors, Anaximander and Anaximenes, sought to solve the problem of the nature of matter, the constitution of the world or universe. In a sense, then, they were what we might call to-day physicists, rather than philosophers, and their inquiries usually resulted in the conclusion that all matter could be reduced to one or more fundamental elements as substrata from which the external world or universe was ultimately derived. Typical of this tendency is Thales who conceived water to be that fundamental element, or Anaximander whose principle was the 'infinite'; or Anaximenes whose principle was air. Later we meet Heraclitus who believed fire to be the source of all being and that all things are in flux, in a continual state of change or becoming.

While these men were obviously preoccupied with the problems relevant to the nature of the external world, contemporaneous with them and with the dawn of the so-called 'historical' epoch in Greece, a group of lyric poets appeared. Their works exhibit an orientation towards the inner nature of man's being, in rather sharp contrast to the direction which the physical philosophers' thought was taking. The poets were exploring the feelings, emotions, the states of self-awareness, the inner springs of action, in short, all the complex structure of man's inner spiritual nature. For example, no one can read the fragmentary remains of Sappho without becoming overwhelmingly impressed with her sensitiveness to and consciousness of this rich and varied inner realm. The great Greek tragedians of the fifth century B.C., whose deep insights into human life have rarely been equalled in history, are under no small obligation to the earlier lyric poets. To make, then, a somewhat sweeping generalization which needs to be explored and carefully ramified, one might conclude that in the fifth century the dominating tendency of poetry was towards the inner world, while that of philosophy was externally directed. To be sure, in philosophy one sees signs of inner awareness, and on the other hand the brilliant theological vision of an Aeschylus emerges from the field of poetry.

Perhaps one of the greatest single events in the history of our culture is the appearance of Socrates in this milieu of fifth-century Greece. For here is a philosopher, a speculative thinker, not a poet, who cuts directly across the general tendency of contemporary philosophizing, and redirects its emphases to the inner nature of man. From that time on philosophy has always been concerned not only with the nature of the physical world, but also with man from the psychological, ethical, and epistemological points of view. Consideration of the problem of value, the development of logic, investigation into the ways of knowing, all actually assume their proper significance after Socrates had made his astounding contribution of re-orientation.

We now know Socrates chiefly through the pages of his great disciple Plato. This is not the time to go into the much-vexed question concerning the relation of the 'Platonic Socrates' and the so-called 'historical Socrates', the two really being, as Professor Shorey has pointed out in his book, *What Plato Said*, 'a double-star which not even the spectrum analysis of the latest philology has been able to resolve.' Suffice it to say that in the Platonic Socrates we have the most complete characterization that has come down to us from antiquity and that the Platonic philosophy constitutes a development of a basic view of life and the world ultimately derivative from Socrates. This is to derogate in no sense from the magnitude of Plato's philosophical achievements.

For our purposes in the consideration of ancient Epicureanism and Stoicism, both of which stem in curious and important ways from Socrates and Plato, it is necessary to have before us the main tenets of Platonism, a body of thought which perhaps is inaccurately described as a philosophical 'system', though of course we must admit that any philosophy must be more or less systematic. For us the most significant feature of Platonism is its pervasive dualism.[1] Plato recognized basically two modes of being, one the phenomenal realm, the world of 'sights and sounds' as he described it, and the other the realm of the ideas or forms, non-spatial, non-temporal entities, which exist 'apart' from the realm of phenomena. The phenomenal world is characterized as impermanent, fraught with changes—things continually come into being and pass out of being, whereas the ideal realm is the realm of permanence and timelessness. Reality in the full sense is to be found only in the world of ideas, while the phenomenal world gets such reality as it has in direct proportion to the degree in which it 'participates' in the world of the ideas. Another way of stating the view would be that the universal is the only real, whereas the particular is real only in so far as it 'participates' in the universal. The most difficult aspect of the Platonic meta-

persuasive dualism - phenomenal world - appearances
2 ideas

physic, as thus far described, obviously lies in the problem of the exact relation obtaining between particular and universal, between things and ideas. 'Participation', as it is used technically by Plato, remains a mysterious phenomenon, and as a result in his 'later' dialogues he tends to designate this relationship as that of model and copy. In the final analysis, this Theory of Ideas, as it is called, is a more precise metaphysical formulation of the view widely held by many men that underlying the world of change and uncertainty about them there is a factor which does not admit of change, that is abiding and eternal, that gives reality to the world in which they live, and which gives purpose and meaning to human existence.

The Theory of Ideas is all the more remarkable when one considers its philosophical scope. Four major functions which it performs can readily be distinguished. From the logical point of view it provides a theory of universals on the basis of which the phenomena of predication can be explained. Secondly, it offers an answer to the ontological problem when it says that the ideas are real, and that all else, in varying degrees, is relatively less real. Thirdly, in the face of the epistemological problem, it holds that knowledge, strictly speaking, is possible only of the ideas, that is, of that which does not change, while it is only possible to have opinion with regard to objects in the phenomenal world which are in continual flux. And lastly, the theory submits an answer to the problem of value, for indeed there are ethical and aesthetic ideas, such as courage and beauty, which function as objective norms in the realm of value. Or to put it another way, an act of courage is such as it is to the extent to which it 'imitates' successfully the idea of courage.

Plato, as his thought developed, became more and more interested in the religious or theological implications of his Theory of Ideas. He conceived of the ideas as hierarchically arranged and at their apex he placed the Idea of the Good as the 'super-transcendent' entity in the universe. So lofty is his conception that many Platonists have found no difficulty in identifying the Idea of the Good with God, though the balance of criticism rightly contends that there are insurmountable difficulties in the way of such a conclusion. Plato's answer to the theological problem is in essence rather to be found in his great cosmological myth in the *Timaeus*, where he sharply distinguishes between God and the ideas. God or the Demiurge there creates the world, fashioning it by keeping his eye on the eternal ideas and by using them as models in the process. He introduces in this way principles of order into the 'disordered motion' or the 'matrix', as the material is called upon which he must work as he creates the world. In this myth, one must not overlook the solution offered to the problem of evil, for here it is said that, though no positive principle of evil is postulated, there is a certain inherent, blind resistance in the 'matrix' which stubbornly keeps the Demiurge from being completely successful in his task, and as a result the world as created contains the various imperfections of which men are aware. But the important point for us to note is that both in the Theory of Ideas and in his theology Plato maintains his dualism, whether between universals and particulars in logic, between ideas and things in ontology or in the realm of value, or between the Divine realm, in which is found both God and the ideas, and this created world in which we live.

This very brief examination of Plato's thought has been included partly to show how his metaphysics is so constructed as to meet all major philosophical problems, and partly to show by contrast how both Epicureanism and Stoicism are comparatively limited in scope. Furthermore, in order to understand the two later philosophies, some knowledge of Plato is essential, since they both in their distinctive ways represent a reaction against his basic dualism. Plato was to some extent a rationalist, by which is meant that he relied heavily upon the reason in the development of his position, but it may be argued that ultimately it is a semi-mystical faculty, a 'higher reason' which finally enables him to reach his conclusions. Certainly the presence of the myths in his *Dialogues* alone is ample evidence that Plato realized the limits of normal human reason, and that he believed that man had a higher intuitive power by which he could achieve a more penetrating insight into the nature of the world. Oddly enough, the reliance upon this 'higher reason' enabled Plato to accept and maintain a radical dualism, for everyone would admit that 'rationalism', that is the use of normal human reason, drives inevitably towards a monism. The history of Western European philosophy can supply us with adequate testimony for this conclusion. In any event, in the various philosophies which appear immediately after Plato, 'rationalism', as we have just attempted to define it, clearly held the field. Certainly one could say that the essential 'irrationality' of postulating the existence of a non-spatial, non-temporal realm of ideas drove Aristotle away from the Platonic position which he indubitably held at the outset of his philosophical career. It might be urged likewise that the same kind of 'rationality' led him to construct his very complex and in many ways magnificent monism. It is then in the same spirit of reaction to dualism that we see the development of the two great schools of Epicureanism and Stoicism in the fourth and the third centuries before Christ. Each possessed its contacts with Platonism, each expresses in its nature the growing tendency towards individualism, the outstanding feature of Hellenistic as opposed to Hellenic culture, each is a rational monism, several doctrines are held in common by both, and yet they are violently opposed to one another. Their importance is considerably enhanced when one remembers that these schools between them

4-3 B.C.

probably commanded the allegiance of the great majority of those who sought a way of life in philosophy in the Hellenistic or subsequently in the Graeco-Roman world.

The details of the life of Epicurus, the first author whose works are included in this volume, are not apposite here. Most of them derive from the *Life,* written by Diogenes Laertius probably in the second century after Christ, which is printed as Part VI of the extant remains of the philosopher. In fact, it is to Diogenes that we owe the preservation of the three letters and the collection of *Principal Doctrines,* all of which he has quoted *in extenso* in his biography. Epicurus was born in 341 B.C., about five years after the death of Plato. After a life spent in a wandering teacher's career he returned to Athens, whence he had set out on his travels, to remain there for the rest of his life. He established his school in a garden outside the city walls, and taught there until his death in 270 B.C. Divers influences brought themselves to bear upon his thought. Ultimately one might contend that his hedonism stems out of certain Platonic notions with respect to pleasure as they are expressed in such Platonic *Dialogues* as the *Protagoras* or *Philebus.*[2] The Cyrenaic hedonism of Aristippus certainly exerted its power on Epicurus, though he could not accept that creed of the crude voluptuary without having submitted it to a thoroughgoing purification. Atomism, which tradition says was founded by Leucippus and subsequently developed by Democritus, provided Epicurus with the requisite physics and finally the necessary metaphysic out of which he could construct his hedonistic materialism. Such cardinal beliefs as that 'nothing can come from nothing' and that 'all that exists is atoms and void' had strong empirical sanction and by very convincing rational arguments integrated well with the notion that pleasure is the highest human good.

Various philosophers and critics in the history of Western European thought have made the mistake of supposing that the materialistic monism of Epicurus is an ignoble philosophy. It can confidently be asserted that such is not the case, for what Epicurus sought primarily to do was to rid men from certain besetting fears which tainted their lives, namely the fear of the gods which led to superstitious enormities, and fear of death with all its concomitants. Once rid of these fears by an increasing consciousness of what is implied in the view that everything consists of atoms and void, man is able to achieve peace of mind—inner calm and security[3]—which is his final desideratum, the best of pleasures. Epicurus also urges a careful discrimination among the several pleasures and categorically rejects such pleasures as may be momentarily intense but which are followed by attendant pain. Hence he argues for the principle of the mean, or moderation, the joys that accrue from friendship, and the advantages of living a simple life, even a withdrawal from active participation in life, as is summed up in the famous maxim, λάθε βιώσας, 'Live unknown'.[4] Only by a rigorous development and discipline of the will can these precepts be followed. Therefore one must conclude that, far from being an ignoble philosophy, Epicureanism is an enlightened creed, within its materialistic limits as enlightened as it could possibly be.

We are unfortunate that we possess such a slight fraction of the voluminous writings of Epicurus, but our loss is greatly compensated by the presence in Latin literature of Lucretius' famous philosophic poem, the *De Rerum Natura*. Of Lucretius we know but little beyond the dates of his birth and death, ca. 99 B.C. to 55 B.C. Tradition records a curious assortment of 'facts', namely, that while he was writing his poem he suffered from intermittent insanity as a result of an amatory potion, that he committed suicide, and that his work was edited by Cicero. The *De Rerum Natura* itself, which shows unmistakable signs of needing a final revision, is in the opinion of many critics the greatest monument in Latin poetry. In it we have a most complete exposition of the Epicurean system, which is all the more valuable to us as evidence on that subject because, though it was written two centuries after the death of Epicurus, the system itself exhibits only slight signs of any change or development in its tenets. The *dicta* of the master were always regarded as final and completely decisive in case of any doctrinal disputes among the members of the sect. Lucretius perhaps derived most of his data from Epicurus' work *On Nature*, but he was probably influenced by a didactic poem of Empedocles to put his own writings in verse. So far as versification goes, Lucretius obviously is most indebted to the Latin poet, Ennius. But there can be no doubt that he venerated above all the master, Epicurus, whom he praises without stint in several passages of the *De Rerum Natura*.[5]

A brief summary of the contents of the poem[6] may serve to indicate those aspects of Epicureanism which Lucretius chose to expound. He devotes Book I to an explanation of the atoms and void, followed by an attempt to refute the physical systems presented by Heraclitus, Empedocles and Anaxagoras. In Book II the poet presents what has been called the 'kinetics of the atomic theory' with special emphasis upon the qualities attributed to the atom. Book III contains a discussion of the material composition of the human soul to which is added a long series of arguments for its mortality. In Book IV we find the Epicurean theories of sense-perception, psychology and the will, with a concluding section of brutal satire on love. In Book V, in many ways the most fascinating of the whole poem, Lucretius treats the origin of the world, astronomical phenomena, the origin and development of the species, the growth of human institutions, language, art and religion. The sixth book contains a conglomeration of topics and shows most signs of being unfinished. In it all sorts of natural phenomena are explained, such as thunder, lightning, the periodic rising of the Nile, the magnet and the like. The book ends abruptly with a description of the famous plague at Athens early in the Peloponnesian War.[7] It is noteworthy that Lucretius devotes no specific section to the Epicurean moral theory, a fact which may explain why the poem attracted slight attention among his contemporaries. The Romans apparently had little interest in 'theoretical physics'.

The whole work, however, is dominated by the Epicurean desire to free mankind from superstition and the fear of death. Death is nothing more than the dispersion of the particular combination of atoms which go to make up the human soul, hence is really nothing and cannot be feared. The gods, on the other hand, exist, but they have nothing to do with human affairs, for if they did they would be troubled, and a god by his very nature cannot have his blessedness marred by trouble. Hence they are not to be feared, but rather they function in the system as ideal Epicureans whose peace of mind should be emulated by every member of the sect. Thus then, starting from the premisses that nothing can come from nothing, and that nothing exists save atoms and void, by a rational process the monism is constructed which will liberate man from fear.

Rarely, if ever, has a system been built which is so nearly water-tight. If one grants Epicurus and Lucretius two or three assumptions, he has difficulty in puncturing their defences. Lucretius too has evinced extraordinary powers of observation, and has marshalled an imposing amount of empirical documentation for his atomic hypothesis, and in a surprising number of instances has anticipated the discoveries of modern science. Unquestionably the weakest link in the chain of his argument lies in his having attributed to the atom the capacity to swerve, the so-called *clinamen*. He is, of course, unable to produce any supporting evidence for his assumption, and indeed the whole construct falls if one refuses to accept it. How crucial it is to the system can be realized when we remember that it is the capacity to swerve which in the first place brings the atoms into contact with one another and, secondly, it is this capacity which accounts for the phenomena of free will, the atom of the innermost soul 'swerving' and, by a transmission of this motion, putting the body in action. One further difficulty deserves mention. The Epicurean must always be embarrassed by the problem of quality. It can never be an easy task to explain how an object which has such a quality as colour can possess it if it is composed of atoms which merely have weight, shape, and solidity.

Critics have always been impressed by the sheerly 'poetic' powers of Lucretius. He himself explains his use of verse on the ground that it is simply to 'sugar-coat the pill of instruction'. In certain of the more technical passages the reader may well feel the inappropriateness of the poetic vehicle, but in the more imaginative parts Lucretius exploits to the full his medium, and one feels his missionary zeal, his comprehension of his material, the depth of his meanings, more than would have been possible had he confined himself to 'prose'. Perhaps this quality is to be seen most clearly in the beautiful symbolic image of Venus, *Aeneadum genetrix,* whom the poet invokes at the opening of Book I. Happily not a little of Lucretius' poetic power has been transmitted into English in the masterful version of Munro.

In considerable contrast to the highly systematized character of Epicureanism, we find Stoicism, which is shot through with most violent and distressing paradoxes. Stoicism, like Epicureanism, takes at least some part of its origin from Plato. Some of this influence is undoubtedly mediated through to the Stoics by way of the Cynic School of Antisthenes with which they always felt themselves in close contact. Zeno, Cleanthes, and Chrysippus are the great names in early Stoicism, Zeno, who was born in the latter part of the fourth century B.C., being the founder of the School. In it the strain of the rationalism which resents dualism is clearly to be found. The Stoic argument seems to have run in some such way as this: Holding firmly to the notion that 'self-sufficiency' is of supreme value, a conception to be found in Plato, they insisted that any theory that the cosmos was radically dualistic was not tenable. The universe, if it is of any value at all, must be self-sufficient; hence if self-sufficient, it must be untainted with dualism, and therefore monistic. If then the universe is self-sufficient the whole must be good. One should not be surprised at the factor of circularity in this argument, for such seems to be perfectly characteristic of Stoic thought.

With these predispositions firmly established, the Stoic took up the Heraclitean theory that fire was the ultimate principle in things, and in the physical aspect of the philosophy we have a straight materialism. All things were once fire, but by a gradual process the world as we know it evolved, and in the future the process will reverse and all will be returned to fire, after which the whole sequence will be repeated. So then the Stoics viewed the cosmos as a great machine which worked in this fashion from fire to fire again with awe-inspiring regularity. It seems as though from this very regularity with which the machine operated, the Stoics conceived the idea that it must be permeated with some divine power, a power they labelled somewhat indiscriminately as God, the Logos, Fate, Providence, Destiny and so on. In any event, here we are face to face with the root paradox of the system. Here is a machine, philosophically a materialistic monism, and by some unexplained means there is attached to it a pantheism.

If this be a fair summary of Stoic physical theory, there immediately appears to be a grave question as to how a moral theory can be made to integrate with this mechanistic determinism. How can the will in any sense be free if its milieu is in a universe all of whose operations are fatally predetermined? The Stoic argued that since the universe was good, there was actually no evil in it.[8] Morally virtue was proclaimed to be the highest good, and virtue was defined as living κατὰ φύσιν, 'according to nature'. Living 'according to nature' then means that man must accept everything that takes place as good or 'indifferent'; if he interprets anything as evil he is obviously wrong, and in making such an erroneous judgment, he is not by any means 'living according to nature' in the full sense. Hence he must endure whatever comes to him in the way of pain, suffering, and all other things that are normally accounted evil, and consequently there is great emphasis laid upon the virtue of καρτερία, 'endurance', which gives, of course, the major connotation to the modern use of the word stoic. If, then, it constitutes a misinterpretation of the data of experience to call them evil, it is surely incumbent upon man to use his 'impressions' (a technical Stoic term) of that experience correctly, and it is here that the Stoic introduces the factor of free will. Though everything in the universe is determined, nevertheless there remains to the individual the power to use correctly or incorrectly his impressions. If he concludes that there is no evil in the universe, he has used his impressions correctly and he is 'living in accordance with nature' in the deepest sense. To be sure, there are many 'indifferent' things in the universe which the individual may identify by determining that they are not 'in his power'. These indifferent things are neither good nor evil, and hence the only evil in the universe lies in the misinterpretation of impressions, *viz.*, that something indifferent is good or evil, or that something good is evil.

The foregoing moral theory is obviously not without very painful metaphysical difficulties. However paradoxical it may be, yet it obviously had a wide, not only rational, but also emotional appeal to the earlier adherents of the philosophy. Evidence for this is to be found in the development of the somewhat vague pantheism into a strong doctrine of God, or the Logos, which in all probability is a precursor of the Logos doctrine of the opening chapters of the *Fourth Gospel,* and which finds beautiful expression in Cleanthes' *Hymn to Zeus,* which is included in the appendix to this volume. As time passed, however, the paradoxes became more and more intolerable to the spirit of rational metaphysics, and though the creed continued to exert its emotional and moral appeal, frequent efforts were made to mend the rational inconsistencies. Doctrines were borrowed from this and that school with the result that the Stoicism of the first century B.C., for example, presents an incredible patch-work of beliefs. But in the first century after Christ, when other philosophies and the so-called 'orthodox' religions were losing their power, there emerged an impatience with this metaphysical morass, and there was a determined effort on the part of the Stoics to cut away these extraneous accretions of doctrine and return to the original form of the creed as presented by the great early Stoics: Zeno, Cleanthes and Chrysippus. So it is that Epictetus is most important for us since he appears in the first century after Christ when this conscious archaizing was going on. He therefore gives us far more of the original Stoicism than one might expect to discover in a writer who lived some centuries after its founding. It is all the more fortunate, for, owing to the accidents of the preservation of ancient texts, Epictetus must remain one of the most important sources for our knowledge of Stoicism.[9]

The so-called *Discourses* of Epictetus are not actually the writings of the philosopher himself, but are apparently almost a stenographic record of his lectures and informal discussions taken down and compiled by one of his pupils, Arrian the imitator of Xenophon, who is distinguished for his famous history of the expedition of Alexander. Epictetus was born a slave and ultimately became a freedman of one Epaphroditus, who in turn was a freedman of the Emperor Nero. In his youth he was allowed to study philosophy under the great Stoic teacher, Musonius Rufus, but when Domitian exiled the philosophers from Rome, Epictetus left the city, established a school at Nicopolis in Epirus, and taught there for the remainder of his long life. The *Discourses* themselves are almost entirely devoted to the moral aspects of Stoicism, having little or nothing to say of physics or logic. Like Epicurus and Lucretius, Epictetus is attacking the persistent fears of man, and in common with all Stoics holds up internal calm and peace of mind as that which is finally to be desired. The peace of mind can be attained only by the proper use of impressions, which involves the keen discrimination between things in our power and those not in our power, a point which Epictetus never tires of stressing, and which is stated with great clarity in the opening section of his *Manual*. Corollary to this notion is the extreme emphasis upon the will and its discipline, and it is probably because of this aspect of Epictetus' thought that a few scholars have attempted to establish some kind of contact between it and the early Christian writings.

The disarming informality of many passages in the *Discourses* engages easily a reader's attention, yet there are some very arid stretches. The sections which exhort to self-control and the like rarely fail to be inspiring, as well as those places which point to the community of human kind and the obligations that are entailed therein, or the eloquent insistence that somehow or other God is in each man. There is clearly evident the influence of Platonic dialectic, and Socrates appears again and again as the supreme example of a man who lived his life well. On many occasions Epictetus says that the study of philosophy or logic is worth nothing if it is but dry theoretical speculation without any reference or applicability to the actual business of living. Yet permeating the whole is a kind of pessimism, which almost takes one by surprise when Epictetus periodically inserts his advice that if one is weary of life, the door is open, and he is free to depart when he wills.

Epictetus probably lived into the reign of Antoninus Pius and certainly his *Discourses* were predominantly influential in moulding the thought and character of that worthy Emperor's successor, Marcus Aurelius. The significant details of Marcus' life are recorded in Matthew Arnold's famous essay which is printed in the appendix to this volume. There can be no doubt that Marcus Aurelius was one of the finest and greatest men who ever lived. When he came to the imperial throne in A.D. 161, many of his subjects felt that actually Plato's prime requisite for political Utopia had come to pass, for a philosopher had become king. Yet within Marcus' reign until his death in A.D. 180 disaster followed disaster. There were wars against barbarian enemies, the economic structure was tottering, there was a violent internal revolt, and finally a devastating plague swept through the empire. Marcus held his post bravely in the face of these calamities and recorded his reactions in his so-called *Meditations*. In them we are allowed to see his inner being in a way rarely vouchsafed to posterity in the case of a famous man.

If one is to read the *Meditations* effectively, he must always bear in mind how they were written and for what purpose. Apparently they were composed by the Emperor as periodic observations or reminders of his thoughts as he faced his varied duties. They were in all probability intended for no eye but his own, and certainly they have the character of being self-administered exhortations to the highest fulfilment of his obligations as an emperor and a man. It is not at all surprising, then, that they are somewhat disjointed and repetitious. Furthermore, these faults are aggravated by the fact that the text is so corrupt in several places that editors seem to have little chance of solving the manuscript difficulties. Therefore it is advisable to read the *Meditations* in small sections and at intervals, if their full power is to be comprehended.

The Emperor has restated many of the major beliefs of Stoicism which we find in Epictetus. He is fond of putting the doctrines of Epicurus and their implications over against the contrasting Stoic views, always, of course, declaring finally for the latter, though on several occasions he does express profound admiration for Epicurus. Most interesting perhaps is Marcus' emphasis upon the Stoic position of the universal brotherhood of man. This is clearly an implication of the belief that the cosmos is a vast machine, ultimately good, all of whose parts are intimately connected with one another. As such, then, human individuals are joined together as brothers, all fellow members of the city of the world. As Marcus says in Book VI, chapter 44, 'but my nature is rational and social; and my city and country, so far as I am Antoninus, is Rome, but so far as I am a man, it is the world'.[10] Throughout the whole we seem to feel a tension, that Marcus is doing his best to make himself a good Stoic, to adhere to the creed's cardinal dogmas, and most of all to the belief that the universe is good, that there is no evil in it. But when Marcus had to face his disintegrating world, torn with war and disease, he struggled hard to resolve the anomaly between his theory and what he saw. As a result there is infused into his writings a rending sadness, a defeatism which sometimes he specifically articulates as in Book VI, chapter 46 when he writes, 'As it happens to thee in the amphitheatre and such places, that the continual sight of the same things and the uniformity make the spectacle wearisome, so it is in the whole of life; for all things above, below, are the same and from the same. How long then?' It is fundamentally this tension which makes the *Meditations* one of the saddest and most moving books in all of literature.

So we have Epicureanism and Stoicism each presented by two eloquent spokesmen. The two systems are alike in that they attempt to give men peace and inner calm. But it is an extraordinary paradox that the hedonistic system should recommend an ascetic withdrawal from the world, a retirement 'into the Garden', in order to gain that peace, while in contrast the Stoic system, a stern and rigid moralism, maintains that the peace must be found in the midst of the world's confusions, for after all, all men are brothers. And in this connection it should not be overlooked that by urging withdrawal from life Epicureanism rendered itself valueless as a basis for any kind of adequate political philosophy. In contrast, the Stoic doctrine of the universal brotherhood of man has been of incalculable importance in the evolution of democratic theory, particularly in the liberal thought of the French eighteenth century and in the formation of the political institutions of the United States. In the Stoics we find a lack of systematic completeness, and a kind of rigour which often seems to advise men to curb and outlaw some of their most valued human emotions and relationships. Perhaps this goes back to their inadequate theory of evil and the impossibility of their attempt to weld a physical materialism with a pantheism, whose theistic implications they found they had to exploit. On the other hand, Epicureanism is systematically far more satisfying, yet it falls down in the face of such crucial questions as the problem of value and the ultimate sanction for some of the most important assumptions held by the school. Both systems are essentially individualistic, though Epicureanism evinces far more self-centredness than is to be found amongst the Stoics. Both systems are finally rational monisms which have explored large and important areas in the data of human experience with almost unrivalled clarity, yet each system likewise leaves equally important areas untouched. The purview of Stoicism is the wider, and this accounts undoubtedly for its having exerted a more powerful influence on the subsequent development of Western European thought. Each system, then, plays its important part in the Greek tradition though neither is as comprehensive as its Platonic ancestor. All who are vitally interested in the beginnings of the Christian tradition, that is, the dominating strain in the history of our Western culture, must know these Stoics and Epicureans along with the other masters of ancient thought if they are to understand the development of that tradition, and particularly if they are to know the meaning of Matthew Arnold's brilliant words, 'The paramount virtue of religion is, that it has *lighted up* morality'.

Whitney J. Oates

NOTES

[1] There are scholars and thinkers who would ultimately deny dualism to Plato, largely on the ground of their interpretations of the so-called 'later' dialogues. Their conclusions are by no means completely compelling, and one is justified, I believe, in saying that the dominant trend among Platonic critics declares for a fundamental dualism inherent throughout his thought.

[2] Obviously he was unmoved by the virtually irrefutable argument against pleasure as the *summum bonum* as Plato presents it in the *Gorgias*. The position is simple, *viz.*, that admittedly there are bad pleasures, and if so, anything of which bad can be predicated in any circumstance, *ipso facto* loses its claim to be considered as a valid *summum bonum*. Plato's thought clearly has room for the so-called 'good pleasures', but does not regard pleasure as such as a possible philosophical ultimate.

[3] Epicurus, as well as the Stoics, seems to have anticipated by better than two thousand years our contemporary psychologists and psychiatrists who seek to restore nervous balance in their patients by attacking their fear complexes and anxiety neuroses.

[4] Fragment 86.

[5] Cf. Lucretius, Book I, note 1.

[6] The whole poem is dedicated to a certain Memmius, who has been conjecturally identified with the governor in whose suite Catullus went to Bithynia. Memmius had none too excellent a reputation and on this ground it is somewhat difficult to explain Lucretius' laudatory words. He was probably a very adequate potential literary patron. See Walter Allen, *Class. Phil.*, XXXIII (1938) pp. 167-181.

[7] Cf. Lucretius, Book VI, note 4.

[8] Cf. Epictetus, *Manual,* section 27.

[9] I am indebted throughout this section on Stoicism to the excellent chapters dealing with the Stoics and Epictetus in P. E. More, *Hellenistic Philosophies,* Princeton, Princeton University Press, 1923.

[10] Cf. also *Meditations,* Book IV, chapter 4.

THE EXTANT WRITINGS
OF
EPICURUS

THE EXTANT WRITINGS OF EPICURUS

I

EPICURUS TO HERODOTUS

For those who are unable, Herodotus, to work in detail through all that I have written about nature, or to peruse the larger books which I have composed, I have already prepared at sufficient length an epitome of the whole system, that they may keep adequately in mind at least the most general principles in each department, in order that as occasion arises they may be able to assist themselves on the most important points, in so far as they undertake the study of nature. But those also who have made considerable progress in the survey of the main principles ought to bear in mind the scheme of the whole system set forth in its essentials. For we have frequent need of the general view, but not so often of the detailed exposition. Indeed it is necessary to go back on the main principles, and constantly to fix in one's memory enough to give one the most essential comprehension of the truth. And in fact the accurate knowledge of details will be fully discovered, if the general principles in the various departments are thoroughly grasped and borne in mind; for even in the case of one fully initiated the most essential feature in all accurate knowledge is the capacity to make a rapid use of observation and mental apprehension, and this can be done if everything is summed up in elementary principles and formulae. For it is not possible for any one to abbreviate the complete course through the whole system, if he cannot embrace in his own mind by means of short formulae all that might be set out with accuracy in detail. Wherefore since the method I have described is valuable to all those who are accustomed to the investigation of nature, I who urge upon others the constant occupation in the investigation of nature, and find my own peace chiefly in a life so occupied, have composed for you another epitome on these lines, summing up the first principles of the whole doctrine.

First of all, Herodotus, we must grasp the ideas attached to words, in order that we may be able to refer to them and so to judge the inferences of opinion or problems of investigation or reflection, so that we may not either leave everything uncertain and go on explaining to infinity or use words devoid of meaning. For this purpose it is essential that the first mental image associated with each word should be regarded, and that there should be no need of explanation, if we are really to have a standard to which to refer a problem of investigation or reflection or a mental inference. And besides we must keep all our investigations in accord with our sensations, and in particular with the immediate apprehensions whether of the mind or of any one of the instruments of judgement, and likewise in accord with the feelings existing in us, in order that we may have indications whereby we may judge both the problem of sense-perception and the unseen.

Having made these points clear, we must now consider things imperceptible to the senses. First of all, that nothing is created out of that which does not exist: for if it were, everything would be created out of everything with no need of seeds. And again, if that which disappears were destroyed into that which did not exist, all things would have perished, since that into which they were dissolved would not exist. Furthermore, the universe always was such as it is now, and always will be the same. For there is nothing into which it changes: for outside the universe there is nothing which could come into it and bring about the change.

Moreover, the universe is bodies and space: for that bodies exist, sense itself witnesses in the experience of all men, and in accordance with the evidence of sense we must of necessity judge of the imperceptible by reasoning, as I have already said. And if there were not that which we term void and place and intangible existence, bodies would have nowhere to exist and nothing through which to move, as they are seen to move. And besides these two nothing can even be thought of either by conception or on the analogy of things conceivable such as could be grasped as whole existences and not spoken of as the accidents or properties of such existences. Furthermore, among bodies some are compounds, and others those of which compounds are formed. And these latter are indivisible and unalterable (if, that is, all things are not to be destroyed into the non-existent, but something permanent is to remain behind at the dissolution of compounds): they are completely solid in nature, and can by no means be dissolved in any part. So it must needs be that the first-beginnings are indivisible corporeal existences.

Moreover, the universe is boundless. For that which is bounded has an extreme point: and the extreme point is seen against something else. So that as it has no extreme point, it has no limit; and as it has no limit, it must be boundless and not bounded. Furthermore, the infinite is boundless both in the number of the bodies and in the extent of the void. For if on the one hand the void were boundless, and the bodies limited in number, the bodies could not stay anywhere, but would be carried about and scattered through the infinite void, not having other bodies to support them and keep them in place by means of collisions. But if, on the other hand, the void were limited, the infinite bodies would not have room wherein to take their place.

Besides this the indivisible and solid bodies, out of which too the compounds are created and into which they are dissolved, have an incomprehensible number of varieties in shape: for it is not possible that such great varieties of things should arise from the same atomic shapes, if they are limited in number. And so in each shape the atoms are quite infinite in number, but their differences of shape are not quite infinite, but only incomprehensible in number.

And the atoms move continuously for all time, some of them falling straight down, others swerving, and others recoiling from their collisions. And of the latter, some are borne on, separating to a long distance from one another, while others again recoil and recoil, whenever they chance to be checked by the interlacing with others, or else shut in by atoms interlaced around them. For on the one hand the nature of the void which separates each atom by itself brings this about, as it is not able to afford resistance, and on the other hand the hardness which belongs to the atoms makes them recoil after collision to as great a distance as the interlacing permits separation after the collision. And these motions have no beginning, since the atoms and the void are the cause.

These brief sayings, if all these points are borne in mind, afford a sufficient outline for our understanding of the nature of existing things.

Furthermore, there are infinite worlds both like and unlike this world of ours. For the atoms being infinite in number, as was proved already, are borne on far out into space. For those atoms, which are of such nature that a world could be created out of them or made by them, have not been used up either on one world or on a limited number of worlds, nor again on all the worlds which are alike, or on those which are different from these. So that there nowhere exists an obstacle to the infinite number of the worlds.

Moreover, there are images like in shape to the solid bodies, far surpassing perceptible things in their subtlety of texture. For it is not impossible that such emanations should be formed in that which surrounds the objects, nor that there should be opportunities for the formation of such hollow and thin frames, nor that there should be effluences which preserve the respective position and order which they had before in the solid bodies: these images we call idols.

Next, nothing among perceptible things contradicts the belief that the images have unsurpassable fineness of texture. And for this reason they have also unsurpassable speed of motion, since the movement of all their atoms is uniform, and besides nothing or very few things hinder their emission by collisions, whereas a body composed of many or infinite atoms is at once hindered by collisions. Besides this, nothing contradicts the belief that the creation of the idols takes place as quick as thought. For the flow of atoms from the surface of bodies is continuous, yet it cannot be detected by any lessening in the size of the object because of the constant filling up of what is lost. The flow of images preserves for a long time the position and order of the atoms in the solid body, though it is occasionally confused. Moreover, compound idols are quickly formed in the air around, because it is not necessary for their substance to be filled in deep inside: and besides there are certain other methods in which existences of this sort are produced. For not one of these beliefs is contradicted by our sensations, if one looks to see in what way sensation will bring us the clear visions from external objects, and in what way again the corresponding sequences of qualities and movements.

Now we must suppose too that it is when something enters us from external objects that we not only see but think of their shapes. For external objects could not make on us an impression of the nature of their own colour and shape by means of the air which lies between us and them, nor again by means of the rays or effluences of any sort which pass from us to them—nearly so well as if models, similar in colour and shape, leave the objects and enter according to their respective size either into our sight or into our mind; moving along swiftly, and so by this means reproducing the image of a single continuous thing and preserving the corresponding sequence of qualities and movements from the original object as the result of their uniform contact with us, kept up by the vibration of the atoms deep in the interior of the concrete body.

And every image which we obtain by an act of apprehension on the part of the mind or of the sense-organs, whether of shape or of properties, this image is the shape or the properties of the concrete object, and is produced by the constant repetition of the image or the impression it has left. Now falsehood and error always lie in the addition of opinion with regard to what is waiting to be confirmed or not contradicted, and then is not confirmed or is contradicted. For the similarity between the things which exist, which we call real and the images received as a likeness of things and produced either in sleep or through some other acts of apprehension on the part of the mind or the other instruments of judgement, could never be, unless there were some effluences of this nature actually brought into contact with our senses. And error would not exist unless another kind of movement too were produced inside ourselves, closely linked to the apprehension of images, but differing from it; and it is owing to this, supposing it is not confirmed, or is contradicted, that

measure of size for the atoms, both for the smaller and the greater, in our contemplation of these unseen bodies by means of thought. For the affinity which the least parts of the atom have to the homogeneous parts of sensible things is sufficient to justify our conclusion to this extent: but that they should ever come together as bodies with motion is quite impossible.

Furthermore, in the infinite we must not speak of 'up' or 'down', as though with reference to an absolute highest or lowest—and indeed we must say that, though it is possible to proceed to infinity in the direction above our heads from wherever we take our stand, the absolute highest point will never appear to us—nor yet can that which passes beneath the point thought of to infinity be at the same time both up and down in reference to the same thing: for it is impossible to think this. So that it is possible to consider as one single motion that which is thought of as the upward motion to infinity and as another the downward motion, even though that which passes from us into the regions above our heads arrives countless times at the feet of beings above and that which passes downwards from us at the head of beings below; for none the less the whole motions are thought of as opposed, the one to the other, to infinity.[1]

Moreover, the atoms must move with equal speed, when they are borne onwards through the void, nothing colliding with them. For neither will the heavy move more quickly than the small and light, when, that is, nothing meets them: nor again the small more quickly than the great, having their whole course uniform, when nothing collides with them either: nor is the motion upwards or sideways owing to blows quicker, nor again that downwards owing to their own weight. For as long as either of the two motions prevails, so long will it have a course as quick as thought, until something checks it either from outside or from its own weight counteracting the force of that which dealt the blow. Moreover, their passage through the void, when it takes place without meeting any bodies which might collide, accomplishes every comprehensible distance in an inconceivably short time. For it is collision and its absence which take the outward appearance of slowness and quickness. Moreover, it will be said that in compound bodies too one atom is faster than another, though as a matter of fact all are equal in speed: this will be said because even in the least period of continuous time all the atoms in aggregate bodies move towards one place, even though in moments of time perceptible only by thought they do not move towards one place but are constantly jostling one against another, until the continuity of their movement comes under the ken of sensation. For the addition of opinion with regard to the unseen, that the moments perceptible only by thought will also contain continuity of motion, is not true in such cases;

for we must remember that it is what we observe with the senses or grasp with the mind by an apprehension that is true. Nor must it either be supposed that in moments perceptible only by thought the moving body too passes to the several places to which its component atoms move (for this too is unthinkable, and in that case, when it arrives all together in a sensible period of time from any point that may be in the infinite void, it would not be taking its departure from the place from which we apprehend its motion); for the motion of the whole body will be the outward expression of its internal collisions, even though up to the limits of perception we suppose the speed of its motion not to be retarded by collision. It is of advantage to grasp this first principle as well.

Next, referring always to the sensations and the feelings, for in this way you will obtain the most trustworthy ground of belief, you must consider that the soul is a body of fine particles distributed throughout the whole structure, and most resembling wind with a certain admixture of heat, and in some respects like to one of these and in some to the other. There is also the part which is many degrees more advanced even than these in fineness of composition, and for this reason is more capable of feeling in harmony with the rest of the structure as well. Now all this is made manifest by the activities of the soul and the feelings and the readiness of its movements and its processes of thought and by what we lose at the moment of death. Further, you must grasp that the soul possesses the chief cause of sensation: yet it could not have acquired sensation, unless it were in some way enclosed by the rest of the structure. And this in its turn having afforded the soul this cause of sensation acquires itself too a share in this contingent capacity from the soul. Yet it does not acquire all the capacities which the soul possesses: and therefore when the soul is released from the body, the body no longer has sensation. For it never possessed this power in itself, but used to afford opportunity for it to another existence, brought into being at the same time with itself: and this existence, owing to the power now consummated within itself as a result of motion, used spontaneously to produce for itself the capacity of sensation and then to communicate it to the body as well, in virtue of its contact and correspondence of movement, as I have already said. Therefore, so long as the soul remains in the body, even though some other part of the body be lost, it will never lose sensation; nay more, whatever portions of the soul may perish too, when that which enclosed it is removed either in whole or in part, if the soul continues to exist at all, it will retain sensation. On the other hand the rest of the structure, though it continues to exist either as a whole or in part, does not retain sensation, if it has once lost that sum of atoms, however small it be, which together goes to produce the nature of the soul. Moreover, if the whole structure is dissolved, the soul is dispersed and no longer has the same powers nor performs its movements, so that it does not possess sensation either. For it is impossible to imagine it with sensation, if it is not in this organism and cannot effect these movements, when what encloses and surrounds it is no longer the same as the surroundings in which it now exists and performs these movements. Furthermore, we must clearly comprehend as well, that the incorporeal in the general acceptation of the term is applied to that which could be thought of as such as an independent existence. Now it is impossible to conceive the incorporeal as a separate existence, except the void: and the void can neither act nor be acted upon, but only provides opportunity of motion through itself to bodies. So that those who say that the soul is incorporeal are talking idly. For it would not be able to act or be acted on in any respect, if it were of this nature. But as it is, both these occurrences are clearly distinguished in respect of the soul. Now if one refers all these reasonings about the soul to the standards of feeling and sensation and remembers what was said at the outset, he will see that they are sufficiently embraced in these general formulae to enable him to work out with certainty on this basis the details of the system as well.

Moreover, as regards shape and colour and size and weight and all other things that are predicated of body, as though they were concomitant properties either of all things or of things visible or recognizable through the sensation of these qualities, we must not suppose that they are either independent existences (for it is impossible to imagine that), nor that they absolutely do not exist, nor that they are some other kind of incorporeal existence accompanying body, nor that they are material parts of body: rather we should suppose that the whole body in its totality owes its own permanent existence to all these, yet not in the sense that it is composed of properties brought together to form it (as when, for instance, a larger structure is put together out of the parts which compose it, whether the first units of size or other parts smaller than itself, whatever it is), but only, as I say, that it owes its own permanent existence to all of them. All these properties have their own peculiar means of being perceived and distinguished, provided always that the aggregate body goes along with them and is never wrested from them, but in virtue of its comprehension as an aggregate of qualities acquires the predicate of body.

Furthermore, there often happen to bodies and yet do not permanently accompany them accidents, of which we must suppose neither that they do not exist at all nor that they have the nature of a whole body, nor that they can be classed among unseen things nor as incorporeal. So that when according to the most general usage we employ this name, we make it clear that accidents have neither the nature of the whole, which we comprehend in its aggregate and call body, nor that of the qualities which permanently accompany it, without which a given body cannot be conceived. But as the result of certain acts of apprehension, provided the aggregate body goes along with them, they might each be given this name, but only on occasions when each one of them is seen to occur, since accidents are not permanent accompaniments. And we must not banish this clear vision from the realm of existence, because it does not possess the nature of the whole to which it is joined nor that of the permanent accompaniments, nor must we suppose that such contingencies exist independently (for this is inconceivable both with regard to them and to the permanent properties), but, just as it appears in sensation, we must think of them all as accidents occurring to bodies, and that not as permanent accompaniments, or again as having in themselves a place in the ranks of material existence; rather they are seen to be just what our actual sensation shows their proper character to be.

Moreover, you must firmly grasp this point as well; we must not look for time, as we do for all other things which we look for in an object, by referring them to the general conceptions which we perceive in our own minds, but we must take the direct intuition, in accordance with which we speak of 'a long time' or 'a short time', and examine it, applying our intuition to time as we do to other things. Neither must we search for expressions as likely to be better, but employ just those which are in common use about it. Nor again must we predicate of time anything else as having the same essential nature as this special perception, as some people do, but we must turn our thoughts particularly to that only with which we associate this peculiar perception and by which we measure it. For indeed this requires no demonstration, but only reflection, to show that it is with days and nights and their divisions that we associate it, and likewise also with internal feelings or absence of feeling, and with movements and states of rest; in connexion with these last again we think of this very perception as a peculiar kind of accident, and in virtue of this we call it time.

And in addition to what we have already said we must believe that worlds, and indeed every limited compound body which continuously exhibits a similar appearance to the things we see, were created from the infinite, and that all such things, greater and less alike, were separated off from individual agglomerations of matter; and that all are again dissolved, some more quickly, some more slowly, some suffering from one set of causes, others from another. And further we must believe that these worlds were neither created all of necessity with one configuration nor yet with every kind of shape. Furthermore, we must believe that in all worlds there are living creatures and plants and other things we see in this world; for indeed no one could prove that in a world of one kind there might or might not have been included the kinds of seeds from which living things and plants and all the rest of the things we see are composed, and that in a world of another kind they could not have been.

Moreover, we must suppose that human nature too was taught and constrained to do many things of every kind merely by circumstances; and that later on reasoning elaborated what had been suggested by nature and made further inventions, in some matters quickly, in others slowly, at some epochs and times making great advances, and lesser again at others. And so names too were not at first deliberately given to things, but men's natures according to their different nationalities had their own peculiar feelings and received their peculiar impressions, and so each in their own way emitted air formed into shape by each of these feelings and impressions, according to the differences made in the different nations by the places of their abode as well. And then later on by common consent in each nationality special names were deliberately given in order to make their meanings less ambiguous to one another and more briefly demonstrated. And sometimes those who were acquainted with them brought in things hitherto unknown and introduced sounds for them, on some occasions being naturally constrained to utter them, and on others choosing them by reasoning in accordance with the prevailing mode of formation, and thus making their meaning clear.

Furthermore, the motions of the heavenly bodies and their turnings and eclipses and risings and settings, and kindred phenomena to these, must not be thought to be due to any being who controls and ordains or has ordained them and at the same time enjoys perfect bliss together with immortality (for trouble and care and anger and kindness are not consistent with a life of blessedness, but these things come to pass where there is weakness and fear and dependence on neighbours). Nor again must we believe that they, which are but fire agglomerated in a mass, possess blessedness, and voluntarily take upon themselves these movements. But we must preserve their full majestic significance in all expressions which we apply to such conceptions, in order that there may not arise out of them opinions contrary to this notion of majesty. Otherwise this very contradiction will cause the greatest disturbance in men's souls. Therefore we must believe that it is due to the original inclusion of matter in such agglomerations during the birth-process of the world that this law of regular succession is also brought about.

Furthermore, we must believe that to discover accurately the cause of the most essential facts is the function of the science of nature, and that blessedness for us in the knowledge of celestial phenomena lies in this and in the understanding of the nature of the existences seen in these celestial phenomena, and of all else that is akin to the exact knowledge requisite for our happiness: in knowing too that what occurs in several ways or is capable of being otherwise has no place here, but that nothing which suggests doubt or alarm can be included at all in that which is naturally immortal and blessed. Now this we can ascertain by our mind is absolutely the case. But what falls within the investigation of risings and settings and turnings and eclipses, and all that is akin to this, is no longer of any value for the happiness which knowledge brings, but persons who have perceived all this, but yet do not know what are the natures of these things and what are the essential causes, are still in fear, just as if they did not know these things at all: indeed, their fear may be even greater, since the wonder which arises out of the observation of these things cannot discover any solution or realize the regulation of the essentials. And for this very reason, even if we discover several causes for turnings and settings and risings and eclipses and the like, as has been the case already in our investigation of detail, we must not suppose that our inquiry into these things has not reached sufficient accuracy to contribute to our peace of mind and happiness. So we must carefully consider in how many ways a similar phenomenon is produced on earth, when we reason about the causes of celestial phenomena and all that is imperceptible to the senses; and we must despise those persons who do not recognize either what exists or comes into being in one way only, or that which may occur in several ways in the case of things which can only be seen by us from a distance, and further are not aware under what conditions it is impossible to have peace of mind. If, therefore, we think that a phenomenon probably occurs in some such particular way, and that in circumstances under which it is equally possible for us to be at peace, when we realize that it may occur in several ways, we shall be just as little disturbed as if we know that it occurs in some particular way.

And besides all these matters in general we must grasp this point, that the principal disturbance in the minds of men arises because they think that these celestial bodies are blessed and immortal, and yet have wills and actions and motives inconsistent with these attributes; and because they are always expecting or imagining some everlasting misery, such as is depicted in legends, or even fear the loss of feeling in death as though it would concern them themselves; and, again, because they are brought to this pass not by reasoned opinion, but rather by some irrational presentiment, and therefore, as they do not know the limits of pain, they suffer a disturbance equally great or even more extensive than if they had reached this belief by opinion. But peace of mind is being delivered from all this, and having a constant memory of the general and most essential principles.

Wherefore we must pay attention to internal feelings and to external sensations in general and in particular, according as the subject is general or particular, and to every immediate intuition in accordance with each of the standards of judgement. For if we pay attention to these, we shall rightly trace the causes whence arose our mental disturbance and fear, and, by learning the true causes of celestial phenomena and all other occurrences that come to pass from time to time, we shall free ourselves from all which produces the utmost fear in other men.

Here, Herodotus, is my treatise on the chief points concerning the nature of the general principles, abridged so that my account would be easy to grasp with accuracy. I think that, even if one were unable to proceed to all the detailed particulars of the system, he would from this obtain an unrivalled strength compared with other men. For indeed he will clear up for himself many of the detailed points by reference to our general system, and these very principles, if he stores them in his mind, will constantly aid him. For such is their character that even those who are at present engaged in working out the details to a considerable degree, or even completely, will be able to carry out the greater part of their investigations into the nature of the whole by conducting their analysis in reference to such a survey as this. And as for all who are not fully among those on the way to being perfected, some of them can from this summary obtain a hasty view of the most important matters without oral instruction so as to secure peace of mind.

ANALYSIS

(The numbers refer to the original text of Diogenes Laertius)

Introduction. (35-37) Need of this epitome for advanced students.

I. *Methods of Procedure.* (37-38)
  1. Words to be used in their first meaning.
  2. The standards of judgement.

II. *The Universe and its Constituents.* (38-45)
  A. Imperceptible things.
    1. Nothing is created out of nothing.
    2. Nothing is destroyed into nothing.
    3. The universe is ever the same.
  B. Bodies and space. The universe consists of bodies and space. There is no other independent existence. Body exists in the form of indivisible particles.
  C. Infinity of the universe. The universe is infinite, both in the number of atoms and in the extent of space.
  D. Differences of shape in the atoms but not infinite differences.
  E. Motion of the atoms.
  F. Infinite number of worlds.

III. *Sense-perception.* (46-53)
  A. Sight.
    1. The 'images'.
    2. Their subtlety and speed.
    3. Their immediate creation.
    4. The method of sight and thought.
    5. Truth and falsehood in vision.
  B. Hearing. Hearing is due to an effluence from the object, which splits up into similar particles, which preserve the character of the original.
  C. Smell is similarly caused by effluences.

IV. *The Atoms.* (54-62)
  A. Their properties: shape, weight and size.
    1. Other qualities change, but there must be something constant to prevent complete destruction.
    2. The atoms have varieties of size, but not all sizes: for then some would become visible.
  B. The parts of the atoms.
    1. The parts of a limited body cannot be infinite in number or infinitely small. For, if they are, (*a*) the body cannot be limited in size, and (*b*) in the enumeration of extreme points it is not possible to continue to infinity.

2. The *minimum visible* has extension without parts, and is the ultimate measure of size. Similarly, there are least indivisible parts in the atom, which are the units of measurement. (In what sense there is motion upward and downward in the infinite.)

C. The motions of the atoms. All move always at equal rate 'as quick as thought', neither weight nor direction making any difference. Their speed is inconceivably great. In compound bodies too all atoms really move at the same pace, though an inference from perception might deny this. Nor of course does the whole body perform the trajects of all its component atoms.

V. *The Soul.* (63-68)

1. It is composed of fine atoms, like the wind and heat, and of the third, more subtle, element.
2. The soul has sensation owing to its protection within the body, to which it then communicates sensation.
3. Even though parts of the body be lost, the soul still has sensation; but if the soul be lost, the body ceases to feel; and so does the soul when the body is broken up.
4. The soul cannot be incorporeal, for if it were like the only incorporeal independent existence, the void, it could not act or be acted on.

VI. *Properties and Accidents.* (68-73)

1. Properties are not independent corporeal existences or parts of body, but the inseparable physical constituents of body, but body owes its essential nature to an aggregate of properties, always existing in it, not uniting to form it.
2. Accidents are not incorporeal existences, etc., but qualities and so on attached to body, but not permanently. Both their existence and their transitory character must be recognized.
3. Time is not recognizable by a concept, as are concrete things and qualities, but is a special kind of accident.

VII. *Worlds, their Creation, Destruction, Shapes and Contents.* (73-74)

1. Worlds are created out of the void by means of separate aggregations of matter and are similarly dissolved.
2. Worlds are of various shapes.
3. In them all there are animals, etc., as in ours.

VIII. *The Growth of Civilization and the Origin of Language.* (75-76)

1. The arts were taught by nature and developed by reason.
2. Language thus originated from natural sounds, caused by feelings and impressions, and was subsequently developed deliberately. New names were introduced in both these ways.

IX. *Celestial Phenomena.* (76-82)

1. Their causes:
   (*a*) The motions of the heavenly bodies are not controlled by any immortal blessed being.
   (*b*) Nor are they divine beings themselves. We must not in either of these ways derogate from the majesty of the gods.
2. The knowledge of the nature of the heavenly bodies, etc., is certain and essential for our happiness, but not the knowledge of the detailed causes of their working. We must therefore be content even if we find several causes for the same phenomenon. We must reason about celestial phenomena on the analogy of things on earth, and not be disturbed, if we find several causes at work.
3. The causes of men's fears. The two chief causes of unrest of mind are (*a*) the belief that the heavenly bodies are divine, and (*b*) the fear of eternal punishment or of annihilation after death. Peace of mind is freedom from these fears.
4. Trust in the senses. To be quit of our fears, we must always attend to the direct evidence of feelings and sensations, and of the other criteria of judgement.

Conclusion. (82-83)

This summary will be of value both to the advanced student and to the more general inquirer.

II - Epicurus infers what is in agreement w/ phenomena to determine causes of various things in heavens-sky -it is an escape from superstition- in just believing what is observable phenomena

phenomena of sky

II

EPICURUS TO PYTHOCLES

CLEON brought me a letter from you in which you continue to express a kindly feeling towards me, which is a just return for my interest in you, and you attempt with some success to recall the arguments which lead to a life of blessedness. You ask me to send you a brief argument about the phenomena of the sky in a short sketch, that you may easily recall it to mind. For you say that what I have written in my other works is hard to remember, even though, as you state, you constantly have them in your hands. I was glad to receive your request and felt constrained to answer it by pleasant expectations for the future. Therefore, as I have finished all my other writings I now intend to accomplish your request, feeling that these arguments will be of value to many other persons as well, and especially to those who have but recently tasted the genuine inquiry into nature, and also to those who are involved too deeply in the business of some regular occupation. Therefore lay good hold on it, keep it in mind, and go through it all keenly, together with the rest which I sent in the small epitome to Herodotus.

First of all then we must not suppose that any other object is to be gained from the knowledge of the phenomena of the sky, whether they are dealt with in connexion with other doctrines or independently, than peace of mind and a sure confidence, just as in all other branches of study. We must not try to force an impossible explanation, nor employ a method of inquiry like our reasoning either about the modes of life or with respect to the solution of other physical problems: witness such propositions as that 'the universe consists of bodies and the intangible', or that 'the elements are indivisible', and all such statements in circumstances where there is only one explanation which harmonizes with phenomena. For this is not so with the things above us: they admit of more than one cause of coming into being and more than one account of their nature which harmonizes with our sensations. For we must not conduct scientific investigation by means of empty assumptions and arbitrary principles, but follow the lead of phenomena: for our life has not now any place for irrational belief and groundless imaginings, but we must live free from trouble. Now all goes on without disturbance as far as regards each of those things which may be explained in several ways so as to harmonize with what we perceive, when one admits, as we are bound to do, probable theories about them. But when one accepts one theory and rejects another, which harmonizes just as well with the phenomenon, it is obvious that he altogether leaves the path of scientific inquiry and has recourse to myth. Now we can obtain indications of what happens above from some of the phenomena on earth: for we can observe how they come to pass, though we cannot observe the phenomena in the sky: for they may be produced in several ways. Yet we must never desert the appearance of each of these phenomena, and further, as regards what is associated with it, must distinguish those things whose production in several ways is not contradicted by phenomena on earth.

A world is a circumscribed portion of sky, containing heavenly bodies and an earth and all the heavenly phenomena, whose dissolution will cause all within it to fall into confusion: it is a piece cut off from the infinite and ends in a boundary either rare or dense, either revolving or stationary: its outline may be spherical or three-cornered, or any kind of shape. For all such conditions are possible, seeing that no phenomenon is evidence against this in our world, in which it is not possible to perceive an ending. And that such worlds are infinite in number we can be sure, and also that such a world may come into being both inside another world and in an interworld, by which we mean a space between worlds; it will be in a place with much void, and not in a large empty space quite void, as some say: this occurs when seeds of the right kind have rushed in from a single world or interworld, or from several: little by little they make junctions and articulations, and cause changes of position to another place, as it may happen, and produce irrigations of the appropriate matter until the period of completion and stability, which lasts as long as the underlying foundations are capable of receiving additions. For it is not merely necessary for a gathering of atoms to take place, nor indeed for a whirl and nothing more to be set in motion, as is supposed, by necessity, in an empty space in which it is possible for a world to come into being, nor can the world go on increasing until it collides with another world, as one of the so-called physical philosophers says. For this is a contradiction of phenomena.

Sun and moon and the other stars were not created by themselves and subsequently taken in by the world, but were fashioned in it from the first and gradually grew in size by the aggregations and whirlings of bodies of minute parts, either windy or fiery or both; for this is what our sensation suggests. The size of sun and moon and the other stars is for us what it appears to be; and in reality it is either slightly greater than what we see or slightly less or the same size: for so too fires on earth when looked at from a distance seem to the senses. And every objection at this point will easily be dissipated, if we pay attention to the clear vision, as I show in my books about nature. The risings and settings of the sun, moon, and other heavenly bodies may be due to kindling and anything seems possible

extinction, the composition of the surrounding matter at the places of rising and setting being such as to lead to these results: for nothing in phenomena is against it. Or again, the effect in question might be produced by their appearance over the top of the earth, and again the interposition of the earth in front of them: for once more nothing in phenomena is against it. Their motions may not impossibly be due to the revolution of the whole heaven, or else it may remain stationary, and they may revolve owing to the natural impulse towards the east, which was produced at the beginning of the world[1] by an excessive heat owing to a spreading of the fire which is always moving on to the regions nearest in succession. The tropics of sun and moon may be caused owing to an obliquity of the whole heaven, which is constrained into this position in the successive seasons; or equally well by an outward impulsion of a current of air, or because the appropriate material successively catches fire, as the former fails; or again, from the beginning this particular form of revolution may have been assigned to these stars, so that they move in a kind of spiral. For all these and kindred explanations are not at variance with any clear-seen facts, if one always clings in such departments of inquiry to the possible and can refer each point to what is in agreement with phenomena without fearing the slavish artifices of the astronomers.

The wanings of the moon and its subsequent waxings might be due to the revolution of its own body, or equally well to successive conformations of the atmosphere, or again to the interposition of other bodies; they may be accounted for in all the ways in which phenomena on earth invite us to such explanations of these phases; provided only one does not become enamoured of the method of the single cause and groundlessly put the others out of court, without having considered what it is possible for a man to observe and what is not, and desiring therefore to observe what is impossible. Next the moon may have her light from herself or from the sun. For on earth too we see many things shining with their own, and many with reflected light. Nor is any celestial phenomenon against these explanations, if one always remembers the method of manifold causes and investigates hypotheses and explanations consistent with them, and does not look to inconsistent notions and emphasize them without cause and so fall back in different ways on different occasions on the method of the single cause. The impression of a face in the moon may be due to the variation of its parts or to interposition or to any one of many causes which might be observed, all in harmony with phenomena. For in the case of all celestial phenomena this process of investigation must never be abandoned: for if one is in opposition to clear-seen facts, he can never have his part in true peace of mind.

The eclipse of sun and moon may take place both owing to their ex-

Observe all possible phenomena; divine doesn't control nature cuz unobservable, it only is in pure blessedness

tinction, as we see this effect is produced on earth, or again by the interposition of some other bodies, either the earth or some unseen body or something else of this sort. And in this way we must consider together the causes that suit with one another and realize that it is not impossible that some should coincide at the same time. Next the regularity of the periods of the heavenly bodies must be understood in the same way as such regularity is seen in some of the events that happen on earth. And do not let the divine nature be introduced at any point into these considerations, but let it be preserved free from burdensome duties and in entire blessedness. For if this principle is not observed, the whole discussion of causes in celestial phenomena is in vain, as it has already been for certain persons who have not clung to the method of possible explanations, but have fallen back on the useless course of thinking that things could only happen in one way, and of rejecting all other ways in harmony with what is possible, being driven thus to what is inconceivable and being unable to compare earthly phenomena, which we must accept as indications.

The successive changes in the length of nights and days may be due to the fact that the sun's movements above the earth become fast and then slow again because he passes across regions of unequal length or because he traverses some regions more quickly or more slowly, or again to the quicker or slower gathering of the fires that make the sun, as we observe occurs with some things on earth, with which we must be in harmony in speaking of celestial phenomena. But those who assume one cause fight against the evidence of phenomena and fail to ask whether it is possible for men to make such observations.

Signs of the weather may occur owing to the coincidence of occasions, as happens with animals we can all see on earth, and also through alterations and changes in the atmosphere. For both these are in accordance with phenomena. But under what circumstances the cause is produced by this or that, we cannot perceive.

Clouds may be produced and formed both by the condensation of the atmosphere owing to compression by winds and by the interlacing of atoms clinging to one another and suitable for producing this result, and again by the gathering of streams from earth and the waters: and there are several other ways in which the formation of such things may not impossibly be brought about. And from them again rain may be produced if they are squeezed in one part or changed in another, or again by a downward current of wind moving through the atmosphere from appropriate places, a more violent shower being produced from certain conglomerations of atoms suited to create such downfalls.

Thunder may be produced by the rushing about of wind in the hollows of the clouds, as happens in vessels on earth, or by the reverberation of fire filled with wind inside them, or by the rending and tearing of clouds, or by the friction and bursting of clouds when they have been congealed into a form like ice: phenomena demand that we should say that this department of celestial events, just like them all, may be caused in several ways.

And lightnings too are produced in several ways: for both owing to the friction and collision of clouds a conformation of atoms which produces fire slips out and gives birth to the lightning, and owing to wind bodies which give rise to this flash are dashed from the clouds: or compression may be the cause, when clouds are squeezed either by one another or by the wind. Or again it may be that the light scattered abroad from the heavenly bodies is taken in by the clouds, and then is driven together by the movement of the clouds and wind, and falls out through the clouds; or else light composed of most subtle particles may filter through the clouds, whereby the clouds may be set on fire by the flame and thunder produced by the movement of the fire. Or the wind may be fired owing to the strain of motion and its violent rotation: or clouds may be rent by wind and atoms fall out which produce fire and cause the appearance of lightning. And several other methods may easily be observed, if one clings always to phenomena and can compare what is akin to these things. Lightning precedes thunder in such a conformation of the clouds, either because at the moment when the wind dashes in, the formation of atoms which gives rise to lightning is driven out, but afterwards the wind whirls about and produces the reverberation; or because they both dash out at the same moment, but lightning moves at a higher speed towards us, and thunder comes after, as in the case of some things seen at a distance and producing blows.

Thunderbolts may occur because there are frequent gatherings of wind, which whirls about and is fanned into a fierce flame, and then a portion of it breaks off and rushes violently on the places beneath, the breaking taking place because the regions approached are successively denser owing to the condensation of clouds: or as the result of the actual outburst of the whirling fire, in the same way that thunder may be produced, when the fire becomes too great and is too violently fanned by wind and so breaks through the cloud, because it cannot retreat to the next regions owing to the constant condensation of clouds one on the other. And thunderbolts may be produced in other ways too. Only superstition must be excluded, as it will, if one successfully follows the lead of seen phenomena to gain indications about the invisible.

Cyclones may be produced either by the driving down of a cloud into the regions below in the form of a pillar, because it is pushed by the wind gathered inside it and is driven on by the violence of the wind, while at the same time the wind outside impels it sideways; or by wind forming into circular motion, while mist is simultaneously thrust down from above; or when a great rush of wind takes place and cannot pass through sideways owing to the surrounding condensation of the atmosphere. And when the spout is let down on to the land, whirlwinds are produced in all the various ways in which their creation may occur owing to the movement of the wind, but if it reaches the sea it produces waterspouts.

Earthquakes may be brought about both because wind is caught up in the earth, so that the earth is dislocated in small masses and is continually shaken, and that causes it to sway. This wind it either takes into itself from outside, or else because masses of ground fall in into cavernous places in the earth and fan into wind the air that is imprisoned in them. And again, earthquakes may be brought about by the actual spreading of the movement which results from the fall of many such masses of ground and the return shock, when the first motion comes into collision with more densely packed bodies of earth. There are also many other ways in which these motions of the earth may be caused.

The winds may be produced when from time to time some alien matter is continually and gradually forcing its way in, or owing to the gathering of a vast quantity of water. The other winds arise when a few currents of air fall into many hollow spaces, and cause a spreading of wind.

Hail is produced both by a powerful congelation, when certain windy bodies form together from all sides and split up: also by a more moderate congelation of watery bodies and their simultaneous division, which causes at one and the same time their coagulation and separation, so that they cling together as they freeze in their separate parts as well as in their whole masses. Their circular shape may possibly arise because the corners melt off all round or because at their conformation bodies, whether watery or windy, come together evenly from all directions part by part, as is alleged.

Snow may be produced when fine particles of rain are poured out of the clouds owing to the existence of pores of suitable shape and the strong and constant compression by winds of clouds of the right kind; and then the water is congealed in its descent owing to some conformation of excessive coldness in the clouds in the lower regions. Or else owing to congelation in clouds of uniform thinness an exudation of this kind might arise from watery clouds lying side by side and rubbing against one another: for they produce hail by causing coagulation, a process most frequent in the atmosphere. Or else, owing to the friction of congealed clouds, these nuclei of snow may find occasion to break off. And there are many other ways in which snow may be produced.

Dew may be produced both when such particles as are productive of this kind of moisture issue from the atmosphere and meet one another, and also when particles rise from moist regions or regions containing water, in which dew is most naturally produced, and then meet together and cause moisture to be produced, and afterwards fall back on the ground below, as is frequently seen to be the case in phenomena on earth as well. And frost is produced by a change in the dew-particles, when such particles as we have described undergo a definite kind of congelation owing to the neighbourhood of a cold atmosphere.

Ice is caused both by the squeezing out from the water of particles of round formation and the driving together of the triangular and acute-angled particles which exist already in the water, and again by the addition from without of particles of this kind, which when driven together produce a congelation in the water, by squeezing out a certain number of the round particles.

The rainbow is caused by light shining from the sun on to watery atmosphere: or else by a peculiar union of light and air, which can produce the special qualities of these colours whether all together or separately; from it as it reflects back again the neighbouring regions of the air can take the tint which we see, by means of the shining of the light on to its various parts. The appearance of its round shape is caused because it is perceived by our sight at equal distance from all its points, or else because the atoms in the air or those in the clouds which are derived from the same air, are pressed together in this manner, and so the combination spreads out in a round shape.

A halo round the moon is caused either when air is carried towards the moon from all sides, or when the air checks the effluences carried from the moon so equably that it forms them into this cloudy ring all round without any gaps or differences, or else when it checks the air round the moon uniformly on all sides so as to make that which encircles it round and thick in texture. This comes to pass in different parts either because some current outside forces the air or because heat blocks the passages in such a way as to produce this effect.

Comets occur either when fire is collected together in certain regions at certain intervals of time in the upper air because some gathering of matter takes place, or when at certain intervals the heaven above us has some peculiar movement, so that stars of this nature are revealed, or when they themselves at certain seasons start to move on account of some gathering of matter and come into the regions within our ken and appear visible. And their disappearance occurs owing to the opposite causes to these.

Some stars 'revolve in their place' (as Homer says), which comes to pass not only because this part of the world is stationary and round it the rest revolves, as some say, but also because a whirl of air is formed in a ring round it, which prevents their moving about as do the other stars.

or else it is because there is not a succession of appropriate fuel for them, but only in this place in which they are seen fixed. And there are many other ways in which this may be brought about, if one is able to infer what is in agreement with phenomena.

That some of the stars should wander in their course, if indeed it is the case that their movements are such, while others do not move in this manner, may be due to the reason that from the first as they moved in their circles they were so constrained by necessity that some of them move along the same regular orbit, and others along one which is associated with certain irregularities: or it may be that among the regions to which they are carried in some places there are regular tracts of air which urge them on successively in the same direction and provide flame for them regularly, while in other places the tracts are irregular, so that the aberrations which we observe result. But to assign a single cause for these occurrences, when phenomena demand several explanations, is madness, and is quite wrongly practised by persons who are partisans of the foolish notions of astrology, by which they give futile explanations of the causes of certain occurrences, and all the time do not by any means free the divine nature from the burden of responsibilities.

That some stars should be seen to be left behind by others is caused because though they move round in the same orbit they are carried along more slowly, and also because they really move in the opposite direction though they are dragged back by the same revolution: also because some are carried round through a greater space and some through a lesser, though all perform the same revolution. But to give a single explanation of these occurrences is only suitable to those who wish to make a show to the many.

What are called falling stars may be produced in part by the rubbing of star against star, and by the falling out of the fragments wherever an outburst of wind occurs, as we explained in the case of lightning-flashes: or else by the meeting of atoms productive of fire, when a gathering of kindred material occurs to cause this, and a movement in the direction of the impulse which results from the original meeting; or else by a gathering of wind in certain dense and misty formations, and its ignition as it whirls round, and then its bursting out of what encloses it and its rush towards the spot to which the impulse of its flight tends. And there are other ways in which this result may be brought about, quite free from superstition.

The signs of the weather which are given by certain animals result from mere coincidence of occasion. For the animals do not exert any compulsion for winter to come to an end, nor is there some divine nature which sits and watches the outgoings of these animals and then fulfils the signs they give. For not even the lowest animal, although 'a small thing gives the greater pleasure', would be seized by such foolishness, much less one who was possessed of perfect happiness.

All these things, Pythocles, you must bear in mind; for thus you will escape in most things from superstition and will be enabled to understand what is akin to them. And most of all give yourself up to the study of the beginnings and of infinity and of the things akin to them, and also of the criteria of truth and of the feelings, and of the purpose for which we reason out these things. For these points when they are thoroughly studied will most easily enable you to understand the causes of the details. But those who have not thoroughly taken these things to heart could not rightly study them in themselves, nor have they made their own the reason for observing them.

ANALYSIS

Introduction. (84-88)

Pythocles' request. Epicurus' consent: general usefulness of the letter. Purpose of investigation: the quiet life. Its principles: investigation of heavenly phenomena differs from that of ethics or physics, for more than one cause may produce the same effect. Such plurality of causes is not a disturbing element, if we do not make arbitrary decisions. Things on earth may help us to explain heavenly phenomena.

I. *Worlds.* (88-90)

Definition of a world: its boundary and shape. Worlds infinite in number. Place of formation. Manner of formation and endurance. False idea of formation and destruction of worlds.

II. *The Heavenly Bodies.* (90-99)

1. Creation, in the world.
2. Constitution.
3. Size: nearly what we see it.
4. Their rising and setting.
5. Their motions.
6. The tropics.
7. The moon:
   a. its phases
   b. its light
   c. the face in the moon.
8. Eclipses.
9. Periods.
10. Length of nights and days.
11. Weather-signs.

III. *Meteorology.* (99-104)

1. Clouds.
2. Rain.
3. Thunder.
4. Lightning.
5. Why lightning precedes thunder.
6. Thunderbolts.

IV. *Atmospheric and Terrestrial Phenomena.* (104-111)

1. Cyclones.
2. Earthquakes.
3. (? Volcanoes.)
4. Hail.
5. Snow.

6. Dew and frost.
7. Ice.
8. The rainbow; its shape.
9. The moon's halo.

V. *Further Celestial Phenomena.* (111-116)

1. Comets.
2. Fixed stars.
3. Planets and regular stars.
4. Difference of speed in orbits of stars.
5. Falling stars.
6. Weather-signs from animals.

Conclusion. (116)

maybe a paper comparing Epicurus's idea of death to Plato's in the Crito

III

EPICURUS TO MENOECEUS

Let no one when young delay to study philosophy, nor when he is old grow weary of his study. For no one can come too early or too late to secure the health of his soul. And the man who says that the age for philosophy has either not yet come or has gone by is like the man who says that the age for happiness is not yet come to him, or has passed away. Wherefore both when young and old a man must study philosophy, that as he grows old he may be young in blessings through the grateful recollection of what has been, and that in youth he may be old as well, since he will know no fear of what is to come. We must then meditate on the things that make our happiness, seeing that when that is with us we have all, but when it is absent we do all to win it.

The things which I used unceasingly to commend to you, these do and practise, considering them to be the first principles of the good life. First of all believe that god is a being immortal and blessed, even as the common idea of a god is engraved on men's minds, and do not assign to him anything alien to his immortality or ill-suited to his blessedness: but believe about him everything that can uphold his blessedness and immortality. For gods there are, since the knowledge of them is by clear vision. But they are not such as the many believe them to be: for indeed they do not consistently represent them as they believe them to be. And the impious man is not he who denies the gods of the many, but he who attaches to the gods the beliefs of the many. For the statements of the many about the gods are not conceptions derived from sensation, but false suppositions, according to which the greatest misfortunes befall the wicked and the greatest blessings the good by the gift of the gods. For men being accustomed always to their own virtues welcome those like themselves, but regard all that is not of their nature as alien.

Become accustomed to the belief that death is nothing to us. For all good and evil consists in sensation, but death is deprivation of sensation. And therefore a right understanding that death is nothing to us makes the mortality of life enjoyable, not because it adds to it an infinite span of time, but because it takes away the craving for immortality. For there is nothing terrible in life for the man who has truly comprehended that there is nothing terrible in not living. So that the man speaks but idly who says that he fears death not because it will be painful when it comes, but because it is painful in anticipation. For that which gives no trouble when it comes, is but an empty pain in anticipation. So death, the most terrifying of ills, is nothing to us, since so long as we exist, death is not with us; but when death comes, then we do not exist. It does not then concern either the living or the dead, since for the former it is not, and the latter are no more.

But the many at one moment shun death as the greatest of evils, at another yearn for it as a respite from the evils in life. But the wise man neither seeks to escape life nor fears the cessation of life, for neither does life offend him nor does the absence of life seem to be any evil. And just as with food he does not seek simply the larger share and nothing else, but rather the most pleasant, so he seeks to enjoy not the longest period of time, but the most pleasant.

And he who counsels the young man to live well, but the old man to make a good end, is foolish, not merely because of the desirability of life, but also because it is the same training which teaches to live well and to die well. Yet much worse still is the man who says it is good not to be born, but

'once born make haste to pass the gates of Death'.

[Theognis, 427]

For if he says this from conviction why does he not pass away out of life? For it is open to him to do so, if he had firmly made up his mind to this. But if he speaks in jest, his words are idle among men who cannot receive them.

We must then bear in mind that the future is neither ours, nor yet wholly not ours, so that we may not altogether expect it as sure to come, nor abandon hope of it, as if it will certainly not come.

We must consider that of desires some are natural, others vain, and of the natural some are necessary and others merely natural; and of the necessary some are necessary for happiness, others for the repose of the body, and others for very life. The right understanding of these facts enables us to refer all choice and avoidance to the health of the body and the soul's freedom from disturbance, since this is the aim of the life of blessedness. For it is to obtain this end that we always act, namely, to avoid pain and fear. And when this is once secured for us, all the tempest of the soul is dispersed, since the living creature has not to wander as though in search of something that is missing, and to look for some other thing by which he can fulfil the good of the soul and the good of the body. For it is then that we have need of pleasure, when we feel pain owing to the absence of pleasure; but when we do not feel pain, we no longer need pleasure. And for this cause we call pleasure the beginning and end of the blessed life. For we recognize pleasure as the first good innate in us, and from pleasure we begin every act of choice and avoid-

pleasure = innate good

ance, and to pleasure we return again, using the feeling as the standard by which we judge every good.

And since pleasure is the first good and natural to us, for this very reason we do not choose every pleasure, but sometimes we pass over many pleasures, when greater discomfort accrues to us as the result of them: and similarly we think many pains better than pleasures, since a greater pleasure comes to us when we have endured pains for a long time. Every pleasure then because of its natural kinship to us is good, yet not every pleasure is to be chosen: even as every pain also is an evil, yet not all are always of a nature to be avoided. Yet by a scale of comparison and by the consideration of advantages and disadvantages we must form our judgement on all these matters. For the good on certain occasions we treat as bad, and conversely the bad as good.

And again independence of desire we think a great good—not that we may at all times enjoy but a few things, but that, if we do not possess many, we may enjoy the few in the genuine persuasion that those have the sweetest pleasure in luxury who least need it, and that all that is natural is easy to be obtained, but that which is superfluous is hard. And so plain savours bring us a pleasure equal to a luxurious diet, when all the pain due to want is removed; and bread and water produce the highest pleasure, when one who needs them puts them to his lips. To grow accustomed therefore to simple and not luxurious diet gives us health to the full, and makes a man alert for the needful employments of life, and when after long intervals we approach luxuries, disposes us better towards them, and fits us to be fearless of fortune.

When, therefore, we maintain that pleasure is the end, we do not mean the pleasures of profligates and those that consist in sensuality, as is supposed by some who are either ignorant or disagree with us or do not understand, but freedom from pain in the body and from trouble in the mind. For it is not continuous drinkings and revellings, nor the satisfaction of lusts, nor the enjoyment of fish and other luxuries of the wealthy table, which produce a pleasant life, but sober reasoning, searching out the motives for all choice and avoidance, and banishing mere opinions, to which are due the greatest disturbance of the spirit.

Of all this the beginning and the greatest good is prudence. Wherefore prudence is a more precious thing even than philosophy: for from prudence are sprung all the other virtues, and it teaches us that it is not possible to live pleasantly without living prudently and honourably and justly, nor, again, to live a life of prudence, honour, and justice without living pleasantly. For the virtues are by nature bound up with the pleasant life, and the pleasant life is inseparable from them. For indeed who, think you, is a better man than he who holds reverent opinions concerning the gods, and is at all times free from fear of death, and has reasoned out the end ordained by nature? He understands that the limit of good things is easy to fulfil and easy to attain, whereas the course of ills is either short in time or slight in pain: he laughs at destiny, whom some have introduced as the mistress of all things. He thinks that with us lies the chief power in determining events, some of which happen by necessity and some by chance, and some are within our control; for while necessity cannot be called to account, he sees that chance is inconstant, but that which is in our control is subject to no master, and to it are naturally attached praise and blame. For, indeed, it were better to follow the myths about the gods than to become a slave to the destiny of the natural philosophers: for the former suggests a hope of placating the gods by worship, whereas the latter involves a necessity which knows no placation. As to chance, he does not regard it as a god as most men do (for in a god's acts there is no disorder), nor as an uncertain cause of all things: for he does not believe that good and evil are given by chance to man for the framing of a blessed life, but that opportunities for great good and great evil are afforded by it. He therefore thinks it better to be unfortunate in reasonable action than to prosper in unreason. For it is better in a man's actions that what is well chosen should fail, rather than that what is ill chosen should be successful owing to chance.

Meditate therefore on these things and things akin to them night and day by yourself, and with a companion like to yourself, and never shall you be disturbed waking or asleep, but you shall live like a god among men. For a man who lives among immortal blessings is not like to a mortal being.

pleasure is an end = freedom from pain in body + from trouble in mind

prudence

ANALYSIS

Introduction. (122) Both young and old must study philosophy.

I *First Principles.* (123-127)

1. The nature of the gods. The gods exist, immortal and blessed, but their nature is not such as is popularly supposed.
2. Death. Death is nothing to us. This makes life pleasant and death no terror. Nor its anticipation painful: it is nothing to living or dead. We should not shun life or fear death: we want a pleasant life, not a long one. To live well is to learn to die well. It is foolish to say it is good to die at once. The future is neither ours nor not ours.

II. *The Moral Theory.* (127-135)

1. Division of desires. Health of body and repose of soul the motive of action. Hence pleasure the standard of the good.
2. Pleasure is in itself always good, but not all pleasures are to be chosen because of accompanying pain. We must judge by comparison.
3. We must be content with a little, and so shall enjoy luxury more, if it comes. Simple diet secures health and alertness.
4. Pleasure does not then mean sensual enjoyment, but health of body and the exercise of the mind on philosophy.
5. The greatest thing is prudence, which teaches all other virtues, and they secure a pleasant life. The prudent man is superior to all others. He knows the limits of good and evil, and is not the slave of necessity, which is worse than belief in popular religion. He regards chance, too, as an opportunity for good, but prefers prudence with misfortune, to prosperity with folly.

Peroration. (135)

The practice of these precepts will make you a god among men.

IV
PRINCIPAL DOCTRINES

I. The blessed and immortal nature knows no trouble itself nor causes trouble to any other, so that it is never constrained by anger or favour. For all such things exist only in the weak.

II. Death is nothing to us: for that which is dissolved is without sensation; and that which lacks sensation is nothing to us.

III. The limit of quantity in pleasures is the removal of all that is painful. Wherever pleasure is present, as long as it is there, there is neither pain of body nor of mind, nor of both at once.

IV. Pain does not last continuously in the flesh, but the acutest pain is there for a very short time, and even that which just exceeds the pleasure in the flesh does not continue for many days at once. But chronic illnesses permit a predominance of pleasure over pain in the flesh.

V. It is not possible to live pleasantly without living prudently and honourably and justly, nor again to live a life of prudence, honour, and justice without living pleasantly. And the man who does not possess the pleasant life, is not living prudently and honourably and justly, and the man who does not possess the virtuous life, cannot possibly live pleasantly.

VI. To secure protection from men anything is a natural good, by which you may be able to attain this end.

VII. Some men wished to become famous and conspicuous, thinking that they would thus win for themselves safety from other men. Wherefore if the life of such men is safe, they have obtained the good which nature craves; but if it is not safe, they do not possess that for which they strove at first by the instinct of nature.

VIII. No pleasure is a bad thing in itself: but the means which produce some pleasures bring with them disturbances many times greater than the pleasures.

IX. If every pleasure could be intensified so that it lasted and influenced the whole organism or the most essential parts of our nature, pleasures would never differ from one another.

X. If the things that produce the pleasures of profligates could dispel the fears of the mind about the phenomena of the sky and death and its pains, and also teach the limits of desires and of pains, we should never have cause to blame them: for they would be filling themselves full with pleasures from every source and never have pain of body or mind, which is the evil of life.

XI. If we were not troubled by our suspicions of the phenomena of the sky and about death, fearing that it concerns us, and also by our failure to grasp the limits of pains and desires, we should have no need of natural science.

XII. A man cannot dispel his fear about the most important matters if he does not know what is the nature of the universe but suspects the truth of some mythical story. So that without natural science it is not possible to attain our pleasures unalloyed.

XIII. There is no profit in securing protection in relation to men, if things above and things beneath the earth and indeed all in the boundless universe remain matters of suspicion.

XIV. The most unalloyed source of protection from men, which is secured to some extent by a certain force of expulsion, is in fact the immunity which results from a quiet life and the retirement from the world.

XV. The wealth demanded by nature is both limited and easily procured; that demanded by idle imaginings stretches on to infinity.

XVI. In but few things chance hinders a wise man, but the greatest and most important matters reason has ordained and throughout the whole period of life does and will ordain.

XVII. The just man is most free from trouble, the unjust most full of trouble.

XVIII. The pleasure in the flesh is not increased, when once the pain due to want is removed, but is only varied: and the limit as regards pleasure in the mind is begotten by the reasoned understanding of these very pleasures and of the emotions akin to them, which used to cause the greatest fear to the mind.

XIX. Infinite time contains no greater pleasure than limited time, if one measures by reason the limits of pleasure.

XX. The flesh perceives the limits of pleasure as unlimited and unlimited time is required to supply it. But the mind, having attained a reasoned understanding of the ultimate good of the flesh and its limits and having dissipated the fears concerning the time to come, supplies us with the complete life, and we have no further need of infinite time: but neither does the mind shun pleasure, nor, when circumstances begin to bring about the departure from life, does it approach its end as though it fell short in any way of the best life.

XXI. He who has learned the limits of life knows that that which removes the pain due to want and makes the whole of life complete is easy to obtain; so that there is no need of actions which involve competition.

XXII. We must consider both the real purpose and all the evidence of direct perception, to which we always refer the conclusions of opinion; otherwise, all will be full of doubt and confusion.

XXIII. If you fight against all sensations, you will have no standard by which to judge even those of them which you say are false.

XXIV. If you reject any single sensation and fail to distinguish between the conclusion of opinion as to the appearance awaiting confirmation and that which is actually given by the sensation or feeling, or each intuitive apprehension of the mind, you will confound all other sensations as well with the same groundless opinion, so that you will reject every standard of judgement. And if among the mental images created by your opinion you affirm both that which awaits confirmation and that which does not, you will not escape error, since you will have preserved the whole cause of doubt in every judgement between what is right and what is wrong.

XXV. If on each occasion instead of referring your actions to the end of nature, you turn to some other nearer standard when you are making a choice or an avoidance, your actions will not be consistent with your principles.

XXVI. Of desires, all that do not lead to a sense of pain, if they are not satisfied, are not necessary, but involve a craving which is easily dispelled, when the object is hard to procure or they seem likely to produce harm.

XXVII. Of all the things which wisdom acquires to produce the blessedness of the complete life, far the greatest is the possession of friendship.

XXVIII. The same conviction which has given us confidence that there is nothing terrible that lasts for ever or even for long, has also seen the protection of friendship most fully completed in the limited evils of this life.

XXIX. Among desires some are natural and necessary, some natural but not necessary, and others neither natural nor necessary, but due to idle imagination.

XXX. Wherever in the case of desires which are physical, but do not lead to a sense of pain, if they are not fulfilled, the effort is intense, such pleasures are due to idle imagination, and it is not owing to their own nature that they fail to be dispelled, but owing to the empty imaginings of the man.

XXXI. The justice which arises from nature is a pledge of mutual advantage to restrain men from harming one another and save them from being harmed.

XXXII. For all living things which have not been able to make compacts not to harm one another or be harmed, nothing ever is either just or unjust; and likewise too for all tribes of men which have been unable or unwilling to make compacts not to harm or be harmed.

XXXIII. Justice never is anything in itself, but in the dealings of men with one another in any place whatever and at any time it is a kind of compact not to harm or be harmed.

XXXIV. Injustice is not an evil in itself, but only in consequence of the fear which attaches to the apprehension of being unable to escape those appointed to punish such actions.

XXXV. It is not possible for one who acts in secret contravention of the terms of the compact not to harm or be harmed, to be confident that he will escape detection, even if at present he escapes a thousand times. For up to the time of death it cannot be certain that he will indeed escape.

XXXVI. In its general aspect justice is the same for all, for it is a kind of mutual advantage in the dealings of men with one another: but with reference to the individual peculiarities of a country or any other circumstances the same thing does not turn out to be just for all.

XXXVII. Among actions which are sanctioned as just by law, that which is proved on examination to be of advantage in the requirements of men's dealings with one another, has the guarantee of justice, whether it is the same for all or not. But if a man makes a law and it does not turn out to lead to advantage in men's dealings with each other, then it no longer has the essential nature of justice. And even if the advantage in the matter of justice shifts from one side to the other, but for a while accords with the general concept, it is none the less just for that period in the eyes of those who do not confound themselves with empty sounds but look to the actual facts.

XXXVIII. Where, provided the circumstances have not been altered, actions which were considered just, have been shown not to accord with the general concept in actual practice, then they are not just. But where, when circumstances have changed, the same actions which were sanctioned as just no longer lead to advantage, there they were just at the time when they were of advantage for the dealings of fellow-citizens with one another; but subsequently they are no longer just, when no longer of advantage.

XXXIX. The man who has best ordered the element of disquiet arising from external circumstances has made those things that he could akin to himself and the rest at least not alien: but with all to which he could not do even this, he has refrained from mixing, and has expelled from his life all which it was of advantage to treat thus.

XL. As many as possess the power to procure complete immunity from their neighbours, these also live most pleasantly with one another, since they have the most certain pledge of security, and after they have enjoyed the fullest intimacy, they do not lament the previous departure of a dead friend, as though he were to be pitied.

V

FRAGMENTS

A. VATICAN COLLECTION

'Epicurus' Exhortation'

IV. All bodily suffering is negligible: for that which causes acute pain has short duration, and that which endures long in the flesh causes but mild pain.

VII. It is hard for an evil-doer to escape detection, but to obtain security for escaping is impossible.

IX. Necessity is an evil, but there is no necessity to live under the control of necessity.

X. Remember that you are of mortal nature and have a limited time to live and have devoted yourself to discussions on nature for all time and eternity and have seen 'things that are now and are to come and have been'.

XI. For most men rest is stagnation and activity madness.

XIV. We are born once and cannot be born twice, but for all time must be no more. But you, who are not master of to-morrow, postpone your happiness: life is wasted in procrastination and each one of us dies without allowing himself leisure.

XV. We value our characters as something peculiar to ourselves, whether they are good and we are esteemed by men, or not; so ought we to value the characters of others, if they are well-disposed to us.

XVI. No one when he sees evil deliberately chooses it, but is enticed by it as being good in comparison with a greater evil and so pursues it.

XVII. It is not the young man who should be thought happy, but an old man who has lived a good life. For the young man at the height of his powers is unstable and is carried this way and that by fortune, like a headlong stream. But the old man has come to anchor in old age as though in port, and the good things for which before he hardly hoped he has brought into safe harbourage in his grateful recollections.

XVIII. Remove sight, association and contact, and the passion of love is at an end.

XIX. Forgetting the good that has been he has become old this very day.

XXI. We must not violate nature, but obey her; and we shall obey her if we fulfil the necessary desires and also the physical, if they bring no harm to us, but sternly reject the harmful.

XXIII. All friendship is desirable in itself, though it starts from the need of help.

XXIV. Dreams have no divine character nor any prophetic force, but they originate from the influx of images.

XXV. Poverty, when measured by the natural purpose of life, is great wealth, but unlimited wealth is great poverty.

XXVI. You must understand that whether the discourse be long or short it tends to the same end.

XXVII. In all other occupations the fruit comes painfully after completion, but in philosophy pleasure goes hand in hand with knowledge; for enjoyment does not follow comprehension, but comprehension and enjoyment are simultaneous.

XXVIII. We must not approve either those who are always ready for friendship, or those who hang back, but for friendship's sake we must even run risks.

XXIX. In investigating nature I would prefer to speak openly and like an oracle to give answers serviceable to all mankind, even though no one should understand me, rather than to conform to popular opinions and so win the praise freely scattered by the mob.

XXX. Some men throughout their lives gather together the means of life, for they do not see that the draught swallowed by all of us at birth is a draught of death.

XXXI. Against all else it is possible to provide security, but as against death all of us mortals alike dwell in an unfortified city.

XXXII. The veneration of the wise man is a great blessing to those who venerate him.

XXXIII. The flesh cries out to be saved from hunger, thirst and cold. For if a man possess this safety and hope to possess it, he might rival even Zeus in happiness.

XXXIV. It is not so much our friends' help that helps us as the confidence of their help.

XXXV. We should not spoil what we have by desiring what we have not, but remember that what we have too was the gift of fortune.

XXXVI. Epicurus' life when compared to other men's in respect of gentleness and self-sufficiency might be thought a mere legend.

XXXVII. Nature is weak towards evil, not towards good: because it is saved by pleasures, but destroyed by pains.

XXXVIII. He is a little man in all respects who has many good reasons for quitting life.

XXXIX. He is no friend who is continually asking for help, nor he who never associates help with friendship. For the former barters kindly feeling for a practical return and the latter destroys the hope of good in the future.

XL. The man who says that all things come to pass by necessity cannot criticize one who denies that all things come to pass by necessity: for he admits that this too happens of necessity.

XLI. We must laugh and philosophize at the same time and do our household duties and employ our other faculties, and never cease proclaiming the sayings of the true philosophy.

XLII. The greatest blessing is created and enjoyed at the same moment.

XLIII. The love of money, if unjustly gained, is impious, and, if justly, shameful; for it is unseemly to be merely parsimonious even with justice on one's side.

XLIV. The wise man when he has accommodated himself to straits knows better how to give than to receive: so great is the treasure of self-sufficiency which he has discovered.

XLV. The study of nature does not make men productive of boasting or bragging nor apt to display that culture which is the object of rivalry with the many, but high-spirited and self-sufficient, taking pride in the good things of their own minds and not of their circumstances.

XLVI. Our bad habits, like evil men who have long done us great harm, let us utterly drive from us.

XLVII. I have anticipated thee, Fortune, and entrenched myself against all thy secret attacks. And we will not give ourselves up as captives to thee or to any other circumstance; but when it is time for us to go, spitting contempt on life and on those who here vainly cling to it, we will leave life crying aloud in a glorious triumph-song that we have lived well.

XLVIII. We must try to make the end of the journey better than the beginning, as long as we are journeying; but when we come to the end, we must be happy and content.

LI. You tell me that the stimulus of the flesh makes you too prone to the pleasures of love. Provided that you do not break the laws or good customs and do not distress any of your neighbours or do harm to your body or squander your pittance, you may indulge your inclination as you please. Yet it is impossible not to come up against one or other of these barriers: for the pleasures of love never profited a man and he is lucky if they do him no harm.

LII. Friendship goes dancing round the world proclaiming to us all to awake to the praises of a happy life.

LIII. We must envy no one: for the good do not deserve envy and the bad, the more they prosper, the more they injure themselves.

LIV. We must not pretend to study philosophy, but study it in reality: for it is not the appearance of health that we need, but real health.

LV. We must heal our misfortunes by the grateful recollection of what has been and by the recognition that it is impossible to make undone what has been done.

LVI-LVII. The wise man is not more pained when being tortured himself, than when seeing his friend tortured: but if his friend does him wrong, his whole life will be confounded by distrust and completely upset.[1]

LVIII. We must release ourselves from the prison of affairs and politics.

LIX. It is not the stomach that is insatiable, as is generally said, but the false opinion that the stomach needs an unlimited amount to fill it.

LX. Every man passes out of life as though he had just been born.

LXI. Most beautiful too is the sight of those near and dear to us, when our original kinship makes us of one mind; for such sight is a great incitement to this end.

LXII. Now if parents are justly angry with their children, it is certainly useless to fight against it and not to ask for pardon; but if their anger is unjust and irrational, it is quite ridiculous to add fuel to their irrational passion by nursing one's own indignation, and not to attempt to turn aside their wrath in other ways by gentleness.

LXIII. Frugality too has a limit, and the man who disregards it is in like case with him who errs through excess.

LXIV. Praise from others must come unasked: we must concern ourselves with the healing of our own lives.

LXV. It is vain to ask of the gods what a man is capable of supplying for himself.

LXVI. Let us show our feeling for our lost friends not by lamentation but by meditation.

LXVII. A free life cannot acquire many possessions, because this is not easy to do without servility to mobs or monarchs, yet it possesses all things in unfailing abundance; and if by chance it obtains many possessions, it is easy to distribute them so as to win the gratitude of neighbours.

LXVIII. Nothing is sufficient for him to whom what is sufficient seems little.

LXIX. The ungrateful greed of the soul makes the creature everlastingly desire varieties of dainty food.

LXX. Let nothing be done in your life, which will cause you fear if it becomes known to your neighbour.

LXXI. Every desire must be confronted with this question: what will happen to me, if the object of my desire is accomplished and what if it is not?

LXXIII. The occurrence of certain bodily pains assists us in guarding against others like them.

LXXIV. In a philosophical discussion he who is worsted gains more in proportion as he learns more.

LXXV. Ungrateful towards the blessings of the past is the saying, 'Wait till the end of a long life'.

LXXVI. You are in your old age just such as I urge you to be, and you have seen the difference between studying philosophy for oneself and proclaiming it to Greece at large: I rejoice with you.

LXXVII. The greatest fruit of self-sufficiency is freedom.

LXXVIII. The noble soul occupies itself with wisdom and friendship: of these the one is a mortal good, the other immortal.

LXXIX. The man who is serene causes no disturbance to himself or to another.

LXXX. The first measure of security is to watch over one's youth and to guard against what makes havoc of all by means of pestering desires.

LXXXI. The disturbance of the soul cannot be ended nor true joy created either by the possession of the greatest wealth or by honour and respect in the eyes of the mob or by anything else that is associated with causes of unlimited desire.

B. REMAINS ASSIGNED TO CERTAIN BOOKS

I. Concerning Choice and Avoidance

1. Freedom from trouble in the mind and from pain in the body are static pleasures, but joy and exultation are considered as active pleasures involving motion.

II. Problems

2. Will the wise man do things that the laws forbid, knowing that he will not be found out? A simple answer is not easy to find.

III. The Shorter Summary

3. Prophecy does not exist, and even if it did exist, things that come to pass must be counted nothing to us.

IV. Against Theophrastus

4. But even apart from this argument I do not know how one should say that things in the dark have colour.

V. Symposium

5. Polyaenus: Do you, Epicurus, deny the existence of the warmth produced by wine? (Someone interrupted:) It does not appear that wine is unconditionally productive of heat.

(And a little later:) It seems that wine is not unconditionally productive of heat, but wine of a certain quantity might be said to produce heat in a certain body.

6. Therefore we must not speak of wine as unconditionally productive of heat, but rather say that a certain quantity of wine will produce heat in a certain body which is in a certain disposition, or that a different quantity will produce cold in a different body. For in the compound body of wine there are certain particles out of which cold might be produced, if, as need arises, united with different particles they could form a structure which would cause cold. So that those are deceived who say that wine is unconditionally heating or cooling.

7. Wine often enters the body without exerting any power either of heating or of cooling, but when the structure is disturbed and an atomic re-arrangement takes place, the atoms which create heat at one time come together and by their number give heat and inflammation to the body, at another they retire and so cool it.

8. Sexual intercourse has never done a man good, and he is lucky if it has not harmed him.

9. It is strange indeed that you were not at all impeded by your youth, as you would say yourself, from attaining, young as you were, a distinction in the art of rhetoric far above all your contemporaries, even the experienced and famous. It is strange indeed, I say, that you were not at all impeded by your youth from winning distinction in the art of rhetoric, which seems to require much practice and habituation, whereas youth can be an impediment to the understanding of the true nature of the world, towards which knowledge might seem to contribute more than practice and habituation.

VI. On the End of Life

10. I know not how I can conceive the good, if I withdraw the pleasures of taste, and withdraw the pleasures of love, and withdraw the pleasures of hearing, and withdraw the pleasurable emotions caused to sight by beautiful form.

11. The stable condition of well-being in the body and the sure hope of its continuance holds the fullest and surest joy for those who can rightly calculate it.

12. Beauty and virtue and the like are to be honoured, if they give pleasure; but if they do not give pleasure, we must bid them farewell.

VII. On Nature

BOOK I

13. The nature of the universe consists of bodies and void.

14. The nature of all existing things is bodies and space.

BOOK XI

15. For if it (*sc.* the sun) had lost its size through the distance, much more would it have lost its colour: for there is no other distance better adapted for such loss than that of the sun.

FROM UNCERTAIN WORKS

16. The atom is a hard body free from any admixture of void; the void is intangible existence.

17. Away with them all: for he (Nausiphanes), like many another slave, was in travail with that wordy braggart, sophistic.

C. REMAINS OF LETTERS

18. If they have this in mind, they are victorious over the evils of want and poverty.

19. Even if war comes, he would not count it terrible, if the gods are propitious. He has led and will lead a pure life in Matro's company, by favour of the gods.

20. Tell me, Polyaenus, do you know what has been a great joy to us?

LETTERS TO SEVERAL PERSONS

To the Philosophers in Mytilene

21. This drove him to such a state of fury that he abused me and ironically called me master.

22. I suppose that those grumblers will believe me to be a disciple of The Mollusc and to have listened to his teaching in company with a few bibulous youths. For indeed the fellow was a bad man and his habits such as could never lead to wisdom.

LETTERS TO INDIVIDUALS

To Anaxarchus

23. But I summon you to continuous pleasures and not to vain and empty virtues which have but disturbing hopes of results.

To Apelles

24. I congratulate you, Apelles, in that you have approached philosophy free from all contamination.

To Themista

25. If you two don't come to me, I am capable of arriving with a hop, skip, and jump, wherever you and Themista summon me.

To Idomeneus

26. Send us therefore offerings for the sustenance of our holy body on behalf of yourself and your children: this is how it occurs to me to put it.

27. O thou who has from thy youth regarded all my promptings as sweet.

28. If you wish to make Pythocles rich, do not give him more money, but diminish his desire.

29. We think highly of frugality not that we may always keep to a cheap and simple diet, but that we may be free from desire regarding it.

30. On this truly happy day of my life, as I am at the point of death, I write this to you. The disease in my bladder and stomach are pursuing their course, lacking nothing of their natural severity: but against all this is the joy in my heart at the recollection of my conversations with you. Do you, as I might expect from your devotion from boyhood to me and to philosophy, take good care of the children of Metrodorus.

To Colotes

31. In your feeling of reverence for what I was then saying you were seized with an unaccountable desire to embrace me and clasp my knees and show me all the signs of homage paid by men in prayers and sup-

plications to others; so you made me return all these proofs of veneration and respect to you.

Go on thy way as an immortal and think of us too as immortal.

To Leontion

32. Lord and Saviour, my dearest Leontion, what a hurrahing you drew from us, when we read aloud your dear letter.

To Pythocles

33. Blest youth, set sail in your bark and flee from every form of culture.

34. I will sit down and wait for your lovely and godlike appearance.

LETTERS TO UNCERTAIN PERSONS

To a Boy or Girl

35. We have arrived at Lampsacus safe and sound, Pythocles and Hermarchus and Ctesippus and I, and there we found Themista and our other friends all well. I hope you too are well and your mamma, and that you are always obedient to pappa and Matro, as you used to be. Let me tell you that the reason that I and all the rest of us love you is that you are always obedient to them.

Letter Written in His Last Days

36. Seven days before writing this the stoppage became complete and I suffered pains such as bring men to their last day. If anything happens to me, do you look after the children of Metrodorus for four or five years, but do not spend any more on them than you now spend each year on me.

Letters to Unknown Recipients

37. I am thrilled with pleasure in the body, when I live on bread and water, and I spit upon luxurious pleasures not for their own sake, but because of the inconveniences that follow them.

38. As I said to you when you were going away, take care also of his brother Apollodorus. He is not a bad boy, but causes me anxiety, when he does what he does not mean to do.

39. Send me some preserved cheese, that when I like I may have a feast.

40. You have looked after me wonderfully generously in sending me food, and have given proofs heaven-high of your good will to me.

41. The only contribution I require is that which . . . ordered the disciples to send me, even if they are among the Hyperboreans. I wish to receive from each of you two a hundred and twenty drachmae a year and no more.

Ctesippus has brought me the annual contribution which you sent for your father and yourself.

42. He will have a valuable return in the instruction which I have given him.

43. I was never anxious to please the mob. For what pleased them, I did not know, and what I did know, was far removed from their comprehension.

44. Think it not unnatural that when the flesh cries aloud, the soul cries too. The flesh cries out to be saved from hunger, thirst, and cold. It is hard for the soul to repress these cries, and dangerous for it to disregard nature's appeal to her because of her own wonted independence day by day.

45. The man who follows nature and not vain opinions is independent in all things. For in reference to what is enough for nature every possession is riches, but in reference to unlimited desires even the greatest wealth is (not riches but poverty).

46. In so far as you are in difficulties, it is because you forget nature; for you create for yourself unlimited fears and desires.

48. It is better for you to be free of fear lying upon a pallet, than to have a golden couch and a rich table and be full of trouble.

49. . . . remembering your letter and your discussion about the men who are not able to see the analogy between phenomena and the unseen nor the harmony which exists between sensations and the unseen and again the contradiction . . .

50. Sweet is the memory of a dead friend.

51. Do not avoid conferring small favours: for then you will seem to be of like character towards great things.

52. If your enemy makes a request to you, do not turn from his petition: but be on your guard; for he is like a dog.

D. FRAGMENTS FROM UNCERTAIN SOURCES

ON PHILOSOPHY

54. Vain is the word of a philosopher which does not heal any suffering of man. For just as there is no profit in medicine if it does not expel

the diseases of the body, so there is no profit in philosophy either, if it does not expel the suffering of the mind.

Physics

55. Nothing new happens in the universe, if you consider the infinite time past.

56. We shall not be considering them any happier or less destructible, if we think of them as not speaking nor conversing with one another, but resembling dumb men.

57. Let us at least sacrifice piously and rightly where it is customary, and let us do all things rightly according to the laws not troubling ourselves with common beliefs in what concerns the noblest and holiest of beings. Further let us be free of any charge in regard to their opinion. For thus can one live in conformity with nature . . .

58. If God listened to the prayers of men, all men would quickly have perished: for they are for ever praying for evil against one another.

Ethics

59. The beginning and the root of all good is the pleasure of the stomach; even wisdom and culture must be referred to this.

60. We have need of pleasure when we are in pain from its absence: but when we are not feeling such pain, though we are in a condition of sensation, we have no need of pleasure. For the pleasure which arises from nature does not produce wickedness, but rather the longing connected with vain fancies.

61. That which creates joy insuperable is the complete removal of a great evil. And this is the nature of good, if one can once grasp it rightly, and then hold by it, and not walk about babbling idly about the good.

62. It is better to endure these particular pains so that we may enjoy greater joys. It is well to abstain from these particular pleasures in order that we may not suffer more severe pains.

63. Let us not blame the flesh as the cause of great evils, nor blame circumstances for our distresses.

64. Great pains quickly put an end to life; long-enduring pains are not severe.

65. Excessive pain will bring you to death.

66. Through love of true philosophy every disturbing and troublesome desire is ended.

67. Thanks be to blessed Nature because she has made what is necessary easy to supply, and what is not easy unnecessary.

68. It is common to find a man who is poor in respect of the natural

end of life and rich in empty fancies. For of the fools none is satisfied with what he has, but is grieved for what he has not. Just as men with fever through the malignance of their disease are always thirsty and desire the most injurious things, so too those whose mind is in an evil state are always poor in everything and in their greed are plunged into ever-changing desires.

69. Nothing satisfies the man who is not satisfied with a little.

70. Self-sufficiency is the greatest of all riches.

71. Most men fear frugality and through their fear are led to actions most likely to produce fear.

72. Many men when they have acquired riches have not found the escape from their ills but only a change to greater ills.

73. By means of occupations worthy of a beast abundance of riches is heaped up, but a miserable life results.

74. Unhappiness comes either through fear or through vain and unbridled desire: but if a man curbs these, he can win for himself the blessedness of understanding.

75. It is not deprivation of these things which is pain, but rather the bearing of the useless pain that arises from vain fancies.

76. The mean soul is puffed up by prosperity and cast down by misfortune.

77. Nature teaches us to pay little heed to what fortune brings, and when we are prosperous to understand that we are unfortunate, and when we are unfortunate not to regard prosperity highly, and to receive unmoved the good things which come from fortune and to range ourselves boldly against the seeming evils which it brings: for all that the many regard as good or evil is fleeting, and wisdom has nothing in common with fortune.

78. He who least needs to-morrow, will most gladly go to meet to-morrow.

79. I spit upon the beautiful and those who vainly admire it, when it does not produce any pleasure.

80. The greatest fruit of justice is serenity.

81. The laws exist for the sake of the wise, not that they may not do wrong, but that they may not suffer it.

82. Even if they are able to escape punishment, it is impossible to win security for escaping: and so the fear of the future which always presses upon them does not suffer them to be happy or to be free from anxiety in the present.

83. The man who has attained the natural end of the human race will be equally good, even though no one is present.

84. A man who causes fear cannot be free from fear.

85. The happy and blessed state belongs not to abundance of riches

or dignity of position or any office or power, but to freedom from pain and moderation in feelings and an attitude of mind which imposes the limits ordained by nature.

86. Live unknown.

87. We must say how best a man will maintain the natural end of life, and how no one will willingly at first aim at public office.

VI

THE LIFE OF EPICURUS

By Diogenes Laertius

EPICURUS, son of Neocles and Chaerestrata, was an Athenian of the deme of Gargettus, and the family of the Philaidae, as Metrodorus says in his work on *Nobility of Birth*. Heraclides in his epitome of Sotion, and others say that the Athenians having colonized Samos, Epicurus was brought up there. In his eighteenth year, as they say, he came to Athens, when Xenocrates was at the Academy and Aristotle was living in Chalcis. After the death of Alexander of Macedon, when the Athenians were driven out of Samos by Perdiccas, he went to join his father in Colophon. Having stayed there some time and gathered disciples he returned again to Athens in the archonship of Anaxicrates. For a while he joined with others in the study of philosophy, but later taught independently, when he had founded the school called after him. He tells us himself that he first made acquaintance with philosophy at the age of fourteen. Apollodorus the Epicurean in the first book of his *Life of Epicurus* says that he took to philosophy because he despised the teachers of literature, since they were not able to explain to him the passage about Chaos in Hesiod. Hermippus says that Epicurus was at one time a schoolmaster and then after he met with the writings of Democritus, he took eagerly to philosophy. And this is why Timon says about him,

'Last and most shameless of the scientists, infant school teacher from Samos, the most stubborn of all living beings'.

His three brothers, Neocles, Chaeredemus, and Aristobulus joined him in studying philosophy at his suggestion, according to Philodemus the Epicurean in the tenth book of his *Comparison of Philosophies*. Also a slave called Mys, as Muronianus says in his chapters on historical coincidences.

Diotimus the Stoic, who is ill-disposed to Epicurus, has calumniated him most bitterly by producing fifty lewd letters as Epicurus' work; so has the writer who has assigned to Epicurus the collection of 'billets-doux' which were attributed to Chrysippus, and also Posidonius the Stoic and his followers, as well as Nicolaus and Sotion in the twelve books of the 'Arguments of Diocles' which are named after the Epicurean celebration of The Twentieth; [1] also Dionysius of Halicarnassus. For they say that he used to go round from house to house with his mother reading out the purification prayers, and assisted his father in elementary teaching for a miserable pittance. They add that one of his brothers prostituted himself and kept company with Leontion, the hetaera. Also that he took Democritus' atomic theory and Aristippus' theory of pleasure and taught them as his own. Further, that he was not an Athenian born, as Timocrates says, and Herodotus too in his book, *The Youth of Epicurus*. He is also said to have used degrading flattery towards Mithres, the steward of Lysimachus, calling him in his letters both 'Saviour' and 'My lord'. Idomeneus too and Herodotus and Timocrates, who divulged his secrets, he is said to have praised and flattered all the same. And in his letters he wrote to Leontion, 'Lord and Saviour, my dearest Leontion, what a hurrahing you drew from us, as we read aloud your dear letter', and to Themista, Leonteus' wife, 'If you two don't come to me, I am capable of arriving with a hop, skip and jump, wherever you and Themista summon me'. And to Pythocles who was young and beautiful he writes, 'I will sit down and wait for your lovely and god-like appearance'. And again in writing to Themista he calls her by a most flattering name, as Theodorus says in the fourth book of his attack on Epicurus. They say that he wrote to many other women of pleasure and particularly to Leontion, with whom Metrodorus was also in love; and that in the treatise *On the End of Life* he wrote, 'I know not how I can conceive the good, if I withdraw the pleasures of taste and withdraw the pleasures of love and those of hearing and sight'. Again in the letter to Pythocles they say he wrote 'Blest youth, set sail in your bark and flee from every form of culture'. Epictetus moreover calls him a filthy talker and abuses him roundly. And even Timocrates, who was the brother of Metrodorus and a disciple of Epicurus, after he had abandoned the school, wrote in a book with the title *Pleasant Things* that Epicurus used to vomit twice a day owing to his luxurious living, and that he himself was scarcely able to escape from his philosophical disquisitions during the night and from the community of the initiates. He adds that Epicurus was profoundly ignorant of philosophy and still more so of practical life, that his body was miserably weak, so that for many years he was unable to rise from his portable couch: further, that he spent no less than a mina a day on his food, as Epicurus writes himself in the letter to Leontion and in the letters to the philosophers in Mytilene: moreover, there were other women who lived with him and Metrodorus, named Mammarion and Hedeia and Erotion and Nicidion. He adds that in the thirty-seven books *On Nature* he repeats himself for the most part and attacks many other philosophers in them but Nausiphanes most of all, saying in his own words, 'Away with them all: for Nausiphanes, like many another slave, was in travail with that wordy braggart, sophistic'. He says that Epicurus himself in his letters about Nausiphanes said, 'This drove him to such a state of fury that he abused me and ironically called me "Master" '. He used to call Nausiphanes 'The mollusc', 'The illiterate', 'The cheat', 'The harlot'. The followers of Plato he called 'Flatterers of Dionysus' and Plato himself 'The golden man', and Aristotle 'The debauchee', saying that he devoured his inheritance and then enlisted and sold drugs. Protagoras he called 'Porter' or 'Copier of Democritus', saying that he taught in the village schools. Heraclitus he called 'The Muddler', Democritus Lerocritus ('Judge of nonsense'), Antidorus Sannidorus ('Maniac'), the Cynics 'Enemies of Hellas', the Logicans 'The destroyers', and Pyrrho 'The uneducated fool'.

But these calumniators are all mad. For Epicurus has witnesses enough and to spare to his unsurpassed kindness to all men. There is his country which honoured him with bronze statues, his friends so numerous that they could not even be reckoned by entire cities, and his disciples who all remained bound for ever by the charm of his teaching, except Metrodorus, son of Stratoniceus, who went over to Carneades, overweighted perhaps by Epicurus' excessive goodness. There is also the permanent continuance of the school after almost all the others had come to an end, and that though it had a countless succession of heads from among the disciples. There is again his grateful devotion to his parents, his generosity to his brothers, and his gentleness towards his servants, of whom the most notable was Mys already mentioned, as is proved by his will and the part they took in his philosophical discussions. In short there is his benevolence to all. Of his reverence towards the gods and his love of his country it would be impossible to speak adequately. But from excess of modesty he would not take any part in politics. Yet although Greece was at that time in great straits he continued to live there, and only once or twice made a voyage to Ionia and the neighbourhood to see his friends. But they came to him from all quarters, and took up their abode with him in the garden, as Apollodorus says, who adds that he bought it for eighty minae: Diocles in the third book of his *Course in Philosophy* confirms this, living a most frugal and simple life. Indeed, he says, they were satisfied with half a pint of wine, and for the most part drank water. He adds that Epicurus did not recommend them to put their belongings into a common stock, as did Pythagoras, who said that 'Friends have all in common'. For to do so implied distrust: and distrust could not go with friendship. Epicurus himself says in his letters that he was content with nothing but water and a bit of bread. 'Send me', he says, 'some preserved cheese, that when I like I may have a feast.' Such was the man who taught that the end is pleasure. Athenaeus sings his praise in an epigram:

Men toil at mean pursuits, for love of gain
  Insatiate they welcome war and strife;
Their idle fancies lead on endless paths,
  But nature's wealth is set in narrow bounds.
This truth the prudent son of Neocles
  Learnt from the Muses or Apollo's shrine.

[Athenaeus, *Anth. Plan.*, IV. 43]

The truth of this we shall know better as we go on from his own words and teaching.

Diocles says that of the earlier philosophers he showed most sympathy with Anaxagoras, though on certain points he opposed him, and with Archelaus, the master of Socrates. And, he adds, he used to practise his disciples in getting his writings by heart. Apollodorus in his *Chronicles* asserts that he listened to the teaching of Nausiphanes and Praxiphanes. Epicurus himself denies this in his letter to Eurylochus and says he was his own teacher. And indeed both Epicurus and Hermarchus deny that there ever was such a philosopher as Leucippus, whom Apollodorus the Epicurean and others say was the master of Democritus. Demetrius of Magnesia says that he was also a follower of Xenocrates.

He uses current diction to expound his theory, but Aristophanes the grammarian censures it as being too peculiar. But he was clear in expression, just as in his book on *Rhetoric* he insists on clearness above everything. In his letters he used to say 'Prosper' or 'Live well', instead of the conventional introduction 'Be happy'.

Ariston in his *Life of Epicurus* says that he borrowed *The Canon* from the *Tripod* of Nausiphanes, whose pupil he says he was, as well as being a disciple of Pamphilus the Platonist in Samos. He states that Epicurus began philosophy at the age of twelve, and was at the head of his School at thirty-two.

He was born, says Apollodorus in the *Chronicles*, in the third year of the 109th Olympiad in the archonship of Sosigenes on the seventh day of the month Gamelion, seven years after the death of Plato. When he was thirty-two he started his school first for five years at Mytilene and Lampsacus and then he migrated to Athens. There he died in the second year of the 127th Olympiad in the archonship of Pytharatus, at the age of seventy-two. Hermarchus of Mytilene, son of Agemortus, succeeded to the headship of the school. Epicurus died of a stone in the bladder, as Hermarchus also says in his letters, after an illness of fourteen days. Hermippus tells us that as he was dying he got into a bronze bath filled with hot water, and asked for a cup of unmixed wine, which he gulped down. Then having adjured his friends to remember his teaching he expired. I have composed the following epigram on him:

'Farewell, remember my sayings.' Thus spake at his death Epicurus,
These the last words as he died spake he aloud to his friends.
Then in a hot bath he laid him, a goblet of wine he demanded,
Quaffed it, and soon the cold air quaffed he of Hades below.

Such was Epicurus' life and such his death.

His will was as follows:

EPICURUS' WILL

I hereby leave all my possessions to Amynomachus, son of Philocrates, of the deme of Bate, and Timocrates, son of Demetrius, of the deme of Potamos, according to the form of gift to each registered in the Metroum, on condition that they make over the garden and all that goes with it to Hermarchus, son of Agemortus, of Mytilene, and to those who study philosophy with him and to those whom Hermarchus may leave as his successors in the school, for them to live there in the pursuit of philosophy. And to those who hereafter follow my philosophy I assign the right to live in the garden, that they may assist Amynomachus and Timocrates to maintain it to the best of their power, and to their heirs, in whatever way may give the securest possession, that they too may preserve the garden, and after them those to whom the disciples of my school may hand it on.

The house in Melite Amynomachus and Timocrates shall assign for a dwelling to Hermarchus and to those who study philosophy with him, as long as Hermarchus shall live.

The income of the property left by me to Amynomachus and Timocrates shall be divided by them as far as possible, with the advice of Hermarchus, for the offerings in honour of my father and mother and brothers, and for the customary celebration of my birthday every year on the tenth of Gamelion, and likewise for the assembly of my disciples which takes place on the twentieth of each month, having been established in recollection of myself and Metrodorus. Let them also keep the day of my brothers in Poseideon and the day of Polyaenus in Metageitnion, as I have done myself.

Amynomachus and Timocrates shall take care of Epicurus, the son of Metrodorus, and of the son of Polyaenus, provided they devote themselves to philosophy and live with Hermarchus. Likewise they shall take care of Metrodorus' daughter, and when she comes of age shall give her in marriage to one of his disciples whom Hermarchus shall choose, provided she is well-behaved and obedient to Hermarchus.

Amynomachus and Timocrates shall set aside for the maintenance of these children such sum out of the revenues of my estate as shall seem good to them each year in consultation with Hermarchus.

They shall give Hermarchus authority with themselves over the income, in order that everything may be done in consultation with the man who has grown old with me in the study of philosophy and has been left by me head of the school. The dowry for the girl, when she comes of age, shall be apportioned by Amynomachus and Timocrates, who shall take a suitable sum from the capital with the approval of Hermarchus. They shall also take care of Nicanor, as I have done, to show that those who have studied with me and have met my needs from their own resources and shown me every mark of friendship and elected to grow old with me in the study of philosophy, may not lack for anything that is necessary, as far as lies in my power.

They are to give all the books that belong to me to Hermarchus. And if any mortal chance befall Hermarchus before Metrodorus' children come of age, Amynomachus and Timocrates shall as far as possible provide all that is necessary from the income of my estate, if the children are well-behaved. They shall carefully carry out all my other arrangements, so that each may be fulfilled as far as possible. Of my slaves I set free Mys, Nicias and Lycon, and I also set Phaedrium free.

When he was on the point of death he wrote the following letter to Idomeneus: 'On this truly happy day of my life, as I am at the point of death, I write this to you. The disease in my bladder and stomach are pursuing their course, lacking nothing of their natural severity: but against all this is the joy in my heart at the recollection of my conversations with you. Do you, as I might expect from your devotion from boyhood to me and to philosophy, take good care of the children of Metrodorus.' Such then was his will.

He had many disciples, but among the most distinguished was first Metrodorus, son of Athenaeus (or Timocrates) and Sande, of Lampsacus. From the time when he first came to know Epicurus he never left him, except when he went to his native city for six months, and then he came back. He was a good man in all respects, as Epicurus too bears witness in prologues to his writings and in the third book of his *Timocrates*. Such was his character: his sister Batis he married to Idomeneus, and had for his own mistress Leontion the Athenian hetaera. He was imperturbable in the face of trouble and of death, as Epicurus says in the first book of his *Metrodorus*. They say that he died at the age of fifty-two, seven years before Epicurus, and of this Epicurus gives evidence, since in the will already quoted he makes provision for the care of his children, implying that he had already died. He had also as a disciple Timocrates, Metrodorus' brother, who has been mentioned already, an aimless person. Metrodorus' writings were as follows: Three books *Against the Physicians. About Sensations. To Timocrates. Concerning Magnanimity. About Epicurus' Ill-health. Against the Logicians.* Nine books *Against the Sophists. Concerning the Path to Wisdom. Concerning Change. Concerning Wealth. Against Democritus. Concerning Nobility of Birth.*

There was also Polyaenus, son of Athenodorus, of Lampsacus, a modest and friendly man, as Philodemus and his followers say.

Also Hermarchus, Epicurus' successor, son of Agemortus, of Mytilene, the son of a poor father, and at first a student of rhetoric. His best books are said to be these: twenty-two essays in the form of letters *On Empedocles. On Science. Against Plato. Against Aristotle.* He was a good man and died of paralysis.

Likewise there was Leonteus of Lampsacus and his wife Themista, to whom Epicurus addressed one of his letters.

Also Colotes and Idomeneus, both of Lampsacus. They too were distinguished, as was also Polystratus who succeeded Hermarchus; then followed Dionysius and after him Basilides. Apollodorus the 'King of the Garden' was also famous, and wrote over four hundred volumes. There were also the two Ptolemies of Alexandria, the Black and the White, Zeno of Sidon, a pupil of Apollodorus, a prolific writer, Demetrius called the Laconian, Diogenes of Tarsus who wrote *Selected Lessons,* Orion, and others whom the genuine Epicureans call Sophists.

There were three other Epicuruses, the son of Leonteus and Themista, another, who was a Magnesian, while the fourth was a drill-sergeant.

Epicurus was a very prolific writer and exceeded all others in the bulk of his works, of which there are more than three hundred rolls. There is not in them one single citation from another author: it is all Epicurus' own words. Chrysippus tried to rival him in the amount of his writings, as Carneades tells us, calling him the parasite who fed on Epicurus' books. 'Whenever Epicurus wrote anything Chrysippus felt bound in rivalry to write the equivalent; and this is why he often repeats himself and says whatever occurs to him, and has left a great deal uncorrected in his hurry; moreover, he has so many quotations that his books are filled with them and nothing else, a characteristic which one may observe also in the writings of Zeno and Aristotle.' Such are the numerous and important works of Epicurus, of which the best are the following: 1. *On Nature,* thirty-seven books, 2. *On Atoms and Void,* 3. *On Love,* 4. Epitome of the books *Against the Physicists,* 5. *Against the Megarians,* 6. *Problems,* 7. *Principal Doctrines,* 8. *On Choice and Avoidance,* 9. *On the End,* 10. *On the Criterion,* or *The Canon,* 11. *Chaeredemus,* 12. *On the Gods,* 13. *On Religion,* 14. *Hegesianax,* 15.

On Lives, four books, 16. *On Just Action,* 17. *Neocles,* addressed to Themista, 18. *Symposium,* 19. *Eurylochus,* addressed to Metrodorus, 20. *On Vision,* 21. *On the Corner in the Atom,* 22. *On Touch,* 23. *On Fate,* 24. *On Internal Sensations,* maxims addressed to Timocrates, 25. *Prognostic,* 26. *The Protreptic,* 27. *On Images,* 28. *On Perception,* 29. *Aristobulus,* 30. *On Music,* 31. *On Justice and the other Virtues,* 32. *On Gifts and Gratitude,* 33. *Polymedes,* 34. *Timocrates,* three books, 35. *Metrodorus,* five books, 36. *Antidorus,* two books, 37. *On Disease,* maxims addressed to Mithras, 38. *Callistolas,* 39. *On Royal Power,* 40. *Anaximenes,* 41. *Letters.*

I will now endeavour to expound the doctrines which he sets forth in these works and will put before you three of his letters, in which he has abridged his whole philosophy. I will also give you the *Principal Doctrines,* and a selection from his sayings which seem most worthy of mention. You will thus be able to understand Epicurus from every point of view and could form a judgement on him. The first letter he writes to Herodotus and it deals with Physics; the second is to Pythocles, and it deals with Celestial Phenomena; the third is to Menoeceus, and contains the moral teaching. We must begin with the first letter, but I will first speak briefly about the divisions of his philosophy.

It is divided into three parts, the Canonicon (or Procedure), the Physics and the Ethics. The Canonicon gives the method of approach to the system, and is contained in the work called *The Canon.* The Physics contains all the investigation into nature, and is contained in the thirty-seven books *On Nature* and in an abridged form in the letters. The Ethics deals with choice and avoidance, and is contained in the books *On Lives* and the letters and the book on *The End.* The Epicureans usually group the Canonicon with the Physics and state that it deals with the criterion of truth and the fundamental principles and contains the elements of the system. The Physics deals with creation and dissolution and with nature; the Ethics with things to be chosen or avoided, with the conduct of life and its purpose.

Logic they reject as misleading. For they say it is sufficient for physicists to be guided by what things say of themselves. Thus in *The Canon* Epicurus says that the tests of truth are the sensations and concepts and the feelings; the Epicureans add to these the intuitive apprehensions of the mind. And this he says himself too in the summary addressed to Herodotus and in the *Principal Doctrines.* For, he says, all sensation is irrational and does not admit of memory; for it is not set in motion by itself, nor when it is set in motion by something else, can it add to it or take from it. Nor is there anything which can refute the sensations. For a similar sensation cannot refute a similar because it is equivalent in validity; nor a dissimilar a dissimilar, for the objects of which they are the criteria are not the same; nor again can reason, for all reason is dependent upon sensations; nor can one sensation refute another, for we attend to them all alike. Again, the fact of apperception confirms the truth of the sensations. And seeing and hearing are as much facts as feeling pain. From this it follows that as regards the imperceptible we must draw inferences from phenomena. For all thoughts have their origin in sensations by means of coincidence and analogy and similarity and combination, reasoning too contributing something. And the visions of the insane and those in dreams are true, for they cause movement, and that which does not exist cannot cause movement.

The concept they speak of as an apprehension or right opinion or thought or general idea stored within the mind, that is to say a recollection of what has often been presented from without, as for instance 'Such and such a thing is a man': for the moment the word 'man' is spoken, immediately by means of the concept his form too is thought of, as the senses give us the information. Therefore the first signification of every name is immediate and clear evidence. And we could not look for the object of our search, unless we have first known it. For instance we ask 'Is that standing yonder a horse or a cow?': to do this we must know by means of a concept the shape of horse and of cow. Otherwise we could not have named them, unless we previously knew their appearance by means of a concept. So the concepts are clear and immediate evidence.

Further, the decision of opinion depends on some previous clear and immediate evidence, to which we refer when we express it: for instance, How do we know whether this is a man? Opinion they also call supposition, and say that it may be true or false: if it is confirmed or not contradicted, it is true; if it is not confirmed or is contradicted, it is false. For this reason was introduced the notion of the problem awaiting confirmation: for example, waiting to come near the tower and see how it looks to the near view.

The internal sensations they say are two, pleasure and pain, which occur to every living creature, and the one is akin to nature and the other alien: by means of these two choice and avoidance are determined. Of investigations some concern actual things, others mere words. This is a brief summary of the division of their philosophy and their views on the criterion of truth.

Now we must proceed to the letter.

(Here follows the *Letter to Herodotus.*)

Such was his letter on Physics: then follows his letter on Celestial Things.

(Here follows the *Letter to Pythocles.*)

Such was his teaching on things celestial. As regards the principles of living and the grounds on which we ought to choose some things and avoid others, he writes the following letter. But before considering it let us explain what he and his followers think about the wise man. Injuries are done by men either through hate or through envy or through contempt, all of which the wise man overcomes by reasoning. When once a man has attained wisdom, he no longer has any tendency contrary to it or willingly pretends that he has. He will be more deeply moved by feelings, but this will not prove an obstacle to wisdom. A man cannot become wise with every kind of physical constitution, nor in every nation. And even if the wise man be put on the rack, he is happy. Only the wise man will show gratitude, and will constantly speak well of his friends alike in their presence and their absence. Yet when he is on the rack, then he will cry out and lament. The wise man will not have intercourse with any woman with whom the law forbids it, as Diogenes says in his summary of Epicurus' moral teaching. Nor will he punish his slaves, but will rather pity them and forgive any that are deserving. They do not think that the wise man will fall in love, or care about his burial. They hold that love is not sent from heaven, as Diogenes says in his . . . book, nor should the wise man make elegant speeches. Sexual intercourse, they say, has never done a man good, and he is lucky if it has not harmed him.

Moreover, the wise man will marry and have children, as Epicurus says in the *Problems* and in the work *On Nature*. But he will marry according to the circumstances of his life. He will feel shame in the presence of some persons, and certainly will not insult them in his cups, so Epicurus says in the *Symposium*. Nor will he take part in public life, as he says in the first book *On Lives*. Nor will he act the tyrant, or live like the Cynics, as he writes in the second book *On Lives*. Nor will he beg. Moreover, even if he is deprived of his eyesight, he will not end his whole life, as he says in the same work. Also the wise man will feel grief, as Diogenes says in the fifth book of the *Miscellanies*. He will engage in lawsuits and will leave writings behind him, but will not deliver speeches on public occasions. He will be careful of his possessions and will provide for the future. He will be fond of the country. He will face fortune and never desert a friend. He will be careful of his reputation in so far as to prevent himself from being despised. He will care more than other men for public spectacles. He will erect statues of others, but whether he had one himself or not, he would be indifferent. Only the wise man could discourse rightly on music and poetry, but in practice he would not compose poems. One wise man is not wiser than another. He will be ready to make money, but only when he is in straits and by means of his philosophy. He will pay court to a king, if occasion demands. He will rejoice at another's misfortunes, but only for his correction. And he will gather together a school, but never so as to become a popular leader. He will give lectures in public, but never unless asked; he will give definite teaching and not profess doubt. In his sleep he will be as he is awake, and on occasion he will even die for a friend.

They hold that faults are not all of equal gravity, that health is a blessing to some, but indifferent to others, that courage does not come by nature, but by a calculation of advantage. That friendship too has practical needs as its motive: one must indeed lay its foundations (for we sow the ground too for the sake of crops), but it is formed and maintained by means of community of life among those who have reached the fullness of pleasure. They say also that there are two ideas of happiness, complete happiness, such as belongs to a god, which admits of no increase, and the happiness which is concerned with the addition and subtraction of pleasures. Now we must proceed to the letter.

(Here follows the *Letter to Menoeceus.*)

In several works he rejects all kinds of prophecy, and specially in the *Shorter Summary*. He says, 'Prophecy does not exist, and even if it did exist, things that come to pass must be counted nothing to us'. So much for his theory of morals, which he has discussed more fully elsewhere.

Epicurus differs from the Cyrenaics about pleasure. For they do not admit static pleasure, but only that which consists in motion. But Epicurus admits both kinds both in the soul and in the body, as he says in the work on *Choice and Avoidance* and in the book on *The End of Life* and in the first book *On Lives* and in the letter to his friends in Mytilene. Similarly, Diogenes in the 17th book of *Miscellanies* and Metrodorus in the *Timocrates* speak thus: 'Pleasure can be thought of both as consisting in motion and as static'. And Epicurus in the work *On Choice* speaks as follows: 'Freedom from trouble in the mind and from pain in the body are static pleasures, but joy and exultation are considered as active pleasures involving motion'.

A further difference from the Cyrenaics: they thought that bodily pains were worse than those of the soul, and pointed out that offences are visited by bodily punishment. But Epicurus held that the pains of the soul are worse: for the flesh is only troubled for the moment, but the soul for past, present, and future. In the same way the pleasures of the soul are greater. As proof that pleasure is the end he points out that all living creatures as soon as they are born take delight in pleasure, but resist pain by a natural impulse apart from reason. Therefore we avoid pain by instinct, just as Heracles, when he is being devoured by the shirt of Nessus, cries aloud,

With tears and groans: the rocks re-echoed far
From Locris' mountain peaks, Euboea's hills.

[Sophocles, *The Trachinian Women*, 787-788]

He says that virtue is preferred for the sake of pleasure, and not for its own sake, just as the doctor's art is employed for the sake of health. So Diogenes says too in the 20th book of *Miscellanies*, and he adds that education is a 'way of life'. Epicurus says also that virtue alone is inseparable from pleasure, but that other things may be separated, such as things to eat.

Come, then, let us put the crown, as it were, to the whole work and to the life of our philosopher, in setting out his *Principal Doctrines* and closing the whole work with them, thus using as our conclusion the starting-point of happiness.

NOTES

I. The Letter to Herodotus.

Herodotus, about whom we have no information, save that he was a disciple of Epicurus, and wrote a treatise on his master's youth, receives in the letter a compact digest of the principal theories of Epicureanism. It is by no means intended for the neophyte, but much rather for the well-advanced student of the system, and is marked by a profusion of technical terms and references, which makes the letter somewhat difficult to understand. However, it is most valuable for our knowledge of Epicurus' philosophy, and should prove most interesting to read after having completed a study of Lucretius' *De Rerum Natura.*

[1] There is some doubt as to whether this paragraph is in its proper position in the letter. Bailey prefers to keep it here on the ground that it treats material somewhat relevant to the discussion of the motion of the atoms which follows immediately.

II. The Letter to Pythocles.

This letter, which is somewhat disjointed in structure, is interesting primarily because it gives us additional information on the Epicurean views with respect to natural phenomena, over and above that which is contained in the sixth book of Lucretius' poem. The confused character of the letter has frequently called its authenticity into question. For Pythocles, a favourite disciple of Epicurus, cf. Bailey, pp. 275-276.

[1] Bailey points out that probably several lines have been lost here.

III. The Letter to Menoeceus.

In distinct contrast to the *Letter to Herodotus,* the *Letter to Menoeceus* is a carefully composed and lucid exposition of the Epicurean moral theory, not intended for the professional philosopher, but for the ordinary 'layman'. As Bailey indicates, the master, in writing to his disciple Menoeceus, repeats the well-known Epicurean attitude with regard to the importance of (a) 'the right understanding of the nature of the gods', and (b) 'the freedom from the fear of death' for the moral life. The letter concludes with a clear statement of the place and meaning of pleasure in the Epicurean system.

IV. Principal Doctrines.

The series of sayings, known as the *Principal Doctrines,* deal, as Bailey says, 'with Epicurus' ethical theory, and in particular with the conditions requisite for the tranquil life of the Epicurean philosopher'. Their genuineness has been frequently attacked. For a summary of the arguments pro and con, cf. Bailey, *Epicurus,* pp. 344-347, who declares for their authenticity.

V. Fragments.

The first collection derives from a Vatican MS. discovered and published near the close of the nineteenth century. Several of them coincide with selections from the principal doctrines and practically all treat the Epicurean moral theory. A number of the passages probably come not from Epicurus himself but from his immediate disciples. The remaining fragments are in the majority from Usener's *Epicurea,* to which have been added some from other sources.

The following table shows the coincidences between the *Vatican Collection* and the *Principal Doctrines*:

Vatican Collection		*Principal Doctrines*
I	=	I
II	=	II
III	=	IV
V	=	V
VI	=	XXXV
VIII	=	XV
XII	=	XVII
XIII	=	XXVII
XX	=	XXIX
XXII	=	XIX
XLIX	=	XII
L	=	VIII
LXXII	=	XIII

Of the remaining fragments, number 47 corresponds to *Vatican Collection* XIV and number 53 to *Vatican Collection* LIV.

[1] These two fragments appear in the MS. as one imperfect sentence. Cf. Bailey, *Epicurus,* p. 384.

VI. Life of Epicurus.

This curious document is the tenth book of the *History of the Philosophers* by Diogenes Laertius, and as has already been pointed out in the General Introduction, included within it the three letters and the *Principal Doctrines*. The *Life* exhibits all the typical characteristics of Diogenes Laertius' extraordinary and in the main uncritical compilations.

[1] The reference is probably, if the MS. text has been properly emended, to the Epicurean festival which took place on the twentieth of each month to commemorate the founder of the system.

LUCRETIUS

On the Nature of Things

(De Rerum Natura)

LUCRETIUS

On the Nature of Things

BOOK I

Mother of the Aeneadae, darling of men and gods, increase-giving Venus, who beneath the gliding signs of heaven fillest with thy presence the ship-carrying sea, the corn-bearing lands, since through thee every kind of living things is conceived, rises up and beholds the light of the sun. Before thee, goddess, flee the winds, the clouds of heaven; before thee and thy advent; for thee earth manifold in works puts forth sweet-smelling flowers; for thee the levels of the sea do laugh and heaven propitiated shines with outspread light. For soon as the vernal aspect of day is disclosed, and the birth-favouring breeze of Favonius unbarred is blowing fresh, first the fowls of the air, O lady, show signs of thee and thy entering in, throughly smitten in heart by thy power. Next the wild herds bound over the glad pastures and swim the rapid rivers: in such wise each made prisoner by thy charms follows thee with desire, whither thou goest to lead it on. Yes, throughout seas and mountains and sweeping rivers and leafy homes of birds and grassy plains, striking fond love into the breasts of all thou constrainest them each after its kind to continue their races with desire. Since thou then art sole mistress of the nature of things and without thee nothing rises up into the divine borders of light, nothing grows to be glad or lovely, fain would I have thee for a helpmate in writing the verses which I essay to pen on the nature of things for our own son of the Memmii, whom thou, goddess, hast willed to have no peer, rich as he ever is in every grace. Wherefore all the more, O lady, lend my lays an everliving charm. Cause meanwhile the savage works of war to be lulled to rest throughout all seas and lands; for thou alone canst bless mankind with calm peace, seeing that Mavors lord of battle controls the savage works of war, Mavors who often flings himself into thy lap quite vanquished by the never-healing wound of love; and then with upturned face and shapely neck thrown back feeds with love his greedy sight gazing. goddess, open-mouthed on thee; and as backward he reclines, his breath stays hanging on thy lips. While then, lady, he is reposing on thy holy body, shed thyself about him and above, and pour from thy lips sweet discourse, asking, glorious dame, gentle peace for the Romans. For neither can we in our country's day of trouble with untroubled mind think only of our work, nor can the illustrious offset of Memmius in times like these be wanting to the general weal. . . . for what remains to tell, apply to true reason unbusied ears and a keen mind withdrawn from cares, lest my gifts set out for you with steadfast zeal you abandon with disdain, before they are understood. For I will essay to discourse to you of the most high system of heaven and the gods and will open up the first beginnings of things, out of which nature gives birth to all things and increase and nourishment, and into which nature likewise dissolves them back after their destruction. These we are accustomed in explaining their reason to call matter and begetting bodies of things and to name seeds of things and also to term first bodies, because from them as first elements all things are.

When human life to view lay foully prostrate upon earth crushed down under the weight of religion, who showed her head from the quarters of heaven with hideous aspect lowering upon mortals, a man of Greece[1] ventured first to lift up his mortal eyes to her face and first to withstand her to her face. Him neither story of gods nor thunderbolts nor heaven with threatening roar could quell: they only chafed the more the eager courage of his soul, filling him with desire to be the first to burst the fast bars of nature's portals. Therefore the living force of his soul gained the day: on he passed far beyond the flaming walls of the world and traversed throughout in mind and spirit the immeasurable universe; whence he returns a conqueror to tell us what can, what cannot come into being; in short on what principle each thing has its powers defined, its deepset boundary mark. Therefore religion is put under foot and trampled upon in turn; us his victory brings level with heaven.

This is what I fear herein, lest haply you should fancy that you are entering on unholy grounds of reason and treading the path of sin; whereas on the contrary often and often that very religion has given birth to sinful and unholy deeds. Thus in Aulis the chosen chieftains of the Danai, foremost of men, foully polluted with Iphianassa's blood the altar of the Trivian maid.[2] Soon as the fillet encircling her maiden tresses shed itself in equal lengths adown each cheek, and soon as she saw her father standing sorrowful before the altars and beside him the ministering priests hiding the knife and her countrymen at sight of her shedding tears, speechless in terror she dropped down on her knees and sank to the ground. Nor aught in such a moment could it avail the luckless girl that she had first bestowed the name of father on the king. For lifted up in the hands of the men she was carried shivering to the altars, not after due performance of the customary rites to be escorted by the clear-ringing bridal song, but in the very season of marriage, stainless maid mid the stain of blood, to fall a sad victim by the sacrificing stroke of a father, that thus a happy and prosperous departure might be granted to the fleet. So great the evils to which religion could prompt!

You yourself some time or other overcome by the terror-speaking tales of the seers will seek to fall away from us. Ay indeed for how many dreams may they now imagine for you, enough to upset the calculations of life and trouble all your fortunes with fear! And with good cause; for if men saw that there was a fixed limit to their woes, they would be able in some way to withstand the religious scruples and threatenings of the seers. As it is, there is no way, no means of resisting, since they must fear after death everlasting pains. For they cannot tell what is the nature of the soul, whether it be born or on the contrary find its way into men at their birth, and whether it perish together with us when severed from us by death or visit the gloom of Orcus and wasteful pools or by divine decree find its way into brutes in our stead, as sang our Ennius who first brought down from delightful Helicon a crown of unfading leaf, destined to bright renown throughout Italian clans of men. And yet with all this Ennius sets forth that there are Acherusian quarters, publishing it in immortal verses; though in our passage thither neither our souls nor bodies hold together, but only certain idols pale in wondrous wise. From these places he tells us the ghost of everliving Homer uprose before him and began to shed salt tears and to unfold in words the nature of things. Wherefore we must well grasp the principle of things above, the principle by which the courses of the sun and moon go on, the force by which every thing on earth proceeds, but above all we must find out by keen reason what the soul and the nature of the mind consist of, and what thing it is which meets us when awake and frightens our minds, if we are under the influence of disease; meets and frightens us too when we are buried in sleep; so that we seem to see and hear speaking to us face to face them who are dead, whose bones earth holds in its embrace. Nor does my mind fail to perceive how hard it is to make clear in Latin verses the dark discoveries of the Greeks, especially as many points must be dealt with in new terms on account of the poverty of the language and the novelty of the questions. But yet your worth and the looked-for pleasure of sweet friendship prompt me to undergo any labour and lead me on to watch the clear nights through, seeking by what words and in what verse I may be able in the end to shed on your mind so clear a light that you can thoroughly scan hidden things.

This terror then and darkness of mind must be dispelled not by the rays of the sun and glittering shafts of day, but by the aspect and the law of nature;[3] the warp of whose design we shall begin with this first principle, nothing is ever gotten out of nothing by divine power. Fear in sooth holds so in check all mortals, because they see many operations go on in earth and heaven, the causes of which they can in no way understand, believing them therefore to be done by power divine. For these reasons when we shall have seen that nothing can be produced from nothing, we shall then more correctly ascertain that which we are seeking, both the elements out of which every thing can be produced and the manner in which all things are done without the hand of the gods.

If things came from nothing, any kind might be born of any thing, nothing would require seed. Men for instance might rise out of the sea, the scaly race out of the earth, and birds might burst out of the sky; horned and other herds, every kind of wild beasts would haunt with changing brood tilth and wilderness alike. Nor would the same fruits keep constant to trees, but would change; any tree might bear any fruit. For if there were not begetting bodies for each, how could things have a fixed unvarying mother? But in fact because things are all produced from fixed seeds, each thing is born and goes forth into the borders of light out of that in which resides its matter and first bodies; and for this reason all things cannot be gotten out of all things, because in particular things resides a distinct power. Again why do we see the rose put forth in spring, corn in the season of heat, vines yielding at the call of autumn, if not because, when the fixed seeds of things have streamed together at the proper time, whatever is born discloses itself, while the due seasons are there and the quickened earth brings its weakly products in safety forth into the borders of light? But if they came from nothing, they would rise up suddenly at uncertain periods and unsuitable times of year, inasmuch as there would be no first-beginnings to be kept from a begetting union by the unpropitious season. No nor would time be required for the growth of things after the meeting of the seed, if they could increase out of nothing. Little babies would at once grow into men and trees in a moment would rise and spring out of the ground. But none of these events it is plain ever comes to pass, since all things grow step by step at a fixed time, as is natural, since they all grow from a fixed seed and in growing preserve their kind; so that you may be sure that all things increase in size and are fed out of their own matter. Furthermore without fixed seasons of rain the earth is unable to put forth its gladdening produce, nor again if kept from food could the nature of living things continue its kind and sustain life; so that you may hold with greater truth that many bodies are common to many things, as we see letters common to different words, than that any thing could come into being without first-beginnings. Again why could not nature have produced men of such a size and strength as to be able to wade on foot across the sea and rend great mountains with their hands and outlive many generations of living men, if not because an unchanging matter has been assigned for begetting things and what can arise out of this matter is fixed? We must admit therefore that nothing can come from nothing, since things require seed before they can severally be born and be brought out into the buxom fields of air. Lastly since we see that tilled grounds surpass untilled and yield a better produce by the labour of hands, we may infer that there are in the earth first-beginnings of things which by turning up the fruitful clods with the share and labouring the soil of the earth we stimulate to rise. But if there were not such, you would see all things without any labour of ours spontaneously come forth in much greater perfection.

Moreover nature dissolves every thing back into its first bodies and does not annihilate things. For if aught were mortal in all its parts alike, the thing in a moment would be snatched away to destruction from before our eyes; since no force would be needed to produce disruption among its parts and undo their fastenings. Whereas in fact, as all things consist of an imperishable seed, nature suffers the destruction of nothing to be seen, until a force has encountered it sufficient to dash things to pieces by a blow or to pierce through the void places within them and break them up. Again if time, whenever it makes away with things through age, utterly destroys them eating up all their matter, out of what does Venus bring back into the light of life the race of living things each after its kind, or, when they are brought back, out of what does earth manifold in works give them nourishment and increase, furnishing them with food each after its kind? Out of what do its own native fountains and extraneous rivers from far and wide keep full the sea? Out of what does ether feed the stars? For infinite time gone by and lapse of days must have eaten up all things which are of mortal body. Now if in that period of time gone by those things have existed, of which this sum of things is composed and recruited, they are possessed no doubt of an imperishable body, and cannot therefore any of them return to nothing. Again the same force and cause would destroy all things without distinction, unless everlasting matter held them together, matter more or less closely linked in mutual entanglement: a touch in sooth would be sufficient cause of death, inasmuch as any amount of force must of course undo the texture of things in which no parts at all were of an everlasting body. But in fact, because the fastenings of first-beginnings one with the other are unlike and matter is everlasting, things continue with body uninjured, until a force is found to encounter them strong enough to overpower the texture of each. A thing therefore never returns to nothing, but all things after disruption go back into the first bodies of matter. Lastly rains die, when father ether has tumbled them into the lap of mother earth; but then goodly crops spring up and boughs are green with leaves upon the trees, trees themselves grow and are laden with fruit; by them in turn our race and the race of wild beasts are fed, by them we see glad towns teem with children and the leafy forests ring on all sides with the song of new birds; through them cattle wearied with their load of fat lay their bodies down about the glad pastures and the white milky stream pours from the distended udders; through them a new brood with weakly limbs frisks and gambols over the soft grass, rapt in their young hearts with the pure new milk None of the things therefore which seem to be lost is utterly lost, since nature replenishes one thing out of another and does not suffer any thing to be begotten, before she has been recruited by the death of some other.

Now mark me: since I have taught that things cannot be born from nothing, cannot when begotten be brought back to nothing, that you may not haply yet begin in any shape to mistrust my words, because the first-beginnings of things cannot be seen by the eyes, take moreover this list of bodies which you must yourself admit are in the number of things and cannot be seen. First of all the force of the wind when aroused beats on the harbours and whelms huge ships and scatters clouds; sometimes in swift whirling eddy it scours the plains and straws them with large trees and scourges the mountain summits with forest-rending blasts: so fiercely does the wind rave with a shrill howling and rage with threatening roar. Winds therefore sure enough are unseen bodies which sweep the seas, the lands, ay and the clouds of heaven, tormenting them and catching them up in sudden whirls. On they stream and spread destruction abroad in just the same way as the soft liquid nature of water, when all at once it is borne along in an overflowing stream, and a great downfall of water from the high hills augments it with copious rains, flinging together fragments of forests and entire trees; nor can the strong bridges sustain the sudden force of coming water: in such wise turbid with much rain the river dashes upon the piers with mighty force: makes havoc with loud noise and rolls under its eddies huge stones: wherever aught opposes its waves, down it dashes it. In this way then must the blasts of wind as well move on, and when they like a mighty stream have borne down in any direction, they push things before them and throw them down with repeated assaults, sometimes catch them up in curling eddy and carry them away in swift-circling whirl. Wherefore once and again I say winds are unseen bodies, since in their works and ways they are found to rival great rivers which are of a visible body. Then again we perceive the different smells of things, yet never see them coming to our nostrils; nor do we behold heats nor can we observe cold with the eyes nor are we used to see voices. Yet all these things must consist of a bodily nature, since they are able to move the senses; for nothing but body can touch and be touched. Again clothes hung up on a shore which waves break upon become moist, and then get dry if spread out in the sun. Yet is has not been seen in what way the moisture of water has sunk into them nor again in what way this has been dispelled by heat.

The moisture therefore is dispersed into small particles which the eyes are quite unable to see. Again after the revolution of many of the sun's years a ring on the finger is thinned on the under side by wearing, the dripping from the eaves hollows a stone, the bent ploughshare of iron imperceptibly decreases in the fields, and we behold the stone-paved streets worn down by the feet of the multitude; the brass statues too at the gates show their right hands to be wasted by the touch of the numerous passers by who greet them. These things then we see are lessened, since they have been thus worn down; but what bodies depart at any given time the nature of vision has jealously shut out our seeing. Lastly the bodies which time and nature add to things by little and little, constraining them to grow in due measure, no exertion of the eyesight can behold; and so too wherever things grow old by age and decay, and when rocks hanging over the sea are eaten away by the gnawing salt spray, you cannot see what they lose at any given moment. Nature therefore works by unseen bodies.

And yet all things are not on all sides jammed together and kept in by body: there is also void in things. To have learned this will be good for you on many accounts; it will not suffer you to wander in doubt and be to seek in the sum of things and distrustful of our words. If there were not void, things could not move at all; for that which is the property of body, to let and hinder, would be present to all things at all times; nothing therefore could go on, since no other thing would be the first to give way. But in fact throughout seas and lands and the heights of heaven we see before our eyes many things move in many ways for various reasons, which things, if there were no void, I need not say would lack and want restless motion: they never would have been begotten at all since matter jammed on all sides would have been at rest. Again however solid things are thought to be, you may yet learn from this that they are of rare body: in rocks and caverns the moisture of water oozes through and all things weep with abundant drops; food distributes itself through the whole body of living things; trees grow and yield fruit in season, because food is diffused through the whole from the very roots over the stem and all the boughs. Voices pass through walls and fly through houses shut, stiffening frost pierces to the bones. Now if there are no void parts, by what way can the bodies severally pass? You would see it to be quite impossible. Once more, why do we see one thing surpass another in weight though not larger in size? For if there is just as much body in a ball of wool as there is in a lump of lead, it is natural it should weigh the same, since the property of body is to weigh all things downwards, while on the contrary the nature of void is ever without weight. Therefore when a thing is just as large, yet is found to be lighter, it proves sure enough that it has more of void in it; while on the other hand that which is heavier shows that there is in it more of body and that it contains within it much less of void. Therefore that which we are seeking with keen reason exists sure enough, mixed up in things; and we call it void.

And herein I am obliged to forestall this point which some raise, lest it draw you away from the truth. The waters they say make way for the scaly creatures as they press on, and open liquid paths, because the fish leave room behind them, into which the yielding waters may stream; thus other things too may move and change place among themselves, although the whole sum be full. This you are to know has been taken up on grounds wholly false. For on what side I ask can the scaly creatures move forwards, unless the waters have first made room? again on what side can the waters give place, so long as the fish are unable to go on? Therefore you must either strip all bodies of motion or admit that in things void is mixed up from which every thing gets its first start in moving. Lastly if two broad bodies after contact quickly spring asunder, the air must surely fill all the void which is formed between the bodies. Well, however rapidly it stream together with swift-circling currents, yet the whole space will not be able to be filled up in one moment; for it must occupy first one spot and then another, until the whole is taken up. But if haply any one supposes that, when the bodies have started asunder, that result follows because the air condenses, he is mistaken; for a void is then formed which was not before, and a void also is filled which existed before; nor can the air condense in such a way, nor supposing it could, could it methinks without void draw into itself and bring its parts together.

Wherefore, however long you hold out by urging many objections, you must needs in the end admit that there is a void in things. And many more arguments I may state to you in order to accumulate proof on my words; but these slight footprints are enough for a keen-searching mind to enable you by yourself to find out all the rest. For as dogs often discover by smell the lair of a mountain-ranging wild beast though covered over with leaves, when once they have got on the sure tracks, thus you in cases like this will be able by yourself alone to see one thing after another and find your way into all dark corners and draw forth the truth. But if you lag or swerve a jot from the reality, this I can promise you, Memmius, without more ado: such plenteous draughts from abundant wellsprings my sweet tongue shall pour from my richly furnished breast, that I fear slow age will steal over our limbs and break open in us the fastnesses of life, ere the whole store of reasons on any one question has by my verses been dropped into your ears.

But now to resume the thread of the design which I am weaving in verse: all nature then, as it exists by itself, is founded on two things: there are bodies and there is void in which these bodies are placed and through which they move about. For that body exists by itself the general feeling of mankind declares; and unless at the very first belief in this be firmly grounded, there will be nothing to which we can appeal on hidden things in order to prove anything by reasoning of mind. Then again, if room and space which we call void did not exist, bodies could not be placed anywhere nor move about at all to any side; as we have demonstrated to you a little before. Moreover there is nothing which you can affirm to be at once separate from all body and quite distinct from void, which would so to say count as the discovery of a third nature. For whatever shall exist, this of itself must be something or other. Now if it shall admit of touch in however slight and small a measure, it will, be it with a large or be it with a little addition, provided it do exist, increase the amount of body and join the sum. But if it shall be intangible and unable to hinder any thing from passing through it on any side, this you are to know will be that which we call empty void. Again whatever shall exist by itself, will either do something or will itself suffer by the action of other things, or will be of such a nature as things are able to exist and go on in. But no thing can do and suffer without body, nor aught furnish room except void and vacancy. Therefore beside void and bodies no third nature taken by itself can be left in the number of things, either such as to fall at any time under the ken of our senses or such as any one can grasp by the reason of his mind.

For whatever things are named, you will either find to be properties linked to these two things or you will see to be accidents of these things. That is a property which can in no case be disjoined and separated without utter destruction accompanying the severance, such as the weight of a stone, the heat of fire, the fluidity of water. Slavery on the other hand, poverty and riches, liberty, war, concord, and all other things which may come and go while the nature of the thing remains unharmed, these we are wont, as it is right we should, to call accidents. Time also exists not by itself, but simply from the things which happen the sense apprehends what has been done in time past, as well as what is present and what is to follow after. And we must admit that no one feels time by itself abstracted from the motion and calm rest of things. So when they say that the daughter of Tyndarus was ravished and the Trojan nations were subdued in war, we must mind that they do not force us to admit that these things are by themselves, since those generations of men, of whom these things were accidents, time now gone by has irrevocably swept away. For whatever shall have been done may be termed an accident in one case of the Teucran people, in another of the countries simply. Yes for if there had been no matter of things and no room and space in which things severally go on, never had the fire, kindled by love of the beauty of Tyndarus' daughter, blazed beneath the Phrygian breast of Alexander and lighted up the famous struggles of cruel war, nor had the timber horse unknown to the Trojans wrapt Pergama in flames by its night-issuing brood of sons of the Greeks; so that you may clearly perceive that all actions from first to last exist not by themselves and are not by themselves in the way that body is, nor are terms of the same kind as void is, but are rather of such a kind that you may fairly call them accidents of body and of the room in which they severally go on.

Bodies again are partly first-beginnings of things, partly those which are formed of a union of first-beginnings. But those which are first-beginnings of things no force can quench: they are sure to have the better by their solid body. Although it seems difficult to believe that aught can be found among things with a solid body. For the lightning of heaven passes through the walls of houses, as well as noise and voices; iron grows red-hot in the fire and stones burn with fierce heat and burst asunder; the hardness of gold is broken up and dissolved by heat; the ice of brass melts vanquished by the flame; warmth and piercing cold ooze through silver, since we have felt both, as we held cups with the hand in due fashion and the water was poured down into them. So universally there is found to be nothing solid in things. But yet because true reason and the nature of things constrains, attend until we make clear in a few verses that there are such things as consist of solid and everlasting body, which we teach are seeds of things and first-beginnings, out of which the whole sum of things which now exists has been produced.

First of all then since there has been found to exist a two-fold and widely dissimilar nature of two things, that is to say of body and of place in which things severally go on, each of the two must exist for and by itself and quite unmixed. For wherever there is empty space which we call void, there body is not; wherever again body maintains itself, there empty void no wise exists. First bodies therefore are solid and without void. Again since there is void in things begotten, solid matter must exist about this void, and no thing can be proved by true reason to conceal in its body and have within it void, unless you choose to allow that that which holds it in is solid. Again that can be nothing but a union of matter which can keep in the void of things. Matter therefore, which consists of a solid body, may be everlasting, though all things else are dissolved. Moreover if there were no empty void, the universe would be solid; unless on the other hand there were certain bodies to fill up whatever places they occupied, the existing universe would be empty and void space. Therefore sure enough body and void are marked off in alternate layers, since the universe is neither of a perfect fullness nor a perfect void. There are therefore certain bodies which can vary void space with full. These can neither be broken in pieces by the stroke of blows from without nor have their texture undone by aught piercing to their core nor give way before any other kind of assault; as we have proved to you a little before. For without void nothing seems to admit of being crushed in or broken up or split in two by cutting, or of taking in wet or permeating cold or penetrating fire, by which all things are destroyed. And the more anything contains within it of void, the more thoroughly it gives way to the assault of these things. Therefore if first bodies are as I have shown solid and without void, they must be everlasting. Again unless matter had been eternal, all things before this would have utterly returned to nothing and whatever things we see would have been born anew from nothing. But since I have proved above that nothing can be produced from nothing, and that what is begotten cannot be recalled to nothing, first-beginnings must be of an imperishable body into which all things can be dissolved at their last hour, that there may be a supply of matter for the reproduction of things. Therefore first-beginnings are of solid singleness, and in no other way can they have been preserved through ages during infinite time past in order to reproduce things.

Again if nature had set no limit to the breaking of things, by this time the bodies of matter would have been so far reduced by the breaking of past ages that nothing could within a fixed time be conceived out of them and reach its utmost growth of being. For we see that anything is more quickly destroyed than again renewed; and therefore that which the long, the infinite duration of all bygone time had broken up demolished and destroyed, could never be reproduced in all remaining time. But now sure enough a fixed limit to their breaking has been set, since we see each thing renewed, and at the same time definite periods fixed for things each after its kind to reach the flower of their age. Moreover while the bodies of matter are most solid, it may yet be explained in what way all things which are formed soft, as air, water, earth, fires, are so formed and by what force they severally go on, since once for all there is void mixed up in things. But on the other hand if the first-beginnings of things be soft, it cannot be explained out of what enduring basalt and iron can be produced; for their whole nature will utterly lack a first foundation to begin with. First-beginnings therefore are strong in solid singleness, and by a denser combination of these all things can be closely packed and exhibit enduring strength.

Again if no limit has been set to the breaking of bodies, nevertheless the several bodies which go to things must survive from eternity up to the present time, not yet assailed by any danger. But since they are possessed of a frail nature, it is not consistent with this that they could have continued through eternity harassed through ages by countless blows. Again too since a limit of growing and sustaining life has been assigned to things each after its kind, and since by the laws of nature it stands decreed what they can each do and what they cannot do, and since nothing is changed, but all things are so constant that the different birds all in succession exhibit in their body the distinctive marks of their kind, they must sure enough have a body of unchangeable matter also. For if the first-beginnings of things could in any way be vanquished and changed, it would then be uncertain too what could and what could not rise into being, in short on what principle each thing has its powers defined, its deepset boundary mark; nor could the generations reproduce so often each after its kind the nature habits, way of life and motions of the parents.

Then again since there is ever a bounding point to bodies, which appears to us to be a least, there ought in the same way to be a bounding point the least conceivable[4] to that first body which already is beyond what our senses can perceive: that point sure enough is without parts and consists of a least nature and never has existed apart by itself and will not be able in future so to exist, since it is in itself a part of that other; and so a first and single part and then other and other similar parts in succession fill up in close serried mass the nature of the first body; and since these cannot exist by themselves, they must cleave to that from which they cannot in any way be torn. First-beginnings therefore are of solid singleness, massed together and cohering closely by means of least parts, not compounded out of a union of those parts, but, rather, strong in everlasting singleness. From them nature allows nothing to be torn, nothing further to be worn away, reserving them as seeds for things. Again unless there shall be a least, the very smallest bodies will consist of infinite parts, inasmuch as the half of the half will always have a half and nothing will set bounds to the division. Therefore between the sum of things and the least of things what difference will there be? There will be no distinction at all; for how absolutely infinite soever the whole sum is, yet the things which are smallest will equally consist of infinite parts. Now since on this head true reason protests and denies that the mind can believe it, you must yield and admit that there exist such things as are possessed of no parts and are of a least nature. And since these exist, those first bodies also you must admit to be solid and everlasting. Once more, if nature creatress of things had been wont to compel all things to be broken up into least parts, then too she would be unable to reproduce anything out of those parts, because those things which are enriched with no parts cannot have the properties which begetting matter ought to have, I mean the various entanglements, weights, blows, clashings, motions, by means of which things severally go on.

For which reasons they who have held fire to be the matter of things and the sum to be formed out of fire alone, are seen to have strayed most widely from true reason. At the head of whom enters Heraclitus to do battle, famous for obscurity more among the frivolous than the earnest Greeks who seek the truth. For fools admire and like all things the more which they perceive to be concealed under involved language, and determine things to be true which can prettily tickle the ears and are varnished over with finely sounding phrase.

For I want to know how things can be so various, if they are formed out of fire one and unmixed: it would avail nothing for hot fire to be condensed or rarefied, if the same nature which the whole fire has, belonged to the parts of fire as well. The heat would be more intense by compression of parts, more faint by their severance and dispersion. More than this you cannot think it in the power of such causes to effect, far less could so great a diversity of things come from mere density and rarity of fires. Observe also, if they suppose void to be mixed up in things, fire may then be condensed and left rare; but because they see many things rise up in contradiction to them and shrink from leaving unmixed void in things, fearing the steep, they lose the true road, and do not perceive on the other hand that if void is taken from things, all things are condensed and out of all things is formed one single body, which cannot briskly radiate anything from it, in the way heat-giving fire emits light and warmth, letting you see that it is not of closely compressed parts. But if they haply think that in some other way fires may be quenched in the union and change their body, you are to know that if they shall scruple on no side to do this, all heat sure enough will be utterly brought to nothing, and all things that are produced will be formed out of nothing. For whenever a thing changes and quits its proper limits, at once this change of state is the death of that which was before. Therefore something or other must needs be left to those fires of theirs undestroyed, that you may not have all things absolutely returning to nothing, and the whole store of things born anew and flourishing out of nothing. Since then in fact there are some most unquestionable bodies which always preserve the same nature, on whose going or coming and change of order things change their nature and bodies are transformed, you are to know that these first bodies of things are not of fire. For it would matter nothing that some should withdraw and go away and others should be added on and some should have their order changed, if one and all they yet retained the nature of heat; for whatever they produced would be altogether fire. But thus methinks it is: there are certain bodies whose clashings, motions, order, positon, and shapes produce fires, and which by a change of order change the nature of the things and do not resemble fire nor anything else which has the power of sending bodies to our senses and touching by its contact our sense of touch.

Again to say that all things are fire and that no real thing except fire exists in the number of things, as this same man does, appears to be sheer dotage. For he himself takes his stand on the side of the senses to fight against the senses and shakes their authority, on which rests all our belief, ay from which this fire as he calls it is known to himself; for he believes that the senses can truly perceive fire, he does not believe they can perceive all other things which are not a whit less clear. Now this appears to me to be as false as it is foolish; for to what shall we appeal? what surer test can we have than the senses, whereby to note truth and falsehood? Again why should any one rather abolish all things and choose to leave the single nature of heat, than deny that fires exist, while he allows anything else to be? it seems to be equal madness to affirm either this or that.

For these reasons they who have held that fire is the matter of things and that the sum can be formed out of fire, and they who have determined air to be the first-beginning in begetting things, and all who have held that water by itself alone forms things, or that earth produces all things and changes into all the different natures of things, appear to have strayed exceedingly wide of the truth; as well as they who make the first-beginnings of things twofold coupling air with fire and earth with water, and they who believe that all things grow out of four things, fire, earth and air and water. Chief of whom is Agrigentine Empedocles: him within the three-cornered shores of its lands that island bore, about which the Ionian sea flows in large cranklings, and splashes up brine from its green waves. Here the sea racing in its straitened frith divides by its waters the shores of Italia's lands from the other's coasts; here is wasteful Charybdis and here the rumblings of Aetna threaten anew to gather up such fury of flames, as again with force to belch forth the fires bursting from its throat and carry up to heaven once more the lightnings of flame. Now though this great country is seen to deserve in many ways the wonder of mankind and is held to be well worth visiting, rich in all good things, guarded by large force of men, yet seems it to have held within it nothing more glorious than this man, nothing more holy, marvellous and dear. The verses too of his godlike genius cry with a loud voice and set forth in such wise his glorious discoveries that he hardly seems born of a mortal stock.

Yet he and those whom we have mentioned above immeasurably inferior and far beneath him, although, the authors of many excellent and godlike discoveries, they have given responses from so to say their hearts' holy of holies with more sanctity and on much more unerring grounds than the Pythia who speaks out from the tripod and laurel of Phoebus, have yet gone to ruin in the first-beginnings of things: it is there they have fallen, and, great themselves, great and heavy has been that fall; first because they have banished void from things and yet assign to them motions, and allow things soft and rare, air, sun, fire, earth, living things and corn, and yet mix not up void in their body; next because they suppose that there is no limit to the division of bodies and no stop set to their breaking and that there exists no least at all in things; though we see that that is the bounding point of any thing which seems to be least to our senses, so that from this you may infer that because the things which you do not see have a bounding point, there is a least in them. Moreover since they assign soft first-beginnings of things, which we see to have birth and to be of a body altogether mortal, the sum of things must in that case revert to nothing and the store of things be born anew and flourish out of nothing: how wide now of the truth both these doctrines are you will already comprehend. In the next place these bodies are in many ways mutually hostile and poisonous; and therefore they will either perish when they have met, or will fly asunder just as we see, when a storm has gathered, lightnings and rains and winds fly asunder.

Again if all things are produced from four things and all again broken up into those things, how can they be called first-beginnings of things any more than things be called their first-beginnings, the supposition being reversed? For they are begotten time about and interchange colour and their whole nature without ceasing. But if haply you suppose that the body of fire and of earth and air and the moisture of water meet in such a way that none of them in the union changes its nature, no thing I tell you can be then produced out of them, neither living thing nor thing with inanimate body, as a tree; in fact each thing amid the medley of this discordant mass will display its own nature and air will be seen to be mixed up with earth and heat to remain in union with moisture. But first-beginnings ought in begetting things to bring with them a latent and unseen nature in order that no thing stand out, to be in the way and prevent whatever is produced from having its own proper being.

Moreover they go back to heaven and its fires for a beginning, and first suppose that fire changes into air, next that from air water is begotten and earth is produced out of water, and that all in reverse order come back from earth, water first, next air, then heat, and that these cease not to interchange, to pass from heaven to earth, from earth to the stars of ether. All which first-beginnings must on no account do; since something unchangeable must needs remain over, that things may not utterly be brought back to nothing. For whenever a thing changes and quits its proper limits, at once this change of state is the death of that which was before. Wherefore since those things which we have mentioned a little before pass into a state of change, they must be formed out of others which cannot in any case be transformed, that you may not have things returning altogether to nothing. Why not rather hold that there are certain bodies possessed of such a nature, that, if they have haply produced fire, the same may, after a few have been taken away and a few added on and the order and motion changed, produce air; and that all other things may in the same way interchange with one another?

'But plain matter of fact clearly proves' you say 'that all things grow up into the air and are fed out of the earth; and unless the season at the propitious period send such abundant showers that the trees reel beneath the soaking storms of rain, and unless the sun on its part foster them and supply heat, corn, trees, and living things could not grow.' Quite true, and unless solid food and soft water should recruit us, our substance would waste away and life break wholly up out of all the sinews and bones; for we beyond doubt are recruited and fed by certain things, this and that other thing by certain other things. Because many first-beginnings common to many things in many ways are mixed up in things, therefore sure enough different things are fed by different things. And it often makes a great difference with what things and in what position the same first-beginnings are held in union and what motions they mutually impart and receive; for the same make up heaven, sea, lands, rivers, sun, the same make up corn, trees, and living things; but they are mixed up with different things and in different ways as they move. Nay you see throughout even in these verses of ours many elements common to many words, though you must needs admit that the lines and words differ one from the other both in meaning and in sound wherewith they sound. So much can elements effect by a mere change of order; but those elements which are the first-beginnings of things can bring with them more combinations out of which different things can severally be produced.

Let us now also examine the homoeomeria of Anaxagoras as the Greeks term it, which the poverty of our native speech does not allow us to name in our own tongue; though it is easy enough to set forth in words the thing itself. First of all then, when he speaks of the homoeomeria of things, you must know he supposes bones to be formed out of very small and minute bones and flesh of very small and minute fleshes and blood by the coming together of many drops of blood, and gold he thinks can be composed of grains of gold and earth be a concretion of small earths, and fires can come from fires and water from waters, and everything else he fancies and supposes to be produced on a like principle. And yet at the same time he does not allow that void exists anywhere in things, or that there is a limit to the division of things. Wherefore he appears to me on both these grounds to be as much mistaken as those whom we have already spoken of above. Moreover the first-beginnings which he supposes are too frail; if first-beginnings they be which are possessed of a nature like to the things themselves and are just as liable to suffering and death, and which nothing reins back from destruction. For which of them will hold out, so as to escape death, beneath so strong a pressure within the very jaws of destruction? fire or water or air? which of these? blood or bones? Not one methinks, where everything will be just as essentially mortal as those things which we see with the senses perish before our eyes vanquished by some force. But I appeal to facts demonstrated above for proof that things cannot fall away to nothing nor on the other hand grow from nothing. Again since food gives increase and nourishment to the body, you are to know that our veins and blood and bones and the like are formed of things foreign to them in kind;[5] or if they shall say that all foods are of a mixed body and contain in them small bodies of sinews and bones and veins as well and particles of blood, it will follow that all food, solid as well as liquid, must be held to be composed of things foreign to them in kind, of bones that is and sinews and matter and blood mixed up. Again if all the bodies which grow out of the earth, are in the earths, the earth must be composed of things foreign to it in kind which grow out of these earths. Apply again this reasoning to other things, and you may use just the same words. If flame and smoke and ash are latent in woods, woods must necessarily be composed of things foreign to them in kind. Again all those bodies, to which the earth gives food, it increases out of things foreign to them in kind which rise out of the earth: thus too the bodies of flame which issue from the woods, are fed[6] out of things foreign to them in kind which rise out of these woods.

Here some slight opening is left for evasion, which Anaxagoras avails himself of, choosing to suppose that all things though latent are mixed up in things, and that is alone visible of which there are the largest number of bodies in the mixture and these more ready to hand and stationed in the first rank. This however is far banished from true reason. For then it were natural that corn too should often, when crushed by the formidable force of the stone, show some mark of blood or some other of the things which have their nourishment in our body. For like reasons it were fitting that from grasses too, when we rub them between two stones, blood should ooze out; that waters should yield sweet drops, in flavour like to the udder of milk in sheep; yes and that often, when clods of earth have been crumbled, kinds of grasses and corn and leaves should be found to lurk distributed among the earth in minute quantities; and lastly that ash and smoke and minute fires should be found latent in woods, when they were broken off. Now since plain matter of fact teaches that none of these results follows, you are to know that things are not so mixed up in things; but rather seeds common to many things must in many ways be mixed up and latent in things.

'But it often comes to pass on high mountains' you say 'that contiguous tops of tall trees rub together, the strong southwinds constraining them so to do, until the flower of flame has broken out and they have burst into a blaze.' Quite true and yet fire is not innate in woods; but there are many seeds of heat, and when they by rubbing have streamed together, they produce conflagrations in the forests. But if the flame was stored up ready made in the forests, the fire could not be concealed for any length of time, but would destroy forests, burn up trees indiscriminately. Do you now see, as we said a little before, that it often makes a very great difference with what things and in what position the same first-beginnings are held in union and what motions they mutually impart and receive, and that the same may when a little changed in arrangement produce say fires and a fir? just as the words too consist of elements only a little changed in arrangement, though we denote firs and fires with two quite distinct names. Once again, if you suppose that whatever you perceive among visible things cannot be produced without imagining bodies of matter possessed of a like nature, in this way, you will find, the first-beginnings of things are destroyed: it will come to this that they will be shaken by loud fits of convulsive laughter and will bedew with salt tears face and cheeks.

Now mark and learn what remains to be known and hear it more distinctly. Nor does my mind fail to perceive how dark the things are; but the great hope of praise has smitten my heart with sharp thyrsus, and at the same time has struck into my breast sweet love of the Muses, with which now inspired I traverse in blooming thought the pathless haunts of the Pierides never yet trodden by sole of man. I love to approach the untasted springs and to quaff, I love to cull fresh flowers and gather for my head a distinguished crown from spots whence the Muses have yet veiled the brows of none; first because I teach of great things and essay to release the mind from the fast bonds of religious scruples, and next because on a dark subject I pen such lucid verses o'erlaying all with the Muses' charm. For that too would seem to be not without good grounds: just as physicians when they purpose to give nauseous wormwood to children, first smear the rim round the bowl with the sweet yellow juice of honey, that the unthinking age of children may be fooled as far as the lips, and meanwhile drink up the bitter draught of wormwood and though beguiled yet not be betrayed, but rather by such means recover health and strength; so I now, since this doctrine seems generally somewhat bitter to those by whom it has not been handled, and the multitude shrinks back from it in dismay, have resolved to set forth to you our doctrine in sweet-toned Pierian verse and o'erlay it as it were with the pleasant honey of the Muses, if haply by such means I might engage your mind on my verses, till you clearly perceive the whole nature of things, its shape and frame.

But since I have taught that most solid bodies of matter fly about for ever unvanquished through all time, mark now, let us unfold whether there is or is not any limit to their sum; likewise let us clearly see whether that which has been found to be void, or room and space, in which things severally go on, is all of it altogether finite or stretches without limits and to an unfathomable depth.

Well then the existing universe is bounded in none of its dimensions; for then it must have had an outside. Again it is seen that there can be an outside of nothing, unless there be something beyond to bound it, so that that is seen, farther than which the nature of this our sense does not follow the thing. Now since we must admit that there is nothing outside the sum, it has no outside, and therefore is without end and limit. And it matters not in which of its regions you take your stand; so invariably, whatever position any one has taken up, he leaves the universe just as infinite as before in all directions. Again if for the moment all existing space be held to be bounded, supposing a man runs forward to its outside borders, and stands on the utmost verge and then throws a winged javelin, do you choose that when hurled with vigorous force it shall advance to the point to which it has been sent and fly to a distance, or do you decide that something can get in its way and stop it? for you must admit and adopt one of the two suppositions; either of which shuts you out from all escape and compels you to grant that the universe stretches without end. For whether there is something to get in its way and prevent its coming whither it was sent and placing itself in the point intended, or whether it is carried forward, in either case it has not started from the end. In this way I will go on and, wherever you have placed the outside borders, I will ask what then becomes of the javelin. The result will be that an end can nowhere be fixed, and that the room given for flight will still prolong the power of flight. Lastly one thing is seen by the eyes to end another thing; air bounds off hills, and mountains air, earth limits sea and sea again all lands; the universe however there is nothing outside to end.

Again if all the space of the whole sum were enclosed within fixed borders and were bounded, in that case the store of matter by its solid weights would have streamed together from all sides to the lowest point nor could anything have gone on under the canopy of heaven, no nor would there have been a heaven nor sunlight at all, inasmuch as all matter, settling down through infinite time past, would lie together in a heap. But as it is, sure enough no rest is given to the bodies of the first-beginnings, because there is no lowest point at all, to which they might stream together as it were, and where they might take up their positions. All things are ever going on in ceaseless motion on all sides and bodies of matter stirred to action are supplied from beneath out of infinite space. Therefore the nature of room and the space of the unfathomable void are such as bright thunderbolts cannot race through in their course though gliding on through endless tract of time, no nor lessen one jot the journey that remains to go by all their travel: so huge a room is spread out on all sides for things without any bounds in all directions round.

Again nature keeps the sum of things from setting any limit to itself, since she compels body to be ended by void and void in turn by body, so that either she thus renders the universe infinite by this alternation of the two, or else the one of the two, in case the other does not bound it, with its single nature stretches nevertheless immeasurably. But void I have already proved to be infinite; therefore matter must be infinite: for if void were infinite, and matter finite[7] neither sea nor earth nor the glittering quarters of heaven nor mortal kind nor the holy bodies of the gods could hold their ground one brief passing hour; since forced asunder from its union the store of matter would be dissolved and borne along the mighty void, or rather I should say would never have combined to produce any thing, since scattered abroad it could never have been brought together. For verily not by design did the first-beginnings of things station themselves each in its right place guided by keen intelligence, nor did they bargain sooth to say what motions each should assume, but because many in number and shifting about in many ways throughout the universe they are driven and tormented by blows during infinite time past, after trying motions and unions of every kind at length they fall into arrangements such as those out of which this our sum of things has been formed, and by which too it is preserved through many great years when once it has been thrown into the appropriate motions, and causes the streams to replenish the greedy sea with copious river waters and the earth, fostered by the heat of the sun, to renew its produce, and the race of living things to come up and flourish, and the gliding fires of ether to live: all which these several things could in no wise bring to pass, unless a store of matter could rise up from infinite space, out of which store they are wont to make up in due season whatever has been lost. For as the nature of living things when robbed of food loses its substance and wastes away, thus all things must be broken up, as soon as matter has ceased to be supplied, diverted in any way from its proper course. Nor can blows from without hold together all the sum which has been brought into union. They can, it is true, frequently strike upon and stay a part, until others come and the sum can be completed. At times however they are compelled to rebound and in so doing grant to the first-beginnings of things room and time for flight, to enable them to get clear away from the mass in union. Wherefore again and again I repeat many bodies must rise up; nay for the blows themselves not to fail, there is need of an infinite supply of matter on all sides.

And herein, Memmius, be far from believing this, that all things as they say press to the centre of the sum, and that for this reason the nature of the world stands fast without any strokes from the outside and the uppermost and lowest parts cannot part asunder in any direction, because all things have been always pressing towards the centre (if you can believe that anything can rest upon itself); or that the heavy bodies which are beneath the earth all press upwards and are at rest on the earth, turned topsy-turvy, just like the images of things we see before us in the waters. In the same way they maintain that living things walk head downwards and cannot tumble out of earth into the parts of heaven lying below them any more than our bodies can spontaneously fly into the quarters of heaven; that when those see the sun, we behold the stars of night; and that they share with us time about the seasons of heaven and pass nights equal in length to our days. But groundless error has devised such dreams for fools, because they have embraced false principles of reason. For there can be no centre where the universe is infinite; no nor, even if there were a centre, could anything take up a position there any more on that account than for some quite different reason be driven away.[8] For all room and space, which we term void, must through centre, through no-centre alike give place to heavy bodies, in whatever directions their motions tend. Nor is there any spot of such a sort that when bodies have reached it, they can lose their force of gravity and stand upon void; and that again which is void must not serve to support anything, but must, as its nature craves, continually give place. Things cannot therefore in such a way be held in union, o'ermastered by love of a centre.

Again since they do not suppose that all bodies press to the centre, but only those of earth, and those of water, both such as descend to the earth in rain[9] and those which are held in by the earth's body, so to say, the fluid of the sea and great waters from the mountains; while on the other hand they teach that the subtle element of air and hot fires at the same time are carried away from the centre and that for this reason the whole ether round bickers with signs and the sun's flame is fed throughout the blue of heaven, because heat flying from the centre all gathers together there, and that the topmost boughs of trees could not put forth leaves at all, unless from time to time nature supplied food from the earth to each throughout both stem and boughs, their reasons are not only false, but they contradict each other. Space I have already proved to be infinite; and space being infinite matter as I have said must also be infinite[10] lest after the winged fashion of flames the walls of the world should suddenly break up and fly abroad along the mighty void, and all other things follow for like reasons and the innermost quarters of heaven tumble in from above and the earth in an instant withdraw from beneath our feet and amid the commingled ruins of things in it and of heaven, ruins unloosing the first bodies, should wholly pass away along the unfathomable void, so that in a moment of time not a wrack should be left behind, nothing save untenanted space and viewless first-beginnings. For on whatever side you shall first determine first bodies to be wanting, this side will be the gate of death for things, through this the whole crowd of matter will fling itself abroad.

If you will thoroughly con these things, then carried to the end with slight trouble you will be able by yourself to understand all the rest.[11] For one thing after another will grow clear and dark night will not rob you of the road and keep you from surveying the utmost ends of nature: in such wise things will light the torch for other things.

BOOK II

It is sweet, when on the great sea the winds trouble its waters, to behold from land another's deep distress; not that it is a pleasure and delight that any should be afflicted, but because it is sweet to see from what evils you are yourself exempt. It is sweet also to look upon the mighty struggles of war arrayed along the plains without sharing yourself in the danger. But nothing is more welcome than to hold the lofty and serene positions well fortified by the learning of the wise, from which you may look down upon others and see them wandering all abroad and going astray in their search for the path of life, see the contest among them of intellect, the rivalry of birth, the striving night and day with surpassing effort to struggle up to the summit of power and be masters of the world. O miserable minds of men! O blinded breasts! in what darkness of life and in how great dangers is passed this term of life whatever its duration! not choose to see that nature craves for herself no more than this, that pain hold aloof from the body, and she in mind enjoy a feeling of pleasure exempt from care and fear? Therefore we see that for the body's nature few things are needed at all, such and such only as take away pain. Nay, though more gratefully at times they can minister to us many choice delights, nature for her part wants them not, when there are no golden images of youths through the house holding in their right hands flaming lamps for supply of light to the nightly banquet, when the house shines not with silver nor glitters with gold nor do the panelled and gilded roofs reecho to the harp, what time, though these things be wanting, they spread themselves in groups on the soft grass beside a stream of water under the boughs of a high tree and at no great cost pleasantly refresh their bodies, above all when the weather smiles and the seasons of the year besprinkle the green grass with flowers. Nor do hot fevers sooner quit the body, if you toss about on pictured tapestry and blushing purple, than if you must lie under a poor man's blanket. Wherefore since treasures avail nothing in respect of our body nor birth nor the glory of kingly power, advancing farther you must hold that they are of no service to the mind as well; unless may be when you see your legions swarm over the ground of the campus waging the mimicry of war, strengthened flank and rear by powerful reserves and great force of cavalry, and you marshall them equipped in arms and animated with one spirit, thereupon you find that religious scruples scared by these things fly panic-stricken from the mind; and that then fears of death leave the breast unembarrassed and free from care, when you see your fleet swarm forth and spread itself far and wide. But if we see that these things are food for laughter and mere mockeries, and in good truth the fears of men and dogging cares dread not the clash of arms and cruel weapons, if unabashed they mix among kings and kesars and stand not in awe of the glitter from gold nor the brilliant sheen of the purple robe, how can you doubt that this is wholly the prerogative of reason, when the whole of life withal is a struggle in the dark? For even as children are flurried and dread all things in the thick darkness, thus we in the daylight fear at times things not a whit more to be dreaded than those which children shudder at in the dark and fancy sure to be. This terror therefore and darkness of mind must be dispelled not by the rays of the sun and glittering shafts of day, but by the aspect and law of nature.

Now mark and I will explain by what motion the begetting bodies of matter do beget different things and after they are begotten again break them up, and by what force they are compelled so to do and what velocity is given to them for travelling through the great void: do you mind to give heed to my words. For verily matter does not cohere inseparably massed together, since we see that everything wanes and perceive that all things ebb as it were by length of time and that age withdraws them from our sight, though yet the sum is seen to remain unimpaired by reason that the bodies which quit each thing, lessen the things from which they go, gift with increase those to which they have come, compel the former to grow old, the latter to come to their prime, and yet abide not with these. Thus the sum of things is ever renewed and mortals live by a reciprocal dependency. Some nations wax, others wane, and in a brief space the races of living things are changed and like runners hand over the lamp of life.

If you think that first-beginnings of things can lag and by lagging give birth to new motions of things, you wander far astray from the path of true reason: since they travel about through void, the first-beginnings of things must all move on either by their own weight or haply by the stroke of another. For when during motion they have, as often happens, met and clashed, the result is a sudden rebounding in an opposite direction; and no wonder, since they are most hard and of weight proportioned to their solidity and nothing behind gets in their way. And that you may more clearly see that all bodies of matter are in restless movement, remember that there is no lowest point in the sum of the universe, and that first bodies have not where to take their stand, since space is without end and limit and extends immeasurably in all directions round, as I have shown in many words and as has been proved by sure reason. Since this then is a certain truth, sure enough no rest is given to first bodies throughout the unfathomable void, but driven on rather in ceaseless and varied motion they partly, after they have pressed together, rebound leaving great spaces between, while in part they are so dashed away after the stroke as to leave but small spaces between. And all that form a denser aggregation when brought together and rebound leaving trifling spaces between, held fast by their own close-tangled shapes, these form enduring bases of stone and unyielding bodies of iron and the rest of their class, few in number, which travel onward along the great void. All the others spring far off and rebound far leaving great spaces between: these furnish us with thin air and bright sunlight. And many more travel along the great void, which have been thrown off from the unions of things or though admitted have yet in no case been able likewise to assimilate their motions. Of this truth, which I am telling, we have a representation and picture always going on before our eyes and present to us: observe whenever the rays are let in and pour the sunlight through the dark chambers of houses: you will see many minute bodies in many ways through the apparent void mingle in the midst of the light of the rays, and as in never-ending conflict skirmish and give battle combating in troops and never halting, driven about in frequent meetings and partings; so that you may guess from this, what it is for first-beginnings of things to be ever tossing about in the great void. So far as it goes, a small thing may give an illustration of great things and put you on the track of knowledge. And for this reason too it is meet that you should give greater heed to these bodies which are seen to tumble about in the sun's rays, because such tumblings imply that motions also of matter latent and unseen are at the bottom. For you will observe many things were impelled by unseen blows to change their course and driven back to return the way they came now this way now that way in all directions round. All you are to know derive this restlessness from the first-beginnings. For the first-beginnings of things move first of themselves; next those bodies which form a small aggregate and come nearest so to say to the powers of the first-beginnings, are impelled and set in movement by the unseen strokes of those first bodies, and they next in turn stir up bodies which are a little larger. Thus motion mounts up from the first-beginnings and step by step issues forth to our senses, so that those bodies also move, which we can discern in the sunlight, though it is not clearly seen by what blows they so act.

Now what velocity is given to bodies of matter, you may apprehend, Memmius, in few words from this: when morning first sprinkles the earth with fresh light and the different birds flitting about the pathless woods through the buxom air fill all places with their clear notes, we see it to be plain and evident to all how suddenly the sun after rising is wont at such a time to overspread all things and clothe them with his light. But that heat which the sun emits and that bright light pass not through empty void; and therefore they are forced to travel more slowly, until they cleave through the waves so to speak of air. Nor do the several minute bodies of heat pass on one by one, but closely entangled and massed together; whereby at one and the same time they are pulled back by one another and are impeded from without, so that they are forced to travel more slowly. But the first-beginnings which are of solid singleness, when they pass through empty void and nothing delays them from without and they themselves, single from the nature of their parts, are borne with headlong endeavour towards the one single spot to which their efforts tend, must sure enough surpass in velocity and be carried along much more swiftly than the light of the sun, and race through many times the extent of space in the same time in which the beams of the sun fill the heaven throughout. . . .[1] nor follow up the several first-beginnings to see by what law each thing goes on.

But some in opposition to this, ignorant of matter, believe that nature cannot without the providence of the gods in such nice conformity to the ways of men vary the seasons of the year and bring forth crops, ay and all the other things, which divine pleasure the guide of life prompts men to approach, escorting them in person and enticing them by her fondlings to continue their races through the arts of Venus, that mankind may not come to an end. Now when they suppose that the gods designed all things for the sake of men, they seem to me in all respects to have strayed most widely from true reason. For even if I did not know what first-beginnings are, yet this, judging by the very arrangements of heaven, I would venture to affirm, and led by many other circumstances to maintain, that the nature of the world has by no means been made for us by divine power: so great are the defects with which it stands encumbered. All which, Memmius, we will hereafter make clear to you: we will now go on to explain what remains to be told of motions.

Now methinks is the place, herein to prove this point also that no bodily thing can by its own power be borne upwards and travel upwards; that the bodies of flames may not in this manner lead you into error. For they are begotten with an upward tendency, and in the same direction receive increase, and goodly crops and trees grow upwards, though their weights, so far as in them is, all tend downwards. And when fires leap to the roofs of houses and with swift flame lick up rafters and beams, we are not to suppose that they do so spontaneously without a force pushing them up. Even thus blood discharged from our body spirts out and springs up on high and scatters gore about. See you not too with what force the liquid of water spits out logs and beams?

The more deeply we have pushed them sheer down and have pressed them in, many of us together, with all our might and much painful effort, with the greater avidity it vomits them up and casts them forth, so that they rise and start out more than half their length. And yet methinks we doubt not that these, so far as in them is, are all borne downwards through the empty void. In the same way flames also ought to be able, when squeezed out, to mount upward through the air, although their weights, so far as in them is, strive to draw them down. See you not too that the nightly meteors of heaven as they fly aloft draw after them long trails of flames in whatever direction nature has given them a passage? Do you not perceive stars and constellations fall to the earth? The sun also from the height of heaven sheds its heat on all sides and sows the fields with light; to the earth therefore as well the sun's heat tends. Lightnings also you see fly athwart the rains: now from this side now from that fires burst from the clouds and rush about; the force of flame falls to the earth all round.

This point too herein we wish you to apprehend: when bodies are borne downwards sheer through void by their own weights, at quite uncertain times and uncertain spots they push themselves a little from their course: you just and only just can call it a change of inclination.[2] If they were not used to swerve, they would all fall down, like drops of rain, through the deep void, and no clashing would have been begotten nor blow produced among the first-beginnings: thus nature never would have produced aught.

But if haply any one believes that heavier bodies, as they are carried more quickly sheer through space, can fall from above on the lighter and so beget blows able to produce begetting motions, he goes most widely astray from true reason. For whenever bodies fall through water and thin air, they must quicken their descents in proportion to their weights, because the body of water and subtle nature of air cannot retard everything in equal degree, but more readily give way, overpowered by the heavier: on the other hand empty void cannot offer resistance to anything in any direction at any time, but must, as its nature craves, continually give way; and for this reason all things must be moved and borne along with equal velocity though of unequal weights through the unresisting void. Therefore heavier things will never be able to fall from above on lighter nor of themselves to beget blows sufficient to produce the varied motions by which nature carries on things. Wherefore again and again I say bodies must swerve a little; and yet not more than the least possible; lest we be found to be imagining oblique motions and this the reality should refute. For this we see to be plain and evident, that weights, so far as in them is, cannot travel obliquely, when they fall from above, at least so far as you can perceive; but that nothing swerves in any case from the straight course, who is there that can perceive?

Again if all motion is ever linked together and a new motion ever springs from another in a fixed order and first-beginnings do not by swerving make some commencement of motion to break through the decrees of fate, that cause follow not cause from everlasting, whence have all living creatures here on earth, whence, I ask, has been wrested from the fates the power by which we go forward whither the will leads each, by which likewise we change the direction of our motions neither at a fixed time nor fixed place; but when and where the mind itself has prompted? For beyond a doubt in these things his own will makes for each a beginning and from this beginning motions are welled through the limbs. See you not too, when the barriers are thrown open at a given moment, that yet the eager powers of the horses cannot start forward so instantaneously as the mind itself desires? the whole store of matter through the whole body must be sought out, in order that stirred up through all the frame it may follow with undivided effort the bent of the mind; so that you see the beginning of motion is born from the heart, and the action first commences in the will of the mind and next is transmitted through the whole body and frame. Quite different is the case when we move on propelled by a stroke inflicted by the strong might and strong compulsion of another; for then it is quite clear that all the matter of the whole body moves and is hurried on against our inclination, until the will has reined it in throughout the limbs. Do you see then in this case that, though an outward force often pushes men on and compels them frequently to advance against their will and to be hurried headlong on, there yet is something in our breast sufficient to struggle against and resist it? And when too this something chooses the store of matter is compelled sometimes to change its course through the limbs and frame, and after it has been forced forward, is reined in and settles back into its place. Wherefore in seeds too you must admit the same, admit that besides blows and weights there is another cause of motions, from which this power of free action has been begotten in us, since we see that nothing can come from nothing. For weight forbids that all things be done by blows through as it were an outward force; but that the mind itself does not feel an internal necessity in all its actions and is not as it were overmastered and compelled to bear and put up with this, is caused by a minute swerving of first-beginnings at no fixed part of space and no fixed time.

Nor was the store of matter ever more closely massed nor held apart by larger spaces between; for nothing is either added to its bulk or lost to it. Wherefore the bodies of the first-beginnings in time gone by moved in the same way in which now they move, and will ever hereafter be borne along in like manner, and the things which have been wont to be begotten will be begotten after the same law and will be and will grow and will wax in strength so far as is given to each by the decrees of nature. And no force can change the sum of things; for there is nothing outside, either into which any kind of matter can escape out of the universe or out of which a new supply can arise and burst into the universe and change all the nature of things and alter their motions.

And herein you need not wonder at this, that though the first-beginnings of things are all in motion, yet the sum is seen to rest in supreme repose, unless where a thing exhibits motions with its individual body. For all the nature of first things lies far away from our senses beneath their ken; and therefore since they are themselves beyond what you can see, they must withdraw from sight their motion as well; and the more so that the things which we can see, do yet often conceal their motions when a great distance off. Thus often the woolly flocks as they crop the glad pastures on a hill, creep on whither the grass jewelled with fresh dew summons and invites each, and the lambs fed to the full gambol and playfully butt; all which objects appear to us from a distance to be blended together and to rest like a white spot on a green hill. Again when mighty legions fill with their movements all parts of the plains waging the mimicry of war, the glitter then lifts itself up to the sky and the whole earth round gleams with brass and beneath a noise is raised by the mighty trampling of men and the mountains stricken by the shouting reecho the voices to the stars of heaven, and horsemen fly about and suddenly wheeling scour across the middle of the plains, shaking them with the vehemence of their charge. And yet there is some spot on the high hills, seen from which they appear to stand still and to rest on the plains as a bright spot.

Now mark and next in order apprehend of what kind and how widely differing in their forms are the beginnings of all things, how varied by manifold diversities of shape; not that a scanty number are possessed of a like form, but because as a rule they do not all resemble one the other. And no wonder; for since there is so great a store of them that, as I have shown, there is no end or sum, they must sure enough not one and all be marked by an equal bulk and like shape, one with another. Let the race of man pass before you in review, and the mute swimming shoals of the scaly tribes and the blithe herds and wild beasts and the different birds which haunt the gladdening watering spots about river-banks and springs and pools, and those which flit about and throng the pathless woods: then go and take any one you like in any one kind, and you will yet find that they differ in their shapes, every one from every other. And in no other way could child recognise mother or mother child; and this we see that they all can do, and that they are just as well known to one another as human beings are. Thus often in front of the beauteous shrines of the gods a calf falls sacrificed beside the incense-burning altars, and spirts from its breast a warm stream of blood; but the bereaved mother as she ranges over the green lawns knows the footprints stamped on the ground by the cloven hoofs, scanning with her eyes every spot to see if she can anywhere behold her lost youngling: then she fills with her moanings the leafy wood each time she desists from her search and again and again goes back to the stall pierced to the heart by the loss of her calf; nor can the soft willows and grass quickened with dew and yon rivers gliding level with their banks comfort her mind and put away the care that has entered into her, nor can other forms of calves throughout the glad pastures divert her mind and ease it of its care: so persistently she seeks something special and known. Again the tender kids with their shaking voices know their horned dams and the butting lambs the flocks of bleating sheep; thus they run, as nature craves, each without fail to its own udder of milk. Lastly in the case of any kind of corn you like you will yet find that any one grain is not so similar to any other in the same kind, but that there runs through them some difference to distinguish the forms. On a like principle of difference we see the class of shells paint the lap of earth, where the sea with gentle waves beats on the thirsty sand of the winding shore. Therefore again and again I say it is necessary for like reasons that first-beginnings of things, since they exist by nature and are not made by hand after the exact model of one, should fly about with shapes in some cases differing one from the other.

It is right easy for us on such a principle to explain why the fire of lightning has much more power to pierce than ours which is born of earthly pinewood: you may say that the heavenly fire of lightning subtle as it is is formed of smaller shapes and therefore passes through openings which this our fire cannot pass born as it is of woods and sprung from pine. Again light passes through horn, but rain is thrown off. Why? but that those first bodies of light are smaller than those of which the nurturing liquid of water is made. And quickly as we see wines flow through a strainer, sluggish oil on the other hand is slow to do so, because sure enough it consists of elements either larger in size or more hooked and tangled in one another, and therefore it is that the first-beginnings of things cannot so readily be separated from each other and severally stream through the several openings of any thing.

Moreover the liquids honey and milk excite a pleasant sensation of tongue when held in the mouth; but on the other hand the nauseous nature of wormwood and of harsh centaury writhes the mouth with a noisome flavour: so that you may easily see that the things which are able to affect the senses pleasantly, consist of smooth and round elements; while all those on the other hand which are found to be bitter and harsh, are held in connexion by particles that are more hooked and for this reason are wont to tear open passages into our senses and in entering in to break through the body.

All things in short which are agreeable to the senses and all which are unpleasant to the feeling are mutually repugnant, formed as they are out of an unlike first shape; lest haply you suppose that the harsh grating of the creaking saw consists of elements as smooth as those of tuneful melodies which musicians wake into life with nimble fingers and give shape to on strings; or suppose that the first-beginnings are of like shape which pass into the nostrils of men, when noisome carcases are burning, and when the stage is fresh sprinkled with Cilician saffron, while the altar close by exhales Panchaean odours; or decide that the pleasant colours of things which are able to feast the eyes are formed of a seed like to the seed of those which make the pupil smart and force it to shed tears or from their disgusting aspect look hideous and foul. For every shape which gratifies the senses has been formed not without a smoothness in its elements; but on the other hand whatever is painful and harsh, has been produced not without some roughness of matter. There are too some elements which are with justice thought to be neither smooth nor altogether hooked with barbed points, but rather to have minute angles slightly projecting, so that they can tickle rather than hurt the senses; of which class tartar of wine is formed and the flavours of elecampane. Again that hot fires and cold frost have fangs of a dissimilar kind wherewith to pierce the senses, is proved to us by the touch of each. For touch, touch, ye holy divinities of the gods, the body's feeling is, either when an extraneous thing makes its way in, or when a thing which is born in the body hurts it, or gives pleasure as it issues forth by the birth-bestowing ways of Venus, or when from some collision the seeds are disordered within the body and distract the feeling by their mutual disturbance; as if haply you were yourself to strike with the hand any part of the body you please and so make trial. Wherefore the shapes of the first-beginnings must differ widely, since they are able to give birth to different feelings.

Again things which look to us hard and dense must consist of particles more hooked together, and be held in union because welded all through with branch-like elements. In this class first of all diamond stones stand in foremost line inured to despise blows, and stout blocks of basalt and the strength of hard iron and brass bolts which scream out as they hold fast to their staples. Those things which are liquid and of fluid body ought to consist more of smooth and round elements; for the several drops have no mutual cohesion and their onward course too has a ready flow downwards. All things lastly which you see disperse themselves in an instant, as smoke mists and flames, if they do not consist entirely of smooth and round, must yet not be held fast by closely tangled elements, so that they may be able to pierce the body and enter it with biting power, yet not stick together: thus you may easily know, that whatever we see the senses have been able to allay, consists not of tangled but of pointed elements. Do not however hold it to be wonderful that some things which are fluid you see to be likewise bitter, for instance the sea's moisture: because it is fluid, it consists of smooth and round particles, and many rough bodies mixed up with these produce pains; and yet they must not be hooked so as to hold together: you are to know that though rough, they are yet spherical, so that while they roll freely on, they may at the same time hurt the senses. And that you may more readily believe that with smooth are mixed rough first-beginnings from which Neptune's body is made bitter, there is a way of separating these, and of seeing how the fresh water, when it is often filtered through the earth, flows by itself into a trench and sweetens; for it leaves above the first-beginnings of the nauseous saltness, inasmuch as the rough particles can more readily stay behind in the earth.

And now that I have shown this, I will go on to link to it a truth which depends on this and from this draws its proof: the first-beginnings of things have different shapes, but the number of shapes is finite. If this were not so, then once more it would follow that some seeds must be of infinite bulk of body. For in the same seed, in the single small size of any first body you like the shapes cannot vary much from one another: say for instance that first bodies consist of three least parts, or augment them by a few more; when to wit in all possible ways, by placing each in turn at the top and at the bottom, by making the right change places with the left, you shall have tried all those parts of one first body and found what manner of shape each different arrangement gives to the whole of that body, if after all this haply you shall wish still to vary the shapes, you will have to add other parts; it will next follow that for like reasons the arrangement will require other parts, if haply you shall wish still again to vary the shapes. From all this it results that increase of bulk in the body follows upon newness of the shapes. Wherefore you cannot possibly believe that seeds have an infinite variety of forms, lest you force some to be of a monstrous hugeness, which as I have above shown cannot be proved. Moreover I tell you barbaric robes and radiant Meliboean purple dipped in Thessalian dye of shells and the hues which are displayed by the golden brood of peacocks steeped in laughing beauty would all be thrown aside surpassed by some new colour of things; the smell of myrrh would be despised and the flavours of honey, and the melodies of the swan and Phoebean tunes set off by the varied play of strings would in like sort be suppressed and silenced; for something ever would arise more surpassing than the rest. All things likewise might fall back into worse states, even as we have said they might advance to better; for reversely too one thing would be more noisome than all other things to nostril, ear and eye and taste. Now since these things are not so, but a fixed limit has been assigned to things which bounds their sum on each side, you must admit that matter also has a finite number of different shapes. Once more from summer fires to chill frosts a definite path is traced out and in like manner is again travelled back; for every degree of cold and heat and intermediate warmths lie between those extremes, filling up in succession the sum. Therefore the things produced differ by finite degrees, since at both ends they are marked off by points, one at one, another at the other, molested on the one hand by flames, on the other by stiffening frosts.

And now that I have shown this, I will go on to link to it a truth which depends on this and from this draws its proof: the first-beginnings of things which have a like shape one with the other, are infinite in number. For since the difference of forms is finite, those which are like must be infinite or the sum of matter will be finite, which I proved not to be the case, when I showed in my verses that the minute bodies of matter from everlasting continually uphold the sum of things through an uninterrupted succession of blows on all sides. For though you see that some animals are rarer than others and discern a less fruitful nature in them, yet in another quarter and spot and in distant lands there may be many of that kind and the full tale may be made up; just as we see that in the class of four-footed beasts snake-handed elephants are elsewhere especially numerous; for India is so fenced about with an ivory rampart made out of many thousands of these, that its inner parts cannot be reached, so great is the quantity of brutes, of which we see but very few samples. But yet though I should grant this point too: be there even as you will some one thing sole in its kind existing alone with a body that had birth, and let no other thing resemble it in the whole world; yet unless there shall be an infinite supply of matter out of which it may be conceived and brought into being, it cannot be produced, and, more than this, it cannot have growth and food. For though I should assume this point also that birth-giving bodies of some one thing are tossed about in finite quantity throughout the universe, whence, where, by what force and in what way shall they meet together and combine in so vast a sea, such an alien medley of matter? They have methinks no way of uniting; but even as when great and numerous shipwrecks have occurred, the great sea is wont to tumble about banks, rudders, yards, prow, masts and swimming oars, so that poop-fittings are seen floating about along every shore and utter to mortals a warning to try to shun the snares and violence and guile of the faithless sea, and never at any time to trust to it, when the winning face of calm ocean laughs treacherously; thus too if you shall once decide that certain first-beginnings are finite, different currents of matter must scatter and tumble them about through all time, so that they can never be brought into union and combine, nor abide in any union nor grow up and increase. But plain matter of fact shows that each of these results manifestly does take place, that things can be brought into being and when begotten advance in growth. It is clear then that in any class you like the first-beginnings of things are infinite, out of which all supplies are furnished.

Thus neither can death-dealing motions keep the mastery always nor entomb existence for evermore, nor on the other hand can the birth and increase giving motions of things preserve them always after they are born. Thus the war of first-beginnings waged from eternity is carried on with dubious issue: now here now there the life-bringing elements of things get the mastery and are o'ermastered in turn: with the funeral wail blends the cry which babies raise when they enter the borders of light; and no night ever followed day nor morning night that heard not mingling with the sickly infant's cries wailings the attendants on death and black funeral.

And herein it is proper you should keep under seal, and guard, there consigned, in faithful memory this truth, that there is nothing whose nature is apparent to sense, which consists of one kind of first-beginnings; nothing which is not formed by a mixing of seed. And whenever a thing possesses in itself in larger measure many powers and properties, in that measure it shows that there are in it the greatest number of different kinds and varied shapes of first-beginnings. First of all the earth has in her first bodies out of which springs rolling coolness along replenish without fail the boundless sea, she has bodies out of which fires rise up; for in many spots the earth's crust is on fire and burns, though headstrong Aetna rages with fire of surpassing force. Then too she has bodies out of which she can raise for mankind goodly crops and joyous trees, out of which too she can supply to the mountain-ranging race of wild beasts rivers, leaves, and glad pastures. Wherefore she has alone been named great mother of gods and mother of beasts and parent of our body.

Of her the old and learned poets of the Greeks have sung, that borne aloft on high raised [3] seat in a chariot she drives a pair of lions, teaching that the great earth hangs in the expanse of air and that earth cannot rest on earth. To her chariot they have yoked wild beasts, because a brood however savage ought to be tamed and softened by the kind offices of parents. They have encircled the top of her head with a mural crown, because fortified in choice positions she sustains towns; adorned with which emblem the image of the divine mother is carried now-a-days through wide lands in awe-inspiring state. Her different nations after old-established ritual term Idaean mother, and give for escort Phrygian bands, because they tell that from those lands corn first began to be produced throughout the world. They assign her Galli,[4] because they would show by this type that they who have done violence to the divinity of the mother and have proved ungrateful to their parents, are to be deemed unworthy to bring a living offspring into the borders of light. Tight-stretched tambourines and hollow cymbals resound all round to the stroke of their open hands, and horns menace with hoarse-sounding music, and the hollow pipe stirs their minds in Phrygian mood. They carry weapons before them, emblems of furious rage, meet to fill the thankless souls and godless breasts of the rabble with terror for the divinity of the goddess. Therefore when first borne in procession through great cities she mutely enriches mortals with a blessing not expressed in words, they strew all her path with brass and silver presenting her with bounteous alms, and scatter over her a snow-shower of roses, o'ershadowing the mother and her troops of attendants. Here an armed band to which the Greeks give the name of Phrygian Curetes, in that it haply joins in the game of arms and springs up in measure all dripping with blood, shaking with its nodding the frightful crests upon the head, represents the Dictaean Curetes who, as the story is, erst drowned in Crete that infant cry of Jove, when the young band about the young babe in rapid dance arms in hand to measured tread beat brass on brass, that Saturn might not get him to consign to his devouring jaws and stab the mother to the heart with a never-healing wound. For these reasons they escort in arms the great mother, or else because they mean by this sign that the goddess preaches to men to be willing with arms and valour to defend their country and be ready to be a safeguard and an ornament to their parents. All which, well and beautifully as it is set forth and told, is yet widely removed from true reason. For the nature of gods must ever in itself of necessity enjoy immortality together with supreme of repose, far removed and withdrawn from our concerns; since exempt from every pain, exempt from all dangers, strong in its own resources, not wanting aught of us, it is neither gained by favours nor moved by anger. And here if any one thinks proper to call the sea Neptune and corn Ceres and chooses rather to misuse the name of Bacchus than to utter the term that belongs to that liquor, let us allow him to declare that the earth is mother of the gods, if he only forbear in earnest to stain his mind with foul religion. The earth however is at all time without feeling, and because it receives into it the first-beginnings of many things, it brings them forth in many ways into the light of the sun.

And so the woolly flocks and the martial breed of horses and horned herds, though often cropping the grass from one field beneath the same canopy of heaven and slaking their thirst from one stream of water, yet have all their life a dissimilar appearance and retain the nature of their parents and severally imitate their ways each after its kind: so great is the diversity of matter in any kind of herbage, so great in every river. And hence too any one you please out of the whole number of living creatures is made up of bones, blood, veins, heat, moisture, flesh, sinews; and these things again differ widely from one another and are composed of first-beginnings of unlike shape. Furthermore whatever things are set on fire and burned, store up in their body, if nothing else, at least those particles, out of which they may radiate fire and send out light and make sparks fly and scatter embers all about. If you will go over all other things by a like process of reasoning, you will thus find that they conceal in their body the seeds of many things and contain elements of various shapes. Again you see many things to which are given at once both colour and taste together with smell; especially those many offerings which are burned on the altars.[5] These must therefore be made up of elements of different shapes; for smell enters in where colour passes not into the frame, colour too in one way, taste in another makes its entrance into the senses; so that you know they differ in the shapes of their first elements. Therefore unlike forms unite into one mass and things are made up of a mixture of seed. Throughout moreover these very verses of ours you see many elements common to many words, though yet you must admit that the verses and words one with another are different and composed of different elements; not that but few letters which are in common run through them or that no two words or verses one with another are made up entirely of the same, but because as a rule they do not all resemble one the other. Thus also though in other things there are many first-beginnings common to many things, yet they can make up one with the other a quite dissimilar whole; so that men and corn and joyous trees may fairly be said to consist of different elements.

And yet we are not to suppose that all things can be joined together in all ways; for then you would see prodigies produced on all hands, forms springing up half man half beast and sometimes tall boughs sprouting from the living body, and many limbs of land-creatures joined with those of sea-animals, nature too throughout the all-bearing lands feeding chimeras which breathed flames from noisome mouth. It is plain however that nothing of the sort is done, since we see that all things produced from fixed seeds and a fixed mother can in growing preserve the marks of their kind. This you are to know must take place after a fixed law. For the particles suitable for each thing from all kinds of food when inside the body pass into the frame and joining on produce the appropriate motions; but on the other hand we see nature throw out on the earth those that are alien, and many things with their unseen bodies fly out of the body impelled by blows: those I mean which have not been able to join on to any part nor when inside to feel in unison with and adopt the vital motions. But lest you haply suppose that living things alone are bound by these conditions, such a law keeps all things within their limits. For even as things begotten are in their whole nature all unlike one the other, thus each must consist of first-beginnings of unlike shape; not that a scanty number are possessed of a like form, but because as a rule they do not all resemble one the other. Again since the seeds differ, there must be a difference in the spaces between, the passages, the connexions, the weights, the blows, the clashings, the motions; all which not only disjoin living bodies, but hold apart the lands and the whole sea, and keep all heaven away from the earth.

Now mark, and apprehend precepts amassed by my welcome toil, lest haply you deem that those things which you see with your eyes to be bright, because white are formed of white principles, or that the things which are black are born from black seed; or that things which are steeped in any other colour, bear that colour because the bodies of matter are dyed with a colour like to it. For the bodies of matter have no colour at all either like to the things or unlike. But if haply it seems to you that no impression of the mind can throw itself into these bodies, you wander far astray. For since men born blind who have never beheld the light of the sun, yet recognise bodies by touch, though linked with no colour for them from their first birth, you are to know that bodies can fall under the ken of our mind too, though stained with no colour. Again whatever things we ourselves touch in the thick darkness, we do not perceive to be dyed with any colour. And since I prove that this is the case, I will now show that there are things which are possessed of no colour.[6] Well, any colour without any exception changes into any other; and this first-beginnings ought in no wise to do: something unchangeable must remain over, that all things be not utterly reduced to nothing. For whenever a thing changes and quits its proper limits, at once this change of state is the death of that which was before. Therefore mind not to dye with colour the seeds of things, that you may not have all things altogether returning to nothing.

Moreover if no quality of colour is assigned to first-beginnings and they are yet possessed of varied shapes out of which they beget colours of every kind and change them about by reason that it makes a great difference with what other seeds and in what position the seeds are severally held in union and what motions they mutually impart and receive, you can explain at once with the greatest ease why those things which just before were of a black colour, may become all at once of marble whiteness; as the sea, when mighty winds have stirred up its waters, is changed into white waves of the brightness of marble: you may say that when the matter of that which we often see to be black, has been mixed up anew and the arrangement of its first-beginnings has been changed and some have been added and some been taken away, the immediate result is that it appears bright and white. But if the waters of the sea consisted of azure seeds, they could in no wise become white; for however much you jumble together seeds which are azure, they can never pass into a marble colour. But if the seeds which make up the one unmixed brightness of the sea are dyed some with one, some with other colours, just as often out of different forms and varied shapes something square and of a uniform figure is made up, in that case it were natural that as we see unlike forms contained in the square, so we should see in the water of the sea or in any other one and unmixed brightness colours widely unlike and different to one another. Moreover the unlike figures do not in the least hinder or prevent the whole figure from being a square on the outside; but the various colours of things are a let and hindrance to the whole things being of a uniform brightness.

Then too the reason which leads and draws us on sometimes to assign colours to the first-beginnings of things, falls to the ground, since white things are not produced from white, nor those which are black from black, but out of things of various colours. For white things will much more readily rise up and be born from no colour than from a black or any other colour which thwarts and opposes it.

Moreover since colours cannot exist without light and first-beginnings of things do not come out into the light, you may be sure they are clothed with no colour. For what colour can there be in total darkness? nay it changes in the light itself according as its brightness comes from a straight or slanting stroke of light. After this fashion the down which encircles and crowns the nape and throat of doves shows itself in the sun: at one time it is ruddy with the hue of bright pyropus; at another it appears by a certain way of looking at it to blend with coral-red green emeralds. The tail of the peacock when it is saturated with abundant light, changes in like fashion its colours as it turns about. And since these colours are begotten by a certain stroke of light, sure enough you must believe that they cannot be produced without it. And since the pupil receives into it a kind of blow, when it is said to perceive a white colour, and then another, when it perceives black or any other colour, and since it is of no moment with what colour the things which you touch are provided, but rather with what sort of shape they are furnished, you are to know that first-beginnings have no need of colours, but produce sensations of touch varying according to their various shapes.

Moreover since no particular kind of colour is assigned to particular shapes and every configuration of first-beginnings can exist in any colour, why on a like principle are not the things which are formed out of them in every kind o'erlaid with colours of every kind? For then it were natural that crows too in flying should often display a white colour from white wings and that swans should come to be black from a black seed, or of any other different colour you please.

Again the more minute the parts are into which any thing is rent, the more you may perceive the colour fade away by little and little and become extinct; as for instance if a piece of purple is torn into small shreds: when it has been plucked into separate threads, the purple, and the scarlet far the most brilliant of colours, are quite effaced; from which you may infer that the shreds part with all their colour before they come back to the seeds of things.

Lastly since you admit that all bodies do not utter a voice nor emit a smell, for this reason you do not assign to all sounds and smells. So also since we cannot perceive all things with the eyes, you are to know that some things are as much denuded of colour as others are without smell and devoid of sound, and that the keen-discerning mind can just as well apprehend these things as it can take note of things which are destitute of other qualities.

But lest haply you suppose that first bodies remain stripped of colour alone, they are also wholly devoid of warmth and cold and violent heat, and are judged to be barren of sound and drained of moisture, and emit from their body no scent of their own. Just as when you set about preparing the balmy liquid of sweet marjoram and myrrh and the flower of spinkenard which gives forth to the nostrils a scent like nectar, before all you should seek, so far as you may and can find it, the substance of scentless oil, such as gives out no perfume to the nostrils, that it may as little as possible meddle with and destroy by its own pungency the odours mixed in its body and boiled up with it; for the same reason the first-beginnings of things must not bring to the begetting of things a smell or sound of their own, since they cannot discharge anything from themselves, and for the same reason no taste either nor cold nor any heat moderate or violent, and the like. For as these things, be they what they may, are still such as to be liable to death, whether pliant with a soft, brittle with a crumbling, or hollow with a porous body, they must all be withdrawn from the first-beginnings, if we wish to assign to things imperishable foundations for the whole sum of existence to rest upon: that you may not have things returning altogether to nothing.

To come to another point, whatever things we perceive to have sense, you must yet admit to be all composed of senseless first-beginnings: manifest tokens which are open to all to apprehend, so far from refuting or contradicting this, do rather themselves take us by the hand and constrain us to believe that, as I say, living things are begotten from senseless things. We may see in fact living worms spring out of stinking dung, when the soaked earth has gotten putridity after excessive rains; and all things besides change in the same way: rivers, leaves, and glad pastures change into cattle, cattle change their substance into our bodies, and often out of these the powers of wild beasts and the bodies of the strong of wing are increased. Therefore nature changes all foods into living bodies and engenders out of them all the senses of living creatures, much in the same way as she dissolves dry woods into flames and converts all things into fires. Now do you see that it is of great moment in what sort of arrangement the first-beginnings of things are severally placed and with what others they are mixed up, when they impart and receive motions?

Then again what is that which strikes your mind, affects that mind and constrains it to give utterance to many different thoughts, to save you from believing that the sensible is begotten out of senseless things? Sure enough it is because stones and wood and earth however mixed together are yet unable to produce vital sense. This therefore it will be well to remember herein, that I do not assert that the sensible and sensations are forthwith begotten out of all elements without exception which produce things; but that it is of great moment first how minute the particles are which make up the sensible thing and then what shape they possess and what in short they are in their motions, arrangements and positions. None of which conditions we find in woods and clods; and yet even these when they have so to speak become rotten through the rains, bring forth worms, because bodies of matter driven from their ancient arrangements by a new condition are combined in the manner needed for the begetting of living creatures. Next they who hold that the sensible can be produced out of sensible elements, accustomed thus to derive their own sense from elements which are sensible in their turn, do thus render their own seeds mortal,[7] when they make them soft; for all sense is bound up with flesh, sinews and veins; which in everything we see to be soft and formed of a mortal body. But even suppose that these things can remain eternal: they must yet I presume either have the sense of some part or else be deemed to possess a sense similar to the entire living creatures. But the parts cannot possibly have sense by themselves alone; for all sense of the different members has reference to something else; nor can the hand when severed from us nor any other part of the body whatever by itself maintain sensation. It remains to assume that they resemble the entire living creatures. In this case it is necessary that they should feel the things which we feel in the same way as we do, in order that they may be able in all points to work in concert with the vital sense. How then can they be called first-beginnings of things and shun the paths of death, seeing that they are living things, and that living things are one and the same with mortal things? Nay granting they could do this, yet by their meeting and union they will make nothing but a jumble and medley of living things; just, you are to know, as men, cattle, and wild beasts would be unable to beget any other thing by all their mixing with one another. But if haply they lose from their body their own sense and adopt another, what use was it to assign what is again withdrawn? moreover, the instance to which we had before recourse, inasmuch as we see the eggs of fowls change into living chicks and worms burst forth, when putridity has seized on the earth after excessive rains, you are to know that sensations can be begotten out of no-sensations.

But if haply any one shall say that sense so far may arise from no-sensation by a process of change, or because it is brought forth by a kind of birth, it will be enough to make plain and to prove to him that no birth takes place until a union of elements has first been effected, and that nothing changes without their having been united. Above all senses cannot exist in any body before the nature itself of the living thing has been begotten, because sure enough the matter remains scattered about in air, rivers, earth, and things produced from earth, and has not met together and combined in appropriate fashion the vital motions by which the all-discerning senses are kindled into action in each living thing.

Again a blow more severe than its nature can endure, prostrates at once any living thing and goes on to stun all the senses of body and mind. For the positions of the first-beginnings are broken up and the vital motions entirely stopped, until the matter, disordered by the shock through the whole frame, unties from the body the vital fastenings of the soul and scatters it abroad and forces it out through all the pores. For what more can we suppose the infliction of a blow can do, than shake from their place and break up the union of the several elements? Often too when the blow is inflicted with less violence, the remaining vital motions are wont to prevail, ay, prevail and still the huge disorders caused by the blow and recall each part into its proper channels and shake off the motion of death now reigning as it were paramount in the body and kindle afresh the almost lost senses. For in what other way should the thing be able to gather together its powers of mind and come back to life from the very threshold of death, rather than pass on to the goal to which it had almost run and so pass away?

Again since there is pain when the bodies of matter are disordered by any force throughout the living flesh and frame and quake in their seats within, and as when they travel back into their place, a soothing pleasure ensues, you are to know that first-beginnings can be assailed by no pain and can derive no pleasure from themselves; since they are not formed of any bodies of first-beginnings, so as to be distressed by any novelty in their motion or derive from it any fruit of fostering delight; and therefore they must not be possessed of any sense.

Again if in order that living creatures may severally have sense, sense is to be assigned to their first-beginnings as well, what are we to say of those of which mankind is specifically made? Sure enough they burst into fits of shaking laughter and sprinkle with dewy tears face and cheeks and have the cunning to say much about the composition of things and to enquire next what their own first-beginnings are; since like in their natures to the entire mortals they must in their turn be formed out of other elements, then those others out of others, so that you can venture nowhere to come to a stop: yes, whatever you shall say speaks and laughs and thinks, I will press you with the argument that it is formed of other things performing these same acts. But if we see these notions to be sheer folly and madness, and a man may laugh though not made of laughing things, and think and reason in learned language though not formed of thoughtful and eloquent seeds, why cannot the things which we see to have sense, just as well be made up of a mixture of things altogether devoid of sense?

Again we are all sprung from a heavenly seed, all have that same father, by whom mother earth the giver of increase, when she has taken in from him liquid drops of moisture, conceives and bears goodly crops and joyous trees and the race of man, bears all kinds of brute beasts, in that she supplies food with which all feed their bodies and lead a pleasant life and continue their race; wherefore with good cause she has gotten the name of mother. That also which before was from the earth, passes back into the earth, and that which was sent from the borders of ether, is carried back and taken in again by the quarters of heaven. Death does not extinguish things in such a way as to destroy the bodies of matter, but only breaks up the union amongst them, and then joins anew the different elements with others; and thus it comes to pass that all things change their shapes and alter their colours and receive sensations and in a moment yield them up; so that from all this you may know it matters much with what others and in what position the same first-beginnings of things are held in union and what motions they do mutually impart and receive, and you must not suppose that that which we see floating about on the surface of things and now born, then at once perishing, can be a property inherent in everlasting first bodies. Nay in our verses themselves it matters much with what other elements and in what kind of order the several elements are placed. If not all, yet by far the greatest number are alike; but the totals composed of them are made to differ by the position of these elements. Thus in actual things as well when the clashings, motions, arrangement, position, and shapes of matter change about, the things must also change.

Apply now, we entreat, your mind to true reason. For a new question struggles earnestly to gain your ears, a new aspect of things to display itself. But there is nothing so easy as not to be at first more difficult to believe than afterwards; and nothing too so great, so marvellous, that all do not gradually abate their admiration of it. Look up at the bright and unsullied hue of heaven and the stars which it holds within it, wandering all about, and the moon and the sun's light of dazzling brilliancy: if all these things were now for the first time, if I say they were now suddenly presented to mortals beyond all expectation, what could have been named that would be more marvellous than these things, or that nations beforehand would less venture to believe could be? Nothing, methinks: so wondrous strange had been this sight. Yet how little, you know, wearied as all are to satiety with seeing, any one now cares to look up into heaven's glittering quarters! Cease therefore to be dismayed by the mere novelty and so to reject reason from your mind with loathing: weigh the questions rather with keen judgement and if they seem to you to be true, surrender, or if they are a falsehood, gird yourself to the encounter. For since the sum of space is unlimited outside beyond these walls of the world, the mind seeks to apprehend what there is yonder there, to which the spirit ever yearns to look forward, and to which the mind's immission reaches in free and unembarrassed flight.

In the first place we see that round in all directions, about, above, and underneath, throughout the universe there is no bound, as I have shown and as the thing of itself proclaims with loud voice and as clearly shines out in the nature of bottomless space. In no wise then can it be deemed probable, when space yawns illimitable towards all points and seeds in number numberless and sum unfathomable fly about in manifold ways driven on in ceaseless motion, that this single earth and heaven have been brought into being, that those bodies of matter so many in number do nothing outside them; the more so that this world has been made by nature, just as the seeds of things have chanced spontaneously to clash, after being brought together in manifold wise without purpose, without foresight, without result, and at last have filtered through such seeds as, suddenly thrown together, were fitted to become on each occasion the rudiments of great things, of earth, sea, and heaven and the race of living things. Wherefore again and again I say you must admit that there are elsewhere other combinations of matter like to this which ether holds in its greedy grasp.

Again when much matter is at hand, when room is there and there is no thing, no cause to hinder, things sure enough must go on and be completed. Well then if on the one hand there is so great a store of seeds as the whole life of living creatures cannot reckon up, and if the same force and nature abide in them and have the power to throw the seeds of things together into their several places in the same way as they are thrown together into our world, you must admit that in other parts of space there are other earths and various races of men and kinds of wild beasts.

Moreover in the sum of all there is no one thing which is begotten single in its kind and grows up single and sole of its kind; but a thing always belongs to some class and there are many other things in the same kind. First in the case of living things, most noble Memmius, you will find that in this sort has been begotten the mountain-ranging race of wild beasts, in this sort the breed of men, in this sort too the mute shoals of scaly creatures and all bodies of fowls. Wherefore on a like principle you must admit that earth and sun, moon, sea, and all things else that are, are not single in their kind, but rather in number past numbering; since the deep-set boundary-mark of life just as much awaits these and they are just as much of a body that had birth, as any class of things which here on earth abounds in samples of its kind.

If you well apprehend and keep in mind these things, nature free at once and rid of her haughty lords is seen to do all things spontaneously of herself without the meddling of the gods. For I appeal to the holy breasts of the gods who in tranquil peace pass a calm time and an unruffled existence, who can rule the sum, who hold in his hand with controlling force the strong reins, of the immeasurable deep? who can at once make all the different heavens to roll and warm with ethereal fires all the fruitful earths, or be present in all places at all times, to bring darkness with clouds and shake with noise the heaven's serene expanse, to hurl lightnings and often throw down his own temples, and withdrawing into the deserts there to spend his rage in practising his bolt which often passes the guilty by and strikes dead the innocent and unoffending?

And since the birth-time of the world and first day of being to sea and earth and the formation of the sun many bodies have been added from without, many seeds added all round, which the great universe in tossing to and fro has contributed; that from them the sea and lands might increase and from them heaven's mansion might enlarge its expanse and raise its high vaults far above earth, and that air might rise up around. For all bodies from all quarters are assigned by blows each to its appropriate thing and all withdraw to their proper classes; moisture passes to moisture, from an earthy body earth increases and fires forge fires and ether ether, until nature, parent of things, with finishing hand has brought all things on to their utmost limit of growth. And this comes to pass when that which is infused into the life-arteries is no more than that which ebbs from them and withdraws: at this point the life-growth in all things must stop, at this point nature by her powers checks further increase. For whatever things you see grow in size with joyous increase and mount by successive steps to mature age, take to themselves more bodies than they discharge from themselves, while food is readily infused into all the arteries and the things are not so widely spread out as to throw off many particles and occasion more waste than their age can take in as nourishment. For no doubt it must be conceded that many bodies ebb away and withdraw from things; but still more must join them, until they have touched the utmost point of growth. Then piece by piece age breaks their powers and matured strength and wastes away on the side of decay. For the larger a thing is and the wider, as soon as its growth is stopped, at once it sheds abroad and discharges from it more bodies in all directions round; and its food is not readily transmitted into all its arteries and is not enough, in proportion to the copious exhalations which the thing throws off, to enable a like amount to rise up and be supplied. For food must keep all things entire by renewing them, food must uphold, food sustain all things: all in vain, since the arteries refuse to hold what is sufficient, and nature does not furnish the needful amount. With good reason therefore all things perish, when they have been rarefied by the ebb of particles and succumb to blows from without, since food sooner or later fails advanced age, and bodies never cease to destroy a thing by thumping it from without and to overpower it by aggressive blows. In this way then the walls too of the great world around shall be stormed and fall to decay and crumbling ruin. Yes and even now the age is enfeebled and the earth exhausted by bearing scarce produces little living creatures, she who produced all races and gave birth to the huge bodies of wild beasts. For methinks no golden chain let down to earth from heaven above the races of mortal beings, nor did the sea and waves which lash the rocks produce them, but the same earth bare them which now feeds them out of herself. Moreover she first spontaneously of herself produced for mortals goodly corn-crops and joyous vineyards; of herself gave sweet fruits and glad pastures; which now-a-days scarce attain any size when furthered by our labour: we exhaust the oxen and the strength of the husband-men; we wear out our iron, scarcely fed after all by the tilled fields; so niggardly are they of their produce and after so much labour do they let it grow. And now the aged ploughman shakes his head and sighs again and again to think that the labours of his hands have come to nothing; and when he compares present times with times past, he often praises the fortunes of his sire and harps on the theme, how the men of old rich in piety comfortably supported life on a scanty plot of ground, since the allotment of land to each man was far less of yore than now. The sorrowful planter too of the exhausted and shrivelled vine impeaches the march of time and wearies heaven, and comprehends not that all things are gradually wasting away and passing to the grave, quite forspent by age and length of days.

BOOK III

Thee, who first wast able amid such thick darkness to raise on high so bright a beacon and shed a light on the true interests of life, thee I follow, glory of the Greek race, and plant now my footsteps firmly fixed in thy imprinted marks, not so much from a desire to rival thee as that from the love I bear thee I yearn to imitate thee; for why need the swallow contend with swans, or what likeness is there between the feats of racing performed by kids with tottering limbs and by the powerful strength of the horse? Thou, father, art discoverer of things, thou furnishest us with fatherly precepts, and like as bees sip of all things in the flowery lawns, we, O glorious being, in like manner feed from out thy pages upon all the golden maxims, golden I say, most worthy ever of endless life. For soon as thy philosophy issuing from a godlike intellect has begun with loud voice to proclaim the nature of things, the terrors of the mind are dispelled, the walls of the world part asunder, I see things in operation throughout the whole void: the divinity of the gods is revealed and their tranquil abodes which neither winds do shake nor clouds drench with rains nor snow congealed by sharp frosts harms with hoary fall: an ever cloudless ether o'ercanopies them, and they laugh with light shed largely round. Nature too supplies all their wants and nothing ever impairs their peace of mind. But on the other hand the Acherusian quarters are nowhere to be seen, though earth is no bar to all things being descried, which are in operation underneath our feet throughout the void. At all this a kind of godlike delight mixed with shuddering awe comes over me to think that nature by thy power is laid thus visibly open, is thus unveiled on every side.

And now since I have shown what-like the beginnings of all things are and how diverse with varied shapes as they fly spontaneously driven on in everlasting motion, and how all things can be severally produced out of these, next after these questions the nature of the mind and soul should methinks be cleared up by my verses and that dread of Acheron be driven headlong forth, troubling as it does the life of man from its inmost depths and overspreading all things with the blackness of death, allowing no pleasure to be pure and unalloyed. For as to what men often give out that diseases and a life of shame are more to be feared than Tartarus, place of death, and that they know the soul to be of blood or it may be of wind, if haply their choice so direct, and that they have no need at all of our philosophy, you may perceive for the following reasons that all these boasts are thrown out more for glory's sake than because the thing is really believed. These very men, exiles from their country and banished far from the sight of men, live degraded by foul charge of guilt, sunk in a word in every kind of misery, and whithersoever the poor wretches are come, they yet do offer sacrifices to the dead and slaughter black sheep and make libations to the gods Manes and in times of distress turn their thoughts to religion much more earnestly. Wherefore you can better test the man in doubts and dangers and mid adversity learn who he is; for then and not till then the words of truth are forced out from the bottom of his heart: the mask is torn off, the reality is left. Avarice again and blind lust of honours which constrain unhappy men to overstep the bounds of right and sometimes as partners and agents of crimes to strive night and day with surpassing effort to struggle up to the summit of power,—these sores of life are in no small measure fostered by the dread of death. For foul scorn and pinching want in every case are seen to be far removed from a life of pleasure and security and to be a loitering so to say before the gates of death. And while men driven on by an unreal dread wish to escape far away from these and keep them far from them, they amass wealth by civil bloodshed and greedily double their riches piling up murder on murder; cruelly triumph in the sad death of a brother and hate and fear the tables of kinsfolk. Often likewise from the same fear envy causes them to pine: they make moan that before their very eyes he is powerful, he attracts attention, who walks arrayed in gorgeous dignity, while they are wallowing in darkness and dirt. Some wear themselves to death for the sake of statues and a name. And often to such a degree through dread of death does hate of life and of the sight of daylight seize upon mortals, that they commit self-murder with a sorrowing heart, quite forgetting that this fear is the source of their cares, this fear which urges men to every sin, prompts this one to put all shame to rout, another to burst asunder the bonds of friendship, and in fine to overturn duty from its very base; since often ere now men have betrayed country and dear parents in seeking to shun the Acherusian quarters. For even as children are flurried and dread all things in the thick darkness, thus we in the daylight fear at times things not a whit more to be dreaded than what children shudder at in the dark and fancy sure to be. This terror therefore and darkness of mind must be dispelled not by the rays of the sun and glittering shafts of day, but by the aspect and law of nature.

First then I say that the mind which we often call the understanding, in which dwells the directing and governing principle of life, is no less part of the man, than hand and foot and eyes are parts of the whole living creature. Some however affirm [1] that the sense of the mind does not dwell in a distinct part, but is a certain vital state of the body, which the Greeks call harmonia, because by it, they say, we live with sense, though the understanding is in no one part; just as when good health is said to belong to the body, though yet it is not any one part of the man in health. In this way they do not assign a distinct part to the sense of the mind; in all which they appear to me to be grievously at fault in more ways than one. Oftentimes the body which is visible to sight, is sick, while yet we have pleasure in another hidden part; and oftentimes the case is the very reverse, the man who is unhappy in mind feeling pleasure in his whole body; just as if, while a sick man's foot is pained, the head meanwhile should be in no pain at all. Moreover when the limbs are consigned to soft sleep and the burdened body lies diffused without sense, there is yet a something else in us which during that time is moved in many ways and admits into it all the motions of joy and unreal cares of the heart. Now that you may know that the soul as well is in the limbs and that the body is not wont to have sense by any harmony, this is a main proof: when much of the body has been taken away, still life often stays in the limbs; and yet the same life, when a few bodies of heat have been dispersed abroad and some air has been forced out through the mouth, abandons at once the veins and quits the bones: by this you may perceive that all bodies have not functions of like importance nor alike uphold existence, but rather that those seeds which constitute wind and heat, cause life to stay in the limbs. Therefore vital heat and wind are within the body and abandon our frame at death. Since then the nature of the mind and that of the soul have been proved to be a part as it were of the man, surrender the name of harmony, whether brought down to musicians from high Helicon, or whether rather they have themselves taken it from something else and transferred it to that thing which then was in need of a distinctive name; whatever it be, let them keep it: do you take in the rest of my precepts.

Now I assert that the mind and the soul are kept together in close union and make up a single nature, but that the directing principle which we call mind and understanding, is the head so to speak and reigns paramount in the whole body. It has a fixed seat in the middle region of the breast: here throb fear and apprehension, about these spots dwell soothing joys; therefore here is the understanding or mind. All the rest of the soul disseminated through the whole body obeys and moves at the will and inclination of the mind. It by itself alone knows for itself, rejoices for itself, at times when the impression does not move either soul or body together with it. And as when some part of us, the head or the eye, suffers from an attack of pain, we do not feel the anguish at the same time over the whole body, thus the mind sometimes suffers pain by itself or is inspirited with joy, when all the rest of the soul throughout the limbs and frame is stirred by no novel sensation. But when the mind is excited by some more vehement apprehension, we see the whole soul feel in unison through all the limbs, sweats and paleness spread over the whole body, the tongue falter, the voice die away, a mist cover the eyes, the ears ring, the limbs sink under one; in short we often see men drop down from terror of mind; so that anybody may easily perceive from this that the soul is closely united with the mind, and, when it has been smitten by the influence of the mind, forthwith pushes and strikes the body.

This same principle teaches that the nature of the mind and soul is bodily; for when it is seen to push the limbs, rouse the body from sleep, and alter the countenance and guide and turn about the whole man, and when we see that none of these effects can take place without touch nor touch without body, must we not admit that the mind and the soul are of a bodily nature? Again you perceive that our mind in our body suffers together with the body and feels in unison with it. When a weapon with a shudder-causing force has been driven in and has laid bare bones and sinews within the body, if it does not take life, yet there ensues a faintness and a lazy sinking to the ground and on the ground the turmoil of mind which arises, and sometimes a kind of undecided inclination to get up. Therefore the nature of the mind must be bodily, since it suffers from bodily weapons and blows.

I will now go on to explain in my verses of what kind of body the mind consists and out of what it is formed. First of all I say that it is extremely fine and formed of exceedingly minute bodies. That this is so you may, if you please to attend, clearly perceive from what follows: nothing that is seen takes place with a velocity equal to that of the mind when it starts some suggestion and actually sets it agoing; the mind therefore is stirred with greater rapidity than any of the things whose nature stands out visible to sight. But that which is so passing nimble, must consist of seeds exceedingly round and exceedingly minute, in order to be stirred and set in motion by a small moving power. Thus water is moved and heaves by ever so small a force, formed as it is of small particles apt to roll. But on the other hand the nature of honey is more sticky, its liquid more sluggish and its movement more dilatory; for the whole mass of matter coheres more closely, because sure enough it is made of bodies not so smooth, fine, and round. A breeze however gentle and light can force, as you may see, a high heap of poppy seed to be blown away from the top downwards; but on the other hand Eurus itself cannot move a heap of stones. Therefore bodies possess a power of moving in proportion to their smallness and smoothness; and on the other hand the greater weight and roughness bodies prove to have, the more stable they are. Since then the nature of the mind has been found to be eminently easy to move, it must consist of bodies exceedingly small, smooth, and round. The knowledge of which fact, my good friend, will on many accounts prove useful and be serviceable to you. The following fact too likewise demonstrates how fine the texture is of which its nature is composed, and how small the room is in which it can be contained, could it only be collected into one mass: soon as the untroubled sleep of death has gotten hold of a man and the nature of the mind and soul has withdrawn, you can perceive then no diminution of the entire body either in appearance or weight: death makes all good save the vital sense and heat. Therefore the whole soul must consist of very small seeds and be inwoven through veins and flesh and sinews; inasmuch as, after it has all withdrawn from the whole body, the exterior contour of the limbs preserves itself entire and not a tittle of the weight is lost. Just in the same way when the flavour of wine is gone or when the delicious aroma of a perfume has been dispersed into the air or when the savour has left some body, yet the thing itself does not therefore look smaller to the eye, nor does aught seem to have been taken from the weight, because sure enough many minute seeds make up the savours and the odour in the whole body of the several things. Therefore, again and again I say, you are to know that the nature of the mind and the soul has been formed of exceedingly minute seeds, since at its departure it takes away none of the weight.

We are not however to suppose that this nature is single. For a certain subtle spirit mixed with heat quits men at death, and then the heat draws air along with it; there being no heat which has not air too mixed with it: for since its nature is rare, many first-beginnings of air must move about through it. Thus the nature of the mind is proved to be threefold; and yet these things all together are not sufficient to produce sense; since the fact of the case does not admit that any of these can produce sense-giving motions and the thoughts which a man turns over in mind. Thus some fourth nature too must be added to these: it is altogether without name; than it nothing exists more nimble or more fine, or of smaller or smoother elements: it first transmits the sense-giving motions through the frame; for it is first stirred, made up as it is of small particles; next the heat and the unseen force of the spirit receive the motions, then the air; then all things are set in action, the blood is stirred, every part of the flesh is filled with sensation; last of all the feeling is transmitted to the bones and marrow, whether it be one of pleasure or an opposite excitement. No pain however can lightly pierce thus far nor any sharp malady make its way in, without all things being so thoroughly disordered that no room is left for life and the parts of the soul fly abroad through all the pores of the body. But commonly a stop is put to these motions on the surface as it were of the body: for this reason we are able to retain life.

Now though I would fain explain in what way these are mixed up together, by what means united, when they exert their powers, the poverty of my native speech deters me sorely against my will: yet will I touch upon them and in summary fashion to the best of my ability: the first-beginnings by their mutual motions are interlaced in such a way that none of them can be separated by itself, nor can the function of any go on divided from the rest by any interval; but they are so to say the several powers of one body. Even so in any flesh of living creature you please without exception there is smell and some colour and a savour, and yet out of all these is made up one single bulk of body. Thus the heat and the air and the unseen power of the spirit mixed together produce a single nature, together with that nimble force which transmits to them from itself the origin of motion; by which means sense-giving motion first takes its rise through the fleshly frame. For this nature lurks secreted in its inmost depths, and nothing in our body is farther beneath all ken than it, and more than this it is the very soul of the whole soul. Just in the same way as the power of the mind and the function of the soul are latent in our limbs and throughout our body, because they are each formed of small and few bodies: even so, you are to know, this nameless power made of minute bodies is concealed and is moreover the very soul so to say of the whole soul, and reigns supreme in the whole body. On a like principle the spirit and air and heat must, as they exert their powers, be mixed up together through the frame, and one must ever be more out of view or more prominent than another, that a single substance may be seen to be formed from the union of all, lest the heat and spirit apart by themselves and the power of the air apart by itself should destroy sense and dissipate it by their disunion. Thus the mind possesses that heat which it displays when it boils up in anger and fire flashes from the keen eyes; there is too much cold spirit comrade of fear, which spreads a shivering over the limbs and stirs the whole frame; yes and there is also that condition of still air which has place when the breast is calm and the looks cheerful. But they have more of the hot whose keen heart and passionate mind lightly boil up in anger. Foremost in this class comes the fierce violence of lions who often as they chafe break their hearts with their roaring and cannot contain within their breast the billows of their rage. Then the chilly mind of stags is fuller of the spirit and more quickly rouses through all the flesh its icy currents which cause a shivering motion to pass over the limbs. But the nature of oxen has its life rather from the still air, and never does the smoky torch of anger applied to it stimulate it too much, shedding over it the shadow of murky gloom, nor is it transfixed and stiffened by the icy shafts of fear: it lies between the other two, stags and cruel lions. And thus it is with mankind: however much teaching renders some equally refined, it yet leaves behind those earliest traces of the nature of each mind; and we are not to suppose that evil habits can be so thoroughly plucked up by the roots, that one man shall not be more prone than another to keen anger, a second shall not be somewhat more quickly assailed by fear, a third shall not take some things more meekly than is right. In many other points there must be differences between the varied natures of men and the tempers which follow upon these; though at present I am unable to set forth the hidden causes of these or to find names enough for the different shapes which belongs to the first-beginnings, from which shapes arises this diversity of things. What herein I think I may affirm is this: traces of the different natures left behind, which reason is unable to expel from us, are so exceedingly slight that there is nothing to hinder us from living a life worthy of gods.

Well this nature is contained by the whole body and is in turn the body's guardian and the cause of its existence; for the two adhere together with common roots and cannot it is plain be riven asunder without destruction. Even as it is not easy to pluck the perfume out of lumps of frankincense without quite destroying its nature as well; so it is not easy to withdraw from the whole body the nature of the mind and soul without dissolving all alike. With first-beginnings so interlaced from their earliest birth are they formed and gifted with a life of joint partnership, and it is plain that the faculty of the body and of the mind cannot feel separately, each alone without the other's power, but sense is kindled throughout our flesh and blown into flame between the two by the joint motions on the part of both. Moreover the body by itself is never either begotten or grows or, it is plain, continues to exist after death. For not in the way that the liquid of water often loses the heat which has been given to it, yet is not for that reason itself riven in pieces, but remains unimpaired,—not in this way, I say, can the abandoned frame endure the separation of the soul, but riven in pieces it utterly perishes and rots away. Thus the mutual connexions of body and soul from the first moment of their existence learn the vital motions even while hid in the body and womb of the mother, so that no separation can take place without mischief and ruin. Thus you may see that, since the cause of existence lies in their joint action, their nature too must be a joint nature.

Furthermore if any one tries to disprove that the body feels and believes that the soul mixed through the whole body takes upon it this motion which we name sense, he combats even manifest and undoubted facts. For who will ever bring forward any explanation of what the body's feeling is, except that which the plain fact of the case has itself given and taught to us? But when the soul it is said has departed, the body throughout is without sense; yes, for it loses what was not its own peculiar property in life; ay and much else it loses, before that soul is driven out of it.

Again to say that the eyes can see no object, but that the soul discerns through them as through an open door, is far from easy, since their sense contradicts this; for this sense e'en draws it and forces it out to the pupil: nay often we are unable to perceive shining things, because our eyes are embarrassed by the lights. But this is not the case with doors; for, because we ourselves see, the open doors do not therefore undergo any fatigue. Again if our eyes are in the place of doors, in that case when the eyes are removed the mind ought it would seem to have more power of seeing things, after doors, jambs and all, have been taken out of the way.

And herein you must by no means adopt the opinion which the revered judgement of the worthy man Democritus lays down, that the first-beginnings of body and mind placed together in successive layers come in alternate order and so weave the tissue of our limbs. For not only are the elements of the soul much smaller than those of which our body and flesh are formed, but they are also much fewer in number and are disseminated merely in scanty number through the frame, so that you can warrant no more than this: the first-beginnings of the soul keep spaces between them at least as great as are the smallest bodies which, if thrown upon it, are first able to excite in our body the sense-giving motions. Thus at times we do not feel the adhesion of dust when it settles on our body, nor the impact of chalk when it rests on our limbs, nor do we feel a mist at night nor a spider's slender threads as they come against us, when we are caught in its meshes in moving along, nor the same insect's flimsy web when it has fallen on our head, nor the feathers of birds and down of plants as it flies about, which commonly from exceeding lightness does not lightly fall, nor do we feel the tread of every creeping creature whatsoever nor each particular foot-print which gnats and the like stamp on our body. So very many first-beginnings must be stirred in us, before the seeds of the soul mixed up in our bodies feel that these have been disturbed, and by thumping with such spaces between can clash, unite, and in turn recoil.

The mind has more to do with holding the fastnesses of life and has more sovereign sway over it than the power of the soul. For without the understanding and the mind no part of the soul can maintain itself in the frame the smallest fraction of time, but follows at once in the other's train and passes away into the air and leaves the cold limbs in the chill of death. But he abides in life whose mind and understanding continue to stay with him: though the trunk is mangled with its limbs shorn all round about it, after the soul has been taken away on all sides and been severed from the limbs, the trunk yet lives and inhales the ethereal airs of life. When robbed, if not of the whole, yet of a large portion of the soul, it still lingers in and cleaves to life; just as, after the eye has been lacerated all round if the pupil has continued uninjured, the living power of sight remains, provided always you do not destroy the whole ball of the eye and pare close round the pupil and leave only it; for that will not be done even to the ball without the entire destruction of the eye. But if that middle portion of the eye, small as it is, is eaten into, the sight is gone at once and darkness ensues, though a man have the bright ball quite unimpaired. On such terms of union soul and mind are ever bound to each other.

Now mark me: that you may know that the minds and light souls of living creatures have birth and are mortal, I will go on to set forth verses worthy of your attention, got together by long study and invented with welcome effort. Do you mind to link to one name both of them alike, and when for instance I shall choose to speak of the soul, showing it to be mortal, believe that I speak of the mind as well, inasmuch as both make up one thing and are one united substance. First of all then since I have shown the soul to be fine and to be formed of minute bodies and made up of much smaller first-beginnings than is the liquid of water or mist or smoke:—for it far surpasses these in nimbleness and is moved, when struck by a far slenderer cause; inasmuch as it is moved by images of smoke and mist; as when for instance sunk in sleep we see altars steam forth their heat and send up their smoke on high; for beyond a doubt images are begotten for us from these things:—well then since you see on the vessels being shattered the water flow away on all sides, and since mist and smoke pass away into air, believe that the soul too is shed abroad and perishes much more quickly and dissolves sooner into its first bodies, when once it has been taken out of the limbs of a man and has withdrawn. For, when the body that serves for its vessel cannot hold it, if shattered from any cause and rarefied by the withdrawal of blood from the veins, how can you believe that this soul can be held by any air? How can that air which is rarer than our body hold it in?

Again we perceive that the mind is begotten along with the body and grows up together with it and becomes old along with it. For even as children go about with a tottering and weakly body, so slender sagacity of mind follows along with it; then when their life has reached the maturity of confirmed strength, the judgement too is greater and the power of the mind more developed. Afterwards when the body has been shattered by the mastering might of time and the frame has drooped with its forces dulled, then the intellect halts, the tongue dotes, the mind gives way, all faculties fail and are found wanting at the same time. It naturally follows then that the whole nature of the soul is dissolved, like smoke, into the high air; since we see it is begotten along with the body and grows up along with it and, as I have shown, breaks down at the same time worn out with age.

Moreover we see that even as the body is liable to violent diseases and severe pain, so is the mind to sharp cares and grief and fear; it naturally follows therefore that it is its partner in death as well. Again in diseases of the body the mind often wanders and goes astray; for it loses its reason and drivels in its speech and often in a profound lethargy is carried into deep and never-ending sleep with drooping eyes and head; out of which it neither hears the voices nor can recognise the faces of those who stand round calling it back to life and bedewing with tears, face and cheeks. Therefore you must admit that the mind too dissolves, since the infection of disease reaches to it; for pain and disease are both forgers of death: a truth we have fully learned ere now by the death of many. Again, when the pungent strength of wine has entered into a man and its spirit has been infused into and transmitted through his veins, why is it that a heaviness of the limbs follows along with this, his legs are hampered as he reels about, his tongue falters, his mind is besotted, his eyes swim, shouting, hiccuping, wranglings are rife, together with all the other usual concomitants, why is all this, if not because the overpowering violence of the wine is wont to disorder the soul within the body? But whenever things can be disordered and hampered, they give token that if a somewhat more potent cause gained an entrance, they would perish and be robbed of all further existence. Moreover it often happens that some one constrained by the violence of disease suddenly drops down before our eyes, as by a stroke of lightning, and foams at the mouth, moans and shivers through his frame, loses his reason, stiffens his muscles, is racked, gasps for breath fitfully, and wearies his limbs with tossing. Sure enough, because the violence of the disease spreads itself through his frame and disorders him, he foams as he tries to eject his soul, just as in the salt sea the waters boil with the mastering might of the winds. A moan too is forced out, because the limbs are seized with pain, and mainly because seeds of voice are driven forth and are carried in a close mass out by the mouth, the road which they are accustomed to take and where they have a well-paved way. Loss of reason follows, because the powers of the mind and soul are disordered and, as I have shown, are riven and forced asunder, torn to pieces by the same baneful malady. Then after the cause of the disease has bent its course back and the acrid humours of the distempered body return to their hiding-places, then he first gets up like one reeling, and by little and little comes back into full possession of his senses and regains his soul. Since therefore even within the body mind and soul are harassed by such violent distempers and so miserably racked by sufferings, why believe that they without the body in the open air can continue existence battling with fierce winds? And since we perceive that the mind is healed like the sick body, and we see that it can be altered by medicine, this too gives warning that the mind has a mortal existence. For it is natural that whosoever essays and attempts to change the mind or seeks to alter any other nature you like, should add new parts or change the arrangement of the present, or withdraw in short some tittle from the sum. But that which is immortal wills not to have its parts transposed nor any addition to be made nor one tittle to ebb away; for whenever a thing changes and quits its proper limits, this change is at once the death of that which was before. Therefore the mind, whether it is sick or whether it is altered by medicine, alike, as I have shown, gives forth mortal symptoms. So invariably is truth found to make head against false reason and to cut off all retreat from the assailant and by a two-fold refutation to put falsehood to rout.

Again we often see a man pass gradually away and limb by limb lose vital sense; first the toes of his feet and the nails turn livid, then the feet and shanks die, then next the steps of chilly death creep with slow pace over the other members. Therefore since the nature of the soul is rent and passes away and does not at one time stand forth in its entireness, it must be reckoned mortal. But if haply you suppose that it can draw itself in through the whole frame and mass its parts together and in this way withdraw sense from all the limbs, yet then that spot into which so great a store of soul is gathered, ought to show itself in possession of a greater amount of sense. But as this is nowhere found, sure enough as we said before, it is torn in pieces and scattered abroad, and therefore dies. Moreover if I were pleased for the moment to grant what is false and admit that the soul might be collected in one mass in the body of those who leave the light dying piecemeal, even then you must admit the soul to be mortal; and it makes no difference whether it perish dispersed in air, or gathered into one lump out of all its parts lose all feeling, since sense ever more and more fails the whole man throughout and less and less of life remains throughout.

And since the mind is one part of a man which remains fixed in a particular spot, just as are the ears and eyes and the other senses which guide and direct life; and just as the hand or eye or nose when separated from us cannot feel and exist apart, but in however short a time wastes away in putrefaction, thus the mind cannot exist by itself without the body and the man's self which as you see serves for the mind's vessel or any thing else you choose to imagine which implies a yet closer union with it, since the body is attached to it by the nearest ties.

Again the quickened powers of body and mind by their joint partnership enjoy health and life; for the nature of the mind cannot by itself alone without the body give forth vital motions nor can the body again bereft of the soul continue to exist and make use of its senses: just, you are to know, as the eye itself torn away from its roots cannot see anything when apart from the whole body, thus the soul and mind cannot it is plain do anything by themselves. Sure enough, because mixed up through veins and flesh, sinews and bones, their first-beginnings are confined by all the body and are not free to bound away leaving great spaces between, therefore thus shut in they make those sense-giving motions which they cannot make after death when forced out of the body into the air by reason that they are not then confined in a like manner; for the air will be a body and a living thing, if the soul shall be able to keep itself together and to enclose in it those motions which it used before to perform in the sinews and within the body. Moreover even while it yet moves within the confines of life, often the soul shaken from some cause or other is seen to wish to pass out and be loosed from the whole body, the features are seen to droop as at the last hour and all the limbs to sink flaccid over the bloodless trunk: just as happens, when the phrase is used, the mind is in a bad way, or the soul is quite gone; when all is hurry and every one is anxious to keep from parting the last tie of life; for then the mind and the power of the soul are shaken throughout and both are quite loosened together with the body; so that a cause somewhat more powerful can quite break them up. Why doubt I would ask that the soul when driven forth out of the body, when in the open air, feeble as it is, stript of its covering, not only cannot continue through eternity, but is unable to hold together the smallest fraction of time? Therefore, again and again I say, when the enveloping body has been all broken up and the vital airs have been forced out, you must admit that the senses of the mind and the soul are dissolved, since the cause of destruction is one and inseparable for both body and soul.

Again since the body is unable to bear the separation of the soul without rotting away in a noisome stench, why doubt that the power of the soul gathering itself up from the inmost depths of body has oozed out and dispersed like smoke, and that the crumbling body has changed and tumbled in with so total a ruin for this reason because its foundations throughout are stirred from their places, the soul oozing out abroad through the frame, through all the winding passages which are in the body, and all openings? So that in ways manifold you may learn that the nature of the soul has been divided piecemeal and gone forth throughout the frame, and that it has been torn to shreds within the body, ere it glided forth and swam out into the air. For no one when dying appears to feel the soul go forth entire from his whole body or first mount up to the throat and gullet, but all feel it fail in that part which lies in a particular quarter; just as they know that the senses as well suffer dissolution each in its own place. But if our mind were immortal, it would not when dying complain so much of its dissolution, as of passing abroad and quitting its vesture, like a snake.

Again why are the mind's understanding and judgement never begotten in the head or feet or hands, but cling in all alike to one spot and fixed quarter, if it be not that particular places are assigned for the birth of everything, and nature has determined where each is to continue to exist after it is born? Our body then must follow the same law [2] and have such a manifold organisation of parts, that no perverted arrangement of its members shall ever show itself: so invariably effect follows cause, nor is flame wont to be born in rivers nor cold in fire.

Again if the nature of the soul is immortal and can feel when separated from our body, methinks we must suppose it to be provided with five senses; and in no other way can we picture to ourselves souls below flitting about Acheron. Painters therefore and former generations of writers have thus represented souls provided with senses. But neither eyes nor nose nor hand can exist for the soul apart from the body nor can tongue, nor can ears perceive by the sense of hearing or exist for the soul by themselves apart from the body.

And since we perceive that vital sense is in the whole body and we see that it is all endowed with life, if on a sudden any force with swift blow shall have cut it in twain so as quite to dissever the two halves, the power of the soul will without doubt at the same time be cleft and cut asunder and dashed in twain together with the body. But that which is cut and divides into any parts, you are to know disclaims for itself an everlasting nature. Stories are told how scythed chariots reeking with indiscriminate slaughter often lop off limbs so instantaneously that that which has fallen down lopped off from the frame is seen to quiver on the ground, while yet the mind and faculty of the man from the suddenness of the mischief cannot feel the pain; and because his mind once for all is wholly given to the business of fighting, with what remains of his body he mingles in the fray and carnage, and often perceives not that the wheels and devouring scythes have carried off among the horses' feet his left arm shield and all; another sees not that his right arm has dropped from him, while he mounts and presses forward. Another tries to get up after he has lost his leg, while the dying foot quivers with its toes on the ground close by. The head too when cut off from the warm and living trunk retains on the ground the expression of life and open eyes, until it has yielded up all the remnants of soul. To take another case, if, as a serpent's tongue is quivering, as its tail is darting out from its long body, you choose to chop with an axe into many pieces both tail and body, you will see all the separate portions thus cut off writhing under the fresh wound and bespattering the earth with gore, the fore part with the mouth making for its own hinder part, to allay with burning bite the pain of the wound with which it has been smitten. Shall we say then that there are entire souls in all those pieces? why from that argument it will follow that one living creature had many souls in its body; and this being absurd, therefore the soul which was one has been divided together with the body; therefore each alike must be reckoned mortal, since each is alike chopped up into many pieces.

Again if the nature of the soul is immortal and makes its way into our body at the time of birth, why are we unable to remember besides the time already gone, and why do we retain no traces of past actions? If the power of the mind has been so completely changed, that all remembrance of past things is lost, that methinks differs not widely from death; therefore you must admit that the soul which was before has perished and that which now is has now been formed.

Again if the quickened power of the mind is wont to be put into us after our body is fully formed, at the instant of our birth and our crossing the threshold of life, it ought agreeably to this to live not in such a way as to seem to have grown with the body and together with its members within the blood, but as in a den apart by and to itself: the very contrary to what undoubted fact teaches; for it is so closely united with the body throughout the veins, flesh, sinews, and bones, that the very teeth have a share of sense; as their aching proves and the sharp twinge of cold water and the crunching of a rough stone, when it has got into them out of bread. Wherefore, again and again I say, we must believe souls to be neither without a birth nor exempted from the law of death; for we must not believe that they could have been so completely united with our bodies, if they found their way into them from without, nor, since they are so closely inwoven with them, does it appear that they can get out unharmed and unloose themselves unscathed from all the sinews and bones and joints. But if haply you believe that the soul finds its way in from without and is wont to ooze through all our limbs, so much the more it will perish thus blended with the body; for what oozes through another is dissolved, and therefore dies. As food distributed through all the cavities of the body, while it is transmitted into the limbs and the whole frame, is destroyed and furnishes out of itself the matter of another nature, thus the soul and mind, though they pass entire into a fresh body, yet in oozing through it are dissolved, whilst there are transmitted so to say into the frame through all the cavities those particles of which this nature of mind is formed, which now is sovereign in our body, being born out of that soul which then perished when dispersed through the frame. Wherefore the nature of the soul is seen to be neither without a birthday nor exempt from death.

Again are seeds of the soul left in the dead body or not? If they are left and remain in it, the soul cannot fairly be deemed immortal, since it has withdrawn lessened by the loss of some parts; but if when taken away from the yet untainted limbs it has fled so entirely away as to leave in the body no parts of itself, whence do carcases exude worms from the now rank flesh and whence does such a swarm of living things, boneless and bloodless, surge through the heaving frame? But if haply you believe that souls find their way into worms from without and can severally pass each into a body and you make no account of why many thousands of souls meet together in a place from which one has withdrawn, this question at least must, it seems, be raised and brought to a decisive test, whether souls hunt out the several seeds of worms and build for themselves a place to dwell in, or find their way into bodies fully formed so to say. But why they should on their part make a body or take such trouble, cannot be explained; since being without a body they are not plagued as they flit about with diseases and cold and hunger, the body being more akin to, more troubled by such infirmities, and by its contact with it the mind suffering many ills. Nevertheless be it ever so expedient for them to make a body, when they are going to enter, yet clearly there is no way by which they can do so. Therefore souls do not make for themselves bodies and limbs; no nor can they by any method find their way into bodies after they are fully formed; for they will neither be able to unite themselves with a nice precision nor will any connexion of mutual sensation be formed between them.

Again why does untamed fierceness go along with the sullen brood of lions, cunning with foxes and proneness to flight with stags? And to take any other instance of the kind, why are all qualities engendered in the limbs and temper from the very commencement of life, if not because a fixed power of mind derived from its proper seed and breed grows up together with the whole body? If it were immortal and wont to pass into different bodies, living creatures would be of interchangeable dispositions; a dog of Hyrcanian breed would often fly before the attack of an antlered stag, a hawk would cower in mid air as it fled at the approach of a dove, men would be without reason, the savage races of wild beasts would have reason. For the assertion that an immortal soul is altered by a change of body is advanced on a false principle. What is changed is dissolved, and therefore dies: the parts are transposed and quit their former order; therefore they must admit of being dissolved too throughout the frame, in order at last to die one and all together with the body. But if they shall say that souls of men always go into human bodies, I yet will ask how it is a soul can change from wise to foolish, and no child has discretion, and why the mare's foal is not so well trained as the powerful strength of the horse. You may be sure they will fly to the subterfuge that the mind grows weakly in a weakly body. But granting this is so, you must admit the soul to be mortal, since changed so completely throughout the frame it loses its former life and sense. Then too in what way will it be able to grow in strength uniformly with its allotted body and reach the coveted flower of age, unless it shall be its partner at its first beginning? Or what means it by passing out from the limbs when decayed with age? Does it fear to remain shut up in a crumbling body, fear that its tenement, worn out by protracted length of days, bury it in its ruins? Why an immortal being incurs no risks.

Again for souls to stand by at the unions of Venus and the birth-throes of beasts seems to be passing absurd, for them the immortals to wait for mortal limbs in number numberless and struggle with one another in forward rivalry, which shall first and by preference have entrance in; unless haply bargains are struck among the souls on these terms, that whichever in its flight shall first come up, shall first have right of entry, and that they shall make no trial at all of each other's strength.[3]

Again a tree cannot exist in the ether, nor clouds in the deep sea nor can fishes live in the fields nor blood exist in woods nor sap in stones. Where each thing can grow and abide is fixed and ordained. Thus the nature of the mind cannot come into being alone without the body nor exist far away from the sinews and blood. But if (for this would be much more likely to happen than that) the force itself of the mind might be in the head or shoulders or heels or might be born in any other part of the body, it would after all be wont to abide in one and the same man or vessel. But since in our body even it is fixed and seen to be ordained where the soul and the mind can severally be and grow, it must still more strenuously be denied that it can abide and be born out of the body altogether. Therefore when the body has died, we must admit that the soul has perished, wrenched away throughout the body. To link forsooth a mortal thing with an everlasting and suppose that they can have sense in common and can be reciprocally acted upon, is sheer folly; for what can be conceived more incongruous, more discordant and inconsistent with itself, than a thing which is mortal, linked with an immortal and everlasting thing, trying in such union to weather furious storms? But if haply the soul is to be accounted immortal for this reason rather, because it is kept sheltered from death-bringing things, either because things hostile to its existence do not approach at all, or because those which do approach, in some way or other retreat discomfited before we can feel the harm they do, manifest experience proves that this can not be true.[4] For besides that it sickens in sympathy with the maladies of the body, it is often attacked by that which frets it on the score of the future and keeps it on the rack of suspense and wears it out with cares; and when ill deeds are in the past, remorse for sins yet gnaws: then there is madness peculiar to the mind and forgetfulness of all things; then too it often sinks into the black waters of lethargy.

Death therefore to us is nothing, concerns us not a jot, since the nature of the mind is proved to be mortal; and as in time gone by we felt no distress, when the Poeni from all sides came together to do battle, and all things shaken by war's troublous uproar shuddered and quaked beneath high heaven, and mortal men were in doubt which of the two peoples it should be to whose empire all must fall by sea and land alike, thus when we shall be no more, when there shall have been a separation of body and soul, out of both of which we are each formed into a single being, to us, you may be sure, who then shall be no more, nothing whatever can happen to excite sensation, not if earth shall be mingled with sea and sea with heaven. And even supposing the nature of the mind and power of the soul do feel, after they have been severed from our body, yet that is nothing to us who by the binding tie of marriage between body and soul are formed each into one single being. And if time should gather up our matter after our death and put it once more into the position in which it now is, and the light of life be given to us again, this result even would concern us not at all, when the chain of our self-consciousness has once been snapped asunder. So now we give ourselves no concern about any self which we have been before, nor do we feel any distress on the score of that self. For when you look back on the whole past course of immeasurable time and think how manifold are the shapes which the motions of matter take, you may easily credit this too, that these very same seeds of which we now are formed, have often before been placed in the same order in which they now are; and yet we cannot recover this in memory: a break in our existence has been interposed, and all the motions have wandered to and fro far astray from the sensations they produced. For he whom evil is to befall, must in his own person exist at the very time it comes, if the misery and suffering are haply to have any place at all; but since death precludes this, and forbids him to be, upon whom the ills can be brought, you may be sure that we have nothing to fear after death, and that he who exists not, cannot become miserable, and that it matters not a whit whether he has been born into life at any other time, when immortal death has taken away his mortal life.

Therefore when you see a man bemoaning his hard case, that after death he shall either rot with his body laid in the grave or be devoured by flames or the jaws of wild beasts, you may be sure that his ring betrays a flaw and that there lurks in his heart a secret goad, though he himself declare that he does not believe that any sense will remain to him after death. He does not methinks really grant the conclusion which he professes to grant nor the principle on which he so professes, nor does he take and force himself root and branch out of life, but all unconsciously imagines something of self to survive. For when any one in life suggests to himself that birds and beasts will rend his body after death, he makes moan for himself: he does not separate himself from that self, nor withdraw himself fully from the body so thrown out, and fancies himself that other self and stands by and impregnates it with his own sense. Hence he makes much moan that he has been born mortal, and sees not that after real death there will be no other self to remain in life and lament to self that his own self has met death, and there to stand and grieve that his own self there lying is mangled or burnt. For if it is an evil after death to be pulled about by the devouring jaws of wild beasts, I cannot see why it should not be a cruel pain to be laid on fires and burn in hot flames, or to be placed in honey and stifled, or to stiffen with cold, stretched on the smooth surface of an icy slab of stone, or to be pressed down and crushed by a load of earth above.

'Now no more shall thy house admit thee with glad welcome, nor a most virtuous wife and sweet children run to be the first to snatch kisses and touch thy heart with a silent joy. No more mayst thou be prosperous in thy doings, a safeguard to thine own. One disastrous day has taken from thee luckless man in luckless wise all the many prizes of life.' This do men say; but add not thereto 'and now no longer does any craving for these things beset thee withal.' For if they could rightly perceive this in thought and follow up the thought in words, they would release themselves from great distress and apprehension of mind. 'Thou, even as now thou art, sunk in the sleep of death, shalt continue so to be all time to come, freed from all distressful pains; but we with a sorrow that would not be sated wept for thee, when close by thou didst turn to an ashen hue on thy appalling funeral pile, and no length of days shall pluck from our hearts our ever-during grief.' This question therefore should be asked of this speaker, what there is in it so passing bitter, if it come in the end to sleep and rest, that any one should pine in never-ending sorrow.

This too men often, when they have reclined at table cup in hand and shade their brows with crowns, love to say from the heart, 'short is this enjoyment for poor weak men; presently it will have been and never after may it be called back'. As if after their death it is to be one of their chiefest afflictions that thirst and parching drought is to burn them up hapless wretches, or a craving for any thing else is to beset them. What folly! no one feels the want of himself and life at the time when mind and body are together sunk in sleep; for all we care this sleep might be everlasting, no craving whatever for ourselves then moves us. And yet by no means do those first-beginnings throughout our frame wander at that time far away from their sense-producing motions, at the moment when a man starts up from sleep and collects himself. Death therefore must be thought to concern us much less, if less there can be than what we see to be nothing; for a greater dispersion of the mass of matter follows after death, and no one wakes up, upon whom the chill cessation of life has once come.

Once more, if the nature of things could suddenly utter a voice and in person could rally any of us in such words as these, 'what hast thou, O mortal, so much at heart, that thou goest such lengths in sickly sorrows? Why bemoan and bewail death? For say thy life past and gone has been welcome to thee and thy blessings have not all, as if they were poured into a perforated vessel, run through and been lost without avail: why not then take thy departure like a guest filled with life, and with resignation, thou fool, enter upon untroubled rest? But if all that thou hast enjoyed, has been squandered and lost, and life is a grievance, why seek to make any addition, to be wasted perversely in its turn and lost utterly without avail? Why not rather make an end of life and travail? For there is nothing more which I can contrive and discover for thee to give pleasure: all things are ever the same. Though thy body is not yet decayed with years nor thy frame worn out and exhausted, yet all things remain the same, ay though in length of life thou shouldst outlast all races of things now living, nay even more if thou shouldst never die,' what answer have we to make save this, that nature sets up against us a well-founded claim and puts forth in her pleading a true indictment? If however one of greater age and more advanced in years should complain and lament poor wretch his death more than is right, would she not with greater cause raise her voice and rally him in sharp accents, 'Away from this time forth with thy tears, rascal; a truce to thy complainings: thou decayest after full enjoyment of all the prizes of life. But because thou ever yearnest for what is not present, and despisest what is, life has slipped from thy grasp unfinished and unsatisfying, and or ever thou thoughtest, death has taken his stand at thy pillow, before thou canst take thy departure sated and filled with good things. Now however resign all things unsuited to thy age, and with a good grace up and greatly go: thou must.' With good reason methinks she would bring her charge, with reason rally and reproach; for old things give way and are supplanted by new without fail, and one thing must ever be replenished out of other things; and no one is delivered over to the pit and black Tartarus: matter is needed for after generations to grow; all of which though will follow thee when they have finished their term of life; and thus it is that all these no less than thou have before this come to an end and hereafter will come to an end. Thus one thing will never cease to rise out of another, and life is granted to none in fee-simple, to all in usufruct. Think too how the bygone antiquity of everlasting time before our birth was nothing to us. Nature therefore holds this up to us as a mirror of the time yet to come after our death. Is there aught in this that looks appalling, aught that wears an aspect of gloom? Is it not more untroubled than any sleep?

And those things sure enough, which are fabled to be in the deep of Acheron, do all exist for us in this life. No Tantalus, numbed by groundless terror, as the story is, fears poor wretch a huge stone hanging in air; but in life rather a baseless dread of the god vexes mortals: the fall they fear is such fall of luck as chance brings to each. Nor do birds eat a way into Tityos laid in Acheron, nor can they sooth to say find during eternity food to peck under his large breast. However huge the bulk of body he extends, though such as to take up with outspread limbs not nine acres merely, but the whole earth, yet will he not be able to endure everlasting pain and supply food from his own body for ever. But he is for us a Tityos, whom, as he grovels in love, vultures rend and bitter bitter anguish eats up or troubled thoughts from any other passion do rive. In life too we have a Sisyphus before our eyes who is bent on asking from the people the rods and cruel axes, and always retires defeated and disappointed. For to ask for power, which empty as it is is never given, and always in the chase of it to undergo severe toil, this is forcing up-hill with much effort a stone which after all rolls back again from the summit and seeks in headlong haste the levels of the plain. Then to be ever feeding the thankless nature of the mind, and never to fill it full and sate it with good things, as the seasons of the year do for us, when they come round and bring their fruits and varied delights, though after all we are never filled with the enjoyments of life, this methinks is to do what is told of the maidens in the flower of their age, to keep pouring water into a perforated vessel which in spite of all can never be filled full. Moreover Cerberus and the furies and yon privation of light are idle tales, as well as all the rest, Ixion's wheel and black Tartarus belching forth hideous fires from his throat: things which nowhere are nor sooth to say can be. But there is in life a dread of punishment for evil deeds, signal as the deeds are signal, and for atonement of guilt, the prison and the frightful hurling down from the rock, scourgings, executioners, the dungeon of the doomed, the pitch, the metal plate, torches; and even though these are wanting, yet the conscience-stricken mind through boding fears applies to itself goads and frightens itself with whips, and sees not meanwhile what end there can be of ills or what limit at last is to be set to punishments, and fears lest these very evils be enhanced after death. The life of fools at length becomes a hell here on earth.

This too you may sometimes say to yourself, 'even worthy Ancus has quitted the light with his eyes, who was far far better than thou, unconscionable man. And since then many other kings and kesars have been laid low, who lorded it over mighty nations. He [6] too, even he who erst paved a way over the great sea and made a path for his legions to march over the deep and taught them to pass on foot over the salt pools and set at naught the roarings of the sea, trampling on them with his horses, had the light taken from him and shed forth his soul from his dying body. The son of the Scipios, thunderbolt of war, terror of Carthage, yielded his bones to earth just as if he were the lowest menial. Think too of the inventors of all sciences and graceful arts, think of the companions of the Heliconian maids; among whom Homer bore the sceptre without a peer, and he now sleeps the same sleep as others. Then there is Democritus, who, when a ripe old age had warned him that the memory-waking motions of his mind were waning, by his own spontaneous act offered up his head to death. Even Epicurus passed away, when his light of life had run its course, he who surpassed in intellect the race of man and quenched the light of all, as the ethereal sun arisen quenches the stars.' Wilt thou then hesitate and think it a hardship to die? Thou for whom life is well nigh dead whilst yet thou livest and seest the light, who spendest the greater part of thy time in sleep and snorest wide awake and ceasest not to see visions and hast a mind troubled with groundless terror and canst not discover often what it is that ails thee, when besotted man thou art sore pressed on all sides with full many cares and goest astray tumbling about in the wayward wanderings of thy mind.

If, just as they are seen to feel that a load is on their mind which wears them out with its pressure, men might apprehend from what causes too it is produced and whence such a pile, if I may say so, of ill lies on their breast, they would not spend their life as we see them now for the most part do, not knowing any one of them what he means and wanting ever change of place as though he might lay his burden down. The man who is sick of home often issues forth from his large mansion, and as suddenly comes back to it, finding as he does that he is no better off abroad. He races to his country-house, driving his jennets in headlong haste, as if hurrying to bring help to a house on fire: he yawns the moment he has reached the door of his house, or sinks heavily into sleep and seeks forgetfulness, or even in haste goes back again to town. In this way each man flies from himself (but self from whom, as you may be sure is commonly the case, he cannot escape, clings to him in his own despite), hates too himself, because he is sick and knows not the cause of the malady; for if he could rightly see into this, relinquishing all else each man would study to learn the nature of things, since the point at stake is the condition for eternity, not for one hour, in which mortals have to pass all the time which remains for them to expect after death.

Once more what evil lust of life is this which constrains us with such force to be so mightily troubled in doubts and dangers? A sure term of life is fixed for mortals, and death cannot be shunned, but meet it we must. Moreover we are ever engaged, ever involved in the same pursuits, and no new pleasure is struck out by living on; but whilst what we crave is wanting, it seems to transcend all the rest; then, when it has been gotten, we crave something else, and ever does the same thirst of life possess us, as we gape for it open-mouthed. Quite doubtful it is what fortune the future will carry with it or what chance will bring us or what end is at hand. Nor by prolonging life do we take one tittle from the time past in death nor can we fret anything away, whereby we may haply be a less long time in the condition of the dead. Therefore you may complete as many generations as you please during your life; none the less however will that everlasting death await you; and for no less long a time will he be no more in being, who beginning with to-day has ended his life, than the man who has died many months and years ago.

BOOK IV

I TRAVERSE the pathless haunts of the Pierides never yet trodden by sole of man.[1] I love to approach the untasted springs and to quaff, I love to cull fresh flowers and gather for my head a distinguished crown from spots whence the Muses have yet veiled the brows of none; first because I teach of great things and essay to release the mind from the fast bonds of religious scruples, and next because on a dark subject I pen such lucid verses o'erlaying all with the Muses' charm. For that too would seem to be not without good grounds: even as physicians when they propose to give nauseous wormwood to children, first smear the rim round the bowl with the sweet yellow juice of honey, that the unthinking age of children may be fooled as far as the lips, and meanwhile drink up the bitter draught of wormwood and though beguiled yet not be betrayed, but rather by such means recover health and strength: so I now, since this doctrine seems generally somewhat bitter to those by whom it has not been handled, and the multitude shrinks back from it in dismay, have resolved to set forth to you our doctrine in sweet-toned Pierian verse and o'erlay it as it were with the pleasant honey of the Muses, if haply by such means I might engage your mind on my verses, till such time as you apprehend all the nature of things and thoroughly feel what use it has.

And now that I have taught what the nature of the mind is and out of what things it is formed into one quickened being with the body, and how it is dissevered and returns into its first-beginnings, I will attempt to lay before you a truth which most nearly concerns these questions, the existence of things which we call idols of things: these, like films peeled off from the surface of things, fly to and fro through the air, and do likewise frighten our minds when they present themselves to us awake as well as in sleep, what time we behold strange shapes and idols of the light-bereaved, which have often startled us in appalling wise as we lay relaxed in sleep: this I will essay, that we may not haply believe that souls break loose from Acheron or that shades fly about among the living or that something of us is left behind after death, when the body and the nature of the mind destroyed together have taken their departure into their several first-beginnings.

I say then that pictures of things and thin shapes are emitted from things off their surface, to which an image serves as a kind of film, or name it if you like a rind, because such image bears an appearance and form like to the thing whatever it is from whose body it is shed and wanders forth. This you may learn however dull of apprehension from what follows. First of all since among things open to sight many emit bodies, some in a state of loose diffusion, like smoke which logs of oak, heat which fires emit; some of a closer and denser texture, like the gossamer coats which at times cicades doff in summer, and the films which calves at their birth cast from the surface of their body, as well as the vesture which the slippery serpent puts off among the thorns; for often we see the brambles enriched with their flying spoils: since these cases occur, a thin image likewise must be emitted from things off their surface. For why those films should drop off and withdraw from things rather than films which are really thin, not one tittle of proof can be given; especially since there are on the surface of things many minute bodies which may be discharged in the same order they had before and preserve the outline of the shape, and be discharged with far more velocity, inasmuch as they are less liable to get hampered being few in number and stationed in the front rank. For without doubt we see many things discharge and freely give not only from the core and centre, as we said before, but from their surfaces, besides other things colour itself. And this is commonly done by yellow and red and dark-blue awnings, when they are spread over large theatres and flutter and wave as they stretch across their poles and crossbeams; for then they dye the seated assemblage below and all the show of the stage and the richly attired company of the fathers, and compel them to dance about in their colour. And the more these objects are shut in all round by the walls of the theatre the more do all of them within laugh on all hands, o'erlaid with graceful hues, the light of day being, narrowed. Therefore since sheets of canvas emit colour from their surface, all things will naturally emit thin pictures too, since in each case alike they discharge from the surface. There are therefore as now shown sure outlines of shapes, which fly all about possessed of an exquisitely small thickness and cannot when separate be seen one at a time. Again all smell, smoke, heat, and other such-like things stream off things in a state of diffusion, because while they are coming from the depths of the body having arisen within it, they are torn in their winding passage, and there are no straight orifices to the paths, for them to make their way out by in a mass. But on the other hand when a thin film of surface colour is discharged, there is nothing to rend it, since it is ready to hand stationed in front rank. Lastly in the case of all idols which show themselves to us in mirrors, in water or any other shining object, since their outsides are possessed of an appearance like to the things they represent, they must be formed of emitted images of things. There are therefore thin shapes and pictures like to the things, which, though no one can see them one at a time, yet when thrown off by constant and repeated reflexion give back a visible image from the surface of mirrors; and in no other way it would seem can they be kept so entire that shapes are given back so exceedingly like each object.

Now mark, and learn how thin the nature of an image is. And first of all, since the first-beginnings are so far below the ken of our senses and much smaller than the things which our eyes first begin to be unable to see, to strengthen yet more the proof of this also, learn in a few words how minutely fine are the beginnings of all things. First, living things are in some cases so very little, that their third part cannot be seen at all. Of what size are we to suppose any gut of such creatures to be? Or the ball of the heart or the eyes? the limbs? Or any part of the frame? How small they must be! And then further the several first-beginnings of which their soul and the nature of their mind must be formed? Do you not perceive how fine, how minute they are? Again in the case of all things which exhale from their body a pungent smell, all-heal, nauseous wormwood, strong-scented southernwood and the bitter centauries, any one of which, if you happen to feel it lightly between two fingers, will impregnate them with a strong smell. . . .[2] but rather you are to know that idols of things wander about many in number in many ways, of no force, powerless to excite sense.

But lest haply you suppose that only those idols of things which go off from things and no others wander about, there are likewise those which are spontaneously begotten and are formed by themselves in this lower heaven which is called air: these fashioned in many ways are borne along on high and being in a fluid state cease not to alter their appearance and change it into the outline of shapes of every possible kind; as we see clouds sometimes gather into masses on high and blot the calm clear face of heaven, fanning the air with their motion. Thus often the faces of giants are seen to fly along and draw after them a far-spreading shadow; sometimes great mountains and rocks torn from the mountains are seen to go in advance and pass across the sun; and then some huge beast is observed to draw with it and bring on the other storm-clouds.

Now I will proceed to show with what ease and celerity they are begotten and how incessantly they flow and fall away from things. The outermost surface is ever streaming off from things and admits of being discharged: when this reaches some things, it passes through them, glass especially. But when it reaches rough stones or the matter of wood, it is then so torn that it cannot give back any idol. But when objects at once shining and dense have been put in its way, a mirror especially, none of these results has place: it can neither pass through it, like glass, nor can it be torn either; such perfect safety the polished surface minds to ensure. In consequence of this idols stream back to us from such objects; and however suddenly at any moment you place any thing opposite a mirror, an image shows itself: hence you may be sure that thin textures and thin shapes of things incessantly stream from their surface. Therefore many idols are begotten in a short time, so that the birth of such things is with good reason named a rapid one. And as the sun must send forth many rays of light in a short time in order that all things may be continually filled with it, so also for a like reason there must be carried away from things in a moment of time idols of things, many in number, in many ways, in all directions round; since to whatever part of them we present a mirror before their surfaces, other things correspond to these in the mirror of a like shape and like colour. Moreover though the state of heaven has just before been of unsullied purity, with exceeding suddenness it becomes so hideously overcast, that you might imagine all its darkness had abandoned Acheron throughout and filled up the great vaults of heaven: in such numbers do faces of black horror rise up from amid the frightful night of storm-clouds and hang over us on high. Now there is no one who can tell how small a fraction of these an image is, or express that sum in language.

Now mark: how swift the motion is with which idols are borne along, and what velocity is assigned to them as they glide through the air, so that but a short hour is spent on a journey through long space, whatever the spot towards which they go with a movement of varied tendency, all this I will tell in sweetly worded rather than in many verses; as the short song of the swan is better than the loud noise of cranes scattered abroad amid the ethereal clouds of the south. First of all we may very often observe that things which are light and made of minute bodies are swift. Of this kind are the light of the sun and its heat, because they are made of minute first things which are knocked forward so to speak and do not hesitate to pass through the space of air between, ever driven on by a blow following behind; for light on the instant is supplied by fresh light and brightness goaded to show its brightness in what you might call an ever on-moving team. Therefore in like manner idols must be able to scour in a moment of time through space unspeakable, first because they are exceedingly small and there is a cause at their back to carry and impel them far forward; where moreover they move on with such winged lightness; next because when emitted they are possessed of so rare a texture, that they can readily pass through any things and stream as it were through the space of air between. Again if those minute bodies of things which are given out from the inmost depths of these things, as the light and heat of the sun, are seen in a moment of time to glide and spread themselves through the length and breadth of heaven, fly over sea and lands and flood the heaven, what then of those which stand ready posted in front rank, when they are discharged and nothing obstructs their egress? How much faster, you see, and farther must they travel, scouring through many times the same amount of space in the same time that the sunlight takes to spread over heaven! This too appears to be an eminently true proof of the velocity with which idols of things are borne along: as soon as ever the brightness of water is set down in the open air, if the heaven is starry, in a moment the clear radiant constellations of ether imaged in the water correspond to those in the heaven. Now do you see in what a moment of time an image drops down from the borders of heaven to the borders of earth? Therefore again and again I repeat you must admit that bodies capable of striking the eyes and of provoking vision constantly travel with a marvellous velocity. Smells too incessantly stream from certain things; as does cold from rivers, heat from the sun, spray from the waves of the sea, that enter into walls near the shore. Various sounds also cease not to fly through the air. Then too a moist salt flavour often comes into the mouth, when we are moving about beside the sea; and when we look on at the mixing of a decoction of wormwood, its bitterness affects us. In such a constant stream from all things the several qualities are carried and are transmitted in all directions round, and no delay, no respite in the flow is ever granted, since we constantly have feeling, and may at any time see, smell, and hear the sound of anything.

Again since a particular figure felt by the hands in the dark is known to be the same which is seen in the bright light of day, touch and sight must be excited by a quite similar cause. Well then if we handle a square thing and it excites our attention in the dark, in the daylight what square thing will be able to fall on our sight, except the image of that thing? Therefore the cause of seeing, it is plain, lies in images and no thing can be perceived without them. Well the idols of things I speak of are borne along all round and are discharged and transmitted in all directions; but because we can see with the eyes alone, the consequence is that, to whatever point we turn our sight, there all the several things meet and strike it with their shape and colour. And the image gives the power to see and the means to distinguish how far each thing is distant from us; for as soon as ever it is discharged, it pushes before it and impels all the air which lies between it and the eyes; and thus that air all streams through our eyes and brushes so to say the pupils and so passes through. The consequence is that we see how far distant each thing is. And the greater the quantity of air which is driven on before it and the larger the current which brushes our eyes, the more distant each different thing is seen to be. You must know these processes go on with extreme rapidity, so that at one and the same moment we see what like a thing is and how far distant it is. And this must by no means be deemed strange herein that, while the idols which strike the eyes cannot be seen one at a time, the things themselves are seen. For thus when the wind too beats us with successive strokes and when piercing cold streams, we are not wont to feel each single particle of that wind and cold, but rather the whole result; and then we perceive blows take effect on our body just as if something or other were beating it and giving us a sensation of its body outside. Again when we thump a stone with a finger, we touch merely the outermost colour on the surface of the stone, and yet we do not feel that colour by our touch, but rather we feel the very hardness of the stone seated in its inmost depths.

Now mark, and learn why the image is seen beyond the mirror; for without doubt it is seen withdrawn far within. The case is just the same as with things which are viewed in their reality beyond a door, when it offers through it an unobstructed prospect and lets many things outside be seen from a house. That vision too is effected by two separate airs: first there is an air seen in such a case inside the doorway; next come the leaves of the door right and left; next a light outside brushes the eyes, then a second air, then those things outside which are viewed in their reality. Thus when the image of the mirror has first discharged itself, in coming to our sight it pushes forward and impels all the air which lies between it and the eyes, and enables us to see the whole of it before the mirror. But when we have perceived the mirror as well, at once the image which is conveyed from us reaches the mirror and then is reflected and comes back to our eyes, and drives on and rolls in front of it a second air and lets us see this before itself, and for this reason it looks so far withdrawn from the mirror. Wherefore again and again I repeat there is no cause at all to wonder why the images give back the reflexion from the surface of mirrors in the spot they do, since in both the given cases the result is produced by two airs. To proceed, the right side of our body is seen in mirrors to be on the left, because when the image comes and strikes on the plane of the mirror, it is not turned back unaltered, but is beaten out in a right line backwards, just as if you were to take a plaster mask before it is dry and dash it on a pillar or beam, and it forthwith were to preserve the lines of its features undistorted in front and were to strike out an exact copy of itself straight backwards. The result will be that the eye which was right will now be left; and conversely the left become the right. An image may also be so transmitted from one mirror to another that five or six idols are often produced. And thus all the things which lurk in the inmost corners of a house, however far they are withdrawn into tortuous recesses, may yet be all brought out through winding passages by the aid of a number of mirrors and be seen to be in the house. So unfailingly does the image reflect itself from mirror to mirror; and when the left side is presented, it becomes the right in the new image; then it is changed back again and turns round to what it was. Moreover all little sides of mirrors which possess a curvature resembling our side, send back to us idols with their right corresponding to our right either for this reason, because the image is transmitted from one mirror to another, and then after it has been twice struck out flies to us, or else because the image, when it has come to the mirror, wheels about, because the curved shape of the mirror teaches it to turn round and face us. Again you would think that idols step out and put down their foot at the same time with us and mimic our action, because from before whatever part of a mirror you move away, from that part forthwith no idols can be reflected; since nature constrains all things, when they are carried back and recoil from things, to be given back at angles equal to those at which they impinged.

Bright things again the eyes eschew and shun to look upon: the sun even blinds them, if you persist in turning them towards it, because its power is great and idols are borne through the clear air with great downward force from on high, and strike the eyes and disorder their fastenings. Moreover any vivid brightness often burns the eyes, because it contains many seeds of fire which make a way in and beget pain in the eyes. Again whatever the jaundiced look at, becomes a greenish-yellow, because many seeds of greenish-yellow stream from their body and meet the idols of things, and many too are mixed up in their eyes, and these by their infection tinge all things with sallow hues. Again we see out of the dark things which are in the light for this reason: when the black air of darkness being the nearer has first entered and taken possession of the open eyes, the bright white air follows straightway after and cleanses them so to say and dispels the black shadows of the other air; for this is a great deal more nimble, a great deal more subtle and more efficacious. As soon as it has filled with light and opened up the passages of the eyes which the black air had before blocked up, forthwith the idols of things which are situated in the light follow and excite them so that we see. This we cannot do conversely in the dark out of the light, because the grosser air of darkness follows behind and quite fills all the openings and blocks up the passages of the eyes, not letting the idols of any things at all be thrown into the eyes to move them. Again when we descry far off the square towers of a town, they often appear to be round for this reason: all the angles are seen from a distance to look obtuse, or rather are not seen at all, and their blow is lost and their stroke never makes its way to our sight, because while the idols are borne on through much air, the air by repeated collisions blunts the stroke perforce. When in this way all the angles have together eluded the sense, the stone structures are rounded off as if by the lathe; yet they do not look like the things which are close before us and really round, but somewhat resembling them as in shadowy outline. Our shadow likewise seems to move in the sunshine and to follow our steps and mimic our action; if you think forsooth that air deprived of life can step, imitating the motions and the actions of men; for that which we are wont to term shadow can be nothing but air devoid of light. Sure enough because the earth in certain spots successively is deprived of light wherever we intercept it in moving about, while that part of it which we have quitted is filled with light, therefore that which was the shadow of our body, seems to have always followed us unchanged in a direct line with us. For new rays of light ever pour in and the old are lost, just as if wool were drawn into the fire. Therefore the earth is readily stripped of light, and again filled, and cleanses itself from black shadows.

And yet in all this we do not admit that the eyes are cheated one whit. For it is their province to observe in what spot soever light and shade are; but whether the lights are still the same or not, and whether it is the same shadow which was in this spot that is now passing to that, or whether what we said a little before is not rather the fact, this the reason of the mind, and only it, has to determine; nor can the eyes know the nature of things. Do not then fasten upon the eyes this frailty of the mind. The ship in which we are sailing, moves on while seeming to stand still; that one which remains at its moorings, is believed to be passing by. The hills and fields seem to be dropping astern, past which we are driving our ship and flying under sail. The stars all seem to be at rest fast fixed to the ethereal vaults, and yet are all in constant motion, since they rise and then go back to their far-off places of setting, after they have traversed the length of heaven with their bright bodies. In like manner sun and moon seem to stay in one place, bodies which simple fact proves are carried on. And though between mountains rising up afar off from amid the waters there opens out for fleets a free passage of wide extent, yet a single island seems to be formed out of them united into one. When children have stopped turning round themselves, the halls appear to them to whirl about and the pillars to course round to such a degree, that they can scarce believe that the whole roof is not threatening to tumble down upon them. Again when nature begins to raise on high the sun's beam ruddy with bickering fires and to lift it up above the mountains, those hills above which the sun then seems to you to be, as blazing close at hand he dyes them with his own fire, are distant from us scarce two thousand arrow-flights, yea often scarce five hundred casts of a javelin; and yet between them and the sun lie immense levels of sea, spread out below the huge borders of ether, and many thousands of lands are between, held by divers peoples and races of wild beasts. Then a puddle of water not more than a finger-breadth deep, which stands between the stones in the streets, offers a prospect beneath the earth of a reach as vast, as that with which the high yawning maw of heaven opens out above the earth; so that you seem to discern clouds and see the bodies of birds far withdrawn into that wondrous sky beneath the earth. Again when our stout horse has stuck in the middle of a river and we have looked down on the swift waters of the stream, some force seems to carry athwart the current the body of the horse which is standing still and to force it rapidly up the stream; and to whatever point we cast our eyes about all things seem to be carried on and to be flowing in the same way as we are. Again although a portico runs in parallel lines from one end to the other and stands supported by equal columns along its whole extent, yet when from the top of it it is seen in its entire length, it gradually forms the contracted top of a narrowing cone, until uniting roof with floor and all the right side with the left it has brought them together into the vanishing point of a cone. To sailors on the sea the sun appears to rise out of the waters and in the waters to set and bury his light; just because they behold nothing but water and sky; that you may not lightly suppose the credit of the senses to be shaken on all hands. Then to people unacquainted with the sea, ships in harbour seem to be all askew and with poop-fittings broken to be pressing up against the water. For whatever part of the oars is raised above the salt water, is straight, and the rudders in their upper half are straight: the parts which are sunk below the water-level, appear to be broken and bent round and to slope up and turn back towards the surface and to be so much twisted back as well-nigh to float on the top of the water. And when the winds carry the thinly scattered clouds across heaven in the night-time, then do the glittering signs appear to glide athwart the rack and to be travelling on high in a direction quite different to their real course. Then if our hand chance to be placed beneath one eye and press it below, through a certain sensation all things which we look at appear then to become double as we look; the light of lamps brilliant with flames to be double, double too the furniture through the whole house, double men's faces and men's bodies. Again when sleep has chained down our limbs in sweet slumber and the whole body is sunk in profound repose, yet then we seem to ourselves to be awake and to be moving our limbs, and mid the thick darkness of night we think we see the sun and the daylight; and though in a confined room, we seem to be passing to new climates, seas, rivers, and mountains, and to be crossing plains on foot and to hear noises, though the austere silence of night prevails all round, and to be uttering speech though quite silent. Many are the other marvels of this sort we see, which all seek to shake as it were the credit of the senses: quite in vain, since the greatest part of these cases cheats us on account of the mental suppositions which we add of ourselves, taking those things as seen which have not been seen by the senses. For nothing is harder than to separate manifest facts from doubtful which straightway the mind adds on of itself.

Again if a man believe that nothing is known, he knows not whether this even can be known, since he admits he knows nothing. I will therefore decline to argue the case against him who places himself with head where his feet should be. And yet granting that he knows this, I would still put this question, since he has never yet seen any truth in things, whence he knows what knowing and not knowing severally are, and what it is that has produced the knowledge of the true and the false and what has proved the doubtful to differ from the certain. You will find that from the senses first has proceeded the knowledge of the true and that the senses cannot be refuted. For that which is of itself to be able to refute things false by true things must from the nature of the case be proved to have the higher certainty. Well then what must fairly be accounted of higher certainty than sense? Shall reason founded on false sense be able to contradict them, wholly founded as it is on the senses? And if they are not true, then all reason as well is rendered false. Or shall the ears be able to take the eyes to task, or the touch the ears? Again shall the taste call in question this touch, or the nostrils refute or the eyes controvert it? Not so, I guess; for each apart has its own distinct office, each its own power; and therefore we must perceive what is soft and cold or hot by one distinct faculty, by another perceive the different colours of things and thus see all objects which are conjoined with colour. Taste too has its faculty apart; smells spring from one source, sounds from another. It must follow therefore that any one sense cannot confute any other. No nor can any sense take itself to task, since equal credit must be assigned to it at all times. What therefore has at any time appeared true to each sense, is true. And if reason shall be unable to explain away the cause why things which close at hand were square, at a distance looked round, it yet is better, if you are at a loss for the reason, to state erroneously the causes of each shape, than to let slip from your grasp on any side things manifest and ruin the groundwork of belief and wrench up all the foundations on which rest life and existence. For not only would all reason give way, life itself would at once fall to the ground, unless you choose to trust the senses and shun precipices and all things else of this sort that are to be avoided, and to pursue the opposite things. All that host of words then be sure is quite unmeaning, which has been drawn out in array against the senses. Once more, as in a building, if the rule first applied is wry, and the square is untrue and swerves from its straight lines, and if there is the slightest hitch in any part of the level, all the construction must be faulty, all must be wry, crooked, sloping, leaning forwards, leaning backwards, without symmetry, so that some parts seem ready to fall, others do fall, ruined all by the first erroneous measurements; so too all reason of things must needs prove to you distorted and false, which is founded on false senses.

And now to explain in what way the other senses do each perceive their several objects, is the nowise arduous task which is still left.

In the first place all sound and voice is heard when they have made their way into the ears and have struck with their body the sense of hearing. For voice too and sound you must admit to be bodily, since they are able to act upon the senses. Again voice often abrades the throat, and shouting in passing forth makes the windpipe more rough: when to wit the first-beginnings of voices have risen up in larger mass and commenced to pass abroad through their strait passage, you are to know the door of the mouth now crammed itself is abraded. There is no doubt then that voices and words consist of bodily first-beginnings, with the power to hurt; nor can you fail to know how much of body is taken away and how much is withdrawn from men's very sinews and strength by a speech continued without interruption from the dawning brightness of morning to the shadow of black night, above all if it has been poured forth with much loud shouting. Voice therefore must be bodily, since a man by much speaking loses a portion from his body. Next roughness of voice comes from roughness of first-beginnings, as smoothness is produced from smoothness. Nor are the first-beginnings of like shape which pierce the ears in these two cases: when the trumpet brays dully in deep low tones, the barbarian country roused echoing back the hoarse hollow sound, and when swans from the headstrong torrents of Helicon raise their clear-toned dirge with plaintive voice.

When therefore we force these voices forth from the depths of our body and discharge them straight out at the mouth, the pliant tongue deft fashioner of words gives them articulate utterance and the structure of the lips does its part in shaping them. Therefore when the distance is not long between the point from which each several voice has started and that at which it arrives, the very words too must be plainly heard and distinguished syllable by syllable; for each voice retains its structure and retains its shape. But if the space between be more than is suitable, the words must be huddled together in passing through much air and the voice be disorganised in its flight through the same. Therefore it is that you can hear a sound, yet cannot distinguish what the meaning of the words is: so huddled and hampered is the voice when it comes. Again a single word often stirs the ears of a whole assembly of people, when uttered by the crier's mouth. One voice therefore in a moment starts asunder into many voices, since it distributes itself separately into all the ears, stamping upon them the form and distinct sound of the word. But such of the voices as do not fall directly on the ears, are carried past and lost, fruitlessly dispersed in air: some striking upon solid spots are thrown back and give back a sound and sometimes mock by an echo of the word. When you fully perceive all this, you may explain to yourself and others how it is that in lonely spots rocks give back in regular succession forms of words like to those sent forth, as we seek our comrades straying about among the darkened hills and with loud voice call upon them scattered abroad. I have seen places give back as many as six or seven voices, when you sent forth one: in such wise did the very hills dash back on hills and repeat the words thus trained to come back. These spots the people round fancy that the goat-footed satyrs and nymphs inhabit, and tell that they are the fauns by whose night-pervading noise and sportive play as they declare the still silence is broken and sounds produced of stringed instruments and sweet plaintive melodies, such as the pipe pours forth when beaten by the fingers of the players, the country-people hearing far and wide, what time Pan nodding the piny covering of his head half a beast's oft runs over the gaping reeds with curved lip, making the pipe without ceasing to pour forth its woodland song. Other such like prodigies and marvels they tell of, that they may not haply be thought to inhabit lonely places, abandoned even by the gods. On this account they vaunt such wonders in their stories or are led on by some other reason; inasmuch as the whole race of man is all too greedy after listening ears.

To proceed, you need not wonder how it is that through places, through which the eyes cannot see plain things, voices come and strike the ears. We often see a conversation go on even through closed doors, sure enough because the voice can pass uninjured through the winding openings of things, while idols refuse to pass: they are torn to shreds, if the openings through which they glide are not straight, like those of glass, through which every image passes. Again a voice distributes itself in all directions, since voices are begotten one out of another, when a single voice has once gone forth and sprung into many, as a spark of fire is often wont to distribute itself into its constituent fires. Therefore places are filled with voices, which though far withdrawn out of view yet are all in commotion and stirred by sound. But idols all proceed in straight courses as soon as they have been discharged; and therefore you can never see beyond a wall, but you may hear voices outside it. And yet this very voice even in passing through the walls of houses is blunted and enters the ears in a huddled state, and we seem to hear the sound rather than the actual words.

The tongue and palate whereby we perceive flavour, have not in them anything that calls for longer explanation or offers more difficulty.

In the first place we perceive flavour in the mouth when we press it out in chewing our food, in the same way as when one haply begins to squeeze with his hand and dry a sponge full of water. Next the whole of what we press out distributes itself through the cavities of the palate and the intricate openings of the porous tongue. Therefore when the bodies of oozing flavour are smooth, they pleasantly touch and pleasantly feel all the parts about the moist exuding quarters of the palate. But on the other hand when they rise in a mass they puncture and tear the sense according to the degree in which they are pervaded by roughness. Next the pleasure from the flavour reaches as far as the palate; when however it has passed down through the throat, there is no pleasure while it is all distributing itself into the frame. And it makes no matter what the food is with which the body is nurtured, provided you can digest what you take and transmit it into the frame and keep the stomach in an equable condition of moistness.

I will now explain how it is that different food is pleasant and nutritious for different creatures; also why that which to some is nauseous and bitter, may yet to others seem passing sweet; and why in these matters the difference and discrepancy is so great that what to one man is food, to another is rank poison; and there is actually a serpent which on being touched by a man's spittle wastes away and destroys itself by gnawing its body. Again hellebore for us is rank poison, but helps to fatten goats and quails. That you may know how this comes to pass, first of all you must remember what we have said before, that the seeds which are contained in things are mixed up in manifold ways. Again all living creatures soever which take food, even as they are unlike on the outside, and, differing in each after its kind, an exterior contour of limbs bounds them, so likewise are they formed of seeds of varying shape. Again since the seeds differ, there must be a discrepancy in the spaces between and the passages, which we name openings, in all the limbs and mouth and palate as well. Some openings therefore must be smaller, some larger; some things must have them three-cornered, others square; many must be round, some many-angled after many fashions. For as the relation between the shapes of seeds and their motions require, the openings also must differ accordingly in their shapes; and the passages must vary, as varies the texture formed by the seeds which bound them. For this reason when that which is sweet to some becomes bitter to others, for that creature to whom it is sweet the smoothest bodies must enter the cavities of the palate with power to feel them all over; but on the other hand in the case of those to whom the same thing is bitter within, rough and barbed seeds sure enough pass down the throat. It is easy now from these principles to understand all particular cases: thus when a fever has attacked anyone from too great a flow of bile, or a violent disease has been excited in any other way, thereupon the whole body is disordered and all the arrangements of particles then and there changed; the consequence of which is that the bodies which before were suited to excite sensation, suit no more; and those fit it better, which are able to make their way in and beget a bitter sense. Both kinds for instance are mixed up in the flavour of honey: a point we have often proved before.

Now mark me, and I will discuss the way in which the contact of smell affects the nostrils: and first there must be many things from which a varied flow of smells streams and rolls on; and we must suppose that they thus stream and discharge and disperse themselves among all things alike; but one smell fits itself better to one creature, another to another on account of their unlike shapes; and therefore bees are drawn on by the smell of honey through the air to a very great distance, and so are vultures by carcases. Also the onward-reaching power of scent in dogs leads them whithersoever the cloven hoof of wild beasts has carried them in their course; and the smell of man is felt far away by the saviour of the Romans' citadel, the bright white goose.[3] Thus different scents assigned to different creatures lead each to its appropriate food and constrain them to recoil from nauseous poison, and in this way the races of beasts are preserved.

Of all these different smells then which strike the nostrils one may reach to a much greater distance than another; though none of them is carried so far as sound, as voice, to say nothing of things which strike the eyesight and provoke vision. For in its mazy course each comes slowly on and is sooner lost, being gradually dispersed into the readily receiving expanse of air; first because coming out of its depths it with difficulty discharges itself from the thing: for the fact that all things are found to have a stronger smell when crushed, when pounded, when broken up by fire, shows that odours stream and withdraw from the inner parts of things: next you may see that smell is formed of larger first-beginnings than voice, since it does not pass through stone walls, through which voice and sound are borne without fail. For this reason also you will find that it is not so easy to trace out in what quarter a thing which smells is situated; for the blow cools down as it loiters through the air, and the courier particles of things are no longer hot when they finish their race to sense; for which reason dogs are often at fault and lose the scent.

But what I have said is not found in smells and in the class of flavours only, but also the forms and colours of things are not all so well suited to the senses of all, but that some will be more distressing to the sight than others. Moreover ravenous lions cannot face and bear to gaze upon a cock with flapping wings putting night to rout and wont to summon morning with shrill voice: in such wise they at once bethink themselves of flight, because sure enough in the body of cocks are certain seeds, and these, when they have been discharged into the eyes of lions, bore into the pupils and cause such sharp pain that courageous though they be, they cannot continue to face them; while at the same time these things cannot hurt at all our sight either because they do not enter in or because the moment they enter, a free passage out of the eyes is granted them, so that they cannot by staying behind hurt the eyes in any part.

Now mark, and hear what things move the mind, and learn in a few words whence the things which come into it do come. I say first of all that idols of things wander about many in number, in many ways, in all directions round, extremely thin; and these when they meet, readily unite, like a cobweb or piece of gold-leaf. For these idols are far thinner in texture than those which take possession of the eyes and provoke vision; since these enter in through the porous parts of the body and stir the fine nature of the mind within and provoke sensation. Therefore we see Centaurs and limbs of Scyllas and Cerberus-like faces of dogs and idols of those who are dead whose bones earth holds in its embrace; since idols of every kind are everywhere borne about, partly those which are spontaneously produced within the air, partly all those which withdraw from various things and those which are formed by compounding the shapes of these. For assuredly no image of Centaur is formed out of a live one, since no such nature of living creature ever existed; but when images of a horse and a man have by chance come together, they readily adhere at once, as we said before, on account of their fine nature and thin texture. All other things of the kind are produced in like fashion. And when these from extreme lightness are borne on with velocity, as I showed before, any one subtle composite image you like readily moves the mind by a single stroke; for the mind is fine and is itself wondrously nimble.

That all this is done as I relate you may easily learn from what follows. So far as the one is like the other, seeing with the mind and seeing with the eyes must be produced in a like way. Well then since I have shown that I perceive for instance a lion by means of idols which provoke the eyes, you may be sure that the mind is moved in a like way, which by means of idols sees a lion or anything else just as well as the eyes, with this difference that it perceives much thinner idols. And when sleep has prostrated the body, for no other reason does the mind's intelligence wake, except because the very same idols provoke our minds which provoke them when we are awake, and to such a degree that we seem without a doubt to perceive him whom life has left and death and earth gotten hold of. This nature constrains to come to pass because all the senses of the body are then hampered and at rest throughout the limbs and cannot refute the unreal by real things. Moreover memory is prostrate and relaxed in sleep and protests not that he has long been in the grasp of death and destruction whom the mind believes it sees alive. Furthermore it is not strange that idols move and throw about their arms and other limbs in regular measure: for sometimes in sleep an image is seen to do this: when the first to wit has gone and a second then been born in another posture, that former one seems to have altered its attitude. This remember you must assume to take place with exceeding celerity: so great is the velocity, so great the store of things; so great in any one unit of time that sense can seize is the store of particles, out of which the supply may go on.

And here many questions present themselves and many points must be cleared up by us, if we desire to give a plain exposition of things. The first question is why, when the wish has occurred to any one to think of a thing, his mind on the instant thinks of that very thing. Do idols observe our will, and so soon as we will does an image present itself to us, if sea, if earth, ay or heaven is what we wish? Assemblies of men, a procession, feasts, battles, everything in short does nature at command produce and provide? And though to increase the marvel the mind of others in the same spot and room is thinking of things all quite different. What again are we to say, when we see in sleep idols advance in measured tread and move their pliant limbs, when in nimble wise they put out each pliant arm in turn and represent to the eyes over and over again an action with foot that moves in time? Idols to wit are imbued with art and move about well-trained, to be able in the night-time to exhibit such plays. Or will this rather be the truth? Because in one unit of time, when we can perceive it by sense and while one single word is uttered, many latent times are contained which reason finds to exist, therefore in any time you please all the several idols are at hand ready prepared in each several place. And because they are so thin, the mind can see distinctly only those which it strains itself to see; therefore all that there are besides are lost, save only those for which it has made itself ready. Moreover it makes itself ready and hopes to see that which follows upon each thing; therefore the result does follow. Do you not see that the eyes also, when they essay to discern things which are thin and fine, strain themselves and make themselves ready, and without that we cannot see distinctly? And yet you may observe even in things which are plain before us, that if you do not attend, it is just as if the thing were all the time away and far distant. What wonder then, if the mind loses all other things save those with which it is itself earnestly occupied? Then too from small indications we draw the widest inferences and by our own fault entangle ourselves in the meshes of self-delusion.

Sometimes it happens too that an image of the same kind is not supplied, but what before was a woman, turns out in our hands to have changed into a man; or a different face and age succeed to the first. But sleep and forgetfulness prevent us from feeling surprise at this.

And herein you should desire with all your might to shun the weakness, with a lively apprehension to avoid the mistake of supposing that the bright lights of the eyes were made in order that we might see; and that the tapering ends of the shanks and hams are attached to the feet as a base in order to enable us to step out with long strides; or again that the forearms were slung to the stout upper arms and ministering hands given us on each side, that we might be able to discharge the needful duties of life. Other explanations of like sort which men give, one and all put effect for cause through wrongheaded reasoning; since nothing was born in the body that we might use it, but that which is born begets for itself a use: thus seeing did not exist before the eyes were born, nor the employment of speech ere the tongue was made; but rather the birth of the tongue was long anterior to language and the ears were made long before sound was heard, and all the limbs, I trow, existed before there was any employment for them: they could not therefore have grown for the purpose of being used. But on the other hand engaging in the strife of battle and mangling the body and staining the limbs with gore were in vogue long before glittering darts ever flew; and nature prompted to shun a wound or ever the left arm by the help of art held up before the person the defence of a shield. Yes and consigning the tired body to rest is much older than a soft-cushioned bed, and the slaking of thirst had birth before cups. These things therefore which have been invented in accordance with the uses and wants of life, may well be believed to have been discovered for the purpose of being used. Far otherwise is it with all those things which first were born, then afterwards made known the purposes to which they might be put; at the head of which class we see the senses and the limbs. Wherefore again and again I repeat, it is quite impossible to believe that they could have been made for the duties which they discharge.

It ought likewise to cause no wonder that the nature of the body of each living creature absolutely requires food. I have shown that bodies ebb away and withdraw from things, many in number in many ways; but most numerous must be those which withdraw from living things; for because these are tried by active motion, and many particles are pressed out from the depths of the frame and carried off by sweating, many breathed out through the mouth, when they pant from exhaustion, from such causes the body becomes rarefied and the whole nature undermined; and this state is attended by pain. Food therefore is taken in order to give support to the frame and recruit the strength by its infusion, and to close up the open-mouthed craving for meat throughout limbs and veins. The moisture too passes into all the parts which call for moisture; and many accumulated bodies of heat which cause a burning in our stomach, the approach of liquid scatters and quenches as if they were fire, so that dry heat can no longer parch the frame. In this way then you see gasping thirst is drenched out of our body, in this way the hungry craving is satisfied.

Now how it comes to pass that we are able to step out when we please, and how it is given us to move about our limbs, and what cause is wont to push forward the great load of this our body I will tell: do you take in my words. I say that idols of walking first present themselves to our mind and strike on the mind, as we said before: then the will arises; for no one begins to do anything, until his mind has first determined what it wills. From the very fact that it determines such thing, there is an image of that thing. When therefore the mind bestirs itself in such a way as to will to walk and step out, it strikes at the same moment the force of the soul which is spread over the whole body throughout the limbs and frame; and this is easily done, since the whole is held in close union with the mind. Next the soul in its turn strikes the body, and thus the whole mass by degrees is pushed on and set in motion. Then again the body becomes also rarefied, and the air, as you see its nature is, being always so nimble in moving, comes and passes in great quantity through the opened pores and is thus distributed into the most minute parts of the body. In this way then by these two causes acting in two ways the body like a ship is carried on by sails and wind. And herein it need not excite any surprise that such very minute bodies can steer so great a body and turn about the whole of this our load; for wind though fine with subtle body drives and pushes on a large ship of large moving mass and one hand directs it however great the speed at which it is going and one rudder steers it to any point you like; and by means of blocks of pulleys and tread-wheels a machine stirs many things of great weight and raises them up with slight effort.

Now by what means yon sleep lets a stream of repose over the limbs and dispels from the breast the cares of the mind, I will tell in sweetly worded rather than in many verses; as the short song of the swan is better than the loud noise of cranes scattered abroad amid the ethereal clouds of the south. Do you lend me a nice ear and a keen mind, that you may not deny what I say to be possible and secede with breast disdainfully rejecting the words of truth, you yourself being in fault the while and unable to discern. Sleep mainly takes place when the force of the soul has been scattered about through the frame, and in part has been forced abroad and taken its departure, and in part has been thrust back and has withdrawn into the depths of the body: after that the limbs are relaxed and droop. For there is no doubt that this sense exists in us by the agency of the soul; and when sleep obstructs the action of this sense, then we must assume that our soul has been disordered and forced abroad; not indeed all; for then the body would lie steeped in the everlasting chill of death. Where no part of the soul remained behind concealed in the limbs, as fire remains concealed when buried under much ash, whence could sense be suddenly rekindled through the limbs, as flame can spring up from hidden fire?

But by what means this change of condition is accomplished and from what the soul can be disordered and the body grow faint, I will explain: do you mind that I waste not my words on the wind. In the first place the body in its outer side, since it is next to and is touched by the air, must be thumped and beaten by its repeated blows; and for this reason all things as a rule are covered either by a hide or else by shells or by a callous skin or by bark. When creatures breathe, this air at the same time buffets the inner side also, as it is inhaled and exhaled. Therefore since the body is beaten on both sides alike and blows arrive by means of the small apertures at the primal parts and primal elements of our body, there gradually ensues a sort of breaking up throughout our limbs, the arrangements of the first-beginnings of body and mind getting disordered. Then next a part of the soul is forced out and a part withdraws into the inner recesses; a part too scattered about through the frame cannot get united together and so act and be acted upon by motion; for nature intercepts all communication and blocks up all the passages; and therefore sense retires deep into the frame as the motions are all altered. And since there is nothing as it were to lend support to the frame, the body becomes weak and all the limbs are faint, the arms and eyelids droop and the hams even in bed often give way under you and relax their powers. Then sleep follows on food, because food produces just the same effects as air, while it is distributed into all the veins; and that sleep is much the heaviest which you take when full or tired, because then the greatest number of bodies fall into disorder, bruised by much exertion. On the same principle the soul comes in part to be forced more deeply into the frame, and there is also a more copious emission of it abroad, and at the same time it is more divided and scattered in itself within you.

And generally to whatever pursuit a man is closely tied down and strongly attached, on whatever subject we have previously much dwelt, the mind having been put to a more than usual strain in it, during sleep we for the most part fancy that we are engaged in the same; lawyers think they plead causes and draw up covenants of sale, generals that they fight and engage in battle, sailors that they wage and carry on war with the winds, we think we pursue our task and investigate the nature of things constantly and consign it when discovered to writings in our native tongue. So all other pursuits and arts are seen for the most part during sleep to occupy and mock the minds of men. And whenever men have given during many days in succession undivided attention to games, we generally see that after they have ceased to perceive these with their senses, there yet remain passages open in the mind through which the same idols of things may enter. Thus for many days those same objects present themselves to the eyes, so that even when awake they see dancers as they think moving their pliant limbs, and receive into the ears the clear music of the harp and speaking strings, and behold the same spectators and at the same time the varied decorations of the stage in all their brilliancy. So great is the influence of zeal and inclination, so great is the influence of the things in which men have been habitually engaged, and not men only but all living creatures. Thus you will see stout horses, even when their bodies are lying down, yet in their sleep sweat and pant without ceasing and strain their powers to the utmost as if for the prize, or as if the barriers were thrown open. And often during soft repose the dogs of hunters do yet all at once throw about their legs and suddenly utter cries and repeatedly snuff the air with their nostrils, as though they had found and were on the tracks of wild beasts; and after they are awake often chase the shadowy idols of stags, as though they saw them in full flight, until they have shaken off their delusions and come to themselves again. And the fawning brood of dogs brought up tame in the house haste to shake their body and raise it up from the ground, as if they beheld unknown faces and features. And the fiercer the different breeds are, the greater rage they must display in sleep. But the various kinds of birds flee and suddenly in the night-time trouble with their wings the groves of the gods, when in gentle sleep hawks and pursuing birds have appeared to show fight and offer battle. Again the minds of men which pursue great aims under great emotions, often during sleep pursue and carry on the same in like manner; kings take by storm, are taken, join battle, raise a loud cry as if stabbed on the spot. Many struggle hard and utter groans in pain, and as if gnawed by the bite of panther or cruel lion fill all the place with loud cries. Many during sleep speak of important affairs and have often and often disclosed their own guilt. Many meet death; many as if tumbling down from high precipices to the ground with their whole body, are scared with terror and after sleep as if out of their judgement scarce come to themselves again, quite disordered by their body's turmoil. Again a thirsty man sits down beside a river or a pleasant spring and gulps down well-nigh all the stream. Cleanly people often, when sound asleep, believing that they are lifting their dress beside a urinal or the public vessels, pour forth the filtered liquid of their whole body, and the Babylonian coverlets of surpassing brilliancy are drenched. Then too those, into the boiling currents of whose age seed is for the first time passing, when the ripe fulness of days has produced it in their limbs, idols encounter from without from what body soever, harbingers of a glorious face and a beautiful bloom, which stir and excite the frame.

That seed we have spoken of before is stirred up in us, as soon as ripe age fortifies the frame. For as different causes set in motion and excite different things, so from man the sole influence of man draws forth human seed. As soon then as it has been forced out from and quits its proper seats throughout the limbs and frame, it withdraws itself from the whole body and meets together in appropriate places and rouses forthwith the appropriate parts of the body. The places are excited and swell with seed, and the inclination arises to emit the seed towards that to which the fell desire all tends, and the body seeks that object from which the mind is wounded by love; for all as a rule fall towards their wound and the blood spirts out in that direction whence comes the stroke by which we are struck; and if he is at close quarters, the red stream covers the foe. Thus then he who gets a hurt from the weapons of Venus, whatever be the object that hits him, inclines to the quarter whence he is wounded, and yearns to unite with it and join body with body; for a mute desire gives a presage of the pleasure.

This pleasure is for us Venus; from that desire is the Latin name of love, from that desire has first trickled into the heart yon drop of Venus' honeyed joy, succeeded soon by chilly care; for though that which you love is away, yet idols of it are at hand and its sweet name is present to the ears. But it is meet to fly idols and scare away all that feeds love and turn your mind on another object, distract your passion elsewhere and not keep it, with your thoughts once set on one object by love of it, and so lay up for yourself care and unfailing pain. For the sore gathers strength and becomes inveterate by feeding, and every day the madness grows in violence and the misery becomes aggravated, unless you erase the first wounds by new blows and first heal them when yet fresh, roaming abroad after Venus the pandemian, or transfer to something else the emotions of your mind.

Nor is he who shuns love without the fruits of Venus, but rather enjoys those blessings which are without any pain: doubtless the pleasure from such things is more unalloyed for the healthy-minded than for the love-sick; for in the very moment of enjoying the burning desire of lovers wavers and wanders undecided, and they cannot tell what first to enjoy with eyes and hands. What they have sought, they tightly squeeze and cause pain of body and often imprint their teeth on the lips and clash mouth to mouth in kissing, because the pleasure is not pure and there are hidden stings which stimulate to hurt even that whatever it is from which spring those germs of frenzy. But Venus with light hand breaks the force of these pains during love, and the fond pleasure mingled therein reins in the bites. For in this there is hope, that from the same body whence springs their burning desire, their flame may likewise be quenched; though nature protests that the very opposite is the truth; and this is the one thing of all, in which, when we have most of it, then all the more the breast burns with fell desire. Meat and drink are taken into the body; and as they can fill up certain fixed parts, in this way the craving for drink and bread is easily satisfied; but from the face and beautiful bloom of man nothing is given into the body to enjoy save flimsy idols; a sorry hope which is often snatched off by the wind. As when in sleep a thirsty man seeks to drink and water is not given to quench the burning in his frame, but he seeks the idols of waters and toils in vain and thirsts as he drinks in the midst of the torrent stream, thus in love Venus mocks lovers with idols, nor can bodies satisfy them by all their gazing upon them nor can they with their hands rub aught off the soft limbs, wandering undecided over the whole body. At last when they have united and enjoy the flower of age, when the body now has a presage of delights and Venus is in the mood to sow the fields of woman, they greedily clasp each other's body and suck each other's lips and breathe in, pressing meanwhile teeth on each other's mouth; all in vain, since they can rub nothing off nor enter and pass each with his whole body into the other's body; for so sometimes they seem to will and strive to do: so greedily are they held in the chains of Venus, while their limbs melt overpowered by the might of the pleasure. At length when the gathered desire has gone forth, there ensues for a brief while a short pause in the burning passion; and then returns the same frenzy, then comes back the old madness, when they are at a loss to know what they really desire to get, and cannot find what device is to conquer that mischief; in such utter uncertainty they pine away by a hidden wound.

Then too they waste their strength and ruin themselves by the labour, then too their life is passed at the beck of another. Meanwhile their estate runs away and is turned into Babylonian coverlets; duties are neglected and their good name staggers and sickens. On her feet laugh elastic and beautiful Sicyonian shoes, yes, and large emeralds with green light are set in gold and the sea-coloured dress is worn constantly and much used drinks in the sweat. The noble earnings of their fathers are turned into hair-bands, head-dresses; sometimes are changed into a sweeping robe and Alidensian and Cean dresses. Feasts set out with rich coverlets and viands, games, numerous cups, perfumes, crowns, and garlands are prepared; all in vain, since out of the very well-spring of delights rises up something of bitter, to pain amid the very flowers; either when the conscience-stricken mind haply gnaws itself with remorse to think that it is passing a life of sloth and ruining itself in brothels, or because she has launched forth some word and left its meaning in doubt and it cleaves to the love-sick heart and burns like living fire, or because it fancies she casts her eyes too freely about or looks on another, and it sees in her face traces of a smile.

And these evils are found in love that is lasting and highly prosperous; but in crossed and hopeless love are ills such as you may seize with closed eyes, past numbering; so that it is better to watch beforehand in the manner I have prescribed, and be on your guard not to be drawn in. For to avoid falling into the toils of love is not so hard as, after you are caught, to get out of the nets you are in and to break through the strong meshes of Venus. And yet even when you are entangled and held fast you may escape the mischief, unless you stand in your own way and begin by overlooking all the defects of her mind or those of her body, whoever it is whom you court and woo. For this men usually do, blinded by passion, and attribute to the beloved those advantages which are not really theirs. We therefore see women in ways manifold deformed and ugly to be objects of endearment and held in the highest admiration. And one lover jeers at others and advises them to propitiate Venus, since they are troubled by a disgraceful passion, and often, poor wretch, gives no thought to his own ills greatest of all. The black is a brune, the filthy and rank has not the love of order; the cat-eyed is a miniature Pallas, the stringy and wizened a gazelle; the dumpy and dwarfish is one of the Graces, from top to toe all grace; the big and overgrown is awe-inspiring and full of dignity. She is tongue-tied, cannot speak, then she has a lisp; the dumb is bashful; then the fire-spit, the teasing, the gossiping turns to a shining lamp. One becomes a slim darling then when she cannot live from want of flesh; and she is only spare, who is half-dead with cough. Then the fat and big-breasted is a Ceres' self big-breasted from Iacchus; the pug-nosed is a she Silenus and a satyress; the thick-lipped a very kiss. It were tedious to attempt to report other things of the kind. Let her however be of ever so great dignity of appearance; such that the power of Venus goes forth from all her limbs; yet there are others too; yet have we lived without her before; yet does she do, and we know that she does, in all things the same as the ugly woman; and fumigates herself, poor wretch, with nauseous perfumes, her very maids running from her and giggling behind her back. But the lover, when shut out, often in tears covers the threshold with flowers and wreaths, and anoints the haughty doorposts with oil of marjoram and imprints kisses, poor wretch, on the doors. When however he has been admitted, if on his approach but one single breath should come in his way, he would seek specious reasons for departing, and the long-conned deep-drawn complaint would fall to the ground; and then he would blame his folly, on seeing that he had attributed to her more than it is right to concede to a mortal. Nor is this unknown to our Venuses; wherefore all the more they themselves hide with the utmost pains all that goes on behind the scenes of life from those whom they wish to retain in the chains of love; but in vain, since you may yet draw forth from her mind into the light all these things and search into all her smiles; and if she is of a fair mind and not troublesome, overlook them in your turn and make allowance for human failings.

Nor does the woman sigh always with feigned passion, when she locks in her embrace and joins with her body the man's body and holds it, sucking his lips into her lips and drinking in his kisses. Often she does it from the heart, and seeking mutual joys courts him to run the complete race of love. And in no other way could birds, cattle, wild beasts, sheep, and mares submit to bear the males, except because the very exuberance of nature in the females is in heat and burns and joyously draws in the Venus of the covering males. See you not too how those whom mutual pleasure has chained are often tortured in their common chains? How often in the highways do dogs, desiring to separate, eagerly pull different ways with all their might, while all the time they are held fast in the strong fetters of Venus! This they would never do, unless they experienced mutual joys, strong enough to force them into the snare and hold them in its meshes. Wherefore again and again I repeat there is a common pleasure.

And when haply in mixing her seed with the man's the woman by sudden force has overpowered and seized for herself his force, then children are formed from the mothers' seed like to the mothers, as from the fathers' seed like to the fathers. But those whom you see with a share of both forms, blending equally the features of the parents, grow from the union of the father's body and the mother's blood, when the mutual ardour of desire working in concert has brought and clashed together the seeds roused throughout the frame by the goads of Venus; and neither of the two has gotten the mastery nor has been mastered. Sometimes too the children may spring up like their grandfathers and often resemble the forms of their grandfathers' fathers, because the parents often keep concealed in their bodies many first-beginnings mixed in many ways, which first proceeding from the original stock one father hands down to the next father; and then from these Venus produces forms after a manifold chance and repeats not only the features, but the voices and hair of their forefathers. And the female sex equally springs from the father's seed and males go forth equally formed from the mother's body; since these distinctions no more proceed from the fixed seed of one or other parent than our faces and bodies and limbs: the birth is always formed out of the two seeds; and whichever parent that which is produced more resembles, of that parent it has more than an equal share; as you may equally observe, whether it is a male child or a female birth.

Nor do the divine powers debar anybody from the power of begetting, forbidding him ever to receive the name of father from sweet children and forcing him to pass his life in a barren wedlock; as men commonly fancy when in sorrow they drench the altars with much blood and pile the raised altars with offerings, to make their wives pregnant with abundant seed. In vain they weary the divinity of the gods and the sacred lots. They are barren sometimes from the too great thickness of the seed, sometimes from its undue fluidity and thinness: because the thin is unable to get a firm hold on the right spots, it at once passes away and is repelled and withdrawn abortively: since by others again a too thick seed is discharged in a state more solid than is suitable, it either does not fly forth with so prolonged a stroke or cannot equally pass into the proper spots or when it has passed in with difficulty mixes with the woman's seed. For well-assorted matches are found to be of great importance; and some males impregnate some females more readily than others, and other females conceive and become pregnant more readily from other males. And many women have hitherto been barren during several marriages and have yet in the end found mates from whom they could conceive children and be enriched with a sweet offspring. And often even for those, to whom hitherto wives however fruitful had been unable in their house to bear, has been found a compatible nature, enabling them to fortify their age with sons. Of such great importance is it, in order that seeds may agree and blend with seeds in a way to promote birth, whether the thick comes into contact with the fluid and the fluid with the thick. And on this point it matters much on what diet life is supported; for by some foods seed is thickened in the limbs, and by others again is thinned and wasted. And in what modes the intercourse goes on, is likewise of very great moment; for women are commonly thought to conceive more readily after the manner of wild beasts and quadrupeds, because the seeds in this way can find the proper spots in consequence of the position of the body. Nor have wives the least use for effeminate motions: a woman hinders and stands in the way of her own conceiving, when thus she acts; for she drives the furrow out of the direct course and path of the share and turns away from the proper spots the stroke of the seed. And thus for their own ends harlots are wont to move, in order not to conceive and lie in child-bed frequently, and at the same time to render Venus more attractive to men. This our wives have surely no need of.

Sometimes too by no divine grace and arrows of Venus a sorry woman of inferior beauty comes to be loved; for the wife sometimes by her own acts and accommodating manners and by elegant neatness of person readily habituates you to pass your life with her. Moreover custom renders love attractive; for that which is struck by oft-repeated blows however lightly, yet after long course of time is overpowered and gives way. See you not too that drops of water falling on stones after long course of time scoop a hole through these stones?

BOOK V

WHO is able with powerful genius to frame a poem worthy of the grandeur of the things and these discoveries? Or who is so great a master of words as to be able to devise praises equal to the deserts of him who left to us such prizes won and earned by his own genius? None methinks who is formed of mortal body. For if we must speak as the acknowledged grandeur of the things itself demands, a god he was, a god, most noble Memmius, who first found out that plan of life which is now termed wisdom, and who by trained skill rescued life from such great billows and such thick darkness and moored it in so perfect a calm and in so brilliant a light. Compare the godlike discoveries of others in old times: Ceres is famed to have pointed out to mortals corn, and Liber the vine-born juice of the grape; though life might well have subsisted without these things, as we are told some nations even now live without them. But a happy life was not possible without a clean breast; wherefore with more reason this man is deemed by us a god, from whom come those sweet solaces of existence which even now are distributed over great nations and gently soothe men's minds. Then if you shall suppose that the deeds of Hercules surpass his, you will be carried still farther away from true reason. For what would yon great gaping maw of Nemean lion now harm us and the bristled Arcadian boar? Ay or what could the bull of Crete do and the hydra plague of Lerna, fenced round with its envenomed snakes? Or how could the triple-breasted might of threefold Geryon, how could the birds with brazen arrowy feathers [1] that dwelt in the Stymphalian swamps do us such mighty injury, and the horses of Thracian Diomede breathing fire from their nostrils along the Bistonian borders and Ismara? And the serpent which guards the bright golden apples of the Hesperides, fierce, dangerous of aspect, girding the tree's stem with his enormous body, what harm pray could he do us beside the Atlantic shore and its sounding main, which none of us goes near and no barbarian ventures to approach? And all other monsters of the kind which have been destroyed, if they had not been vanquished, what harm could they do, I ask, though now alive? None methinks: the earth even now so abounds to repletion in wild beasts and is filled with troublous terror throughout woods and great mountains and deep forests; places which we have it for the most part in our own power to shun. But unless the breast is cleared, what battles and dangers must then find their way into us in our own despite! What poignant cares inspired by lust then rend the distressful man, and then also what mighty fears! And pride, filthy lust and wantonness? What disasters they occasion, and luxury and all sorts of sloth? He therefore who shall have subdued all these and banished them from the mind by words, not arms, shall he not have a just title to be ranked among the gods? And all the more so that he was wont to deliver many precepts in beautiful and god-like phrase about the immortal gods themselves and to open up by his teachings all the nature of things.

While walking in his footsteps I follow out his reasonings and teach by my verses, by what law all things are made, what necessity there is then for them to continue in that law, and how impotent they are to annul the binding statutes of time: foremost in which class of things the nature of the mind has been proved to be formed of a body that had birth and to be unable to endure unscathed through great time, mere idols being wont to mock the mind in sleep, when we seem to see him whom life has abandoned: to continue, the order of my design has now brought me to this point, where I must proceed to show that the world is formed of a mortal body and at the same time had birth; to show too in what way that union of matter founded earth, heaven, sea, stars, sun, and the ball of the moon; also what living creatures sprang out of the earth, as well as those which never at any time were born; in what way too mankind began to use with one another varied speech by the names conferred on things; and also in what ways yon fear of the gods gained an entry into men's breasts, and now throughout the world maintains as holy fanes, lakes, groves, altars, and idols of the gods. Furthermore I shall make clear by what force piloting nature guides the courses of the sun and the wanderings of the moon; lest haply we imagine that these of their own free will between heaven and earth traverse their everlasting orbits, graciously furthering the increase of crops and living creatures, or we think they roll on by any forethought of the gods. For they who have been rightly taught that the gods lead a life without care, if nevertheless they wonder by what plan all things can be carried on, above all in regard to those things which are seen overhead in the ethereal borders, are borne back again into their old religious scruples and take unto themselves hard taskmasters, whom they poor wretches believe to be almighty, not knowing what can, what cannot be, in short by what system each thing has its powers defined, its deep-set boundary mark.

Well then not to detain you any longer by mere promises, look before all on seas and lands and heaven: their threefold nature, their three bodies, Memmius, three forms so unlike, three such wondrous textures a single day shall give over to destruction; and the mass and fabric of the world upheld for many years shall tumble to ruin. Nor can I fail to perceive with what a novel and strange effect it falls upon the mind, this destruction of heaven and earth that is to be, and how hard it is for me to produce a full conviction of it by words; as is the case when you bring to the ears a thing hitherto unexampled, and yet you cannot submit it to the eyesight nor put it into the hands; through which the straightest highway of belief leads into the human breast and quarters of the mind. But yet I will speak out: it well may be that the reality itself will bring credit to my words and that you will see earthquakes arise and all things grievously shattered to pieces in short time. But this may pilot fortune guide far away from us, and may reason rather than the reality convince that all things may be overpowered and tumble in with a frightful crash.

But before I shall begin on this question to pour forth decrees of fate with more sanctity and much more certainty than the Pythia who speaks out from the tripod and laurel of Phoebus, I will clearly set forth to you many comforting topics in learned language; lest held in the yoke of religion you haply suppose that earth and sun and heaven, sea, stars, and moon must last for ever with divine body; and therefore think it right that they after the fashion of the giants should all suffer punishment for their monstrous guilt, who by their reasoning displace the walls of the world and seek to quench the glorious sun of heaven, branding immortal things in mortal speech; though in truth these things are so far from possessing divinity and are so unworthy of being reckoned in the number of gods, that they may be thought to afford a notable instance of what is quite without vital motion and sense. For it is quite impossible to suppose that the nature and judgement of the mind can exist with any body whatever; even as a tree cannot exist in the ether nor clouds in the salt sea, nor can fishes live in the fields nor blood exist in woods nor sap in stones. Where each thing can grow and abide is fixed and ordained. Thus the nature of the mind cannot come into being alone without the body nor exist far away from the sinews and blood. But if (for this would be much more likely to happen than that) the force itself of the mind might be in the head or shoulders or heels or might be born in any other part of the body, it would after all be wont to abide in one and the same man or vessel. But since in our body even it is fixed and seen to be ordained where the soul and the mind can severally be and grow, it must still more strenuously be denied that it can abide out of the body and the living room altogether in crumbling clods of earth or in the fire of the sun or in water or in the high borders of ether. These things therefore are not possessed of divine sense, since they cannot be quickened with the vital feeling.

This too you may not possibly believe, that the holy seats of the gods exist in any parts of the world: the fine nature of the gods far withdrawn from our senses is hardly seen by the thought of the mind; and since it has ever eluded the touch and stroke of the hands, it must touch nothing which is tangible for us; for that cannot touch which does not admit of being touched in turn. And therefore their seats as well must be unlike our seats, fine, even as their bodies are fine. All which I will prove to you later in copious argument. To say again that for the sake of men they have willed to set in order the glorious nature of the world and therefore it is meet to praise the work of the gods calling as it does for all praise, and to believe that it will be eternal and immortal, and that it is an unholy thing ever to shake by any force from its fixed seats that which by the forethought of the gods in ancient days has been established on everlasting foundations for mankind, or to assail it by speech and utterly overturn it from top to bottom; and to invent and add other figments of the kind, Memmius, is all sheer folly. For what advantage can our gratitude bestow on immortal and blessed beings, that for our sakes they should take in hand to administer aught? And what novel incident should have induced them hitherto at rest so long after to desire to change their former life? For it seems natural he should rejoice in a new state of things, whom old things annoy; but for him whom no ill has befallen in times gone by, when he passed a pleasant existence, what could have kindled in such a one a love of change? Did life lie grovelling in darkness and sorrow, until the first dawn of the birth-time of things? Or what evil had it been for us never to have been born? Whoever has been born must want to continue in life, so long as fond pleasure shall keep him; but for him who has never tasted the love, never been on the lists, of life, what harm not to have been born? Whence again was first implanted in the gods a pattern for begetting things in general as well as the preconception of what men are, so that they knew and saw in mind what they wanted to make? And in what way was the power of first-beginnings ever ascertained, and what they could effect by a change in their mutual arrangements, unless nature herself gave the model for making things? For in suchwise the first-beginnings of things many in number in many ways impelled by blows for infinite ages back and kept in motion by their own weights have been wont to be carried along and to unite in all manner of ways and thoroughly test every kind of production possible by their mutual combinations; that it is not strange if they have also fallen into arrangements and have come into courses like to those out of which this sum of things is now carried on by constant renewing.

But if I did not know what first-beginnings of things are, yet this judging by the very arrangements of heaven I would venture to affirm, and led by many other facts to maintain, that the nature of things has by no means been made for us by divine power: so great are the defects with which it is encumbered. In the first place of all the space which the vast reach of heaven covers, a portion greedy mountains and forests of wild beasts have occupied, rocks and wasteful pools take up and the sea which holds wide apart the coasts of different lands. Next of nearly two thirds burning heat and the constant fall of frost rob mortals. What is left for tillage, even that nature by its power would overrun with thorns, unless the force of man made head against it, accustomed for the sake of a livelihood to groan beneath the strong hoe and to cut through the earth by pressing down the plough. Unless by turning up the fruitful clods with the share and labouring the soil of the earth we stimulate things to rise, they could not spontaneously come up into the clear air; and even then sometimes when things earned with great toil now put forth their leaves over the lands and are all in blossom, either the ethereal sun burns them up with excessive heats or sudden rains and cold frosts cut them off, and the blasts of the winds waste them by a furious hurricane. Again why does nature give food and increase to the frightful race of wild beasts dangerous to mankind both by sea and land? Why do the seasons of the year bring diseases in their train? Why stalks abroad untimely death? Then too the baby, like to a sailor cast away by the cruel waves, lies naked on the ground, speechless, wanting every furtherance of life, soon as nature by the throes of birth has shed him forth from his mother's womb into the borders of light: he fills the room with a rueful wauling, as well he may whose destiny it is to go through in life so many ills. But the different flocks, herds, and wild beasts grow up; they want no rattles; to none of them need be addressed the fond broken accents of the fostering nurse; they ask not different dresses according to the season; no nor do they want arms or lofty walls, whereby to protect their own, the earth itself and nature manifold in her works producing in plenty all things for all.

First of all, since the body of the earth and water and the light breath of air and burning heats, out of which this sum of things is seen to be formed, do all consist of a body that had a birth and is mortal, the whole nature of the world must be reckoned of a like body. For those things whose parts and members we see to be of a body that had a birth and of forms that are mortal, we perceive to be likewise without exception mortal, and at the same time to have had a birth. Since therefore I see that the chiefest members and parts of the world are destroyed and begotten anew, I may be sure that for heaven and earth as well there has been a time of beginning and there will be a time of destruction.

And herein that you may not think I have unfairly seized on this point for myself, because I have assumed that earth and fire are mortal and have not doubted that water and air perish, and have said that these are likewise begotten and grow afresh, mark the proofs: first of all some portion of the earth, burnt up by constant suns, trampled by a multitude of feet, sends forth a cloud and flying eddies of dust, which the strong winds disperse over the whole air. Part too of the soil is put under water by rains, and rivers graze against and eat into the banks. Again whatever increases something else, is in its turn replenished; and since beyond a doubt earth the universal mother is found at the same time to be the general tomb of things, therefore you see she is lessened and increases and grows again.

Furthermore, that sea, rivers, fountains always stream over with new moisture and that waters well up without ceasing, it needs no words to prove: the great flow of waters from all sides clearly shows it. But then the water on the surface is always taken off, and thus it is that on the whole there is no overflow, partly because the seas are lessened by the strong winds sweeping over them and by the ethereal sun decomposing them with his rays; partly, because the water is diffused below the surface over all lands; for the salt is strained off and the matter of liquid streams back again to the source and all meets together at the river-heads, and then flows over the lands in a fresh current, where a channel once scooped out has carried down the waters with liquid foot.

And next I will speak of the air which is changed over its whole body every hour in countless ways. For whatever ebbs from things, is all borne always into the great sea of air; and unless it in return were to give back bodies to things and to recruit them as they ebb, all things ere now would have been dissolved and changed into air. It therefore ceases not to be begotten from things and to go back into things, since it is a fact that all things constantly ebb.

Likewise the abundant source of clear light, the ethereal sun, constantly floods heaven with fresh brightness and supplies the place of light on the instant by new light; for every previous emission of brightness is quite lost to it, wherever it falls. This you may know from the following examples: as soon as ever clouds begin to pass below the sun and to break off so to say the rays of light, forthwith their lower part is wholly lost, and the earth is over-shadowed wherever the clouds pass over; so that you may know that things constantly require new irradiation and that all the preceding emissions of light are lost, and in no other way can things be seen in the sun, unless the fountain head of light itself send a supply. Moreover, you see, nightly lights which belong to earth, such as hanging lamps and torches bright with darting flames, hasten in like fashion amid great darkness with ministering heat to supply new light; are eager to bicker with fires, ay eager; nor is the light ever broken off nor does it quit the spots illuminated: with such suddenness is its destruction concealed by the swift birth of flame from all the fires at once. In the same way then we must believe that sun, moon, and stars emit light from fresh and ever fresh supplies rising up, and always lose every previous discharge of flames; that you may not haply believe that these flourish indestructible.

Again see you not that even stones are conquered by time, that high towers fall and rocks moulder away, that shrines and idols of gods are worn out with decay, and that the holy divinity cannot prolong the bounds of fate or struggle against the fixed laws of nature? Then see we not the monuments of men, fallen to ruin, ask for themselves as well whether you'd believe that *they* decay with years? See we not basalt rocks tumble down riven away from high mountains and unable to endure and suffer the strong might of finite age? Surely they would never fall suddenly thus riven away, if for infinite time past they had held out against all the batteries of age without a crash.

Again gaze on this, which about and above holds in its embrace all the earth: if it begets all things out of itself, as some say, and takes them back when they are destroyed, then the whole of it has had a birth and is of a mortal body; for whatever gives increase and food out of itself to other things, must be lessened; and must be replenished, when it takes things back.

Again if there was no birth-time of earth and heaven and they have been from everlasting, why before the Theban war and the destruction of Troy have not other poets as well sung other themes? Whither have so many deeds of men so often passed away, why live they nowhere embodied in lasting records of fame? The truth methinks is that the sum has but a recent date and the nature of the world is new and has but lately had its commencement. Wherefore even now some arts are receiving their last polish, some are even in course of growth: just now many improvements have been made in ships; only yesterday musicians have given birth to tuneful melodies; then too this nature or system of things has been discovered lately, and I the very first of all have only now been found able to transfer it into native words. But if haply you believe that before this all things have existed just the same, but that the generations of men have perished by burning heat, or that cities have fallen by some great concussion of the world, or that after constant rains devouring rivers have gone forth over the earth and have whelmed towns, so much the more you must yield and admit that there will be entire destruction too of earth and heaven; for when things were tried by so great distempers and so great dangers, at that time had a more disastrous cause pressed upon them, they would far and wide have gone to destruction and mighty ruin. And in no other way are we proved to be mortals, except because we all alike in turn fall sick of the same diseases which those had whom nature has withdrawn from life.

Again whatever things last for ever, must either, because they are of solid body, repel strokes and not suffer aught to pass into them, sufficient to disunite the closely massed parts within: such are the bodies of matter whose nature we have shown before: or they must be able to endure through all time for this reason, because they are exempt from blows, as void is which remains untouched and suffers not a jot from any stroke; or else because there is no extent of room around, into which things so to say may depart and be broken up: in this way the sum of sums is eternal and there is no place outside into which things may spring asunder, nor are there any bodies which can fall upon them and dissolve them by a powerful blow. But the nature of the world, as I have shown, is neither of solid body, since void is mixed up in things, nor is it again like void, no nor is there lack of bodies that may haply rise up in mass out of the infinite and overthrow this sum of things with furious tornado or bring upon them some other perilous disaster; nor further is the nature of room or the space of deep void wanting, into which the walls of the world may be scattered abroad; or they may be assailed and perish by some other force. Therefore the gate of death is not closed against heaven or sun or earth or the deep waters of the sea, but stands open and looks towards them with huge wide-gaping maw. And therefore also you must admit that these things likewise had a birth; for things which are of mortal body could not for an infinite time back up to the present have been able to set at naught the puissant strength of immeasurable age.

Again since the chiefest members of the world fight so hotly together, fiercely stirred by no hallowed civil warfare, see you not that some limit may be set to their long struggle? Either when the sun and all heat shall have drunk up all the waters and gotten the mastery: this they are ever striving to do, but as yet are unable to accomplish their endeavours: such abundant supplies the rivers furnish, and threaten to turn aggressors and flood all things with a deluge from the deep gulfs of ocean; all in vain, since the winds sweeping over the seas and the ethereal sun decomposing them with his rays do lessen them, and trust to be able to dry all things up before water can attain the end of its endeavour. Such a war do they breathe out with undecided issue, and strive with each other to determine it for mighty ends; though once by the way fire got the upper hand and once, as the story goes, water reigned paramount in the fields. Fire gained the mastery and licked and burnt up many things, when the headstrong might of the horses of the sun dashed from the course and hurried Phaethon through the whole sky and over all lands. But the almighty father, stirred then to fierce wrath, with a sudden thunderstroke dashed Phaethon down from his horses to earth, and the sun meeting him as he fell caught from him the ever-burning lamp of the world and got in hand the scattered steeds and yoked them shaking all over; then guided them on their proper course and gave fresh life to all things. Thus to wit have the old poets of the Greeks sung; though it is all too widely at variance with true reason. Fire may gain the mastery when more bodies of matter than usual have gathered themselves up out of the infinite; and then its powers decay, vanquished in some way or other, or else things perish burnt up by the torrid air. Water too of yore gathered itself and began to get the mastery, as the story goes, when it whelmed many cities of men; and then when all that force that had gathered itself up out of the infinite, by some means or other was turned aside and withdrew, the rains were stayed and the rivers abated their fury.

But in what ways yon concourse of matter founded earth and heaven and the deeps of the sea, the courses of the sun and moon, I will next in order describe. For verily not by design did the first-beginnings of things station themselves each in its right place by keen intelligence, nor did they bargain sooth to say what motions each should assume, but because the first-beginnings of things many in number in many ways impelled by blows for infinite ages back and kept in motion by their own weights have been wont to be carried along and to unite in all manner of ways and thoroughly to test every kind of production possible by their mutual combinations, therefore it is that spread abroad through great time after trying unions and motions of every kind they at length meet together in those masses which suddenly brought together become often the rudiments of great things, of earth, sea, and heaven and the race of living things.

At this time then neither could the sun's disc be discerned flying aloft with its abundant light, nor the stars of great ether, nor sea nor heaven, no nor earth nor air, nor could any thing be seen like to our things, but only a strange stormy crisis and medley, gathered together out of first-beginnings of every kind, whose state of discord joining battle disordered their interspaces, passages, connexions, weights, blows, clashings, and motions, because by reason of their unlike forms and varied shapes they could not all remain thus joined together nor fall into mutually harmonious motions. Then next the several parts began to fly asunder and things to be joined like with like and to mark off the world and portion out its members and arrange its mighty parts, that is to say, to separate high heaven from earth, and let the sea spread itself out apart with its unmixed water, and likewise let the fires of ether spread apart pure and unmixed.

For first the several bodies of earth, because they were heavy and closely entangled, met together in the middle and took up all of them the lowest positions; and the more they got entangled and the closer their union, the more they squeezed out those particles which were to make up sea, stars, sun, and moon and the walls of the great world. All these are of smooth and round seeds and of much smaller elements than the earth. Therefore the fire-laden ether first burst out from the different parts of the earth through all the porous openings and lightly bore off with itself many fires; much in the same way as we often see, so soon as the morning light of the beaming sun blushes golden over the grass jewelled with dew, and the pools and the ever-running rivers exhale a mist, and even as the earth itself is sometimes seen to smoke; and when all these are gathered together aloft, then do clouds on high with a now cohering body weave a covering beneath heaven. In this way therefore then the light and expansive ether with its now cohering body swept round and arched itself on all sides and expanding widely in all directions round in this way fenced all other things in with its greedy grasp. After it followed the rudiments of sun and moon, whose spheres turn round in air midway between earth and ether: these neither earth has taken unto itself nor greatest ether, because they were neither heavy enough to sink and settle down nor light enough to glide along the uppermost borders; they yet however are so placed between the two as to wheel along their life-like bodies and still to be parts of the whole world; just as in us some members may be at rest, while others at the same time are in motion. These things then being withdrawn, the earth in those parts where the vast azure level of ocean now spreads, in a moment sank in and drenched with salt flood the hollows. At every day the more the heats of ether round and the rays of the sun on all sides compressed the earth into a close mass by oft-repeated blows on all its outer edges, so that thus buffeted it was condensed and drawn together about its centre, ever the more did the salt sweat squeezed out of its body increase by its oozings the sea and floating fields, and ever the more did those many bodies of heat and air escape and fly abroad and condense far away from earth the high glittering quarters of heaven. The plains sank down, the high hills grew in elevation; for the rocks could not settle down nor all the parts sink to one uniform level.

Thus then the ponderous mass of earth was formed with close-cohering body and all the slime of the world so to speak slid down by its weight to the lowest point and settled at the bottom like dregs. Then the sea, then the air, then the fire-laden ether itself, all are left unmixed with their clear bodies; and some are lighter than others, and clearest and lightest of all ether floats upon the airy currents, and blends not its clear body with the troubled airs; it suffers all these things below to be upset with furious hurricanes, suffer them to be troubled by wayward storms; while it carries along its own fires gliding with a changeless onward sweep. For that ether may stream on gently and with one uniform effort the Pontos shows, a sea which streams with a changeless current, ever preserving one uniform gliding course.

Let us now sing what causes the motions of the stars. In the first place, if the great sphere of heaven revolves, we must say that an air presses on the pole at each end and confines it on the outside and closes it in at both ends; and then that a third air streams above and moves in the same direction in which roll on as they shine the stars of the eternal world; or else that this third air streams below in order to carry up the sphere in the contrary direction; just as we see rivers turn wheels and water-scoops. It is likewise quite possible too that all the heaven remains at rest, while at the same time the glittering signs are carried on; either because rapid heats of ether are shut in and whirl round while seeking a way out and roll their fires in all directions through heaven's Summanian quarters; or else an air streaming from some part from another source outside drives and whirls the fires; or else they may glide on of themselves going withersoever the food of each calls and invites them, feeding their flamy bodies everywhere throughout heaven. For which of these causes is in operation in this world, it is not easy to affirm for certain; but what can be and is done throughout the universe in various worlds formed on various plans, this I teach, and I go on to set forth several causes which may exist throughout the universe for the motions of stars; one of which however must in this world also be the cause that imparts lively motion to the signs; but to dictate which of them it is, is by no means the duty of the man who advances step by step.

And in order that the earth may rest in the middle of the world, it is proper that its weight should gradually pass away and be lessened, and that it should have another nature underneath it conjoined from the beginning of its existence and formed into one being with the airy portions of the world in which it is embodied and lives. For this reason it is no burden and does not weigh down the air; just as his limbs are of no weight to a man nor is his head a burden to his neck, nor do we feel that the whole weight of the body rests on the feet; but whatever weights come from without and are laid upon us, hurt us though they are often very much smaller: of such great moment it is what function each thing has to perform. Thus then the earth is not an alien body suddenly brought in and forced from some other quarter on air alien to it, but was conceived together with it at the first birth of the world and is a fixed portion of that world, just as our limbs are seen to be to us. Again the earth when suddenly shaken by loud thunder shakes by its motion all the things which are above it; and this it could in no wise do, unless it had been fast bound with the airy portions of the world and with heaven. For the earth and they cohere with one another by common roots, conjoined and formed into a single being from the beginning of their existence. See you not too that great as is the weight of our body, the force of the soul, though of the extremest fineness, supports it, because it is so closely conjoined and formed into a single being with it? Then too what is able to lift the body with a nimble bound save the force of the mind which guides the limbs? Now do you see what power a subtle nature may have, when it is conjoined with a heavy body, as the air is conjoined with the earth and the force of the mind with us?

Again the disc of the sun cannot be much larger nor its body of heat much smaller, than they appear to be to our senses. For from whatever distances fires can reach us with their light and breathe on our limbs burning heat, those distances take away nothing by such spaces between from the body of the flames, the fire is not in the least narrowed in appearance. Therefore since the heat of the sun and the light which it sheds reach our senses and stroke the proper places, the form too and size of the sun must be seen from this earth in their real dimensions, so that you may not add anything whatever more or less. And whether the moon as it is borne on illuminates places with a borrowed light, or emits its own light from its own body, whatever that is, the form with which it is thus borne on is not at all larger than the one which it presents to our eyes seems to us to be. For all things which we see at a great distance through much air, look dimmed in appearance before their size is diminished. Therefore since the moon presents a bright aspect and well-defined form, it must be seen on high by us from this earth precisely such as it is in the outline which defines it, and of the size it actually is. Lastly in the case of all those fires of ether which you observe from this earth—since in the case of fires which we see here on earth, so long as their flickering is distinct, so long as their heat is perceived, their size is seen sometimes to change to a very very small extent either way, according to the distance at which they are—you may infer that the fires of ether may be smaller than they look in an extremely minute degree, or larger by a very small and insignificant fraction.

This likewise need not excite wonder, how it is that so small a body as yon sun can emit so great a light, enough to flood completely seas and all lands and heaven and to steep all things in its burning heat. It well may be that a single spring for the whole world may open up from this spot and gush out in plenteous stream and shoot forth light, because elements of heat meet together from all sides out of the whole world in such manner and the mass of them thrown together streams to a point in such manner, that this heat wells forth from a single source. See you not too what a breadth of meadowland a small spring of water sometimes floods, streaming out over the fields? It is likewise possible that heat from the sun's flame though not at all great may infect the whole air with fervent fires, if haply the air is in a suitable and susceptible state, so that it can be kindled when struck by small bodies of heat; thus we see sometimes a general conflagration from a single spark catch fields of corn and stubble. Perhaps too the sun as he shines aloft with rosy lamp has round about him much fire with heats that are not visible, and thus the fire may be marked by no radiance, so that fraught with heat it increases to such a degree the stroke of the rays.

Nor with regard to the sun is there one single explanation, certain and manifest, of the way in which he passes from his summer positions to the midwinter turning-point of Capricorn and then coming back from thence bends his course to the solstitial goal of Cancer, and how the moon is seen once a month to pass over that space, in traversing which the sun spends the period of a year. No single plain cause, I say, has been assigned for these things. It seems highly probable that that may be the truth which the revered judgement of the worthy man Democritus maintains: the nearer the different constellations are to the earth, the less they can be carried along with the whirl of heaven; for the velocity of its force, he says, passes away and the intensity diminishes in the lower parts, and therefore the sun is gradually left behind with the rearward signs, because he is much lower than the burning signs. And the moon more than the sun: the lower her path is and the more distant she is from heaven and the nearer she approaches to earth, the less she can keep pace with the signs. For the fainter the whirl is in which she is borne along, being as she is lower than the sun, so much the more all the signs around overtake and pass her. Therefore it is that she appears to come back to every sign more quickly, because the signs go more quickly back to her. It is quite possible too that from quarters of the world crossing the sun's path two airs may stream each in its turn at a fixed time; one of which may force the sun away from the summer signs so far as his midwinter turning-point and freezing cold, and the other may force him back from the freezing shades of cold as far as the heat-laden quarters and burning signs. And in like manner we must suppose that the moon, and the stars which make revolutions of great years in great orbits may pass by means of airs from opposite quarters in turn. See you not too that clouds from contrary winds pass in contrary directions, the upper in a contrary way to the lower? Why may not yon stars just as well be borne on through their great orbits in ether by currents contrary one to the other?

But night buries the earth in thick darkness, either when the sun after his long course has struck upon the utmost parts of heaven and now exhausted has blown forth all his fires shaken by their journey and weakened by passing through much air: or else because the same force which has carried on his orb above the earth, compels him to change his course and pass below the earth.

At a fixed time too Matuta spreads rosy morning over the borders of ether and opens up her light, either because the same sun, coming back below the earth, seizes heaven before his time trying to kindle it with his rays; or because fires meet together and many seeds of heat are accustomed to stream together at a fixed time, which cause new sunlight to be born every day. Thus they tell that from the high mountains of Ida scattered fires are seen at day-break, that these then unite as it were into a single ball and make up an orb. And herein it ought to cause no surprise that these seeds of fire stream together at a time so surely fixed and reproduce the radiance of the sun. For we see many occurrences which take place at a fixed time in all things. At a fixed time trees blossom and at a fixed time shed their blossoms; and at a time no less surely fixed age bids the teeth be shed and the boy put on the soft dress of puberty and let a soft beard fall down equally from each cheek. Lastly lightnings, snow, rains, clouds, and winds take place at not very irregular seasons of year. For where causes from their very first-beginnings have been in this way and things have thus fallen out from the first birth of the world, in due sequence too they now come round after a fixed order.

Likewise days may lengthen and nights wane, and days shorten when the nights receive increase, either because the same sun running his course below the earth and above in curves of unlike length parts the borders of ether and divides his orbit into unequal halves; and as he comes round adds on in the opposite half just as much as he has subtracted from the other of the two halves, until he has arrived at that sign of heaven, where the node of the year makes the shades of night of the same length as the daylight. For when the sun's course lies midway between the blast of the north and of the south, heaven keeps his two goals apart at distances now rendered exactly equal on account of the position of the whole starry circle, in gliding through which the sun takes up the period of a year, lighting with slanting rays earth and heaven; as is clearly shown by the plans of those who have mapped out all the quarters of heaven as they are set off with their array of signs. Or else because the air is denser in certain parts, therefore the quivering beam of fire is retarded below the earth and cannot easily pass through and force its way out to its place of rising: for this reason in wintertime nights linger long, ere the beamy badge of day arrive. Or else, because in the way just mentioned at alternate parts of the year fires are accustomed to stream together more slowly and more quickly, which cause the sun to rise in a certain point, therefore it is that those appear to speak the truth who suppose a fresh sun to be born every day.[2]

The moon may shine because struck by the sun's rays, and turn that light every day more and more directly towards our sight, in proportion as she recedes from the sun's orb, until just opposite to him she has shone out with full light and at her rising as she soars aloft has beheld his setting; and then by slow steps reversing as it were her course she must in the same way hide her light, the nearer and nearer she now glides to the sun from a different quarter through the circle of the signs; according to the theory of those who suppose the moon to be like a ball and to hold on her course under the sun. She may also very possibly revolve with her own light and display various phases of brightness; for there may well be another body which is carried on and glides in her company getting before her path and obstructing her in all manner of ways and yet cannot be seen, because it glides on without light. She may also revolve, like it may be to a spherical ball steeped over one half in shining light, and as she rolls round this sphere she may present changing phases, until she has turned that half which is illuminated full towards our sight and open eyes; then by slow steps she whirls back and withdraws the light-fraught half of the spherical ball; as the Babylonian science of the Chaldees refuting the system of the astronomers essays to prove in opposition to them; just as though that which each party fights for might not be equally true, or there were any reason why you should venture to embrace the one theory less than the other. Again, why a new moon should not be born every day after a regular succession of forms and regular phases, and each day the one which is born perish and another be produced in its room and stead, it is not easy to teach by reasoning or prove by words, since so many things can be born in such a regular succession. Spring and Venus go their way, and the winged harbinger of Venus steps on before; and close on Zephyr's foot-prints mother Flora strews all the way before them and covers it over with the choicest colours and odours. Next in order follows parching heat, and in its company dusty Ceres and the Etesian blasts of the north winds. Next autumn advances and Euhius Euan steps on together. Then other seasons and winds follow, loud-roaring Volturnus and the south-wind stored with lightning. At last midwinter brings with it snows and gives back benumbing cold; after it follows winter with teeth chattering with cold. It is therefore the less strange that a moon is begotten at a fixed time and at a fixed time is destroyed again, since many things may take place at a time so surely fixed.

The eclipses of the sun likewise and the obscurations of the moon you may suppose to take place from many different causes. For why should the moon be able to shut the earth out from the sun's light and on the earthward side put in his way her high-exalted head, placing her dark orb before his burning rays; and yet at the same time it be thought that another body gliding on ever without light cannot do the same? Why too should not the sun be able, quite exhausted, to lose his fires at a fixed time, and again reproduce his light when in his journey through the air he has passed by spots fatal to his flames, which cause his fires to be quenched and to perish? And why should the earth be able in turn to rob the moon of light and moreover herself to keep the sun suppressed, while in her monthly course she glides through the well-defined shadows of the cone; and yet at the same time another body not be able to pass under the moon or glide above the sun's orb, breaking off its rays and the light it sheds forth? Yes and if the moon shines with her own brightness, why should she not be able to grow faint in a certain part of the world, while she is passing through spots hostile to her own light?

And now further since I have explained in what way everything might take place throughout the blue of the great heaven; how we might know what force and cause set in motion the varied courses of the sun and wanderings of the moon; and in what way their light might be intercepted and they be lost to us and spread darkness over the earth little expecting it, when so to speak they close their eye of light and opening it again survey all places shining in bright radiance, I now go back to the infancy of the world and the tender age of the fields of earth and show what first in their early essays of production they resolved to raise into the borders of light and give in charge to the wayward winds.

In the beginning the earth gave forth all kinds of herbage and verdant sheen about the hills and over all the plains; the flowery meadows glittered with the bright green hue, and next in order to the different trees was given a strong and emulous desire of growing up into the air with full unbridled powers. As feathers and hairs and bristles are first born on the limbs of four-footed beasts and the body of the strong of wing, thus the new earth then first put forth grass and bushes, and next gave birth to the races of mortal creatures springing up many in number in many ways after divers fashions. For no living creatures can have dropped from heaven nor can those belonging to the land have come out of the salt pools. It follows that with good reason the earth has gotten the name of mother, since all things have been produced out of the earth. And many living creatures even now spring out of the earth taking form by rains and the heat of the sun. It is therefore the less strange if at that time they sprang up more in number and larger in size, having come to maturity in the freshness of earth and ether. First of all the race of fowls and the various birds would leave their eggs, hatched in the springtime, just as now in summer the cicades leave spontaneously their gossamer coats in quest of a living and life. Then you must know did the earth first give forth races of mortal men. For much heat and moisture would then abound in the fields; and therefore wherever a suitable spot offered, wombs would grow attached to the earth by roots; and when the warmth of the infants, flying the wet and craving the air, had opened these in the fulness of time, nature would turn to that spot the pores of the earth and constrain it to yield from its opened veins a liquid most like to milk, even as now-a-days every woman when she has borne, is filled with sweet milk, because all that current of nutriment streams towards the breasts. To the children the earth would furnish food, the heat raiment, the grass a bed rich in abundance of soft down. Then the fresh youth of the world would give forth neither severe colds nor excessive heats nor gales of great violence; for all things grow and acquire strength in a like proportion.

Wherefore again and again I say the earth with good title has gotten and keeps the name of mother, since she of herself gave birth to mankind and at a time nearly fixed shed forth every beast that ranges wildly over the great mountains, and at the same time the fowls of the air with all their varied shapes. But because she must have some limit set to her bearing, she ceased like a woman worn out by length of days. For time changes the nature of the whole world and all things must pass on from one condition to another, and nothing continues like to itself: all things quit their bounds, all things nature changes and compels to alter. One thing crumbles away and is worn and enfeebled with age, then another comes unto honour and issues out of its state of contempt. In this way then time changes the nature of the whole world and the earth passes out of one condition into another: what once it could, it can bear no more, in order to be able to bear what before it did not bear.

And many monsters too the earth at that time essayed to produce, things coming up with strange face and limbs, the man-woman, a thing between the two and neither the one sex nor the other, widely differing from both; some things deprived of feet, others again destitute of hands, others too proving dumb without mouth, or blind without eyes, and things bound fast by the adhesion of their limbs over all the body, so that they could not do anything nor go anywhere nor avoid the evil nor take what their needs required. Every other monster and portent of this kind she would produce, but all in vain, since nature set a ban on their increase and they could not reach the coveted flower of age nor find food nor be united in marriage. For we see that many conditions must meet together in things in order that they may beget and continue their kinds; first a supply of food, then a way by which the birth-producing seeds throughout the frame may stream from the relaxed limbs; also in order that the woman may be united with the male, the possession of organs whereby they may each interchange mutual joys.

And many races of living things must then have died out and been unable to beget and continue their breed. For in the case of all things which you see breathing the breath of life, either craft or courage or else speed has from the beginning of its existence protected and preserved each particular race. And there are many things which, recommended to us by their useful services, continue to exist consigned to our protection. In the first place the fierce breed of lions and the savage races their courage has protected, foxes their craft and stags their proneness to fight. But light-sleeping dogs with faithful heart in breast and every kind which is born of the seed of beasts of burden and at the same time the woolly flocks and the horned herds are all consigned, Memmius, to the protection of man. For they have ever fled with eagerness from wild beasts and have ensued peace and plenty of food obtained without their own labour, as we give it in requital of their useful services. But those to whom nature has granted none of these qualities, so that they could neither live by their own means nor perform for us any useful service in return for which we should suffer their kind to feed and be safe under our protection, those, you are to know, would lie exposed as a prey and booty of others, hampered all in their own death-bringing shackles, until nature brought that kind to utter destruction.

But Centaurs never have existed, and at no time can there exist things of twofold nature and double body formed into one frame out of limbs of alien kinds, such that the faculties and powers of this and that portion cannot be sufficiently like. This however dull of understanding you may learn from what follows. To begin, a horse when three years have gone round is in the prime of his vigour, far different the boy: often even at that age he will call in his sleep for the milk of the breast. Afterwards when in advanced age his lusty strength and limbs now faint with ebbing life fail the horse, then and not till then youth in the flower of age commences for that boy and clothes his cheeks in soft down; that you may not haply believe that out of a man and the burden-carrying seed of horses Centaurs can be formed and have being; or that Scyllas with bodies half those of fishes girdled round with raving dogs can exist, and all other things of the kind, whose limbs we see cannot harmonize together; as they neither come to their flower at the same time nor reach the fulness of their bodily strength nor lose it in advanced old age, nor burn with similar passions nor have compatible manners, nor feel the same things give pleasure throughout their frames. Thus we may see bearded goats often fatten on hemlock which for man is rank poison. Since flame moreover is wont to scorch and burn the tawny bodies of lions just as much as any other kind of flesh and blood existing on earth, how could it be that a single chimera with triple body, in front a lion, behind a dragon, in the middle the goat whose name it bears, could breathe out at the mouth fierce flame from its body? Wherefore also he who fables that in the new time of the earth and the fresh youth of heaven such living creatures could have been begotten, resting upon this one futile term new, may babble out many things in like fashion, may say that rivers then ran with gold over all parts of the earth and that trees were wont to blossom with precious stones, or that man was born with such giant force of frame that he could wade on foot across deep seas and whirl the whole heaven about him with his hands. For the fact that there were many seeds of things in the earth what time it first shed forth living creatures, is yet no proof that there could have been produced beasts of different kinds mixed together, and limbs of different living things formed into a single frame, because the kinds of herbage and corn and joyous trees which even now spring in plenty out of the earth yet cannot be produced with the several sorts plaited into one, but each thing goes on after its own fashion, and all preserve their distinctive differences according to a fixed law of nature.

But the race of man then in the fields was much hardier, as beseemed it to be, since the hard earth had produced it; and built on a groundwork of larger and more solid bones within, knit with powerful sinews throughout the frame of flesh; not lightly to be disabled by heat or cold or strange kinds of food or any malady of body. And during the revolution of many lustres of the sun through heaven they led a life after the roving fashion of wild beasts. No one then was a sturdy guider of the bent plough or knew how to labour the fields with iron or plant in the ground young saplings or lop with pruning-hooks old boughs from the high trees. What the sun and rains had given, what the earth had produced spontaneously, was guerdon sufficient to content their hearts. Among acorn-bearing oaks they would refresh their bodies for the most part; and the arbute-berries which you now see in the winter-time ripen with a bright scarlet hue, the earth would then bear in greatest plenty and of a larger size; and many coarse kinds of food besides the teeming freshness of the world then bare, more than enough for poor wretched men. But rivers and springs invited to slake thirst, even as now a rush of water down from the great hills summons with clear plash far and wide the thirsty races of wild beasts. Then too as they ranged about they would occupy the well-known woodland haunts of the nymphs, out of which they knew that smooth-gliding streams of water with a copious gush bathed the dripping rocks, the dripping rocks, trickling down over the green moss; and in parts welled and bubbled out over the level plain. And as yet they knew not how to apply fire to their purposes or to make use of skins and clothe their body in the spoils of wild beasts, but they would dwell in woods and mountain-caves and forests and shelter in the brushwood their squalid limbs when driven to shun the buffeting of the winds and the rains. And they were unable to look to the general weal and knew not how to make a common use of any customs or laws. Whatever prize fortune threw in his way, each man would bear off, trained at his own discretion to think of himself and live for himself alone. And Venus would join the bodies of lovers in the woods; for each woman was gained over either by mutual desire or the headstrong violence and vehement lust of the man or a bribe of some acorns and arbute-berries or choice pears. And trusting to the marvellous powers of their hands and feet they would pursue the forest-haunting races of wild beasts with showers of stones and club of ponderous weight; and many they would conquer, a few they would avoid in hiding-places; and like to bristly swine just as they were they would throw their savage limbs all naked on the ground, when overtaken by night, covering themselves up with leaves and boughs. Yet never with loud wailings would they call for the daylight and the sun, wandering terror-stricken over the fields in the shadows of night, but silent and buried in sleep they would wait, till the sun with rosy torch carried light into heaven; for accustomed as they had been from childhood always to see darkness and light begotten time about, never could any wonder come over them, nor any misgiving that never-ending night would cover the earth and the light of the sun be withdrawn for evermore. But what gave them trouble was rather the races of wild beasts which would often render repose fatal to the poor wretches. And driven from their home they would fly from their rocky shelters on the approach of a foaming bear or a strong lion, and in the dead of night they would surrender in terror to their savage guests their sleeping-places strewn with leaves.

Nor then much more than now would the races of mortal men leave the sweet light of ebbing life. For then this one or that other one of them would be more likely to be seized, and torn open by their teeth would furnish to the wild beasts a living food, and would fill with his moaning woods and mountains and forests as he looked on his living flesh buried in a living grave. But those whom flight had saved with body eaten into, holding ever after their quivering palms over the noisome sores would summon death with appalling cries, until cruel gripings had rid them of life, forlorn of help, unwitting what wounds wanted. But then a single day gave not over to death many thousands of men marching with banners spread, nor did the stormy waters of the sea dash on the rocks men and ships. At this time the sea would often rise up and rage without aim, without purpose, without result, and just as lightly put off its empty threats; nor could the winning wiles of the calm sea treacherously entice any one to his ruin with laughing waters, when the reckless craft of the skipper had not yet risen into the light. Then too want of food would consign to death their fainting frames, now on the contrary 'tis plenty sinks into ruin. They unwittingly would often pour out poison for themselves; now with nicer skill men give it to their son's wife instead.

Next after they had got themselves huts and skins and fire, and the woman united with the man passed with him into one domicile and the duties of wedlock were learnt by the two,[3] and they saw an offspring born from them, then first mankind began to soften. For fire made their chilled bodies less able now to bear the frost beneath the canopy of heaven, and Venus impaired their strength and children with their caresses soon broke down the naughty temper of parents. Then too neighbours began to join in a league of friendship mutually desiring neither to do nor suffer harm; and asked for indulgence to children and womankind, when with cries and gestures they declared in stammering speech that meet it is for all to have mercy on the weak. And though harmony could not be established without exception, yet a very large portion observed their agreements with good faith, or else the race of man would then have been wholly cut off, nor could breeding have continued their generations to this day.

But nature impelled them to utter the various sounds of the tongue and use struck out the names of things, much in the same way as the inability to speak is seen in its turn to drive children to the use of gestures, when it forces them to point with the finger at the things which are before them. For every one feels how far he can make use of his peculiar powers. Ere the horns of a calf are formed and project from his forehead, he butts with it when angry and pushes out in his rage. Then whelps of panthers and cubs of lions fight with claws and feet and teeth at a time when teeth and claws are hardly yet formed. Again we see every kind of fowl trust to wings and seek from pinions a fluttering succour. Therefore to suppose that some one man at that time apportioned names to things and that men from him learnt their first words, is sheer folly. For why should this particular man be able to denote all things by words and to utter the various sounds of the tongue, and yet at the same time others be supposed not to have been able to do so? Again if others as well as he had not made use of words among themselves, whence was implanted in this man the previous conception of its use and whence was given to him the original faculty, to know and perceive in mind what he wanted to do? Again one man could not constrain and subdue and force many to choose to learn the names of things. It is no easy thing in any way to teach and convince the deaf of what is needful to be done; for they never would suffer nor in any way endure sounds of voice hitherto unheard to continue to be dinned fruitlessly into their ears. Lastly what is there so passing strange in this circumstance, that the race of men whose voice and tongue were in full force, should denote things by different words as different feelings prompted? Since dumb brutes, yes and the races of wild beasts are accustomed to give forth distinct and varied sounds, when they have fear or pain and when joys are rife. This you may learn from facts plain to sense: when the large spongy open lips of Molossian dogs begin to growl enraged and bare their hard teeth, thus drawn back in rage they threaten in a tone far different from that in which they bark outright and fill with sounds all the places round. Again when they essay fondly to lick their whelps with their tongue or when they toss them with their feet and snapping at them make a feint with lightly closing teeth of swallowing though with gentle forbearance, they caress them with a yelping sound of a sort greatly differing from that which they utter when, left alone in a house, they bay or when they slink away howling from blows with a crouching body. Again is not the neigh too seen to differ, when a young stallion in the flower of age rages among the mares smitten by the goads of winged love, and when with wide-stretched nostrils he snorts out the signal to arms, and when as it chances on any other occasion he neighs with limbs all shaking? Lastly the race of fowls and various birds, hawks and ospreys and gulls seeking their living in the salt water mid the waves of the sea, utter at a different time noises widely different from those they make when they are fighting for food and struggling with their prey. And some of them change together with the weather their harsh croakings, as the long-lived races of crows and flocks of rooks when they are said to be calling for water and rain and sometimes to be summoning winds and gales. Therefore if different sensations compel creatures, dumb though they be, to utter different sounds, how much more natural it is that mortal men in those times should have been able to denote dissimilar things by many different words!

And lest haply on this head you ask in silent thought this question, it was lightning that brought fire down on earth for mortals in the beginning; thence the whole heat of flames is spread abroad. Thus we see many things shine dyed in heavenly flames, when the stroke from heaven has stored them with its heat. Ay and without this when a branching tree sways to and fro and tosses about under the buffeting of the winds, pressing against the boughs of another tree, fire is forced out by the power of the violent friction, and sometimes the burning heat of flame flashes out, the boughs and stems rubbing against each other. Now either of these accidents may have given fire to men. Next the sun taught them to cook food and soften it with the heat of flame, since they would see many things grow mellow, when subdued by the strokes of the rays and by heat throughout the land.

And more and more every day men who excelled in intellect and were of vigorous understanding, would kindly show them how to exchange their former way of living for new methods. Kings began to build towns and lay out a citadel as a place of strength and of refuge for themselves, and divided cattle and lands and gave to each man in proportion to his personal beauty and strength and intellect; for beauty and vigorous strength were much esteemed. Afterwards wealth was discovered and gold found out, which soon robbed of their honours strong and beautiful alike; for men however valiant and beautiful of person generally follow in the train of the richer man. But were a man to order his life by the rules of true reason, a frugal subsistence joined to a contented mind is for him great riches; for never is there any lack of a little. But men desired to be famous and powerful, in order that their fortunes might rest on a firm foundation and they might be able by their wealth to lead a tranquil life; but in vain, since in their struggle to mount up to the highest dignities they rendered their path one full of danger; and even if they reach it, yet envy like a thunderbolt sometimes strikes and dashes men down from the highest point with ignominy into noisome Tartarus; since the highest summits and those elevated above the level of other things are mostly blasted by envy as by a thunderbolt; so that far better it is to obey in peace and quiet than to wish to rule with power supreme and be the master of kingdoms. Therefore let men wear themselves out to no purpose and sweat drops of blood, as they struggle on along the strait road of ambition, since they gather their knowledge from the mouths of others and follow after things from hearsay rather than the dictates of their own feelings; and this prevails not now nor will prevail by and by any more than it has prevailed before.

Kings therefore being slain the old majesty of thrones and proud sceptres were overthrown and laid in the dust, and the glorious badge of the sovereign head bloodstained beneath the feet of the rabble mourned for its high prerogative; for that is greedily trampled on which before was too much dreaded. It would come then in the end to the lees of uttermost disorder, each man seeking for himself empire and sovereignty. Next a portion of them taught men to elect legal officers, and drew up codes, to induce men to obey the laws. For mankind, tired out with a life of brute force, lay exhausted from its feuds; and therefore the more readily it submitted of its own freewill to laws and stringent codes. For as each one moved by anger took measures to avenge himself with more severity than is now permitted by equitable laws, for this reason men grew sick of a life of brute force. Thence fear of punishment mars the prizes of life; for violence and wrong enclose all who commit them in their meshes and do mostly recoil on him from whom they began; and it is not easy for him who by his deeds trangresses the terms of the public peace to pass a tranquil and a peaceful existence. For though he eludes God and man, yet he cannot but feel a misgiving that his secret can be kept for ever; seeing that many by speaking in their dreams or in the wanderings of disease have often we are told betrayed themselves and have disclosed their hidden deeds of evil and their sins.

And now what cause has spread over great nations the worship of the divinities of the gods and filled towns with altars and led to the performance of stated sacred rites, rites now in fashion on solemn occasions and in solemn places, from which even now is implanted in mortals a shuddering awe which raises new temples of the gods over the whole earth and prompts men to crowd them on festive days, all this it is not so difficult to explain in words. Even then in sooth the races of mortal men would see in waking mind glorious forms, would see them in sleep of yet more marvellous size of body. To these then they would attribute sense, because they seemed to move their limbs and to utter lofty words suitable to their glorious aspect and surpassing powers. And they would give them life everlasting, because their face would ever appear before them and their form abide; yes and yet without all this, because they would not believe that beings possessed of such powers could lightly be overcome by any force. And they would believe them to be preeminent in bliss, because none of them was ever troubled with the fear of death, and because at the same time in sleep they would see them perform many miracles, yet feel on their part no fatigue from the effort. Again they would see the system of heaven and the different seasons of the years come round in regular succession, and could not find out by what causes this was done; therefore they would seek a refuge in handing over all things to the gods and supposing all things to be guided by their nod. And they placed in heaven the abodes and realms of the gods, because night and moon are seen to roll through heaven, moon, day, and night and night's austere constellations and night-wandering meteors of the sky and flying bodies of flame, clouds, sun, rains, snow, winds, lightnings, hail, and rapid rumblings and loud threatful thunderclaps.

O hapless race of men, when that they charged the gods with such acts and coupled with them bitter wrath! What groanings did they then beget for themselves, what wounds for us, what tears for our children's children! No act is it of piety to be often seen with veiled head to turn to a stone and approach every altar and fall prostrate on the ground and spread out the palms before the statues of the gods and sprinkle the altars with much blood of beasts and link vow on to vow, but rather to be able to look on all things with a mind at peace. For when we turn our gaze on the heavenly quarters of the great upper world and ether fast above the glittering stars, and direct our thoughts to the courses of the sun and moon, then into our breasts burdened with other ills that fear as well begins to exalt its reawakened head, the fear that we may haply find the power of the gods to be unlimited, able to wheel the bright stars in their varied motion; for lack of power to solve the question troubles the mind with doubts, whether there was ever a birth-time of the world, and whether likewise there is to be any end; how far the walls of the world can endure this strain of restless motion; or whether gifted by the grace of the gods with an everlasting existence they may glide on through a never-ending tract of time and defy the strong powers of immeasurable ages. Again who is there whose mind does not shrink into itself with fear of the gods, whose limbs do not cower in terror, when the parched earth rocks with the appalling thunderstroke and rattlings run through the great heaven? Do not peoples and nations quake, and proud monarchs shrink into themselves smitten with fear of the gods, lest for any foul transgression or overweening word the heavy time of reckoning has arrived at its fulness? When too the utmost fury of the headstrong wind passes over the sea and sweeps over its waters the commander of a fleet together with his mighty legions and elephants, does he not draw near with vows to seek the mercy of the gods and ask in prayer with fear and trembling a lull in the winds and propitious gales; but all in vain, since often caught up in the furious hurricane he is borne none the less to the shoals of death? so constantly does some hidden power trample on human grandeur and is seen to tread under its heel and make sport for itself of the renowned rods and cruel axes. Again when the whole earth rocks under their feet and towns tumble with the shock or doubtfully threaten to fall, what wonder that mortal men abase themselves and make over to the gods in things here on earth high prerogatives and marvellous powers, sufficient to govern all things?

To proceed, copper and gold and iron were discovered and at the same time weighty silver and the substance of lead, when fire with its heat had burnt up vast forests on the great hills, either by a discharge of heaven's lightning, or else because men waging with one another a forest-war had carried fire among the enemy in order to strike terror, or because drawn on by the goodness of the soil they would wish to clear rich fields and bring the country into pasture, or else to destroy wild beasts and enrich themselves with the booty; for hunting with the pitfall and with fire came into use before the practice of enclosing the lawn with toils and stirring it with dogs. Whatever the fact is, from whatever cause the heat of flame had swallowed up the forests with a frightful crackling from their very roots and had thoroughly baked the earth with fire, there would run from the boiling veins and collect into the hollows of the ground a stream of silver and gold, as well as of copper and lead. And when they saw these afterwards cool into lumps and glitter on the earth with a brilliant gleam, they would lift them up attracted by the bright and polished lustre, and they would see them to be moulded in a shape the same as the outline of the cavities in which each lay. Then it would strike them that these might be melted by heat and cast in any form or shape soever, and might by hammering out be brought to tapering points of any degree of sharpness and fineness, so as to furnish them with tools and enable them to cut the forests and hew timber and plane smooth the planks, and also to drill and pierce and bore. And they would set about these works just as much with silver and gold at first as with the overpowering strength of stout copper, but in vain, since their force would fail and give way and not be able like copper to stand the severe strain. At that time copper was in higher esteem and gold would lie neglected on account of its uselessness, with its dull blunted edge: now copper lies neglected, gold has mounted up to the highest place of honour. Thus time as it goes round changes the seasons of things. That which was in esteem, falls at length into utter disrepute; and then another thing mounts up and issues out of its degraded state and every day is more and more coveted and blossoms forth high in honour when discovered and is in marvellous repute with men.

And now, Memmius, it is easy for you to find out by yourself in what way the nature of iron was discovered. Arms of old were hands, nails, and teeth and stones and boughs broken off from the forests, and flame and fire, as soon as they had become known. Afterwards the force of iron and copper was discovered; and the use of copper was known before that of iron, as its nature is easier to work and it is found in greater quantity. With copper they would labour the soil of the earth, with copper stir up the billows of war and deal about wide-gaping wounds and seize cattle and lands; for every thing defenceless and unarmed would readily yield to them with arms in hand. Then by slow steps the sword of iron gained ground and the make of the copper sickle became a byword; and with iron they began to plough through the earth's soil, and the struggles of wavering war were rendered equal. And the custom of mounting in arms on the back of a horse and guiding him with reins and showing prowess with the right hand is older than that of tempting the risks of war in a two-horsed chariot; and yoking a pair of horses is older than yoking four or mounting in arms scythed chariots. Next the Poeni taught the lucan kine [4] with towered body, hideous of aspect, with snake-like hand, to endure the wounds of war and to disorder the mighty ranks of Mars. Thus sad discord begat one thing after another, to affright nations of men under arms, and every day made some addition to the terrors of war.

They made trial of bulls too in the service of war and essayed to send savage boars against the enemy. And some sent before them valorous lions with armed trainers and courageous keepers to guide them and to hold them in chains; but in vain, since heated with promiscuous slaughter they would disorder in their rage the troops without distinction, shaking all about the frightful crests upon their heads; and the horsemen were not able to calm the breasts of the horses scared by the roaring and turn them with the bridle upon the enemy. The lionesses with a spring would throw their enraged bodies on all sides and would attack in the face those who met them, and others off their guard they would tear down from behind and twining round them would bring them to the ground overpowered by the wound, fastening on them with firm bite and with hooked claws. The bulls would toss their own friends and trample them under foot, and gore with their horns the flanks and bellies of the horses underneath and turn up the earth with threatening front. The boars too would rend their friends with powerful tusks, in their rage dyeing with their blood the weapons broken in them, ay dyeing with their blood the weapons broken in their own bodies; and would put to promiscuous rout horse and foot; for the tame beasts would try to avoid by shying to the side the cruel push of the tusk, or would rear up and paw the winds, all in vain, since you might see them tumble down with their tendons severed and strew the ground in their heavy fall. Those whom they believed before to have been sufficiently broken in at home, they would see lash themselves into fury in the heat of action from wounds and shouting, flight, panic, and uproar; and they could not rally any portion of them; for all the different kinds of wild beasts would fly all abroad; just as now the lucan kine when cruelly mangled by the steel fly often all abroad, after inflicting on their friends many cruel sufferings. But men chose thus to act not so much in any hope of victory, as from a wish to give the enemy something to rue at the cost of their own lives, when they mistrusted their numbers and were in want of arms.

A garment tied on the body was in use before a dress of woven stuff. Woven stuff comes after iron, because iron is needed for weaving a web; and in no other way can such finely polished things be made, as heddles and spindles, shuttles and ringing yarn-beams. And nature impelled men to work up the wool before womankind: for the male sex in general far excels the other in skill and is much more ingenious: until the rugged countrymen so upbraided them with it, that they were glad to give it over into the hands of the women and take their share in supporting hard toil, and in such hard work hardened body and hands.

But nature parent of things was herself the first model of sowing and first gave rise to grafting, since berries and acorns dropping from the trees would put forth in due season swarms of young shoots underneath; and hence also came the fashion of inserting grafts in their stocks and planting in the ground young saplings over the fields. Next they would try another and yet another kind of tillage for their loved piece of land and would see the earth better the wild fruits through genial fostering and kindly cultivation. And they would force the forests to recede every day higher and higher up the hill-side and yield the ground below to tilth, in order to have on the uplands and plains meadows, tanks, runnels, corn-fields, and glad vineyards, and allow a grey-green strip of olives to run between and mark the divisions, spreading itself over hillocks and valleys and plains; just as you now see richly dight with varied beauty all the ground which they lay out and plant with rows of sweet fruit-trees and enclose all round with plantations of other goodly trees.

But imitating with the mouth the clear notes of birds was in use long before men were able to sing in tune smooth-running verses and give pleasure to the ear. And the whistlings of the zephyr through the hollows of reeds first taught peasants to blow into hollow stalks. Then step by step they learned sweet plaintive ditties, which the pipe pours forth pressed by the fingers of the players, heard through pathless woods and forests and lawns, through the unfrequented haunts of shepherds and abodes of unearthly calm. These things would soothe and gratify their minds when sated with food; for then all things of this kind are welcome. Often therefore stretched in groups on the soft grass beside a stream of water under the boughs of a high tree at no great cost they would pleasantly refresh their bodies, above all when the weather smiled and the seasons of the year painted the green grass with flowers. Then went round the jest, the tale, the peals of merry laughter; for the peasant muse was then in its glory; then frolick mirth would prompt to entwine head and shoulders with garlands plaited with flowers and leaves, and to advance in the dance out of step and move the limbs clumsily and with clumsy foot beat mother earth; which would occasion smiles and peals of merry laughter, because all these things then from their greater novelty and strangeness were in high repute. And the wakeful found a solace for want of sleep in this, in drawing out a variety of notes and going through tunes and running over the reeds with curving lip; whence even at the present day watchmen observe these traditions and have lately learned to keep the proper tune; and yet for all this receive not a jot more of enjoyment, than erst the rugged race of sons of earth received. For that which we have in our hands, if we have known before nothing pleasanter, pleases above all and is thought to be the best; and as a rule the later discovery of something better spoils the taste for the former things and changes the feelings in regard to all that has gone before. Thus began distaste for the acorn, thus were abandoned those sleeping-places strewn with grass and enriched with leaves. The dress too of wild beasts' skin fell into neglect; though I can fancy that in those days it was found to arouse such jealousy that he who first wore it met his death by an ambuscade, and after all it was torn in pieces among them and drenched in blood was utterly destroyed and could not be turned to any use. In those times therefore skins now gold and purple plague men's lives with cares and wear them out with war. And in this methinks the greater blame rests with us; for cold would torture the naked sons of earth without their skins; but us it harms not in the least to do without a robe of purple, spangled with gold and large figures, if only we have a dress of the people to protect us. Mankind therefore ever toils vainly and to no purpose and wastes life in groundless cares, because sure enough they have not learnt what is the true end of getting and up to what point genuine pleasure goes on increasing: this by slow degrees has carried life out into the deep sea and stirred up from their lowest depths the mighty billows of war.

But those watchful guardians, sun and moon, traversing with their light all round the great revolving sphere of heaven taught men that the seasons of the year came round and that the system was carried on after a fixed plan and fixed order.

Already they would pass their life fenced about with strong towers, and the land, portioned out and marked off by boundaries, be tilled; the sea would be filled with ships scudding under sail; towns have auxiliaries and allies as stipulated by treaty, when poets began to consign the deeds of men to verse; and letters had not been invented long before. For this reason our age cannot look back to what has gone before, save where reason points out any traces.

Ships and tillage, walls, laws, arms, roads, dress, and all such like things, all the prizes, all the elegancies too of life without exception, poems, pictures, and the chiselling of fine-wrought statues, all these things practiced together with the acquired knowledge of the untiring mind taught men by slow degrees as they advanced on the way step by step. Thus time by degrees brings each several thing forth before men's eyes and reason raises it up into the borders of light; for things must be brought to light one after the other and in due order in the different arts, until these have reached their highest point of development.

BOOK VI

IN DAYS of yore Athens of famous name first imparted corn-producing crops to suffering mankind, and modelled life anew and passed laws; and first too bestowed sweet solaces of existence, when she gave birth to a man who showed himself gifted with such a genius and poured forth all knowledge of old from his truth-telling mouth; whose glory, even now that he is dead, on account of his godlike discoveries confirmed by length of time is spread abroad among men and reaches high as heaven. For when he saw that the things which their needs imperiously demand for subsistence, had all without exception been already provided for men, and that life, so far as was possible, was placed on a sure footing, that men were great in affluence of riches and honours and glory and swelled with pride in the high reputation of their children, and yet that none of them at home for all that had a heart the less disquieted, and that this heart in despite of the understanding plagued life without any respite and was constrained to rave with distressful complainings, he then perceived that the vessel itself did cause the corruption and that by its corruption all the things that came into it and were gathered from abroad, however salutary were spoilt within it; partly because he saw it to be leaky and full of holes so that it could never by any means be filled full; partly because he perceived that it befouled so to say with a nauseous flavour everything within it, which it had taken in. He therefore cleansed men's breasts with truth-telling precepts and fixed a limit to lust and fear and explained what was the chief good which we all strive to reach, and pointed out the road along which by a short cross-track we might arrive at it in a straightforward course; he showed too what evils existed in mortal affairs throughout, rising up and manifoldly flying about by a natural—call it chance or force, because nature had so brought it about; and from what gates you must sally out duly to encounter each; and he proved that mankind mostly without cause arouse in their breast the melancholy tumbling billows of cares. For even as children are flurried and dread all things in the thick darkness, thus we in the daylight fear at times things not a whit more to be dreaded than what children shudder at in the dark and fancy sure to be. This terror therefore and darkness of mind must be dispelled not by the rays of the sun and glittering shafts of day, but by the aspect and law of nature Wherefore the more readily I will go on in my verses to complete the web of my design.

And since I have shown that the quarters of ether are mortal and that heaven is formed of a body that had a birth, and since of all the things which go on and must go on in it, I have unravelled most, hear further what remains to be told; since once for all I have willed to mount the illustrious chariot of the Muses, and ascending to heaven [1] to explain the true law of winds and storms, which men foolishly lay to the charge of the gods, telling how, when they are angry, they raise fierce tempests; and, when there is a lull in the fury of the winds, how that anger is appeased, how the omens which have been are again changed, when their fury has thus been appeased: I have willed at the same time to explain all the other things which mortals observe to go on upon earth and in heaven, when often they are in anxious suspense of mind, and which abase their souls with fear of the gods and weigh and press them down to earth, because ignorance of the causes constrains them to submit things to the empire of the gods and to make over to them the kingdom. For they who have been rightly taught that the gods lead a life without care, if nevertheless they wonder on what plan all things can be carried on, above all in regard to those things which are seen overhead in the ethereal borders, are borne back again into their old religious scruples and take unto themselves hard taskmasters, whom they poor wretches believe to be almighty, not knowing what can, what cannot be, in short on what principle each thing has its powers defined, its deep-set boundary mark; and therefore they are led all the farther astray by blind reason. Now unless you drive from your mind with loathing all these things, and banish far from you all belief in things degrading to the gods and inconsistent with their peace, then often will the holy deities of the gods, having their majesty lessened by you, do you hurt; not that the supreme power of the gods can be so outraged, that in their wrath they shall resolve to exact sharp vengeance, but because you will fancy to yourself that they, though they enjoy quiet and calm peace, do roll great billows of wrath; nor will you approach the sanctuaries of the gods with a calm breast nor will you be able with tranquil peace of mind to take in those idols which are carried from their holy body into the minds of men, as heralds of their divine form. And what kind of life follows after this, may be conceived. But in order that most veracious reason may drive it far away from us, though much has already gone forth from me, much however still remains and has to be embellished in smooth-polished verses; the law and aspect of heaven have to be grasped; storms and bright lightnings, what they do and from what cause they are borne along, all this has to be sung; that you may not mark out the heaven into quarters and be startled and distracted on seeing from which of them the volant fire has come or to which of the two halves it has betaken itself, in what way it has gained an entrance within walled places, and how after lording it with tyrant sway, it has gotten itself out from these. Do thou, deft muse Calliope, solace of men and joy of gods, point out the course before me as I race to the white boundary-line of the final goal, that under thy guidance I may win the crown with signal applause.

In the first place the blue of heaven is shaken with thunder, because the ethereal clouds clash together as they fly aloft when the winds combat from opposite quarters. For no sound ever comes from a cloudless part of heaven, but wheresoever the clouds are gathered in a denser mass, from that part with greater frequency comes a clap with a loud growl. Again clouds cannot be either of so dense a body as stones and timbers, nor again so fine as mists and flying bodies of smoke; for then they must either fall borne down by their dead weight like stones, or like smoke they would be unable to keep together and hold within frozen snows and hail-showers. They also give forth a sound over the levels of the wide-stretching upper world, just as at times a canvas-awning stretched over large theatres makes a creaking noise, when it tosses about among the poles and beams; sometimes, too, rent by the boisterous gales it madly howls and closely imitates the rasping noise of pieces of paper: for this kind of noise too you may observe in thunder: you may observe again the sound which is heard when the winds whirl about with their blows and buffet through the air either a hanging cloth or flying bits of paper. For sometimes the clouds cannot meet front to front in direct collision, but must rather move from the flank and so with contrary motions graze leisurely along each other's bodies; whence comes that dry sound which brushes the ears and is long drawn out, until they have made their way out of their confined positions.

In this way also all things appear to quake often from the shock of heavy thunder, and the mighty walls of the far-stretching ether seem in an instant to have been riven and to have sprung asunder; when a storm of violent wind has suddenly gathered and worked itself into the clouds and, there shut in, with its whirling eddy ever more and more on all sides forces the cloud to become hollow with a thick surrounding crust of body; afterwards when its force and impetuous onset have split it, then the cloud thus rent gives forth a crash with a frightful hurtling noise. And no wonder, when a small bladder filled with air often emits a hideous sound if suddenly burst.

It can also be explained how the winds, when they blow through the clouds, make noises: we see branching and rough clouds often borne along in many ways; thus, you are to know, when the blasts of the northwest blow through a dense forest, the leaves give forth a rustling and the boughs a crashing. Sometimes too the force of the strong wind in rapid motion rends the cloud, breaking through it by an assault right in front: what a blast of wind can do there, is shown by facts plain to sense, when here on earth where it is gentler it yet twists out tall trees and tears them up from their deepest roots. There are also waves among the clouds and they give a kind of roar as they break heavily; just as in deep rivers and on the great sea when the surf breaks. Sometimes too when the burning force of thunder has fallen out of one cloud into another, if haply the latter contains much moisture when it has taken the fire into it, it drowns it at once with a loud noise; just so iron glowing hot from the fiery furnaces sometimes hisses, when we have plunged it quickly into cold water. Again if the cloud which receives the fire is drier, it is set on fire in an instant and burns with a loud noise; just as if a flame should range over the laurel-covered hills through a whirlwind and burn them up with its impetuous assault; and there is not anything that burns in the crackling flame with a more startling sound than the Delphic laurel of Phoebus. Then often too much crashing of ice and tumbling in of hail make a noise in the great clouds on high; for when the wind packs them together into a confined space, the mountains of storm-clouds congealed and mixed with hail break up.

It lightens too, when the clouds have struck out by their collision many seeds of fire; just as if a stone were to strike another stone or a piece of iron; for then too light bursts out and fire scatters about bright sparks. But we hear the thunder with our ears after the eyes see the flash of lightning, because things always travel more slowly to the ears than those which excite vision travel to the eyes. This you may perceive from the following instance as well: when you see a man at a distance cutting with a double-edged axe a large tree, you perceive the stroke before the blow carries the sound to the ear: thus we see lightning too before we hear the thunder, which is discharged at the same time as the fire from the same cause, being born indeed from the same collision.

Also in the following manner clouds dye places with winged light and the storm flashes out with a rapid quivering movement. When the wind has made its way into a cloud and whirling about in it has, as I have shown above, made the cloud hollow with a dense crust, it becomes hot by its own velocity: thus you see all things thoroughly heated and fired by motion; nay a leaden ball in whirling through a long course even melts. When therefore this wind now on fire has rent the black cloud, it scatters abroad at once seeds of fire pressed out by force so to speak, and these produce the throbbing flashes of flame; then follows a sound which strikes on the ears more slowly than the things which travel to our eyes strike on them. This you are to know takes place when the clouds are dense and at the same time piled up on high one above the other in marvellous accumulation; that you be not led into error, because we see how great their breadth is below, rather than to how great a height they are piled up. Observe, at a time when the winds shall carry clouds like to mountains with a slanting course through the air, or when you shall see them piled on the sides of great mountains one on the top of the other and pressing down from above perfectly at rest, the winds being buried on all sides: you will then be able to observe their great masses and to see caverns as it were built of hanging rocks; and when a storm has gathered and the winds have filled these, they chafe with a loud roaring shut up in the clouds, and bluster in their dens after the fashion of wild beasts: now from this point, now from that the winds send their growlings through the clouds, and seeking a way out whirl about and roll together seeds of fire out of the clouds and then gather many into a mass and make flame rotate in the hollow furnaces within, until they have burst the cloud and shone forth in forked flashes.

From this cause again yon golden colour of clear bright fire flies down with velocity to the earth: the clouds must themselves have very many seeds of fire; for when they are without any moisture, they are mostly of a brilliant flame colour. Moreover they must take in many from the sun's light, so that with good cause they are ruddy and shed forth fires. When therefore the wind has driven, thrust, squeezed together, and collected into one spot these clouds, they press out and shed forth seeds which cause the colours of flame to flash out. It also lightens, when the clouds of heaven are rarefied as well. For when the wind lightly unravels them and breaks them up as they move, those seeds which produce the lightning must fall perforce; and then it lightens without a hideous startling noise and without any uproar.

Well, to proceed, what kind of nature thunderbolts possess, is shown by their strokes and the traces of their heat which have burnt themselves into things and the marks which exhale the noxious vapours of sulphur: all these are signs of fire, not of wind or rain. Again they often set on fire even the roofs of houses and with swift flame rule resistless within the house. This fire subtle above all fires nature, you are to know, forms of minute and lightly moving bodies, and it is such as nothing whatever can withstand. The mighty thunderbolt passes through the walls of houses, like a shout and voices, passes through stones, through brass, and in a moment of time melts brass and gold; and causes wine too in an instant to disappear, while the vessels are untouched, because sure enough its heat on reaching it readily loosens and rarefies all the earthen material of the vessel on every side and forcing a way within lightly separates and disperses the first-beginnings of the wine. This the sun's heat would be unable to accomplish in an age, though beating on it incessantly with its quivering heat: so much more nimble and overpowering is this other force.

And now in what way these are begotten and are formed with a force so resistless as to be able with their stroke to burst asunder towers, throw down houses, wrench away beams and rafters, and cast down and burn up the monuments of men, to strike men dead, prostrate cattle far and near, by what force they can do all this and the like, I will make clear and will not longer detain you with mere professions.

Thunderbolts we must suppose to be begotten out of dense clouds piled up high; for they are never sent forth at all when the sky is clear or when the clouds are of a slight density. That this is so beyond all question is proved by facts evident to sense: clouds at such times form so dense a mass over the whole sky that we might imagine all its darkness had abandoned Acheron throughout and filled up the great vaults of heaven: in such numbers, gathering up out of the frightful night of storm-clouds, do faces of black horror hang over us on high; what time the storm begins to forge its thunderbolts. Very often again a black storm-cloud too out at sea, like a stream of pitch sent down from heaven, falls in such wise upon the waters heavily charged with darkness afar off and draws down a black tempest big with lightnings and storms, itself so fraught above all the rest with fires and winds, that even on land men shudder and seek shelter. Thus then we must suppose that the storm above our head reaches high up; for the clouds would never bury the earth in such thick darkness, unless they were built up high heap upon heap, the sunlight totally disappearing; nor could the clouds when they descend drown it with so great a rain, as to make rivers overflow and put fields under water, if they were not piled high up in the sky. In this case then all things are filled with winds and fire; therefore thunderings and lightnings go on all about. For I have shown above that hollow clouds have very many seeds of heat, and they must also take many in from the sun's rays and their heat. On this account when the same wind which happens to collect them into any one place, has forced out many seeds of heat and has mixed itself up with that fire, then the eddy of wind forces a way in and whirls about in the straitened room and points the thunderbolt in the fiery furnaces within; for it is kindled in two ways at once: it is heated by its own velocity and from the contact of fire. After that when the force of the wind has been thoroughly heated and the impetuous power of the fire has entered in, then the thunderbolt fully forged as it were suddenly rends the cloud, and the heat put in motion is carried on traversing all places with flashing lights. Close upon it falls so heavy a clap that it seems to crush down from above the quarters of heaven which have all at once sprung asunder. Then a trembling violently seizes the earth and rumblings run through high heaven; for the whole body of the storm then without exception quakes with the shock and loud roarings are aroused. After this shock follows so heavy and copious a rain that the whole ether seems to be turning into rain and then to be tumbling down and returning to a deluge: so great a flood of it is discharged by the bursting of the cloud and the storm of wind, when the sound flies forth from the burning stroke. At times too the force of the wind set in motion from without falls on a cloud hot with a fully forged thunderbolt; and when it has burst it, forthwith there falls down yon fiery eddying whirl which in our native speech we call a thunderbolt. The same takes place on every other side towards which the force in question has borne down. Sometimes too the power of the wind though discharged without fire, yet catches fire in the course of its long travel, and while it is passing on, it loses on the way some large bodies which cannot like the rest get through the air; and gathers together out of the air itself and carries along with it other bodies of very small size which mix with it and produce fire by their flight; very much in the same way as a leaden ball becomes hot during its course, when it loses many bodies of cold and has taken up fire in the air. Sometimes too the force of the blow itself strikes out fire, when the force of wind discharged in a cold state without fire has struck, because sure enough, when it has smitten with a powerful stroke, the elements of heat are able to stream together out of the wind itself and at the same time out of the thing which then encounters the stroke. Thus, when we strike a stone with iron, fire flies out; and none the less, because the force of the iron is cold, do its seeds of fiery brightness meet together upon the stroke. Therefore in the same way too a thing ought to be set on fire by the thunderbolt, if it has happened to be in a state suited to receive and susceptible of the flames. At the same time the might of the wind cannot lightly be thought to be absolutely and decidedly cold, seeing that it is discharged with such force from above; but if it is not already set on fire during its course, it yet arrives in a warm state with heat mixed up in it.

But the velocity of thunderbolts is great and their stroke powerful, and they run through their course with a rapid descent, because their force when set in motion first in all cases collects itself in the clouds and gathers itself up for a great effort at starting; then when the cloud is no longer able to hold the increased moving power, their force is pressed out and therefore flies with a marvellous moving power, like to that with which missiles are carried when discharged from powerful engines. Then too the thunderbolt consists of small and smooth elements, and such a nature it is not easy for anything to withstand; for it flies between and passes in through the porous passages; therefore it is not checked and delayed by many collisions, and for this reason it glides and flies on with a swift moving power. Next, all weights without exception naturally pressing downward, when to this a blow is added, the velocity is doubled and yon moving power becomes so intense that the thunderbolt dashes aside more impetuously and swiftly whatever gets in its way and tries to hinder it, and pursues its journey. Then too as it advances with a long-continued moving power, it must again and again receive new velocity which ever increases as it goes on and augments its powerful might and gives vigour to its stroke; for it forces all the seeds of the thunder to be borne right onward to one spot so to speak, throwing them all together, as on they roll, into that single line. Perhaps too as it goes on it attracts certain bodies out of the air itself, and these by their blows kindle apace its velocity. It passes too through things without injuring them, and leaves many things quite whole after it has gone through, because the clear bright fire flies through by the pores. And it breaks to pieces many things, when the first bodies of the thunderbolt have fallen exactly on the first bodies of these things, at the points where they are intertwined and held together. Again it easily melts brass and fuses gold in an instant, because its force is formed of bodies minutely small and of smooth elements, which easily make their way in and when they are in, in a moment break up all the knots and untie the bonds of union. And more especially in autumn the mansion of heaven studded with glittering stars and the whole earth are shaken on all sides, and also when the flowery season of spring discloses itself. For during the cold fires are wanting and winds fail during the heat, and the clouds then are not of so dense a body. When therefore the seasons of heaven are between the two extremes, the different causes of thunder and lightning all combine; for the very cross-current of the year mixes up cold and heat, both of which a cloud needs for forging thunderbolts; so that there is great discord in things and the air raving with fires and winds heaves in mighty disorder. The first part of heat and the last of cold is the spring-time; therefore unlike things must battle with one another and be turbulent when mixed together. And when the last heat mixed with the first cold rolls on its course, a time which goes by the name of autumn, then too fierce winters are in conflict with summers. Therefore these seasons are to be called the cross-seas of the year; and it is not wonderful that in that season thunderbolts are most frequent and troublous storms are stirred up in heaven; since both sides then engage in the troublous medley of dubious war, the one armed with flames, the other with winds and water commingled.

This is the way to see into the true nature of the thunderbolt and to understand by what force it produces each effect, and not the turning over the scrolls of Tyrrhene charms and vainly searching for tokens of the hidden will of the gods, in order to know from what quarter the volant fire has come or to which of the two halves it has betaken itself, in what way it has gained an entrance within walled places, and how after lording it with tyrant sway it has gotten itself out from these; also what harm the thunderstroke from heaven can do. But if Jupiter and other gods shake with an appalling crash the glittering quarters of heaven, and hurl their fire whither each is so minded, why strike they not those whoever they be who have recked not of committing some abominable sin and make them give forth the flames of lightning from breast pierced through and through, a sharp lesson to men? and why rather is he whose conscience is burdened with no foul offence, innocent though he be, wrapped and enveloped in the flames, in a moment caught up by the whirlwind and fire of heaven? Why too aim they at solitary spots and spend their labour in vain? Or are they then practising their arms and strengthening their sinews? And why do they suffer the father's bolt to be blunted on the earth? Why does he allow it himself, and not spare it for his enemies? Why again, when heaven is unclouded on all sides, does Jupiter never hurl a bolt on the earth or send abroad his claps? Or does he, so soon as clouds have spread under, then go down in person into them, that from them he may aim the strokes of his bolt near at hand? Ay and for what reason does he hurl into the sea? Of what has he to impeach its waters and liquid mass and floating fields? Again if he wills us to avoid the thunderstroke, why fears he to let us see it discharged? Or if he wills to crush us off our guard with his fire, why thunders he from that side, to enable us to shun it? Why stirs he up beforehand darkness and roarings and rumblings? And how can you believe that he hurls at many points at the same time? Or would you venture to maintain that it never has happened that more than one stroke was made at one time? Nay often and often it has happened and must happen that, even as it rains and showers fall in many different quarters, so many thunderings go on at one time. Once more why does he dash down the holy sanctuaries of the gods and his own gorgeous seats with the destroying thunderbolt, and break the finewrought idols of the gods, and spoil his own images of their glory by an overbearing wound? and why does he mostly aim at lofty spots, and why do we see most traces of his fire on the mountain tops?

To proceed, it is easy from these facts to understand in what way those things, which the Greeks from their nature have named presteres, come down from above into the sea. For sometimes a pillar so to speak is let down from heaven and descends into the sea, and round about it the surges boil, stirred up by heavy blasts of winds; and all ships caught in that turmoil are dashed about and brought into extreme danger. This takes place when at times the force of the wind put in motion cannot burst the cloud which it essays to burst, but weighs it down, so that it is like a pillar let down from heaven into the sea, yet gradually, just as if a thing were thrust down from above and stretched out to the level of the waters by the fist and push of the arm; and when the force of the wind has rent this cloud, it bursts out from it into the sea and occasions a marvellous boiling in the waters; for the whirling eddy descends and brings down together with it yon cloud of limber body; and as soon as it has forced it down full-charged as it is to the levels of the sea, the eddy in a moment plunges itself entire into the water, and stirs up the whole sea with a prodigious noise and forces it to boil. Sometimes too the eddy of wind wraps itself up in clouds and gathers out of the air seeds of cloud and imitates in a sort the prester let down from heaven. When this prester has let itself down to the land and has burst, it belches forth a whirlwind and storm of enormous violence; but as it seldom takes place at all and as mountains cannot but obstruct it on land, it is seen more frequently on the sea with its wide prospect and unobstructed horizon.

Clouds are formed, when in this upper space of heaven many bodies flying about have in some one instant met together, of a rougher sort, such as are able, though they have got the very slightest holds of each other, to catch together and be held in union. These bodies first cause small clouds to form; and these next catch together and collect into masses and increase by joining with each other and are carried on by the winds continually until a fierce storm has gathered. The nearer too the tops of a mountain in each case are to heaven, the more constantly at this elevation they smoke with the thick darkness of a swarthy cloud, because, as soon as clouds form, before the eyes can see them, thin as they are, the winds carry and bring them together to the highest summits of a mountain; and then at last when they have gathered in a greater mass, being now dense they are able to make themselves visible and at the same time they are seen to rise up from the very top of the mountain into the ether: the very fact of the case and our sensations, when we climb high mountains, prove that the regions which stretch up on high are windy. Again clothes hung up on the shore, when they drink in the clinging moisture, prove that nature takes up many bodies over the whole sea as well. This makes it still more plain that many bodies may likewise rise up out of the salt heaving sea to add to the bulk of clouds; for the two liquids are near akin in their nature. Again we see mists and steam rise out of all rivers and at the same time from the earth as well; and they forced out like a breath from these parts are then carried upwards and overcast heaven with their darkness and make up clouds on high as they gradually come together; for the heat of starry ether at the same time presses down too on them and by condensing as it were weaves a web of clouds below the blue. Sometimes there come here into heaven from without those bodies which form clouds and the flying storm-rack; for I have shown that their number passes numbering and that the sum of the deep is infinite; and I have proved with what velocity bodies fly and how in a moment of time they are wont to pass through space unspeakable. It is not therefore strange that a tempest and darkness often in a short time cover over with such great mountains of clouds seas and lands, as they hang down upon them overhead, since on all sides through all the cavities of ether and as it were through the vents of the great world around the power of going out and coming in is accorded to the elements.

Now mark and I will explain in what way the rainy moisture is formed in the clouds above and then is sent down and falls to the earth in the shape of rain. And first I will prove that many seeds of water rise up together with the clouds themselves out of all things and that both the clouds and the water which is in the clouds thus increase together; just as our body increases together with the blood, as well as the sweat and all the moisture which is in the frame. The clouds likewise imbibe much sea-water as well, like hanging fleeces of wool, when the winds carry them over the great sea. In like manner moisture is taken up out of all rivers into the clouds; and when the seeds of waters full many in number in many ways have met in them, augmented from all sides, then the close-packed clouds endeavour to discharge their moisture from two causes: the force of the wind drives them together, and likewise the very abundance of the rain-clouds, when a greater mass than usual has been brought together, pushes down, presses from above and forces the rain to stream out. Again when the clouds are also rarefied by the winds, or are dispersed, being smitten at the same time by the heat of the sun, they discharge a rainy moisture and trickle down, just as wax over a hot fire melts away and turns fast into liquid. But a violent rain follows, when the clouds are violently pressed upon by both causes, by their own accumulated weight and by the impetuous assault of the wind. And rains are wont to hold out and to last long, when many seeds of waters are stirred to action, and clouds upon clouds and rack upon rack welling forth from all quarters round about are borne along, and when the reeking earth steams moisture back again from its whole surface. When in such a case the sun has shone with his rays amid the murky tempest right opposite the dripping rain-clouds, then the colour of the rainbow shows itself among the black clouds.

As to the other things which grow by themselves and are formed by themselves, as well as the things which are formed within the clouds, all, without exception all, snow, winds, hail, and cold hoarfrosts and the great force of ice, the great congealing power of waters, and the stop which everywhere curbs running rivers, it is yet most easy to find out and apprehend in mind how all these things take place and in what way they are formed, when you have fully understood the properties assigned to elements.

Now mark and learn what the law of earthquakes is. And first of all take for granted that the earth below us as well as above is filled in all parts with windy caverns and bears within its bosom many lakes and many chasms, cliffs and craggy rocks; and you must suppose that many rivers hidden beneath the crust of the earth roll on with violence, waves, and submerged stones; for the very nature of the case requires it to be throughout like to itself. With such things then attached and placed below, the earth quakes above from the shock of great falling masses, when underneath time has undermined vast caverns; whole mountains indeed fall in, and in an instant from the mighty shock tremblings spread themselves far and wide from that centre. And with good cause, since buildings beside a road tremble throughout when shaken by a waggon of not such very great weight; and they rock no less, where any sharp pebble on the road jolts up the iron tires of the wheels on both sides. Sometimes too, when an enormous mass of soil through age rolls down from the land into great and extensive pools of water, the earth rocks and sways with the undulation of the water; just as a vessel at times cannot rest, until the liquid within has ceased to sway about in unsteady undulations.

Again when the wind gathering itself together in the hollow places underground bears down on one point and pushing on presses with great violence the deep caverns, the earth leans over on the side to which the headlong violence of the wind presses. Then all buildings which are above ground, and ever the more, the more they tower up towards heaven, lean over and bulge out yielding in the same direction, and the timbers wrenched from their supports hang over ready to give way. And yet men shrink from believing that a time of destruction and ruin awaits the nature of the great world, though they see so great a mass of earth hang ready to fall! And if the winds did not abate their blowing, no force could rein things in or hold them up on their road to destruction. As it is, because by turns they do abate and then increase in violence, and so to speak rally and return to the charge, and then are defeated and retire, for this reason the earth oftener threatens to fall than really falls: it leans over and then sways back again, and after tumbling forward recovers in equal poise its fixed position. For this reason the whole house rocks, the top more than the middle, the middle than the bottom, the bottom in a very very slight degree.

The same great quaking likewise arises from this cause, when on a sudden the wind and some enormous force of air gathering either from without or within the earth have flung themselves into the hollows of the earth, and there chafe at first with much uproar among the great caverns and are carried on with a whirling motion, and when their force afterwards stirred and lashed into fury bursts abroad and at the same moment cleaves the deep earth and opens up a great yawning chasm. This fell out in Syrian Sidon and took place at Aegium in the Peloponnese, two towns which an outbreak of wind of this sort and the ensuing earthquake threw down. And many walled places besides fell down by great commotions on land and many towns sank down engulfed in the sea together with their burghers. And if they do not break out, still the impetuous fury of the air and the fierce violence of the wind spread over the numerous passages of the earth like a shivering-fit and thereby cause a trembling; just as cold when it has pierced into our frames to the very marrow, sets them a-shivering in spite of themselves, forcing them to shake and move. Men are therefore disturbed by a twofold terror throughout their cities: they fear the roofs above their heads, they dread lest the nature of the earth in a moment break up her caverns underneath, and rent asunder display her own wide-gaping maw and wildly tumbled together seek to fill it up with her own ruins. Let them then fancy as much as they please that heaven and earth shall be incorruptible and consigned to an everlasting exemption from decay; and yet sometimes the very present force of danger applies on some side or other this goad of fear among others, that the earth shall in an instant be withdrawn from under their feet and carried down into the pit, and that the sum of things shall utterly give way and follow after and a jumbled wreck of world ensue.

First of all they wonder that nature does not increase the bulk of the sea, when there is so great a flow of water into it, when all rivers from all quarters fall into it. Add to these passing rains and flying storms, which bespatter every sea and moisten every land; add its own springs; yet all these compared with the sum of the sea will be like an addition of bulk hardly amounting to a single drop; it is therefore the less wonderful that the great sea does not increase. Again the sun absorbs a great deal with his heat: we see him with his burning rays thoroughly dry clothes dripping with wet: but we know seas to be many in number and to stretch over a wide surface. Therefore however small the portion of moisture which the sun draws off the surface from any one spot, it will yet in so vast an expanse take largely from its waters. Then again the winds too may withdraw a great deal of moisture as they sweep over the surface, since we very often see the roads dried by the winds in a single night and the soft mud form into hard crusts. Again I have shown that the clouds take off much moisture too imbibed from the great surface of the sea and scatter it about over the whole earth, when it rains on land and the winds carry on the clouds. Lastly since the earth is of a porous body and is in contact with the sea, girding its shores all round, just as water comes from the earth into the sea, in the same way it must ooze into the land out of the salt sea; for the salt is strained off and the matter of liquid streams back again to the source and all flows together to the river-heads, and then passes anew over the lands in a fresh current, where a channel once scooped out has carried down the waters with liquid foot.

And now I will explain why it is that fires breathe forth at times through the gorges of Mount Aetna with such hurricane-like fury; for with a destroying force of no ordinary kind the flame-storm gathered itself up and lording it over the lands of the Sicilians drew on itself the gaze of neighbouring nations, when seeing all the quarters of heaven smoke and sparkle men were filled in heart with awe-struck apprehension, not knowing what strange change nature was travailing to work.

In these matters you must look far and deep and make a wide survey in all directions, in order to bear in mind that the sum of things is unfathomable and to perceive how very small, how inconceivably minute a fraction of the whole sum one heaven is, not so large a fraction of it as one man is of the whole earth. If you should clearly comprehend, clearly see this point well put, you would cease to wonder at many things. Does any one among us wonder if he has gotten into his frame a fever that has broken out with burning heat, or into his body the pains of any other disease? The foot suddenly swells, sharp pain often seizes the teeth, or else attacks the eyes; the holy fire breaks out and creeping over the body burns whatever part it has seized upon, and spreads over the frame, because sure enough there are seeds of many things, and this earth and heaven bring to us evil enough to allow of a measureless amount of disease springing up. In this way then we must suppose that all things are supplied out of the infinite to the whole heaven and earth in quantity sufficient to allow the earth in a moment to be shaken and stirred, and a rapid hurricane to scour over sea and land, the fire of Aetna to overflow, the heaven to be in flames; for that too is seen and the heavenly quarters are on fire; and rain-storms gather in a heavier mass, when the seeds of water have haply come together for such an end. 'Ay but the stormy rage of the conflagration is too too gigantic.' Yes and so any river you like is greatest to him who has never before seen any greater, and thus a tree and a man seem gigantic, and in the case of all things of all kinds the greatest a man has seen he fancies to be gigantic, though yet all things with heaven and earth and sea included are nothing to the whole sum of the universal sum.

And now at last I will explain in what ways yon flame roused to fury in a moment blazes forth from the huge furnaces of Aetna. And first the nature of the whole mountain is hollow underneath, under-propped throughout with caverns of basalt rocks. Furthermore in all caves are wind and air; for wind is produced, when the air has been stirred and put in motion. When this air has been thoroughly heated and raging about has imparted its heat to all the rocks round, wherever it comes in contact with them, and to the earth, and has struck out from them fire burning with swift flames, it rises up and then forces itself out on high straight through the gorges; and so carries its heat far and scatters far its ashes and rolls on smoke of a thick pitchy blackness and flings out at the same time stones of prodigious weight; leaving no doubt that this is the stormy force of air. Again the sea to a great extent breaks its waves and sucks back its surf at the roots of that mountain. Caverns reach from this sea as far as the deep gorges of the mountain below. Through these you must admit that air mixed up with water passes; and the nature of the case compels this air to enter in from that [2] open sea and pass right within and then go out in blasts and so lift up flame and throw out stones and raise clouds of sand; for on the summit are craters, as they name them in their own language; what we call gorges and mouths.

There are things too not a few for which it is not sufficient to assign one cause; you must give several, one of which at the same time is the real cause. For instance should you see the lifeless body of a man lying at some distance, it would be natural to mention all the different causes of death, in order that the one real cause of that man's death be mentioned among them. Thus you may be able to prove that he has not died by steel or cold or from disease or haply from poison; yet we know that it is something of this kind which has befallen him; and so in many other cases we may make the same remark.

The Nile rises every summer and overflows the plains, that one sole river throughout the whole land of Egypt. It waters Egypt often in the middle of the hot season, either because in summer there are north winds opposite its mouths, which at that time of year go by the name of Etesian winds. Blowing up the river they retard it and driving the waters backwards fill its channel full and force the river to stand still; for beyond a doubt these blasts which start from the icy constellations of the pole are carried right up the stream. That river comes from the south out of the heat-fraught country, rising far up from the central region of day among races of men black in their sun-baked complexion. It is quite possible too that the great accumulation of sand may bar up the mouths against the opposing waves, when the sea stirred up by the winds throws up the sand within the channel; whereby the outlet of the river is rendered less free and the current of the waters at the same time less rapid in its downward flow. It may be also that the rains are more frequent at its source in that season, because the Etesian blasts of the north winds drive all the clouds together into those parts at that time. And, you are to know, when they have been driven on to the central region of day and have gathered together, then the clouds jammed close against the high mountains are massed together and violently compressed. Perhaps too it gets its increase high up from the lofty mountains of the Ethiopians, when the all-surveying sun with his thawing rays constrains the white snows to descend into the plains.

Now mark, and I will make clear to you what kind of nature the several Avernian places and lakes possess. First of all, as to the name Avernian by which they are called, it has been given to them from their real nature, because they are noxious to all birds; for when they have arrived in flight just opposite those spots, they forget to row with their wings, they drop their sails and fall with soft neck outstretched headlong to the earth, if so be that the nature of the ground admit of that, or into the water, if so be that a lake of Avernus spreads below. There is such a spot at Cumae, where the mountains are charged with acrid sulphur, and smoke enriched with hot springs. Such a spot there also is within the Athenian walls, on the very summit of the citadel, beside the temple of bountiful Tritonian Pallas; which croaking crows never come near on the wing; no not when the high altars smoke with offerings: so constantly they fly, not before the sharp wrath of Pallas for the sake of yon vigil kept, as the poets of the Greeks have sung, but the nature of the place suffices by its own proper power. In Syria too as well a spot, we are told, is found to exist of such a sort that as soon as ever even four-footed beasts have entered in, its mere natural power forces them to fall down heavily, just as if they were felled in a moment as sacrifices to the Manes gods. Now all these things go on by a natural law, and it is quite plain whence spring the causes from which they are produced; that the gate of Orcus be not haply believed to exist in such spots; and next we imagine that the Manes gods from beneath do haply draw souls down from them to the borders of Acheron; as wing-footed stags are supposed often by their scent to draw out from their holes the savage serpent-tribes. How widely opposed to true reason this is, now learn; for now I essay to tell of the real fact.

First of all I say, as I have often said before, that in the earth are elements of things of every kind: many, which serve for food, helpful to life; and many whose property it is to cause diseases and hasten death. And we have shown before that one thing is more adapted to one, another thing to another living creature for the purposes of life, because of their natures and their textures and their primary elements being all unlike the one to the other. Many which are noxious pass through the ears, many make their way too through the nostrils, dangerous and harsh when they come in contact; and not a few are to be shunned by the touch, and not a few to be avoided by the sight, and others are nauseous in taste.

Again you may see how many things are for man of a virulently noxious sensation and are nauseous and oppressive; to certain trees for instance has been given so very oppressive a shade that they often cause headaches when a man has lain down under them extended on the grass. There is a tree too on the great hills of Helicon which has the property of killing a man by the noisome scent of its flower. All these things you are to know rise up out of the earth, because it contains many seeds of many things in many ways mixed up together and gives them out in a state of separation. Again when a newly extinguished night-light encounters the nostrils with its acrid stench, it sends to sleep then and there a man who from disease is subject to falling down and foaming at the mouth. A woman is put to sleep by oppressive castor and falls back in her seat, and her gay work drops out of her soft hands, if she has smelt it at the time when she has her monthly discharges. And many things besides relax through all the frame the fainting limbs and shake the soul in its seats within. Then too if you linger long in the hot baths when you are somewhat full and do bathe, how liable you are to tumble down in a fit while seated in the midst of the hot water! Again how readily do the oppressive power and fumes of charcoal make their way into the brain, if we have not first taken water! But when burning violently it has filled the chambers of a house, the fumes of the virulent substance act on the nerves like a murderous blow. See you not too that even within the earth sulphur is generated and asphalt forms incrustations of a noisome stench? See you not, when they are following up the veins of silver and gold and searching with the pick quite into the bowels of the earth, what stenches Scaptensula exhales from below? Then what mischief do gold mines exhale! To what state do they reduce men's faces and what a complexion they produce! Know you not by sight or hearsay how they commonly perish in a short time and how all vital power fails those whom the hard compulsion of necessity confines in such an employment? All such exhalations then the earth steams forth and breathes out into the open air and light of heaven.

Thus too the Avernian spots must send up some power deadly to birds, which rises up from the earth into the air so as to poison a certain portion of the atmosphere; in such a way that a bird as soon as ever it is borne on its wings into it, is then attacked by the unseen poison and so palsied that it tumbles plump down on the spot where this exhalation has its course. And when it falls into it, then the same power of that exhalation robs all its limbs of the remnants of life: first of all it causes a sort of dizziness; but afterwards, when the birds have tumbled into the very springs of the poison, then life too has to be vomited forth, because all round rises up large store of mischievous matter.

Sometimes too this power and exhalation of Avernus dispels whatever air lies between the birds and earth, so that almost a void is left there. And when the birds have arrived in their flight just opposite this spot, at once the buoyant force of their pinions is crippled and rendered vain and all the sustaining efforts of their wings are lost on both sides. So when they are unable to buoy themselves up and lean upon their wings, nature, you know, compels them by their weight to tumble down to earth, and lying stark through what is now almost a void they disperse their soul through all the openings of their body.[3] Again during summer the water in wells becomes colder, because the earth is rarefied by heat and rapidly sends out into the air whatever seeds of heat it happens to have. The more then the earth is drained of heat, the colder becomes the water which is hidden in the earth. Again when all the earth is compressed by cold and contracts and so to say congeals, then, you are to know, while it contracts, it presses out into the wells whatever heat it contains itself.

At the fane of Hammon there is said to be a fountain which is cold in the daylight and hot in the night-time. This fountain men marvel at exceedingly and suppose that it suddenly becomes hot by the influence of the fierce sun below the earth, when night has covered the earth with awful darkness. But this is far far removed from true reason. Why when the sun though in contact with the uncovered body of the water has not been able to make it hot on its upper side, though his light above possesses such great heat, how can he below the earth which is of so dense a body boil the water and glut it with heat? above all when he can scarcely with his burning rays force his heat through the walls of houses. What then is the cause? this sure enough: the earth is more porous and warmer round the fountain than the rest of the earth, and there are many seeds of fire near the body of water. For this reason when night has buried the earth in its dewy shadows, the earth at once becomes quite cold and contracts: in this way just as if it were squeezed by the hand it forces out into the fountain whatever seeds of fire it has; and these make the water hot to the touch and taste. Next when the sun has risen and with his rays has loosened the earth and has rarefied it as his heat waxes stronger, the first-beginnings of fire return back to their ancient seats and all the heat of the water withdraws into the earth: for this reason the fountain becomes cold in the daylight. Again the liquid of water is played upon by the sun's rays and in the daytime is rarefied by his throbbing heat; and therefore it gives up whatever seeds of fire it has; just as it often parts with the frost which it holds in itself, and thaws the ice and loosens its bonds.

There is also a cold fountain of such a nature that tow often when held over it imbibes fire forthwith and emits flame; a pine-torch in like manner is lighted and shines among the waters, in whatever direction it swims under the impulse of the winds. Because sure enough there are in the water very many seeds of heat, and from the earth itself at the bottom must rise up bodies of fire throughout the whole fountain and at the same time pass abroad in exhalations and go forth into the air, not in such numbers however that the fountain can become hot, for these reasons a force compels those seeds to burst out through the water and disperse abroad and to unite when they have mounted up. In the sea at Aradus is a fountain of this kind, which wells up with fresh water and keeps off the salt waters all round it; and in many other quarters the sea affords a seasonable help in need to thirsting sailors, vomiting forth fresh waters amid the salt. In this way then those seeds may burst forth through that fountain and well out; and when they are met together in the tow or cohere in the body of the pine-torch, they at once readily take fire, because the tow and pinewood contain in them likewise many seeds of latent fire. See you not too that, when you bring a newly extinguished wick near night-lamps it catches light before it has touched the flame; and the same with the pinewood? And many things beside catch fire at some distance touched merely by the heat, before the fire in actual contact infects them. This therefore you must suppose to take place in that fountain as well.

Next in order I will proceed to discuss by what law of nature it comes to pass that iron can be attracted by that stone which the Greeks call the Magnet from the name of its native place, because it has its origin within the bounds of the country of the Magnesians. This stone men wonder at; as it often produces a chain of rings hanging down from it. Thus you may see sometimes five and more suspended in succession and tossing about in the light airs, one always hanging down from one and attached to its lower side, and each in turn one from the other experiencing the binding power of the stone: with such a continued current its force flies through all.

In things of this kind many points must be established before you can assign the true law of the thing in question, and it must be approached by a very circuitous road; wherefore all the more I call for an attentive ear and mind.

In the first place from all things whatsoever which we see there must incessantly stream and be discharged and scattered abroad such bodies as strike the eyes and provoke vision. Smells too incessantly stream from certain things; as does cold from rivers, heat from the sun, spray from the waves of the sea, that eat into walls near the shore. Various sounds too cease not to stream through the air. Then a moist salt flavour often comes into the mouth, when we are moving about beside the sea; and when we look on at the mixing of a decoction of wormwood, its bitterness affects us. In such a constant stream from all things the several qualities of things are carried and are transmitted in all directions round, and no delay, no respite in the flow is ever granted, since we constantly have feeling, and may at any time see, smell and hear the sound of anything.

And now I will state once again how rare a body all things have: a question made clear in the first part of my poem also: although the knowledge of this is of importance in regard to many things, above all in regard to this very question which I am coming to discuss, at the very outset it is necessary to establish that nothing comes under sense save body mixed with void. For instance in caves rocks overhead sweat with moisture and trickle down in oozing drops. Sweat too oozes out from our whole body; the beard grows, and hairs over all our limbs and frame. Food is distributed through all the veins, gives increase and nourishment to the very extremities and nails. We feel, too, cold and heat pass through brass, we feel them pass through gold and silver, when we hold full cups. Again voices fly through the stone partitions of houses; smell passes through and cold, and the heat of fire which is wont ay to pierce even the strength of iron, where the Gaulish cuirass girds the body round. And when a storm has gathered in earth and heaven, and when along with it the influence of disease makes its way in from without, they both withdraw respectively to heaven and earth and there work their wills, since there is nothing at all that is not of a rare texture of body.

Furthermore all bodies whatever which are discharged from things are not qualified to excite the same sensations nor are adapted for all things alike. The sun for instance bakes and dries up the earth, but thaws ice, and forces the snows piled up high on the high hills to melt away beneath his rays; wax again turns to liquid when placed within reach of his heat. Fire also melts brass and fuses gold, but shrivels up and draws together hides and flesh. The liquid of water after fire hardens steel, but softens hides and flesh hardened by heat. The wild olive delights the bearded she-goats as much as if the flavour it yielded were of ambrosia and steeped in nectar; but nothing that puts forth leaf is more bitter to man than this food. Again a swine eschews marjoram-oil and dreads all perfumes; for they are rank poison to bristly swine, though they are found at times to give us as it were fresh life. But on the other hand though mire is to us the nastiest filth, it is found to be so welcome to swine that they wallow in it all over with a craving not to be satisfied.

There is still one point left which it seems proper to mention, before

I come to speak of the matter in hand. Since many pores are assigned to various things, they must possess natures differing the one from the other and must have each its own nature, its own direction: thus there are in living creatures various senses, each of which takes into it in its own peculiar way its own special object; for we see that sounds pass into one thing, taste from different flavours into another thing, smells into another. Again one thing is seen to stream through stones and another thing to pass through woods, another through gold, and another still to go out through silver and brass; for form is seen to stream through this passage, heat through that, and one thing is seen to pass through by the same way more quickly than other things. The nature of the passages, you are to know, compels it so to be, varying in manifold wise, as we have shown a little above, owing to the unlike nature and textures of things.

Therefore now that these points have all been established and arranged for us as premisses ready to our hand, for what remains, the law will easily be explained out of them, and the whole cause be laid open which attracts the strength of iron. First of all there must stream from this stone very many seeds or a current if you will which dispels with blows all the air which lies between the stone and iron. When this space is emptied and much room left void between, forthwith the first-beginnings of iron fall headlong forward into the void in one mass, and in consequence the ring itself follows and then goes on with its whole body. And nothing has its primal elements more intricately entangled or coheres in closer connexion than the nature of stubborn iron and its coldness that makes you shiver. Therefore what I say is the less strange, that from among such elements as these bodies cannot gather in large numbers out of the iron and be carried into the void without the whole ring following. This it does do, and follows on until it has quite reached the stone and fastened on it with unseen bonds of connexion. The same thing takes place in all directions: on whatever side a void is formed, whether athwart or from above the first bodies next it are at once carried on into the void; for they are set in motion by blows from another source and cannot by their own free act rise up into the air. Moreover (to render it more feasible, this thing also is helped on by external aid and motion) as soon as the air in front of the ring has been made rarer and the space more empty and void, it follows at once that all the air which lies behind, carries and pushes it on as it were at its back. For the air which lies around them always beats on things; but at such a time as this it is able to push on the iron, because on one side a space is void and receives the iron into it. This air of which I am speaking to you makes its way with much subtlety through the frequent pores of the iron to its minute parts and then thrusts and pushes it on, as the wind a ship and its sails. Again all things must have air in their body, since they are of a rare body and air surrounds and is in contact with all things. This air therefore which is in the inmost recesses of the iron, is ever stirred in restless motion and therefore beats the ring without a doubt and stirs it within, you know: the ring is carried in the direction in which it has once plunged forward, and into the void part towards which it has made its start.

Sometimes too it happens that the nature of iron is repelled from this stone, being in the habit of flying from and following it in turns. I have seen Samothracian iron rings even jump up, and at the same time filings of iron rave within brass basins, when this Magnet stone had been placed under: such a strong desire the iron seems to have to fly from the stone. So great a disturbance is raised by the interposition of the brass, because sure enough when the current of the brass has first seized on and taken possession of the open passages of the iron, the current of the stone comes after and finds all things full in the iron and has no opening to swim through as before. It is forced therefore to dash against and beat with its wave the iron texture; by which means it repels from it and sets in motion through the brass that which without the brass it often draws to itself. And forbear herein to wonder that the current from this stone is not able to set in motion other things as well as iron: some of these stand still by the power of their own weight; for instance gold; and others, because they are of so rare a body that the current flies through them uninterrupted, cannot in any case be set in motion; to which class wood is found to belong. When therefore the nature of iron lying between the two has received into it certain first bodies of brass, then do the Magnet stones set it in motion with their stream.

And yet these cases are not so much at variance with other things, that I have only a scanty store of similar instances to relate of things mutually fitted one for the other and for nothing else: stones for instance you see are cemented by mortar alone; wood is united with wood so firmly by bulls' glue only, that the veins of boards often gape in cracks before the binding power of the glue can be brought to loosen its hold. Vine-born juices venture to mix with streams of water, though heavy pitch and light oil cannot. Again the purple dye of the shellfish so unites with the body of wool alone, that it cannot in any case be severed, not were you to take pains to undo what is done with Neptune's wave, not if the whole sea were willed to wash it out with all its waters. Then too is there not one thing only that fastens gold to gold, and is not brass soldered to brass by tin? and how many other cases of the kind might one find! What then? You have no need whatever of such long circuitous roads, nor is it worth my while to spend so much pains on this, but it is better briefly to comprise many things in few words: things whose textures have such a mutual correspondence, that cavities fit solids, the cavities of the first the solids of the second, the cavities of the second the solids of the first, form the closest union. Again some things may be fastened together and held in union with hooks and eyes as it were; and this seems rather to be the case with this stone and iron.

And now I will explain what the law of diseases is and from what causes the force of disease may suddenly gather itself up and bring death-dealing destruction on the race of man and the troops of brute beasts. And first I have shown above that there are seeds of many things helpful to our life; and on the other hand many must fly about conducing to disease and death. When these by chance have happened to gather together and have disordered the atmosphere, the air becomes distempered. And all that force of disease and that pestilence come either from without down through the atmosphere in the shape of clouds and mists, or else do gather themselves up and rise out of the earth, when soaked with wet it has contracted a taint, being beaten upon by unseasonable rains and suns. See you not too that all who come to a place far away from country and home are affected by the strangeness of climate and water, because there are wide differences in such things? For what a difference may we suppose between the climate of the Briton and that of Egypt where the pole of heaven slants askew, and again between that in Pontus and that of Gades and so on to the races of men black with sun-baked complexion? Now as we see these four climates under the four opposite winds and quarters of heaven all differing from each other, so also the complexions and faces of the men are seen to differ widely and diseases varying in kind are found to seize upon the different races. There is the elephant disease which is generated beside the streams of Nile in the midst of Egypt and nowhere else. In Attica the feet are attacked and the eyes in Achaean lands. And so different places are hurtful to different parts and members: the variations of air occasion that. Therefore when an atmosphere which happens to put itself in motion unsuited to us and a hurtful air begin to advance, they creep slowly on in the shape of mist and cloud and disorder everything in their line of advance and compel all to change; and when they have at length reached our atmosphere, they corrupt it too and make it like to themselves and unsuited to us. This new destroying power and pestilence therefore all at once either fall upon the waters or else sink deep into the corn-crops or other food of man and provender of beast; or else their force remains suspended within the atmosphere, and when we inhale from it mixed airs, we must absorb at the same time into our body those things as well. In like manner pestilence often falls on kine also and a distemper too on the silly sheep. And it makes no difference whether we travel to places unfavourable to us and change the atmosphere which wraps us round, or whether nature without our choice brings to us a tainted atmosphere or something to the use of which we have not been accustomed, and which is able to attack us on its first arrival.

Such a form of disease and a death-fraught miasm erst within the borders of Cecrops defiled the whole land with dead, and dispeopled the streets, drained the town of burghers.[4] Rising first and starting from the inmost corners of Egypt, after traversing much air and many floating fields, the plague brooded at last over the whole people of Pandion; and then they were handed over in troops to disease and death. First of all they would have the head seized with burning heat and both eyes blood-shot with a glare diffused over; the livid throat within would exude blood and the passage of the voice be clogged and choked with ulcers, and the mind's interpreter the tongue drip with gore, quite enfeebled with sufferings, heavy in movement, rough to touch. Next when the force of disease passing down the throat had filled the breast and had streamed together even into the sad heart of the sufferers, then would all the barriers of life give away. The breath would pour out at the mouth a noisome stench, even as the stench of rotting carcases thrown out unburied. And then the powers of the entire mind, the whole body would sink utterly, now on the very threshold of death. And a bitter bitter despondency was the constant attendant on insufferable ills and complaining mingled with moaning. An ever-recurring hiccup often the night and day through, forcing on continual spasms in sinews and limbs, would break men quite, forwearying those forspent before. And yet in none could you perceive the skin on the surface of the body burn with any great heat, but the body would rather offer to the hand a lukewarm sensation and at the same time be red all over with ulcers burnt into it so to speak, like unto the holy fire as it spreads over the frame. The inward parts of the men however would burn to the very bones, a flame would burn within the stomach as within furnaces. Nothing was light and thin enough to apply to the relief of the body of any one; ever wind and cold alone. Many would plunge their limbs burning with disease into the cool rivers, throwing their body naked into the water. Many tumbled headforemost deep down into the wells, meeting the water straight with mouth wide-agape. Parching thirst with a craving not to be appeased, drenching their bodies, would make an abundant draught no better than the smallest drop. No respite was there of ill: their bodies would lie quite spent. The healing art would mutter low in voiceless fear, as again and again they rolled about their eyeballs wide open, burning with disease, never visited by sleep. And many symptoms of death besides would then be given, the mind disordered in sorrow and fear, the clouded brow, the fierce delirious expression, the ears too troubled and filled with ringings, the breathing quick or else strangely loud and slow-recurring, and the sweat glistening wet over the neck, the spittle in thin small flakes, tinged with a saffron-colour, salt, scarce forced up the rough throat by coughing. The tendons of the hands ceased not to contract, the limbs to shiver, a coldness to mount with slow sure pace from the feet upwards. Then at their very last moments they had nostrils pinched, the tip of the nose sharp, eyes deep-sunk, temples hollow, the skin cold and hard, on the grim mouth a grin, the brow tense and swollen; and not long after their limbs would be stretched stiff in death: about the eighth day of bright sunlight or else on the ninth return of his lamp they would yield up life. And if any of them at that time had shunned the doom of death, yet in after time consumption and death would await him from noisome ulcers and the black discharge of the bowels, or else a quantity of purulent blood accompanied by headache would often pass out by the gorged nostrils: into these the whole strength and substance of the man would stream. Then too if any one had escaped the acrid discharge of noisome blood, the disease would yet pass into his sinews and joints and onward even into the sexual organs of the body; and some from excessive dread of the gates of death would live bereaved of these parts by the knife; and some though without hands and feet would continue in life, and some would lose their eyes: with such force had the fear of death come upon them. And some were seized with such utter loss of memory that they did not know themselves. And though bodies lay in heaps above bodies unburied on the ground, yet would the race of birds and beasts either scour far away, to escape the acrid stench, or where any one had tasted, it drooped in near-following death. Though hardly at all in those days would any bird appear, or the sullen breeds of wild beasts quit the forests. Many would droop with disease and die: above all faithful dogs would lie stretched in all the streets and yield up breath with a struggle; for the power of disease would wrench life from their frame. Funerals lonely, unattended, would be hurried on with emulous haste. And no sure and general method of cure was found; for that which had given to one man the power to inhale the vital air and to gaze on the quarters of heaven, would be destruction to others and would bring on death. But in such times this was what was deplorable and above all eminently heart-rending: when a man saw himself enmeshed by the disease, as though he were doomed to death, losing all spirit he would lie with sorrow-stricken heart, and with his thoughts turned on death would surrender his life then and there. Ay for at no time did they cease to catch from one another the infection of the devouring plague, like to woolly flocks and horned herds. And this above all heaped death on death: whenever any refused to attend their own sick, killing neglect soon after would punish them for their too great love of life and fear of death by a foul and evil death, abandoned in turn, forlorn of help. But they who had stayed by them, would perish by infection and the labour which shame would then compel them to undergo and the sick man's accents of affection mingled with those of complaining: this kind of death the most virtuous would meet. . . .[5] and different bodies on different piles, struggling as they did to bury the multitude of their dead: then spent with tears and grief they would go home; and in great part they would take to their bed from sorrow. And none could be found whom at so fearful a time neither disease nor death nor mourning assailed.

Then too every shepherd and herdsman, ay and sturdy guider of the bent plough sickened; and their bodies would lie huddled together in the corners of a hut, delivered over to death by poverty and disease. Sometimes you might see lifeless bodies of parents above their lifeless children, and then the reverse of this, children giving up life above their mothers and fathers. And in no small measure that affliction streamed from the land into the town, brought thither by the sickening crowd of peasants meeting plague-stricken from every side. They would fill all places and buildings: wherefore all the more the heat would destroy them and thus close-packed death would pile them up in heaps. Many bodies drawn forth by thirst and tumbled out along the street would lie extended by the fountains of water, the breath of life cut off from their too great delight in water; and over all the open places of the people and the streets you might see many limbs drooping with their half-lifeless body, foul with stench and covered with rags, perish away from filth of body, with nothing but skin on their bones, now nearly buried in noisome sores and dirt. All the holy sanctuaries of the gods too death had filled with lifeless bodies, and all the temples of the heavenly powers in all parts stood burdened with carcases: all which places the wardens had thronged with guests. For now no longer the worship of the gods or their divinities were greatly regarded: so overmastering was the present affliction. Nor did those rites of sepulture continue in force in the city, with which that pious folk had always been wont to be buried; for the whole of it was in dismay and confusion, and each man would sorrowfully bury as the present moment allowed. And the sudden pressure and poverty prompted to many frightful acts; thus with a loud uproar they would place their own kinsfolk upon the funeral piles of others, and apply torches, quarrelling often with much bloodshed sooner than abandon the bodies.

NOTES

Book I.

[1] The reference is to Epicurus, who is devoutly praised by Lucretius in his poem. Cf. especially the opening lines of Books III, V, and VI.

[2] Here follows Lucretius' famous account of the sacrifice of Iphigenia by her father Agamemnon at Aulis that the Greek ships might sail on their expedition against Troy.

[3] These lines are frequently repeated by Lucretius and give obviously the clue to his rational and scientific mode of attack.

[4, 5, 6, 7] A lacuna here has been filled by Munro.

[8] The text is mutilated here, but Munro has filled the gaps in his translation.

[9, 10, 11] A lacuna here has been filled by Munro.

Book II.

[1] A lacuna occurs here.

[2] The capacity to swerve, gratuitously attributed to the atom, undoubtedly marks the weakest point in the structure of Lucretius' philosophical system.

[3] A lacuna here has been filled by Munro.

[4] I.e., the eunuch priests of Cybele.

[5, 6, 7] A lacuna here has been filled by Munro.

Book III.

[1, 2] A lacuna here has been filled by Munro.

[3] Cf. Plato, the vision of Er in *Republic*, X.

[4, 5] A lacuna here has been filled by Munro.

[6] The reference is to Xerxes.

Book IV.

[1] The opening twenty-five lines of this book are found likewise in Book I, lines 926-950.

[2] There is a lacuna here which has been partly filled by Munro.

[3] The reference is to the traditional story which told how the sacred geese on the Capitoline cackled and thus spread the alarm when the Gauls sacked Rome in 390 B.C.

Book V.

[1, 2, 3] A lacuna here has been filled by Munro.

[4] I.e., elephants.

Book VI.

[1, 2, 3] A lacuna here has been filled by Munro.

[3] There is a gap here in the text.

[4] Here follows Lucretius' famous description of the plague which swept Athens in the early years of the Peloponnesian War. The poet follows closely, and in parts even translates, Thucydides' account in his history, Book II, 47-54. There is no agreement among medical scientists as to the exact identification of the disease.

[5] There is a gap here in the text.

ARRIAN'S DISCOURSES OF EPICTETUS

ARRIAN'S DISCOURSES OF EPICTETUS

PREFACE

ARRIANUS TO LUCIUS GELLIUS GREETING

I DID not write down the Lectures of Epictetus in the form of a book, as one might do with such utterances as his, nor did I of my own will give them to the public, for, as I say, I did not write them down for publication. What I tried to do was to make notes of all that I used to hear him say word for word in the very language he used, so far as possible, and to preserve his sayings as reminders for myself hereafter of the nature of his mind and the directness of his speech. It follows then, as is natural, that the words are just such as a man might use to another on the impulse of the moment, not such as he would write for formal publication, with a view to a circle of readers hereafter. Moreover, such as they are, somehow or other they were put abroad among men without my consent and without my knowledge. Well, to me it is no great matter, if I appear in the world's eyes incapable of writing a book; and to Epictetus it will not matter in the least if men despise his lectures, for in the very act of giving them he made it plain that his one and only desire was to impel the minds of his hearers towards the noblest objects. If then these lectures should accomplish this result and no other, I take it they would be just what the lectures of philosophers ought to be; and if they fail, yet I would have those who read them understand that when Epictetus himself was speaking, his hearers were forced to feel just what he would have them feel. If the words read by themselves do not achieve this result, it may be that I am to blame, but it may be also that it could not be otherwise. Farewell.

BOOK I

CHAPTER I

ON THINGS IN OUR POWER AND THINGS NOT IN OUR POWER

Of our faculties in general you will find that none can take cognizance of itself; none therefore has the power to approve or disapprove its own action. Our grammatical faculty for instance: how far can that take cognizance? Only so far as to distinguish expression. Our musical faculty? Only so far as to distinguish tune. Does any one of these then take cognizance of itself? By no means. If you are writing to your friend, when you want to know what words to write grammar will tell you; but whether you should write to your friend or should not write grammar will not tell you. And in the same way music will tell you about tunes, but whether at this precise moment you should sing and play the lyre or should not sing nor play the lyre it will not tell you. What will tell you then? That faculty which takes cognizance of itself and of all things else. What is this? The reasoning faculty: for this alone of the faculties we have received is created to comprehend even its own nature; that is to say, what it is and what it can do, and with what precious qualities it has come to us, and to comprehend all other faculties as well. For what else is it that tells us that gold is a goodly thing? For the gold does not tell us. Clearly it is the faculty which can deal with our impressions.[1] What else is it which distinguishes the faculties of music, grammar, and the rest, testing their uses and pointing out the due seasons for their use? It is reason and nothing else.

The gods then, as was but right, put in our hands the one blessing that is best of all and master of all, that and nothing else, the power to deal rightly with our impressions, but everything else they did not put in our hands. Was it that they would not? For my part I think that if they could have entrusted us with those other powers as well they would have done so, but they were quite unable. Prisoners on the earth and in an earthly body and among earthly companions, how was it possible that we should not be hindered from the attainment of these powers by these external fetters?

But what says Zeus? 'Epictetus, if it were possible I would have made your body and your possessions (those trifles that you prize) free and untrammelled. But as things are—never forget this—this body is not yours, it is but a clever mixture of clay. But since I could not make it free, I gave you a portion in our divinity, this faculty of impulse to act and not to act, of will to get and will to avoid,[2] in a word the faculty which can turn impressions to right use. If you pay heed to this, and put your affairs in its keeping, you will never suffer let nor hindrance, you will not groan, you will blame no man, you will flatter none. What then? Does all this seem but little to you?'

Heaven forbid!

'Are you content then?'

So surely as I hope for the gods' favour.

But, as things are, though we have it in our power to pay heed to one thing and to devote ourselves to one, yet instead of this we prefer to pay heed to many things and to be bound fast to many—our body, our property, brother and friend, child and slave. Inasmuch then as we are bound fast to many things, we are burdened by them and dragged down. That is why, if the weather is bad for sailing, we sit distracted and keep looking continually and ask, 'What wind is blowing?' 'The north wind.' What have we to do with that? 'When will the west wind blow?' When it so chooses, good sir, or when Aeolus chooses. For God made Aeolus the master of the winds, not you. What follows? We must make the best of those things that are in our power, and take the rest as nature gives it. What do you mean by 'nature'? I mean, God's will.

'What? Am I to be beheaded now, and I alone?'

Why? Would you have had all beheaded, to give you consolation? Will you not stretch out your neck as Lateranus did in Rome when Nero ordered his beheadal? For he stretched out his neck and took the blow, and when the blow dealt him was too weak he shrank up a little and then stretched it out again. Nay more, on a previous occasion, when Nero's freedman Epaphroditus came to him and asked him the cause of his offence, he answered, 'If I want to say anything, I will say it to your master.'

What then must a man have ready to help him in such emergencies? Surely this: he must ask himself, 'What is mine, and what is not mine? What may I do, what may I not do?'

I must die. But must I die groaning? I must be imprisoned. But must I whine as well? I must suffer exile. Can any one then hinder me from going with a smile, and a good courage, and at peace?

'Tell the secret!'

I refuse to tell, for this is in my power.

'But I will chain you.'

What say you, fellow? Chain me? My leg you will chain—yes, but my will—no, not even Zeus can conquer that.

'I will imprison you.'

My bit of a body, you mean.

'I will behead you.'

Why? When did I ever tell you that I was the only man in the world that could not be beheaded?

These are the thoughts that those who pursue philosophy should ponder, these are the lessons they should write down day by day, in these they should exercise themselves.

Thrasea used to say 'I had rather be killed to-day than exiled to-morrow'. What then did Rufus say to him? 'If you choose it as the harder, what is the meaning of your foolish choice? If as the easier, who has given you the easier? Will you not study to be content with what is given you?'

It was in this spirit that Agrippinus used to say—do you know what? 'I will not stand in my own way!' News was brought him, 'Your trial is on in the Senate!' 'Good luck to it, but the fifth hour is come'—this was the hour when he used to take his exercise and have a cold bath—'let us go and take exercise.' When he had taken his exercise they came and told him, 'You are condemned.' 'Exile or death?' he asked. 'Exile.' 'And my property?' 'It is not confiscated.' 'Well then, let us go to Aricia and dine.'

Here you see the result of training as training should be, of the will to get and will to avoid, so disciplined that nothing can hinder or frustrate them. I must die, must I? If at once, then I am dying: if soon, I dine now, as it is time for dinner, and afterwards when the time comes I will die. And die how? As befits one who gives back what is not his own.

CHAPTER II

HOW ONE MAY BE TRUE TO ONE'S CHARACTER IN EVERYTHING

To THE rational creature that which is against reason is alone past bearing; the rational he can always bear. Blows are not by nature intolerable.

'What do you mean?'

Let me explain; the Lacedaemonians bear flogging, because they have learnt that it is in accord with reason.

'But is it not intolerable to hang oneself?'

At any rate, when a man comes to feel that it is rational, he goes and hangs himself at once. In a word, if we look to it we shall see that by nothing is the rational creature so distressed as by the irrational, and again to nothing so much attracted as to the rational.

But rational and irrational mean different things to different persons, just as good and evil, expedient and inexpedient, are different for different persons. That is the chief reason why we need education, that we may learn so to adjust our preconceptions [3] of rational and irrational to particular conditions as to be in harmony with nature. But to decide what is rational and irrational we not only estimate the value of things external, but each one of us considers what is in keeping with his character. For one man thinks it reasonable to perform the meanest office[4] for another; for he looks merely to this, that if he refuses he will be beaten and get no food, while if he does it nothing hard or painful will be done to him. To another it seems intolerable not only to do this service himself, but even to suffer another to do it. If then you ask me, 'Am I to do it or not?' I shall say to you, to get food is worth more than to go without it, and to be flogged is worth less than to escape flogging: therefore, if you measure your affairs by this standard, go and do it.

'But I shall be false to myself.'

That is for you to bring into the question, not for me. For it is you who know yourself; you know at how much you put your worth, and at what price you sell yourself. For different men sell at different prices.

That is why Agrippinus, when Florus was considering whether he should go down to Nero's shows, to perform some part in them himself, said to him, 'Go down.' And when he asked, 'Why do you not go down yourself?' said, 'Because I do not even consider the question.' For when a man once lowers himself to think about such matters, and to value external things and calculate about them he has almost forgotten his own character. What is it you ask me? 'Is death or life to be preferred?' I say 'life'. 'Pain or pleasure?' I say 'pleasure'.

'But, if I do not act in the tragedy, I shall be beheaded.'

Go then and act your tragedy, but I will not do so. You ask me, 'Why?' I answer, 'Because you count yourself to be but an ordinary thread in the tunic.' What follows then? You ought to think how you can be like other men, just as one thread does not wish to have something special to distinguish it from the rest: but I want to be the purple, that touch of brilliance which gives distinction and beauty to the rest. Why then do you say to me, 'Make yourself like unto the many?' If I do that, I shall no longer be the purple.

Priscus Helvidius too saw this, and acted on it. When Vespasian sent to him not to come into the Senate he answered, 'You can forbid me to be a senator; but as long as I am a senator I must come in.'

'Come in then,' he says, 'and be silent.'

'Question me not and I will be silent.'

'But I am bound to question you.'

'And I am bound to say what seems right to me.'

'But, if you say it, I shall kill you.'

'When did I tell you, that I was immortal? You will do your part, and I mine. It is yours to kill, mine to die without quailing: yours to banish, mine to go into exile without groaning.'

What good, you ask, did Priscus do, being but one? What good does the purple do to the garment? Just this, that being purple it gives distinction and stands out as a fine example to the rest. Another man, had Caesar in such circumstances told him not to come into the Senate, would have said, 'Thank you for sparing me.' Such a one he would never have forbidden to come in; he would know that he would either sit silent like a pipkin or if he spoke would say what he knew Caesar wished and pile on more besides.

This spirit too was shown by a certain athlete, who was threatened with death if he did not sacrifice his virility. When his brother, who was a philosopher, came to him and said, 'Brother, what will you do? Are we to let the knife do its work and still go into the gymnasium?' he would not consent, but endured to meet his death. (*Here some one asked,* 'How did he do so, as an athlete or as a philosopher?')[5] He did so as a man, and a man who had wrestled at Olympia and been proclaimed victor, one who had passed his days in such a place as that, not one who anoints himself at Bato's. Another man would have consented to have even his head cut off, if he could have lived without it.

That is what I mean by keeping your character: such is its power with those who have acquired the habit of carrying it into every question that arises.

'Go to, Epictetus, have yourself shaved.'

If I am a philosopher I say, 'I will not be shaved.'

'I must behead you then.'

Behead me, if it is better for you so.

One asked, 'How then shall we discover, each of us, what suits his character?'

How does the bull, he answered, at the lion's approach, alone discover what powers he is endowed with, when he stands forth to protect the whole herd? It is plain that with the possession of his power the consciousness of it also is given him. So each of us, who has power of this sort, will not be unaware of its possession. Like the bull, the man of noble nature does not become noble of a sudden; he must train through the winter, and make ready, and not lightly leap to meet things that concern him not.

Of one thing beware, O man; see what is the price at which you sell your will. If you do nothing else, do not sell your will cheap. The great, heroic style, it may be, belongs to others, to Socrates and men like him.

'If then this is our true nature, why do not all men, or many, show it?'

What? Do all horses turn out swift, are all dogs good at the scent?

'What am I to do then? Since I have no natural gifts, am I to make no effort for that reason?'

Heaven forbid. Epictetus is not better than Socrates: if only he is as good as Socrates I am content. For I shall never be a Milo, yet I do not neglect my body; nor a Croesus, and yet I do not neglect my property; nor, in a word, do we abandon our effort in any field because we despair of the first place.

CHAPTER III

WHAT CONCLUSIONS MAY BE DRAWN FROM THE FACT THAT GOD IS FATHER OF MEN

If a man could only take to heart this judgement, as he ought, that we are all, before anything else, children of God and that God is the Father of gods and men, I think that he will never harbour a mean or ignoble thought about himself. Why, if Caesar adopts you, your arrogance will be past all bearing; but if you realize that you are a son of Zeus, will you feel no elation? We ought to be proud, but we are not; as there are these two elements mingled in our birth, the body which we share with the animals, and the reason and mind which we share with the gods, men in general decline upon that wretched and dead kinship with the beasts, and but few claim that which is divine and blessed.

And so, since every one, whoever he be, must needs deal with each person or thing according to the opinion that he holds about them, those few who think that they have been born to be faithful, born to be honourable, born to deal with their impressions without error, have no mean or ignoble thought about themselves. But the thoughts of most men are just the opposite to this. 'What am I? A miserable creature of a man'; and 'my wretched rags of flesh'. Wretched indeed, but you have too something better than your 'rags of flesh'. Why then do you discard the better and cling to your rags?

By reason of this lower kinship some of us fall away and become like wolves, faithless and treacherous and mischievous, others like lions, savage and brutal and untameable, but the greater part of us become foxes and the most god-forsaken creatures in the animal world. For a foul-mouthed and wicked man is no better than a fox or the meanest and most miserable of creatures. Look to it then and beware lest you turn out to be one of these god-forsaken creatures.

CHAPTER IV

ON PROGRESS, OR MORAL ADVANCE

How shall we describe 'progress'?[6] It is the state of him who having learnt from philosophers that man wills to get what is good, and wills to avoid what is evil, and having learnt also that peace and calm come to a man only if he fail not to get what he wills, and if he fall not into that which he avoids, has put away from him altogether the will to get anything and has postponed it to the future, and wills to avoid only such things as are dependent on his will. For if he tries to avoid anything beyond his will, he knows that, for all his avoidance, he will one day come to grief and be unhappy. And if this is the promise that virtue makes to us—the promise to produce happiness and peace and calm, surely progress toward virtue is progress toward each of these. For to whatever end the perfection of a thing leads, to that end is progress an approach.

How is it then that, though we admit that this is the nature of virtue, we search elsewhere for progress and display it elsewhere?

What does virtue produce?

Peace of mind.

Who then makes progress? Is it he who has read many treatises of Chrysippus? Can this be virtue—to have understood Chrysippus? For if this be so, we must admit that progress is nothing but to understand a lot of sayings of Chrysippus. But, the fact is, we admit that virtue tends to one result, and yet declare that progress, the approach to virtue, tends to another.

'Yonder man', he says, 'can already read Chrysippus by himself.'

Bravo, by the gods, you make progress, fellow. Progress indeed! Why do you mock him? Why do you draw him away from the sense of his own shortcomings? Will you not show him what virtue really means, that he may learn where to seek for progress? Miserable man, there is only one place to seek it—where your work lies. Where does it lie? It lies in the region of will; that you may not fail to get what you will to get, nor fall into what you will to avoid; it lies in avoiding error in the region of impulse, impulse to act and impulse not to act: it lies in assent and the withholding of assent, that in these you may never be deceived.[7] But the first department I have named comes first and is most necessary. If you merely tremble and mourn and seek to escape misfortune, progress is of course impossible.

Show me your progress then in this field. You act as though when I was talking to an athlete and said, 'Show me your shoulders', he answered, 'Look at my leaping-weights.' That is for you and your leaping-weights to look to; I want to see the final result of your leaping-weights.

'Take the treatise on "Impulse" and learn how I have read it.'

Slave, that is not what I am looking for—I want to know what impulses you have, for action and against it, to know what you will to get and will to avoid; how you plan and purpose and prepare—whether in harmony with nature, or out of harmony with nature. Show me that you act in harmony with nature, and I will tell you that you are making progress; act out of harmony with nature, and I bid you begone and write books on such things and not merely expound them. What good, I ask, will they do you? Do not you know that the whole book is worth but five pence? Do you think then that the man who expounds it is worth more? Therefore never seek your work in one place and progress in another.

Where then is progress?

If any one of you, dismissing things without, has brought his mind to bear on his own will, to work out its full development, that he may bring it into perfect harmony with nature—lofty, free, unhindered, untrammelled, trustworthy, self-respecting; if he has learnt that he that wills to get or to avoid what is not in his power cannot be trustworthy nor free, but must needs himself change as they change, fitful as the winds, and must needs have made himself subservient to others, who can procure or hinder such things; and if, in a word, when he rises in the morning he guards and keeps these principles, washes as one that is trustworthy, eats as one that is self-respecting, and on each occasion that arises labours to achieve his main tasks, even as the runner makes running his one aim and the voice-trainer his training—he is the man who is indeed in the path of progress and who has not travelled to no purpose.

But if all his efforts are turned to the study of books, if on this he spends his labour, and for this has gone abroad, then I bid him go straight home and not neglect what he finds there; for this that he has gone abroad for is nothing; his true work is to study to remove from his life mourning and lamentation, the 'ah me' and 'alas for my misery', the talk of 'bad fortune' and 'misfortune'; and to learn, what is death, what is exile, what is imprisonment, what is the cup of hemlock; that he may be able to say in prison, 'My dear Crito, if it pleases the gods, so be it', and not such words as 'miserable old man that I am, is it for this I kept my grey hairs?' (Plato, *Crito,* 43d) Whose words are they? Do you think I shall name to you a mean man of no reputation? Are they not the words of Priam and of Oedipus? Are they not the words of all kings that are? For what else are tragedies but a portrayal in such metrical form of the sufferings of men who have set their admiration on outward things? If delusion after all were the only means for a man to learn this lesson—the lesson that not one of the things beyond the compass of our will concerns us, then I for my part would choose a delusion such as this, if it should procure me a life of undisturbed tranquillity; I leave it to you to see what you choose.

What then does Chrysippus offer us?

'That you may know', he says, 'that these truths from which tranquillity and peace of mind come to men are not false—take my books and you shall find that what gives me peace of mind is true and in harmony with nature.'

O great good fortune! O great benefactor, who shows us the way! And yet—though all men have raised temples and altars to Triptolemus, for teaching us the cultivation of the crops, yet what man of you ever set up an altar in honour of him who found the truth and brought it to light and published it among all men—not the truth of mere living, but the truth that leads to right living? Who ever dedicated a shrine or an image for this gift, or worships God for it? I say shall we, who offer sacrifices because the gods gave us wheat or the vine, never give thanks to God that they produced this manner of fruit in the mind of men, whereby they were to show us the true way of happiness?

CHAPTER V

AGAINST FOLLOWERS OF THE ACADEMY

If a man, says Epictetus, objects to what is manifestly clear, it is not easy to find an argument against him, whereby one shall change his mind. And this is not because of his power, nor because of the weakness of him that is instructing him; but, when a man, worsted in argument, becomes hardened like a stone, how can one reason with him any more?

Now there are two ways in which a man may be thus hardened: one when his reasoning faculty is petrified, and the other when his moral sense is petrified, and he sets himself deliberately not to assent to manifest arguments, and not to abandon what conflicts with them. Now most of us fear the deadening of the body and would take all possible means to avoid such a calamity, yet we take no heed of the deadening of the mind and the spirit. When the mind itself is in such a state that a man can follow nothing and understand nothing, we do indeed think that he is in a bad condition; yet, if a man's sense of shame and self-respect is deadened, we even go so far as to call him 'a strong man'.

Do you comprehend that you are awake?

'No,' he says, 'no more than I comprehend it, when I seem to be awake in my dreams.'

Is there no difference then between the one sort of impression and the other?

'None.'

Can I argue with him any longer? What fire or sword, I say, am I to bring to bear on him, to prove that his mind is deadened? He has sensation and pretends that he has not; he is worse than the dead. One man does not see the battle; he is ill off. This other sees it but stirs not, nor advances; his state is still more wretched. His sense of shame and self-respect is cut out of him, and his reasoning faculty, though not cut away, is brutalized. Am I to call this 'strength'? Heaven forbid, unless I call it 'strength' in those who sin against nature, that makes them do and say in public whatever occurs to their fancy.

CHAPTER VI

ON PROVIDENCE

EACH single thing that comes into being in the universe affords a ready ground for praising Providence, if one possesses these two qualities—a power to see clearly the circumstances of each, and the spirit of gratitude therewith. Without these, one man will fail to see the usefulness of nature's products and another though he see it will not give thanks for them. If God had created colours and, in general, all visible things, but had not created a faculty to behold them, of what use would they be? None at all. If on the other hand He had created this faculty, but had not created objects of such a nature as to fall under the faculty of vision, even so of what use would it be? None at all. If again He had created both these, and had not created light, even so there would be no use in them. Who is it then that has adapted this to that, and that to this? Who is it that has fitted the sword to the scabbard and the scabbard to the sword? Is there no one? Surely the very structure of such finished products leads us commonly to infer that they must be the work of some craftsman, and are not constructed at random. Are we to say then that each of these products points to the craftsman, but that things visible and vision and light do not? Do not male and female and the desire of union and the power to use the organs adapted for it—do not these point to the craftsman? But if these things are so, then the fact that the intellect is so framed that we are not merely the passive subjects of sensations, but select and subtract from them and add to them, and by this means construct particular objects, nay more, that we pass from them to others which are not in mere juxtaposition—I say are not these facts sufficient to rouse men's attention and to deter them from leaving out the craftsman? If it be not so, let them explain to us what it is which makes each of these things, or how it is possible that objects so marvellously designed should have come into being by chance and at random?

Again, are these faculties found in us alone? Many in us alone—faculties which the rational creature had special need of—but many you will find that we share with irrational creatures. Do they also then understand events and things? No—for using is one thing, and understanding is another. God had need of them as creatures dealing with impressions, and of us as dealing with them and understanding them as well. That is why it is enough for them to eat and drink and rest and breed, and every function is theirs which each irrational creature fulfils; while we, to whom He gave also the power of understanding, cannot be satisfied with these functions, but, unless we act with method and order and consistently with our respective natures and constitutions, we shall no longer attain to our end. For those whose constitutions are different have also different functions and different ends. Therefore that which by constitution is capable only of using things, is satisfied to use them anyhow; but that which by constitution is capable of understanding things as well as using them, will never attain its end, unless to use it adds method also. What is my conclusion? God makes one animal for eating, and another for service in farming, another to produce cheese, and others for different uses of a like nature, for which there is no need of understanding impressions and being able to distinguish them; but He brought man into the world to take cognizance of Himself and His works, and not only to take cognizance but also to interpret them. Therefore it is beneath man's dignity to begin and to end where the irrational creatures do: he must rather begin where they do and end where nature has ended in forming us; and nature ends in contemplation and understanding and a way of life in harmony with nature. See to it then that ye do not die without taking cognizance of these things.

You travel to Olympia, that you may see the work of Phidias, and each of you thinks it a misfortune to die without visiting these sights, and will you have no desire to behold and to comprehend those things for which there is no need of travel, in the presence of which you stand here and now, each one of you? Will you not realize then who you are and to what end you are born and what that is which you have received the power to see?

'Yes, but there are unpleasant and hard things in life.'

Are there none such at Olympia? Are you not scorched with heat? Are you not cramped for room? Is not washing difficult? Are you not wet through when it is wet? Do you not get your fill of noise and clamour and other annoyances? Yet I fancy that when you set against all these hardships the magnificence of the spectacle you bear them and put up with them. And have you not received faculties, which will enable you to bear all that happens to you? Have you not received greatness of spirit? Have you not received courage? Have you not received endurance? If I am of a great spirit what concern have I in what may happen? What shall shake me or confound me or seem painful to me? Instead of using my faculty for the purpose for which I have received it, am I to mourn and lament at the events of fortune?

'Yes, but my rheum flows.'

Slave! What have you hands for then? Is it not to wipe your rheum away?

'Is it reasonable then that there should be rheum in the world?'

Well, how much better it is to wipe your rheum away than to complain! What do you think would have become of Heracles if there had not been a lion, as in the story, and a hydra and a stag and a boar and unjust and brutal men, whom he drove forth and cleansed the world of them? What would he have done, if there had been nothing of this sort? Is it not plain that he would have wrapped himself up and slept? Nay to begin with he would never have been a Heracles at all, had he slumbered all this life in such ease and luxury; and if by any chance he had been, of what good would he have been? What use would he have made of his arms and his might and his endurance and noble heart as well, had not he been stimulated and trained by such perils and opportunities?

'Was it his duty then to contrive these occasions for himself and to seek means to bring a lion, a boar, or a hydra into his country?'

That were madness and folly; but as they had come into being and were found in the world these monsters were of service to display Heracles' powers and to train them.

It is for you then, when you realize this, to look to the faculties you possess, and considering them to say, 'Zeus, send me what trial Thou wilt; for I have endowments and resources, given me by Thee, to bring myself honour through what befalls.' Nay, instead, you sit trembling for fear of what may happen, or lamenting, mourning, and groaning for what does happen, and then you reproach the gods. What else but impiety indeed can attend upon so ignoble a spirit as yours? And yet God not only gave us these faculties, which will enable us to bear all the issue of events without being humiliated or broken down by it, but, as became a good king and a true father, He gave us this gift free from all let or hindrance or compulsion—nay, He put it wholly in our hands, not even leaving Himself any power to let or hinder us. Yet possessing these powers in freedom for your own you refuse to use them and will not realize what gifts you have received and from whose hand, but you sit mourning and grieving, some of you blinded to the giver Himself and refusing to recognize your benefactor, and some from meanness of spirit turning to reproaches and complaints against God. Yet I will show you that you have resources and endowment to fit you for a noble and courageous spirit: show me, if you can, what endowments you have for complaining and reproach.

CHAPTER VII

ON THE USE OF VARIABLE PREMISSES AND HYPOTHETICAL ARGUMENTS AND THE LIKE[8]

MOST men ignore the fact that the treatment of variable premisses and hypothetical arguments and again of syllogisms that conclude by way of question, and, in a word, of all such arguments is concerned with conduct. For really, whatever subject we are dealing with, our aim is to find how the good man may fitly deal with it and fitly behave towards it. It follows then that either they must say that the virtuous man will not condescend to question and answer, or that if he does he will take no care to avoid behaving lightly and at random in questioning and answering; or else, if they accept neither alternative, they must admit that we have to investigate those subjects round which question and answer chiefly turn. For what do we promise in a discussion? To establish what is true, to remove what is false, to withhold assent in what is uncertain. Is it enough then merely to learn that this is so?

'It is enough.'

Is it enough then for him who wishes not to go wrong in the use of coin merely to be told why you accept genuine drachmas and reject spurious ones?

'It is not enough.'

What then must you acquire besides? Surely you must have a faculty to test and distinguish genuine drachmas from spurious. Is it not true then in regard to argument also that merely to hear what is said is not enough; a man must acquire the faculty to test and distinguish the true from the false and the uncertain?

'It must be so.'

This being so, what is required in argument?

'Accept what follows from the premisses you have duly granted.'

Here again, is it enough merely to know this? No, you must learn how a conclusion follows from the premisses, and how sometimes one proposition follows from one other, and sometimes from many together.

May we say then that this faculty too must be acquired by him who is to behave with good sense in discussion, and who is himself to prove each point in his demonstration and to follow the demonstrations of others, and to avoid being led astray by sophistical arguments, posing as demonstrations? Thus it comes about that we are led to think it really necessary to discuss and to practise the arguments and moods which are conclusive.

But note this: there are cases where we have granted the premisses properly, and such and such a conclusion follows which, though it follows, is none the less false. What then is it fitting for me to do? Must I accept the false conclusion? How can I do that? Must I say I was wrong in granting the premisses?

'No, you may not do this either.'

That it does not follow from the premisses granted?

'No, you may not do this.'

What then is one to do in these circumstances? May we not say that just as in order to be in debt it is not enough merely to borrow, but one must remain a borrower and not have paid off the loan, so in order to be bound to admit an inference it is not enough to have granted the premisses, but one must abide by having granted them?

In a word, if they remain to the end as we granted them, we are absolutely bound to remain by our concessions and accept what follows the premisses; if, on the other hand, they do not remain as they were granted, we are also absolutely bound to abandon the concession and no longer to accept what is inconsistent with the premisses; for since we have abandoned our agreement as to the premisses, this inference which is drawn no longer concerns us or touches us. We must then examine into premisses of this sort and into such changes and alterations in them, by which they are changed in the actual process of question or answer or syllogism or the like, and so afford occasion to the foolish to be troubled because they do not see the sequence of the argument. Why must we do so? That in this sphere we may do what is fitting by avoiding what is random or confused in argument.

And we ought to do the same with hypotheses and hypothetical arguments. For it is necessary sometimes to assume a hypothesis as a step to the next argument. Must we then concede every given hypothesis or not? And if not every one, which? And, having conceded it, must we abide by it once for all and maintain it, or are we sometimes to abandon it, and are we to accept what follows from it and reject what conflicts with it?

'Yes.'

But a man says, 'If you accept a hypothesis of what is possible, I will reduce you in argument to what is impossible.'

Will the prudent man refuse to meet him in argument, and avoid examination and discussion with him? Nay, it is just the prudent man who is capable of reasoning logically and who is expert at questioning and answering, yes and who is proof against deception and sophistry. Will he then consent to argue, but take no pains to avoid being careless and casual in argument? If so, will he not cease to be the man we consider him to be? But without some such training and preparation as I suggest can he guard the sequence of his argument? Let them show that he can, and then all these speculations are idle; they were absurd and inconsistent with the conception we have formed of the good man.

Why do we persist in being lazy and indolent and sluggish, why do we seek excuses to enable us to avoid toiling early and late to perfect ourselves in logical theory?

'Do you call it parricide if I go wrong in logic?'

Slave, here is no father for you to kill. You ask what you have done; you have committed the one error which was possible in this field. Your answer is the very one I made myself to Rufus when he rebuked me because I could not find the one missing step in a syllogism. 'Well,' said I, 'I suppose I have not burnt the Capitol down'; and he answered, 'Slave, the missing step here is the Capitol.'

You are not going to tell me, are you, that setting fire to the Capitol and killing one's father are the only forms of wrongdoing? To deal with one's impressions without thought or method, to fail to follow argument or demonstration or sophism, in a word, to be unable to see what concerns himself and what does not in question and answer—is there no wrongdoing, I ask, in any of these?

CHAPTER VIII

THAT FACULTIES ARE FRAUGHT WITH DANGER FOR THE UNEDUCATED

Just as it is possible to interchange terms which are equivalent to one another, so and in just as many ways it is allowable to vary in argument the types of disputative argument and enthymeme. Take for instance this kind of argument: 'If you borrowed and did not repay, you owe me the money. You did not borrow without repaying; therefore you do not owe me the money.' And the philosopher above all others is the proper person to handle such arguments with skill. For if enthymeme is imperfect syllogism, plainly he who is trained in perfect syllogism would be equally capable in dealing with imperfect.

Why then, you ask, do we not train ourselves and one another in this style of argument? Because even now, though we do not devote ourselves to training in these matters and though we are not drawn away, so far as I have any influence, from cultivating character, nevertheless we make no advance towards goodness. What should we have to expect then, if we should add this business to our other employments? And there is more—not only should we have less leisure for more necessary things, but we should give uncommon occasion for conceit and vanity. For the faculty of disputative and plausible reasoning is a powerful one, especially if it should be developed by training and gain further dignity from mastery of language. For indeed generally every faculty is dangerous when it comes into the hands of those who are without education and without real force, for it tends to exalt and puff them up. For how would it be possible to persuade the young man who excels in these arguments that he ought not to become dependent upon them, but to make them depend upon him? Instead of this he tramples under foot all we say to him and walks among us in a high state of elation, so puffed up that he cannot bear that any one should remind him how far he has fallen short and into what errors he has lapsed.

'What do you mean? Was not Plato a philosopher?'

I reply, Was not Hippocrates a physician? But you see how eloquent Hippocrates was. Was Hippocrates so eloquent by virtue of being a physician? Why then do you mix qualities, which are casually united in the same persons? Suppose Plato was handsome and strong; ought I also to set to and strive to become handsome or strong, as though this were necessary for philosophy, just because one philosopher was handsome as well? Will you not have the discernment to see what makes men philosophers and what qualities are accidental in them? Suppose now I were a philosopher, ought you to become lame?

You ask me, do I then count these faculties as of no effect?

Heaven forbid! no more than I ignore the faculty of vision. Nevertheless if you ask me what is the true good of man, I can only say to you that it lies in a certain disposition of the will.

CHAPTER IX

HOW ONE MAY DRAW CONCLUSIONS FROM THE FACT THAT WE ARE GOD'S KINSMEN

IF THESE statements of the philosophers are true, that God and men are akin, there is but one course open to men, to do as Socrates did: never to reply to one who asks his country, 'I am an Athenian', or 'I am a Corinthian', but 'I am a citizen of the universe.' For why do you say that you are an Athenian, instead of merely a native of the little spot on which your bit of a body was cast forth at birth? Plainly you call yourself Athenian or Corinthian after that more sovereign region which includes not only the very spot where you were born, and all your household, but also generally that region from which the race of your forbears has come down to you. When a man therefore has learnt to understand the government of the universe and has realized that there is nothing so great or sovereign or all-inclusive as this frame of things wherein men and God are united, and that from it come the seeds from which are sprung not only my own father or grandfather, but all things that are begotten and that grow upon earth, and rational creatures in particular—for these alone are by nature fitted to share in the society of God, being connected with Him by the bond of reason—why should he not call himself a citizen of the universe and a son of God? Why should he fear anything that can happen to him among men? When kinship with Caesar or any other of those who are powerful in Rome is sufficient to make men live in security, above all scorn and free from every fear, shall not the fact that we have God as maker and father and kinsman relieve us from pains and fears?

'And where am I to find food to eat, if I have nothing?' says one.

Well, what do slaves do when they leave their masters, or what do they rely on? Do they rely on fields, or servants, or silver plate? No, on nothing but themselves; nevertheless sustenance does not fail them. And shall our philosopher in his wanderings have to rest his confidence in others, instead of taking care of himself? Is he to be baser and more cowardly than the unreasoning beasts? For each one of them is content with itself, and lacks not its proper sustenance nor the way of life that is naturally suited to it.

I think that the old man who sits here to teach you ought to devote his skill not to save you from being low-minded, and from reasoning about yourselves in a low and ignoble spirit, but rather to prevent young men from arising of the type who, discovering their kinship with the gods, and seeing that we have these fetters attached to us in the shape of the body and its possessions and all that we find necessary for the course and management of our life by reason of the body, may desire to fling all these away as vexatious and useless burdens and so depart to the gods their kindred.

And so your teacher and instructor, if he were a true teacher, should engage in this conflict of argument:

You come saying, 'Epictetus, we can bear no longer to be bound with the fetters of this wretched body, giving it meat and drink and rest and purgation, and by reason of the body having to adapt ourselves to this or that set of circumstances. Are not these things indifferent and as nothing to us, and death no evil thing? Are we not kinsmen of the gods, from whom we have come hither? Suffer us to depart to the place whence we have come, suffer us to be released from these bonds that are fastened to us and weigh us down. Here are robbers and thieves and law-courts and so-called kings, who by reason of our poor body and its possessions are accounted to have authority over us. Suffer us to show them that they have authority over nothing.'

Hereupon I answer: 'Men as you are, wait upon God. When He gives the signal and releases you from this service, then you shall depart to Him; but for the present be content to dwell in this country wherein He appointed you to dwell. Short indeed is the time of your dwelling here, and easy for them whose spirit is thus disposed. What manner of tyrant or what thief or what law-courts have any fears for those who have thus set at nought the body and its possessions? Stay where you are, and depart not without reason.' Such should be the answer of the teacher to his gifted pupils. How different is what we see! There is no life in your master, and no life in you. When you have had your fill to-day, you sit groaning about the morrow, and how you are to find food. Slave, if you get food, you will have it; if not, you will depart: the door is open. Why do you whine? What room is there for tears any more? What occasion for flattery any more? Why should one envy another? Why should he gaze with wonder on them that are rich or powerful, especially if they be strong and quick to anger? For what will they do with us? We will pay no heed to what they have power to do, what we really care for they cannot touch. Who, I ask you, will be master over one who is of this spirit?

How did Socrates approach these matters? Surely as one should who is convinced of his kinship with the gods. 'If you tell me,' he says, ' "We acquit you on condition that you discourse no longer as you have done hitherto, and that you do not annoy young or old among us" ', I shall answer, 'It is absurd for you to suppose that, while I am bound to maintain and guard any post to which your general appointed me, and should rather die ten thousand times than abandon it, yet if God has appointed us to a certain place and way of life we ought to abandon that.' [Plato, *Apology,* 29c, 28e] Here you see a man who is a kinsman of the gods in very truth. But as for us—we think of ourselves as if we were all belly and flesh and animal desire; such are our fears, such our passions; those that can help us to these ends we flatter, and at the same time fear.

Some one has asked me to write for him to Rome, one who, as the world thought, had had misfortunes; he had once been famous and rich, and had now lost everything and was living here. So I wrote for him in a humble tone. And he read my letter and gave it me back and said, 'I wanted your help, not your pity.' So, too, Rufus, to try me, used to say,

'Your master will do this or that to you'; and when I answered him, 'This is the lot of man', 'Why then', said he, 'do I appeal to your master when I can get everything from you?' for, indeed, it is true that what a man has of himself it is idle and futile for him to receive from another. Am I then, who can get from myself the gift of a noble and lofty spirit, to get from you a field or money or office? Heaven forbid! I will not be so blind to my true possessions. But when a man is mean and cowardly, for him one must needs write letters as for one that is dead. 'Make us a present of the corpse of so and so and his miserable quart of blood.' For indeed such a one is a mere corpse and a quart of blood and nothing more. If he were anything more, he would have realized that one man cannot make another miserable.

CHAPTER X

TO THOSE WHO HAVE SPENT THEIR ENERGIES ON ADVANCEMENT IN ROME

IF WE had been as earnest and serious about our work as old men in Rome are about their concerns, we too might perhaps have achieved something. I know what was said to me by a man older than myself who is now in charge of the corn-supply in Rome, when he passed through here on his way back from exile; he ran down his former life and made great professions for the future, saying that when once he was back he would have no other interest except to live out the rest of his life in peace and tranquillity, 'For how little I have still left me', said he.

And I said to him, 'You will not do it; so soon as you sniff the air of Rome you will forget all your professions'; and I told him that if he got a chance of entering the Palace, he would thrust his way in and give God thanks.

'Epictetus,' he answered, 'if you find me putting one foot in the Palace, believe what you like of me.'

Well, what did he do? Before he came to Rome, a dispatch from the Emperor met him, and as soon as he got it he forgot all he had said and has gone on adding to his heap ever since. I should like to stand by him now and remind him of the words he used as he passed through, and say to him, 'How much more clever a prophet am I than you!'

What conclusion do I draw? Do I say that the creature man is not to be active? Heaven forbid! But what is it that fetters our faculty of action? Take myself first: when day comes, I remind myself a little as to what lesson I ought to read to my pupils. Then in a moment I find myself saying, 'But what do I really care what sort of lesson I give to this man or that? The first thing is for me to sleep.' And yet how can their business be compared in importance with ours? If you attend to what they are doing you will see the difference. They do nothing all day long except vote, dispute, deliberate about a handful of corn or an acre of land, and petty profits of this sort. Is there any resemblance between receiving and reading a petition such as this: 'I beg you to let me export a little corn', and a petition such as, 'I beg you to inquire from Chrysippus how the universe is governed and what position the rational creature holds in it; inquire too who you are and what is good for you, and what is evil'? What have these petitions in common? Do both demand the same attention? Is it equally shameful to neglect one and to neglect the other?

What is my conclusion? Are we elders alone indolent and sleepy? Nay, the fault is much rather with you young men. For indeed, we old folk, when we see young men playing, are only too eager and ready to join their play. Much more, if I saw them thoroughly awakened and eager to share my studies, should I be eager myself to take my studies seriously too.

CHAPTER XI

ON FAMILY AFFECTION

WHEN an official came to Epictetus and inquired for special directions he asked whether he had a wife and children; and when the man said, 'Yes', he asked again, How do you get on?

'Miserably', he said.

What do you mean? said he; Men do not marry and have children to the end that they may be miserable, but rather that they may be happy.

'Ah', said he, 'but I am so miserable about my poor children, that lately when my daughter was ill and was thought to be in danger I could not bear to be near her, but fled away from her, until some one brought me news that she was well.'

Well, do you think you were right to do it?

'It was natural', he said.

Nay, said the master, only convince me that it was natural, and I will convince you that everything that is natural is right.

'All fathers', he said, 'or most of us, at least, feel like that.'

I do not deny, said Epictetus, that parents feel so, but the real question is whether it is right. No doubt as far as that goes, we must say that even tumours come into being for the good of the body, and in a word that error is natural, for nearly all, or most of us at least, are prone to error. Prove to me then how it is natural.

'I cannot'; he said, 'rather do you prove to me how it is wrong or unnatural.'

He answered, Suppose we were discussing black and white, what test should we call in to distinguish between them?

'The sight', he said.

What if we were discussing things hot or cold, hard and soft, what test should we use?

'Touch.'

Well then, as we are discussing what is natural and right and the opposite, what test would you have us take?

'I do not know', said he.

Look here, it is no great loss perhaps not to know the proper test for colours and smells, nay, and flavours too, but do you think it is a small loss to man not to know what is good and what is evil, what is natural and what is unnatural?

'No, the greatest possible loss.'

Tell me now, is everything right which seems noble and fitting to certain people? To-day, for instance, are the opinions of Jews and Syrians, Egyptians and Romans, as to food all of them right?

'How can they be?'

No, I suppose if the Egyptians' views are right the other nations' must of necessity be wrong; if the Jews' opinions are good, other people's must be bad.

'Of course.'

And where there is ignorance, there is also want of insight and education as to necessary things.

'Yes.'

When once you have realized this, then, said Epictetus, you will make this your one interest in the future, and to this alone devote your mind—to discover the means of judging what is natural and to use your criterion to distinguish each particular case as it arises.

For the present I can help you just so far as this in regard to what you wish: do you think family affection is natural and good?

'Of course.'

Again, is it true that affection is natural and good, and reason not good?

'Certainly not.'

Is there a conflict then between reason and affection?

'I think not.'

If there were a conflict, then, as one of the two is natural, the other must needs be unnatural?

'Certainly', he said.

It follows then that whenever we find reason and affection united in an action, we confidently affirm that it is right and good.

'Granted', he said.

Mark what follows. I do not think you will deny that it is not reasonable to leave one's child when it is ill and to go away. The only question left for us is to consider whether it is affectionate.

'Let us consider it then.'

Was it right, I ask, for you, being affectionately disposed to your child, to run away and leave her? Is her mother not fond of the child?

'She is indeed.'

Should the mother then have left her too, or should she not?

'She should not.'

What of the nurse? Is she fond of the child?

'She is', he said.

Ought she then to have left her?

'By no means.'

Again, is not the child's attendant fond of her?

'He is.'

Ought he then to have gone away and left her? Was it right that as a consequence the child should be thus left desolate and helpless because of the great affection of you its parents and of those about it, or should die in the hands of those who had no love or care for it?

'Heaven forbid!'

Once more, it is not fair or reasonable, is it, that a man should not allow others equally affectionate with himself to do what, because he is affectionate, he thinks proper for himself. It is absurd. Tell me, would you have liked, if you were ill, your relations and every one else, even your wife and children, to show their affection for you in such a way as to leave you alone and desolate?

'Certainly not.'

Would you pray to be so loved by your own people, as to be always left alone by them when you were ill, because of their exceeding affection, or would you, if it were a question of being left alone, rather pray, supposing that were possible, to have the affection of your enemies? And if that is so, we are forced to the conclusion that your conduct was not that of affection.

What reason had you then? Was there nothing which moved and impelled you to abandon the child? How is that possible? It must have been the same sort of motive, which once made a man in Rome cover his eyes when the horse he had backed was running, and then again when the horse unexpectedly won made him faint so that he needed sponges to recover him. What is the motive? This perhaps is not the moment to define it; but it is enough that we should be convinced of this—if what philosophers say is sound—that we must not look for it somewhere outside us, but that it is always one and the same motive which causes us to do or not to do a thing, to speak or not to speak, to be elated or depressed, to fly or to pursue—the very motive which has moved you and me at this moment, you to come and sit and listen to me, and me to say what I do. What is the motive? Surely it is nothing but this—that we are so minded?

'Nothing else.'

And if things had looked different to us, we should still have done what we were minded to do and nothing else. So when Achilles mourned, his reason was, not the death of Patroclus—for another man, when his comrade dies, is not thus affected—but that he was so minded. So in your case, you ran away just because you were so minded; and again, if you stay it will be because you are so minded. And now you return to Rome, because you have a mind to do so; and if your mind changes, you will not depart thither. And in a word it is not death nor exile nor pain nor any such thing which is the cause of our action or inaction, but thoughts and judgements of the mind. Are you convinced of this or not?

'I am', he said.

Then on each occasion the effects of an action correspond to the causes. So henceforward whenever we do a thing wrong, we shall blame nothing else but the judgement which led us to do it, and we shall try to remove and extirpate this even more than we do tumours and abscesses from the body. And so also we shall assert that our right actions are determined in the same way; and we shall no longer blame neighbour or wife or children as though they caused evils to befall us, being convinced that, unless we make up our mind that things are such, we do not act as though they were, but that whether we judge them to be so or not depends upon ourselves and not on anything outside us.

'True', he said.

From this day forward then we shall not investigate or examine the nature or condition of anything else—whether it be land or slaves or horses or dogs—but only our own judgements.

'I hope so', said he.

You see then that you must become a student—that creature whom all mock at—if you really wish to investigate your judgements. That this is not the work of an hour or a day you fully understand without my telling you.

CHAPTER XII

ON CONTENTMENT

CONCERNING the gods there are some who say that the Divine does not exist, others that it exists but is inactive and indifferent and takes no thought for anything, others again that God does exist and take thought but only for great things and things in the heavens, but for nothing on earth; and a fourth class say that God takes thought also for earthly and human things, but only in a general way, and has no care for individuals: and there is a fifth class, to whom belong Odysseus and Socrates, who say

where'er I move
Thou seest me.

[Homer, *Iliad*, X. 279]

Before all things then it is necessary to examine each of these views, to see whether it is true or untrue. For if there are no gods, how can following the gods be the end of man? If again there are gods, but they care for nothing, in that case too what good will it be to follow them? But once more, if they exist and do care, yet if there is no communication between them and men, nay what is more, if there is none between them and me, to follow them cannot be a true end. The good man then, having examined into all these questions, has submitted his mind to Him that orders the universe, as good citizens submit to the law of the city. The man who is under education ought to approach education with this purpose in his mind: 'How can I follow the gods in everything, and how can I be content with the divine governance and how can I become free?' For he is free, for whom all things happen according to his will and whom no one can hinder.

'What then? Is freedom the same as madness?'

Heaven forbid! frenzy and freedom have nothing in common.

'But', you say, 'I want everything to happen as I think good, whatever that may be.'

Then you are in a state of madness, you are out of your mind. Do you not know that freedom is a noble thing, and worthy of regard? But merely to want one's chance thoughts to be realized, is not a noble thing; it comes perilously near being the most shameful of all things. How do we act in matters of grammar? Do I want to write Dion's name as I will? No, I am taught to will the right way of writing. How is it in music? Just the same. So it is universally, in every region of art or science. Otherwise it would not be worth while to know anything, if everything conformed itself to each man's will.

Are we to say then that in this sphere alone, the greatest and most momentous of all, the sphere of freedom, it is permitted me to indulge chance desires? By no means: education is just this—learning to frame one's will in accord with events. How do events happen? They happen as the Disposer of events has ordained them. He ordained summer and winter, fruitful and barren seasons, virtue and vice and all such opposites for the sake of the harmony of the universe, and gave to each one of us a body and bodily parts and property and men to associate with.

Remembering then that things are thus ordained we ought to approach education, not that we may change the conditions of life, that is not given to us, nor is it good for us—but that, our circumstances being as they are and as nature makes them, we may conform our mind to events.

I ask you, is it possible to avoid men? How can we? Can we change their nature by our society? Who gives us that power? What is left for us then, or what means do we discover to deal with them? We must so act as to leave them to do as seems good to them, while we remain in accord with nature.

But you are impatient and discontented; if you are alone you call it a wilderness, and if you are with men you describe them as plotters and robbers, and you find fault even with your own parents and children and brothers and neighbours.

Why, when you are alone you ought to call it peace and freedom and consider yourself the equal of the gods; when you are in a large company you should not call it a crowd or a mob or a nuisance, but a high-day and a festival, and so accept all things in a spirit of content.

What punishment is there, you ask, for those who do not accept things in this spirit? Their punishment is to be as they are. Is one discontented with being alone? Let him be deserted. Is one discontented with his parents? Let him be a bad son, and mourn his lot. Is one discontented with his children? Let him be a bad father.

'Cast him into prison.'

What do you mean by prison? he is in prison already; for a man's prison is the place that he is in against his will, just as, conversely, Socrates was not in prison, for he chose to be there.

'Am I then to have a maimed leg?'

Slave, do you mean to arraign the universe for one wretched leg? Will you not make a gift of it to the sum of things? Will you not resign it? Will you not joyfully yield it up to Him who gave it? Will you be vexed and discontented with the ordinances of Zeus, laid down and ordained by Him with the Fates who were present at your birth and span your thread of life? Do you not know, what a little part you are, compared with the universe? I say this of your body, for in reason you are not inferior to the gods nor less than they; for the greatness of reason is judged not by length or height but by its judgements.

Will you not then set your good in that region where you are equal to the gods?

'Alas, but look what a father and mother I have got!'

Why? was it given you on entering life to choose and say, 'Let such an one marry such an one at this hour, that I may be born?' No such choice was given you: your parents had to be in existence first, and your birth had to follow. Of what parents? Of such as they were.

Well then, as your parents are what they are, is no resource left you? Surely if you did not know to what end you possess the faculty of vision, you would be unhappy and miserable if you closed your eyes, when colours were brought near you; but are you not more wretched and unhappy still for not knowing that you have a high and noble spirit to face each occasion as it arises? The objects which correspond to the faculty that you have are brought near you: yet you turn away your faculty just at the very moment when you ought to keep it open-eyed and alert. Rather give thanks to the gods that they set you above those things which they put out of your power, and made you responsible only for what is within your control. For your parents they left you without responsibility; and the same is true of brothers, body, property, death, life. For what then did they make you responsible? For that which alone is in your power, the proper handling of your impressions. Why then do you insist on dragging in these things for which you are not responsible? That is to make trouble for yourself.

CHAPTER XIII

HOW ONE MAY ACT IN ALL THINGS SO AS TO PLEASE THE GODS.

WHEN some one asked Epictetus how one may eat so as to please the gods, he said, If you can eat justly, and with good feeling and, it may be, with self-control and modesty, may you not also eat so as to please the gods? And when you call for hot water and the slave does not answer, or answers and brings it luke-warm, or is not to be found in the house, is it not pleasing to the gods that you should not be angry nor break into a passion?

'How then is one to bear with such persons?'

Slave, will you not bear with your own brother, who has Zeus for his forefather, and is born as a son of the same seed as you and of the same heavenly descent? You were appointed to a place of superiority like this, and are you straightway going to constitute yourself a despot? Will you not remember what you are and whom you are ruling? that they are kinsmen, born your brothers, children of Zeus?

'But I have bought them, and they have not bought me.'

Do you see where your eyes are looking? You are looking at the earth, at what is lowest and basest,[9] at these miserable laws of the dead, and you regard not the laws of the gods.

CHAPTER XIV

THAT GOD BEHOLDS ALL MEN

When one asked him how a man may be convinced that every one of his acts is seen by God, Do you not think, he said, that all things are united together?

'I do', he said.

Again, do you think that things on earth feel the influence of things in heaven?

'I do', he said.

Whence comes it that in such perfect order as at God's command, when He bids the plants to flower, they flower, when He bids them grow, they grow, when He bids them to bear fruit, they bear, when to ripen, they ripen; when again He bids them drop their fruit, they drop it, and when to let fall their leaves, they let them fall, and when He bids them gather themselves up and be still and take their rest, they are still and take their rest? Whence is it that as the moon waxes and wanes and as the sun draws near and departs afar we behold so great a change and transformation of things on the earth? If the plants then and our own bodies are so closely bound up with the universe, and so share its affections, is it not much more so with our minds? And if our minds are so bound up with God and in such close touch with Him as being part and portion of His very being, does not God perceive their every movement as closely akin to Him?

Consider this: you, a man, have power to reflect on the divine governance and on each divine operation as well as upon things human, you have the faculty of being moved in your senses and your intelligence by countless objects, sometimes assenting, sometimes rejecting, sometimes doubting; you guard in your own mind these many impressions derived from so many and various objects, and moved by them you conceive thoughts corresponding to those objects which have first impressed you, and so from countless objects you derive and maintain one after another the products of art and memory.

All this you do, and is God not able to behold all things and be present with all and to have some communication with all? Why, the sun is able to illuminate so large a part of the universe, and to leave unilluminated only so much as the shadow which the earth makes can cover: and cannot He who has created the sun itself, and who makes it to revolve—a small part of Himself as compared with the whole—has not He, I say, the power to perceive all things?

'But', says one, 'I cannot comprehend all these things at once.'

Of course no one tells you that in faculty you are equal to Zeus.[10] Nevertheless He has set by each man his genius[11] to guard him, and committed each man to his genius to watch over, ay and a genius which sleeps not and is not to be beguiled. To what other guardian, better or more attentive, could He have committed each one of us? Therefore, when you close your doors and make darkness within, remember never to say that you are alone: you are not alone, God is within, and your genius. What need have they of light to see what you are doing? To this God you ought to swear allegiance from the first as the soldiers swear to Caesar. They are paid servants, yet they swear that they will put the safety of Caesar above all things: and shall you not swear too, who have been counted worthy of so many and so great blessings, or having sworn shall you not keep your oath? And what shall your oath be? Never to disobey, never to accuse, never to find fault with any of God's gifts, never to let your will rebel, when you have to do or to bear what necessity demands. Can the soldier's oath be compared with ours? The soldiers swear to respect no man above Caesar, but we to respect ourselves first of all.

CHAPTER XV

WHAT PHILOSOPHY PROFESSES

WHEN a man consulted Epictetus how to persuade his brother to be angry with him no longer, he replied, 'Philosophy does not promise to secure to man anything outside him. If it did it would be admitting something beyond its subject-matter. For as wood is the material dealt with by the carpenter, bronze by the statuary, so the subject-matter of each man's art of living is his own life. What are we to say then of your brother's life? That again is the concern of his art of living: to yours it is a thing external, like land, health, good repute. Philosophy makes no promises about such things.'

'In all circumstances' (says philosophy), 'I will keep the Governing Principle [12] in accord with nature.'

Whose Governing Principle?

'His, in whom I am.'

How then am I to prevent my brother from being angry with me? Bring him to me and I will tell him, but I have nothing to say to you about his anger.

When the man who consulted him said, 'What I am looking for is this—how I may be in accord with nature, even though he be not reconciled with me', he replied, No great thing comes suddenly into being, any more than a cluster of grapes or a fig. If you say to me now, 'I want a fig', I shall answer that it needs time. Let it flower first, then put forth its fruit and then ripen. I say then, if the fig tree's fruit is not brought to perfection suddenly in a single hour, would you gather fruit of men's minds so soon and so easily? I tell you, you must not expect it.

CHAPTER XVI

ON PROVIDENCE

MARVEL not that the other creatures have their bodily needs supplied—not only meat and drink, but a bed to lie on—and that they want no shoes nor rugs nor clothes, while we want all these things. For it would not have been a good thing that these creatures, born not for themselves but for service, should have been created liable to wants. Consider what it would be for us to have to take thought not only for ourselves but for sheep and asses, how they were to dress and what shoes they were to put on, and how they should find meat and drink. But just as soldiers when they appear before their general are ready shod, and clothed and armed, and it would be a strange thing indeed if the tribune had to go round and shoe or clothe his regiment, so also nature has made the creatures that are born for service ready and prepared and able to dispense with any attention. So one small child can drive sheep with a rod.

Yet we forbear to give thanks that we have not to pay the same attention to them as to ourselves, and proceed to complain against God on our own account. I declare, by Zeus and all the gods, one single fact of nature would suffice to make him that is reverent and grateful realize the providence of God: no great matter, I mean; take the mere fact that milk is produced from grass and cheese from milk and wool from skin. Who is it that has created or contrived these things?

'No one', he says.

Oh, the depth of man's stupidity and shamelessness!

Come, let us leave the chief works of nature, and behold what she works by the way. Is anything more useless than the hairs upon the chin? Did she not use even these in the most suitable way she could? Did she not by these means distinguish male and female? Does not the nature of each one of us cry aloud from afar, 'I am a man: on these terms approach me and address me; seek nothing else. Behold the signs.' Again, in women nature took the hair from their face, even as she mingled in their voice a softer note. What! You say the creature ought to have been left undistinguished and each of us to have proclaimed, 'I am a man'? Nay, but how noble and comely and dignified is this sign, how much more fair than the cock's crest, how much more magnificent than the lion's mane! Therefore we ought to preserve the signs God has given; we ought not to abandon them, nor, so far as in us lies, to confound the sexes which have been distinguished.

Are these the only works of Providence in us? Nay, what words are enough to praise them or bring them home to us? If we had sense we ought to do nothing else, in public and in private, than praise and bless God and pay Him due thanks. Ought we not, as we dig and plough and eat, to sing the hymn to God? 'Great is God that He gave us these instruments wherewith we shall till the earth. Great is God that He has given us hands, and power to swallow, and a belly, and the power to grow without knowing it, and to draw our breath in sleep.' At every moment we ought to sing these praises and above all the greatest and divinest praise, that God gave us the faculty to comprehend these gifts and to use the way of reason.

More than that: since most of you are walking in blindness, should there not be some one to discharge this duty and sing praises to God for all? What else can a lame old man as I am do but chant the praise of God? If, indeed, I were a nightingale I should sing as a nightingale, if a swan, as a swan: but as I am a rational creature I must praise God. This is my task, and I do it: and I will not abandon this duty, so long as it is given me; and I invite you all to join in this same song.

CHAPTER XVII

THAT THE PROCESSES OF LOGIC ARE NECESSARY

SINCE it is reason which makes all other things articulate and complete, and reason itself must be analysed and made articulate, what is it that shall effect this? Plainly, reason itself or something else. That something else either is reason or it will be something superior to reason, which is impossible. If it is reason, who again will analyse that reason? For if it analyses itself, so can the reason with which we started. If we are going to call in something else, the process will be endless and unceasing.

'Yes,' says one, 'but the more pressing need is not logic but the discipline of men's thoughts and feelings', and the like.

If you want to hear about moral improvement, well and good. But if you say to me, 'I do not know whether you argue truly or falsely', and if I use an ambiguous word and you say to me 'distinguish', I shall grow impatient and say to you, 'this is the more pressing need.' It is for this reason, I suppose, that men put the processes of logic in the forefront, just as we put the testing of the measure before the measuring of the corn. And if we do not determine first what is the bushel and what is the scale, how shall we be able to measure or weigh anything? So in the sphere of thought if we have not fully grasped and trained to perfection the instrument by which we judge other things and understand other things, shall we ever be able to arrive at accurate knowledge? Of course, it is impossible.

'Yes,' they say, 'but the bushel is a mere thing of wood and bears no fruit.'

True, but it can measure corn.

'The processes of logic, too, are unfruitful.'

This we will consider presently: but even if one should concede this, it is enough that logic has the power to analyse and distinguish other things and in fact, as one might say, has the power to weigh and measure. Who asserts this? Is it only Chrysippus and Zeno and Cleanthes? Does not Antisthenes agree? Why, who is it that has written, 'The beginning of education is the analysis of terms'? Does not Socrates too say the same? Does not Xenophon write of him that he began with the analysis of terms, to discover what each means?

Is this then what you call great and admirable—to understand or interpret Chrysippus? Nay, no one says that. What is admirable then? To understand the will of Nature. Very well: do you understand it of yourself? If so, what more do you need? For if it is true that all error is involuntary and you have learnt the truth, you must needs do rightly hereafter.

'But,' you may say, 'I do not understand the will of Nature.'

Who then expounds it? They say 'Chrysippus.' I come and inquire what this interpreter of Nature says. I begin not to understand what he means and I seek some one to interpret. The interpreter says, 'Let us examine the sense of this phrase, as if it were Latin.'

Why, pray, should the interpreter put on airs? Even Chrysippus has no right to do so, if he is only expounding the will of Nature, and does not follow it himself: how much less his interpreter. For we have no need of Chrysippus for his own sake, but only to enable us to follow

Nature: just as we have no need, for himself, of the priest who offers sacrifice, but because we think that through him we shall understand the signs which the gods give of the future, nor do we need the sacrifice for itself, but because through it the sign is given, nor do we marvel at the crow or the raven but at God who gives His signs by them.

So I come to this interpreter and priest and say, 'Examine the victim's flesh to see what sign is given me.' He takes and opens the flesh and interprets, 'Man, you have a will unhindered and unconstrained by nature. This is written here in the flesh of the sacrifice. I will show you the truth of it first in the sphere of assent. Can any one prevent you from agreeing to what is true? No one. Can any one compel you to accept the false? No one. Do you see that in this sphere your faculty is free from let and hindrance and constraint and compulsion? Is it any different in the sphere of will and impulse? What, I ask, can overcome impulse except another impulse? And what can overcome the will to get or will to avoid except another will to get or to avoid?'

'If he threatens me with death,' one says, 'he compels me.'

No, it is not what he threatens you with which compels you, but your decision that it is better to do what you are bidden than to die. Once more then it is your own judgement which compels you—that is, will puts pressure on will. For if God had so created that portion of His own being which He has taken from Himself and given to us, that it could suffer hindrance or compulsion from another, He would cease to be God and to care for us as He must needs do. 'This', says the priest, 'is what I find in the sacrifice: this is God's sign to you: if you will, you are free: if you will, you will blame no one, you will accuse no one: everything shall be in accordance with your own mind and the mind of God.'

This is the prophecy which draws me to consult this seer and philosopher, and his interpretation makes me admire not him but the truths which he interprets.

CHAPTER XVIII

THAT WE SHOULD NOT BE ANGRY AT MEN'S ERRORS

If what philosophers say is true, that in all men action starts from one source, feeling, as in assent it is the feeling that a thing is so, and in denial the feeling that it is not so, yes, by Zeus, and in withholding judgement, the feeling that it is uncertain: so also impulse towards a thing is originated by the feeling that it is fitting, and will to get a thing by the feeling that it is expedient for one, and it is impossible to judge one thing expedient and will to get another, and to judge one thing fitting and be impelled to another. If all this be true, why are we angry with the multitude?

'They are thieves', he says, 'and robbers.'

What do you mean by thieves and robbers?

'They are gone astray and know not what is good and what is evil.'

Ought we then to be angry with them or to pity them? Only show them their error and you will see how they desist from their faults. But if their eyes are not opened, they regard nothing as superior to their own judgement.

'What!' you say. 'Ought not this robber and this adulterer to be put to death?'

Nay, say not so, but rather, 'Should I not destroy this man who is in error and delusion about the greatest matters and is blinded not merely in the vision which distinguishes white and black, but in the judgement which distinguishes good and evil?' If you put it this way, you will recognize how inhuman your words are; that it is like saying, 'Should I not kill this blind man, or this deaf one?' For if the greatest harm that can befall one is the loss of what is greatest, and a right will is the greatest thing in every one, is it not enough for him to lose this, without incurring your anger besides? Man, if you must needs harbour unnatural feelings at the misfortune of another, pity him rather than hate him; give up this spirit of offence and hatred: do not use these phrases which the backbiting multitude use, 'These accursed and pestilent fools'.

Very well. How are you suddenly converted to wisdom? What an angry temper you show!

Why then are we angry? Because we admire the material things of which they rob us. For only cease to admire your clothes, and you are not angry with him who steals them: cease to admire your wife's beauty, and you cease to be angry with the adulterer. Know that the thief and adulterer have no place among things that are your own, but only among things that are another's and beyond your power. If you let them alone and count them as nothing you have no one to be angry with any more. But as long as you admire these things you must be angry with yourself rather than with them. For, look you, you have fine clothes, your neighbour has none: you have a window, you wish to air them. He does not know what is the true good of man, but fancies, as you do too, that it is to have fine clothes. Is he not to come then and carry them off? Why, if you show a cake to greedy men, and gobble it down all to yourself, do you expect them not to snatch at it? Do not provoke them, do not have a window, do not air your clothes.

For my part, yesterday I had an iron lamp beside my household gods, and hearing a noise I rushed to the window. I found the lamp had been carried off. I reasoned with myself, that the man who took it yielded to some plausible feeling. What do I conclude? To-morrow, I say, you will find one of earthenware. The truth is, a man loses only what he has. 'I have lost my cloak.' Yes, for you had one. 'I have got a headache.' Have you a horn-ache too? Why then are you vexed? Your losses and your pains are concerned only with what you possess.

'But the tyrant will chain me.'

Yes, your leg.

'But he will cut off.'

What? Your neck. But what will he fail to bind or cut off? Your will. That is why the men of old enjoined 'Know thyself.' What follows? You ought to practise in small things and go on from them to greater.

'I have a headache.'

Then do not say, 'Ah me!'

'I have earache.'

Do not say, 'Ah me!' And I do not mean that you may not groan, but do not groan in spirit. And if the boy brings you your leg-bands slowly, do not cry out loud and pull a long face and say, 'Every one hates me.' Who is not likely to hate such an one?

Put confidence in these thoughts for the future and walk erect and free, not relying on bulk of body like an athlete. For you do not need to be invincible by brute force like an ass.

Who then is the man who is invincible? He whom nothing beyond his will can dismay. So I go on observing him in each set of circumstances as if he were an athlete. He has overcome the first round. What will he do in the second? What if it be a hot sun, and the struggle is in Olympia?

So it is in life. If you offer a man a trifle of silver, he will scorn it. What will happen if you offer him a young maid? What if you do it in the dark? What happens if you ply him with reputation, or abuse, or praise, or death? All these he can conquer. What will he do if he is wrestling in the hot sun, I mean, if he has drunk too much? What if he is in a frenzy, or in sleep? The man who can overcome in all these circumstances is what I mean by the invincible athlete.

CHAPTER XIX

HOW ONE SHOULD BEHAVE TOWARDS TYRANTS

If a man possesses some advantage, or thinks he does though he does not, he is bound, if he be uneducated, to be puffed up because of it. The tyrant, for instance, says, 'I am mightiest of all men.'

Well, and what can you give me? Can you enable me to get what I will to get? How can you? Can you avoid what you will to avoid, independent of circumstances? Is your impulse free from error? How can you claim any such power?

Tell me, on shipboard, do you put confidence in yourself or in the man who knows? And in a chariot? Surely in him who knows. How is it in other arts? Exactly the same. What does your power come to then?

'All men pay me attention.'

Yes, and I pay attention to my platter and work it and polish it and I fix up a peg for my oil-flask. Does that mean that these are superior to me? No, but they do me some service, and for this reason I pay them attention. Again: do I not pay attention to my ass? Do I not wash his feet? Do I not curry him? Do you not know that every man pays regard to himself, and to you only as to his ass? For who pays regard to you as a man? Show me. Who wishes to become like you? Who regards you as one like Socrates to admire and follow?

'But I can behead you.'

Well said. I forgot, of course, one ought to pay you worship as if you were fever or cholera, and raise an altar to you, like the altar to Fever in Rome.

What is it then which disturbs and confounds the multitude? Is it the tyrant and his guards? Nay, God forbid! It is impossible for that which is free by nature to be disturbed or hindered by anything but itself. It is a man's own judgements which disturb him. For when the tyrant says to a man, 'I will chain your leg,' he that values his leg says, 'Nay, have mercy,' but he that values his will says, 'If it seems more profitable to you, chain it.'

'Do you pay no heed?'

No, I pay no heed.

'I will show you that I am master.'

How can you? Zeus gave me my freedom. Or do you think that he was likely to let his own son be enslaved? You are master of my dead body, take it.

'Do you mean that when you approach me, you pay no respect to me?'

No, I only pay respect to myself: if you wish me to say that I pay respect to you too, I tell you that I do so, but only as I pay respect to my water-pot.

This is not mere self-love: for it is natural to man, as to other creatures, to do everything for his own sake; for even the sun does everything for its own sake, and in a word so does Zeus himself. But when he would be called 'The Rain-giver' and 'Fruit-giver' and 'Father of men and gods', you see that he cannot win these names or do these works unless he does some good to the world at large: and in general he has so created the nature of the rational animal, that he can attain nothing good for himself, unless he contributes some service to the community. So it turns out that to do everything for his own sake is not unsocial. For what do you expect? Do you expect a man to hold aloof from himself and his own interest? No: we cannot ignore the one principle of action which governs all things—to be at unity with themselves.

What follows? When men's minds harbour wrong opinions on things beyond the will, counting them good and evil, they are bound to pay regard to tyrants. Would that it were only tyrants, and not chamberlains too! How can a man possibly grow wise of a sudden, when Caesar appoints him to the charge of the privy? How is it we straightway say, 'Felicio has spoken wisely to me'? I would fain have him deposed from the dung-heap, that he may seem foolish to you again. Epaphroditus had a shoemaker, whom he sold because he was useless: then by some chance he was bought by one of Caesar's officials, and became Caesar's shoemaker. If you could have seen how Epaphroditus honoured him. 'How is my good Felicio, I pray you?' Then if some one asked us, 'What is your master doing?' the answer was, 'He is consulting Felicio about something.' What, had he not sold him for useless? Who has suddenly made a wise man of him? This is what comes of honouring anything outside one's will.

He has been honoured with a tribuneship. All who meet him congratulate him; one kisses his eyes, another his neck, his slaves kiss his hands. He comes into his house and finds lamps being lighted. He goes up to the Capitol and offers sacrifice. Who, I ask you, ever offered sacrifice in gratitude for right direction of the will or for impulse in accordance with nature? For we give thanks to the gods for what we think our good!

To-day one spoke to me about the priesthood of Augustus. I told him, 'Fellow, leave the thing alone; you will spend a great deal on nothing.'

'Well, but those who draw up contracts will record my name.'

Can you be there when men read it and say to them, 'That is my name,' and even supposing you can be there now, what will you do if you die?

'My name will remain.'

Write it on a stone and it will remain. But who will remember you outside Nicopolis?

'But I shall wear a golden crown.'

If you desire a crown at all, take a crown of roses and wear that: you will look smarter in that.

CHAPTER XX

HOW REASON HAS THE FACULTY OF TAKING COGNIZANCE OF ITSELF

EVERY art and faculty has certain principal things of which it is to take cognizance. When therefore the faculty itself is of like kind with the objects of which it takes cognizance, it must of necessity have power to take cognizance of itself: when it is of unlike kind, it cannot take cognizance of itself. For instance, the shoemaker's art is concerned with hides, but itself is absolutely different from the material of hides: for this reason it does not take cognizance of itself. Grammar again is concerned with written speech: is it then written speech itself? Certainly not: therefore it cannot take cognizance of itself.

For what purpose then have we received reason from nature?

That we may deal with impressions aright.

What then is reason itself?

A system framed from impressions of a certain kind. Thus it naturally has the power to take cognizance of itself.

Again, sagacity has been given us. To take cognizance of what?

Things good and bad and indifferent.

What is it then itself?

Good.

And what is folly?

Bad. Do you see then that of necessity sagacity has the power of taking cognizance of itself and its opposite? Therefore the primary and highest task of the philosopher is to test impressions and distinguish them and to make use of none which is untested. Consider how we have invented an art to test the currency, in which we are admitted to have some interest. Look how many means the assayer uses to test the coin —sight, touch, smell, finally hearing: he breaks the penny and attends to the sound, and is not content with hearing its note once, but by much attention gets an ear for music.

Thus, where we think it makes a serious difference to us whether we are right or wrong, we take great pains to distinguish the possible sources of error, and yet when we have to do with our Governing Principle itself, poor thing, we gape and sleep and are ready to accept any impression that comes: for we do not notice our loss.

When you wish, therefore, to realize how little concerned you are about good and evil, and how eager about things indifferent, consider how you regard physical blindness on the one hand, and mental delusion on the other, and you will recognize that you are far from having a proper feeling in regard to things good and evil.

'Yes, but it needs much preparation and much toil and study.'

What of that? Do you expect that a brief study will enable you to acquire the greatest art? Yet the principal doctrine of philosophers itself is brief enough. If you will learn it, read Zeno's words and you will see. For it is no long matter to say man's end is to follow the gods, and the essence of good is the power of dealing rightly with impressions.

'Tell us then what is "God," and what is "impression," and what is nature in the individual, and what in the universe'.

That is a long story.

Again, if Epicurus should come and say, that the good must be in the flesh, that too means a long discussion; it means we must be taught what is the commanding faculty in us, what constitutes our substantial and true nature. If it is not probable that the good of the snail is in the shell, is it probable that man's good is in his body? Take yourself, Epicurus. What is the more masterful faculty you possess? What is it in you which deliberates, which examines everything, which examines the flesh itself and decides that it is the principal thing? Why do you light a lamp and toil for us, and write such big volumes? Is it that we may not be ignorant of the truth? Who are we? What concern have we with you? So the argument becomes a long one.

CHAPTER XXI

TO THOSE WHO WISH TO BE ADMIRED

When a man has his proper station in life, he does not hanker after what is beyond him.

What is it, man, that you wish to have?

'I am content if I am in accord with Nature in what I will to get and will to avoid, if I follow Nature in impulse to act and to refrain from action, in purpose, and design and assent.'

Why then do you walk about as if you had swallowed a poker?

'I would fain that they who meet me should admire me, and cry aloud, "What a great philosopher!" '

Who are these by whom you wish to be admired? Are not these the men whom you generally describe as mad? What do you want then? Do you want to be admired by madmen?

CHAPTER XXII

ON PRIMARY CONCEPTIONS [13]

Primary conceptions are common to all men, and one does not conflict with another. Who among us, for instance, does not assume that the good is expedient and desirable and that we ought in all circumstances to follow and pursue it? Which of us does not assume that the just is noble and becoming?

At what moment then does conflict arise? It arises in the application of primary conceptions to particular facts; when for instance one says, 'He has done well: he is brave,' and another, 'Nay, he is out of his mind.' Hence arises the conflict of men with one another. Such is the conflict between Jews and Syrians and Egyptians and Romans—not the question whether holiness must be put before all things and must in all circumstances be pursued, but whether it is holy or unholy to eat of swine's flesh. Such you will find is the conflict between Agememnon and Achilles. Call them to come forward.

What do you say, Agamemnon? Do you say that what is right and noble ought not to be done?

'Of course it ought.'

And what do you say, Achilles? Do you not approve of doing what is noble?

'Nay, I approve of it above all things.'

Now apply these primary notions: and here the conflict begins. One says, 'I ought not to give back Chryseis to her father.' The other says, 'Nay, you ought.' Certainly one or other of them wrongly applies the primary notion of right. Again one says, 'Well, if I must give back Chryseis, I must take the prize from one of you': the other says, 'What, take away my beloved?' 'Yes, yours,' he says. 'Am I alone then to be the loser?' 'But am I alone to have nothing?' So a conflict arises.

In what then does education consist? In learning to apply the natural primary conceptions to particular occasions in accordance with nature, and further to distinguish between things in our power and things not in our power. In our power are will and all operations of the will, and beyond our power are the body, the parts of the body, possessions, parents, brothers, children, country, in a word—those whose society we share. Where then are we to place 'the good'? To what class of things shall we apply it?

'To what is in our power.'

Does it follow then that health and a whole body, and life are not good, nor children, parents, and country? No one will bear with you if you say that. Let us then transfer the name 'good' to this class of things. Is it possible for a man to be happy if he is injured and fails to win good things?

'It is impossible.'

Can he also find the proper way to live with his fellows? Nay, how is it possible? For instance, I incline by nature to my true interest. If it is my interest to have a field, it is also my interest to take it away from my neighbour: if it is my interest to have a robe, it is my interest also to steal it from the bath. This is the source of wars, factions, tyrannies, plots.

Again, how shall I be able to observe what is fitting towards Zeus, for if I am injured or unfortunate, he heeds me not? So one hears, 'What have I to do with him, if he cannot help me?' and again, 'What have I to do with him, if he wills that I should be as I am now?' It follows that I begin to hate him. Why then do we build temples and make images to Zeus as if he were an evil genius, as if he were Fever? How can we give him any more the name Saviour, Rain-giver, and Fruit-giver? Surely if we place the true nature of the good in outward things, all these consequences follow.

What are we to do then? This is the search to be made by the true student of philosophy, who is in travail with truth. These are his thoughts: 'I do not see what is good and what evil. Am I not mad? I am.' But if I put 'the good' in the region of things that my will controls, every one will laugh at me. Some grey-haired old man will arrive, with many gold rings on his fingers: then he will shake his head and say, 'Listen to me, my child: you must study philosophy, but you must keep a cool head too. All that talk is folly. You learn the syllogism from philosophers, but you know better than the philosophers what you ought to do.'

Fellow, why do you rebuke me then, if I know it? What am I to say to this slave? If I am silent, he bursts with anger. One ought to say, 'Pardon me as you would pardon lovers. I am not my own master. I am mad.'

CHAPTER XXIII

AGAINST EPICURUS

Epicurus understands as well as we do that we are by nature social beings, but having once placed our good not in the spirit but in the husk which contains it he cannot say anything different. On the other hand he firmly grasps the principle that one must not admire nor accept anything which is severed from the nature of the good: and he is quite right.

How can we be social beings, if (as you say) we have no natural affection for our offspring? Why do you advise the wise man not to bring up children? Why are you afraid that they may bring him into troubles? Does the mouse he rears indoors cause him trouble? What does he care then, if a tiny mouse begins crying in his house? But he knows that if once a child is born, it will not be in our power not to love it nor care for it.

Epicurus says that the man who is wise does not enter into politics, for he knows what sort of things the politician has to do. Of course if you are going to live among men as if they were flies, what is to prevent you? But Epicurus, as though he did not know what natural affection is, says 'Let us not bring up children.'

If a sheep does not abandon its offspring, nor a wolf, does a man abandon his? What would you have us do? Would you have us foolish as sheep? Even they do not abandon their young. Would you have us savage as wolves? Even they do not abandon theirs. Nay, who takes your advice when he sees his child fallen on the ground and crying? Why, I think that if your father and mother had foreseen that you were going to talk thus, even then they would not have cast you away from them.

CHAPTER XXIV

HOW ONE SHOULD CONTEND AGAINST DIFFICULTIES

DIFFICULTIES are what show men's character. Therefore when a difficult crisis meets you, remember that you are as the raw youth with whom God the trainer is wrestling.

'To what end?' the hearer asks.

That you may win at Olympia: and that cannot be done without sweating for it. To my mind no man's difficulties ever gave him a finer trial than yours, if only you will use them for exercise, as the athlete wrestles with the young man. Even now we are sending you to Rome to spy out the land:[14] and no one sends a coward as a spy, for that means that if he but hears a noise or sees a shadow anywhere, he will come running in confusion and saying that the enemy are close at hand. So now if you come and tell us 'The doings in Rome are fearful, death is terrible, exile is terrible, evil-speaking is terrible, poverty is terrible: fly sirs, the enemy is at hand', we shall say to you, 'Begone, prophesy to yourself, the only mistake we made was in sending a man like you to spy out the land'. Diogenes, who was sent scouting before you, has brought us back a different report: he says, 'Death is not evil, for it is not dishonour'; he says, 'Glory is a vain noise made by madmen'. And what a message this scout brought us about pain and pleasure and poverty! 'To wear no raiment', he says, 'is better than any robe with purple hem'; 'to sleep on the ground without a bed', he says, 'is the softest couch.' Moreover he proves each point by showing his own confidence, his tranquillity of mind, his freedom, and withal his body well knit, and in good condition. 'No enemy is near,' he says, 'all is full of peace.'

What do you mean, Diogenes?

'See,' he says, 'have I suffered shot or wound or rout?'

That is the right kind of scouting: but you come back to us and talk at random. Drop your cowardice and go back again, and take a more accurate observation.

What am I to do then?

What do you do, when you disembark from a ship? Do you take the helm and the oars with you? What do you take then? You take what is yours, oil-flask and wallet. So now if you remember what is yours, you will never claim what is another's.

The emperor says to you, 'Lay aside your purple hem.'

See, I wear the narrow one.

'Lay aside this also.'

See, I wear the toga only.

'Lay aside the toga.'

See, I take that off too.

'Ay, but you still rouse my envy.'

Then take my poor body, every bit of it. The man to whom I can throw away my body has no fears for me.

'But he will not leave me as his heir.'

What? Did I forget that none of these things was mine? In what sense do we call them 'mine'? Only as we call 'mine' the pallet in an inn. If then the inn-keeper dies and leaves you the pallets, well and good; if he leaves them to another, that man will have them, and you will look for another. If you do not find one you will sleep on the ground, only do so with a good cheer, snoring the while, and remembering that it is among rich men and kings and emperors that tragedies find room, and that no poor man fills a part in a tragedy except as one of the chorus. But kings begin with a prelude of good things:

Crown high the halls

[Author unknown]

and then about the third or fourth act comes—

O Cithaeron, why didst thou receive me?

[Sophocles, *Oedipus the King*, 1391]

Poor slave, where are your crowns, where your diadem? Your guards avail you naught. Therefore when you come near to one of those great men remember this, that you are meeting a tragic character, no actor, but Oedipus in person.

'Nay, but such a one is blessed, for he has a great company to walk with him.'

I too join the ranks of the multitude and have a large company to walk with.

To sum up: remember that the door is open. Do not be a greater coward than the children, but do as they do. Children, when things do not please them, say, 'I will not play any more'; so, when things seem to you to reach that point, just say, 'I will not play any more,' and so depart, instead of staying to make moan.

CHAPTER XXV

ON THE SAME THEME

IF THIS is true, and if we are not silly and insincere when we say that for men good and evil lies in the region of the will, and that everything else has no concern for us, why are we disturbed or fearful any more? No one has authority over the things in which we are interested: and we pay no regard to the things over which others have authority. What more have we to trouble about?

'Nay, but give me commands' (says the student).

What command should I give you? Has not Zeus laid commands upon you? Has He not given you what is yours, free from hindrance and constraint, and what is not yours subject to hindrance and constraint? What command then have you brought with you into the world, and what manner of ordinance? Guard what is your own by all means, grasp not at the things of others. Your good faith is your own. . . . Who can take these qualities from you? Who shall hinder you from using them but yourself? And how will you do so? When you take no interest in what is your own, you lose it and it ceases to be yours.

When you have instructions and commands from Zeus such as these, what commands would you have from me? Am I greater or more trustworthy than He? Do you need any other commands if you keep these of His? Has He not laid these commands upon you? Look at the primary conceptions. Look at the demonstrations of philosophers. Look at the lessons you have often heard, and the words you have spoken yourself—all you have read, all you have studied.

How long, then, is it right to keep these commands and not break up the game?

As long as it is conducted properly.

Here is a king chosen by lot at the Saturnalia: for they decide to play the game of 'Kings'. He gives his orders: '*You* drink, *you* mix the wine, *you* sing, *you* go, *you* come'. I obey, that I may not break up the game.

'Now believe that you are in evil case.'

I do not believe it, and who will compel me to believe it?

Again, we agree to play 'Agamemnon and Achilles'. He who is given the part of Agamemnon says to me, 'Go to Achilles and drag away Briseis'. I go. 'Come.' I come.

In fact we must behave in life as we do with hypothetical arguments. 'Let us assume it is night.'

Granted.

'What follows? Is it day?'

No, for I have already assented to the assumption that it is night.

'Let us assume that you believe that it is night.'

Granted.

'Now believe that it really *is* night.'

This does not follow from the hypothesis.

So too it is in life. 'Let us assume that you are unfortunate.'

Granted.

'Are you then unfortunate?'

Yes.

'What then, are you in misery?'

Yes.

'Now, believe that you are in evil case.'

This does not follow from the hypothesis: and Another forbids me.

How far, then, must we submit to such commands? So far as is expedient; that is, so far as I am true to what is becoming and consistent. There are, however, some severe and sour-tempered persons who say, 'I cannot dine with this fellow, and put up with his daily narrative of how he fought in Mysia. "I told you, brother, how I mounted the hill: now I begin again at the siege."' Another says, 'I would rather dine and hear him babble on to his heart's content.' It is for you to compare these estimates: only do nothing in the spirit of one burdened and afflicted, who believes himself in evil case: for no one compels you to this. Suppose some one made the room smoke. If the smoke is moderate I will stay: if excessive, I go out: for one must remember and hold fast to this, that the door is open.

The order comes, 'Do not dwell in Nicopolis.'

I will not.

'Nor in Athens.'

I give up Athens.

'Nor in Rome.'

I give up Rome.

'Dwell in Gyara.'

I dwell in Gyara: but this seems to me a very smoky room indeed, and I depart where no one shall hinder me from dwelling: for that dwelling is open to every man. And beyond the last inner tunic, which is this poor body of mine, no one has any authority over me at all. That is why Demetrius said to Nero, 'You threaten me with death, but nature threatens you.' If I pay regard to my poor body, I have given myself over as a slave: and if I value my wretched property I am a slave, for thereby I show at once what power can master me. Just as when the snake draws in its head I say, 'Strike the part of him which he guards,' so you may be sure that your master will trample on that part of you which you wish to guard. When you remember this, whom will you flatter or fear any more?

'Nay, but I want to sit where the senators sit.'

Do you see that you are making a strait place for yourself and squeezing yourself?

'How else then shall I have a good view in the amphitheatre?'

Man, do not go to the show and you will not be crushed. Why do you trouble yourself? Or wait a little, and when the show is done, sit down in the senators' seats and sun yourself. For remember this (and it is true universally) that it is we who straiten and crush ourselves—that is to say, it is our judgements which straiten and crush us. For instance, what does it mean to be slandered? Stand by a stone and slander it: what effect will you produce? If a man then listens like a stone, what advantage has the slanderer? But if the slanderer has the weakness of him that he slanders to work upon, then he does achieve something.

'Tear his toga off him.'

Why bring *him* in? Take his toga. Tear that.

'I have done you an outrage.'

May it turn out to your good.

These were the principles that Socrates practised: that is why his face always wore the same expression. But we are fain to study and practise everything except how to be free men and untrammelled.

'The philosophers talk paradoxes.'

But are there no paradoxes in the other arts? Nay, what is more paradoxical than to lance a man's eye that he may see? If one told this to a person unskilled in the physician's art, would he not laugh at him who said it? Is it surprising then that in philosophy also many truths seem paradoxical to those who are unskilled?

CHAPTER XXVI

WHAT IS THE LAW OF LIFE

WHEN some one was reciting hypothetical arguments, Epictetus said: This also is a law which governs hypothesis, that we must accept what conforms with the hypothesis. But much more important is the law of living, which is this—to act in conformity with nature. For if we wish in every subject and in all circumstances to observe what is natural, it is plain that in everything we must aim at not letting slip what is in harmony with nature nor accepting what is in conflict with it. First, then, philosophers train us in the region of speculation, which is easier, and only then lead us on to what is harder: for in the sphere of speculation there is no influence which hinders us from following what we are taught, but in life there are many influences which drag us the contrary way. We may laugh, then, at him who says that he wants to try living first; for it is not easy to begin with what is harder.

And this is the defence that we must plead with parents who are angered at their children studying philosophy: 'Suppose I am in error, my father, and ignorant of what is fitting and proper for me. If, then, this cannot be taught or learnt, why do you reproach me? If it can be taught, teach me, and, if you cannot, let me learn from those who say that they know. For what think you? That I fall into evil and fail to do well because I wish to? God forbid. What, then, is the cause of my going wrong? Ignorance. Would you not then have me put away my ignorance? Who was ever taught the art of music or of steering by anger? Do you think, then, that your anger will enable me to learn the art of living?' This argument can only be used by one who has entertained the purpose of right living. But if a man studies logic and goes to the philosophers just because he wants to show at a dinner party that he knows hypothetical arguments, is he not merely trying to win the admiration of some senator who sits next him? For in such society the great forces of the world prevail, and what we call wealth here seems child's-play there.

This is what makes it difficult to get the mastery over one's impressions, where distracting forces are strong. I know a man who clung to the knees of Epaphroditus in tears and said he was in distress, for he had nothing left but a million and a half. What did Epaphroditus do? Did he laugh at him, as we should? No, he was astonished, and said, 'Unhappy man, how ever did you manage to keep silence and endure it?'

Once when he put to confusion the student who was reading hypothetical arguments, and the master who had set him to read laughed at his pupil, he said, You are laughing at yourself; you did not give the young man any preliminary training, nor discover whether he can follow the arguments, but just treat him as a reader. Why is it, he said, that when a mind is unable to follow and judge a complex argument we trust to it the task of praise and blame and of deciding on good and bad actions? If he speaks ill of any one, does the man attend to him, and is any one elated by a praise which comes from one who cannot find the logical connexion in such small matters?

This, then, is where the philosophic life begins; in the discovery of the true state of one's own mind: for when once you realize that it is in a feeble state, you will not choose to employ it any more for great matters. But, as it is, some men, finding themselves unable to swallow a mouthful, buy themselves a treatise, and set about eating it whole, and, in consequence they vomit or have indigestion. Hence come colics and fluxes and fevers. They ought first to have considered whether they have the faculty.

It is easy enough in speculation to examine and refute the ignorant, but in practical life men do not submit themselves to be tested, and we hate the man who examines and exposes us. Yet Socrates used to say that a life which was not put to the test was not worth living. [Plato, *Apology*, 38a]

CHAPTER XXVII

ON THE WAYS IN WHICH IMPRESSIONS COME TO US: AND THE AIDS WE MUST PROVIDE FOR OURSELVES TO DEAL WITH THEM

Impressions come to us in four ways: either things are and seem so to us; or they are not and seem not to be; or they are and seem not; or they are not and yet seem to be. Now it is the business of the true philosopher to deal rightly with all these; he ought to afford help at whatever point the pressure comes. If it is the fallacies of Pyrrho and of the Academy which crush us, let us render help against them. If it is the plausibilities of circumstances, which make things seem good which are not, let us seek help against this danger: if it is habit which crushes us, we must try to discover help against that.

What, then, can we discover to help us against habit?

Contrary habit.

You hear ignorant folk saying, 'Unhappy man that he was, he died': 'His father perished, and his mother': 'He was cut off, yes, and untimely and in a foreign land.' Now listen to the arguments on the other side;

draw yourself away from these voices, set against habit the opposite habit. Set against fallacious arguments the processes of reason, training yourself to be familiar with these processes: against the plausibilities of things we must have our primary conceptions clear, like weapons bright and ready for use.

When death appears an evil we must have ready to hand the argument that it is fitting to avoid evils, and death is a necessary thing. What am I to do? Where am I to escape it? Grant that I am not Sarpedon son of Zeus, to utter those noble words, 'I would fain go and achieve glory or afford another the occasion to achieve it: if I cannot win success myself, I will not grudge another the chance of doing a noble deed'. Grant that this is beyond us, can we not compass the other?

I ask you, Where am I to escape death? Point me to the place, point me to the people, among whom I am to go, on whom it does not light, point me to a charm against it. If I have none, what would you have me do? I cannot escape death: am I not to escape the fear of it? Am I to die in tears and trembling? For trouble of mind springs from this, from wishing for a thing which does not come to pass. Wheresoever I can alter external things to suit my own will, I alter them: where I cannot, I am fain to tear any man's eyes out who stands in my way. For man's nature is such that he cannot bear to be deprived of what is good, nor can he bear to be involved in evil. And so the end of the matter is that when I cannot alter things, nor blind him that hinders me, I sit still and moan and revile whom I can—Zeus and the other gods; for if they heed me not, what have I to do with them?

'Yes, but that will be impious of you.'

Well, how shall I be worse off than I am now? In a word, we must remember this, that unless piety and true interest coincide, piety cannot be preserved in a man. Do not these principles seem to you to be urgent?

Let the Pyrrhonist and the disciple of the Academy come and maintain the contrary! For my part I have no leisure for these discussions, nor can I act as advocate to the common-sense view.

If I had some petty action concerned with a plot of land, I should have called in another to be my advocate, how much more in a matter of this concern.

With what argument, then, am I content? With what is appropriate to the subject in hand. How sensation takes place, whether through the whole body or through particular parts, I cannot render a reasoned account, though I find difficulty in both views. But that you and I are not the same persons, I know absolutely and for certain. How is that? When I want to swallow a morsel I never lift it to your mouth, but to mine. When I want to take a piece of bread, I never take rubbish instead, but go to the bread as to a mark. And even you who make nothing of the senses, act just as I do. Which of you when he wants to go to the bath goes to the mill instead?

What follows? Must we not to the best of our power hold fast to this—that is, maintain the view of common sense, and guard ourselves against all that upsets it? Yes, who disputes that? But these are matters for one who has the power and the leisure: the man who trembles, and is disturbed, and whose heart is shaken within him, ought to devote his time to something else.

CHAPTER XXVIII

THAT WE MUST NOT BE ANGRY WITH MEN: AND CONCERNING WHAT THINGS ARE SMALL AND WHAT ARE GREAT AMONG MEN

WHAT is the reason that we assent to a thing? Because it seems to us that it is so. It is impossible that we shall assent to that which seems not to be. Why? Because this is the nature of the mind—to agree to what is true, and disagree with what is false, and withhold judgement on what is doubtful.

What is the proof of this?

'Feel now, if you can, that it is night.'

It is impossible.

'Put away the feeling that it is day.'

It is impossible.

'Assume or put away the feeling that the stars are even in number.'

It is not possible.

When a man assents, then, to what is false, know that he had no wish to assent to the false: 'for no soul is robbed of the truth with its own consent,' as Plato says, but the false seemed to him true.

Now, in the sphere of action what have we to correspond to true and false in the sphere of perception? What is fitting and unfitting, profitable and unprofitable, appropriate and inappropriate, and the like.

Cannot a man, then, think a thing is to his profit, and not choose it?

He cannot.

What of her [15] who says

I know full well what ills I mean to do
But passion overpowers what counsel bids me.

[Euripides, *Medea,* 1078]

Here the very gratification of passion and the vengeance she takes on her husband she believes to be more to her profit than saving her children.

'Yes, but she is deceived.'

Prove to her plainly that she is deceived and she will not do it, but as long as you do not show her, what else can she follow but that which appears to her? Nothing. Why then are you indignant with her, because, unhappy woman, she is deluded on the greatest matters and is transformed from a human being into a serpent? Why do you not rather pity her—if so it may be? As we pity the blind and the lame, so should we pity those who are blinded and lamed in their most sovereign faculties.

We must remember this clearly, that man measures his every action by his impressions; of course they may be good or bad: if good, he is free from reproach; if bad, he pays the penalty in his own person, for it is impossible for one to be deluded and another to suffer for it. The man who remembers this, I say, will be angry with no one, indignant with no one, revile none, blame none, hate none, offend none.

'So you say that deeds so great and awful take their origin from this, the impressions of the mind?'

From this and nothing else. The Iliad is nothing but men's impressions and how they dealt with them. It was impressions that made Paris take away the wife of Menelaus, impressions that drew Helen to follow him. If, then, his impressions had led Menelaus to feel that it was a gain to be robbed of such a wife, what would have happened? We should have lost the Iliad, and not only that but the Odyssey too.

'What? Do these great matters depend on one that is so small?'

What are these you call 'such great matters'? Wars and factions, deaths of many men and destructions of cities. What is there great in this, pray?

'Is there nothing great?'

Why, what is there great in the death of many oxen and many sheep, and the burning and destruction of many nests of swallows and storks?

'Are these like those other horrors?'

Most like: bodies of men perished, so did bodies of oxen and sheep. Huts of men were burnt: so were storks' nests. What is great or awful here? Or if it be so, show me how a man's home differs from a stork's nest, as a dwelling.

'Is a stork, then, like a man?'

What do you say? In respect of his body, very like; save only that men's homes are built of beams and rafters and bricks, and storks' nests of sticks and clay.

'Does a man then differ in nothing from a stork?'

God forbid: but he does not differ in these matters.

'In what then does he differ?'

Search and you will find that he differs in something else. Look whether it be not that he differs in understanding what he does, in his faculty for society, in his good faith, his self-respect, his security of aim, his prudence.

Where then is man's good and man's evil, in the true sense, to be found?

In that faculty which makes men different from all else. If a man preserves this and keeps it safely fortified; if his sense of honour, his good faith, and his prudence are not destroyed, then he too is preserved; but if any of these perish or be taken by storm, then he too perishes with them. And it is on this that great events depend. Was Alexander's great failure when the Hellenes came against the Trojans and sacked Troy and when his brothers perished? By no means: for no one fails by the act of another; yet then there was destruction of storks' nests. Nay, his failure was when he lost the man of honour, the man of good faith, the man who respected manners and the laws of hospitality. When did Achilles fail? Was it when Patroclus died? God forbid: it was when he was angry, when he cried for a trumpery maiden, when he forgot that he was there not to win lady-loves, but to make war. These are man's failures—this is his siege, this is his razed city, when his right judgements are broken to the ground, and when they are destroyed.

'But when women are carried off, and children are made captive, and men themselves are slaughtered—are not these things evil?'

Where do you get this idea from? If it is true, teach it me too.

'No, I cannot: but how can you say that they are not evil?'

Let us turn to our standards, let us look to our primary notions. For I cannot be sufficiently astonished at what men do. When we want to judge weights, we do not judge at random: when we judge things straight and crooked, it is not at random: in a word, when it is important to us to know the truth on any subject, no one of us will ever do anything at random. Yet when we are dealing with the primary and sole cause of right or wrong action, of prosperity or adversity, of good or bad fortune, there alone we are random and headlong: we nowhere have anything like a scale, nowhere anything like a standard: some impression strikes me, and straightway I act on it.

Am I any better than Agamemnon or Achilles, that they should do and suffer such evils because they follow their impressions, and I should be content with mine?

Surely tragedy has no other source but this. What is the 'Atreus' of Euripides? Impressions. What is the 'Oedipus' of Sophocles? Impressions. 'Phoenix'? Impressions. 'Hippolytus'? Impressions. How do you think then we should describe the man who takes no pains to discipline his impressions? What name do we give to those who follow everything that comes into their mind?

'Madmen.'

Well, is not this exactly what we do?

CHAPTER XXIX

ON CONSTANCY

THE essence of good and of evil lies in an attitude of the will.

What are external things then?

They are materials for the will, in dealing with which it will find its own good or evil.

How will it find its good?

If it does not value over much the things that it deals with. For its judgements on matters presented to it, if they be right, make the will good, and if crooked and perverse make it bad. This law God has ordained and says, 'If you want anything good, get it from yourself.'

You say, 'Not so, but from another.'

I say, No, from yourself. So when the tyrant threatens and does not invite me, I say, 'What does he threaten?' If he says, 'I will bind you', I say, 'He threatens my hands and my feet.' If he says, 'I will behead you', I say, 'He threatens my neck'. If he says, 'I will put you in prison', I say, 'He threatens all my poor flesh', and if he threatens banishment, the same.

'Does he then not threaten you at all?'

Not at all, if I feel that these things are nothing to me: but if I fear any of them, he does threaten me. Who is there left for me to fear, and over what has he control? Over what is in my power? No one controls that. Over what is not in my power? I have no concern in that.

'Do you philosophers then teach us to despise kings?'

Heaven forbid! Which of us teaches men to resist them in the matters over which they have authority? Take my bit of a body, take my property, take my good name, take my companions. If I try to persuade any of them to resist, I give him leave to accuse me indeed.

'Yes, but I want to command your judgements.'

Who has given you this authority? How can you conquer another's judgement?

'I will conquer him', he says, 'by bringing fear to bear on him.'

You are not aware that it was the judgement that conquered itself, it was not conquered by another. The will may conquer itself, but nothing else can conquer it. That is the reason too why the noblest and most just law of God is this: 'Let the better always be victorious over the worse.'

'Ten', you say, 'are better than one.'

Better for what? To bind, to slay, to carry off where they will, to take away property. Ten conquer one therefore only in so far as they are better.

'In what then are they worse?'

They are worse if the one has right judgements, and the ten have not. I ask you, can they conquer him in this? How can they? If we weigh them in the balance, must not the heavier pull down the scale?

'This is your outcome then, that Socrates should suffer the fate he did at the hands of the Athenians?'

Slave, why do you say, 'Socrates'? State the fact as it really is, That Socrates' vile body should be arrested and haled to prison by those who are stronger, and that some one should give hemlock to Socrates' vile body and it should die of chill—does this seem to you marvellous, does this seem unjust, is it for this you accuse God? Did Socrates then get nothing in exchange? In what did his true good consist? Which are we to attend to? To you or to him? Nay, what does Socrates say? 'Anytus or Meletus can slay me, but they cannot harm me' [Plato, *Apology,* 30c]: and again, 'If God so will, so be it.' [Plato, *Crito,* 43d] Prove, I say, that one who has worse judgements gains the mastery over him who is his superior in judgements. You will not prove it: far from it. For the law of nature and of God is this, 'Let the better always come out victor over the worse.' Victorious in what? In that wherein it is better. One body is stronger than another, the majority are stronger than one, the thief stronger than he who is not a thief. That is why I too lost my lamp, because in the matter of vigilance the thief was a stronger man than I. But he bought his lamp for this price: for a lamp he became a thief, for a lamp he broke his faith, for a lamp he became a brute. This seemed to his judgement to be profitable.

Very well: but now some one has laid hold on my cloak, and drags me into the market, then others raise a clamour against me, 'Philosopher, what good have your judgements done you? for, see, you are haled to prison, see, you are about to be beheaded.'

And what sort of Introduction to philosophy could I have studied, that would save me from being haled off, if a stronger man seizes my cloak, or, if ten men drag me about and cast me into prison, will save me from being cast there? Have I then learnt nothing else? I have learnt to see that everything that happens, if it is beyond the control of my will, is nothing to me. Have you not gained benefit then in this respect? Why do you seek benefit elsewhere than where you learnt that it is to be found?

I sit on then in prison and say, 'This person who clamours at me has no ear for the true meaning of things, he does not understand what is said, in a word he has taken no pains to know what philosophers do or say. Let him be.'

But the answer comes, 'Come out of your prison.'

If you have no more need of me in prison, I come out: if you need me again, I will come in. For how long? For as long as reason requires that I should abide by my vile body; but when reason demands it no longer, take it from me and good health to you! Only let me not cast it off without reason or from a faint heart, or for a casual pretext. For again God wills it not: for He has need of a world like this, and of such creatures as ourselves to move upon the earth. But if He give the signal of retreat, as He gave it to Socrates, one must obey His signal as that of the general in command.

'What then? must I say these things to the multitude?'

Why should you? Is it not sufficient to believe them yourself? For when children come up to us and clap their hands and say, 'A good Saturnalia to you to-day!' do we say 'These things are not good'? Not at all, we clap with them ourselves. So, when you cannot change a man's opinion, recognize that he is a child, clap with him, and if you do not wish to do this, you have only to hold your peace.

These things we must remember, and when called to face a crisis that is to test us we must realize that the moment is come to show whether we have learnt our lesson. For a young man going straight from his studies to face a crisis may be compared to one who has practised the analysis of syllogisms. If some one offers him one that is easy to analyse, he says, 'Nay, propound me one which is cunningly involved, that I may get proper exercise.' And so wrestlers are discontented if put to wrestle with young men of light weight: 'He cannot lift me', one says. Here is a young man of parts, yet when the crisis calls he must needs weep and say, 'I would fain go on learning.'

Learning what? If you did not learn your lesson to display it in action, what did you learn it for?

I imagine one of those who are sitting here crying out in the travail of his heart, 'Why does not a crisis come to me such as has come to him? Am I to wear my life out idly in a corner, when I might win a crown at Olympia? When will some one bring me news of a contest like that?' Such ought to be the attitude of you all. Why, among Caesar's gladiators there are some who are vexed that no one brings them out or matches them in fight, and they pray to God and go to the managers and implore them to let them fight; and shall no one of you display a like spirit? That is exactly why I should like to take ship for Rome to see how my wrestler puts his lesson into practice.

'I do not want', says he, 'an exercise of this sort.'

What? is it in your power to take the task you choose? No, a body is given you of such a kind, parents of such a kind, brothers of such a kind, a country of such a kind, a position in it of such a kind: and yet you come to me and say, 'Change the task set me.' What! have you not resources, to deal with what is given you? Instead of saying, 'It is yours to set the task, and mine to study it well', you say, 'Do not put before me such a syllogism, but such an one: do not impose on me such a conclusion, but such an one.' A time will soon come when tragic actors will imagine that they are merely mask and shoes and robe, and nothing else. Man, you have these things given you as your subject and task. Speak your part, that we may know whether you are a tragic actor or a buffoon: for except their speech they have all else in common. Does the tragic actor disappear, if you take away his shoes and mask and bring him on the stage in the bare guise of a ghost, or is he there still? If he has a voice he is there still.

So it is in life: 'Take a post of command'; I take it, and taking it show how a philosopher behaves.

'Lay aside the senator's dress, and put on rags and appear in that character.' Very well: is it not given me still to display a noble voice?

In what part then do you appear now?

As a witness called by God: 'Come and bear witness for me, for I count you worthy to come forward as my witness. Is anything good or evil which lies outside the range of the will? Do I harm any one? Do I put each man's advantage elsewhere than in himself?'

What is the witness you now bear to God?

'I am in danger, O Lord, and in misfortune; no man heeds me, no man gives me anything, all blame me and speak evil of me.'

Is this the witness you are going to bear, and so dishonour the calling that he has given you, in that he honoured you thus and counted you worthy to be brought forward to bear such weighty witness?

But suppose that he who has authority pronounces, 'I judge you to be godless and unholy', how does this affect you?

'I am judged to be godless and unholy.'

Nothing more?

'Nothing.'

If he had been giving judgement on a hypothetical proposition and had declared, 'I judge the proposition "if it be day, there is light" to be false', how would it have affected the proposition? Who is judged here? Who is condemned? The proposition or the man who is deluded about it? Who in the world then is this who has authority to pronounce upon you? Does he know what godliness or ungodliness is? Has he made a study of it? Has he learnt it? Where and with what master?

If a musician pays no heed to him when he pronounces that the lowest note is the highest, nor a geometrician when he decides that the lines from the centre of a circle to the circumference are not equal, shall he who is educated in true philosophy pay any heed to an uneducated man when he gives judgement on what is holy and unholy, just and unjust? What a great wrong for philosophers to be guilty of! Is this what you have learnt by coming to school?

Leave other people, persons of no endurance, to argue on these matters to little purpose. Let them sit in a corner and take their paltry fees, or murmur that no one offers them anything, and come forward yourself and practise what you have learnt. For it is not arguments that are wanting nowadays: no, the books of the Stoics are full of them. What then is the one thing wanting? We want the man who will apply his arguments, and bear witness to them by action. This is the character I would have you take up, that we may no longer make use of old examples in the school, but may be able to show an example from our own day.

Whose business then is it to take cognizance of these questions? It is for him that has studied at school; for man is a creature with a faculty of taking cognizance, but it is shameful for him to exercise it in the spirit of runaway slaves. No: one must sit undistracted and listen in turn to tragic actor or harp-player, and not do as the runaways do. At the very moment one of them is attending and praising the actor, he gives a glance all round, and then if some one utters the word 'master' he is fluttered and confounded in a moment. It is shameful that philosophers should take cognizance of the works of nature in this spirit. For what does 'master' mean? No man is master of another man; his masters are only death and life, pleasure and pain. For, apart from them, you may bring me face to face with Caesar and you shall see what constancy I show. But when he comes in thunder and lightning with these in his train, and I show fear of them, I am only recognizing my master as the runaway does. But so long as I have respite from them I am just like the runaway watching in the theatre; I wash, drink, sing, but do everything in fear and misery. But if I once free myself from my masters, that is from those feelings which make masters formidable, my trouble is past, and I have a master no more.

'Should I then proclaim this to all men?'

No! One should study the weakness of the uninstructed and say to them, 'This man advises me what he thinks good for himself, and I excuse him.' For Socrates too excused the gaoler who wept when he was going to drink the poison, and said, 'How nobly he has wept for us!' Does he say to the gaoler, 'That is why we dismissed the women'? No, he says that to his intimate friends, who were fit to hear it, but the gaoler he treats considerately like a child. [Plato, *Phaedo,* 116d]

CHAPTER XXX

WHAT A MAN SHOULD HAVE READY TO HAND IN THE CRISES OF LIFE

WHEN you appear before one of the mighty of the earth, remember that Another looks from above on what is happening and that you must please Him rather than this man. He that is above inquires of you: 'What did you say in the school about exile and prison and bonds and death and dishonour?'

I said they were 'indifferent'.

'What do you call them now, then? Have they changed?'

No.

'Have you changed then?'

No.

'Tell me then what things are indifferent.'

Things which lie outside the will's control.

'Tell me what follows.'

Things indifferent concern me not at all.

'Tell me also what you thought were "good things".'

A right will and a faculty of dealing rightly with impressions.

'And what did you think was the end?'

To follow Thee.

'Do you still say that?'

Yes. I say the same now as before.

Go on then into the palace in confidence and remember these things, and you shall see how a young man who has studied what he ought compares with men who have had no study. By the gods I imagine that you will feel thus: 'Why do we make these many and great preparations for nothing? Is this what authority meant? Are the vestibule, the chamberlains, the guards no more than this? Was it for this that I listened to those long discourses? These terrors were naught, and I made ready for them all the time as though they were great matters.'

BOOK II

CHAPTER I

THAT THERE IS NO CONFLICT BETWEEN CONFIDENCE AND CAUTION

PERHAPS the contention of philosophers that it is possible in everything we do to combine confidence with caution may appear a paradox, but nevertheless we must do our best to consider whether it is true. In a sense, no doubt, caution seems to be contrary to confidence, and contraries are by no means compatible. But I think that what seems to many a paradox in this subject depends on a confusion, and it is this. If we really called upon a man to use caution and confidence in regard to the same things, they might fairly find fault with us as uniting qualities which cannot be united. But as a matter of fact there is nothing strange in the statement: for if it is true, as has often been said and often proved, that the true nature of good and also of evil depends on how we deal with impressions, and if things outside the will's control cannot be described as good or bad, we cannot surely call it a paradoxical demand of the philosophers if they say, 'Be confident in all that lies beyond the will's control, be cautious in all that is dependent on the will.' For if evil depends on evil choice, it is only in regard to matters of will that it is right to use caution; and if things outside the will's control, which do not depend on us, concern us in no way, we should use confidence in regard to these. And in that way we shall be at once cautious and confident and indeed confident because of our caution. For because we are cautious as to things which are really evil we shall get confidence to face things which are not so.

However, we behave like deer: when hinds fear the feathers [1] and fly from them, where do they turn, and in what do they take refuge as a safe retreat? They turn to the nets, and so they perish because they confuse objects of fear with objects of confidence.

So it is with us. Where do we show fear? In regard to things outside our will's control. Again, when do we behave with confidence as though there were nothing to fear? In matters within the will's control. So if only we are successful in things beyond our will's control we think it is of no consequence to us to be deceived or to act rashly, or to do a shameless deed, or to conceive a shameful desire. But where death or exile or pain or infamy confronts us, there we show the spirit of retreat and of wild alarm. Wherefore, as is likely with men who are mistaken in the greatest matters, we convert our natural confidence into something bold, desperate, reckless, shameless, whereas we change our natural caution and modesty into a cowardly and abject quality, full of fears and perturbations. For if a man transfers his caution to the region of the will and the operations of the will, with the will to be cautious he will find that the will to avoid lies in his control: while if he turns his caution to what is beyond the control of our will, inasmuch as his will to avoid will be directed to what depends upon others he will of necessity be subject to fear, inconstancy, and perturbation. For it is not death or pain which is a fearful thing, but the fear of pain or death. Therefore men praise him who said

Not death, but shameful death, is to be feared.

[Author unknown]

We ought then to turn our confidence towards death, and our caution towards the fear of death: what we really do is just the contrary; we fly from death, yet we pay no heed to forming judgements about death, but are reckless and indifferent. Socrates called such fears 'bogies', and rightly too. [Plato, *Phaedo,* 77e] For just as masks seem fearful and terrible to children from want of experience, so we are affected by events for much the same reason as children are affected by 'bogies'. For what makes a child? Want of knowledge. What makes a child? Want of instruction. For so far as a child knows those things he is no worse off than we are. What is death? A bogy. Turn it round and see what it is: you see it does not bite. The stuff of the body was bound to be parted from the airy element, either now or hereafter, as it existed apart from it before. Why then are you vexed if they are parted now? For if not parted now, they will be hereafter. Why so? That the revolution of the universe may be accomplished, for it has need of things present, things future, and things past and done with. What is pain? A bogy. Turn it round and see what it is. The poor flesh is subject to rough movement, then again to smooth. If it is not to your profit, the door stands open: if it is to your profit, bear it. For in every event the door must stand open and then we have no trouble.

What then is the fruit of these judgements? A fruit which must needs be most noble and most becoming to those who are truly being educated —a mind tranquil and fearless and free. For on these matters you must not trust the multitude, who say, 'Only the free may be educated', but rather the philosophers who say, 'Only the educated are free.'

'What do you mean by that?'

I mean this. What else is freedom but power to pass our life as we will?

'True.'

Tell me, fellow men, do you wish to live doing wrong?

'We do not.'

Is no one free who does wrong?

'No one.'

Do you wish to live in fear, in pain, in distress of mind?

'By no means.'

Well, no man who suffers fear or pain or distress of mind is free, but whoever is quit of fears and pains and distresses is by the self-same road quit of slavery. How then shall we go on believing you, dearest lawgivers?

Do we allow none but the free to get education?

Nay! philosophers say that we do not allow any to be free except those whose education is complete: that is, God does not allow it.

'Well then, when a man turns his slave round before the praetor,[2] does he do nothing?'

He does something.

'What?'

He turns his slave round before the praetor.

'Nothing else?'

Yes, he is bound to pay the twentieth for him.

'What follows? Has not the man to whom this is done gained freedom?'

No more than he has gained peace of mind. For do you who can confer this freedom own no master? Have you not a master in money, a girl lover or a boy lover, the tyrant, or a friend of the tyrant? If not, why do you tremble when you go away to face a crisis of this sort? Therefore I say many times over: What you must practise and have at command is to know what you ought to approach with confidence, and what with caution; all that is beyond the control of the will with confidence, and what is dependent on the will with caution.

'But' (says my pupil), 'have I not recited to you? Do you not know what I am doing?'

What are you engaged on? Paltry phrases. Away with your paltry phrases: show me how you stand in regard to the will to get and the will to avoid: if you do not fail to get what you will, or fall into what you will to avoid. As for those paltry periods, if you have sense you will take them away somewhere or other and make away with them.

'What do you mean? Did not Socrates write?'

Yes, who wrote so much as he? But under what conditions? He could not always have some one at hand examining his judgements or to be examined by him in turn, and therefore be examined and questioned himself and was always putting to trial some primary conception or other in a practical way. This is what a philosopher writes: but paltry phrases and periods he leaves to others, to the stupid or the blessed, those whose peace of mind gives them leisure for study or those who can draw no logical conclusions because of their folly.

To-day, when the crisis calls you, will you go off and display your recitation and harp on, 'How cleverly I compose dialogues'? Nay, fellow man, make this your object, 'Look how I fail not to get what I will. Look how I escape what I will to avoid. Let death come and you shall know; bring me pains, prison, dishonour, condemnation.' This is the true field of display for a young man come from school. Leave those other trifles to other men; let no one ever hear you say a word on them, do not tolerate any compliments upon them; assume the air of being no one and of knowing nothing. Show that you know this only, how not to fail and how not to fall. Let others practise law-suits, logical puzzles and syllogisms: let your study be how to suffer death, bondage, the rack, exile: let all this be done with confidence and trust in Him who has called you to face them, and judged you worthy of this place you hold, wherein at your appointed post you shall show what is the power of reason, the Governing Principle, when arrayed against forces which are outside the will. And, if you do this, that paradox will no longer seem impossible or paradoxical—that we must show caution and confidence at the same time, confidence in regard to things beyond the will, caution in things which depend on the will.

CHAPTER II

ON PEACE OF MIND

CONSIDER, you who are going into court, what you want to maintain and where you want to end: for if you want to maintain your freedom of will in its natural condition, you have all security and facility to do so, and your trouble is over. If you wish to maintain authority over what is in your power and to keep it naturally free, and if you are content with this, what more need you attend to? For who is master of this, who can take it away from you? If you wish to be a man of honour and trust, who will forbid you? If you wish not to be hindered or compelled, what man will compel you to will to get what is against your judgement, and to will to avoid things that you do not think proper to avoid?

What can he do then? He will cause you troubles which seem to you formidable: but how can he make you will to avoid what is done to you? As long then as you retain in your control the will to get and the will to avoid, you need attend to nothing else. This is your introduction, this your narrative, this your proof, this your victory, this your peroration, this your ground of boasting.

That is why Socrates, in reply to one who reminded him to make ready for the court, said: 'Do you not think my whole life is a preparation for this?'

What kind of preparation?

'I have maintained', said he, 'what is my own.'

What do you mean?

'I never did an unjust act in my private or in my public life.' [Xenophon, *Apologia Socratis*, 2, 3]

But if you wish to keep what is outside you as well—your paltry body, and goods, and reputation—I advise you to begin this moment to make all possible preparation, and further to study the character of your judge and your opponent. If you must clasp his knees, clasp them; if you must weep, then weep; if you must lament, then lament. For when once you allow outward things to dominate what is your own, you had better become a slave and have done with it. Don't be drawn this way and that, wishing to be a slave one moment and free another, but be this or that simply and with all your mind, free or slave, philosopher or unenlightened, a fighting cock of spirit, or one of no spirit; either bear stroke after stroke patiently till you die, or give way at once. Let it not be your lot to suffer many blows and then give way in the end. If such conduct is shameful, get your own mind clear at once: 'Where is the nature of good and evil to be found? Where truth is. Where truth and nature are, there is caution; where truth and nature are, there is confidence.'

For what think you? If Socrates had wished to keep his outward possessions, would he have come forward and said, 'Anytus and Meletus have power to kill me, but not to harm me'? Was he so foolish as not to see that this road leads not to that end, but elsewhere? Why is it then, that he renders no account to his judges, and adds a word of provocation? Just as my friend Heraclitus, when he had an action in Rhodes concerning a plot of land and had pointed out to the judges that his arguments were just, when he came to his peroration said, 'I will not supplicate you, nor do I regard the judgement you will give; it is you who are on your trial rather than I', and so he made an end of the business. You need not speak like that, only do not supplicate. Do not add the words, 'I do not supplicate', unless, as happened to Socrates, the right time has come deliberately to provoke your judges. If, indeed, you are preparing a peroration of this sort, why do you appear in court? Why do you answer the summons? If you wish to be crucified, wait and the cross will come: but if reason requires that you should answer the summons and do your best to persuade the judge, you must act in accordance with this, but always keeping true to yourself.

On this principle it is ridiculous to say, 'Give me advice.' What advice am I to give you? Say rather, 'Enable my mind to adapt itself to the issue, whatever it may be', for the other phrase is as though a man unskilled in writing should say, 'Tell me what to write, when a name is set me to write.' For if I say 'Dion', and then yonder fellow comes forward and sets him the name not of Dion but of Theon, what is to happen? What is he to write? If you have practised writing, you can prepare yourself for anything that is dictated to you. But if you have not practised, what is the good of my making a suggestion? For if circumstances suggest something different, what will you say or what will you do? Remember then this general principle, and you will need no special suggestion. But if you fix your gaze on outward things, you must needs be tossed up and down, at the will of your master. And who is your master? He who has authority over any of those things on which you set your heart or which you will to avoid.

CHAPTER III

TO THOSE WHO COMMEND PERSONS TO PHILOSOPHERS

THAT is a good answer of Diogenes to one who asked him for letters of introduction: 'You are a man, and that his eyes will tell him; but whether you are good or bad he will discover, if he has skill to distinguish the good from the bad; and if he has not that skill, he will never discover it, though I should write him ten thousand letters. A drachma might just as well ask to be introduced to some one in order to be tested. If the man is a judge of silver, you will introduce yourself. We ought, therefore, to have some faculty to guide us in life, as the assayer has in dealing with silver, that I may be able to say as he does, 'Give me any drachma you please, and I will distinguish.' Now I can deal with a syllogism and say, 'Bring any one you like, and I will distinguish between him who can analyse syllogisms and him who cannot.' Why? Because I know how to analyse them: I have the faculty a man must have who is to recognize those who can handle syllogisms aright. But when I have to deal with life, how do I behave? Sometimes I call a thing good, sometimes evil. And the reason is just this, that whereas I have knowledge of syllogisms, I have no knowledge or experience of life.

CHAPTER IV

TO THE MAN CAUGHT IN ADULTERY

WHEN Epictetus was saying that man is born for mutual trust, and he who overthrows this overthrows the quality peculiar to man, there came in one of those who are reputed scholars, a man who had once been caught committing adultery in the city. If, said Epictetus, we put away this trust, for which we are born, and plot against our neighbour's wife, what are we doing? Are we not pulling down and destroying? Whom? The man of trust, of honour, of piety. Is this all? Are we not overthrowing neighbourly feeling, friendship, the city itself? What position are we taking up?

How am I to treat you, my fellow man? As a neighbour? As a friend? Of what kind? As a citizen? What trust am I to put in you? No doubt, if you were a piece of pottery, so cracked that you could not be used for anything, you would be cast out on the dunghill, and no one would stoop to take you thence: what shall we do with you then, if being a man you can fill no place becoming to a man? Granted that you cannot hold the position of a friend, can you hold that of a slave? And who will trust you? Will you not then consent to be cast upon a dunghill yourself as a useless vessel, as a thing for the dunghill?

Will you complain, 'No man pays any attention to me, a man and a scholar'?

Of course, for you are bad and useless. Wasps might as well be indignant because no one heeds them, but all avoid them and any one who can strikes and crushes them. Your sting is such that you cause pain and trouble to any one you strike with it. What would you have us do to you? There is no place to put you.

What then? Is it not true that 'women are common property by nature'? I agree, for the sucking-pig is the common property of those who are bidden to the feast. Very well, when it has been cut into portions, come, if you see fit, and snatch the portion of the guest who sits next you, steal it secretly or slip your hand over it and taste it, or if you cannot snatch any of the flesh rub your fingers on the fat and lick them. A fine companion you are for a feast or a dinner, worthy of Socrates indeed!

Again, is not the theatre common to all citizens? When they are seated there, come, if you see fit, and turn one of them out. In the same way you may say that women are common property by nature. But when the law-giver, like the giver of the feast, has apportioned them, will you not look for your own portion instead of stealing what is another's and guzzling that?

'Yes, but I am a scholar and understand Archedemus.'

Well then, understand Archedemus, be an adulterer and a man of broken trust, a wolf or an ape instead of a man; for what is there to hinder you?

CHAPTER V

HOW A CAREFUL LIFE IS COMPATIBLE WITH A NOBLE SPIRIT

MATERIAL things are indifferent, but how we handle them is not indifferent.

How then is one to maintain the constant and tranquil mind, and therewith the careful spirit which is not random or hasty?

You can do it if you imitate those who play dice. Counters and dice are indifferent: how do I know what is going to turn up? My business is to use what does turn up with diligence and skill. In like manner this is the principal business of life: distinguish between things, weigh them one against the other, and say, 'External things are not in my power, my will is my own. Where am I to seek what is good and what is evil? Within me, among my own possessions.' You must never use the word good or evil or benefit or injury or any such word, in connexion with other men's possessions.

'Do you mean then that outward things are to be used without care?'

By no means. For this again is evil for the will and unnatural to it. They must be used with care, for their use is not a matter of indifference, but at the same time with constancy and tranquillity, for in themselves they are indifferent. For where the true value of things is concerned, no one can hinder or compel me. I am subject to hindrance and compulsion only in matters which lie out of my power to win, which are neither good nor evil, but they may be dealt with well or ill, and this rests with me.

It is difficult to unite and combine these qualities—the diligence of a man who devotes himself to material things, and the constancy of one who disregards them—yet not impossible. Otherwise it would be impossible to be happy. We act very much as if we were on a voyage. What can I do? I can choose out the helmsman, the sailors, the day, the moment. Then a storm arises. What do I care? I have fulfilled my task: another has now to act, the helmsman. Suppose even the ship goes down. What have I to do then? I do only what lies in my power, drowning, if drown I must, without fear, not crying out or accusing heaven, for I know that what is born must needs also perish. For I am not immortal, but a man, a part of the universe as an hour is part of the day. Like the hour I must be here and like an hour pass away. What matters it then to me how I pass, by drowning or by fever, for by some such means I must needs pass away?

You will see that those who play ball with skill behave so. No one of them discusses whether the ball is good or bad, but only how to strike it and how to receive it. Therefore balanced play consists in this—skill, speed, good judgement consist in this—that while I cannot catch the ball, even if I spread my gown for it, the expert catches it if I throw it. But if we catch or strike the ball with flurry or fear, what is the good of the game? How will any one stick to the game and see how it works out? One will say, 'Strike', and another, 'Do not strike', and another, 'You have had one stroke.' This surely is fighting instead of playing.

In that sense Socrates knew how to play the game.

'What do you mean?'

He knew how to play in the court. 'Tell me, Anytus,' said he, 'in what way you say that I disbelieve in God. What do you think that divinities are? Are they not either children of the gods, or the mixed offspring of men and gods?' And when Anytus agreed, he said, 'Who then do you think can believe in the existence of mules and not in asses?' [Plato, *Apology*, 27c] He was like one playing at ball. What then was the ball that he played with? Life, imprisonment, exile, taking poison, being deprived of his wife, leaving his children orphans. These were the things he played with, but none the less he played and tossed the ball with balance. So we ought to play the game, so to speak, with all possible care and skill, but treat the ball itself as indifferent. A man must certainly cultivate skill in regard to some outward things: he need not accept a thing for its own sake, but he should show his skill in regard to it, whatever it be. In the same way the weaver does not make fleeces, but devotes himself to dealing with them in whatever form he receives them. Sustenance and property are given you by Another, who can take them away from you too, yes and your bit of a body as well.

It is for you, then, to take what is given you and make the most of it. Then if you come off without harm, others who meet you will rejoice with you in your safety, but the man who has a good eye for conduct, if he sees that you behaved here with honour, will praise you and rejoice with you: but if he sees a man has saved his life by acting dishonourably, he will do the opposite. For where a man can rejoice with reason, his neighbour can rejoice with him also.

How is it then that some external things are described as natural and some as unnatural? It is because we regard ourselves as detached from the rest of the universe. For the foot (for instance), I shall say it is natural to be clean, but if you take it as a foot and not as a detached thing, it will be fitting for it to walk in the mud and tread upon thorns and sometimes to be cut off for the sake of the whole body: or else it will cease to be a foot. We must hold exactly the same sort of view about ourselves.

What are you? A man. If you regard man as a detached being, it is natural for him to live to old age, to be rich, to be healthy. But if you regard him as a man and a part of a larger whole, that whole makes it fitting that at one moment you should fall ill, at another go a voyage and risk your life, and at another be at your wit's end, and, it may be, die before your time. Why then are you indignant? Do you not know that, just as the foot spoke of if viewed apart will cease to be a foot, so you will cease to be a man? For what is a man? A part of a city, first a part of the City in which gods and men are incorporate, and secondly of that city which has the next claim to be called so, which is a small copy of the City universal.

'What,' you say, 'am I now to be put on my trial?'

Is another then to have a fever, another to go a voyage, another die, another be condemned? I say it is impossible in a body like ours, in this enveloping space, in this common life, that events of this sort should not happen, one to this man and another to that. It is your business then to take what fate brings and deal with what happens, as is fitting. Suppose then the judge says, 'I will judge you to be a wrongdoer'; you reply, 'May it go well with you! I did my part, and it is for you to see if you have done yours: for the judge's part too, do not forget, has its own danger!'

CHAPTER VI

ON WHAT IS MEANT BY 'INDIFFERENT' THINGS

TAKE a given hypothetical proposition. In itself it is indifferent, but your judgement upon it is not indifferent, but is either knowledge, or mere opinion, or delusion. In the same way though life is indifferent, the way you deal with it is not indifferent. Therefore, when you are told 'These things also are indifferent', do not be careless, and when you are urged to be careful, do not show a mean spirit and be over-awed by material things.

It is a good thing to know what you can do and what you are prepared for, that in matters where you are not prepared, you may keep quiet and not be vexed if others have the advantage of you there. For when it is a question of syllogisms, you in your turn will expect to have the advantage, and if they are vexed with this you will console them with the words, 'I learnt them, but you did not. So when acquired dexterity is needed it is for you in your turn not to seek what only practice can give: leave that to those who have acquired the knack, and be content yourself to show constancy.

'Go and salute such an one.'

I have saluted him.

'How?'

In no mean spirit.

'But his house was shut upon you.'

Yes, for I have not learnt to enter by the window: when I find the door shut, I must either retire or go in by the window.

'But again one says, "Talk to him."'

I do talk to him.

'How?'

In no mean spirit.

Suppose you did not get what you wanted? Surely that was his business and not yours. Why then do you claim what is another's? If you always remember what is yours and what is not yours, you will never be put to confusion. Therefore Chrysippus well says, 'As long as the consequences are unknown to me, I always hold fast to what is better adapted to secure what is natural, for God Himself created me with the faculty of choosing what is natural.' Nay, if I really knew that it was ordained for me now to be ill, I should wish to be ill; for the foot too, if it had a mind, would wish to get muddy.

For instance, why do ears of corn grow? Is it not that they may ripen in the sun? And if they are ripened is it not that they may be reaped, for they are not things apart? If they had feelings then, ought they to pray never to be reaped at any time? But this is a curse upon corn—to pray that it should never be reaped. In like manner know that you are cursing men when you pray for them not to die: it is like a prayer not to be ripened, not to be reaped. But we men, being creatures whose fate it is to be reaped, are also made aware of this very fact, that we are destined for reaping, and so we are angry; for we do not know who we are, nor have we studied human things as those who are skilled in horses study the concerns of horses.

But Chrysantas, when he was about to strike the enemy, and heard the bugle sounding the retreat, desisted: so convinced was he that it was more to his advantage to do the general's bidding than his own. But not a man of us, even when necessity calls, is willing to obey her easily, but we bear what comes upon us with tears and groans, and we call it 'circumstances'.

What do you mean by 'circumstances', fellow men? If you mean by 'circumstances' what surrounds you, everything is circumstance: if you use the term in the sense of hardships, how is it a hardship that what was born should be destroyed? The instrument of destruction is a sword or a wheel or the sea or a potsherd or a tyrant. What matters it to you, by what road you are to go down to Hades? All roads are alike. But, if you will hear the truth, the road the tyrant sends you is shorter. No tyrant ever took six months to execute a man, but a fever often takes a year to kill one. All these complaints are mere noise and vanity of idle phrases.

'In Caesar's presence my life is in danger.'

But am not I in equal danger, dwelling in Nicopolis, where earthquakes are so many? And you too, when you sail across the Adriatic, are you not in danger of your life?

'Yes, but in thought too I am in danger.'

Your thought? How can that be? Who can compel you to think against your will? The thought of others? How can it be any danger to you for others to have false ideas?

'Yes, but I am in danger of being banished.'

What is being banished? Is it being elsewhere than in Rome?

'Yes, suppose I am sent to Gyara?'

If it makes for your good, you will go: if not, you have a place to go to instead of Gyara, a place whither he who is sending you to Gyara will also go whether he will or no. Why then do you go to Rome as though it meant so much? It is not much compared with your preparation for it: so that a youth of fine feeling may say, 'It was not worth this price—to have heard so many lectures and written so many exercises, and sat at the feet of an old man of no great merit.'

There is only one thing for you to remember, that is, the distinction between what is yours and what is not yours. Never lay claim to anything that is not your own. Tribunal and prison are distinct places, one high, the other low; but your will, if you choose to keep it the same in both, may be kept the same. So we shall emulate Socrates, but only when we can write songs of triumph in prison. As for our condition up till now, I doubt whether we should have borne with one who should say to us in prison, 'Would you like me to recite to you songs of triumph?'

'Why do you trouble me? Do you not know the ills which beset me? for this is my state.'

What is it?

'I am at the point of death.'

Yes, but are other men going to be immortal?

CHAPTER VII

HOW TO CONSULT DIVINERS

MANY of us often neglect acts which are fitting because we consult the diviners out of season. What can the diviner see more than death or danger or disease or generally things of that sort? If then I have to risk my life for a friend, if even it is fitting for me to die for him, how can it be in season for me to consult a diviner? Have I not within me the diviner who has told me the true nature of good and evil, who has expounded the signs of both? What need have I then of the flesh of victims or the flight of birds? Can I bear with him when he says, 'This is expedient for you'? Does he know what is expedient, does he know what is good, has he learnt signs to distinguish between good things and bad, like the signs in the flesh of victims? If he knows the signs of good and evil, he knows also the signs of things noble and shameful, just and unjust. It is yours, man, to tell me what is portended—life or death, poverty or wealth; but whether this is expedient or inexpedient I am not going to inquire of you.

Why do you not lay down the law in matters of grammar? Are you going to do it here then, where all mankind are at sea and in conflict with one another? Therefore that was a good answer that the lady made who wished to send the shipload of supplies to Gratilla in exile, when one said, 'Domitian will take them away': 'I would rather', she said, 'that Domitian should take them away than that I should not send them.'

What then leads us to consult diviners so constantly? Cowardice, fear of events. That is why we flatter the diviners.

'Master, shall I inherit from my father?'

'Let us see: let us offer sacrifice.'

'Yes, master, as fortune wills.'

When he says, 'You shall inherit', we give thanks to him as though we had received the inheritance from him. That is why they go on deluding us.

What must we do then? We must come without the will to get or the will to avoid, just as the wayfarer asks the man he meets which of two ways leads anywhere, not wanting the right hand to be the road rather than the left, for he does not wish to go one particular road, but the road which leads to his goal. We ought to approach God as we approach a guide, dealing with Him as we deal with our eyes, not beseeching them to show us one sort of things rather than another, but accepting the impressions of things as they are shown us. But instead of that we tremble and get hold of the augur and appeal to him as if he were a god and say, 'Master, have pity, suffer me to come off safe.'

Slave, do you not wish for what is better for you? Is anything better than what seems good to God? Why do you do all that in you lies to corrupt the judge, and pervert your counsellor?

CHAPTER VIII

WHAT IS THE TRUE NATURE OF THE GOOD

GOD is beneficent, but the good also is beneficent. It is natural therefore that the true nature of the good should be in the same region as the true nature of God. What then is the nature of God? Is it flesh? God forbid. Land? God forbid. Fame? God forbid. It is intelligence, knowledge, right reason. In these then and nowhere else seek the true nature of the good. Do you look for it in a plant? No. Or in an irrational creature? No. If then you seek it in what is rational why do you seek it elsewhere than in what distinguishes it from irrational things? Plants have not the faculty of dealing with impressions; therefore you do not predicate 'good' of them.

The good then demands power to deal with impressions. Is that all it demands? If that be all, you must say that other animals also are capable of good and of happiness and unhappiness. But you do not say so and you are right, for whatever power they may have to deal with impressions, they have not the power to understand how they do so, and with good reason, for they are subservient to others, and are not of primary importance.

Take the ass, for instance, is it born to be of primary importance? No; it is born because we had need of a back able to bear burdens. Nay, more, we had need that it should walk; therefore it has further received the power of dealing with impressions, for else it could not have walked. Beyond that its powers cease. But if the ass itself had received the power to understand how it deals with impressions, then it is plain that reason would have required that it should not have been subject to us or have supplied these needs, but should have been our equal and like ourselves. Will you not then seek the true nature of the good in that, the want of which makes you refuse to predicate good of other things?

'What do you mean? Are not they too God's works?'

They are, but not His principal works, nor parts of the Divine. But you are a principal work, a fragment of God Himself, you have in yourself a part of Him. Why then are you ignorant of your high birth? Why do you not know whence you have come? Will you not remember, when you eat, who you are that eat, and whom you are feeding, and the same in your relations with women? When you take part in society, or training, or conversation, do you not know that it is God you are nourishing and training? You bear God about with you, poor wretch, and know it not. Do you think I speak of some external god of silver or gold? No, you bear Him about within you and are unaware that you are defiling Him with unclean thoughts and foul actions. If an image of God were present, you would not dare to do any of the things you do; yet when God Himself is present within you and sees and hears all things, you are not ashamed of thinking and acting thus: O slow to understand your nature, and estranged from God!

Again, when we send a young man from school to the world of action, why is it that we fear that he may do something amiss—in eating, in relations with women, that he may be humbled by wearing rags, or puffed up by fine clothes?

He does not know the God that is in him, he knows not in whose company he is going. Can we allow him to say, 'I would fain have you with me'? Have you not God there? and, having Him, do you look for any one else? Will He tell you anything different from this? Why, if you were a statue wrought by Phidias—his Zeus or his Athena—you would have remembered what you are and the Craftsman who made you, and if you had any intelligence, you would have tried to do nothing unworthy of him who made you or of yourself, and to bear yourself becomingly in men's eyes. But as it is, do you, whom Zeus has made, for that reason take no thought what manner of man you will show yourself? Yet what comparison is there between the one artificer and the other or the one work and the other? What work of art, for instance, has in itself the faculties of which it gives indication in its structure? Is it not stone or bronze or gold or ivory? Even the Athena of Phidias having once for all stretched out her hand and received the Victory upon it stands thus for all time, but the works of God are endowed with movement and breath, and have the faculty of dealing with impressions and of testing them.

When this Craftsman has made you, do you dishonour his work? Nay, more, He not only made you, but committed you as a trust to yourself and none other. Will you not remember this, but even dishonour the trust committed to you?

If God had committed some orphan to your care, would you have neglected him so? Yet He has entrusted your own self to you and He says, 'I had none other more trustworthy than you: keep this man for me such as he is born to be, modest, faithful, high-minded, undismayed, free from passion and tumult.' After that, do you refuse to keep him so?

But they will say, 'Where has this man got his high looks and his lofty countenance?'

Nay, I have not got them yet as I ought: for as yet I have not confidence in what I have learnt and assented to, I still fear my own weakness. Only let me gain confidence and then you shall see a proper aspect and a proper bearing, then I will show you the statue as it is when it is finished and polished. What think you? That this means proud looks? Heaven forbid! Does Zeus of Olympia wear proud looks? No, but his gaze is steadfast, as his should be who is to say:

For my word cannot be taken back, nor can it deceive.

[Homer, *Iliad,* I. 256]

Such will I show myself to you—faithful, self-respecting, noble, free from tumult.

'Do you mean, free from death and old age and disease?'

No, but as one who dies as a god, and who bears illness like a god. These are my possessions, these my faculties; all others are beyond me. I will show you the sinews of a philosopher.

'What do you mean by sinews?'

Will to achieve that fails not, will to avoid that falls not into evil, impulse to act appropriately, strenuous purpose, assent that is not precipitate. This is what you shall see.

CHAPTER IX

THAT WE ADOPT THE PROFESSION OF THE PHILOSOPHER WHEN WE CANNOT FULFIL THAT OF A MAN

It is no ordinary task merely to fulfil man's promise. For what is Man? A rational animal, subject to death. At once we ask, from what does the rational element distinguish us? From wild beasts. And from what else? From sheep and the like. Look to it then that you do nothing like a wild beast, else you destroy the Man in you and fail to fulfil his promise. See that you do not act like a sheep, or else again the Man in you perishes.

You ask how we act like sheep?

When we consult the belly, or our passions, when our actions are random or dirty or inconsiderate, are we not falling away to the state of sheep? What do we destroy? The faculty of reason. When our actions are combative, mischievous, angry, and rude, do we not fall away and become wild beasts? In a word, some of us are great beasts, and others are small but base-natured beasts, which give occasion to say, 'Nay, rather let me be food for a lion.' All these are actions by which the calling of man is destroyed.

What makes a complex proposition be what it is? It must fulfil its promise: it keeps its character only if the parts it is composed of are true. What makes a disjunctive proposition? It must fulfil its purport. Is not the same true of flutes, lyre, horse, and dog? Is it surprising then that man too keeps or loses his nature on the same principle? Each man is strengthened and preserved by the exercise of the functions that correspond to his nature, the carpenter by carpentering, the grammarian by studies in grammar. If a man gets the habit of writing ungrammatically, his art is bound to be destroyed and perish. In the same way the modest man is made by modest acts and ruined by immodest acts, the man of honour keeps his character by honest acts and loses it by dishonest. So again men of the opposite character are strengthened by the opposite actions: the shameless man by shamelessness, the dishonest by dishonesty, the slanderous by slander, the ill-tempered by ill-temper, the miser by grasping at more than he gives. That is why philosophers enjoin upon us 'not to be content with learning only, but to add practice as well and then training'. For we have acquired wrong habits in course of years and have adopted for our use conceptions opposite to the true, and therefore if we do not adopt true conceptions for our use we shall be nothing else but interpreters of judgements which are not our own.

Of course any one of us can discourse for the moment on what is good and what is bad: as thus, 'Of things that are, some are good, some bad, some indifferent; good are virtues and things that have part in virtues; evil are the opposite; indifferent are wealth, health, reputation.' And then if some loud noise disturbs us while we are speaking or one of the bystanders laughs at us, we are put out of countenance. Philosopher, where are those principles you were talking of? Whence did you fetch them forth to utter? From the lips and no further.

These principles are not your own: why do you make a mess of them? Why do you gamble with things of highest moment? It is one thing (to use an illustration) to put bread and wine away into a store-cupboard, and another thing to eat. What you eat is digested and distributed, and is turned into sinews, flesh, bones, blood, complexion, breath. What you store away you have at hand and can show to others at will, but it does you no good except for the mere name of having it. What is the good of expounding these doctrines any more than those of another school? Sit down now and discourse on the doctrines of Epicurus, and you will soon discourse more effectively than Epicurus himself. Why then do you call yourself a Stoic, why do you deceive the world, why being a Hellene do you act the Jew? [3] Do you not see in what sense a man is called a Jew, in what sense a Syrian, in what an Egyptian? When we see a man trimming between two faiths we are wont to say, 'He is no Jew, but is acting a part', but when he adopts the attitude of mind of him who is baptized and has made his choice, then he is not only called a Jew but is a Jew indeed. So we also are but counterfeit 'baptists', Jews in name only, but really something else, with no feeling for reason, far from acting on the principles we talk of, though we pride ourselves on them as though we knew them. So, being unable to fulfil the calling of Man we adopt that of the Philosopher, a heavy burden indeed! It is as though one who could not lift ten pounds were fain to lift the stone of Ajax!

CHAPTER X

HOW THE ACTS APPROPRIATE TO MAN ARE TO BE DISCOVERED FROM THE NAMES HE BEARS

CONSIDER who you are. First, a Man; that is, one who has nothing more sovereign than will, but all else subject to this, and will itself free from slavery or subjection. Consider then from what you are parted by reason. You are parted from wild beasts, you are parted from sheep. On these terms you are a citizen of the universe and a part of it, not one of those marked for service, but of those fitted for command; for you have the faculty to understand the divine governance of the universe and to reason on its sequence. What then is the calling of a Citizen? To have no personal interest, never to think about anything as though he were detached, but to be like the hand or the foot, which, if they had the power of reason and understood the order of nature, would direct every impulse and every process of the will by reference to the whole. That is why it is well said by philosophers that 'if the good man knew coming events beforehand he would help on nature, even if it meant working with disease, and death and maiming', for he would realize that by the ordering of the universe this task is allotted him, and that the whole is more commanding than the part and the city than the citizen. 'But seeing that we do not know beforehand, it is appropriate that we should hold fast to the things that are by nature more fit to be chosen; for indeed we are born for this.'

Next remember that you are a Son. What part do we expect a son to play? His part is to count all that is his as his father's, to obey him in all things, never to speak ill of him to any, nor to say or do anything to harm him, to give way to him and yield him place in all things, working with him so far as his powers allow.

Next know that you are also a Brother. For this part too you are bound to show a spirit of concession and obedience; and to speak kindly, and not to claim against another anything that is outside the will, but gladly to sacrifice those things, that you may gain in the region where your will has control. For look what a thing it is to gain good nature at the price of a lettuce, if it so chance, or the surrender of a chair: what a gain is that!

Next, if you are a member of a city council, remember that you are a councillor; if young, that you are young; if old, that you are old; if a father, that you are a father. For each of these names, if properly considered, suggests the acts appropriate to it. But if you go and disparage your brother, I tell you that you are forgetting who you are and what is your name. I say, if you were a smith and used your hammer wrong, you would have forgotten the smith; but if you forget the brother's part and turn into an enemy instead of a brother, are you going to imagine that you have undergone no change? If instead of man, a gentle and sociable creature, you have become a dangerous, aggressive, and biting brute, have you lost nothing? Do you think you must lose cash in order to suffer damage? Does no other sort of loss damage man? If you lost skill in grammar or music you would count the loss as damage; if you are going to lose honour and dignity and gentleness, do you count it as nothing? Surely those other losses are due to some external cause outside our will, but these are due to ourselves. Those qualities it is no honour to have and no dishonour to lose, but these you cannot lack or lose without dishonour, reproach, and disaster.

What does he lose who is the victim of unnatural lust? He loses his manhood. And the agent of such lust, what does he lose? He loses his manhood like the other, and much besides. What does the adulterer lose? He loses the man of honour and self-control, the gentleman, the citizen, the neighbour. What does the angry man lose? Something else. The man who fears? Something else. No one is evil without destruction and loss.

If on the other hand you look for loss in paltry pence, all the men I have mentioned are without loss or damage, if it so chance, nay they actually receive gain and profit, when they get cash by any of these actions. But notice, that if you make money the standard in everything, you will not count even the man who loses his nose as having suffered injury.

'Yes, I do,' he says, 'for his body is mutilated.'

Well, but does the man who has lost, not his nose but his sense of smell, lose nothing? Is there no faculty of the mind, which brings gain to him that gets it and hurt to him that loses it?

'What can possibly be the faculty you mean?'

Have we no natural sense of honour?

'We have.'

Does he that destroys this suffer no damage, no deprivation, no loss of what belongs to him? Have we not a natural faculty of trust, a natural gift of affection, of beneficence, of mutual toleration? Are we then to count the man who suffers himself to be injured in regard to these as free from loss and damage?

'What conclusion do you draw? Am I not to harm him who harmed me?'

First consider what 'harm' means and remember what you heard from the philosophers. For if good lies in the will and evil also lies in the will, look whether what you are saying does not come to this: 'What do you mean? As he harmed himself by doing me a wrong, am I not to harm myself by doing him a wrong?' Why then do we not look at things in this light? When we suffer some loss in body or property, we count it hurt: is there no hurt, when we suffer loss in respect of our will?

Of course the man who is deceived or the man who does a wrong has no pain in his head or his eye or his hip, nor does he lose his estate; and these are the things we care for, nothing else. But we take no concern whatever whether our will is going to be kept honourable and trustworthy or shameless and faithless, except only so far as we discuss it in the lecture-room, and therefore so far as our wretched discussions go we make some progress, but beyond them not the least.

CHAPTER XI

WHAT IS THE BEGINNING OF PHILOSOPHY

The beginning of philosophy with those who approach it in the right way and by the door is a consciousness of one's own weakness and want of power in regard to necessary things. For we come into the world with no innate conception of a right-angled triangle, or of a quarter-tone or of a semi-tone, but we are taught what each of these means by systematic instruction; and therefore those who are ignorant of these things do not think that they know them. On the other hand every one has come into the world with an innate conception as to good and bad, noble and shameful, becoming and unbecoming, happiness and unhappiness, fitting and inappropriate, what is right to do and what is wrong. Therefore we all use these terms and try to fit our preconceived notions to particular facts. 'He did nobly', 'dutifully', 'undutifully'. 'He was unfortunate', 'he was fortunate'; 'he is unjust', 'he is just.' Which of us refrains from these phrases? Which of us puts off using them until he is taught them, just as men who have no knowledge of lines or sounds refrain from talking of them? The reason is that on the subject in question we come into the world with a certain amount of teaching, so to say, already given us by nature; to this basis of knowledge we have added our own fancies.

'Why!' says he; 'do I not know what is noble and what is shameful? Have I no conception of them?'

You have.

'Do I not fit my conception to particulars?'

You do.

'Do I not fit them well then?'

There lies the whole question and there fancy comes in. For, starting with these admitted principles, men advance to the matter in dispute, applying these principles inappropriately. For if they really possessed this faculty as well, what would prevent them from being perfect? You think that you apply your preconceptions properly to particular cases; but tell me, how do you arrive at this?

I have such a conviction.

But another has a different conviction, has he not, and yet believes, as you do, that he is applying his conception rightly?

He does.

Is it possible then for you both to apply your conceptions properly in matters on which you hold contrary opinion?

It is impossible.

Can you then point us to anything beyond your own opinion which will enable us to apply our conceptions better? Does the madman do anything else but what he *thinks* right? Is this criterion then sufficient for him too?

It is not.

Come, then, let us look for something beyond personal opinion. Where shall we find it?

Here you see the beginning of philosophy, in the discovery of the conflict of men's minds with one another, and the attempt to seek for the reason of this conflict, and the condemnation of mere opinion, as a thing not to be trusted; and a search to determine whether your opinion is true, and an attempt to discover a standard, just as we discover the balance to deal with weights and the rule to deal with things straight and crooked. This is the beginning of philosophy.

'Are all opinions right which all men hold?'

Nay, how is it possible for contraries to be both right?

'Well, then, not all opinions, but our opinions?'

Why ours, rather than those of the Syrians or the Egyptians, or the personal opinion of myself or of this man or that?

'Why indeed?'

So then, what each man thinks is not sufficient to make a thing so: for in dealing with weights and measures we are not satisfied with mere appearance, but have found a standard to determine each. Is there, then, no standard here beyond opinion? It is impossible surely that things most necessary among men should be beyond discovery and beyond proof?

There is a standard then. Then, why do we not seek it and find it, and having found it use it hereafter without fail, never so much as 'stretching out our finger' without it? For it is this standard, I suppose, the discovery of which relieves from madness those who wrongly use personal opinion as their only measure, and enables us thereafter to start from known principles, clearly defined, and so to apply our conceptions to particulars in definite and articulate form.

What subject, I might ask, lies before us for our present discussion?

'Pleasure.'

Submit it to the rule, put it in the balance. Ought the good to be something which is worthy to inspire confidence and trust?

'It ought.'

Is it proper to have confidence in anything which is insecure?

'No.'

Has pleasure, then, any certainty in it?

'No.'

Away with it then! Cast it from the scales and drive it far away from the region of good things. But if your sight is not keen, and you are not satisfied with one set of scales, try another.

Is it proper to be elated at what is good?

'It is.'

Is it proper, then, to be elated at the pleasure of the moment? Be careful how you say that it is proper. If you do, I shall not count you worthy of the scales.

Thus things are judged and weighed if we have standards ready to test them: and in fact the work of philosophy is to investigate and firmly establish such standards; and the duty of the good man is to proceed to apply the decisions arrived at.

CHAPTER XII

ON THE ART OF DISCUSSION

OUR philosophers have precisely defined what a man must learn in order to know how to argue: but we are still quite unpractised in the proper use of what we have learnt. Give any one of us you like an unskilled person to argue with, and he does not discover how to deal with him: he just rouses the man for a moment, and then if he answers him in the wrong key he cannot deal with him any longer: he either reviles him or laughs at him ever after, and says, 'He is an ignoramus, there is nothing to be got out of him.'

But the true guide, when he finds a man wandering, leads him to the right road, instead of leaving him with a gibe or an insult. So should you do. Only show him the truth and you will see that he follows. But so long as you do not show it him, do not laugh at him, but rather realize your own incapacity.

Now how did Socrates proceed? He compelled the man who was conversing with him to be his witness, and needed no witness besides. Therefore he was able to say: 'I am satisfied with my opponent as a witness, and let every one else alone: and I do not take the votes of other people, but only of him who is arguing with me.' [Plato, *Gorgias*, 474a] For he drew out so clearly the consequences of a man's conceptions that every one realized the contradiction and abandoned it.

'Does the man who envies rejoice in his envy?'

'Not at all; he is pained rather than pleased.'

Thus he rouses his neighbour by contradiction.

'Well, does envy seem to you to be a feeling of pain at evil things? Yet how can there be envy of things evil?'

So he makes his opponent say that envy is pain felt at good things.

'Again, can a man envy things which do not concern him?'

'Certainly not.'

In this way he made the conception full and articulate, and so went away. He did not say, 'Define me envy', and then, when the man defined it, 'You define it ill, for the terms of the definition do not correspond to the subject defined.' Such phrases are technical and therefore tiresome to the lay mind, and hard to follow, yet you and I cannot get away from them. We are quite unable to rouse the ordinary man's attention in a way which will enable him to follow his own impressions and so arrive at admitting or rejecting this or that. And therefore those of us who are at all cautious naturally give the subject up, when we become aware of this incapacity; while the mass of men, who venture at random into this sort of enterprise, muddle others and get muddled themselves, and end by abusing their opponents and getting abused in return, and so leave the field. But the first quality of all in Socrates, and the most characteristic, was that he never lost his temper in argument, never uttered anything abusive, never anything insolent, but bore with abuse from others and quieted strife. If you would get to know what a faculty he had in this matter, read the Banquet of Xenophon and you will see how many strifes he has brought to an end. Therefore the poets too with good reason have praised this gift most highly:

And straightway with skill he brought to rest a mighty quarrel.

[Hesiod, *Theogony*, 87]

What follows? The occupation is not a very safe one nowadays, and especially in Rome. For he who pursues it will certainly not have to do it in a corner, but he must go up to a consular or a rich man, if it so chance, and ask him: 'You there, can you tell me to whose care you trust your horses?'

'Yes.'

Do you trust them to a chance comer and one unskilled in horse-keeping?

'Certainly not.'

Again, tell me to whom you trust your gold or your silver or your clothes.

'Not to a chance comer either.'

And your body—have you ever thought of trusting that to anybody to look after it?

'Certainly.'

He too, no doubt, is one skilled in the art of training or of medicine, is he not?

'Certainly he is.'

Are these then your best possessions or have you got something besides, better than all?

'What can you mean?'

I mean, of course, that which makes use of all these possessions and tests each one, and thinks about them.

'Do you mean the soul?'

You are right; that is exactly what I do mean.

'Yes, I certainly think that this is a better possession than all the rest.'

Can you tell me, then, in what manner you have taken care of your soul? for it is not likely that one so wise as you, and of such position in the state, should lightly and recklessly allow the best possession you have to be neglected and go to ruin.

'Certainly not.'

Well, have you taken care of it yourself? Did any one teach you how, or did you find out for yourself?

When you do this, the danger is, you will find, that first he will say: 'My good sir, what concern is it of yours? Are you my master?' Then, if you persist in annoying him he will lift his hand and give you a drubbing.

That (says Epictetus) was a pursuit I had a keen taste for once, before I was reduced to my present condition.

CHAPTER XIII

CONCERNING ANXIETY

When I see a man in a state of anxiety, I say, 'What can this man want? If he did not want something which is not in his power, how could he still be anxious? It is for this reason that one who sings to the lyre is not anxious when he is performing by himself, but when he enters the theatre, even if he has a very good voice and plays well: for he not only wants to perform well, but also to win a great name, and that is beyond his own control.

In fact, where he has knowledge there he has confidence. Bring in any unskilled person you like, and he pays no heed to him. On the other hand he is anxious whenever he has no knowledge and has made no study of the subject. What does this mean? He does not know what 'the people' is, nor what its praise is worth: he has learnt to strike the bottom note or the top note, but he does not know what the praise of the multitude is, nor what value it has in life; he has made no study of that. So he is bound to tremble and grow pale.

When I see a man, then, in this state of fear I cannot say that he is no performer with the lyre, but I can say something else of him, and not one thing but many. And first of all I call him a stranger and say, This man does not know where in the world he is; though he has been with us so long, he does not know the laws and customs of the City—what he may do and what he may not do—no, nor has he called in a lawyer at any time to tell him and explain to him what are the requirements of the law. Of course he does not draw up a will without knowing how he ought to draw it up, or without calling in one who knows, nor does he lightly put his seal to a guarantee or give a written security; but he calls in no lawyer when he is exercising the will to get and will to avoid, impulse and intention and purpose. What do I mean by 'having no lawyer'? I mean that he does not know that he is wishing to have what is not given him, and wishing not to have what he cannot avoid, and he does not know what is his own and what is not his own. If he did know, he would never feel hindrance or constraint or anxiety; how could he? Does any one fear about things which are not evil?

'No.'

Or again about things which are evil but are in his power to prevent?

'Certainly not.'

If, then, nothing beyond our will's control is either good or evil, and everything within our will's control depends entirely on ourselves, so that no one can take any such thing away from us or win it for us against our will, what room is left for anxiety? Yet we are anxious for our bit of a body, for our bit of property, for what Caesar will think, but are not anxious at all for what is within us. Am I anxious about not conceiving a false thought? No, for that depends on myself.

Or about indulging an impulse contrary to nature?

No, not about this either. So, when you see a man pale, just as the physician, judging from his colour, says, 'This man's spleen is out of order, or that man's liver', so do you say, 'This man is disordered in the will to get and the will to avoid, he is not in the right way, he is feverish'; for nothing else changes the complexion and causes a man to tremble and his teeth to chatter,

and droop the knee and sink upon his feet.

[Homer, *Iliad*, XIII, 281]

Therefore Zeno was not distressed when he was going to meet Antigonus, for Antigonus had no authority over any of the things that Zeno admired, and Zeno paid no attention to the possessions of Antigonus. Antigonus was anxious when he was going to meet Zeno, and with good reason, for he wanted to please him, and this lay beyond his control; but Zeno did not wish to please Antigonus, any more than any artist cares to please one who has no skill.

Do I want to please you? Why should I? Do you know the standards by which man judges man? Have you made it your study to learn what a good man is and what a bad man is, and what makes each of them so? Why, then, are you not good yourself?

'Not good? What do you mean?' he replies.

Why, no good man whines or groans or laments, no good man grows pale or trembles or says, 'How will he receive me? What hearing will he give me?'

Slave, he will do as he thinks good. What concern have you in what does not belong to you? Is it not his fault if he gives a bad reception to what you offer?

'His fault, certainly.'

But can the fault be one man's and the harm another's?

'No.'

Why, then, are you anxious about another's concerns?

'Nay, but I am anxious to know how I am to address him.'

What, is it not in your power to address him as you will?

'Yes, but I am afraid I may lose my self-possession.'

Are you afraid of losing your self-possession when you are going to write the name Dion?

'Certainly not.'

What is the reason? Is it not, that you have practised writing?

Of course it is. Or again, when you are about to read, would you not be in like case?

'Exactly.'

What is the reason? The reason is that every art contains within it an element of strength and confidence. Have you not practised speaking, then? What else did you study at school? You studied syllogisms and variable arguments. What for? Was it not that you might converse with skill, and does not 'with skill' mean in good season, with security and good sense, and, more than that, without failure or hindrance, and, to crown all, with confidence?

'Yes.'

Well, if you are a rider and have to confront a man on foot in the plain, where you have the advantage of practice and he has not, are you anxious?

'Nay, but he has power to put me to death.'

Miserable man, tell the truth and be not a braggart nor claim to be a philosopher. Know who are your masters. As long as you give them this hold over your body, you must follow every one who is stronger than you.

But Socrates, who spoke to the Tyrants, to his judges, and in prison, in the tone we know, had studied speaking to some purpose. So had Diogenes, who spoke in the same tone to Alexander, to Philip, to the pirates, to his purchaser. . . . Leave this to those who have made it their concern, to the confident: and do you go to your own concerns and never leave them again. Go and sit in your corner and weave syllogisms and propound them to others,

No ruler of a state is found in you.

[Author unknown]

CHAPTER XIV

ON NASO

ONCE when a Roman came in with his son and was listening to one of his lectures Epictetus said: 'This is the method of my teaching', and broke off short. And when the Roman begged him to continue, he replied:—Every art, when it is being taught, is tiresome to one who is unskilled and untried in it. The products of the arts indeed show at once the use they are made for, and most of them have an attraction and charm of their own; for though it is no pleasure to be present and follow the process by which a shoemaker learns his art, the shoe itself is useful and a pleasant thing to look at as well. So too the process by which a carpenter learns is very tiresome to the unskilled person who happens to be by, but his work shows the use of his art. This you will see still more in the case of music, for if you are by when a man is being taught you will think the process of all things the most unpleasant, yet the effects of music are pleasant and delightful for unmusical persons to hear.

So with philosophy; we picture to ourselves the work of the philosopher to be something of this sort: he must bring his own will into harmony with events, in such manner that nothing which happens should happen against our will, and that we should not wish for anything to happen that does not happen. The result of this is that those who have thus ordered their life do not fail to get what they will, and do not fall into what they will to avoid: each man spends his own life free from pain, from fear, and from distraction, and maintains the natural and acquired relations which unite him to his fellows—the part of son, father, brother, citizen, husband, wife, neighbour, fellow traveller, ruler, subject.

Such is the business of the philosopher as we picture it. The next thing is that we seek how we are to achieve it. Now we see that the carpenter becomes a carpenter by learning certain things, the helmsman becomes a helmsman by learning certain things. May we, then, infer that in the sphere of conduct too it is not enough merely to wish to become good, but one must learn certain things? We have, then, to look and see what these things are. The philosophers say that the first thing one must learn is this: 'that God exists and provides for the universe, and it is impossible for a man to act or even to conceive a thought or reflection without God knowing. The next thing is to learn the true nature of the gods. For whatever their nature is discovered to be, he that is to please and obey them must needs try, so far as he can, to make himself like them.' If God is faithful, he must be faithful too; if free, he must be free too; if beneficent, he too must be beneficent: if high-minded, he must be high-minded: he must, in fact, as one who makes God his ideal, follow this out in every act and word.

'At what point, then, must we begin?'

If you attempt this task, I will tell you, that you must first understand terms.

'What? Do you imply that I do not understand terms now?'

You do not.

'How then do I use them?'

You use them as illiterate persons deal with written sounds, as cattle deal with impressions: for it is one thing to use them, and another to understand. If you think you understand them, let us take any term you like and put ourselves to the test, to see if we understand.

'But it is vexatious when one is getting old, and has served, if it so chance, one's three campaigns, to be put through an examination.' [4]

I know that as well as you. You have come to me now as if you were in want of nothing: and indeed what could you be imagined as wanting? You are rich, you have children, it may be, and a wife and many servants, the Emperor knows you, you possess many friends in Rome, you perform the acts appropriate to you, you know how to return good for good and evil for evil. What do you lack? If I show you that you lack what is most necessary and important for happiness, and that hitherto you have paid attention to everything rather than to acting appropriately, and if I conclude my criticism by saying that you do not know what God or man is, or what good or evil is, though perhaps you may bear being told of your ignorance in other ways, you cannot bear with me when I say that you do not know your own self; how can you submit to examination and abide my question? You cannot bear it at all: you go away at once in disgust. And yet what evil have I done you? Unless indeed the mirror does harm to the ugly man, by showing him what sort of man he is: unless the physician too insults the sick man, when he says to him, 'Sir, you think there is nothing wrong with you, but you are in a fever; take no food to-day and drink water'; and no one says, 'What shocking insolence!' But if you say to a man, 'There is fever in your will to get, your will to avoid is degraded, your designs are inconsistent, your impulses out of harmony with nature, your conceptions random and false', he goes away at once and says, 'He insulted me!'

Our condition may be compared to the gathering at a public festival. Cattle and oxen are brought thither for sale, and the mass of men come to buy or to sell; only some few come to look at the assembled people and see how and why the assembly gathers and who instituted it and with what object. It is just the same here, in this assembly of the world: some are like cattle and trouble themselves about nothing but their fodder, for you who busy yourselves with property and lands and servants and public offices are busy with fodder and nothing else. There are but few who come to this assembly with a desire to see what really is the meaning of the universe and Who governs it. Does no one govern it? How can that be? A city or a household cannot endure even for a brief span of time without one to govern and take charge of it, and can this great and noble frame of things be administered in such good order by mere random chance?

There is, then, One who governs it. What is His nature and how does He govern? And we, what are we, His creations, and to what work are we born? Have we any connexion and relation with Him or not? Such are the thoughts which occur to these few, and so they devote their time to this and this alone, to investigate the assembly of life before they leave it. What follows? They are laughed at by the multitude, just as in the other assembly those who look on are laughed at by those who buy and sell. Nay, the cattle themselves, if they shared our perception, would laugh at those who have made anything else but fodder the object of their wonder and regard!

CHAPTER XV

ON THOSE WHO CLING STUBBORNLY TO THEIR JUDGEMENTS

THERE are some who when they hear these precepts—that a man must be steadfast, and that the will is by nature a free thing and not subject to compulsion, whereas all else is subject to hindrance and compulsion, being in bondage and dependence—imagine that they must abide without swerving by every judgement that they have formed. No—first of all the judgement arrived at must be sound.

For I would have the body firmly braced, but it must be the firmness of health and good condition; if you show me that you have the firmness of a madman and boast of that, I shall say to you, 'Look, man, for some one to cure you.' This is not firmness, but the opposite.

Let me describe another state of mind to be found in those who hear these precepts amiss. A friend of mine, for instance, determined for no reason to starve himself. I learnt of it when he was in the third day of his fasting, and went and asked him what had happened.

'I have decided', said he.

Yes, but, for all that, say what it was that persuaded you; for if your decision was right, here we are at your side ready to help you to leave this life, but, if your decision was against reason, then change your mind.

'A man must abide by his decisions.'

What are you doing, man? Not all decisions, but right decisions. For instance, if you were convinced at the moment that it was right, abide by that opinion if you think fit, and do not change it, but say, 'one must abide by one's decisions.'

Will you not lay this foundation to begin with—that is, examine your decision and see whether it is sound or unsound, and then afterwards build on it your firmness and unshaken resolve? But if you lay a rotten and crumbling foundation you will not be able to build even a tiny building; the more courses and the stronger that you lay upon it the quicker will it collapse. You are removing from life without any reason our familiar friend, our fellow citizen in the great City and the small, and then, though you are guilty of murder and of killing one who has done no wrong, you say, 'I must abide by my decisions.' If perchance it occurred to you to kill *me*, would you be bound to abide by your decisions?

Well, I had much ado to persuade that friend to change his mind. But it is impossible to move some of the men of to-day, so that I think that I know now what I did not know before, the meaning of the familiar saying, 'A fool is not to be persuaded nor broken of his folly.' May it never be my lot to have for friend a wise fool: nothing is more difficult to handle.

'I have decided.'

So have the madmen, but the more firmly they persist in false judgements the more hellebore [5] do they require. Will you not act as the sick man should, and call in the physician? As he says, 'I am sick, master; help me: consider what I ought to do, it is for me to obey you', so you should say, 'I do not know what I ought to do, but I have come to learn.' Oh no, you say: 'Talk to me about other things; this I have decided.' Other things indeed! What is greater or more to your advantage than that you should be convinced that it is not sufficient to have decided and to refuse all change of mind? This is the firmness of madness, not of health.

'If you force me to this, I would fain die.'

Why, man, what has happened?

'I have decided.'

Lucky for me that you have not decided to kill me.

'I do not take fees.'

Why?

'I have decided.'

Let me tell you that the same energy with which you now refuse to take fees may incline you one day (what is to prevent it?) to take them and to say again, 'I have decided.'

Just as in an ailing body, which suffers from a flux, the flux inclines now to this part and now to that, so it is with a weak mind: no one can tell which way it sways, but when this swaying and drift has energy to back it, then the mischief becomes past help and remedy.

CHAPTER XVI

THAT WE DO NOT PRACTISE APPLYING OUR JUDGEMENTS ABOUT THINGS GOOD AND EVIL

WHERE lies the good?

In a man's will.

Where lies evil?

In the will.

Where is the neutral sphere?

In the region outside the will's control.

Well, now, does any one of us remember these principles outside the lecture-room? Does any man practise by himself to answer facts as he would answer questions? For instance, is it day? 'Yes.' Again, is it night? 'No.' Again, are the stars even in number? 'I cannot say.' When money is shown you have you practised giving the proper answer, that it is not a good thing? Have you trained yourself in answers like this, or only to meet fallacious arguments? Why are you surprised, then, that you surpass yourself in the sphere where you have practised, and make no progress where you are unpractised?

Why is it that the orator, though he knows that he has written a good speech, and has got by heart what he has written, and brings a pleasant voice to his task, still feels anxiety in spite of all? The reason is that merely to declaim his speech does not content him. What does he want then? To be praised by his audience. Now he has been trained to be able to declaim, but he has not been trained in regard to praise and blame. For when did he hear from any one what praise is and what blame is: what is the nature of each, what manner of praise must be pursued, and what manner of blame must be avoided? When did he go through this training in accordance with these principles?

Why, then, are you still surprised that he is superior to others in the things he has been taught, and on a level with the mass of men in the things he has not studied? He is like the singer accompanying the lyre who knows how to play, sings well, and wears a fine tunic, and yet trembles when he comes on; for though he has all this knowledge he does not know what the people is or the clamour or mockery of the people. Nay, he does not even know what this anxiety is that he is feeling, whether it depends on himself or on another, whether it can be suppressed or not. Therefore, if men praise him, he leaves the stage puffed up; if they mock him, his poor bubble of conceit is pricked and subsides.

Very much the same is our position. What do we admire? External things. What are we anxious about? External things. And yet we are at a loss to know how fears or anxiety assail us! What else can possibly happen when we count impending events as evil? We cannot be free from fear, we cannot be free from anxiety. Yet we say, 'O Lord God, how am I to be rid of anxiety?' Fool, have you no hands? Did not God make them for you? Sit still and pray forsooth, that your rheum may not flow. Nay, wipe your nose rather and do not accuse God.

What moral do I draw? Has not God given you anything in the sphere of conduct? Has He not given you endurance, has He not given you greatness of mind, has He not given you manliness? When you have these strong hands to help you, do you still seek for one to wipe your rheum away?

But we do not practise such conduct nor pay attention to it. Find me one man who cares how he is going to do a thing, who is interested not in getting something but in realizing his true nature. Who is there that when walking is interested in his own activity, or when deliberating is interested in the act of deliberation, and not in getting that for which he is planning? And then if he succeeds he is elated and says, 'What a fine plan that was of ours! Did not I tell you, my brother, that if we have thought a thing out it is bound to happen so?' But if he fails he is humbled and miserable, and cannot find anything to say about what has happened. Which of us ever called in a prophet in order to realize his true nature? Which of us ever slept in a temple of dreams for this? Name the man. Give me but one, that I may set eyes on him I have long been seeking for, the man who is truly noble and has fine feeling; be he young or old, give me one.

Why, then, do we wonder any more that, whereas we are quite at home in dealing with material things, when we come to express ourselves in action we behave basely and unseemly, are worthless, cowardly, unenduring, failures altogether? But if we kept our fear not for death or exile, but for fear itself, then we should practise to avoid what we think evil. As it is we are glib and fluent in the lecture-room, and if any paltry question arises about a point of conduct, we are capable of pursuing the subject logically; but put us to the practical test and you will find us miserable shipwrecks. Let a distracting thought occur to us and you will soon find out for what we were studying and training. The result of our want of practice is that we are always heaping up terrors and imagining things bigger than they really are. When I go a voyage, as soon as I gaze down into the deep or look round on the sea and find no land, I am beside myself, imagining that if I am wrecked I must swallow all this sea, for it never occurs to me that three quarts are enough for me. What is it alarms me? The sea? No, but my judgement about it. Again, when an earthquake happens, I imagine that the city is going to fall on me. What! Is not a tiny stone enough to knock my brains out?

What, then, are the burdens that weigh upon us and drive us out of our minds? What else but our judgements? When a man goes away and leaves the companions and the places and the society that he is used to, what else is it that weighs upon him but judgement? Children, when they cry a little because their nurse has left them, forget her as soon as they are given a bit of cake.

'Do you want us to be like children too?'

No, not at all; it is not by cake I would have you influenced, but by true judgements. What do I mean? I mean the judgements that a man must study all day long, uninfluenced by anything that does not concern him, whether it be companion or place or gymnasia, or even his own body; he must remember the law and keep this before his eyes.

What is the law of God?

To guard what is your own, not to claim what is another's; to use what is given you, not to long for anything if it be not given; if anything be taken away, to give it up at once and without a struggle, with gratitude for the time you have enjoyed it, if you would not cry for your nurse and your mammy. For what difference does it make what a man is a slave to, and what he depends on? How are you better than one who weeps for a mistress, if you break your heart for a paltry gymnasium and paltry colonnades and precious young men and that sort of occupation? Here comes a man complaining that he is not to drink the water of Dirce any more.

What! is not the Marcian water [6] as good as that of Dirce?

'Nay, but I was used to the other.'

Yes, and you will get used to this in turn. I say, if such things are going to influence you, go away and cry for it, and try to write a line like that of Euripides,

The baths of Nero and the Marcian spring.

[This line parodies Euripides, *The Phoenissae,* 368]

See how tragedy arises when fools have to face everyday events!

'When shall I see Athens again, then, and the Acropolis?'

Unhappy man, are you not content with what you see day by day? Can you set eyes on anything better or greater than the sun, the moon, the stars, the whole earth, the ocean? And if you really understand Him that governs the universe and if you carry Him about within you, do you still long for paltry stones and pretty rock? What will you do, then, when you are going to leave the very sun and moon? Shall you sit crying like little children? What were you doing, then, at school? What did you hear? What did you learn? Why did you write yourself down a philosopher when you might have written the truth, saying, 'I did a few Introductions and read Chrysippus' sayings, but I never entered the door of a philosopher. What share have I in the calling of Socrates, who lived and died so nobly, or of Diogenes? Can you imagine one of them weeping or indignant, because he is not going to see this man or that or be in Athens or in Corinth, but in Susa, if it so chance, or Ecbatana? Does he who may leave the banquet when he will and play no longer, vex himself while he stays on? Does he not stay at play just as long as it pleases him? Do you suppose the man I describe would endure interminable exile or condemnation to death?

Will you not be weaned at last, as children are, and take more solid food, and cease to cry 'nurse' and 'mammy', cries for old women's ears?

'But I shall distress them', you say, 'by departing.'

You will distress them? No, you will not distress them; what distresses them and you is judgement. What can you do then? Get rid of your judgement: theirs, if they do well, they will get rid of themselves, or they will sorrow for it and have themselves to thank. Man, be bold at last, even to despair, as the phrase is, that you may have peace and freedom and a lofty mind. Lift up your neck at last, as one released from slavery. Have courage to look up to God and say, 'Deal with me hereafter as Thou wilt, I am as one with Thee, I am Thine. I flinch from nothing so long as Thou thinkest it good. Lead me, where Thou wilt, put on me what raiment Thou wilt. Wouldst Thou have me hold office, or eschew it, stay or fly, be poor or rich? For all this I will defend Thee before men. I will show each thing in its true nature, as it is.'

Nay, stay rather in the cow's belly and wait for your mammy's milk to fill you. What would have become of Heracles, if he had stayed at home? He would have been Eurystheus, and no Heracles.

But tell me, how many friends and companions had he, as he went about the world? No nearer friend than God: and that is why he was believed to be son of Zeus, and was so. Obedient to Him, he went about the world, cleansing it of wrong and lawlessness.

Do you say you are no Heracles, nor able to get rid of other men's evils, not even a Theseus, to cleanse Attica of ills?

Cleanse your own heart, cast out from your mind, not Procrustes and Sciron, but pain, fear, desire, envy, ill will, avarice, cowardice, passion uncontrolled. These things you cannot cast out, unless you look to God alone, on Him alone set your thoughts, and consecrate yourself to His commands. If you wish for anything else, with groaning and sorrow you will follow what is stronger than you, ever seeking peace outside you, and never able to be at peace: for you seek it where it is not, and refuse to seek it where it is.

CHAPTER XVII

HOW WE MUST ADJUST OUR PRIMARY CONCEPTIONS TO PARTICULAR THINGS

WHAT is the first business of the philosopher? To cast away conceit: for it is impossible for a man to begin learning what he thinks he knows. When we go to the philosophers we all bandy phrases freely of things to be done and not to be done, of things good and bad, noble and base; we make them the ground of our praise and blame, accusation and disparagement, pronouncing judgement on noble and base conduct and distinguishing between them. But what do we go to the philosophers for? To learn in their school what we think we do not know. What is that? Principles. For we want to learn what the philosophers talk of, some of us because we think their words witty and smart, and others in hope to make profit of them. It is absurd, then, to think that a man will learn anything but what he wishes to learn, or in fact that he will make progress if he does not learn. But the mass of men are under the same delusion as Theopompus the rhetor, when he criticized Plato because he wanted to define every term. What are his words?

'Did none of us before you talk of "good" or "just," or did we use the terms vaguely and idly without understanding what each of them meant?'

Who told you, Theopompus, that we had not natural notions and primary conceptions of each of these? But it is impossible to adjust the primary conceptions to the appropriate facts, without making them articulate and without considering just this—what fact must be ranged under each conception.

You may say just the same thing, for instance, to physicians. Which of us did not use the words 'healthy' and 'diseased' before Hippocrates was born? Were those terms we used mere empty sounds? No, we have a conception of 'healthy', but we cannot apply it. Therefore one physician says, 'Take no food', and another 'Give food', and one says, 'Cut the vein', and another, 'Use the cupping-glass.' What is the reason? Nothing but incapacity to apply the conception of 'the healthy' to particulars in the proper way.

So it is here in life. Which of us does not talk of 'good' and 'bad', 'expedient' and 'inexpedient'? Which of us has not a primary conception of each of these? Is that conception, then, articulate and complete? Prove it. How am I to prove it? Apply it properly to particular facts. To begin with, Plato makes his definitions conform to the conception of 'the useful', you to the conception of 'the useless'. Is it possible, then, for both of you to be right? Of course not. Does not one man apply his primary conception of 'good' to wealth while another does not? Another applies it to pleasure, another to health. To sum up, if all of us who use these terms really know them adequately as well, and if we need take no pains to make our conceptions articulate, why do we quarrel and make war and criticize one another?

Indeed, I need not bring forward our contentions with one another and make mention of them. Take yourself alone; if you apply your preconceptions properly, why do you feel miserable and hampered? Let us dismiss for the moment the Second Department[7] of study, that concerned with impulses and with what is fitting in relation to them. Let us dismiss also the Third Department, that of assents. I grant you all this. Let us confine ourselves to the First Department, where we have almost sensible demonstration that we do not apply our preconceptions properly. Do you now will things possible, and possible for you? Why, then, do you feel hindered and miserable? Do you now refuse to shun what is necessary? Why, then, do you fall into trouble and misfortune? Why does a thing not happen when you will it, and happen when you do not will it, for this is the strongest proof of misery and misfortune? I will a thing, and it does not happen; what could be more wretched than I? I will it not and it happens; again, what is more wretched than I?

It was because she could not endure this that Medea was led to kill her children: and the act showed a great nature; for she had a right conception of what it means for one's will not to be realized. 'Then', said she, 'I shall thus take vengeance on him who did me wrong and outrage. Yet what is the good of putting him in this misery? What am I to do then? I kill my children, but I shall also be punishing myself. What do I care?' This is the aberration of a mind of great force; for she did not know where the power lies to do what we will; that we must not get it from outside, nor by disturbing or disarranging events. Do not will to have your husband, and then nothing that you will fails to happen. Do not will that he should live with you in all circumstances, do not will to stay in Corinth: in a word, will nothing but what God wills. Then who shall hinder you, who compel you? You will be as free as Zeus Himself.

When you have a leader such as this, and identify your will with His, you need never fear failure any more. But, once make a gift to poverty and wealth of your will to get and your will to avoid, and you will fail and be unfortunate. Give them to health and you will be unhappy: or to office, honour, country, friends, children—in a word, if you give them to anything beyond your will's control. But give them to Zeus and to the other gods; hand them to their keeping, let them control them, and command them, and you can never be miserable any more. But if, O man of no endurance, you are envious, pitiful, jealous, timorous, and never go a day without bewailing yourself and the gods, how can you call yourself a philosopher any more? Philosophy indeed! Just because you worked at variable syllogisms? Will you not unlearn all this, if you can, and begin at the beginning again, and realize that so far you never touched the matter, and, beginning here, build further on this foundation, so that nothing shall be when you will it not, nothing shall not be when you will it? Give me one young man who has come to school with this purpose, ready to strive at this, like one at the games, saying, 'For my part let all else go for nothing: I am content if I shall be allowed to spend my life unhindered and free from pain, and to lift my neck like a free man in face of facts, and to look up to heaven as God's friend, fearing nothing that can happen.' Let one of you show himself in this character, that I may say, 'Come to your own, young man: for it is your destiny to adorn philosophy, these possessions are yours, the books and theories are for you.' Then, when he has worked at this subject and made himself master of it, let him come again and say to me, 'I wish to be free from passion and disquiet, and to know in a religious and philosophic and devoted spirit how it is fitting for me to behave towards the gods, towards my parents, my brothers, my country, and towards foreigners.'

Enter now on the Second Department: this is yours too.

'Yes, but now I have studied the Second Department; next I should wish to be secure and unshaken, and that not only in my waking hours, but in my sleep and in my cups and when distraught.'

Man, you are a god, you have great designs!

'No,' he replies, 'I want to understand what Chrysippus says in his treatise on "The Liar".'[8]

That's your design, is it, my poor fellow? Take it and go hang! What good will it do you? You will read all the treatise with sorrow and repeat it to others with trembling.

That is just how you behave. 'Would you like me to read to you, brother, and you to me?' 'Man, you are a wonderful writer': and, 'You have a great turn for Xenophon's style', and, 'You for Plato's', and, 'You for Antisthenes'.' And after all, when you have related your dreams to one another, you return again to the same behaviour as before: the same will to get and will to avoid, the same impulses and designs and purposes, the same prayers, the same interests. Then you never look for any one to remind you of the truth, but are vexed if any one reminds you. Then you say, 'He is an unamiable man; he did not weep when I left home nor say, "What difficulties you are going to! my son, if you return safe, I will light some lamps." This is what an amiable man would say.' Great good you will get if you return safe! It is worth while lighting a lamp for such as you, for you ought no doubt to be free from disease and death!

We must, then, as I say, put off this fancy of thinking that we know anything useful, and we must approach philosophy as we approach the study of geometry and music: otherwise we shall not come near making progress, even if we go through all the Introductions and treatises of Chrysippus and Antipater and Archedemus.

CHAPTER XVIII

HOW WE MUST STRUGGLE AGAINST IMPRESSIONS

Every habit and every faculty is confirmed and strengthened by the corresponding acts, the faculty of walking by walking, that of running by running. If you wish to have a faculty for reading, read; if for writing, write. When you have not read for thirty days on end, but have done something else, you will know what happens. So if you lie in bed for ten days, and then get up and try to take a fairly long walk, you will see how your legs lose their power. So generally if you wish to acquire a habit for anything, do the thing; if you do not wish to acquire the habit, abstain from doing it, and acquire the habit of doing something else instead. The same holds good in things of the mind: when you are angry, know that you have not merely done ill, but that you have strengthened the habit, and, as it were, put fuel on the fire. When you yield to carnal passion you must take account not only of this one defeat, but of the fact that you have fed your incontinence and strengthened it. For habits and faculties are bound to be affected by the corresponding actions; they are either implanted if they did not exist before, or strengthened and intensified if they were there already. This is exactly how philosophers say that morbid habits spring up in the mind. For when once you conceive a desire for money, if reason is applied to make you realize the evil, the desire is checked and the Governing Principle recovers its first power; but if you give it no medicine to heal it, it will not return to where it was, but when stimulated again by the appropriate impression it kindles to desire quicker than before. And if this happens time after time it ends by growing hardened, and the weakness confirms the avarice in a man. For he who has a fever and gets quit of it is not in the same condition as before he had it, unless he has undergone a complete cure. The same sort of thing happens with affections of the mind. They leave traces behind them like weals from a blow, and if a man does not succeed in removing them, when he is flogged again on the same place his weals turn into sores. If, then, you wish not to be choleric, do not feed the angry habit, do not add fuel to the fire. To begin with, keep quiet, and count the days when you were not angry. I used to be angry every day, then every other day, then every three days, then every four. But if you miss thirty days, then sacrifice to God: for the habit is first weakened and then wholly destroyed.

I kept free from distress to-day, and again next day, and for two or three months after; and when occasions arose to provoke it, I took pains to check it.

Know that you are doing well.

To-day when I saw a handsome woman I did not say to myself, 'Would that she were mine!' and 'Blessed is her husband!' For he who says that will say, 'Blessed is the adulterer!' Nor do I picture the next scene: the woman present and disrobing and reclining by my side. I pat myself on the head and say, 'Bravo, Epictetus, you have refuted a pretty fallacy, a much prettier one than the so-called "Master" '.[9] And if, though the woman herself, poor thing, is willing and beckons and sends to me, and even touches me and comes close to me, I still hold aloof and conquer: the refutation of this fallacy is something greater than the argument of 'The Liar', or the 'Resting' argument. This is a thing to be really proud of, rather than of propounding the 'Master' argument.

How, then, is this to be done? Make up your mind at last to please your true self, make up your mind to appear noble to God; set your desires on becoming pure in the presence of your pure self and God. 'Then when an impression of that sort assails you', says Plato [*Laws,* 854b], 'go and offer expiatory sacrifices, go as a suppliant and sacrifice to the gods who avert evil': it is enough even if 'you withdraw to the society of the good and noble' and set yourself to compare them with yourself, whether your pattern be among the living or the dead. Go to Socrates and see him reclining with Alcibiades and making light of his beauty. Consider what a victory, what an Olympic triumph, he won over himself—and knew it—what place he thus achieved among the followers of Heracles! a victory that deserves the salutation, 'Hail, admirable victor, who hast conquered something more than these worn-out boxers and pancratiasts and the gladiators who are like them!' If you set these thoughts against your impression, you will conquer it, and not be carried away by it. But first of all do not be hurried away by the suddenness of the shock, but say, 'Wait for me a little, impression. Let me see what you are, and what is at stake: let me test you'. And, further, do not allow it to go on picturing the next scene. If you do, it straightway carries you off whither it will. Cast out this filthy impression and bring in some other impression, a lovely and noble one, in its place. I say, if you acquire the habit of training yourself thus, you will see what shoulders you get, what sinews, what vigour; but now you have only paltry words and nothing more.

The man who truly trains is he who disciplines himself to face such impressions. Stay, unhappy man! be not carried away. Great is the struggle, divine the task; the stake is a kingdom, freedom, peace, an unruffled spirit. Remember God, call Him to aid and support you, as voyagers call in storm to the Dioscuri. Can any storm be greater than that which springs from violent impressions that drive out reason? For what is storm itself but an impression? Take away the fear of death, and you may bring as much thunder and lightning as you will, and you will discover what deep peace and tranquillity is in your mind. But if you once allow yourself to be defeated and say that you will conquer hereafter, and then do the same again, be sure that you will be weak and miserable; you will never notice hereafter that you are going wrong, but will even begin to provide excuses for your conduct: and then you will confirm the truth of Hesiod's words, 'A dilatory man is ever wrestling with calamities'. [*Works and Days*, 413]

CHAPTER XIX

TO THOSE WHO TAKE UP THE PRINCIPLES OF THE PHILOSOPHERS ONLY TO DISCUSS THEM

THE 'Master' argument appears to have been propounded on some such basis as this.

There are three propositions which are at variance with one another—i.e., any two with the third—namely, these: (1) everything true as an event in the past is necessary; (2) the impossible does not follow from the possible; (3) what neither is true nor will be is yet possible. Diodorus, noticing this conflict of statements, used the probability of the first two to prove the conclusion, 'Nothing is possible which neither is nor will be true'. Some one else, however, will maintain another pair of these propositions. 'What neither is nor will be true is yet possible', and, 'The impossible does not follow from the possible', while rejecting the third, 'Everything true in the past is necessary', as appears to be the view of Cleanthes and his school, who have been supported to a large extent by Antipater. Others maintain the third pair, 'What neither is true nor will be is yet possible', and 'Everything true as an event in the past is necessary', and reject 'The impossible does not follow from the possible'. But to maintain all three propositions at once is impracticable, because every pair is in conflict with the third.

If, then, some one ask me, 'But which of these do you maintain?' I shall answer him that I do not know, but the account I have received is that Diodorus maintained one pair, and the school of Panthoides and Cleanthes, I fancy, the second, and the school of Chrysippus the third.

'What do you hold then?'

I have never given my mind to this, to put my own impression to the test and compare different views and form a judgement of my own on the subject: therefore I am no better than a grammarian.

'Who was Hector's father?'

Priam.

'Who were his brothers?'

Paris and Deiphobus.

'And who was their mother?'

Hecuba. That is the account I have received.

'From whom?'

From Homer: and Hellanicus also writes on the same subject, I believe, and others of the same class.

So it is with me and the 'Master' argument: I go no further. But if I am a vain person I cause the utmost amazement among the company at a banquet by enumerating those who have written on the subject. 'Chrysippus also has written admirably in the first book of his treatise "On the possible". Cleanthes, too, has written a special book on this, and Archedemus. And Antipater also has written, not only in his book on "The possible", but also specially in his work on "the Master" argument. Have you not read the treatise?'

'I have not read it.'

Read it.

And what good will he get from it? He will only be more silly and tiresome than he is now. For what have you got by reading it? What judgement have you formed on the subject? You will only tell us of Helen and Priam and the island of Calypso, which never was nor will be.

And indeed in the field of literature it does not matter much that you should master the received account and have formed no judgement of your own. But we are much more liable to this fault in matters of conduct than in literary matters.

'Tell me about things good and evil.'

Listen.

From Ilion to the Cicones I came,
Wind-borne.

[Homer, *Odyssey*, IX. 39]

'Of things that are, some are good, some bad, some indifferent. The virtues and all that share in them are good, vices and all that share in them are bad, and all that comes between is indifferent—wealth, health, life, death, pleasure, pain.'

How do you know?

'Hellanicus says so in his history of Egypt.' For you might just as well say that as say 'Diogenes or Chrysippus or Cleanthes said so in his Ethics'. I ask, have you put any of these doctrines to the test, and formed a judgement of your own? Show us how you are wont to bear yourself in a storm on shipboard. Do you remember this distinction of good and bad when the sail cracks and you cry aloud to heaven, and some bystander, untimely merry, says 'Tell me, by the gods, what have you been telling us lately? Is it a vice to suffer shipwreck? Does it partake of vice?' Will you not take up a belaying pin and give him a drubbing? 'What have we to do with you, fellow? We are perishing, and you come and mock us.'

Again, if you are sent for by Caesar and are accused, do you remember the distinction? As you enter with a pale face, and trembling withal, suppose some one comes up and says to you, 'Why do you tremble, man? What are you concerned about? Does Caesar put virtue and vice in the hearts of those who come before him?'

'Why do you mock me, as though I had not miseries enough?'

Nay, philosopher, tell me why you tremble. Is it not of death you stand in danger, or prison or pain of body or exile or disgrace, nothing else? Is it wickedness, or anything that partakes of wickedness? And what did you tell us that all these were?

'Man, what have I to do with you? My own evils are enough for me.'

Well said, indeed: for your own evils are indeed enough—meanness, cowardice, the boasting spirit, which you showed when you sat in the lecture-room. Why did you pride yourself on what was not your own? Why did you call yourself a Stoic?

Watch your own conduct thus and you will discover to what school you belong. You will find that most of you are Epicureans and some few Peripatetics, but with all the fibre gone from you. Where have you shown that you really hold virtue to be equal to all else, or even superior? Show me a Stoic if you can! Where or how is he to be found? You can show me men who use the fine phrases of the Stoics, in any number, for the same men who do this can recite Epicurean phrases just as well and can repeat those of the Peripatetics just as perfectly; is it not so?

Who then is a Stoic?

Show me a man moulded to the pattern of the judgements that he utters, in the same way as we call a statue Phidian that is moulded according to the art of Phidias. Show me one who is sick and yet happy, in peril and yet happy, dying and yet happy, in exile and happy, in disgrace and happy. Show him me. By the gods I would fain see a Stoic. Nay you cannot show me a finished Stoic; then show me one in the moulding, one who has set his feet on the path. Do me this kindness, do not grudge an old man like me a sight I never saw till now. What! you think you are going to show me the Zeus of Phidias or his Athena, that work of ivory and gold? It is a soul I want; let one of you show me the soul of a man who wishes to be at one with God, and to blame God or man no longer, to fail in nothing, to feel no misfortune, to be free from anger, envy, and jealousy—one who (why wrap up my meaning?) desires to change his manhood for godhead, and who in this poor dead body of his has his purpose set upon communion with God. Show him to me. Nay, you cannot. Why, then, do you mock yourselves, and trifle with others? Why do you put on a character which is not your own, and walk about like thieves and robbers in these stolen phrases and properties that do not belong to you?

And so now I am your teacher, and you are at school with me: and my purpose is this, to make you my completed work, untouched by hindrance or compulsion, or constraint, free, tranquil, happy, looking to God in everything small or great; and you are here to learn and practise these things. Why, then, do you not finish the work, if indeed you also have the purpose you should have, and if I have the purpose and the proper equipment also? What is it that is wanting? When I see a craftsman and material ready to his hand, I look for the finished work. Now here, too, is the craftsman, and here is the material. What do we lack? Is not the subject teachable? It is teachable. Is it not within our power then? Nay, it is the one thing of all others which is in our power. Wealth is not in our power, nor health, nor anything else, in a word, except the proper use of impressions. This alone, by nature's gift, is unhindered and untrammelled. Why, then, do you not finish the work? Tell me the reason: for it lies either in me or in you or in the nature of the thing. The achievement itself is possible, and rests with us alone. It follows then that the reason lies in me or in you, or, more truly, in both. What is my conclusion? Let us begin, if you only will, to carry out such purpose here and now. Let us leave behind what is past. Only let us begin; have trust in me, and you shall see.

CHAPTER XX

AGAINST FOLLOWERS OF EPICURUS AND OF THE ACADEMY

EVEN those who contradict propositions that are true and evident are obliged to make use of them. And indeed one may almost give as the strongest proof that a thing is evident that even he who contradicts it finds himself obliged to make use of it. For instance, if one should deny that any universal statement is true, plainly he cannot help asserting the contrary.

'No universal statement is true.'

Slave, this is not true either: for what else is your assertion than, 'If a statement is universal, it is false?' Again, if one comes forward and says, 'Know that nothing is knowable, but that everything is unprovable,' or another says, 'Believe me, and it will be to your advantage; you ought not to believe a man at all'; or again, if another says, 'Learn from me, man, that it is impossible to learn anything; I tell you this, and will teach you, if you will.' What difference is there between such persons and—whom shall I say?—those who call themselves Academics? 'Men, give your assent to the statement that no man assents!'

'Believe us that no man believes any one!'

So too Epicurus, when he wishes to get rid of the natural fellowship of men with one another, makes use of the very principle of which he is getting rid. For what does he say? 'Men, be not deceived, be not misled or deluded. There is no natural fellowship of rational beings with one another: believe me. Those who state the contrary deceive you and mislead your reason.'

What concern, then, is it of yours? Let us be deceived. Will you come off any the worse if the rest of us are all convinced that we have a natural fellowship with one another and that we are bound by all means to guard it? Nay, your position will be much better and more secure. Man, why do you take thought for our sake, why do you keep awake for us, why do you light your lamp, why do you rise early, why do you write such big books? Is it to prevent any of us being deluded into thinking that the gods have any care for mankind, or to prevent us from supposing that the nature of the good is anything but pleasure? For if this is so, be off with you and go to sleep; do as the worm does, for this is the life of which you pronounce yourself worthy: eating, drinking, copulation, evacuation, and snoring.

What does it matter to you, what opinions others will hold on these matters, or whether they are right or wrong? What have we to do with you? You take interest in sheep because they offer themselves to be shorn and milked and finally to be slaughtered by us. Would it not be desirable if men could be charmed and bewitched by the Stoics into slumber, and offer themselves to you and those like you to be shorn and milked? These sentiments were proper enough to utter to your fellow Epicureans; ought you not to conceal them from outsiders, and take special pains to convince them before all things that we are born with a sociable nature, that self-control is a good thing, that so you may secure everything for yourself? Or do you say we must maintain this fellowship towards some and not towards others? Towards whom, then, must we observe it? Towards those who observe it in their turn, or towards those who transgress it? And who transgress it more completely than you who have laid down these doctrines?

What, then, was it that roused Epicurus from his slumbers and compelled him to write what he wrote? What else but that which is the most powerful of all human things, Nature, which draws a man to her will though he groan and resist? For (she says), because you hold these unsociable opinions, write them down and bequeath them to others and stay up late for them and by your own act accuse the very principles you maintain. What! we speak of Orestes pursued by the Furies and roused from his slumbers, but are not the Furies and Torments that beset Epicurus more exacting? They roused him from his sleep and would not allow him to rest, but compelled him to announce his miseries, as madness and wine compel the priests of Cybele. So powerful and unconquerable a thing is human nature. How can a vine be moved to act, not as a vine but as an olive, or again an olive not as an olive but as a vine? It is impossible, inconceivable. So it is impossible for man utterly to destroy the instincts of man; even those who have their bodily organs cut off cannot cut off the desires of men. In the same way Epicurus, though he cut off all the attributes of a man and a householder and a citizen and a friend, could not cut off human desires. No, he could not do it, any more than the indolent Academics could cast away or blind their senses, though they have made this the chief object of their life. Is not this sheer misfortune?[10] A man has received from Nature measures and standards for the discovery of truth, and instead of busying himself to add to them and to work out further results, he does exactly the opposite, and tries to remove and destroy any faculty which he possesses for discovering the truth.

What say you, philosopher? What is your view of religion and piety?

'If you will, I will prove that it is good.'

Prove it then, that our fellow citizens may take heed and honour the Divine and cease at last from being indifferent as to the highest matters.

'Have you the proofs then?'

I have, and am thankful for it!

'Since you find such an interest in these things, now hear the contrary: "The gods do not exist, and if they do, they pay no regard to men and we have no communion with them, and thus religion and piety, of which the multitude talk, are a lie of pretentious persons and sophists, or it may be of lawgivers, for the fear and deterrence of wrongdoers." '

Bravo, philosopher! What a service you confer on our citizens! Our young men are already inclining to despise divine things, and you recover them for us!

'What is the matter? Does not this please you? Now learn, how justice is nothing, how self-respect is folly, how "father" and "son" are empty words.'

Bravo, philosopher! Stick to your task, persuade our young men, that we may have more to agree with you and share your views. These, nc doubt, are the arguments which have brought well-governed cities to greatness, these are the arguments which made Lacedaemon, these are the convictions which Lycurgus wrought into the Spartans by his laws and training: that slavery is no more shameful than noble, and freedom no more noble than shameful! For these beliefs no doubt those who died at Thermopylae died! And for what principles but these did the Athenians give up their city?

And yet the men who state these theories marry and beget children and share in city life and appoint themselves priests and prophets. Of what? Of what has no existence! And they question the Pythian prophetess themselves, to learn lies, and they interpret oracles to others. Is not this the height of shameless imposition?

Man, what are you doing? You convict yourself of falsehood day by day: will you not abandon these crude fallacies? When you eat where do you put your hand, to your mouth or to your eye? When you bathe into what do you go? When did you ever call the jug a saucer or the ladle a spit?

If I were slave to one of these men, I would torture him, even if I had to stand a flogging from him every day. 'Put a drop of oil, boy, in the bath.' I would get some fish sauce and pour it over his head. 'What is that? By your fortune I had an impression, very like oil, indistinguishable from it. 'Give me gruel here.' I would fill a dish with vinegar sauce and bring it him.

'Did I not ask for gruel?'

Yes, master, this is gruel.

'Is not this vinegar sauce?'

How is it more that than gruel?

'Take it and smell, take it and taste.'

How can you know if the senses play us false? If I had three or four fellow slaves who shared my mind I should give him such a dressing that he would hang himself, or change his opinion. Such men trifle with us; they take advantage of all the gifts of nature, while in theory they do away with them.

Grateful and self-respecting men indeed! they eat bread every day, to say nothing else, and yet dare to assert that we know not whether there is a Demeter or Kore or Pluto: not to say that they enjoy day and night and the changes of the year, the stars and sea and land and the service that men render, yet not one of these things makes them take notice in the least. No, their only aim is to vomit their paltry problem, and having thus exercised their stomach to go away and have a bath. But they have not given the slightest thought to what they are going to say: what subject they are going to speak about, or to whom, and what they are going to get from these arguments: whether any young man of noble spirit may be influenced by them or has been influenced already and may lose all the germs of nobility in him: whether we may be giving an adulterer opportunity to brazen out his acts: whether one who is embezzling public funds may find some excuse to lay hold of in these theories: whether one who neglects his parents may get from them fresh courage.

What, then, do you hold good or evil, base or noble? Is it this doctrine, or that? It is useless to go on disputing with one of these men, or reasoning with him, or trying to alter his opinion. One might have very much more hope of altering the mind of a profligate than of men who are absolutely deaf and blind to their own miseries.

CHAPTER XXI

CONCERNING INCONSISTENCY OF MIND

THERE are some admissions which men readily make, others they do not. Now no one will admit that he is thoughtless or foolish: on the contrary, you will hear every one say, 'Would that I had luck as I have wits!' But men readily admit that they are cowards and say, 'I am a bit of a coward, I admit, but for the rest you will find me no fool'. A man will not readily own to incontinence, to injustice not at all, never to envy or fussiness, while most men will own to being pitiful. You ask what is the reason? The most vital reason is a confusion and want of consistency in men's views of what is good and evil, but, apart from this, different persons are affected by different motives; speaking generally, people are not ready to own to qualities which to their mind appear base. Cowardice and a sense of pity they imagine show good nature, silliness a slavish mind, and social faults they are least ready to admit. In most of the errors which they are inclined to confess to, it is because they think there is an involuntary element, as in the cowardly and the pitiful. So if any one does own to incontinence, he brings in passion, to give him the excuse of involuntary action. Injustice is in no circumstances conceived as involuntary. There is an involuntary element, they think, in jealousy, and for this reason this too is a fault which men confess.

Moving, then, as we do among men of this character, so bewildered, so ignorant of what they are saying, or of what evil is theirs, or whether they have any, or what is the reason of it, or how they are to be relieved, we ought ourselves, I think, to be constantly on our guard, asking ourselves, 'Am I too perhaps one of them? What impression have I of myself? How do I bear myself? Do I too bear myself as a man of prudence and self-control? Do I too sometimes say that I am educated to meet every emergency? Am I conscious, as the man who knows nothing should be, that I know nothing? Do I come to my teacher as to the oracles, prepared to obey, or do I too come to school like a driveller, to learn nothing but history and to understand the books which I did not understand before, and if it so chance, to expound them to others?'

Man, you have had a boxing match with your slave at home, and turned your house upside down and disturbed your neighbours, and now do you come to me with a solemn air like a wise man and sit and criticize the way I interpret language, and how I rattle out anything that comes into my head? Do you come in a spirit of envy, depressed because nothing is brought you from home, and while the discussion is going on, sit thinking of nothing yourself but how you stand with your father or your brother? 'What are men at home saying about me? They are thinking now that I am making progress and say, "He will come back knowing everything". I did indeed wish to return one day if I could, having learnt everything, but it needs hard work, and no one sends me anything and the baths are shockingly bad in Nicopolis, and I am badly off in my lodgings and in the lecture-room.'

Then they say, 'No one gets any good from the lecture-room!'

Why, who comes to the lecture-room? Who comes to be cured? Who comes to have his judgements purified? Who comes that he may grow conscious of his needs? Why are you surprised, then, that you carry away from school the very qualities you bring there, for you do not come to put away your opinions or to correct them, or to get others in exchange? No, far from it! What you must look to is whether you get what you come for. You wish to chatter about principles. Well, do you not come away with lighter tongues than before? Does not school afford you material for displaying your precious principles? Do you not analyse variable syllogisms? Do you not pursue the assumptions of 'The Liar'[11] and hypothetical propositions? Why then do you go on being vexed at getting what you come for?

'Yes, but if my child or my brother die, or if I must be racked and die myself, what good will such things do me?'

What! is this what you came for? Is this what you sit by me for? Did you ever light your lamp or sit up late for this? Or, when you have gone out for a walk, have you ever put a conception before your mind instead of a syllogism and pursued this with your companion? When have you ever done so? Then you say, 'Principles are useless.' To whom? To those who use them wrongly. For collyrium is not useless to those who anoint themselves at the right time and in the right way, plasters are not useless, leaping-weights are not useless, but only useless to some, and again useful to others.

If you ask me now, 'Are syllogisms useful?' I shall say they are useful, and if you wish I will prove it.

'What good have they done me then?'

Man, did you ask whether they were useful in general, or useful to you? Suppose a man suffering from dysentery asked me, 'Is vinegar useful?' I shall say it is. 'Is it useful to me?' I shall say: 'No; seek first to get your flux stayed, and your ulcerations healed.' It is the same with you. You must first attend to your ulcers, and stay your flux, and arrive at peace in your mind and bring it to school undistracted, and then you will discover how wonderful the power of reason is.

CHAPTER XXII

ON FRIENDSHIP

A MAN naturally loves those things in which he is interested. Now do men take an interest in things evil? Certainly not. Do they take interest in what does not concern them? No, they do not. It follows then that they are interested in good things alone, and if interested in them, therefore love them too. Whoever then has knowledge of good things, would know how to love them; but how could one who cannot distinguish good things from evil and things indifferent from both have power to love? Therefore the wise man alone has power to love.

'Nay, how is this?' says one. 'I am not wise, yet I love my child.'

By the gods, I am surprised, to begin with, at your admission that you are not wise. What do you lack? Do you not enjoy sensation, do you not distinguish impressions, do you not supply your body with the food that is suited to it, and with shelter and a dwelling? How is it then that you admit that you are foolish? I suppose because you are often disturbed and bewildered by your impressions, and overcome by their persuasive powers, so that the very things that at one moment you consider good you presently consider bad and afterwards indifferent; and, in a word, you are subject to pain, fear, envy, confusion, change: that is why you confess yourself to be foolish. And do you not change in your affections? Do you believe at one time that wealth and pleasure and mere outward things are good, and at another time that they are evil, and do you not regard the same persons now as good, now as bad, and sometimes feel friendly towards them, sometimes unfriendly, and now praise, now blame them?

'Yes. I am subject to these feelings.'

Well then; do you think a man can be a friend to anything about which he is deceived?

'Not at all.'

Nor can he whose choice of a friend is subject to change bear good will to him?

'No, he cannot.'

Can he who first reviles a man and then admires him?

'No, he cannot.'

Again, did you never see curs fawning on one another and playing with one another, so that you say nothing could be friendlier? But to see what friendship is, throw a piece of meat among them and you will learn. So with you and your dear boy: throw a bit of land between you, and you will learn how your boy wishes to give you a speedy burial, and you pray for the boy to die. Then you cry out again, 'What a child I have reared! He is impatient to bury me'. Throw a pretty maid between you and suppose you both love her, you the old man, and he the young man. Or suppose you throw a bit of glory between you. And if you have to risk your life, you will use the words of Admetus' father:

You love the light; shall not your father love it?

[Euripides, *Alcestis*, 691]

Do you think that he did not love his own child when it was small, and was not distressed when it had the fever, and did not often say, 'Would it were I who had the fever instead!'? yet when the event came close upon him, see what words they utter! Were not Eteocles and Polynices born of the same mother and the same father? Were they not reared together, did they not live together, drink together, sleep together, often kiss one another, so that if one had seen them he would, no doubt, have laughed at the paradoxes of philosophers on friendship. Yet when the bit of meat, in the shape of a king's throne, fell between them, see what they say:

> E. *Where wilt stand upon the tower?*
> P. *Wherefore dost thou ask me this?*
> E. *I will face thee then and slay thee.*
> P. *I desire thy blood no less.*
>
> [Euripides, *The Phoenissae,* 621]

Yes, such are the prayers they utter!

For be not deceived, every creature, to speak generally, is attached to nothing so much as to its own interest. Whatever then seems to hinder his way to this, be it a brother or a father or a child, the object of his passion or his own lover, he hates him, guards against him, curses him. For his nature is to love nothing so much as his own interest; this is his father and brother and kinsfolk and country and god. At any rate, when the gods seem to hinder us in regard to this we revile even the gods and overthrow their statues and set fire to their temples, as Alexander ordered the shrines of Asclepius to be burnt when the object of his passion died. Therefore if interest, religion and honour, country, parents and friends are set in the same scale, then all are safe; but if interest is in one scale, and in the other friends and country and kindred and justice itself, all these are weighed down by interest and disappear. For the creature must needs incline to that side where 'I' and 'mine' are; if they are in the flesh, the ruling power must be there; if in the will, it must be there; if in external things, it must be there.

If then I identify myself with my will, then and only then shall I be a friend and son and father in the true sense. For this will be my interest—to guard my character for good faith, honour, forbearance, self-control, and service of others, to maintain my relations with others. But if I separate myself from what is noble, then Epicurus' statement is confirmed, which declares that 'there is no such thing as the noble or at best it is but the creature of opinion'.

It was this ignorance that made the Athenians and Lacedaemonians quarrel with one another, and the Thebans with both, and the Great King with Hellas, and the Macedonians with Hellas and the King, and now the Romans with the Getae; and yet earlier this was the reason of the wars with Ilion. Paris was the guest of Menelaus, and any one who had seen the courtesies they used to one another would not have believed one who denied that they were friends. But a morsel was thrown between them, in the shape of a pretty woman, and for that there was war! So now, when you see friends or brothers who seem to be of one mind, do not therefore pronounce upon their friendship, though they swear to it and say it is impossible for them to part with one another. The Governing Principle of the bad man is not to be trusted; it is uncertain, irresolute, conquered now by one impression, now by another. The question you must ask is, not what others ask, whether they were born of the same parents and brought up together and under the charge of the same slave; but this question only, where they put their interest—outside them or in the will. If they put it outside, do not call them friends, any more than you can call them faithful, or stable, or confident, or free; nay, do not call them even men, if you are wise. For it is no human judgement which makes them bite one another and revile one another and occupy deserts or market-places like wild beasts and behave like robbers in the law-courts; and which makes them guilty of profligacy and adultery and seduction and the other offences men commit against one another. There is one judgement and one only which is responsible for all this—that they set themselves and all their interests elsewhere than in their will. But if you hear that these men in very truth believe the good to lie only in the region of the will and in dealing rightly with impressions, you need trouble yourself no more as to whether a man is son or father, whether they are brothers, or have been familiar companions for years; I say, if you grasp this one fact and no more, you may pronounce with confidence that they are friends, as you may that they are faithful and just. For where else is friendship but where faith and honour are, where men give and take what is good, and nothing else?

'But he has paid me attention all this time: did he not love me?'

How do you know, slave, whether he has paid you this attention, as a man cleans his boots, or tends his beast? How do you know whether, when you have lost your use as a paltry vessel, he will not throw you away like a broken plate?

'But she is my wife and we have lived together this long time.'

How long did Eriphyle live with Amphiaraus, ay, and was mother of many children?—But a necklace came between them.

'What do you mean by a necklace?'

Man's judgement about good and evil. This was the brutish element, this was what broke up the friendship, which suffered not the wife to be true to her wedlock, nor the mother to be a mother indeed. So let every one of you, who is anxious himself to be friend to another, or to win another for his friend, uproot these judgements, hate them, drive them out of his mind. If he does that, then first he will never revile himself or be in conflict with himself, he will be free from change of mind, and self-torture; secondly he will be friendly to his neighbour, always and absolutely, if he be like himself, and if he be unlike, he will bear with him, be gentle and tender with him, considerate to him as one who is ignorant and in error about the highest matters; not hard upon any man, for he knows of a certainty Plato's saying, 'No soul is robbed of the truth save involuntarily'.

But if you fail to do this, you may do everything else that friends do —drink together and live under the same roof and sail in the same ship and be born of the same parents; well, the same may be true of snakes, but neither they nor you will be capable of friendship so long as you retain these brutish and revolting judgements.

CHAPTER XXIII

ON THE FACULTY OF EXPRESSION

Every one can read a book with the more pleasure and ease the plainer the letters in which it is written. So too every one can listen more easily to discourse which is expressed in becoming and distinguished language. We must therefore not say that the faculty of expression is nothing. To say so is at once irreligious and cowardly; irreligious because it means disparaging God's gifts, just as though one should deny the usefulness of the faculty of vision or hearing or even the faculty of speech. Was it for nothing then that God gave you your eyes? Was it for nothing He mingled with them a spirit[12] so powerful and cunningly devised, that even from a distance they can fashion the shapes of what they see? And what messenger is so swift and attentive as they? Was it for nothing that He made the intervening air so active and sensitive that vision passes through it as through a tense medium? Was it for nothing that He made light, without the presence of which all the rest would have been useless?

Man, be not ungrateful, nor again forget higher things! Give thanks to God for sight and hearing, yes, and for life itself and what is conducive to life—for grain and fruit, for wine and oil; but remember that He has given you another gift superior to all these, the faculty which shall use them, test them, and calculate the value of each. For what is it that pronounces on each of these faculties, and decides their value? Is it the faculty itself, in each case? Did you ever hear the faculty of vision saying anything about itself, or the faculty of hearing? No, these faculties are ordained as ministers and slaves to serve the faculty which deals with impressions. And if you ask what each is worth, whom do you ask? Who answers you? How then can any other faculty be superior to this, which uses the rest as its servants and itself tests each result and pronounces on it? Which of those faculties knows what it is and what it is worth, which of them knows when it ought to be used and when it ought not? What is the faculty that opens and closes the eyes and brings them near some objects and turns them away, at need, from others? Is it the faculty of vision? No, it is the faculty of will. What is it that closes and opens the ears? What is it that makes us curious and questioning, or again unmoved by discourse? Is it the faculty of hearing? It is no other faculty but that of the will.

I say, when the will sees that all the other faculties which surround it are blind and deaf and are unable to see anything else beyond the very objects for which they are ordained to minister to this faculty and serve it, and this alone has clear sight and surveys the rest and itself and estimates their value, is it likely to pronounce that any other faculty but itself is the highest? What is the function of the eye, when opened, but to see? But what is it tells us whether we ought to look at a man's wife or how? The faculty of will. What tells us whether we ought to believe or disbelieve what we are told, and if we believe whether we are to be excited or not? Is it not the faculty of will? This faculty of eloquence I spoke of, if such special faculty there be, concerned with the framing of fair phrases, does no more than construct and adorn phrases, when there is an occasion for discourse, just as hairdressers arrange and adorn the hair. But whether it is better to speak or be silent, and to speak in this way or that, and whether it is proper or improper—in a word, to decide the occasion and the use for each discourse, all these are questions for one faculty only, that of the will. Would you have it come forward and pronounce against itself?

'But', says the objector, 'what if the matter stands thus, what if that which ministers can be superior to that which it serves, the horse to the horseman, the hound to the hunter, the lyre to him that plays it, the servants to the king they serve?' The answer is: What is it that uses other things? The will. What is it that attends to everything? The will. What is it that destroys the whole man, now by starvation, now by a halter, now by a headlong fall? The will. Is there then anything stronger in men than this? Nay, how can things that are subject to hindrance be stronger than that which is unhindered? What has power to hinder the faculty of vision? Will and events beyond the will. The faculty of hearing and that of speech are subject to the same hindrance. But what can hinder the will? Nothing beyond the will, only the perversion of the will itself. Therefore vice or virtue resides in this alone. Yet being so mighty a faculty, ordained to rule all the rest, you would have it come forward and tell us that the flesh is of all things most excellent. Why, if the flesh itself asserted that it was the most excellent of things, one would not tolerate it even then. But as it is, Epicurus, what is the faculty that pronounces this judgement? Is it the faculty which has written on 'The End' or 'Physics' or 'The Standard'? The faculty which made you grow your beard as a philosopher? which wrote in the hour of death 'I am living my last day and that a blessed one'? [13] Is this faculty flesh or will? Surely it is madness to admit that you have a faculty superior to this. Can you be in truth so blind and deaf?

What follows? Do we disparage the other faculties? God forbid. Do we say that there is no use nor advancement save in the faculty of will? God forbid! That were foolish, irreligious, ungrateful toward God. We are only giving each thing its due. For there is use in an ass, but not so much as in an ox; there is use in a dog, but not so much as in a servant; there is use in a servant, but not so much as in a fellow-citizen; there is use in them too, but not so much as in those who govern them. Yet because other faculties are higher we must not depreciate the use which inferior faculties yield. The faculty of eloquence has its value, but it is not so great as that of the will; but when I say this, let no one suppose that I bid you neglect your manner of speech, any more than I would have you neglect eyes or ears or hands or feet or clothes or shoes.

But if you ask me, 'What then is the highest of all things,' what am I to say? The faculty of speech? I cannot say that. No, the faculty of will, when it is in the right way. For it is this which controls the faculty of speech and all other faculties small and great. When this is set in the right course, a man becomes good; when it fails, man becomes bad; it is this which makes our fortune bad or good, this which makes us critical of one another or well content; in a word, to ignore this means misery, to attend to it means happiness.

Yet to do away with the faculty of eloquence and deny its existence is indeed not only ungrateful to those who have given it, but shows a coward's spirit. For he who denies it seems to me to fear that, if there is a faculty of eloquence, we may not be able to despise it. It is just the same with those who deny that there is any difference between beauty and ugliness. What! are we to believe that the sight of Thersites could move men as much as the sight of Achilles, and the sight of Helen no more than the sight of an ordinary woman? No, these are the words of foolish and uneducated persons, who do not know one thing from another, and who fear that if once one becomes aware of such differences, one may be overwhelmed and defeated.

No, the great thing is this—to leave each in possession of his own faculty, and so leaving him to see the value of the faculty, and to understand what is the highest of all things and to pursue this always, and concentrate your interest on this, counting all other things subordinate to this, yet not failing to attend to them too so far as you may. For even to the eyes you must attend, yet not as though they were the highest, but to these also for the sake of the highest; for the highest will not fulfil its proper nature unless it uses the eyes with reason, and chooses one thing rather than another.

What then do we see men doing? They are like a man returning to his own country who, finding a good inn on his road, stays on there because it pleases him. Man, you are forgetting your purpose! You were not travelling *to* this, but *through* it.

'Yes, but this is a fine inn.'

And how many other fine inns are there, and how many fine meadows? But they are merely to pass through; your purpose is yonder; to return to your country, to relieve your kinsfolk of their fears, to fulfil your own duties as a citizen, to marry, beget children, and hold office in due course. For you have not come into the world to choose your pick of fine places, but to live and move in the place where you were born and appointed to be a citizen. The same principle holds good in what we are discussing. Our road to perfection must needs lie through instruction and the spoken word; and one must purify the will and bring into right order the faculty which deals with impressions; and principles must be communicated in a particular style, with some variety and epigram. But this being so, some people are attracted by the very means they are using and stay where they are, one caught by style, another by syllogisms, a third by variable arguments, and a fourth by some other seductive inn by the way; and there they stay on and moulder away, like those whom the Sirens entertain.

Man, the purpose set before you was to make yourself capable of dealing with the impressions that you meet as nature orders, so as not to fail in what you will to get, nor to fall into what you will to avoid, never suffering misfortune or bad fortune, free, unhindered, unconstrained, conforming to the governance of God, obeying this, well pleased with this, criticizing none, blaming none, able to say these lines with your whole heart,

Lead me, O Zeus, and thou my Destiny.

[Cleanthes]

Having this purpose before you, are you going to stay where you are just because a pretty phrase or certain precepts please you, and choose to make your home there, forgetting what you have left at home, and say, 'These things are fine'? Who says they are not fine? But they are fine as things to pass through, as inns by the way. What prevents you from being unfortunate, though you speak like Demosthenes? Though you can analyse syllogisms like Chrysippus, what prevents you from being wretched, mournful, envious—in a word, bewildered and miserable? Nothing prevents you. Do you see then that these were inns of no value; and the goal set before you was different? Certain persons when I say this think I am disparaging the study of rhetoric or of principles. No, I am not depreciating that, but only the tendency to dwell unceasingly on such matters and to set your hopes on them. If any man does his hearers harm by bringing this truth home to them, count me among those who do this harm. But when I see that what is highest and most sovereign is something different, I cannot say that it is what it is not in order to gratify you.

CHAPTER XXIV

TO ONE WHOM HE DID NOT THINK WORTHY

SOME one said to him, 'I often came to you, desiring to hear you and you never gave me an answer, and now, if it may be, I beg you to say something to me'.

Do you think, he replied, that there is an art of speaking, like other arts, and that he who has it will speak with skill and he who has it not, without skill?

'I think so.'

Is it true then that he who by his speech gains benefit himself and is able to benefit others would speak with skill, and he who tends to be harmed himself and harm others would be unskilled in the art of speaking?

'Yes, you would find that some are harmed, some benefited.'

But what of the hearers? Are they all benefited by what they hear, or would you find that of them too some are benefited and some harmed?

'Yes, that is true of them too', he said.

Here too then it is true that those who hear with skill are benefited, and those who hear without skill are harmed?

He agreed.

Is there then a skill in hearing as well as in speaking?

'So it appears.'

If you will, look at the question thus. Whose part do you think it is to touch an instrument musically?

'The musician's.'

And whose part do you think it is to make a statue properly?

'The sculptor's.'

Does it not seem to you to require any art to look at a statue with skill?

'Yes, this requires art too.'

If then right speaking demands a skilled person, do you see that hearing with profit also demands a skilled person? As for perfection and profit in the full sense, that, if you like, we may for the moment dismiss, as we are both far from anything of that sort; but this I think every one would admit, that he who is to listen to philosophers must have at least some practice in listening. Is it not so?

Show me then what it is you would have me speak to you about. What are you able to hear about? About things good and bad? Good what? A good horse?

'No.'

A good ox?

'No.'

What then? A good man?

'Yes.'

Do we know then what man is, what his nature is, what the notion is? Are our ears open in any degree with regard to this? Nay, do you understand what Nature is, or can you in any measure follow me when I speak? Am I to demonstrate to you? How am I to do it? Do you really understand what demonstration is, or how a thing is demonstrated, or by what means, or what processes are like demonstration without being demonstrations? Do you know what is true or what is false, what follows what, what is in conflict, or disagreement or discord with what? Can I rouse you to philosophy? How can I show you the conflict of the multitude, their disputes as to things good and evil, useful and harmful, when you do not so much as know what conflict is? Show me then what good I shall do you by conversing with you.

'Rouse my interest.'

As the sheep when he sees the grass that suits him has his desire roused to eat, but if you set a stone or loaf by him he will not be roused, so there are in us certain natural inclinations toward discourse, when the appropriate hearer appears and provokes the inclination; but if he lies there like a stone or a piece of grass, how can he rouse a man's will? Does the vine say to the farmer, 'Attend to me'? No, its very appearance shows that it will be to his profit to attend to it and so calls out his energies. Who does not answer the call of winning and saucy children to play with them and crawl with them and talk nonsense with them, but who wants to play or bray with an ass? However small he may be, he is still an ass.

'Why then do you say nothing to me?'

There is only one thing I can say to you, that he who is ignorant who he is and for what he is born and what the world is that he is in and who are his fellows, and what things are good and evil, noble and base; who cannot understand reasoning or demonstration, or what is true or what false, and is unable to distinguish them, such a man will not follow nature in his will to get or to avoid, in his impulses or designs, in assent, refusal, or withholding of assent; to sum up, he will go about the world deaf and blind, thinking himself somebody, when he is really nobody. Do you think there is anything new in this? Ever since the race of men began, have not all errors and misfortunes arisen from this ignorance?

Why did Agamemnon and Achilles quarrel with one another? Was it not because they did not know what was expedient or inexpedient? Did not one say that it was expedient to give back Chryseis to her father, and the other that it was not? Did not one say that he ought to take the other's prize, and the other that he ought not? Did not this too make them forget who they were and for what they had come?

Let be, man, what have you come for? To win women for your love or to make war?

'To make war.'

With whom? Trojans or Greeks?

'Trojans.'

Why then do you leave Hector and draw your sword on your own king? And you, best of men, have you left your duties as a king,

trusted with clans and all their mighty cares,

[Homer, *Iliad*, II. 25]

to fight a duel for a paltry damsel with the most warlike of your allies, whom you ought by all means to respect and guard? Do you show yourself inferior to the courteous high priest who pays all attention to you noble gladiators? Do you see what ignorance as to things expedient leads to?

'But I too am rich.'

Are you any richer than Agamemnon?

'But I am handsome as well.'

Are you any handsomer than Achilles?

'But I have a fine head of hair.'

Had not Achilles a finer, and golden hair too, and he did not comb and smooth it to look fine?

'But I am strong.'

Can you lift a stone as big as Hector or Ajax could?

'But I am noble too.'

Was your mother a goddess, or your father of the seed of Zeus? What good do these things do Achilles, when he sits weeping for his darling mistress?

'But I am an orator.'

And was not he? Do not you see how he handled Odysseus and Phoenix, the most eloquent of the Hellenes, how he shut their mouths?

This is all I can say to you, and even this I have no heart for.

'Why?'

Because you do not excite my interest. Is there anything in you to excite me as men who keep horses are excited at sight of a well-bred horse? Your poor body? You make an ugly figure. Your clothes? They are too luxurious. Your air, your countenance? There is nothing to see. When you wish to hear a philosopher, do not say to him, 'You say nothing to me,' but only show yourself worthy to hear and you will see how you will rouse him to discourse!

CHAPTER XXV

HOW THE ART OF REASONING IS NECESSARY

When one of his audience said, 'Convince me that logic is useful,' he said,

Would you have me demonstrate it?

'Yes.'

Well, then, must I not use a demonstrative argument?

And, when the other agreed, he said, How then shall you know if I impose upon you? And when the man had no answer, he said, You see how you yourself admit that logic is necessary, if without it you are not even able to learn this much—whether it is necessary or not.

CHAPTER XXVI

WHAT IS THE DISTINCTIVE CHARACTER OF ERROR

Every error implies conflict; for since he who errs does not wish to go wrong but to go right, plainly he is not doing what he wishes. For what does the thief wish to do? What is to his interest. If then thieving is against his interest, he is not doing what he wishes. But every rational soul by nature dislikes conflict; and so, as long as a man does not understand that he is in conflict, there is nothing to prevent him from doing conflicting acts, but, whenever he understands, strong necessity makes him abandon the conflict and avoid it, just as bitter necessity makes a man renounce a falsehood when he discovers it, though as long as he has not this impression he assents to it as true.

He then who can show to each man the conflict which causes his error, and can clearly bring home to him how he fails to do what he wishes and does what he does not wish, is powerful in argument and strong to encourage and convict. For if one shows this, a man will retire from his error of himself; but as long as you do not succeed in showing this, you need not wonder if he persists in his error, for he acts because he has an impression that he is right. That is why Socrates too, relying on this faculty, said, 'I am not wont to produce any other witness to support what I say, but am content with him to whom I am talking on each occasion; it is his vote that I take, his evidence that I call, and his sole word suffices instead of all.' For Socrates knew what moves the rational soul, and that it will incline to what moves it, whether it wishes to or not. Show the conflict to the rational Governing Principle and it will desist. If you do not show it, blame yourself rather than him who refuses to obey.

BOOK III

CHAPTER I

ON ADORNMENT

When a young student of rhetoric came into his lecture-room with his hair elaborately arranged and paying great attention to his dress in general: Tell me, said he, do you not think that some dogs and horses are beautiful and some ugly, and is it not so with every creature?

'I think so', he said.

Is not the same true of men, some are beautiful, some ugly?

'Certainly.'

Now do we give the attribute 'beautiful' to each of them in their own kind on the same grounds or on special grounds in each case? Listen and you will see what I mean. Since we see that a dog is born for one thing and a horse for another, and a nightingale, if you like to take that, for another, speaking generally one would not be giving an absurd opinion in saying that each of them was beautiful when it best fulfilled its nature; and since the nature of each is different, I think that each of them would be beautiful in a different way, would it not?

'Yes.'

So that what makes a dog beautiful makes a horse ugly, and what makes a horse beautiful makes a dog ugly, seeing that their natures are different?

'So it seems.'

Yes, for what makes a pancratiast[1] beautiful does not, I imagine, make a good wrestler, and makes a very ridiculous runner; and one who is beautiful for the pentathlon makes a very ugly appearance as a wrestler?

'True', he said.

What then makes a man beautiful if it is not that which in its kind makes dog and horse beautiful?

'It is just that', he said.

What then makes a dog beautiful? The presence of a dog's virtue. What makes a horse beautiful? The presence of a horse's virtue. What makes a man beautiful? Is it the presence of a man's virtue? Therefore, young man, if you would be beautiful, make this the object of your effort, human virtue. And what is human virtue? Consider whom you praise, when you praise men dispassionately; do you praise the just or the unjust?

'The just.'

Do you praise the temperate or the intemperate?

'The temperate.'

The continent or the incontinent?

'The continent.'

Therefore if you make yourself such an one, be sure that you will make yourself beautiful, but as long as you neglect this you cannot help being ugly, though you should use every device to appear beautiful.

But beyond this I do not know what more to say to you; for, if I say what I think, I shall vex you and you will go out and perhaps never return, but if I say nothing, consider what my conduct will be then; you come to me to get good, and I shall be refusing to do you good; you come to me to consult a philosopher, and I shall be refusing you a philosopher's advice. Besides, it is cruelty towards you to leave you uncorrected. If some day hereafter you come to your senses you will accuse me with good reason: 'What did Epictetus find in me, that when he saw me coming in to him in such a shameful state he should do nothing for me and say never a word to me? Did he so utterly despair of me? Was I not young? Was I not fit to listen to discourse? How many other young men make many mistakes like me in their youth? I hear that one Polemo, who had been the most intemperate of young men, underwent such a wonderful change. Grant that he did not think I should be a Polemo: he could have set my hair right, have taken away my bangles, have stopped me pulling my hairs out, but seeing that I had the aspect of—whom shall I say?—he said nothing.' I do not say whose aspect this is, but you will say it for yourself when you come to look into your own heart, and you will learn what it means and what sort of men they are who adopt it.

If hereafter you bring this charge against me, what defence shall I be able to make?

Yes, but suppose I do speak, and he will not obey?

Did Laius obey Apollo? Did he not go away in his drunken stupor and dismiss the oracle from his mind? What then? Did Apollo withhold the truth from him for that reason? Indeed I do not know whether you will obey me or not, but Apollo knew most certainly that Laius would not obey, and yet he spoke. Why did he speak? Nay, why is he Apollo, why does he give oracles, why has he set himself in this position, to be a Prophet and a Fountain of truth, so that men from all the world come to him? Why is 'Know thyself' written up over his shrine, though no one understands it?

Did Socrates persuade all who came to him to attend to their characters? Not one in a thousand! Nevertheless when appointed to this post, as he says, by the ordinance of God, he refused to desert it. Nay, what did he say to his judges? 'If you acquit me', he says, 'on these terms, that I cease to do what I do now, I shall not accept your offer, nor give up my ways, but I shall go to any one I meet, young or old, and put to him these questions that I put now, and I shall question you my fellow citizens far more than any others because you are nearer akin to me.' [Plato, *Apology*, 29c]

Are you so fussy and interfering, Socrates? What do you care what we do?

'What language to use! You are my fellow and kinsman, yet you neglect yourself and provide the city with a bad citizen, your kinsmen with a bad kinsman, and your neighbours with a bad neighbour!'

'Who are you, then?'

To this question it is a weighty answer to say, 'I am he who is bound to take interest in men.' For ordinary cattle dare not resist the lion; but if the bull comes up to withstand him, say to him, if you think fit, 'Who are you?' and 'What do you care?' Man! in every class of creatures nature produces some exceptional specimen; it is so among cattle, dogs, bees, horses. Do not say then to the exception, 'What are you then?' If you do, he will get a voice somehow and say, 'I am like the purple in a garment: do not require me to be like the rest, nor blame my nature, because it made me different from the rest.'

What then? Am I fit to play this part? How can I be? And are you fit to hear the truth? Would that it were so! Nevertheless since I am condemned, it seems, to wear a white beard and a cloak, and since you come to me as to a philosopher, I will not treat you cruelly as though I despaired of you, but will say, Young man, who is it that you want to make beautiful? First get to know who you are and then adorn yourself. You are a man, that is, a mortal creature which has the power to deal with impressions rationally. What does 'rationally' mean? Perfectly, and in accordance with nature. What then is your distinctive possession? Your animal nature? No. Your mortality? No. Your power to deal with impressions? No. Your reasoning faculty is the distinctive one: this you must adorn and make beautiful. Leave your hair to Him that formed it in accordance with His will. Tell me, what other names have you? Are you man or woman?

'Man.'

Adorn Man then, not Woman. Woman is born smooth and tender, and if she has much hair on her body it is a prodigy, and exhibited in Rome as a prodigy. But in a man it is a prodigy not to be hairy: if he is born smooth it is a prodigy, and if he make himself smooth by shaving and plucking, what are we to make of him? Where are we to show him, and what notice are we to put up? 'I will show you a man who prefers to be a woman.' What a shocking exhibition! Every one will be astonished at the notice: by Zeus, I think that even the men who pluck out their hairs do so without understanding that this is what they are doing! Man, what complaint have you to make of Nature? Is it that she made you a man? Ought she to have made all to be women? Why, if all were women, there would be no one to adorn yourself for.

If you are not satisfied with your condition as it is, do the thing completely. Remove—what shall I call it?—that which is the cause of your hairiness; make yourself a woman out and out, and not half-man, half-woman, and then we shall not be misled. Whom do you wish to please? Your darling womenkind? Then please them as a man.

'Yes, but they like smooth men.'

Go and hang yourself! If they liked unnatural creatures, would you become one? Is this your function, is this what you were born for, that profligate women should take pleasure in you? Is it with this character that we are to make you a citizen of Corinth, and, if it so chance, City-warden, or Governor of the Ephebi,[2] or General, or Steward of the games? Well, and when you have married a wife, are you going to pluck yourself smooth? For whom and for what? And when you have begotten boys, are you going to bring them into our citizenship as plucked creatures too? Noble citizen and senator and orator! Is this the kind of young man we are to pray to have bred and reared for us?

Nay, by the gods, young man! but when once you have heard these words, go and say to yourself: 'These are not the words of Epictetus: how could they be? but some kind god speaks through him; for it would never have occurred to Epictetus to say this, as he is not wont to speak to any one. Come then, let us obey God, that we may not incur God's wrath.'

Why, if a raven croaks and gives you a sign, it is not the raven that gives the sign, but God through him: and if He gives you a sign through a human voice, will He not be making man tell you this, that you may learn the power of the divine, and see that it gives signs to some in this way, and to others in that, and of the highest and most sovereign matters gives signs through the noblest messenger? What else is the meaning of the poet, when he says

Since we warned him
By Hermes Argus-slayer, clear of sight,
To slay him not nor woo his wedded wife?

[Homer, *Odyssey*, I. 37]

And as Hermes was sent down to tell him this, so now the gods have sent 'Hermes the Argus-slayer, their messenger,' and tell you this—not to pervert what is good and right, and not to interfere with it, but to leave man man and woman woman, the beautiful person a beautiful person, and the ugly person an ugly person. For you are not flesh, nor hair, but a rational will: if you get this beautiful, then you will be beautiful.

So far I do not dare to tell you that you are ugly, for I think you would hear anything rather than that. But see what Socrates says to Alcibiades, most beautiful and charming of men: 'Strive then to attain beauty.' What does he say to him? Does he say, 'Arrange your hair and smooth your legs'? God forbid! but 'Set your will in order, rid it of bad judgements.'

'How treat the poor body then?'

According to its nature: that is God's concern, trust it to Him.

'What then? Is the body to be unclean?'

God forbid! but cleanse your true, natural self: let man be clean as man, woman as woman, child as child.

Nay, let us pluck out the lion's mane, lest it be unclean, and the cock's comb, for he too must be clean!

Clean? yes, but clean as a cock, and the lion as a lion, and the hound of the chase as such a hound should be.

CHAPTER II

(1) IN WHAT MATTERS SHOULD THE MAN WHO IS TO MAKE PROGRESS TRAIN HIMSELF: AND (2) THAT WE NEGLECT WHAT IS MOST VITAL

THERE are three departments [3] in which a man who is to be good and noble must be trained. The first concerns the will to get and will to avoid; he must be trained not to fail to get what he wills to get nor fall into what he wills to avoid. The second is concerned with impulse to act and not to act, and, in a word, the sphere of what is fitting: that we should act in order, with due consideration, and with proper care. The object of the third is that we may not be deceived, and may not judge at random, and generally it is concerned with assent.

Of these the most important and the most pressing is the first, which is concerned with strong emotions, for such emotion does not arise except when the will to get or the will to avoid fails of its object. This it is which brings with it disturbances, tumults, misfortunes, bad fortunes, mournings, lamentations, envies; which makes men envious and jealous—passions which make us unable to listen to reason.

The second is the sphere of what is fitting: for I must not be without feeling like a statue, but must maintain my natural and acquired relations, as a religious man, as son, brother, father, citizen.

The third department is appropriate only for those who are already making progress, and is concerned with giving certainty in the very things we have spoken of, so that even in sleep or drunkenness or melancholy no untested impression may come upon us unawares.

'This', says a pupil, 'is beyond us.'

But the philosophers of to-day have disregarded the first and second departments, and devote themselves to the third—variable premisses, syllogisms concluding with a question, hypothetical syllogisms, fallacious arguments.

'Of course,' he says, 'when a man is engaged on these subjects he must take pains to escape being deceived.' But whose business is it to do this? It is only for the man who is already good.

In logic then you fall short: but have you reached perfection in other subjects? Are you proof against deceit in regard to money? If you see a pretty girl, do you resist the impression? If your neighbour comes in for an inheritance, do you not feel a twinge? Do you lack nothing now but security of judgement? Unhappy man, even while you are learning this lesson you are in an agony of terror lest some one should think scorn of you, and you ask whether any one is talking about you! And if some one comes and tells you, 'We were discussing who was the best philosopher, and one who was there said, "There is only one philosopher, So-and-so (naming you)"', straightway your poor little four-inch soul shoots up to two cubits! Then if another who is by says, 'Nonsense! It is not worth while to listen to So-and-so: what does he know? He has the first rudiments, nothing more', you are beside yourself, and grow pale and cry out at once, 'I will show him the man I am, he shall see I am a great philosopher.' Why, the facts themselves are evidence; why do you want to show it by something else? Do you not know that Diogenes pointed out one of the sophists thus, making a vulgar gesture? Then, when the man was furious, 'That is So-and-so,' said he, 'I have shown him to you.' A man is not indeed like a stone or a log, that you can show what he is by just pointing a finger, but you show what he is as a man, when you show what are his judgements.

Let us look at your judgements too. Is it not clear that you set no value on your will, but look outside to things beyond your will?—what So-and-so will say, what men will think of you, whether they will think you a scholar, one who has read Chrysippus or Antipater, for if you have read them and Archedemus as well, you have read everything. Why are you still in agony, lest you should fail to show us what manner of man you are? Would you like me to say what manner of man you showed yourself to us? A man who comes before us mean, critical, quick-tempered, cowardly, blaming everything, accusing every one, never quiet, vainglorious—that is what you showed us! Go away now and read Archedemus; then if a mouse fall and make a noise, you die of fright! For the same sort of death awaits you, as—whom shall I say?—Crinis! He too was proud of understanding Archedemus!

Unhappy man, will you not leave these things alone, which do not concern you? They are suited only to those who can learn them without confusion, to those who are able to say, 'I feel no anger, pain, or envy; I am under no hindrance, no constraint. What is left for me to do? I have leisure and peace of mind. Let us see how we ought to deal with logical changes: let us see how one may adopt a hypothesis and not be led to an absurd conclusion.'

These are matters well enough for men like that. It is fitting for sailors who are in good trim to light a fire, and take their dinner, if luck serves, and to sing and dance: but you come to me when the ship is sinking and begin hoisting the topsails!

CHAPTER III

WHAT IS THE MATERIAL WITH WHICH THE GOOD MAN DEALS: AND WHAT SHOULD BE THE OBJECT OF OUR TRAINING

THE material of the good man is his own Governing Principle, as the body is the material of the physician and trainer, the land of the farmer; and it is the function of the good man to deal with his impressions naturally. And just as it is the nature of every soul to assent to what is true and dissent from what is false, and withhold judgement in what is uncertain, so it is its nature to be moved with the will to get what is good and the will to avoid what is evil, and to be neutral towards what is neither good nor evil. For just as neither the banker nor the greengrocer can refuse the Emperor's currency, but, if you show it, he must part, willy-nilly, with what the coin will buy, so it is also with the soul. The very sight of good attracts one towards it, the sight of evil repels. The soul will never reject a clear impression of good, any more than we reject Caesar's currency. On this depends every motion of man and of God. Therefore the good is preferred to every tie of kinship.

I have no concern with my father, but with the good!

'Are you so hard-hearted?'

It is my nature; this is the currency which God has given me. Therefore if the good is different from the noble and just, then father and brother, country and all such things disappear.

I say, am I to neglect my good, that you may get it? am I to make way for you? Why should I?

'I am your father.'

But not my good.

'I am your brother.'

But not my good. If we make the good consist in right will, the mere maintenance of such relations becomes good: further, he who resigns some of his external possessions attains the good.

'My father is taking away my money.'

But he is not harming you.

'My brother will have the greater part of the land.'

Let him have as much as he likes: does he gain in character? Is he more modest, trustworthy, brotherly? Who can eject one from *that* possession? Not even Zeus: nor did He wish to eject me; He put my character in my keeping and gave it me as He had it himself, unhindered, unfettered, unrestrained.

Inasmuch then as different people have a different currency, a man shows his coin and gets what it will buy. A thief has come to the province as Proconsul. What coin does he use? Money. Show him money, and carry off what you will. An adulterer has come. What currency does he use? Pretty girls. 'Take your coin', says he, 'and sell me the thing I want.' Give, and buy. Another's heart is set on minions. Give him the coin and take what you will. Another is a sportsman. Give him a fine horse or dog. With sighs and groans he will sell you what you like for it: for he is constrained from within, by Another, who has ordained this currency.

It is by this principle above all that you must guide yourself in training. Go out as soon as it is dawn and whomsoever you may see and hear, question yourself and answer as to an interrogator.

What did you see? A beautiful woman or boy. Apply the rule: Is this within the will's control or beyond it? Beyond. Away with it then!

What did you see? One mourning at his child's death. Apply the rule: Is death beyond the will, or can the will control it? Death is beyond the will's control. Put it out of the way then!

Did a Consul meet you? Apply the rule: What is a consulship? Is it beyond the will's control or within it? Beyond it. Take it away: the coin will not pass; reject it, you have no concern with it.

I say, if we did this and trained ourselves on this principle every day from dawn to night, we should indeed achieve something. As it is, we are caught open-mouthed by every impression we meet, and only in the lecture-room, if then, does our mind wake up a little. Then we go into the street and if we see a mourner we say, 'He is undone'; if a

Consul, 'Lucky man'; if an outlaw, 'Miserable man'; if a poor man, 'Wretched man, he has nothing to buy food with.'

These mistaken judgements we must eradicate, and concentrate our efforts on doing so. For what is weeping and lamenting? A matter of judgement. What is misfortune? Judgement. What is faction, discord, criticism, accusation, irreligion, foolishness? All these are judgements, nothing else, and judgements passed on things beyond the will, as though they were good and evil. Only let a man turn these efforts to the sphere of the will, and I guarantee that he will enjoy peace of mind, whatever his circumstances may be.

The soul is like a dish full of water, and the impressions like the rays of light which strike the water. Now when the water is disturbed the light seems to be disturbed too, but it is not really disturbed. So when a man has a fit of dizziness, the arts and virtues are not put to confusion, but only the spirit in which they exist: when this is at rest, they come to rest too.

CHAPTER IV

AGAINST ONE WHO WAS INDECOROUSLY EXCITED IN THE THEATRE

WHEN the Procurator of Epirus offended decorum by the way he showed interest in a comedian, the people reviled him for this; thereupon when he brought word of this to Epictetus and expressed annoyance at those who reviled him: Why! he said, what harm were they doing? They too showed their interest as you did!

'What!' said he, 'is this the way they show interest?'

Yes, he said, when they saw you, their Governor, the friend and Procurator of Caesar, showing your interest in this way, would you not expect them to do the same? If it is not right to show interest in that way, leave off doing it yourself: but if it is right, why are you angry at their imitating you? For whom else but you, their superiors, have the people to imitate? Whom are they to look to when they come to the theatre but you? 'See', they say, 'how Caesar's Procurator behaves in the theatre. He cries out: then I will cry out too. He jumps from his seat. I will do so too. His claque of slaves shout from their scattered seats: I have no slaves, I will cry as loud as I can to make up for it.' You ought to know then that when you enter the theatre you enter it as a pattern and example to all other spectators how to behave. Why then did they revile you? Because every man hates what stands in his way. They wanted So-and-so to be crowned, you wanted another; they stood in your way and you in theirs. You were found to be stronger than they; they did what they could, they reviled what stood in their way. What would you have then? That you should do what you wish, and they should not even say what they wish? Nay, what wonder they should talk so? Do not farmers revile Zeus, when He stands in their way? Do not sailors revile Him? Do they not revile Caesar without ceasing? What follows? Does not Zeus know? Does not Caesar have reported to him what men say? What does he do then? He knows that if he punishes all who revile him he will have no one left to rule over. What is my conclusion? When you enter the theatre you ought not to say, 'Let me have Sophron crowned', but, 'Let me keep my will in accord with Nature in this matter, for no one is dearer to me than myself: it is absurd then that I should be injured, that another may be victorious on the stage.'

Whom then do I want to win? The victor: and so the victory will always be in accordance with my wish.

'But I wish Sophron to be crowned.'

Hold as many contests as you please in your own house and proclaim him there victor in the Nemean, Pythian, Isthmian and Olympic games: but in public do not claim more than your share, nor steal what is public property. If you do, you must put up with being reviled: for when you do as the people do, you put yourself on their level.

CHAPTER V

AGAINST THOSE WHO MAKE ILLNESS AN EXCUSE FOR LEAVING THE LECTURE-ROOM

'I AM ill here,' says one, 'and want to go away home.'

What, were you never ill at home? Do you not consider whether you are doing anything here to improve your will, for if you are doing no good, you might just as well never have come? Go away, and attend to your affairs at home: for if your Governing Principle cannot be brought into accord with Nature, no doubt your bit of land will prosper; you will add to your bit of money! You will tend your old father, frequent the market-place, serve as a magistrate, do anything that comes next, poor wretch, in your wretched way. But if you understand that you are getting rid of bad judgements and gaining others in their place, and that you have transferred your attention from things outside the will's control to things within it, and that now if you cry, 'Ah me!' it is not for your father or your brother but for yourself that you cry, then why should you take account of illness any more? Do you not know that disease and death are bound to overtake us whatever we are doing? They overtake the farmer at his farming, the sailor on the seas. What would you like to be doing when they overtake you? For you must needs be overtaken, whatever you are doing. If you can find anything better than this to be doing when you are overtaken, do it by all means!

For my own part I would wish death to overtake me occupied with nothing but the care of my will, trying to make it calm, unhindered, unconstrained, free. I would fain be found so employed, that I may be able to say to God, 'Did I transgress Thy commands? Did I use the faculties Thou gavest me to wrong purpose? Did I use my senses or my primary notions in vain? Did I ever accuse Thee? Did I ever find fault with Thy ordinance? I fell sick, when it was Thy will: so did others, but I rebelled not. I became poor when Thou didst will it, but I rejoiced in my poverty. I held no office, because it was Thy will: I never coveted office. Didst Thou ever see me gloomy for that reason? Did I ever come before Thee but with a cheerful face, ready for any commands or orders that Thou mightest give? Now it is Thy will for me to leave the festival. I go, giving all thanks to Thee, that Thou didst deign to let me share Thy festival and see Thy works and understand Thy government.' May these be my thoughts, these my studies, writing or reading, when death comes upon me!

'But I am ill, and shall not have my mother to hold my head.'

Go to your mother then; for you deserve to be ill, with her to hold your head.

'But I had a nice bed to lie on at home.'

Go to your nice bed then; sick or well you deserve to lie on a bed of that sort! Pray do not lose what you can do there.

But what does Socrates say? 'As one man', he says, 'delights to improve his field, and another his horse, so I delight in following day by day my own improvement.'

'In what? In paltry phrases?'

Man, hold your peace.

'In pretty precepts then?'

Enough of that.

'Nay, but philosophers busy themselves with nothing else, so far as I see.'

Is it nothing (do you think?) never to accuse any one, God or man, never to blame any, to go in and out with the same countenance? These are the things which Socrates knew, and yet he never said that he knew or taught anything; and if any one asked for phrases or precepts, he would take him away to Protagoras or Hippias. In the same way if any one had come looking for greenstuff, he would have taken him to the gardener. Which of you then makes this the purpose of his life? Why, if you did, you would gladly suffer sickness and hunger and death. If any one of you was ever in love with a pretty girl, he knows that I speak true!

CHAPTER VI

SCATTERED SAYINGS

When one of his acquaintances asked why more progress was made in old days, although the processes of reason have been more studied by the men of to-day, he answered, On what has the effort been spent, and in what was the greater progress in the past? For you will find that progress to-day corresponds exactly to the effort spent. The fact is that to-day men have spent their effort on the analysis of syllogisms, and progress is made in that: in old days men spent their effort on maintaining their mind in accord with Nature, and they made progress in that. Therefore do not confound the processes, nor seek to spend effort on one thing and make progress in another. If you look whether any of us who sets himself to keep in accord with Nature and to live his life so, fails to make progress, you will find there is none.

'The good man can suffer no defeat.'

Of course, for he engages in no contest where he is not superior. 'Take my lands, if you will: take my servants, take my office, take my poor body, yet you will not make me fail to get what I will or fall into what I will to avoid.' This is the only contest for which he enters—that which is concerned with the sphere of the will, and therefore he cannot fail to be invincible.

When some one asked him what 'general perception' meant, he replied, You might describe the faculty which only distinguishes sounds as 'general' hearing, but the faculty which distinguishes musical sounds you would not call 'general' but 'technical'. In the same way there are certain things which all men who are not utterly perverted can see in virtue of their general faculties. It is this mental constitution to which the name 'general perception' is given.

It is not easy to give stimulus to young men who have no grit: 'you cannot lift a cream-cheese by a hook' [Musonius Rufus]; but young men of parts hold fast to reason even if you try to deter them. That is why Rufus generally tried to deter them, and made this his test of those who were gifted and those who were not; 'for', said he, 'just as the stone, if you throw it up, will fall to the earth by its own nature, so the gifted soul is all the more inclined towards its natural object, the more you try to beat it off.'

CHAPTER VII

DIALOGUE WITH THE COMMISSIONER[4] OF THE FREE CITIES, WHO WAS AN EPICUREAN

WHEN the Commissioner, who was an Epicurean, came into his lecture-room, It is proper, said Epictetus, that we who are ignorant should inquire of you philosophers what is the Best Thing in the world, just as those who come to a strange city make inquiry of the citizens who know the place; that having learnt what it is we may pursue it for ourselves, and come to the sight of it, as foreigners visit the sights of the cities. For all, one may say, are agreed that man has to do with three things, soul and body and external things; it only remains for you to answer the question, 'What is the *best* in man?' What shall we say to men? Shall we say, 'The flesh'? and was it for this that Maximus sailed as far as Cassiope to see his son on his way? Was it to have pleasure in the flesh? When the Commissioner denied it, saying, 'God forbid!' Epictetus went on, Is it not proper to devote our efforts to what is best in us?

'It is most proper.'

What have we then better than the flesh?

'The soul', he said.

And which are better, the goods of the best element in us or the goods of the inferior?

'Those of the best.'

Are the goods of the soul in the sphere of the will or beyond it?

'Within the sphere of the will.'

Is the pleasure of the soul then within the sphere of the will?

'Yes', he said.

And what gives rise to it? Does it arise of itself? That is inconceivable; for we must assume the existence of the good as something which has value in itself, by partaking in which we shall have pleasure in the soul.

To this too he agreed.

What then will give rise to this pleasure of the soul in us? If the goods of the soul give rise to it, then the nature of the good is discovered; for it is impossible that the good and that which gives us rational delight should be different from one another, or that the consequence should be good unless that on which it depends is good. For the primary end must be good, if that which follows on it is to be rational. But you cannot say this if you have any sense, for you will be saying what is inconsistent with Epicurus, and with the other judgements of your school. You will be reduced to saying that the pleasure of the soul is pleasure in bodily things: these, as it now appears, are of primary value and are identical with the nature of the good.

Therefore Maximus acted foolishly, if he had any motive in sailing but the flesh, that is the highest principle. He acts like a fool too if, as a judge, he refrains from other men's goods when he can take them. If you think fit to do it, the only point for us to look to is that it be done secretly, securely, without any one's knowledge. For even Epicurus himself does not set down stealing as evil, but only detected stealing: and he says 'Do not steal', only because 'it is impossible to be sure of escaping detection'. But I tell you that if it be done cleverly and cautiously, we shall escape detection. Further, we have powerful friends in Rome, both men and women, and the Greeks are feeble folk: no one will have the courage to go to Rome to prosecute. Why do you refrain from your own good? It is foolish and silly. Nay, even if you tell me you refrain, I will not believe you; for just as it is impossible to assent to what appears false and to reject what is true, so it is impossible to hold aloof from what appears good. Now wealth is a good thing, and, so to speak, most productive of pleasure. Why should not one acquire it? Why should we not corrupt our neighbour's wife, if we can do it without detection; and if her husband talks nonsense, why should we not break his neck as well? This, if you wish to be a philosopher of the right sort, to be perfect and consistent with your own judgements. Otherwise you will be no better than we so-called Stoics, for we too say one thing and do another: we say noble words and do shameful deeds! You will be suffering from the opposite perversion, of uttering shameful judgements, and doing noble deeds!

Before God, I ask you, can you imagine a city of Epicureans?

'I shall not marry' (says one).

'Nor shall I,' (says another) 'for it is wrong to marry.'

Yes, and it is wrong to get children, and wrong to be a citizen!

What is to happen then? Where will your citizens come from? Who will educate them? Who will be Governor of the Ephebi? Who will manage the Gymnasia? Yes, and what will be their education? Will it be the education the Lacedaemonians or Athenians received? Take me a young man and bring him up in accordance with your judgements. The judgements are bad, subversive of the city, ruinous to family life, not even fit for women. Man, leave these principles alone. You live in an imperial city: you must hold office, judge justly, refrain from other men's property: no woman but your wife must seem fair in your eyes, no boy, no silver or gold plate. You must look for judgements that will be in keeping with such conduct, and will enable you to refrain with pleasure from things so persuasive to attract and to overcome you. If on the other hand we back up their persuasive power by this philosophy, such as it is, that we have discovered, thrusting us forward and confirming us in the same direction, what is to become of us? What is the best part of a piece of plate, the silver or the art spent on it? The hand in itself is mere flesh, it is the products of the hand that claim precedence. So too appropriate actions are of three kinds: the first class relative to mere existence, the second relative to particular conditions, the third commanding and absolute. On this principle too we ought not to honour man's material being, his rags of flesh, but his leading characteristics. What are these? Citizenship, marriage, procreation of children, worship of God, care of parents, and in general, will to get and to avoid, impulse to act and not to act, each in its proper and natural manner.

What is our nature? To be free, noble, self-respecting. What other animal blushes? What other can have a conception of shame? We must subordinate pleasure to these principles, to minister to them as a servant, to evoke our interests and to keep us in the way of our natural activities.

'But I am rich, and have need of nothing.'

Why then do you still pretend to be a philosopher? Gold and silver plate are enough for you: what need have you of judgements?

'Nay, but I also sit as judge over the Greeks.'

What! you know how to judge? What made you know that?

'Caesar wrote me a patent.'

Let him write to you to judge questions of music: what use will it be to you? But let that pass. How did you get made a judge? Whose hand did you kiss? Was it Symphorus' or Numenius'? [5] In whose antechamber did you sleep? To whom did you send gifts? After all, do you not see that being judge is worth no more nor less than Numenius is worth?

'Well, but I can put any one I wish in prison.'

As you may a stone!

'But I can cudgel to death any one I wish.'

As you can an ass! This is not governing men. Govern us as rational creatures by showing us what is expedient, and we will follow it: show us what is inexpedient and we will turn away from it. Make us admire and emulate you, as Socrates made men do. He was the true ruler of men, for he brought men to submit to him their will to get and to avoid, their impulse to act and not to act.

'Do this, refrain from this, or I will put you in prison.' This is not how rational beings are ruled. But, 'Do this as Zeus ordained: if not, you will suffer penalty and harm.' What kind of harm? No harm but that of failing to do your duty: you will destroy the trustworthy, self-respecting, well-behaved man in you. Look not for any greater harm than this!

CHAPTER VIII

HOW WE SHOULD TRAIN OURSELVES TO DEAL WITH IMPRESSIONS

As WE train ourselves to deal with sophistical questions, so we ought to train ourselves day by day to deal with impressions: for these too propound questions to us.

'The son of So-and-so is dead.'

Answer, That is beyond the will, not an evil.

'So-and-so's father has disinherited him: what do you think?'

It is outside the will, not an evil.

'Caesar has condemned him.'

That is outside the will, not an evil.

'Something has made him grieve.'

That is an act of will, and evil.

'He has endured nobly.'

That is an act of will, and good.

If we acquire this habit, we shall make progress, for we shall never assent to anything but that of which we get a convincing impression.[6]

The son dies. What happens?

The son dies.

Nothing more?

Nothing.

The ship is lost. What happens?

The ship is lost.

He is led to prison. What happens?

He is led to prison. Each man may add, 'He has fared ill', but if so, that is his own affair.

'Still', you say, 'Zeus does wrong to act so.'

Why? Do you mean because He made you patient, noble-minded, because He saved these things from being evil, because He puts it in your power to endure these troubles and still be happy, because He 'opens the door' to you, when your position is impossible? Leave the scene, man, and do not complain.

If you would know the attitude of the Romans to philosophers, listen to this. Italicus, a man of the highest repute as a philosopher among them, in my presence expressed his indignation at his lot, which he thought intolerable, by saying, 'I cannot bear it: you are ruining me, you will make me like him', and pointed to me!

CHAPTER IX

TO A RHETOR GOING UP TO ROME FOR A TRIAL

WHEN a man, who was going to Rome for an action regarding his official position, came in to see him, he inquired the reason for his journey, and when the man went on to ask him his opinion on the matter, 'If you ask me', he said, 'what you will do in Rome, whether you will succeed or fail, I have no precept to offer: but if you ask me how you will do, I can say this, that if your judgements are right you will do well, if wrong, you will do ill. For every man's action is determined by a judgement. What is it that made you desire to be elected patron [7] of the Cnossians?' Judgement.

What is the reason you now go to Rome? Judgement. Yes, and in stormy weather and at your own risk and charges?

'Necessity compels me.'

Who tells you this? Your judgement. If then judgements are the cause of everything and a man has bad judgements, the result resembles the cause, whatever this be. Have we all then sound judgements? Have you and your opponent? Then how are you at variance? Have you sound judgements any more than he? Why? You think so. So does he, and so do madmen. Opinion is a bad criterion. No! Show me that you have examined your judgements and paid attention to them. You are now sailing to Rome to be patron of the Cnossians and are not content to stay at home with the honours you had before, but desire some greater and more distinguished honour. When did you ever take the trouble to sail like this in order to examine your judgements and reject any that are bad? Whom have you ever consulted for this purpose? What time or what part of your life have you charged with this duty? Review the seasons of your life in your own mind, if you respect me. Did you examine your judgements when you were a boy? Did not you do what you did then as you do everything now? And when you grew to be a youth and listened to the teachers of rhetoric and wrote declamations of your own, what did you imagine that you lacked? And when in early manhood you began to enter public life and to plead in cases and to have a reputation, did you ever think any one your equal? Would you ever have let any one examine you and show that your judgements were bad? What then would you have me tell you?

'Give me some help in the matter.'

I have no precepts to offer for your purpose: and if you have come to me for this, you have come to me as you would come to a greengrocer or a shoemaker and not as to a philosopher.

'For what purpose then have philosophers precepts to offer?'

For this: that, whatever the issue may be, we should keep our Governing Principle in accord with Nature to our life's end. Do you think this a small matter?

'No, the greatest of all.'

Well then: will a little time suffice for this, and can it be acquired in a passing visit? Acquire it if you can!

Then you will go away and say, 'I met Epictetus, it was like meeting a stone, or a statue.'

Yes, for you just saw me and no more. Man can only meet man properly when he gets to understand his convictions and shows him his own in turn. Get to know my judgements, and show me yours, and then say that you have met me. Let us question one another: if one of my judgements is bad, remove it: if you have anything to say, put it forward. That is how to meet a philosopher. That's not your way, but 'We are passing through: while we wait to charter our ship, we can see Epictetus; let us see what he is saying.' Then when you leave you say, 'Epictetus was nothing: he talked bad Greek, outlandish stuff.' Of course, of what else are you competent to judge, coming in like that?

'But', he goes on, 'if I let myself be absorbed in these things, I shall be like you without land, like you without silver cups, like you without fine cattle.'

To this perhaps it is sufficient to answer, I have no need of them: but if you get a large property, you still need something else, and willy-nilly you are poorer than I.

'What do you mean that I need?'

You need what you have not got—tranquillity, a mind in accord with Nature, and free from perturbation. Whether I am Patron or not, what does it matter? It does matter to you. I am richer than you: I am not in an agony as to what Caesar will think of me: I do not flatter any one for that. This is what I have instead of your silver and gold plate. You have vessels of gold, but your reason—judgements, assent, impulse, will—is of common clay. But mine are in accord with Nature, and that being so, why should I not make a special study of reasoning? I have leisure, and my mind is not distracted. How can I occupy my mind that is thus free? I cannot find an occupation more worthy of man than that. When you have nothing to do, you are troubled in spirit, and enter a theatre, or wander aimlessly. Why should not the philosopher devote his efforts to developing his own reason? You devote yourself to crystal vases, I to the syllogism called 'the Liar': you to murrhine[8] vessels, I to the syllogism of 'Denial'. To you all that you have appears small: to me all I have appears great. Your desire can never be fulfilled, mine is fulfilled already. Your case is like that of children putting their hand into a narrow-necked jar and pulling out raisins and almonds. If a child fills his hand full, he cannot pull it out and then he cries. Let a few go, child, and you will get it out. So I say to you, 'Let your desire go.' Do not crave much, and you will obtain.

CHAPTER X

HOW ONE SHOULD BEAR ILLNESSES

We should have each judgement ready at the moment when it is needed: judgements on dinner at dinner-time, on the bath at bathing-time, on bed at bedtime.

Admit not sleep into your tender eyelids
Till you have reckoned up each deed of the day—
How have I erred, what done or left undone?
So start, and so review your acts, and then
For vile deeds chide yourself, for good be glad.

[Ascribed to Pythagoras]

Keep hold of these lines for practical use, not to declaim them as a cry like 'Paean Apollo'. Again in a fever we must be ready with judgements for that; if we fall into a fever we must not give up and forget everything, and say, 'If I ever study philosophy again, may the worst befall me! I must go off somewhere and attend to my poor body.' Well, but does not fever come there? What does studying philosophy mean? Does it not mean preparing to face events? Do you not understand then that what you are saying comes to this, 'If I go on preparing to bear events quietly, may the worst befall me'? That is as though a man should give up competing for the pancration because he has been struck. But there it is possible to leave off and so escape a beating: but what profit do we get if we leave off studying philosophy?

What ought one to say then as each hardship comes? 'I was practising for *this*, I was training for *this*.' God says to you, 'Give me a proof, whether you have kept the rules of wrestling—eaten the proper food, trained, and obeyed the trainer.' After that, are you going to play the coward when the moment of action comes? If now is the time for fever, take your fever in the right way; if for thirst, thirst in the right way, if for hunger, hunger aright. Is it not in your power? Who will hinder you? The physician will hinder you from drinking, but he cannot hinder you from thirsting aright: he will hinder you from eating, but he cannot hinder you from hungering in the right way.

'But am I not a student?'

Why are you a student? Slave, is it not that you may be happy and have peace of mind? Is it not that you may conform to nature and so live your life? What hinders you in a fever from keeping your Governing Principle in accord with Nature? Here is the test of the matter, this is how the philosopher is proved. For fever too is a part of life, like walking, sailing, travelling. Do you read when you are walking? No. Nor do you in a fever: but if you walk aright, you have done your part as a walker; if you bear your fever aright, you have done your part as a sick man. What does bearing fever rightly mean? It means not to blame God or man, not to be crushed by what happens, to await death in a right spirit, to do what you are bidden; when the physician comes in, not to be afraid of what he may say, and if he says, 'You are doing well', not to be overjoyed: for what good is there in that? What good had you when you were in health? It means not to be disheartened if he says, 'You are doing badly'; for what does 'doing badly' mean? It means drawing near the dissolution of the soul from the body. What is there to fear in that? If you do not draw near now, shall you not draw near later? Is the world going to be turned upside down by your death? Why then do you coax the physician? Why do you say, 'Master, if you will, I shall get well'? Why do you give him occasion to lift his brow in arrogance? As you give the shoemaker his due in regard to the foot, the builder in regard to the house, why do you not give the physician his due (and no more) in regard to the paltry body, for the body is not mine and is naturally dead? This is what the moment requires from the man in a fever: if he fulfils these requirements, he has what is his own.

It is not the business of the philosopher to guard these outward things—paltry wine or oil or body—but to guard his Governing Principle. How is he to regard outward things? Only so far that he does not concern himself with them unreasonably. What occasion is left then for fear? What occasion for anger, what occasion for fear concerning things that are not our own, nor of any value? For the two principles we must have ready at command are these: that outside the will there is nothing good or evil, and that we must not lead events but follow them. 'My brother ought not to have behaved so to me.' No, but it is his business to look to that; however he may behave, I will deal with him as I ought. This is my part, that is another's: this no one can hinder, that is subject to hindrance.

CHAPTER XI

SCATTERED SAYINGS

THERE are certain punishments ordained as it were by law for those who disobey the government of God. Whoever judges anything to be good except what depends upon the will, let him be liable to envy, desire, flattery, distraction. Whoever judges anything else to be evil (save acts of the will), let distress be his, and mourning, lamentation, misfortune. And yet, though we suffer punishments so severe, we cannot refrain.

Remember what the poet says about the stranger:

Stranger, though baser man than thou should come,
He must be honoured, for the hand of Zeus
Guards stranger folk and poor.

[Homer, *Odyssey*, XIV. 56]

One should be ready to apply this to a father: 'Though a baser one than thou should come, I may not dishonour a father; for all depend on Zeus, God of our fathers', and to a brother, 'for all depend on Zeus, God of kindred'. In the same way we shall find that Zeus is Protector of all other relations of life.

CHAPTER XII

ON TRAINING

WE OUGHT not to train ourselves in unnatural or extraordinary actions, for in that case we who claim to be philosophers shall be no better than mountebanks. For it is difficult to walk on a tight-rope, and not only difficult but dangerous as well: ought we for that reason to practise walking on a tight-rope or setting up a palm-tree, or embracing statues? By no means. Not everything that is difficult and dangerous is suitable for training, but only that which is conducive to what is set before us as the object of our effort. What is set before us as the object of our effort? To move without hindrance in the will to get and the will to avoid. And what does that mean? Not to fail in what we will nor to fall into what we avoid. To this end, therefore, let our training be directed: for since it is impossible without great and continuous effort to secure that the will to get fail not and the will to avoid be not foiled, know that, if you allow training to be directed to things lying outside and beyond the will, you will not get what you will to get nor avoid what you will to avoid.

And since habit has established a strong predominance, because we have acquired the habit of turning our will to get and our will to avoid only to what lies outside our control, we must set a contrary habit to counteract the former, and where impressions are most likely to go wrong there employ training as an antidote.

I am inclined to pleasure: in order to train myself I will incline beyond measure in the opposite direction. I am disposed to avoid trouble: I will harden and train my impressions to this end, that my will to avoid may hold aloof from everything of this kind. For how do we describe the man who trains? He is the man who practises avoiding the use of his will to get, and willing to avoid only what is in the sphere of the will and who exercises himself in what is hard to overcome. And so different men have to train for different objects. What is it to the purpose here to set up a palm-tree, or to carry about a hut of skins or a pestle and mortar? Man, train yourself, if you are arrogant, to bear with being reviled, and not to be annoyed when you are disparaged. Then you will make such progress that, even if you are struck, you will say to yourself, 'Imagine that you have embraced a statue.' Next train yourself to use wine properly, not for heavy drinking—for there are men misguided enough to train for this—but first to abstain from wine, and to leave alone pretty maids and sweet cakes. Then, if the proper time comes, you will enter the lists, if at all, to try yourself and learn whether your impressions overcome you as before. But to begin with, fly far from enemies that are stronger than you. The battle is an unequal one when it is between a pretty maid and a young man beginning philosophy. 'Pot and stone', as the saying is, 'do not agree.'

Next after the will to get and the will to avoid comes the sphere of impulse for action and against action: where the object is to obey reason, not to do anything at the wrong time or place, or offend the harmony of things in any other way.

Third comes the sphere of assents, concerned with things plausible and attractive. For, as Socrates bade men 'not live a life without examination', so you ought not to accept an impression without examination, but say, 'Wait, let me see who you are and whence you come', just as the night-watch say, 'Show me your token.' 'Have you the token given by nature, which the impression that is to be accepted must have?'

And to conclude, the methods which are applied to the body by those who exercise it, may themselves conduce to training, if they tend in this direction, that is, if they bear upon the will to get and the will to avoid. But if their object is display, they are the marks of one who has swerved from the right line, whose aims are alien, one who is looking for spectators to say, 'What a great man!' This is why Apollonius was right in saying, 'If you wish to train for your soul's sake, when you are thirsty in hot weather take a mouthful of cold water and spit it out and tell no one!'

CHAPTER XIII

WHAT A 'FORLORN' CONDITION MEANS, AND A 'FORLORN' MAN

THE 'forlorn' state is the condition of one without help. For a man is not forlorn simply because he is alone, any more than a man in a crowd is unforlorn. At any rate when we lose a brother or a son or a friend, in whom we rest our trust, we say that we have been left forlorn, though often we are in Rome, with that great throng meeting us in the streets, and those numbers living about us, and sometimes we have a multitude of slaves. For according to its conception the term 'forlorn' means that a man is without help, exposed to those who wish to harm him. For this reason, when we are travelling, we call ourselves forlorn most of all, when we fall among robbers. For it is not the sight of a man as such that relieves us from being forlorn, but the sight of one who is faithful and self-respecting and serviceable. For if being alone is enough to make one forlorn, you must say that Zeus Himself is forlorn at the Conflagration of the Universe [9] and bewails Himself: 'Unhappy me! I have neither Hera nor Athena nor Apollo nor, in a word, brother or son or grandson or kinsman.' And in fact this is what some say that He does, when left alone in the Conflagration: for they cannot conceive of the mode of life of a solitary Being: they start with a natural principle, the fact that men are by nature drawn by ties of fellowship and mutual affection, and enjoy converse with their kind. But nevertheless a man must prepare himself for solitude too—he must be able to suffice for himself, and able to commune with himself. Just as Zeus communes with Himself and is at peace with Himself and reflects upon the nature of His government, and occupies Himself with thoughts appropriate to Himself, so should we be able to talk to ourselves, without need of others, or craving for diversion: we should study the divine government and the relation in which we stand to other things: we should consider what was our attitude to events before, and what it is now: what the things are which still afflict us: how they may be cured, how removed: if any things need to be brought to perfection, perfect them as reason requires.

For see: Caesar[10] seems to provide us with profound peace; there are no wars nor battles any more, no great bands of robbers or pirates: we are able to travel by land at every season, and to sail from sunrise to sunset. Can he then provide us also with peace from fever, from shipwreck, from fire or earthquake or thunderbolt? Go to, can he give us peace from love? He cannot. From mourning? He cannot. From envy? No! he cannot give us peace from any of them. But the reasoning of philosophers promises to give us peace from these troubles also. What does it say? 'Men, if you attend to me, wherever you may be, whatever you may be doing, you will feel no distress, no anger, no compulsion, no hindrance, but will live undisturbed and free from all distractions.' When a man has this peace proclaimed to him, not by Caesar (how could *he* proclaim it?) but proclaimed by God, through the voice of reason, is he not content when he is alone? When he considers and reflects, 'Now no evil can befall me, robber exists not for me, earthquake exists not: all is full of peace and tranquillity: every road, every city, every meeting, neighbour, companion—all are harmless.' Another, Who takes care of me, supplies food and raiment; He has given me senses and primary conceptions; and when He does not provide necessaries, He sounds the recall, He opens the door and says, "Come." Where? To nothing you need fear, but to that whence you were born, to your friends and kindred, the elements. So much of you as was fire shall pass into fire, what was earth shall pass into earth, the spirit into spirit, the water into water. There is no Hades, nor Acheron, nor Cocytus, nor Pyriphlegethon, but all is full of gods and divine beings. When one has this to think upon, and when he beholds the sun and moon and stars, and enjoys land and sea, he is not forlorn any more than he is destitute of help.

'Nay,' you say, 'but what if one come upon me alone and murder me?'

Fool, he murders not you, but your paltry body.

How can we speak any more then of being forlorn and helpless? Why do we make ourselves worse than children? For what do children do when they are left alone? They pick up potsherds and dust and build something or other and then pull it down and build something else again, and so they never lack diversion. If you sail away, am I to sit and shed tears because I am left alone and forlorn? Shall I not in that case have my potsherds and my dust? But they do this in their foolishness: do we in our wisdom make ourselves miserable?

Great power is always dangerous in a beginner. We must then bear such things according to our strength, but always according to nature. A certain course may suit a strong man but not a consumptive. Be content to practise the life of an invalid, that you may one day live the life of a healthy man. Take scant food, drink water: refrain from willing to get anything for a while, that you may one day direct your will rationally. If you do so, then, when you have some good in you, you will direct your will aright.

'No,' you say, 'we want at once to live as wise men and benefit mankind.'

Benefit indeed! What are you after? Did you ever benefit yourself?

'But I want to stir them up.'

Have you stirred yourself up first? You want to benefit them; then show them in your own life what sort of men philosophy makes, and cease to talk folly. When you eat, benefit those who eat with you, when you drink, benefit those who drink, by yielding and giving way to all, by bearing with them: that is the way to benefit them and not by venting your own phlegm [11] upon them!

CHAPTER XIV

SCATTERED SAYINGS

As BAD actors cannot sing alone, but only in a large company, so some men cannot walk alone. Man, if you are worth anything, you must walk alone, and talk to yourself and not hide in the chorus. Learn to bear mockery, look about you, examine yourself, that you may get to know who you are.

When a man drinks water, or puts himself in training in any way, he tells everybody at every opportunity, 'I am a water-drinker.' What? Do you drink water for the sake of drinking it? Man, if it is to your profit to drink it, drink; if not, your conduct is absurd. I say, if you drink water because it does you good, say nothing to those who dislike it. What? Are these the people of all others that you wish to please?

Actions have varying degrees of value: some are based on first principles, others are determined by circumstances, or compromise, or compliance, or manner of life.

There are two qualities that men must get rid of—conceit and diffidence. Conceit is to think that one needs nothing beyond oneself: diffidence is to suppose that one cannot live the untroubled life in the midst of so many difficulties. Now conceit is removed by cross-questioning, and that was what Socrates began with: that the thing is not impossible you must discover by thought and search. This search will do you no harm: and indeed philosophy means very little else but this—to search how it is practicable to exercise the will to get and the will to avoid without hindrance.

'I am better than you, for my father is of consular rank.' Another says, 'I have been tribune, and you have not.' If we were horses you would say, 'My sire was swifter', or, 'I have plenty of barley and fodder', or, 'I have fine trappings.' If you said that, you may imagine me replying, 'Very well then, let us try our paces.' Come, is there nothing in men, like the pace of a horse, which will enable us to distinguish the better from the worse? Are there not self-respect, honour, justice? Show yourself superior in these qualities, that you may be superior as a man should be. If you say to me, 'I am great at kicking', I shall answer, 'That is the boast of an ass!'

CHAPTER XV

THAT WE SHOULD APPROACH EVERYTHING WITH CONSIDERATION [12]

IN EVERYTHING you do consider what comes first and what follows, and so approach it. Otherwise you will come to it with a good heart at first because you have not reflected on any of the consequences, and afterwards when difficulties come in sight you will shamefully desist.

'I wish to win at the Olympic games.'

'So do I, by the gods, for it is a fine thing.'

Yes, but consider the first steps to it and what follows: and then, if it is to your advantage, lay your hand to the work. You must be under discipline, eat to order, touch no sweets, train under compulsion, at a fixed hour, in heat and cold, drink no cold water, nor wine, except to order; you must hand yourself over completely to your trainer as you would to a physician. Then, when the contest comes, you get hacked, sometimes dislocate your hand, twist your ankle, swallow plenty of sand, get a flogging, and with all this you are sometimes defeated. First consider these things and then enter on the athlete's career, if you still wish to do so: otherwise, look you, you will be behaving like the children, who one day play at athletes, another at gladiators, then sound the trumpet, next dramatize anything they see and admire. You will be just the same—now athlete, now gladiator, then philosopher, then orator, but nothing with all your soul. Like an ape you imitate everything you see, and one thing after another takes your fancy, but nothing that is familiar pleases you, for you undertake nothing with forethought; you do not survey the whole subject and examine it beforehand, but you take it up half-heartedly and at random. In the same way some people when they see a philosopher, and hear some one speaking like Euphrates (and indeed who can speak as he can?) wish to be philosophers themselves.

Man, consider first, what it is you are undertaking: then consider your own powers, and what you can bear. If you want to be a wrestler, look to your shoulders, your thighs, your loins. For different men are born for different things. Do you suppose that you can be a philosopher if you do as you do now? Do you suppose that you can eat and drink as you do now, and indulge your anger and displeasure just as before? Nay, you must sit up late, you must work hard, conquer some of your desires, abandon your own people, be looked down on by a mere slave, be ridiculed by those who meet you, get the worst of it in everything—in office, in honour, in justice. When you have carefully considered these drawbacks, then come to us, if you think fit: if you are willing to pay this price for peace of mind, freedom, tranquillity. If not, do not come near: do not be like the children, first a philosopher, then a tax-collector, then an orator, then one of Caesar's procurators. These callings do not agree. You must be one man, good or bad: you must develop either your rational soul, or your outward endowments, you must be busy either with your inner man, or with things outside, that is, you must choose between the position of a philosopher and that of an ordinary man.

When Galba was killed some one said to Rufus, 'Now the world is governed by Providence, isn't it?' To which he answered, 'Did I base my proof that the world is governed by Providence upon a casual thing like Galba's death?'

CHAPTER XVI

THAT WE MUST BE CAUTIOUS IN OUR SOCIAL RELATIONS

THE man who mixes with other people a good deal either for talk or for a wine-party or generally for social purposes, must needs either grow like them himself or convert them to his likeness; for if you put a quenched coal by one that is burning, either it will put the burning one out, or will catch fire from it. As the risk then is so serious, you must be cautious in indulging lightly in the society of the untrained, for it is impossible to rub up against one who is covered with soot and not get sooty oneself. What are you going to do, if he talks about gladiators, about horses, about athletes, worse still if he talks about men: 'So-and-so is bad', 'So-and-so is good': 'That was well done', 'That was ill done': again, if he mocks or jeers, or shows a malicious humour? Has any of you the perfect skill of the lyre-player, who takes up his lyre and has only to touch the strings to know which are out of tune and so tune his instrument? Which of you has the faculty that Socrates had, of drawing to his side those who met him in any kind of society?

How could you have? *You* must needs be converted by your untrained companions.

Why then are they stronger than you? It is because these unsound sayings of theirs are based upon judgements, but your fine words come merely from your lips: that is why they are without life or vigour, that is why a man may well loathe the sound of your exhortations and your wretched 'virtue', which you prate of so glibly. That is how the untrained get the better of you: for judgement is powerful everywhere, judgement suffers no defeat. Therefore, until your fine ideas are firmly fastened in you, and until you acquire some power to secure them, I advise you to be cautious in associating with the untrained: otherwise anything you take note of in the lecture-room will melt away day by day like wax in the sun. Therefore go away somewhere far from the sun, as long as your ideas are in this waxen state. For this reason philosophers even advise us to leave our own countries, because old habits are a drag on us and prevent us from beginning to acquire a new set of habits, and we cannot bear men meeting us and saying, 'Look, So-and-so is turning philosopher, behaving like this and like that.' On the same principle physicians send away patients who are ill for long to a new country and a new climate, and rightly so. Do the same. Adopt new habits: fix your opinions, exercise yourselves in them. No, you leave the lecture-room to go to a show, a gladiatorial display, a colonnade, a circus: then you come back here from them and return there again, and nothing affects you. So you acquire no habit that gives you distinction; you pay no regard or attention to yourself: you do not watch yourself and ask, 'How do I deal with the impressions that meet me? Naturally, or unnaturally? How am I to answer their call? Rightly or wrongly? Do I warn things beyond my will that they have no concern with me?' I say, if you are not yet in this state, then fly from your former habits, fly from the uneducated, if you wish to begin at last to be more than ciphers.

CHAPTER XVII

CONCERNING PROVIDENCE

When you accuse Providence, only consider the matter, and you will understand that its action is according to reason.

'But the unjust man', you say, 'is better off.'

In what? In money: for in regard to this he has the advantage over you, because he flatters, is shameless. is vigilant. Is this surprising? But look whether he is better off than you in being trustworthy and self-respecting. You will find that he is not; where you are superior to him, you will find that you are better off. So when some one was indignant once at the prosperity of Philostorgos, I said, 'Would you be willing to share the bed of Suras?' 'May that day never come!' he said. 'Why then are you indignant at his getting a return for what he sells, or how do you come to count him blessed who gets what he has by means that you abhor? Or what is the harm in Providence giving the better lot to those who are better? Is it not better to be self-respecting than to be rich?'

He agreed.

Man, why are you indignant then at having the better lot? Therefore always remember the truth and be ready to apply it—that it is a law of nature for the better to have the advantage of the worse in that in which he is better, and then you will never be indignant.

'But my wife uses me ill.'

Very well: if any one asks you, 'What is the matter?' say, 'My wife uses me ill.'

'Nothing else?'

Nothing.

'My father gives me nothing' . . . but need you go further in your own mind and add this lie, that poverty is evil? For this reason it is not poverty that we must cast out, but our judgement about poverty, and so we shall be at peace.

CHAPTER XVIII

THAT WE MUST NOT ALLOW NEWS TO DISTURB US

WHEN any disturbing news is brought you, bear this in mind, that news cannot affect anything within the region of the will. Can any one bring news to you that you are wrong in your thought or wrong in your will? Surely not: but only that some one is dead; what does that concern you? That some one speaks ill of you; what does that concern you? That your father has some design or other. Against whom? Is it against your will? How can he have? No, it is against your wretched body, or your wretched property; you are safe, it is not against *you*.

But the judge pronounces that you are guilty of impiety. Did not the judges pronounce the same on Socrates? Is it your concern that the judge pronounced on you? No. Why then do you trouble yourself?

Your father has a duty of his own, which he must fulfil, or else lose his character as father, affectionate and gentle. Do not try to make him lose anything else for that reason; for a man never suffers harm except in that in which he is at fault.

Again, it is your duty to make your defence with firmness, self-respect, dispassionately: otherwise you lose your character as son, self-respecting and honourable. What then? Is the judge free from danger? No: he too incurs danger just as much. Why then do you still fear what judgement he will give? What have you to do with another's evil? Your evil is to defend yourself badly: that is the only thing you need be careful about. Whether you are condemned or not condemned is another's business, and the evil in the same way is another's.

'So-and-so threatens you.'

Threatens me? No.

'He blames you.'

It will be for him to see how he does his own business.

'He is going to condemn you unjustly.'

All the worse for him!

CHAPTER XIX

WHAT IS THE DIFFERENCE BETWEEN THE PHILOSOPHER AND THE UNEDUCATED MAN

THE first difference between the philosopher and the uneducated man is that the latter says, 'Woe is me for my child, for my brother, woe is me for my father', and the other, if he is compelled to speak, considers the matter and says, 'Woe is me for myself.' For nothing outside the will can hinder or harm the will; it can only harm itself. If then we accept this, and, when things go amiss, are inclined to blame ourselves, remembering that judgement alone can disturb our peace and constancy, I swear to you by all the gods that we have made progress.

Instead of this we have come the wrong way from the beginning. When we were still children, if we stumbled when we were star-gazing, the nurse, instead of rebuking us, struck the stone. What is wrong with the stone? Was it to move out of the way because of your child's folly? Again, if (when children) we do not find something to eat after our bath our attendant does not check our appetite, but flogs the cook. Man, did we appoint you to attend on the cook? No, on our child: correct him, do him good. So even when we are grown up we appear like children: for it is being a child to be unmusical in musical things, ungrammatical in grammar, uneducated in life.

CHAPTER XX

THAT BENEFIT MAY BE DERIVED FROM ALL OUTWARD THINGS

IN REGARD to intellectual impressions it is generally agreed that good and evil depend upon us and not upon external things. No one calls the proposition, 'It is day', good, or 'It is night', bad, or 'Three is four', the greatest of evils. No, they say that knowledge is good and error evil, so that good may arise even in regard to what is false; that is, the knowledge that it is false. The same ought to be true in practical life.

'Is health good, and disease evil?'

No, man.

'What then?'

To use health well is good, to use it ill is evil.

'Do you mean that benefit can be gained even from disease?'

By heaven, can it not be gained even from death, ay or from lameness? Do you think Menoeceus gained but little good by his death?

'Nay, if any one says that sort of thing, I wish him a benefit like that Menoeceus gained!'

Out upon you, man, did he not preserve the patriot, the man of great mind, trustworthy and noble? And if he had lived on, was he not bound to lose all these, and win their very opposite? Would he not in that case have assumed the character of the coward, the ignoble, the hater of his country and lover of his life? Go to, do you think he gained but little good by his death? Well, did Admetus' father gain great good by living on so ignobly and miserably? Did he not die afterwards? I adjure you by the gods, cease to admire material things, cease to make yourselves slaves, first of things, and next, for their sake, of men who can acquire them or take them away.

'Can we then get benefit from these things?'

From all.

'Even from one who reviles us?'

Why, what good does the athlete get from the man who wrestles with him? The greatest. So my reviler helps to train me for the contest: he trains me to be patient, dispassionate, gentle. You deny it? You admit that the man who grips my neck and gets my loins and shoulders into order does me good, and the trainer does well to bid me 'lift the pestle with both hands', and the more severe he is, the more good do I get: and are you going to tell me that he who trains me to be free from anger does me no good? That means that you do not know how to get any good from humankind.

'He is a bad neighbour', you say?

Yes, for himself: but he is good for me; he trains me to be considerate and fair-minded.

'A bad father.'

Yes, for himself, but not for me. This is the magic wand of Hermes. 'Touch what you will', he says, 'and it will turn to gold.' Nay, bring what you will and I will turn it to good. Bring illness, bring death, bring poverty, bring reviling, bring the utmost peril of the law-court: the wand of Hermes will turn them all to good purpose!

'What will you make of death?'

What else but an adornment for you, what else but a means for you to show in deed what man is when he follows the will of nature?

'What will you make of sickness?'

I will show its nature, I will shine in it. I will be firm and tranquil, I will not flatter my physician nor pray for death. What more do you look for? Whatever you give me I will make it a means of blessedness and happiness, make it dignified and admirable.

That is not your way. You say, 'See you do not fall ill, it is an evil.' It is like saying, 'See you do not get an impression that three is four, it is an evil.' Man, how is it an evil? If I get a right notion of it, it cannot harm me any more. Will it not rather do me good? If then I have proper notions of poverty, of sickness, of life without office, is not that enough for me? Will they not serve my good? How then should I seek any more for good and evil in things external?

But we do not act on this. We carry these views to the lecture-room door, but no one takes them home: as soon as we leave here we are at war with our slave-boy, with our neighbours, with those who jeer and laugh at us. Good luck to the Lesbian,[13] for he convicts me every day of knowing nothing.

CHAPTER XXI

TO THOSE WHO UNDERTAKE THE PROFESSION OF TEACHER WITH A LIGHT HEART

THOSE who have learnt precepts and nothing more are anxious to give them out at once, just as men with weak stomachs vomit food. First digest your precepts, and then you will not vomit them; undigested, they become vomit indeed, impure and uneatable. Show us that you have digested them to some purpose, and that your Governing Principle is changed, as athletes can show their shoulders, as a result of their training and eating, and as those who have acquired the arts can show the result of their learning. The carpenter does not come and say, 'Hear me discourse on carpentry', but he undertakes a contract and builds a house and so shows that he has acquired the art. Do you likewise: eat as a man, drink as a man, adorn yourself, marry, get children, live a citizen's life; endure revilings, bear with an inconsiderate brother, bear with a father, a son, a travelling companion. Show us that you can do this, and then we shall see that you have in truth learnt something from the philosophers. Not you: you say, 'Come and hear me reading out comments!' Away with you, look for some one to disgorge your vomit on.

'I assure you I will expound Chrysippus' doctrines to you as no one else can. I will break up his language and make it quite clear. I will add, it may be, a touch of Antipater's or Archedemus' verve.'

What! is it for this that young men are to leave their countries and their parents, that they may come and hear you expounding petty points of language? Ought they not to return ready to bear with others and work with them, tranquil and free from tumult, furnished with a provision for life's journey, which will enable them to bear what befalls them well and to adorn themselves thereby? And how are you to impart to them what you do not possess yourself? For your sole occupation from the first has been this—how you are to resolve syllogisms and variable arguments, and arguments concluding with a question.

'But So-and-so gives lectures, why should not I?'

Slave, you cannot do this off-hand, and in a random fashion. It demands mature years, and a certain way of life, and the guidance of God.

You say no: but no one sails from harbour without sacrificing to the gods and invoking their help, and men do not sow at random, but only when they have invoked Demeter; and when a man has laid his hand to a task so momentous as this without the gods' help, will he be secure and will those who come to him be fortunate in their coming? Man, what are you doing but making the Mysteries common? You say, 'There is a shrine at Eleusis, lo, here is one also: there is a hierophant there: I too will make a hierophant: there is a herald there, I too will appoint a herald: there is a torch-bearer there, I too will have a torch-bearer: there are torches there, so there are here: the cries are the same. What difference is there between our doings and the Mysteries?'

Most impious of men, is there no difference? The benefit of the Mysteries depends on proper place and time: one must approach with sacrifice and prayer, with body purified and mind ready and disposed to approach holy rites and ancient sanctities. Only so do the Mysteries bring benefit, only so do we arrive at the belief that all these things were established by those of old for our education and the amendment of our life. But you publish and divulge them out of place and out of season, without sacrifices or purifying: you have not the dress which the hierophant should have, nor the proper hair, nor the fillet: you have not the right voice nor age, you have not lived pure as he has, but you have merely learnt off the words and say, 'The words have a holy power in themselves.'

You must approach the task in another fashion: it is momentous and full of mystery, not a chance gift which any one can command. The care of the young demands, it may be, more than wisdom: yes, by Zeus, one must have a certain readiness and special fitness, and a certain habit of body, and above all the counsel of God advising one to discharge this duty, as He counselled Socrates to examine men, and Diogenes to rebuke men in royal fashion, and Zeno to instruct and lay down precepts. You open a doctor's consulting-room with nothing but some drugs, without ever taking the trouble to acquire a knowledge of when or how they are applied. 'See, that's his remedy, eye-salve' (you say): 'I have that too.' Have you also the faculty of using it? Do you know when and how and to whom it will do good? Why then do you play at hazard with matters of highest moment, why are you reckless, why do you take in hand a task unsuited to your powers? Leave it to those who can do it and do it with distinction.

Do not bring disgrace upon philosophy by your personal act, nor join those who disparage the profession; but if the study of precepts really attracts you, sit quietly and turn them over in your mind, but never call yourself a philosopher nor allow any one else to do so, but say: 'He is in error: I am unchanged; my will, my impulses, my assent, are what they were, and, in a word, I have not advanced from my position, but deal with impressions as before.' So think, so speak about yourself, if you would think aright. But if this is beyond you, then play at hazard and do as you are doing, for you will be acting in character.

CHAPTER XXII

ON THE CALLING OF THE CYNIC [14]

WHEN one of his acquaintance, who seemed inclined to the Cynic School, asked him what should be the character of the Cynic, and what was the primary conception of the school, he said, We will consider it at leisure: but this much I can tell you, that he who undertakes so great an enterprise without God's help is under God's wrath, and has no other wish but to disgrace himself in the public eye, for in a well-managed house a man does not come forward and say to himself, 'I ought to be steward': for, if he does, the master of the house takes notice, and when he sees him swaggering and ordering people about, he drags him away and gives him the lash. So it happens also in this great City of the Universe. Here, too, there is a Master of the House who assigns each thing its place.

'You are the sun: your faculty is to revolve and make the year and the seasons, to give growth and increase to the fruits, to rouse the winds and bring them to rest and to give temperate warmth to men's bodies; go, travel on your course and so move all things from the greatest to the least.'

'You are a calf: when a lion appears, do your part, or you will suffer for it.' 'You are a bull, come near and fight: for this is your proper portion and lies within your powers.' 'You can lead the army against Ilion: be Agamemnon.' 'You can fight Hector in single combat: be Achilles.' But if Thersites came forward and claimed the command he would not get it, or if he got it he would be shamed before a multitude of witnesses.

You, like the rest, must give the matter careful thought: it is not what you think. 'I wear a coarse cloak now and shall do so then, I sleep hard now and shall still do so, I shall take to myself a wallet and a staff and begin to go about begging and reviling those I meet, and if I see any one using pitch-plasters, [15] or with his hair finely dressed, or walking in scarlet, I shall rebuke him.'

If that is your impression of the Cynic's calling, give it a wide berth: do not come near it, for you have no concern with it; but if you have a true impression of it and still deem yourself not unworthy, then consider what a great enterprise you are taking in hand.

First, you must show a complete change in your conduct, and must cease to accuse God or man: you must utterly put away the will to get, and must will to avoid only what lies within the sphere of your will: you must harbour no anger, wrath, envy, pity: a fair maid, a fair name, favourites, or sweet cakes, must mean nothing to you. For you must know that other men, when they indulge in such things, have the protection of their walls and houses and darkness. There are many things to hide them: one, may be, has closed the door, or has set some one to guard his chamber: 'If any one comes, say, "He is out" or "He is busy."' But the Cynic, instead of all these, should have self-respect for his shelter: if he has not that, he will be naked and exposed and put to shame. This is his house, his door, this his chamber-guards, this his darkness: for he must not wish to conceal anything that is his: if he does, he disappears; he loses the true Cynic, the free open-air spirit, he has begun to fear outward things, he has begun to have need of concealment, and when he would hide himself he cannot; for he has no place or means to hide himself. But if by chance the public teacher, the 'pedagogue' is caught erring what must be his feelings! Is it possible with these fears before one to be confident with one's whole mind, and command other men? It is impracticable, impossible.

First then you must make your Governing Principle pure, and hold fast this rule of life, 'Henceforth my mind is the material I have to work on, as the carpenter has his timber and the shoemaker his leather: my business is to deal with my impressions aright. My wretched body is nothing to me, its parts are nothing to me. Death? Let it come when it will, whether to my whole body or to a part of it. Exile? Can one be sent into exile beyond the Universe? One cannot. Wherever I go, there is the sun, there is the moon, there are the stars, dreams, auguries, conversation with the gods.'

The true Cynic when he has ordered himself thus cannot be satisfied with this: he must know that he is sent as a messenger from God to men concerning things good and evil, to show them that they have gone astray and are seeking the true nature of good and evil where it is not to be found, and take no thought where it really is: he must realize, in the words of Diogenes when brought before Philip after the battle of Chaeronea, that he is sent 'to reconnoitre'. For indeed the Cynic has to discover what things are friendly to men and what are hostile: and when he has accurately made his observations he must return and report the truth, not driven by fear to point out enemies where there are none, nor in any other way disturbed or confounded by his impressions.

He must then be able, if chance so offer, to come forward on the tragic stage, and with a loud voice utter the words of Socrates: 'O race of men, whither are ye hurrying? What are you doing, miserable creatures? You wander up and down like blind folk: you have left the true path and go away on a vain errand, you seek peace and happiness elsewhere, where it is not to be found, and believe not when another shows the way.' Why do you seek it outside? Do you seek it in the body? It is not there. If you doubt, look at Myron, look at Ophellius. In property? It is not there. If you disbelieve, look at Croesus, look at the rich men of to-day, and see how full their life is of lamentation. In office? It is not there. If it were, then those who have twice or thrice been consuls should be happy, but they are not. Whom shall we trust on this matter? Shall we trust you who look upon their fortune from outside and are dazzled by the outward show, or the men themselves? What do they say? Listen to them, when they lament and sigh, and think their condition to be more miserable and perilous just because of their consulships and glory and distinction. Shall you find it in royalty? It is not there. If it were, Nero would have been happy, and Sardanapalus. Why, even Agamemnon was not happy, though he was a finer fellow than Sardanapalus and Nero. When the rest were snoring what did he do? *'Many hairs he plucked by the roots from his head'*, and what did he say himself? *'Thus do I wander and am in agony of spirit, and my heart leaps from my breast.'* [Homer, *Iliad*, X. 15, 91, 94, 95]

Miserable man, what is wrong with your affairs? Is it your property? No. Your body? No. You have *'store of gold and copper'*. What is wrong with you then? You have neglected and ruined that in you—whatever it be—wherewith we exercise the will to get and to avoid, the impulse to act and not to act. How have you neglected it? It is ignorant of the true nature of the good to which it is born and of the nature of evil, and of what concerns it and what does not. And so when something that does not concern it is in bad case, it says, 'Woe is me, the Hellenes are in peril!' Oh miserable mind of man, alone neglected and uncared for!

'They are going to perish, slain by the Trojans!'

And if the Trojans slay them not, will they not die?

'Yes, but not all at once.'

What does it matter then? If death is evil, it is equally evil, whether men die alone or together. Will anything else happen, but that body and soul will be separated?

Nothing.

And if the Hellenes perish, is *the door closed* to you? Is not death within your power?

'It is.'

Why do you mourn then? Bravo! a king indeed, and holding the sceptre of Zeus!

A king cannot be miserable any more than God can be. What are you then? A shepherd in very truth, for you weep just like shepherds when a wolf carries off one of their sheep: yes and these whom you rule are sheep too. And why did you come here? Was there any danger to your will to get or your will to avoid, your impulse for action and against action?

'No,' he says, 'but my brother's poor wife was carried off.'

It is a great gain to be robbed of an adulterous wife.

'Are we then to suffer the scorn of the Trojans?'

What are they? Are they wise or foolish? If they are wise, why do you make war on them? If they are foolish, what does it matter to you?

In what then does the good reside, since it is not in these things? Tell us, Sir Messenger and Spy.

It is where you think not, and will not seek for it. For if you had wished you would have found it in yourselves and would not have wandered outside and would not have sought the things of others as your own. Turn again to *yourselves,* learn to understand the primary notions which you have. Of what nature do you imagine the good to be?

'Tranquil, fraught with happiness, unhindered.'

Nay, but do you not imagine it as naturally great? Do you not imagine it as precious? Do you not imagine it as free from harm? I ask you then, in what subject must we seek for that which is tranquil and unhindered? In the slavish or the free?

'In the free.'

Your poor body then, is it slavish or free?

'We know not.'

Do you not know that it is a slave to fever, gout, ophthalmia, dysentery, the tyrant, fire, sword, everything stronger than itself?

'Yes, it is a slave.'

How then can any part of the body be still free from hindrance? How can that which is naturally dead—earth and clay—be great or precious? What then? Have you no element of freedom?

'Perhaps none.'

Why, who can compel you to assent to what appears false?

'No one.'

And who to refuse assent to what appears true?

'No one.'

Here then you see that there is something in you which is naturally free. What man among you can have will to get or to avoid, impulse to act or not to act, or can prepare or put an object before himself, without conceiving an impression of what is profitable or fitting?

'No one.'

Here too then you have free and unhindered action. Miserable men, develop this, set your minds on this, seek your good *here.*

'Nay, but how is it possible for a man who has nothing, naked, without home or hearth, in squalor, without a slave, without a city, to live a tranquil life?'

Lo, God has sent you one who shall show indeed that it is possible. 'Look at me, I have no house or city, property or slave: I sleep on the ground, I have no wife or children, no miserable palace, but only earth and sky and one poor cloak. Yet what do I lack? Am I not quit of pain and fear, am I not free? When has any of you ever seen me failing to get what I will to get, or falling into what I will to avoid? When did I blame God or man, when did I accuse any? Has any of you seen me with a gloomy face? How do I meet those of whom you stand in fear and awe? Do I not meet them as slaves? Who that sees me but thinks that he sees his king and master?' There you have the true Cynic's words; this is his character, and scheme of life. No, you say, what makes the Cynic is a little wallet, and a staff and a big pair of jaws; to devour or hoard everything you give him or to revile out of season those who meet him, or to make a show of his fine shoulder!

Is this the spirit in which you mean to take in hand so great an enterprise? Take a mirror first, look at your shoulders, take note of your loins and your thighs. Man, it is an Olympic contest you are about to enter your name for, not a miserable, make-believe match. At Olympia you cannot simply be beaten and leave the grounds; in the first place you must be disgraced in the sight of all the world, not before men of Athens only or of Lacedaemon or of Nicopolis; in the next place the man who lightly enters the lists must be flogged, but before he is flogged he must suffer thirst and scorching heat and swallow plenty of dust. Think it over more carefully, know yourself, inquire of heaven, attempt not the task without God. If He advise you, know that He wishes you to become great or to receive many stripes. For this too is a very fine strand woven into the Cynic's lot: he must suffer strokes like an ass and love the very men that strike him as though he were the father or brother of all.

No, no; if a man flogs you, you must stand in the midst and cry aloud, 'Caesar, what pains I suffer under your rule of peace! Let us go to the proconsul.'

What has the Cynic to do with Caesar or proconsul or any one else but Zeus, Who has sent him upon earth, and Whom he serves? Does he call upon any one but Him? Is he not convinced that whatever pains he suffers are God's training of him? Why, Heracles, when he was being trained by Eurystheus, did not count himself wretched, but fulfilled all his commands without shrinking, and shall this man, who is under the training and discipline of Zeus, cry aloud in indignation, if he be worthy to carry the staff of Diogenes? Listen to what Diogenes said when the fever was on him to those who passed by: 'Base creatures,' he said, 'will you not stay? You go all that way to Olympia to see athletes killed or matched in battle, and yet have you no wish to see a battle between fever and a man?' I suppose you think a man like that would have been very likely to accuse God, Who sent him, of using him hardly? Nay, he was proud of his distresses, and was fain to be the spectacle of passers-by. On what ground is he to accuse God? That he is living a seemly life, and that he is displaying his virtue in a clearer light? But what does he say of poverty, of death, of pain? How did he compare his own happiness with that of the Great King? Nay, he did not so much as think it comparable. For where there are tumults, and distresses, and fears, where the will to get is unfulfilled, and the will to avoid is foiled, a world of envies and jealousies, how can happiness find a way there? But wherever there are unsound judgements, there all these passions must be.

And when the young man asked Epictetus, whether, if he fell sick and a friend asked him to come to his house to be tended in his sickness, he was to consent, he said, Where will you find me a Cynic's friend? For he must be another like himself, that he may be worthy to be counted as his friend; he must share with him the sceptre and the kingdom and be a worthy minister, if he is to be deemed worthy of his friendship, as Diogenes was worthy of Antisthenes, and Crates of Diogenes. Or do you think that if he salutes him as he comes near that makes him his friend, and the Cynic will count him worthy to receive him in his house? Wherefore, if this is your opinion and such your thoughts, look round rather for a fine dunghill to have your fever on, one that shelters you from the north wind, to save you from a chill. But you seem to me to want to get away into some one's house for a time and eat your fill. How comes it then that you should take in hand so great a matter?

'Will the Cynic', said his questioner, 'accept marriage and children as matters of prime importance?'

If, he replied, you grant me a city of wise men, it may be that no one will lightly adopt the Cynic's calling. For what reason should he take upon him this manner of life? But if we assume that he does, there will be nothing to prevent him from marrying and getting children; for his wife will be like himself, and his wife's father will be like him, and his children will be brought up on these lines. But in the present constitution of the world—which is that of the battlefield—it is a question whether the Cynic should not be undistracted entirely, devoted to the service of God, able to go to and fro among men, not tied down to acts that befit private occasions, nor involved in personal relations, which if he violates he will cease to keep his character as a good man, and if he maintains them he will destroy the Messenger and Spy and Herald of the gods that is in him. For he must show services to his father-in-law, and render them to his wife's other relations and to herself; and so he is reduced to being a sick nurse or a general provider. Not to speak of other things, he must needs have a saucepan, to make water hot for the baby, to wash him in the bath; when his wife has had a child he must provide wool and oil for her, and a bed and a cup—the vessels mount up at once—not to mention other business and distraction. What becomes now of that king of ours who watches every interest of the public,

Trusted with clans and full of many cares,

[Homer, *Iliad*, II. 25]

whose duty it is to watch others, those who have married and got children, to see which of them uses his wife well, which ill, who is quarrelsome, which house is prospering and which is not, going about like a physician and feeling men's pulses? 'You have a fever, you a headache, you the gout; I prescribe fasting for you, food for you, no bath for you; you need the surgeon's knife, you the cautery.' How can the man who is involved in the acts appropriate to private life find leisure? Must he not procure clothes for the children? Must he not send them to the schoolmaster with their tablets and note-books, and provide them with beds, for they cannot be Cynics from their mother's womb? If he does not provide for them, it were better to fling them aside as soon as born rather than kill them thus. See to what a pass we bring our Cynic, how we take away his kingdom!

'Yes, but Crates married.'

The case you mention was a special one and a love-match, and you have to assume a wife who was a Crates herself. Our inquiry is concerned with ordinary marriages which are liable to distraction; and from this point of view we do not find that in these circumstances marriage has a primary claim on the Cynic.

'How then', says he, 'will he keep society going?'

By God, do you think that those who bring into the world two or three ugly little squeakers to fill their place do men greater benefit than those who exercise oversight, so far as they can, over all men, to see what they do, how they live, what they attend to, what they undutifully neglect? Do you think the Thebans reaped greater benefit from those who left them children than from Epaminondas who died childless? Did Priam who begat fifty sons, rascals all, or Danaus or Aeolus contribute more to society than Homer? What? Shall a man abstain from marrying or getting children for the sake of acting as general or writing a treatise, and be thought to have got a fair exchange for his childlessness, and shall the kingdom of the Cynic be thought no compensation?

Perhaps we do not realize his greatness nor picture at its true worth the character of Diogenes: we only look at the Cynics of to-day,

Dogs of the table, guardians of the gate,

[Homer, *Iliad,* XXII. 69]

who copy those of old in nothing, except perhaps in dirty habits.

If we knew what a Cynic was we should not be moved or astonished at his not marrying or getting children. Man, he is parent to all men, he has men for his sons, women for his daughters; he approaches all and treats all in the spirit of a father. Do you think he reviles those he meets because he is a busybody? He does it as a father, as a brother, and as servant of Zeus, the Father of all.

Nay, ask me if you think well, whether he will take part in politics.

Fool, do you look for a higher form of politics than those he handles now? Is he to come forward and address an Athenian assembly on revenues or ways and means, when he ought to be discoursing to all mankind, alike to Athenians, to Corinthians, and to Romans, not about ways and means or revenues or peace and war, but about happiness and unhappiness, good fortune and bad fortune, slavery and freedom. When a man is engaged in politics of such moment, do you ask me if he is to be a politician? Nay, ask me if he is to hold office. Fool, what office is greater than this that he holds?

Yet such an one has need also of a body of a certain quality; for if he come forward with a consumptive figure, thin and pale, his testimony no longer carries the same force. For he must not only display mental qualities to convince the lay mind that it is possible to be good and noble without the things that they set store by, but his body must show that the plain and simple life of the open air does no harm to the body—'Look you, how my body and I bear witness to this.' As indeed Diogenes did; for he went about with the glow of health on his face, and attracted the masses by his bodily presence. But a Cynic who excites pity is like a beggar; every one turns from him and takes offence at him; for he ought not to appear dirty, lest he should scare men away thereby; nay his very squalor should be cleanly and attractive.

Further, the Cynic ought to have great natural grace and quickness of wit (without this he is a driveller, nothing more) that he may be able to give a ready and apposite answer to each question that arises: as Diogenes answered him who said, 'Are you the Diogenes who disbelieves in the gods?' by saying, 'How can I be when I think the gods hate you?' or again, when Alexander stood over him as he slept and said:

Sleep all night long becomes not men of counsel,

[Homer, *Iliad,* II. 24]

replied, still in his sleep,

Trusted with clans and full of many cares.

[Homer, *Iliad,* II. 25]

But above all, his Governing Principle must be purer than the sun; otherwise he must needs be a gambler and a reckless person; he will be rebuking others when he is involved in evil himself. See what this means. The kings and tyrants of this world have their armed bodyguard which enables them to rebuke certain persons and to punish those who do wrong even though they are wicked themselves, but the Cynic's conscience takes the place of arms and bodyguard and furnishes him with this authority. When he sees that he has watched and toiled for men, and that his sleep has been pure, and that when sleep leaves him he is purer still, and that all the thoughts of his heart have been those of one who is a friend and servant of the gods, and who shares the rule of Zeus, and that everywhere he is ready to say:

Lead me, O Zeus, and lead me, Destiny,

[Cleanthes]

and 'If thus the gods would have it, be it so'—then, I ask, why should he not have confidence to speak freely to his brothers, to his children, and in a word to his kinsfolk?

Therefore the man whose mind is thus disposed is not fussy nor impertinent, for when he is inspecting the affairs of men, he is concerned with what is not another's but his own, unless you are to call the general too a busybody, when he inspects and reviews and keeps watch over his soldiers, and punishes those who offend against discipline. But if you rebuke others when you are carrying a nice cake hid under your arm, I shall say to you, 'Would not you rather go off into a corner and eat what you have stolen?' What have you to do with other men's concerns? Who are you? Are you the bull or the queen bee? Show me the tokens of your royalty, like those which nature gives her. But if you are only a drone claiming the kingdom of the bees, do not you think that your fellow citizens will make an end of you, as the bees do to the drones?

The Cynic must have the spirit of patience in such measure as to seem to the multitude as unfeeling as a stone. Reviling or blows or insults are nothing to him; he has given his bit of a body to any one who will, to treat it as he pleases. For he remembers that the inferior must needs be conquered by the superior, where it is inferior, and the body is inferior to the multitude, the weaker inferior to them that are stronger. He therefore never enters upon this contest, where he may be conquered, but at once resigns what does not belong to him and does not claim power over slaves. But when it comes to the will and the power of dealing with impressions then you will see what eyes he has, so that you will say, 'Argus was blind in comparison.' Is there reckless assent, is there vain impulse, will to get which fails, will to avoid which is foiled, purpose incomplete, blame, disparagement or envy? It is on these he concentrates his attention and energy; for the rest he snores and takes his ease, and all is peace. No one robs him of his will or masters that.

Do they master his bit of a body?

Yes.

And his bit of property?

Yes.

And offices and honours?

What does he care for these? When any one tries to frighten him with these fears he says to him, 'Get away, look for children to frighten. They think masks fearsome, but I know that they are made of pot, and have nothing inside.'

So momentous is the profession you are thinking of. Before God I beg you to wait if you will, and look first to your equipment; for mark what Hector says to Andromache: 'Go rather to the house', he says, 'and weave':

War shall be men's concern,
All men's, and mine in chief.

[Homer, *Iliad*, VI. 492]

So truly did he realize his own endowment and her incapacity.

CHAPTER XXIII

TO THOSE WHO READ AND DISCOURSE FOR DISPLAY

FIRST say to yourself, what manner of man you want to be; when you have settled this, act upon it in all you do; for in pretty nearly all pursuits we see that done. Athletes first decide what they want to be, and then they act accordingly. If a man is to be a long-distance runner, he takes the diet, the walking, the rubbing, and the gymnastic suited to that; if he is going in for the short course, he alters all this to suit his aim, if for the pentathlon he alters his training still more. You will find the same done in the arts. If you are a carpenter you will have this kind of work; if a smith, you will have that kind. For in everything we do, if we have no standard to go by, we shall do it ineffectively; if we use the wrong standard, we shall fail completely.

Now we have two standards to go by, one general and one special. The first is that we must act as human beings. What does this include? We must not act like a sheep, at random, nor like a brute, destructively. The special standard is relative to each man's occupation and purpose. The lyre-player must act as a lyre-player, the carpenter as a carpenter, the philosopher as a philosopher, the orator as an orator. When therefore you say, 'Come and hear me lecturing to you', see to it first that you are not acting without aim. Then if you find you have a standard, see to it that it is the right one.

Do you wish to do men good or to receive compliments?

At once you have the answer, 'What account do I take of the praise of the multitude?'

An excellent answer. Nor does the musician heed the multitude, so far as he is a true musician, nor the geometrician. Do you wish then to do good? What are you aiming at? Tell us, that we too may run to your lecture-room. Now can any one do good to others unless he has received good himself? No, no more than the man who is no carpenter can help others in carpentry, or he who is no shoemaker in shoemaking.

Would you really know then whether you have received any good? Produce your judgements, my philosopher. What does the will to get profess? Success in getting. And the will to avoid? Escape from what it avoids. Well, do we fulfil their profession? Tell me the truth, and if you lie, I will tell you myself. When lately your audience were slack in their attendance, and did not applaud you, you went away in low spirits. Again when you were lately praised you went round and said to every one, 'What did you think of me?'

'I thought you wonderful, master, as I live.'

'How did I give that passage?'

'Which do you mean?'

'Where I described Pan and the Nymphs.'

'Superlatively.'

And yet you tell me that in respect to that will to get and will to avoid you behave in a natural way. Go to, get some one else to believe you! Did you not lately praise So-and-so against your real opinion? Did you not flatter So-and-so, the senator's son? Did you want your children to be like that?

'Heaven forbid!'

Why then did you praise him and pay him attention?

'He is a young man of parts, and ready to listen to arguments.'

How do you know that?

'He admires me.'

Now you have stated the true reason. After all, what do you think? Do not these very admirers secretly despise you? When a man who is conscious of no good action or good thought meets a philosopher who says, 'Here is a genius, frank and unspoilt', do not you think he is bound to say to himself, 'This man wants something from me'? Tell me, what sign of genius has he displayed? Why, he has been with you all this long time, he has heard you discoursing, he has heard you lecturing. Has he grown modest? Has he returned to himself? Has he realized what misery he is in? Has he cast away his vanity? Is he looking for some one to teach him?

'He is.'

Some one to teach him how he should live? No, you fool, but how he should speak, for that is what he admires you for. Listen and hear what he says: 'This man is a perfect artist in style, his style is much finer than Dio's.' That's a different thing altogether. Does he say, 'This man has self-respect, he is trustworthy and tranquil-minded'? If he did say so, I should say, 'Since he is trustworthy, tell me what you mean by this "trustworthy" man', and if he could not answer I should add, 'First learn what your words mean, and then speak.'

If you are in this sorry state, gaping for men to praise you, and counting your audience, do you really want to do others good?

'To-day I had a much larger audience.'

'Yes, it was a large one.'

'I suppose five hundred.'

'Nonsense! put them at a thousand.'

'Dio never had so large an audience.'

'How is that?'

'Why, they have a fine turn for understanding arguments.'

'Noble teaching, master, can move even a stone.'

There you have the words of a philosopher! These are the feelings of one who is to benefit mankind, there you have a man who has listened to reason, who has read the teaching of Socrates in the spirit of Socrates, and not as so much Lysias or Isocrates! ' "I have often wondered by what arguments"—no, "by what argument"—the singular is smoother than the plural.' [16] Did you ever read the words except as one reads paltry songs? If you had read them properly you would not have dwelt on these points of language, but would rather have studied the passage, 'Anytus and Meletus can kill me, but they cannot harm me', and this, 'My nature is such that I cannot attend to my affairs, but only to the argument which appears best to me when I reflect.' That was why no one ever heard Socrates say, 'I know and teach'; no, he sent one man here, another there; and therefore they used to come to him, asking to be introduced by him to philosophers, and he took and introduced them. No, of course, as he went with them he would say, 'Come and hear me discourse to-day in the house of Quadratus'!

What am I to hear from you? Do you want to display to me your fine composition? Man, you compose well enough, and what good does it do you?

'Do praise me, I beg.'

What do you mean by praise?

'Say "Bravo!" to me, or "Marvellous!" '

Very well, I say it; but if praise is what philosophers put in the category of the good, what praise can I give you? If correct speaking is a good thing, teach me that, and I will praise you.

'What? are you bound to dislike listening to fine oratory?'

Heaven forbid! I do not dislike listening to a harp-player, but am I therefore bound to stand and play the harp? Hear what Socrates says,

'It would not be seemly for me, sir, at this time of life, to come before you like a youth framing fine phrases.' [Plato, *Apology,* 17c] 'Like a youth', he says. Yes, it is indeed a pretty art, to select fine phrases and put them together, and then come forward and read them or recite them with ability, and as one reads to add, 'There are not many that can understand what I say, as sure as you hope to live.'

Does the philosopher invite men to a lecture? Does he not draw to him those who are going to get good from him, as the sun draws sustenance to itself? No physician worth the name invites men to come and be healed by him, though I hear that in Rome to-day physicians do invite them; in my day physicians were called in by their patients.

'I bid you to come and hear that you are in a bad way, that you attend to everything rather than what you should attend to, and that you do not know what is good and what is evil, and are unhappy and miserable.'

A fine invitation!

Surely, unless the philosopher's words force home this lesson, they are dead and so is he. Rufus was wont to say, 'If you find leisure to praise me, my words are spoken in vain.' Wherefore he spoke in such fashion that each of us as he sat there thought he was himself accused: such was his grip of men's doings, so vividly did he set each man's ills before his eyes. The philosopher's school, sirs, is a physician's consulting-room. You must leave it in pain, not in pleasure; for you come to it in disorder, one with a shoulder put out, another with an ulcer, another with fistula, another with headache. And then you would have me sit there and utter fine little thoughts and phrases, that you may leave me with praise on your lips, and carrying away, one his shoulder, one his head, one his ulcer, one his fistula, exactly in the state he brought them to me. Is it for this you say that young men are to go abroad and leave their parents and friends and kinsmen and property, that they may say, 'Ye gods!' to you when you deliver your phrases? Was this what Socrates did, or Zeno, or Cleanthes?

You ask, 'Is there not the hortatory style?'

Yes—no one denies it—just as there is the style for proof and the style for teaching. Who has ever named a fourth style along with them, the ostentatious? What is the hortatory style? The power of showing to one and to many what a sordid struggle they are plunged in, and how they pay regard to everything rather than to what they want. For they want what tends to happiness, but they seek it in the wrong place. Is it for this that you must set up a thousand benches and invite men to come and hear you, and then mount the rostrum in a fine robe or an elegant cloak and describe the death of Achilles? Cease, by all your gods, to dishonour noble words and subjects, so far as in you lies.

Nothing is more effective in exhortation than when the speaker makes plain to his hearers that he has need of them. Tell me, in all your readings or discourses, did you ever make one of your audience anxious about himself or rouse him to a sense of his position? Did you ever send one away saying, 'The philosopher has got a good grip of me: I must act so no more'? Why, even if your fame is at its height, he only says to some one, 'A pretty description that about Xerxes!' while another puts in, 'No, the battle of Thermopylae.' Is this what a philosopher's lecture comes to?

CHAPTER XXIV

THAT WE OUGHT NOT TO SPEND OUR FEELINGS ON THINGS BEYOND OUR POWER

If a thing goes against another's nature, you must not take it as evil for you; for you are born not to share humiliation or evil fortune, but to share good fortune. And if a man is unfortunate, remember that his misfortune is his own fault; for God created all men for happiness and peace of mind. To this end He gave men resources, giving each man some things for his own, and some not for his own, things subject to hindrance and deprivation and compulsion not for his own, but things beyond hindrance for his own. The true nature of good and evil He gave man for his own, as was natural for Him to do, Who cares for us and protects us as a Father.

'Oh, but I have just parted from such an one, and he is distressed!'

Why did he count as his own what was not his? When he rejoiced to look on you why did he not reflect that you are mortal, and that you may go on a journey? Wherefore he pays the penalty for his own foolishness. But why do you bewail yourself, and to what end? Did not you study this distinction either? Did you, as worthless women do, regard all the things in which you took pleasure—places, persons, ways of life—as though they would always be with you? And so now you sit and weep because you do not see the same persons and pass your time in the same place. No doubt you deserve this fate—to be more wretched than rooks and ravens, who may fly where they will and change their nests, and cross the seas, without lamenting or longing for their first possessions.

'Yes, but this happens to them because they have no reason.'

Is our reason then given us by the gods for misfortune and misery, that we may continue in wretchedness and mourning? Or would you have all men to be immortal, and no one go abroad? Are we never to go away but all to stay rooted like plants, and if one of our close friends goes abroad are we to sit and weep: and again, if he return, are we to dance and clap like little children?

Shall we not at last give up the milk of babes, and remember what we heard from the philosophers, unless we took what they said for enchanters' tales? 'This world is one city, and the substance of which it is constructed is one; and things must needs move in a cycle, one thing giving way to another, and some things must pass away, and others come into being, some must abide as they are and others must move; and the universe is full of friends—the gods first, and after them men, whom nature has made akin to one another; some of them must be with one another and others must go away, and we should rejoice in those that are with us, yet not be sad at those who go away. And man, besides being born to a high courage, and to despise all that is beyond his will, has this too for his own, that he is not rooted nor attached to the earth, but goes now to one place, now to another, at one time under the pressure of business, at another merely to see the world.' Such indeed was the lot of Odysseus:

> *Cities of many men he saw, and learnt*
> *Their mind;*
>
> [Homer, *Odyssey*, I. 3]

and yet earlier it was the lot of Heracles to go about all the inhabited world,

> *Beholding laws and insolence of men,*
>
> [Homer, *Odyssey*, XVII. 487]

cleansing the world and casting forth the insolent, and bringing in the rule of law. Yet how many friends, think you, had he in Thebes, how many in Argos, how many in Athens, and how many did he win for himself as he went about, seeing that he married a wife, where he thought fit, and got children, and forsook his children, with no mourning nor longing, nor as one leaving them orphans? For he knew that no man is an orphan, but that all men have always the Father Who cares for them continually; for to him it was no mere tale that he had heard that Zeus is the Father of men, for he believed Him to be his own father and called Him so, and all that he did he did as looking to Him, wherefore it was in his power to live happily everywhere. But happiness and longing for what is absent can never be united; for that which is happy must needs have all that it will, and be as it were in a state of satisfaction; no thirst or hunger must come near it. But Odysseus, you say, had a sense of longing for his wife, and sat upon a rock and wept. Do you take Homer for your authority in everything, and Homer's stories? If Odysseus really wept, was he not miserable, and what good man is ever miserable? The universe is indeed managed ill if Zeus does not take care of His citizens, that they may be happy as He is. It is not lawful or right even to think of such a thing, and if Odysseus wept and lamented, he was no good man. For how can a man be good, when he knows not who he is, and how can he know this when he has forgotten that all things that have come into being are perishable, and that it is impossible for man to be with man for ever? Now to desire what is impossible is slavish and silly; it is to make oneself a stranger in the world, and to fight against God with one's own judgements, as alone one can.

'But my mother mourns because she does not see me.'

Why does she not take to heart these lessons? Yet I do not say that we must not take pains to prevent her lamenting; but that we must not wish absolutely for what is not ours. Another's sorrow is no concern of mine, my sorrow is my own; and so I shall absolutely check my own sorrow, for it is in my power, but another's I shall try to check only so far as I can, but not absolutely; otherwise I shall fight against God, I shall set myself against Zeus and array myself against His conduct of the universe, and the penalty for this battling with God and this disobedience will be paid not only by 'children's children', but by me in my own person, by day and by night, when I start in my dreams and am disturbed, when I tremble at every message, when my peace of mind hangs upon another's letters.

Some one is come from Rome.

'If only it be no ill news!'

What ill can happen to you in a place where you are not?

From Greece.

'If only it be no ill news!'

On this principle, every place can cause you misery. Is it not enough that you should be miserable where you are yourself? Must you needs be miserable overseas, and by letter? Is this what you mean by being secure?

What happens then if your friends there die?

What else except that mortal men have died? How can you wish at the same time to grow old and not to see the death of any that you love? Do you not know that in the long course of time many events of divers sorts must happen? One man must be overcome by fever, another by a robber, a third by a despot. For such is the nature of the atmosphere about us, and of our companions; cold and heat and unsuitable food, and travel by land, and sea, and winds and manifold perils destroy one man and send another into exile, and another they send on an embassy or as a soldier. Sit still then with your wits dazed at all these things—mourning, unfortunate, miserable, depending on something other than yourself—not one thing or two, but things innumerable.

Is this what your lesson comes to, is this what you learnt in the philosopher's school? Do you not know that life is a soldier's service? One man must keep guard, another go out to reconnoitre, another take the field. It is not possible for all to stay where they are, nor is it better so. But you neglect to fulfil the orders of the general and complain, when some severe order is laid upon you; you do not understand to what a pitiful state you are bringing the army so far as in you lies; you do not see that if all follow your example there will be no one to dig a trench, or raise a palisade, no one to keep night watch or fight in the field, but every one will seem an unserviceable soldier.

Again, if you go as a sailor on shipboard, keep to one place and hold fast to that; if you are called on to climb the mast, refuse, if to run out on the bows, refuse that. Why, what ship's master will put up with you, and not fling you overboard like a useless bit of furniture, a mere hindrance and bad example to the other sailors? So too it is in the world; each man's life is a campaign, and a long and varied one. It is for you to play the soldier's part—do everything at the General's bidding, divining His wishes, if it be possible. For there is no comparison between that General and the ordinary one in power and superiority of character. You are set in an imperial City and not in some humble town; you are always a senator. Do you not know that such an one can attend but little to his own household? He must spend most of his time abroad, in command or under command, or as subordinate to some officer, or as soldier or judge? And yet you tell me you want to be attached like a plant and rooted in the same place?

'Yes, for it is pleasant.'

Who denies it? Dainties are pleasant too, and a beautiful woman is a pleasant thing. Your talk is the talk of those who make pleasure their end.

Do you not realize whose language you are using, the language of Epicureans and abandoned creatures? and yet though your actions and your principles are theirs, you quote to us the words of Zeno and Socrates? Fling away from you, as far as may be, these alien properties that you adorn yourself with, and that do not fit you! People of that sort have no wish except to sleep without hindrance or compulsion, and then to get up and yawn at their ease and wash their face, then to write and read at their pleasure, then to talk nonsense and be complimented by their friends, whatever they say, then to go out for a walk and after a little walk to have a bath, then to eat, and then go to sleep—the sort of sleep men of that kind are likely to indulge in—I need say no more—you may judge what it is.

Come, now, tell me the way of life your heart is set on—you who profess to admire truth and Socrates and Diogenes. What do you want to do in Athens? Just what you are doing? Nothing else? Then why do you call yourself a Stoic? If those who speak falsely of the Roman constitution are seriously punished, are those who speak falsely of so great and serious a subject and a name to get off scot free? That cannot be; none may escape this divine and mighty law, which exacts the greatest punishments from those whose offence is greatest. What does it say? 'He that pretends to qualities that concern him not, let him be given to vanity and arrogance; let him that disobeys the divine government be an abject slave, let him be subject to pain, envy, pity, in a word, let him be miserable and full of lamentations.'

'What is your conclusion? Would you have me court this great man or that and frequent his doorstep?'

If reason so determine, for country's sake or kindred or mankind, why should you not go to him? You are not ashamed to go to the shoemaker when you want shoes, nor to the market-gardener when you want lettuces. Are you ashamed to go to the rich when you want something they can give?

'Yes, but I do not admire the shoemaker.'

Do not admire the rich man either.

'I shall not flatter the market-gardener.'

Do not flatter the rich man either.

'How then am I to get what I want?'

Do I say to you, 'Go, and you will get what you want', or only, 'Go, and act up to your character'?

'Why do I go then?'

That you may come away feeling that you have fulfilled the acts required of a citizen, a brother, a friend. But remember that you have gone to a shoemaker, a greengrocer, one who has no authority over great or high matters, though he sell what he has for a big price. You are going as it were to fetch lettuces; they are worth an obol, but not a talent.

Apply this principle. The business is worth going to a man's door for. Very well, I will go. It is worth an interview. Very well, I will have an interview with him. But if I must kiss his hand and flatter him with compliments, that is like paying a talent. I will have none of it. It is not to my profit, nor to the profit of the city or my friends to ruin a good citizen and a friend.

'But men will think you took no pains if you fail.'

Have you again forgotten why you went there? Do you not know that a good man does nothing for the sake of what men think, but only for the sake of doing right?

'What does he gain by doing right?'

What does a man gain who writes Dio's name correctly? The gain of writing.

'Is there no further reward?'

Do you look for any greater reward for a good man than to do what is noble and right? At Olympia you do not want anything else; you are content to have been crowned at Olympia. Does it seem to you so small and worthless a thing to be noble and good and happy? Therefore, since the gods have made you a citizen of this city and you are bound to set your hand betimes to a man's work, why hanker after nurses and the breast, and allow silly women to soften you and make you effeminate with their tears? Will you then never cease to be a babe? Do you not know that he who acts like a child is ridiculous in proportion to his years?

Did you not see any one in Athens, or go to any one's house?

'Yes, the man I wanted to see.'

Do the same here; choose to see the man you want, and you will see him; only do it in no abject spirit, without will to get or to avoid, and all will be well with you; but it does not depend on going or standing at the door, but on the judgements that are within you. When you have come to despise things without you and beyond your will's control, and have come to regard none of them as your own, but only this—to be right in judgement, in thought, in impulse, in will to get and to avoid, what room is left for flattery or abjectness of mind? Why do you still long for the peace of your home, and for your familiar haunts? Wait a little and these places will become familiar to you in their turn. Then if your spirit is as degenerate as this, go weep and mourn as soon as you are again parted from these.

'How then am I to prove myself affectionate?'

In a noble and not a miserable spirit. For it is against all reason to be of an abject and broken spirit and to depend on another and to blame God or man. Prove yourself affectionate, but see that you observe these rules; if this affection of yours, or whatever you call it, is going to make you a miserable slave, it is not for your good to be affectionate. Nay, what prevents you loving a man as one who is mortal and bound to leave you? Did not Socrates love his children? Yes, but as one who is free and bears in mind that the love of the gods stands first, and therefore he failed in none of the duties of a good man, either in his defence, or in assessing his penalty, or earlier still as a member of the council or a soldier in the field. But we abound in every kind of excuse for a mean spirit; with some of us it is a child, with others our mother or our brothers. We ought not to let any one make us miserable, but let every one make us happy, and God above all, Who created us for this. Go to, did Diogenes love no one, he who was so gentle and kind-hearted that he cheerfully took upon him all those troubles and distresses of body for the general good of men? But how did he love? As the servant of Zeus should love, caring for his friends, but submitting himself to God. That was why he alone made the whole world his country, and no special land, and when he was made prisoner he did not long for Athens or for his friends and companions there, but made himself at home with the pirates who took him and tried to make them better, and afterwards when he was sold he lived in Corinth just as he lived before in Athens; yes, and if he had gone away to the Perrhaebians it would have been just the same. That is how freedom is achieved. That is why he said, 'Since Antisthenes freed me, I have ceased to be a slave.' How did he free him? Hear what he says: 'He taught me what is mine and what is not mine; property is not mine; kinsfolk, relations, friends, reputation, familiar places, converse with men—none of these is my own.'

What is yours then?

'Power to deal with impressions. He showed me that I possess this beyond all hindrance and compulsion; no one can hamper me, no one can compel me to deal with them otherwise than I will. Who then has authority over me any more? Has Philip, or Alexander, or Perdiccas, or the Great King? How can they? for he who is to be mastered by men, must first—long before—allow himself to be mastered by things. When a man is not overcome by pleasure, or pain, or reputation, or wealth, and, when it seems good to him, can spit his whole body in the tyrant's face,[17] and so leave this world, whose slave can you call him any more? To whom is he subject? But if he had sought his pleasure by living in Athens, and had allowed life in Athens to have the mastery over him, he would have been in every man's control, and any one who was stronger than he would have had power to cause him pain. You can imagine how he would have flattered the pirates to sell him to an Athenian, that he might one day see the beautiful Peiraeus and the Long Walls and the Acropolis.

Slave, who are you that want to see them? If you are servile and abject what good will they do you?

'Nay, I shall be free.'

Show me how you are free. Suppose some one, no matter who, takes you away from your familiar course of life; he has laid hands on you and says, 'You are my slave, for it is in my power to prevent you from living as you will, it rests with me to relax your servitude, or to humiliate you; when I choose you can put on a glad face again and go off in high spirits to Athens.' What do you say to this man who leads you captive? Whom do you produce to set you free from him? Or do you refuse to look him in the face, and cutting arguments short implore him to let you go? Man, you ought to go to prison rejoicing, hastening thither before your gaoler can lay hands on you. What! You decline to live in Rome, and long for Hellas? I suppose you will weep in our faces again, when you have to die, because you are not going to see Athens and have a walk in the Lyceum?

Is this what you went abroad for? Is this why you sought converse with a teacher who might do you good? Good forsooth! Was your object to analyse syllogisms more readily or track out hypothetical propositions? Was it for this reason that you left brother, country, friends, relations, that you might learn this lesson and return? It was not then to secure constancy or peace of mind that you went abroad; it was not that you might be set beyond harm's reach and never blame or accuse any one any more, it was not that no one should be able to injure you, and that so you might maintain your life unhindered in all its relations. A fine traffic this that you have achieved by your travels—syllogisms and shifting terms and hypothetical arguments! Yes, you had better sit in the market if you think fit, and post up a notice like the druggists. Nay! will you not rather deny knowledge of what you learnt, that you may not get your precepts condemned as useless? What harm has philosophy done you, how has Chrysippus wronged you, that you should prove his labours to be useless by your own act? Not content with the ills you had at home, which were enough to cause you pain and sorrow, even if you had not gone abroad, did you acquire new ills besides? Yes, and if again you have other friends and companions, and if you attach yourself to another country you will only multiply your causes for lamentation. Why then do you live, only to involve yourself in trouble after trouble and make yourself miserable? What, man! You call this 'affection'? Affection indeed! If affection is good, it can cause no evil. If it is evil, I have no concern with it. I am born for what is good for me, not for what is evil.

What then is the proper training for this? In the first place, the principal and most important thing, on the very threshold so to speak, is that when you are attached to a thing, not a thing which cannot be taken away but anything like a ewer, or a crystal cup, you should bear in mind what it is, that you may not be disturbed when it is broken. So should it be with persons; if you kiss your child, or brother, or friend, never allow your imagination to range at large, nor allow your exultation to go as far as it will, but pluck it back, keep it in check like those who stand behind generals driving in triumph and remind them that they are men. In like manner you must remind yourself that you love a mortal, and that nothing that you love is your very own; it is given you for the moment, not for ever nor inseparably, but like a fig or a bunch of grapes at the appointed season of the year, and if you long for it in winter you are a fool. So too if you long for your son or your friend, when it is not given you to have him, know that you are longing for a fig in winter time. For as winter is to the fig, so is the whole pressure of the universe to that which it destroys. And therefore in the very moment that you take pleasure in a thing, set before your mind the opposite impressions. What harm is there in whispering to yourself as you kiss your child, 'To-morrow you will die', and to your friend in like manner, 'To-morrow you or I shall go away, and we shall see one another no more'?

'But such words are of ill omen.'

Yes, and so are some incantations, but because they do good, I do not mind, if only they do good. But do you give the name 'ill-omened' to anything but what signifies evil? Cowardice is an ill-omened thing, and so is a mean spirit, mourning, sorrow, shamelessness; these are ill-omened words, yet even these we must not hesitate to utter, that we may guard against the things themselves. Do you call any word ill-omened that signifies a process of nature? Say that harvesting ears of corn is ill-omened, for it means destruction of the ears; yes, but not the destruction of the world. Say that the fall of the leaf is ill-omened and the change of the fresh fig into the dry and of grapes into raisins; for all these are changes from a previous state into a new one. This is not destruction but an ordered dispensation and government of things. Going abroad is a slight change; death is a greater change—from what now is, not to what is not, but to what is not now.

'Shall I then be no more?'

You will not be, but something else will be, of which the world now has need; for indeed you came into being, not when you willed it, but when the world had need. For this reason the good man, remembering who he is and whence he has come, and by whom he was created, sets his mind on this alone, how he shall fill his place in an orderly fashion with due obedience to God. To God he says, 'Dost Thou want me still to live? I will live as one who is free and noble, in accordance with Thy will; for Thou didst give me freedom from hindrance in what was mine. Hast Thou no more need of me? Then may it be well with Thee; I stayed here until now for Thee and for none other, and so now I obey Thee and depart.'

'How do you depart?'

Again, as Thou willest, as a free man, as Thy servant, as one who has learnt what Thou dost command and forbid. But as long as I continue among Thy creatures, whom wouldst Thou have me be? A magistrate or a private person, a senator or a commoner, a soldier or a general, a teacher or the head of a household? Whatever place or post Thou dost commit to my charge, 'I will die ten thousand times', to use Socrates' words, 'sooner than abandon it.' Where wouldst Thou have me be? In Rome or Athens or Thebes or Gyara? Only remember me there. If Thou dost send me to a place where men cannot live as their nature requires, I shall go away, not in disobedience but believing that Thou dost sound the note for my retreat. I do not abandon Thee; heaven forbid! but I recognize that Thou hast no need of me. But if it be given me to live in accordance with nature, I shall not seek another place than where I am or other society than that in which I am.

Let these thoughts be at your command by night and day: write them, read them, talk of them, to yourself and to your neighbour. Go first to one and then to another, asking him, 'Can you help me towards this?' Then if some so-called 'undesirable' event befall you, the first immediate relief to you will be, that it was not unexpected. For in all matters it is a great thing to say, 'I knew that I had begotten a mortal.'[18] For this is what you will say, and again, 'I knew that I was mortal. I knew that I might have to go away, that I might be cast into exile. I knew that I might be thrown into prison.' Then if you reflect within yourself and ask from what quarter the event has come, you will at once remember, 'It comes from the region of things outside my will, which are not mine; how then does it concern me?' Then comes the most commanding question of all: 'Who has sent it me?'

The Prince or the General, the City or the Law of the City.

Give it me then, for I must always obey the law in everything.

And further, when your imagination (which is not in your control) bites deep into your soul, struggle against it with your reason, fight it down, suffer it not to grow strong nor to advance the next step, calling up at pleasure what pictures it will. If you are in Gyara do not imagine your way of life in Rome, and the great delights you enjoyed when you lived there and that you would enjoy on your return. No, make your one effort there, to live a brave life in Gyara, as one who lives in Gyara should; and if you are in Rome do not imagine life in Athens, but make life in Rome your one study.

Further, you should put this delight first in place of all others, the delight that comes from understanding that you are obeying God, that not in word but in deed you are fulfilling the part of the good man. What a fine thing it is to be able to say to myself, 'I am now putting into action what other men talk big of in the lecture-room, and win a name for paradox. As they sit there it is my virtues they are expounding, it is about me they are inquiring, it is my praise they are singing. I say, Zeus wished to make my experience prove this truth to me, and He wished to discover for Himself, whether He had a soldier in the true sense, a citizen in the true sense, and to put me forward as a witness to the rest of mankind of what does and does not depend on man's will. "Behold,"

He says, "your fears are idle and your desires vain. Do not seek good things outside you but within, or you will not find them." It is on these terms that now He brings me here, and again sends me thither; He shows me to men poor, without office, sick, sends me to Gyara, puts me in prison; not that He hates me—heaven forbid! who hates his best servant?—nor that He takes no thought of me, for He takes thought of the lowliest, but because He is training me and using me as a witness to other men. When I am appointed to such a service as this, it is not for me to consider where or in whose company I am or what they say of me, but rather to spend all my effort on God and His commands and ordinances.'

If you always have these thoughts at hand, and make yourself familiar with them and keep them at command, you will never want for one to comfort and strengthen you. For dishonour consists not in having nothing to eat, but in not having reason sufficient to secure you from fear and pain. But if you once win yourself freedom from fear and pain, then tyrants and their guards, and the Emperor's household, will cease to exist for you; you, who have received this high office from Zeus, will not feel the sting of an imperial appointment or of those who offer sacrifice on the Capitol in virtue of their offices.

Only make no display of your office, and boast not yourself in it, but prove it by your conduct; be content, even if no one observes you, to live in true health and happiness.

CHAPTER XXV

TO THOSE WHO FAIL TO ACHIEVE WHAT THEY SET BEFORE THEM

CONSIDER which of the aims that you set before you at the first you have achieved, and which you have not, and how some things give you pleasure to remember and some give you pain; and if possible, recover what you failed to obtain. For those who are entering on the greatest of all struggles must not shrink, but must be ready to endure stripes; for the struggle they are concerned with is not wrestling or the pancration, in which a man may succeed or fail, and yet be worth little or worth very much—nay more, he may be most fortunate or most miserable; no, his struggle is for good fortune and happiness itself.

What follows? In this competition, even if we give in for the moment, nothing prevents us from returning to the struggle; we have not to wait for another four years for the next Olympic Games to come. At once you may recover yourself, and pull yourself together, and renew the struggle with the same energy as before; and if you grow faint again, you may renew it again, and if you once attain to victory you are as one who has never failed. Only do not begin to take a pleasure in failing from sheer force of habit, and go about as a sorry athlete defeated in the whole round of all the Games, for all the world like quails that have escaped!

'I am overpowered by the impression of a pretty maid. Well! was I not overpowered lately? I am eager to find fault with some one. Did I not do so lately?'

You talk lightly to us, as though you had got off scot-free. It is as though a man, when his doctor forbade him to bathe, should say, 'Why, did not I bathe quite lately?' What if the doctor can answer him, 'Well, what effect did bathing have on you? Did you not fall into a fever? Did you not get a headache?' So when you found fault with some one lately, was it not the act of a bad man, and of a foolish one? Did you not feed this habit, by putting before it acts which were congenial to it? And when the pretty girl was too much for you, did you get away unpunished? What do you mean then by talking of what you did lately? Nay, you ought rather, I think, to have remembered, as slaves remember their floggings, and to have refrained from repeating the same offence. But it is not the same thing: pain makes the memory of the slave, but what pain or penalty attends your offences? When did you acquire the habit of avoiding evil activities?

CHAPTER XXVI

TO THOSE WHO FEAR WANT

Are you not ashamed of being more cowardly and mean-spirited than runaway slaves? How do they leave their masters when they run away? What lands or servants have they to trust to? Do not they steal just a morsel to last them for the first days, and then go on their way over land or it may be sea, contriving one resource after another to keep themselves alive? And when did a runaway slave ever die of hunger? Yet you are all of a flutter and keep awake at nights for fear you should run short of necessaries. Miserable man, are you so blind as not to see the road, to which want of necessaries leads you? Where does it lead? The same way as fever, the same way as a falling stone—to death. Well, and is not this exactly the situation you often described to your companions? Many a passage did you read and write about it. How often did you boast that you could face death at any rate with a quiet mind!

'Yes, but my family will starve.'

What of that? Does their hunger lead in a different direction? Is not the way that leads below the same, and the world it leads to the same? Will you then not have courage to face every form of want and necessity, and to look on that world whither even the richest and those who have held the highest offices must descend, nay even kings and emperors themselves? Only you will descend hungry, if it so chance, and they will burst with over-eating and over-drinking.

Did you ever by chance see a beggar who was not old? They are all far gone in years; yet they bear the pinch of cold night and day, and lie forlorn upon the ground, and their food is what bare necessity demands and no more, but they almost arrive at immortality, and yet you who are sound in hand and foot are so afraid of starving!

Can you not draw water, or write, or take charge of children, or be another man's doorkeeper?

But it is disgraceful, you say, to be reduced to this necessity.

First learn then what is disgraceful, and then tell us that you are a philosopher; but for the present, if another call you so, do not allow him.

When a thing is not your business, when you are not responsible for it, when it has befallen you without your own act, like a headache or a fever, can it disgrace you? If your parents were poor, or if they made others their heirs instead of you, if they give you no help while they are alive, is this any disgrace to you? Is this what you learnt with the philosophers? Did you never hear that what is disgraceful is blameable, and the blameable is what deserves blame, and it is absurd to blame a man for what is not his own act, done by himself? Well, did you make your father what he is, or is it in your power to mend his character? Is this given you? What follows? Ought you to desire what is not given you, or to be ashamed if you do not attain to it? Is this all the habit you acquired when you studied philosophy, to look to others and to hope for nothing from yourself and your own acts? Lament therefore and mourn, and when you eat be fearful that you will have nothing to eat to-morrow. Tremble for your wretched slaves, lest they should steal, or run away, or die. Live in this spirit, and never cease to live so, you who never came near philosophy, except in name, and disgraced its principles so far as in you lies, by showing them to be useless and unprofitable to those who take them up. You never set your will to gain constancy, tranquillity, and peace of mind; you never paid regard to any master for this end, though you attended to many for the sake of syllogisms. You never tested any of these impressions thoroughly for yourself, asking, 'Can I bear it or can I not? What have I to look to?' No, you assumed that all was well with you, and that you were quite secure, and devoted your efforts to the final study of all, how to be immovable. And in what were you to make yourself immovable? Cowardice, a base spirit, admiration of the rich, failure to get what you will, defeat of your will to avoid. It was to secure these results that you spent all your care.

Ought you not to win some possession from philosophy, before you try to make it secure? Did you ever see any one build a coping, unless he had a wall round which to build it? Who ever appoints a door-keeper where there is no door to guard?

Again, you make it your study to be able to demonstrate. Demonstrate what? You study not to be shaken by fallacies. Shaken from what position? Show me first what you are guarding, what you are measuring, or what you are weighing; then it is time enough to show me the balance or the bushel. How long do you mean to measure dust and ashes? Ought you not to demonstrate those principles which make men happy, which make things prosper as they wish, principles which make them not blame any one or accuse any one, but acquiesce in the government of the universe? Show me these.

'See, I do show them', he says. 'I will analyse syllogisms for you.'

Slave, this is the measuring instrument, not that which is measured. That is why you now pay the penalty for your neglect of philosophy; you tremble, you lie awake, you take counsel with every one, and unless your plans promise to please every one you think you have taken bad counsel.

Then you fear starvation, as you think; but what you really fear is not starvation; you are afraid that you may not have a cook, that you may not have another to cater for you, another to shoe you, another to dress you, others to rub you, others to follow you; when you have stripped in the bath and stretched yourself out like the crucified, you want to be rubbed on this side and that, and then you want the masseur to stand by and say, 'Turn, and give me his side, take his head, hand me his shoulder'; and then when you have left the bath and gone home you expect to cry out, 'Will no one bring me something to eat?' and then, 'Remove the tables, and wipe them.' What you really fear is that you may not be able to live the life of an invalid; for the life of healthy men you have only to see how slaves and labourers and true philosophers live; the life of Socrates, though he had a wife and children to live with, the life of Diogenes, and of Cleanthes, who combined philosophy with drawing water. If this is what you want to have, you will have it everywhere, and will live with confidence. Confidence in what? In that which alone it is possible to confide in, what is trustworthy, and cannot be hindered or taken away, that is, your own will. Why have you made yourself so useless and unprofitable that no one is willing to take you into his house and take care of you? Every one will pick up a vessel that is whole and fit for use if it is flung aside and will count it gain; but every one will count you loss, not gain. Cannot you even serve the purpose of a dog or a cock? Why then do you wish to live any more, if this is your character?

Does a good man ever fear that food may fail him? It does not fail the blind, it does not fail the lame, will it fail the good man? There is no want of some one to give pay to the good soldier, or workman, or shoemaker: will the good man find none? Does God so disregard His own principles, His servants, His witnesses, whom alone He uses as examples to the untaught, to show 'that He exists and orders the universe well, and does not disregard human things, and that for the good man nothing is evil, whether he lives or dies'? [Plato, *Apology*, 41d] What if He does not provide food? It only means that, like a good general, He has given me the signal to retire. I obey, I follow, I praise my Commander, and laud His acts. For I came when He thought fit, and again shall go when He thinks fit; and while I lived this was the work I had to do, to praise God in my own heart, and to others, be it to one or to many. If He does not provide me with much or with abundance, His will is for me to live simply; for He did not give abundance to Heracles, His own son; another than he was king of Argos and Mycenae, and he was subject to him and suffered toils and discipline. Yet Eurystheus was the man he was, no true king of Argos and Mycenae, for he was not king over himself, while Heracles was ruler and commander of all land and sea, cleansing them from lawlessness and wrong, and bringing in justice and righteousness, and this he did unarmed and single-handed.

And when Odysseus was shipwrecked and cast ashore, his necessity never broke his spirit, or made it abject. Nay, how did he approach the maidens to ask of them the necessaries of life, which men think it most shameful to beg from another?

Like hill-bred lion, trusting in his might.

[Homer, *Odyssey*, VI. 130]

Trusting in what? Not in reputation, not in money, nor office, but in his own might, that is in judgements on things within our power and beyond it. For it is these alone that make free men, whom nothing can hinder, which lift up the neck of those who are in humiliation, and make them look with unwavering eyes upon rich men and upon despots.

And this was what the philosopher had to give, but you are going to leave him, it seems, not with courage but trembling for your pitiful clothes and plate. Miserable man! have you so wasted your time until now?

'What then, if I fall ill?'

You shall bear illness well.

'Who shall tend me?'

God, and your friends.

'I shall lie on a hard bed.'

But you can do it like a man.

'I shall not have a proper house.'

If you have one, you will be ill all the same.

'Who will give me food?'

Those who find it for others; you will be no worse off than Manes [19] on your sick-bed. And what is the end of the illness? Nothing worse than death. Will you realize once for all that it is not death that is the source of all man's evils, and of a mean and cowardly spirit, but rather the fear of death? Against this fear then I would have you discipline yourself; to this let all your reasonings, your lectures, and your trainings be directed; and then you will know that only so do men achieve their freedom.

BOOK IV

CHAPTER I

ON FREEDOM

THAT man is free, who lives as he wishes, who is proof against compulsion and hindrance and violence, whose impulses are untrammelled, who gets what he wills to get and avoids what he wills to avoid.

Who then would live in error?

No one.

Who would live deceived, reckless, unjust, intemperate, querulous, abject?

No one.

No bad man then lives as he would, and so no bad man is free.

Who would live in a state of distress, fear, envy, pity, failing in the will to get and in the will to avoid?

No one.

Do we then find any bad man without distress or fear, above circumstance, free from failure?

None. Then we find none free.

If a man who has been twice consul hear this, he will forgive you if you add, 'But *you* are wise, this does not concern you.' But if you tell him the truth, saying, 'You are just as much a slave yourself as those who have been thrice sold', what can you expect but a flogging?

'How can I be a slave?' he says; 'my father is free, my mother is free, no one has bought me; nay, I am a senator, and a friend of Caesar, I have been consul and have many slaves.'

In the first place, most excellent senator, perhaps your father too was a slave of the same kind as you, yes and your mother and your grandfather and the whole line of your ancestors. And if really they were ever so free, how does that affect you? What does it matter if they had a fine spirit, when you have none, if they were fearless and you are a coward, if they were self-controlled and you are intemperate?

'Nay, what has this to do with being a slave?' he replies.

Does it seem to you slavery to act against your will, under compulsion and with groaning?

'I grant you that,' he says, 'but who can compel me except Caesar, who is lord of all?'

Why, then, your own lips confess that you have one master: you must not comfort yourself with the thought that he is, as you say, the common master of all, but realize that you are a slave in a large household. You are just like the people of Nicopolis, who are wont to cry aloud, 'By Caesar's fortune, we are free.'

However, let us leave Caesar for the moment if you please, but tell me this: Did you never fall in love with any one, with a girl, or a boy, or a slave, or a free man?

'What has that to do with slavery or freedom?'

Were you never commanded by her you loved to do anything you did not wish? Did you never flatter your precious slave-boy? Did you never kiss his feet? Yet if any one compel you to kiss Caesar's, you count it an outrage, the very extravagance of tyranny. What is this if not slavery? Did you never go out at night where you did not wish, and spend more than you wished and utter words of lamentation and groaning? Did you put up with being reviled and shut out? If you are ashamed to confess your own story, see what Thrasonides says and does: he had served in as many campaigns or more perhaps than you and yet, first of all, he has gone out at night, at an hour when Getas does not dare to go, nay, if he were forced by his master to go, he would have made a loud outcry and have gone with lamentations over his cruel slavery, and then, what does he say?

A worthless girl has made a slave of me,
Whom never foe subdued.

[Menander, Fragment 338, Koch]

Poor wretch, to be slave to a paltry girl and a worthless one too! Why do you call yourself free then any more? Why do you boast of your campaigns? Then he asks for a sword, and is angry with the friend who refuses it out of goodwill, and sends gifts to the girl who hates him, and falls to praying and weeping, and then again when he has a little luck he is exultant. How can we call him free when he has not learnt to give up desire and fear?

Now look at the lower animals and see how we apply the notion of freedom to them. Men put lions in cages and rear them as tame creatures and feed them, and sometimes even take them about with them. Yet who will call a lion like that 'free'? The softer he lives, the worse is his slavery. What lion, if he got sense or reason, would wish to be a lion of that sort? Look at the birds yonder and see what lengths they go in striving to escape, when they are caught and reared in cages; why, some of them actually starve themselves rather than endure that sort of life; and even those that do not die, pine away and barely keep alive, and dash out if they find any chance of an opening. So strong is their desire for natural freedom, an independent and unhindered existence.

Why, what ails you in your cage?

'What a question! I am born to fly where I will, to live in the air, to sing when I will; you take all this away from me, and say, "What ails you?"'

Therefore we will call only those creatures free, that do not endure captivity, but escape by death as soon as they are caught. So too Diogenes says somewhere, 'A quiet death is the one sure means of freedom', and he writes to the Persian king, 'You cannot enslave the city of the Athenians any more than you can enslave fishes.'

'What! shall I not capture them?'

'If you capture them,' he says, 'they will straightway leave you and be gone, like fishes; for when you take one of them, he dies. So if the Athenians die as soon as you take them, what is the good of your armament?' These are the words of a free man who has seriously examined the question and found the truth, as is reasonable; but if you look for it elsewhere than where it is, what wonder if you never find it?

The slave is anxious to be set free at once. Why? Do you think it is because he is anxious to pay the tax on his manumission? No! the reason is he imagines that up till now he is hampered and ill at ease because he has not got his freedom. 'If I am enfranchised,' he says, 'at once all will be well, I heed nobody, I talk to all men as an equal and one of their quality, I go where I will, I come whence I will and where I will.' Then he is emancipated, and having nothing to eat he straightway looks for some one to flatter and to dine with; then he either has to sell his body to lust and endure the worst, and if he gets a manger to eat at, he has plunged into a slavery much severer than the first; or if perchance he grows rich, being a low-bred fellow he dotes on some paltry girl and gets miserable and bewails himself and longs to be a slave again.

'What ailed me in those days? Another gave me clothes and shoes, another fed me and tended me in sickness, and the service I did him was a small matter. Now, how wretched and miserable I am, with many masters instead of one! Still, if I can get rings [1] on my fingers I shall live happily and prosperously enough.'

And so first, to get them, he puts up with what he deserves, and having got them repeats the process. Next he says, 'If I go on a campaign I am quit of all my troubles.' He turns soldier and endures the lot of a criminal, but all the same he begs for a second campaign and a third.[2] Lastly, when he gets the crown to his career and is made a senator, once more he becomes a slave again as he goes to the senate; then he enjoys the noblest and the sleekest slavery of all.

Let him not be foolish, let him learn, as Socrates said, what is the true nature of everything, and not apply primary conceptions at random to particular facts. For this is the cause of all the miseries of men, that they are not able to apply their common primary conceptions to particular cases. One of us fancies this, another that. One fancies he is ill. Not at all; it is only that he does not apply his primary conceptions. Another fancies that he is poor, that his father or mother is cruel, another that Caesar is not gracious. But really it is one thing, and one thing only; they do not know how to adjust their primary conceptions. For who has not a primary notion of evil—that it is harmful, to be shunned, by every means to be got rid of? One primary notion does not conflict with another, the conflict is in the application.

What then is this evil which is harmful and to be shunned?

'Not to be Caesar's friend', he says.

He has gone out of his way, he has failed to apply his notions, he is in sore distress, he is seeking for what is nothing to the purpose; for when he has got Caesar's friendship he has equally failed of his object. For what is the object of every man's search? To have a quiet mind, to be happy, to do everything as he will, to be free from hindrance and compulsion. Very well: when he becomes Caesar's friend is he relieved from hindrance and compulsion, is he in peace and happiness? Of whom are we to inquire? Whom can we better trust than the very man who has become Caesar's friend?

Come forward and tell us! when was your sleep more tranquil, now or before you became Caesar's friend?

At once the answer comes, 'Cease, by the gods I beg you, to mock at my fortune; you do not know what a miserable state is mine; no sleep comes near to me, but in comes some one to say, "Now he's awake, now he'll be coming out"; then troubles and cares assail me.'

Tell me, when did you dine more agreeably, now or before?

Hear again what he says about this: if he is not invited, he is distressed, and if he is invited he dines as a slave with his lord, anxious all the while for fear he should say or do something foolish. And what do you think he fears? To be flogged like a slave? How should he come off so well? No, so great a man as he, and Caesar's friend, must fear to lose his neck; nought less were fitting. When did you bathe with more peace of mind, or exercise yourself more at your ease? In a word, which life would you rather live, to-day's or the old life? No one, I can swear, is so wanting in sense or feeling, that he does not lament his lot the louder the more he is Caesar's friend.

Inasmuch then as neither those who bear the name of kings nor kings' friends live as they will, what free men are left? Seek, and you shall find, for nature supplies you with means to find the truth. If, with these means and no more to guide you, you cannot find the answer for yourself, then listen to those who have made the search. What do they say?

Does freedom seem to you a good thing?

'The greatest good.'

Can any one who attains the greatest good be miserable or fare badly?

'No.'

Whensoever then you see men unhappy, miserable, mourning, you may declare with confidence that they are not free.

'I do declare it.'

Well then, we have got away from buying and selling, and that kind of disposal of property which they deal with. For if you are right in making these admissions, no one who is miserable can be free, whether he be a great king or a little one, a consular or one who has twice been consul.

'Granted.'

Answer me once more. Does freedom seem to you a great and noble and precious thing?

'Certainly.'

Can then one who possesses so great and precious and noble a thing be of a humble spirit?

'He cannot.'

Therefore when you see a man cringing to another or flattering him against his true opinion, you may say with confidence that he too is not free, and not only if he does it for a paltry dinner, but even if he does it for a province or a consulship. But those who do it for small objects you may call slaves on a small scale, and the others, as they deserve, slaves on a large scale.

'I grant you this too.'

Again, does freedom seem to you to be something independent, owning no authority but itself?

'Certainly.'

Then whenever a man can be hindered or compelled by another at will, assert with confidence that he is not free. Do not look at his grandfathers and great grandfathers and search whether he was bought or sold, but if you hear him say 'Master' from the heart and with feeling, then call him slave, though twelve fasces go before him; [3] and if you hear him say, 'Wretched am I, that I am so treated', call him slave; in a word, if you see him bewailing himself, complaining, miserable, call him slave, though he wears the purple hem. If, however, he does not behave like this, call him not free yet, but get to know his judgements and see whether they are liable to compulsion or hindrance or unhappiness, and if you find any such, call him a slave on holiday at the Saturnalia; say that his master is away; he will presently return and then you will learn his true condition.

'In what form will he return?'

In the form of every one who has authority over the things that a man wishes for, to get them for him or to take them away.

'Have we then so many masters?'

Yes, for even before these personal masters, we have masters in circumstance, and circumstances are many. It must needs follow then that those who have authority over any of these are our masters. For no one really fears Caesar himself; men fear death, exile, deprivation of property, prison, disfranchisement. Nor does any one love Caesar, unless he has great merit; we love wealth, the tribunate, the praetorship, the consulship. When we love and hate and fear these, the men who have authority over them are bound to be our masters, and that is why we worship them like gods; for we consider that that which has authority over the greatest benefit is divine; and then if we make a false minor premiss, 'this man has control over the greatest benefit', our conclusion is bound to be wrong too.

What is it then which makes man his own master and free from hindrance? Wealth does not make him so, nor a consulship, nor a province, nor a kingdom; we must find something else. Now what is it which makes him unhindered and unfettered in writing?

'Knowledge of how to write.'

What makes him so in flute-playing?

'Knowledge of flute-playing.'

So too in living, it is knowledge of how to live. You have heard this as a general principle; consider it in detail. Is it possible for one who aims at an object which lies in the power of others to be unhindered? Is it possible for him to be untrammelled?

'No.'

It follows that he cannot be free. Consider then: have we nothing which is in our power alone, or have we everything? Or only some things in our power, and some in that of others?

'How do you mean?'

When you wish your body to be whole, is it in your power or not?

'It is not.'

And when you wish it to be healthy?

'That is not in my power.'

And when you wish it to be beautiful?

'That is not in my power.'

And to live or die?

'That is not mine either.'

The body then is something not our own and must give an account to any one who is stronger than ourselves.

'Granted.'

Is it in your power to have land when you will, and as long as you will, and of the quality you will?

'No.'

And slaves?

'No.'

And clothes?

'No.'

And your bit of a house?

'No.'

And horses?

'None of these things.'

And if you wish your children or your wife or your brother or your friends to live, whatever happens, is that in your power?

'No, that is not either.'

Have you nothing then which owns no other authority, nothing which you alone control, or have you something of that sort?

'I do not know.'

Look at the matter thus and consider it. Can any one make you assent to what is false?

'No one.'

Well, then, in the region of assent you are unhindered and unfettered.

'Granted.'

Again, can any one force your impulse towards what you do not wish?

'He can; for when he threatens me with death or bonds, he forces my impulse.'

Well now, if you despise death and bonds, do you heed him any longer?

'No.'

Is it your doing then to despise death, or is it not yours?

'Mine.'

It rests with you then to be impelled to action, does it not?

'I grant it rests with me.'

And impulse not to act, with whom does that rest? It is yours too.

'Supposing that my impulse is to walk, and he hinders me, what then?'

What part of you will he hinder? Your assent?

'No, but my poor body.'

Yes, as a stone is hindered.

'Granted; but I do not walk any more.'

Who told you that it is your business to walk unhindered? The only thing I told you was unhindered was your impulse; as to the service of the body, and its cooperation, you have heard long ago that it is no affair of yours.

'I grant you this too.'

Can any one compel you to will to get what you do not wish?

'No one.'

Or to purpose or to plan, or in a word to deal with the impressions that you meet with?

'No one can do this either; but if I will to get something a man will hinder me from obtaining it.'

How will he hinder you, if you set your will upon things which are your own and beyond hindrance?

'Not at all.'

But no one tells you that he who wills to get what is not his own is unhindered.

'Am I then not to will to get health?'

Certainly not, nor anything else that is not your own. For nothing is your own, that it does not rest with you to procure or to keep when you will. Keep your hands far away from it; above all, keep your will away, or else you surrender yourself into slavery, you put your neck under the yoke, if you admire what is not your own, and set your heart on anything mortal, whatever it be, or anything that depends upon another.

'Is not my hand my own?'

It is a part of you, but by nature a thing of clay, subject to hindrance and compulsion, slave to everything that is stronger than itself. Nay, why do I name you the hand? You must treat your whole body like a poor ass, with its burden on its back, going with you just so far as it may, and so far as it is given you; but if the king's service calls, and a soldier lays hands on it, let it go, do not resist or murmur; if you do, you will only get a flogging and lose your poor ass all the same.

But when this is your proper attitude to your body, consider what is left for you to do with other things that are procured for the body's sake. As the body is the poor ass, other things become the ass's bridle and pack-saddle, shoes and barley and fodder. Give them up too, let them go quicker and with a lighter heart than the ass itself.

And when you have prepared and trained yourself thus to distinguish what is your own from what is not your own, things subject to hindrance from things unhindered, to regard these latter as your concern, and the former as not, to direct your will to gain the latter and to avoid the former, then have you any one to fear any more?

'No one.'

Of course. What should you fear for? Shall you fear for what is your own, that is, for what makes good and evil for you? Nay, who has authority over what is yours? Who can take it away, who can hinder it, any more than they can hinder God? Is it your body and your property that you fear for? Are you afraid for what is not your own, for what does not concern you at all?

Why, what have you been studying all along but to distinguish what is yours from what is not yours, what is in your power from what is not in your power, things subject to hindrance from things unhindered? Why did you go to the philosophers? Was it that you might be just as unfortunate and miserable as ever? I say that so trained you will be free from fear and perturbation. What has pain to do with you now, for it is only things that cause fear in expectation which cause pain when they come? What shall you have desire for any longer, for your will is tranquil and harmonious, set on objects within its compass to obtain, objects that are noble and within your reach, and you have no wish to get what is beyond your will, and you give no scope to that jostling element of unreason which breaks all bounds in its impatience?

When once you adopt this attitude towards things, no man can inspire fear in you any longer. For how can man cause fear in man by his aspect or his talk or by his society generally, any more than fear can be roused by horse or dog or bee in another horse or dog or bee? No, it is *things* which inspire fear in every man; it is the power of winning things for another or of taking them away from him, that makes a man feared.

How then is the citadel destroyed? Not by fire or sword, but by judgements. For if we pull down the citadel in the city, we have not got rid of the citadel which is held by fever or by fair women, in a word the citadel in ourselves and the tyrants who are within us, who threaten each one of us day by day, now in new forms, now in old. This is the point where we must begin, this is where the citadel must be destroyed, and the tyrants cast forth; we must give up our body, and all that belongs to it —faculties, property, reputation, offices, honours, children, brothers, friends—all these we must regard as having no concern for us.

If the tyrants are cast forth from this, what need is there for me to blockade the outward citadel? What harm does it do to me by standing? Why do I try and cast forth the guards? I feel them no longer; their rods and their spears and swords are pointed against others. I was never hindered in my will or compelled against my wish.

Nay, how can this be?

I have submitted my will to God. He wills that I should have a fever; I will it too. He wills that I should have an impulse. I will it too. He wills that I should will to get a thing. I too will it. He wills that I should get something, and I wish it; He wills that I should not, I wish it no more. I am willing then (if He wills it) to die or be put on the rack. Who can hinder me any more against my own judgement or put compulsion on me? I am as safe as Zeus.

I act as the more cautious travellers do. A man has heard that the road is infested by robbers; he does not dare to venture on it alone, but waits for company—a legate, or a quaestor, or a proconsul—and joining him he passes safely on the road. The prudent man does the same in the world; in the world are many haunts of robbers, tyrants, storms, distresses, chances of losing what is dearest. 'Where is a man to escape? How is he to go on his way unrobbed? What company is he to wait for that he may pass through in safety? To whom is he to join himself? To this or that rich man, or consular? What is the good of that? Your great man himself is stripped, and utters mourning and lamentation. What if my fellow traveller turns against me himself to rob me? What am I to do? I will be "a friend of Caesar"; if I am his companion no one will do me wrong. But first, how many things must I endure and undergo, to become a distinguished person! How often must I suffer robbery and from how many! And then, if I rise to distinction, even Caesar is mortal. And if some circumstance lead him to become my enemy, where, I ask, is it better for me to retire? To the wilderness? Why, does not fever come there? What is to become of me then? Is it impossible to find a travelling-companion who is safe, trustworthy, strong, proof against attack?' Thus he reflects and comes to understand that if he attaches himself to God, he will pass through the world in safety.

'What do you mean by "attach" himself?'

That what God wills, he may will too, and what God wills not, he may not will either.

How then is this to be done?

How else, but by examining the purposes of God and His governance of the world. What has He given me to be my own, and independent, what has He reserved for Himself? He has given me all that lies within the sphere of my choice, and has put it in my hands, unfettered, unhindered. How could He make my clay body free from hindrance? My property, my chattels, my honour, my children, my wife, He made subject to the revolution of the universe. Why then do I fight against God? Why do I will what is not for me to will, what is not given me to hold under all conditions, but to hold only as it is given and so far as it is given?

Suppose He that gave takes away. Why then do I resist? I shall not merely be silly, if I try to compel Him that is stronger; first of all I shall be doing wrong. For whence did I bring what I have into the world? My father gave them me. And who gave them him? Who is it that has made the sun, and the fruits of the earth, and the seasons, and the union and fellowship of men with one another?

You have received everything, nay your very self, from Another, and yet you complain and blame the Giver, if He takes anything away from you. Who are you and for what have you come? Did not He bring you into the world? Did not He show you the light? Has He not given you fellow workers? Has He not given you senses too, and reason? And in what character did He bring you into life? Was it not as a mortal, one who should live upon earth with his little portion of flesh and behold God's governance and share for a little while in His pageant and His festival? Will you not then look at the pageant and the festal gathering as long as it is given you, and then, when God leads you forth, go away with an obeisance to Him and thanksgiving for what you have heard and seen?

'No, I wanted to go on feasting.'

Yes, those at the Mysteries too want to go on with the ceremony, and those at Olympia to see fresh competitors, but the festival is at an end. Leave it and depart, in a thankful and modest spirit; make room for others. Others must come into being, even as you did, and being born must have room and dwellings and necessaries. But if the first comers do not retire, what is left for them? Why will nothing satisfy or content you? Why do you crowd the world's room?

'Yes, but I want my wife and my children to be with me.'

Are they yours? Are they not His who gave them? Are they not His who has made you? Will you not give up what it not yours, and give way to Him who is stronger than you?

'Why then did He bring me into the world on these terms?'

Depart, if it does not suit you. God has no need of a querulous spectator. He needs men who join in the feast and in the dance, ready to applaud and glorify and praise the festival. But the impatient and miserable He will gladly see left outside the festival: for even when they were there they did not behave as at a festival nor fill the place appropriate to them, but were peevish and complained of fate and fortune and their company: insensible to fortune's gifts and to their own faculties, which they have received for just the opposite—a great heart, a noble spirit, and the very freedom we are now in search of.

'For what then have I received these gifts?'

To use them.

'For how long?'

Just so long as He who lent them wills.

'But what if they are necessary for me?'

Do not set your heart on them, and they will not be. Do not tell yourself that they are necessary, and they are not.

This is what you ought to practise from sunrise to sunset, beginning with the meanest things and those most subject to injury—a jug or a cup. From this go on to a tunic, a dog, a horse, a field; and from that to yourself, your body and its members, your children, your wife, your brothers. Look carefully on all sides and fling them away from you. Purify your judgements, and see that nothing that is not your own is attached to you or clings to you, that nothing shall give you pain if it is torn from you. And as you train yourself day by day, as in the lecture-room, say not that you are a philosopher (I grant you that would be arrogant), but that you are providing for your enfranchisement; for this is freedom indeed. This was the freedom which Diogenes won from Antisthenes, and said that no one could enslave him any more. That explains his bearing as a captive, and his behaviour to the pirates: did he call any of them master? I do not mean the mere name (I have no fear of that), but the state of mind, of which it is the expression. Think how he rebukes them for feeding their prisoners badly. Think how he was sold: did he look for a master? No, for a slave.[4] And when he was sold, think how he bore himself towards his master: he began talking to him at once, telling him that he ought not to dress as he did, or shave as he did, and what life his sons ought to lead. What wonder in that? For if he had bought a slave skilled in gymnastic would he have used him as a servant in the palaestra or as a master? As a master; and in the same way if he had bought a man skilled in medicine or in architecture. And on this principle the man with skill is bound in every subject to be superior to the man without skill. Whoever then possesses knowledge of life in general must be master. For who is master on shipboard?

'The helmsman.'

Why? Is it because any one who disobeys him is punished? No! but because he possesses skill in steering.

'But my master can flog me.'

Can he do it with impunity?

'So I thought.'

But as he cannot do it with impunity, therefore he has no authority to do it. No one can do wrong acts with impunity.

'What penalty falls on the man who imprisons his own slave, if he think fit?'

The very act of imprisoning him is his penalty, and this you will admit yourself, if you will hold fast the principle that man is not a brute but a civilized creature. For when does a vine do badly? When it acts against its nature. When does a cock do badly? In the same conditions. The same is true of a man. What is his nature then? Is it to bite and kick and cast into prison and behead? No, but to do good, to work with others and pray for them. Therefore, whether you will or no, man does badly when he acts without sense.

'Did not Socrates then do badly?'

No, but his judges and accusers did.

'Did not Helvidius in Rome do badly?'

No, but his murderer did.

'What do you mean?'

Just as you do not say the fighting-cock has done badly when it has won and been wounded, but when it has been beaten without a scratch, and you do not count a hound happy when he does not strain in the pursuit, but when you see him sweating, in distress, his flanks bursting with the chase. What is there incredible in the statement that every man's evil is that which contradicts his nature? Is this incredible? Is it not what you say in every other sphere? Why then do you take another line only when man is in question? Is our other statement then incredible—that man's nature is civilized and affectionate and trustworthy?

'No, this is not, either.'

How comes it then, further, that he suffers no harm though he be flogged or imprisoned or beheaded? Is not it true that, if he suffer these things in a noble spirit, he goes away the gainer, and is profited, whereas he who suffers harm is the man who undergoes the most pitiful and shameful fate, the man who changes from a man into a wolf or a serpent or a wasp?

Come now and let us review the conclusions we have agreed to. He is free, whom none can hinder, the man who can deal with things as he wishes. But the man who can be hindered or compelled or fettered or driven into anything against his will, is a slave. And who is he whom none can hinder? The man who fixes his aim on nothing that is not his own. And what does 'not his own' mean? All that it does not lie in our power to have or not to have, or to have of a particular quality or under particular conditions. The body then does not belong to us, its parts do not belong to us, our property does not belong to us. If then you set your heart on one of these as though it were your own, you will pay the penalty deserved by him who desires what does not belong to him. The road that leads to freedom, the only release from slavery is this, to be able to say with your whole soul:

Lead me, O Zeus, and lead me, Destiny,
Whither ordainèd is by your decree.

[Cleanthes]

But, what say you, my philosopher, suppose the tyrant call on you to say something unworthy of you? Do you assent or refuse? Tell me.

'Let me think it over.'

You will think it over now, will you? And what, pray, did you think over when you were at lecture? Did you not study what things are good and what are evil, and what are neither?

'Yes, I did.'

What conclusion did you approve then?

'That things right and noble were good, things wrong and shameful bad.'

Is life a good thing?

'No.'

Is death evil?

'No.'

Is prison?

'No.'

And what did you think of ignoble and faithless speech, and treachery to a friend and flattery of a tyrant?

'We thought them evil.'

Why do you ask the question now, then? You should have asked it and made up your mind long ago. It is nonsense to question now whether, when I can win the greatest goods, it is fitting for me not to win the greatest evils? A fine and necessary question forsooth, needing a deal of thought! Man, why do you mock us?

That is not the sort of thing that men 'question'. If you really imagined shameful acts to be bad, and noble acts good, and all else to be indifferent, you would not have proceeded to raise this question: not at all: you would at once have been able to decide the question by intuition, as an act of sight. For when do you question whether black things are white, or heavy things light, instead of following the obvious conclusions of your senses? Why then do you talk now of considering whether things indifferent are more to be shunned than things evil? These are not your judgements: prison and death do not seem to you indifferent, but the greatest evils, nor do base words and acts seem evil, they seem not to matter for us.

This is the habit to which you have trained yourself from the first. 'Where am I? In the lecture-room. And who are listening to me? I am talking to philosophers. But now I have left the lecture-room. Away with those sayings of pedants and fools!' That is how a philosopher gives witness against a friend, that is how a philosopher turns parasite: that is how he hires himself out at a price, and speaks against his real opinion in the Senate, while in his heart his judgement cries aloud, not a flat and miserable apology for an opinion, hanging to idle discussions as by a hair-thread, but a judgement strong and serviceable, trained by actions, which is the true initiation. Watch yourself and see how you take the news, I do not say that your child is dead (how should that befall you?), but that your oil is spilt, or your wine drunk up: well may one who stands by, as your temper rises high, say just this to you, 'Philosopher, you use different language in the lecture-room: why do you deceive us? Why, worm that you are, do you call yourself a man?' I would fain stand by one of these men when he is indulging his lust, that I might see how eager he is, and what words he utters, and whether he remembers his own name, or the discourses which he hears or delivers or reads.

'Yes, but what has this to do with freedom?'

Nay! what else but this has to do with it, whether you rich people agree, or not?

'And who is your witness to this?'

Why, it is none other than your very selves. You who own that great master, and live at his nod and motion, and your blood runs cold if he so much as look at one of you with a sour face: you who pay court to old women and old men, and say, 'I cannot do that, I am not allowed.' Why are you not allowed? Did you not just now contend with me and assert you were free?

'Yes, but Aprulla has forbidden me.'

Tell the truth then, slave that you are, and do not run away from your masters, nor disown your slavery, nor dare to claim your enfranchisement, when you have so many proofs of slavery against you. I declare that the man who is compelled by love to act against his opinion, seeing the better course all the time, but wanting the strength to follow it, one might be more inclined to think deserving pardon, as overpowered by an influence violent and in a way divine. But who can bear with you, whose love is all for old women and old men, wiping their faces clean and washing them and giving them presents, and tending them like a slave in their illness, while all the time you are praying for them to die, and questioning the doctors, whether they are sick unto death at last? Or again, when you kiss the hands of other people's slaves in order to get those great and splendid offices and honours, becoming the slave of men who are not even free? Then, if you please, you walk in splendour as praetor or consul. Do I not know how you became praetor, where you got the consulship, who gave it you? For my part I would not wish to live, if I had to owe my life to Felicio, and put up with his contempt and slavish arrogance; for I know what a slave is who is prosperous as the world thinks and puffed up with vanity.

'Are you then free?' says one.

By the gods, I wish to be and pray to be, but I cannot yet look in the face of my masters, I still set store by my poor body, I count it of great moment to keep it sound, yes though I have not a sound body to begin with. But I can show you one who is free, that you may not have to look for your example. Diogenes was free. How came he by this? Not because he was of free parents (he was not), but because he was free himself, had cast away all the weakness that might give slavery a hold on him, and so no one could approach or lay hold on him to enslave him. Everything he had he was ready to let go, it was loosely attached to him. If you had laid hold on his property, he would have let it go rather than have followed you for it; if you seized his leg, he would have let that go; if his whole poor body, he would have let his whole body go; and the same with kinsfolk, friends, and country. For he knew whence he had them and from whom, and on what conditions he received them. His true ancestors, the gods, and his true Country he would never have deserted, nor have suffered another to yield them more obedience or attention, nor would another have died for his Country more cheerfully. For he never sought to get the reputation of acting for the universe, but he remembered that everything that comes to pass has its source there and is done for that true Country's sake and is entrusted to us by Him that governs it. Wherefore look what he says and writes himself: 'Therefore, Diogenes,' he says, 'you have power to converse as you will with the king of the Persians and with Archidamus, king of the Lacedaemonians.' Was it because he was the son of free parents? When all the men of Athens and Lacedaemon and Corinth were unable to converse with them as they wished, and feared and flattered them instead, was it because they were sons of slaves? 'Why have I the power to do it then?' he says. 'Because I count my poor body not my own, because I need nothing, because law and nothing else is all in all to me.' These were the things which left him free.

And that you may not think that I point you to the example of a man alone in the world, with no wife or children or country or friends or kindred, who might have bent his will and drawn him from his purpose, take Socrates and look at him: he had wife and children, but regarded them as not his own; a country, in such manner and so far as duty allowed: friends, kinsmen, all these things he had made subject to law and obedience to law. For this reason, when duty called him to take the field, he was the first to leave Athens and ran all risks of battle most ungrudgingly, but when he was sent by the Tyrants to fetch Leon, he never entertained the idea, because he thought it shameful, though he knew that he would have to die, if it so chanced. And what did it matter to him? Why, he wanted to preserve something else—not his poor flesh, but his honour and self-respect. These are things which cannot be trusted to another or made subject to another. Afterwards when he had to plead for his life, did he behave as one who had children or as one who had a wife? No, but as one alone in the world. And again, when he had to drink the poison, how did he behave? When he might have saved himself, and when Crito said to him, 'Escape, for the sake of your children', what did he say? Did he think the chance a godsend? No, he looked at what was fitting, and had no eye, no thought for anything besides. For he wished to save not his poor body, but 'that which right increases and preserves, and wrong diminishes and makes to wither'. Socrates refuses to save himself with dishonour: he who would not put the question to the vote, when the Athenians bade him, who despised the Tyrants, who held such noble discourse on virtue and goodness—it is impossible to save him with dishonour: his safety is secured by death, not by flight. For the good actor too, if he stops when he ought, has more chance of safety than one who acts out of season.

What will your children do then?

'If I had gone away to Thessaly you would have looked after them: and when I have gone away to Hades, will there be no one to look after them?' [Plato, *Crito,* 54a]

See how he calls death by smooth names and scoffs at it. But if you and I had been in his place, we should at once have argued that we ought to repay injury with injury: and we should have added, 'I shall be useful to many men if I keep alive, but to no one if I die.' Nay, had it been necessary to creep out through a hole in the rock to escape, we should have done so. And yet how could we have been of use to any one? For those we were trying to help would not have stood fast. Or again, if we did good by living, should we not have done much more good to men by dying when and as we ought? Even so now that Socrates is dead, the memory of what he did or said in his lifetime is no less useful to men, or it may be even more useful than before.

Make this your study, study these judgements, and these sayings: fix your eyes on these examples, if you wish to be free, if you set your desires on freedom as it deserves. It is no wonder that you pay this great, this heavy price for so vast an object. Men hang themselves, or cast themselves down headlong, nay sometimes whole cities perish for the sake of what the world calls 'freedom', and will you not repay to God what He has given, when He asks it, for the sake of true freedom, the freedom which stands secure against all attack? Shall you not practise, as Plato says, not death only, but torture and exile and flogging, in a word practise giving back all that is not yours? If not, you will be a slave among slaves, even if you are consul ten thousand times, and no less, if you go up into Caesar's Palace; and you will discover that 'what philosophers say may be contrary to opinion', as Cleanthes said, 'but not contrary to reason'. For you will really get to know that what they say is true, and that none of these objects that men admire and set their hearts on is of any use to those who get them, though those who have never chanced to have them get the impression, that if only these things were theirs their cup of blessings would be full, and then, when they get them, the sun scorches them and the sea tosses them no less, and they feel the same boredom and the same desire for what they have not got. For freedom is secured not by the fulfilling of men's desires, but by the removal of desire. To learn the truth of what I say, you must spend your pains on these new studies instead of your studies in the past: sit up late that you may acquire a judgement that makes you free: pay your attentions not to a rich old man, but to a philosopher, and be seen about his doors: to be so seen will not do you discredit: you will not depart empty or without profit, if you approach in the right spirit. If you doubt my word, do but try: there is no disgrace in trying.

CHAPTER II

ON INTERCOURSE WITH MEN

THE one thing to be careful about beyond all others is this—not to get so involved with any of your former companions or friends, as to compromise your character for his sake, for if you do this you will destroy yourself. If the thought slips in, 'I shall seem rude to him, and he will not be the same to me as before', remember that nothing is done without paying for it, and that it is not possible to be the same man that you once were, unless you do as you did before. Choose then which you will —to be like your former self and be loved as before by those who loved you, or to be better than before, and so miss what they once gave you. For if this is the better choice, then incline to this, and let no irrelevant arguments distract you, for no one can make progress by facing both ways. No; if you have chosen this course before all, if you wish to devote yourself to this and nothing else, and to spend all your labour on this, then dismiss all other thoughts, or else this facing both ways will produce a double result—you will not make progress as you ought, and you will fail to get what you got before; for before, when you frankly set your desires on worthless objects, you were agreeable to your companions. You cannot excel both ways; in proportion as you succeed on the one side, you must needs fall short on the other. When you do not drink with those whom you used to drink with, you cannot seem as agreeable to them as of old; choose then, whether you wish to be a drinker and gratify them, or sober and displease them. If you do not sing with those that you sang with, you cannot win their affection as before: here too then you must choose which you prefer. For if it is better to have self-respect and self-control, than to have it said of one, 'What a charming fellow!', then give up all other considerations, put them from you, turn away from them, and have nothing to do with them. But if this is not going to satisfy you, then turn round completely, and practise the very opposite—unnatural lust, adultery, and all that is in keeping with them, and you shall get what you want. Yes, jump up and shriek applause over your dancer.

But characters so opposite do not mix: you cannot act both Thersites and Agamemnon. If you want to be Thersites you must be humpbacked and bald, if Agamemnon, you must be handsome and tall, and love your subjects.

CHAPTER III

WHAT TO AIM AT IN EXCHANGE

If you give up any external possession, mind you see what you are to get in exchange for it: and if it is worth more, then never say, 'I have been a loser.' You will not lose if you get a horse for an ass, an ox for a sheep, a noble action for a piece of money, true peace instead of pedantry, self-respect instead of foul language. If you remember this you will everywhere preserve your character as it ought to be: if you do not remember it, I warn you that your time perishes for nought, and you will waste and overthrow all the pains that you now spend upon yourself. It needs but a little to overthrow and destroy everything—just a slight aberration from reason. For the helmsman to wreck his vessel, he does not need the same resources, as he needs to save it: if he turn it but a little too far to the wind, he is lost; yes, and if he do it not deliberately but from mere want of attention, he is lost all the same. It is very much the same in life: if you doze but a little, all that you have amassed up till now leaves you. Keep awake then and watch your impressions: it is no trifle you have in keeping, but self-respect, honour, constancy, a quiet mind, untouched by distress, or fear, or agitation—in a word, freedom.

What are you going to sell all this for? Look and see what your purchase is worth.

'But I am not going to sell my freedom for anything of that kind.'

Well, suppose you waive external gain, consider what the exchange is that you are making. It is yours to say, 'Self-control for me, a tribunate for him: a praetorship for him, self-respect for me. I do not clamour, when to do so is unseemly, I will not jump from my seat, when I ought not, for I am free and God's friend, to obey Him of my own free will. I must not lay claim to anything else—body, property, office, reputation, anything in short, for He does not wish me to lay claim to them: had He wished it, He would have made them good for me, but He has not done so, and therefore I cannot transgress any of His commands.' In everything you do, guard what is your own good: for the rest, be content just to take anything that is given you, so far as you may use it rationally. Otherwise you will be wretched and miserable, hampered and hindered. These are the laws that are sent you from God, these are His ordinances. These you must expound, and these obey, not those of Masurius and Cassius.

CHAPTER IV

TO THOSE WHOSE HEART IS SET ON A QUIET LIFE

REMEMBER that it is not only desire of office and of wealth that makes men abject and subservient to others, but also desire of peace and leisure and travel and learning. Regard for any external thing, whatever it be, makes you subservient to another. What difference does it make then whether you desire to be a senator, or not to be a senator, to be in office, or to be out of office? What difference is there between saying, 'I am miserable, I don't know what to do, I am tied to my books like a corpse', and saying, 'I am miserable, I have no leisure to read'? For books, like salutations and office, belong to the outer world which is beyond your own control. If you deny it, tell me why do you want to read? If you are drawn by the mere pleasure of reading, or by curiosity, you are a trifler, without perseverance: but if you judge it by the true standard, what is that but peace of mind? If reading does not win you peace of mind, what is the good of it?

'Nay,' he says, 'it does, and that is just why I am vexed at being deprived of it.'

And what, pray, is this peace of mind, which any one can hinder—I do not mean Caesar, or Caesar's friend, but a raven, a flute-player, a fever, countless other things? Nothing is so characteristic of peace of mind as that it is continuous and unhindered. Suppose now I am called away to do something: I shall go and attend to the limits which one must observe—acting with self-respect and security, with no will to get or to avoid external things, watching men also to see what they say and how they move, and that not from ill nature, nor to blame or mock at them, but looking at myself all the time to see if I am making the same mistakes too.

'How then shall I cease to err?' you ask.

Time was when I made the same mistakes as others, but I do so no more, thanks be to God. If you have acted thus and devoted yourself to this, have you done worse than if you had read a thousand lines or written as many? When you eat, are you vexed that you are not reading? Are you not content with eating as your reading bids you? And the same when you wash and take exercise? Why, then, do you not keep an equable tenor always, even when you approach Caesar or this or that great man? What do you lack, if you keep yourself free from passion, undismayed, modest, if you are rather a spectator of events than a spectacle to others, if you do not envy those preferred to you, if you are not dazzled by material things?

You say you lack books? How, or to what end? Books are, no doubt, a preparation for life, but life itself is made up of things different from books. To ask for books is as though an athlete should complain, as he enters the arena, that he is not training outside. Life is what you were training for all along, this is what the leaping-weights, and the sawdust, and the young men you wrestled with were leading up to. What? Are you hankering after them, when the time for action is come? It is as if in the sphere of assent, when impressions are presented to us, some which are 'apprehensive', and some which have no such power, we should refuse to distinguish between them and should prefer to read the theory of apprehensive impressions.

What, then, is the reason of our failure?

The reason is that we never directed our reading or our writing to the right object—that is, to dealing naturally with the impressions that come upon us, when we have to act. We are content to go thus far and no farther—to understand what is said, and to be able to explain it to another, to analyse the syllogism and trace out the hypothetical argument. Therefore hindrance besets us in the sphere where our pains are spent.

Do you want things which are not always in your power?

Be condemned, then, to hindrance, obstruction, failure. But if we were to study the doctrine of impulse, not to see what is said about impulse but to make our own impulses good, if we were to study the will to get and the will to avoid to the end that we may never fail to get what we will nor fall into what we avoid, and study the doctrine of what is fitting that we may remember our true relations and may do nothing irrationally or contrary to what is fitting—then we should not have to suffer vexation at being hindered in regard to the principles we have studied, but should find contentment in acting in accordance with them, and we should cease to calculate as we have been wont to do till to-day, 'To-day I read so many lines, wrote so many', and should reckon thus, 'To-day I governed my impulse by the precepts of the philosophers, I did not entertain desire, I avoided only things within the compass of my will, I was not awed by this man, or over-persuaded by that man, but trained my faculty of patience, of abstinence, of co-operation': and then we should give thanks to God, for the gifts for which our thanks are due.

As it is, we do not realize that we too, with a difference, behave like the multitude. Another man fears that he may not become a magistrate, you fear that you may be one. Man, act not so. Nay, just as you laugh at him who fears he may not hold office, so laugh at yourself too. There is nothing to choose between being thirsty with fever, and shunning water like a madman. If you act thus, how shall you be able to say, as Socrates did, 'If God so wills, so be it'? Do you think that, if Socrates had set his desire on a life of leisure and daily conversation with young men in the

Lyceum or the Academy, he would have cheerfully gone on all the campaigns in which he served? Would he not have groaned and lamented, 'Unhappy that I am, wretched and miserable in the field, when I might be sunning myself in the Lyceum.' What? Was this your task in life, to sun yourself? Was it not to have a mind at peace, to be free from hindrance and encumbrance? Nay, how would he have been Socrates any more, if he had lamented like that? How could he have written songs of triumph in prison?

In a word, then, remember this, that, whenever you pay regard to anything outside your will's control, you so far destroy your will. And freedom from office lies outside your will just as much as office, leisure just much as business.

'Am I, then, to pass my life amid this tumult?'

What do you mean by 'tumult'?

'Amid a multitude of men.'

Well, and what is there hard in that? Imagine you are at Olympia, make up your mind that it is a festival. There, too, one cries this, another that, one does this, another that, and one man jostles another. The public baths, too, are thronged, yet which of us does not enjoy this assemblage, and leave it with pain? Be not dissatisfied nor peevish at what happens. 'Vinegar disgusts me, for it is acid; honey disgusts me, for it upsets my tone; I dislike green stuff.' In the same way you say, 'I dislike retirement, it means solitude; I dislike a crowd, it means disturbance.'

Say not so, but, if things so turn out, that you live alone or in a small company, call it 'peace' and make a proper use of it: converse with yourself, train your impressions, develop your primary notions. If you chance on a crowd, call it 'games', 'assembly', 'festival', and try to share the feast with your fellow men. For what sight is pleasanter for the man who loves his kind than a multitude of men? We are pleased to see troops of horses or oxen, we delight to see a multitude of ships: does the sight of a multitude of men vex us?

'Nay, but their clamour overwhelms me.'

Well, that is only a hindrance to your hearing: how does it affect you? Does it affect your faculty of dealing with your impressions? Who can hinder you from dealing naturally with the will to get and the will to avoid, the impulse to act and not to act? What tumult can avail to touch these?

Only remember these general principles: 'What is mine, what is not mine? What is given me? What does God wish me to do now? What does He not wish?' A little while ago His will was that you should live a quiet life in converse with yourself, and write on these matters, read, listen, prepare yourself: you had sufficient time for this. Now He says to you,

'Now come into the conflict, show us what you have learnt, how you have trained. How long are you going to exercise yourself in solitude? The time has now come for you to discover whether you are an athlete worthy of victory, or one of those who go about the world suffering continual defeat.' Why, then, are you vexed? There is no conflict without a crowd: there must be many to train beforehand, many to cry applause, many stewards, many spectators.

'Yes, but I wanted to live a quiet life.'

Lament and mourn, then, as you deserve: for what greater penalty than this can fall on him who is uninstructed and disobedient to the ordinances of God than to be distressed, to mourn, to envy, in a word, to be unhappy and miserable? Have you no wish to free yourself from these ills?

'And how shall I free myself?'

Have you not often heard, that you must get rid of the will to get altogether, and must will to avoid only those things which are within your control? That you must give up everything—body, property, reputation, books, the throng, office, private life? For if once you swerve from this path you become a slave and a subject, you are liable to hindrance and compulsion, and completely at the mercy of others. But the saying of Cleanthes is ready to our need,

Lead me, O Zeus, and lead me, Destiny.

Will you have me go to Rome? To Rome then. To Gyara? I will go to Gyara. To Athens? I will go to Athens. To prison? I will go to prison. If once you say, 'When are we to get away to Athens?' you are lost. That wish, if unfulfilled, must make you miserable, and, if fulfilled, it must make you puffed up, elated on false grounds: again, if you are hindered, it must make you unhappy, at the conflict between circumstances and your will. Give up all these things then.

'Athens is beautiful.'

Yes, but happiness is far more beautiful—freedom from passion and disturbance, the sense that your affairs depend on no one.

'In Rome there is crowd and salutations.'

Yes, but peace of mind outweighs all discomforts. If, then, the time for these has come, why do you not get rid of your will to avoid them? Why must you bear your burden like a cudgelled ass? If you do this, you must needs (look you) be the perpetual slave of him who has power to accomplish your departure, or him who can in any way hinder it, and you are bound to pay respect to him as to an Evil Genius.

There is but one way to peace of mind (keep this thought by you at dawn and in the day-time and at night)—to give up what is beyond your control, to count nothing your own, to surrender everything to heaven and fortune, to leave everything to be managed by those to whom Zeus has given control, and to devote yourself to one object only, that which is your own beyond all hindrance, and in all that you read and write and hear to make this your aim. Therefore I cannot call a man industrious, if I am merely told that he reads or writes, no, not even if one adds 'he is at work all night', unless I know what he is working for. You do not call a man industrious who keeps late hours for the sake of a mistress: neither do I. But if he does it for glory, I call him ambitious; if for money, I call him fond of money, not fond of work. But if the object of his work is his own Governing Principle, if he is working to make this live a natural life, then and then only I call him industrious. You must never praise or blame men for qualities that are indifferent, but for their judgements. For it is these which are each man's property, these which make their actions base or noble. Bear this in mind and rejoice in what is at hand and be content with what the moment brings. If you see any of the principles that you have learnt and thought over being realized by you in action, rejoice over them. If you have put away bad nature, and evil-speaking, or made them less, if you have got rid of wantonness, foul speaking, recklessness, slackness, if you are not excited by things that once excited you, or at least not as before, then you can keep festival day by day, to-day because you behaved well in this action, to-morrow because you did well in another. How much greater cause is this for offering sacrifice than if you were made consul or prefect! These things come to you from your own self and from the gods. Remember Who is the Giver, and to whom He gives and why. If you are brought up to reason thus, you need no longer raise the question, 'Where shall I be happy?' and 'Where shall I please God?' Do not men have their equal portion in all places? Do they not everywhere alike behold what comes to pass?

CHAPTER V

TO THOSE THAT ARE CONTENTIOUS AND BRUTAL

THE good and noble man does not contend with any one, and to the best of his power does not suffer others to contend. We have an illustration of this, as of other qualities, set out for us in the life of Socrates, who not only avoided contention himself on all occasions, but tried to prevent the contentions of others. Look at the *Symposium* of Xenophon and see how many contentions he has reconciled, and again how patient he was with Thrasymachus, with Polus, with Callicles, and how patient always with his wife, and with his son, when his son tried to convict him of fallacious arguments. For he remembered to hold fast the truth that no man is master of another's Governing Principle. Therefore he wished to do nothing that was not his own. What does that mean? Not to move other people to act naturally, for that is not his to do: but to let others act for themselves, as they think fit, and himself none the less to live and spend his days in accord with nature, only doing his own business in such a way that they, too, should follow nature. For this is the conduct which the good and noble man always has set before him.

Is it his will to become praetor?

No, but if this is given him, to keep his own Governing Principle in these circumstances.

To marry?

No, but if marriage is given him, to keep himself in a natural state in those circumstances. But if he wills that his son or his wife should not go wrong, then he wills to make his own what is not his own. In fact education is this, to learn what is one's own and what is not.

Where, then, is there any room for contention if a man bears himself thus? Is he amazed at anything that happens? Does anything take him by surprise? Does he not expect the wicked to deal worse and more severely with him than the event turns out? Does he not count everything gain in which they fall short of the worst?

'Such a one reviled you.'

Many thanks to him for not striking.

'But he did strike too.'

Many thanks to him for not wounding.

'But he did wound.'

Many thanks to him for not killing. For when, or in whose school, did he learn 'that man is a gentle and sociable creature and that wrongdoing in itself does great harm to the wrongdoer'?

If, then, he has not learnt this or been convinced of it, why should he not follow what appears to be his interest?

'My neighbour has thrown stones.'

Is that any offence on your part?

'But my crockery is broken.'

You are no piece of crockery: you are a rational will. You ask what is given you to meet this attack? If you want to act the wolf, you may bite back, and throw more stones at him than he threw: but if you seek to act as a man, then examine your store and see what faculties you have brought into the world with you. Have you brought the faculty of a brute, the faculty of revenging wrongs? When is a horse miserable? When it is deprived of its natural faculties, not when it is unable to crow like a cock, but when it is unable to run. And the dog? Not when it cannot fly, but when it cannot follow a trail. On the same principle a man is wretched, not when he cannot throttle lions or embrace statues (for he has not been endowed by nature with faculties for this), but when he has lost his rational and trustworthy faculty. This is he for whom men

should meet and mourn
The miseries he has come to,

not, by Zeus, the man who is born or dies, but he whose lot it is to lose while he lives what is his own—not his patrimony, his paltry field or house or inn or slaves (for none of these is man's own, but all are alien to him, all are subject and subservient to their Masters, who give them now to one now to another)—to lose the qualities that make him man, the distinctive stamp impressed upon his mind: like the stamp we look for on coins, which if we find we pass them, and if we do not, fling them away.

Whose imprint does this sesterce bear?

'Trajan's.'

Here with it.

'Nero's.'

Fling it away, it will not pass, it is good for nothing.

So, too, it is with man. What stamp have his judgements? 'Gentle, sociable, patient, affectionate.' Good, I accept him, I make him a citizen, I accept him as a neighbour and fellow voyager. Only beware that he has not the stamp of Nero. Is he hot-tempered, is he wrathful, is he querulous? 'If it takes his fancy, he cuffs the heads of those he meets.' Why, then, did you say that he is a man? Is everything judged by its outward form alone? On that principle you must call your waxen apple an apple. No, it must smell and taste like an apple: the outward semblance is not enough. So, when you judge man, nose and eyes are not sufficient, you must see if he has the judgements of a man. Here is one who does not listen to reason, does not understand when his fallacies are exposed; he is an ass. Here is one whose self-respect is deadened: he is useless, anything rather than a man. Here is one looking to find some one he can kick or bite; it follows he is not even a sheep or an ass, but some savage beast or other.

'What then? Do you want me to be despised?'

By whom? By those who know? Nay, how will those who know despise one who is gentle and self-respecting? By those who do not know? What do you care for them? No craftsman cares for those who have no skill!

'Yes, but they will attack me much more.'

What do you mean by 'me'? Can any one injure your will or hinder you from dealing with the impressions you meet with in a natural way?

'No.'

Why, then, do you persist in being troubled and want to show yourself a man of fears? Why do you not come forward and openly proclaim that you are at peace with all men, whatever they do, and that you laugh above all at those who think that they are harming you? saying, 'These slaves do not know who I am, nor where to find what is good or bad for me, for they have no way of getting at my position.' In the same way those who inhabit a strong city laugh at those who besiege it. 'Why are these men troubling themselves for nothing? Our wall is secure, we have food for a long time, and all other supplies.' These are the things that make a city secure against capture; the soul of man is made secure by judgements alone. For what wall is so strong, or what substance so impenetrable, or what property so secure against robbery, or what reputation so unassailable? When the objects that a man sets his mind on are bound to bring him trouble of mind, sick hopes, fear, mourning, disappointment of the will to get, failure of the will to avoid, they are always subject to death and to capture.

If this be so, are we not willing to make the one means of safety which is given us secure, and, abandoning what is mortal and slavish, to spend our efforts on what is immortal and free by nature? Do we not remember that one man does not harm nor benefit another? It is man's judgement on each situation that harms him. It is this which overthrows him, this is contention, this is faction, this is war. The conflict of Eteocles and Polynices was caused by nothing else but this judgement, the judgement on kingship, the judgement on exile—that exile is the worst of evils, kingship the greatest good: and the nature of every man is this—to pursue the good, to avoid the evil, to consider him who takes away from one's good and who involves one in evil as an enemy and aggressor, even though he be a brother, a son, a father, for no kinship is closer than that of the good. Wherefore, if these outward things are reckoned good and evil, there is no love between father and sons or between brother and brother, but the whole world is full of enemies, aggressors, malicious persons. But if a right will is the only good thing, and a wrong will the only evil, what becomes of conflict and reviling? How can it arise? Over things that do not concern us? With whom should we contend? With the ignorant, the miserable, with those who are deluded in regard to the highest matters?

Socrates remembered this when he lived in his own house and bore with a most shrewish wife and an unfeeling son. For what did her shrewishness mean? Pouring water at will over his head, and trampling on his cake. What is that to me, if I make up my mind that it is nothing to me? This is what I have to do, and no king nor master shall hinder me against my will, the many shall not prevail against the one, nor the stronger against the weaker: for God has given each man his reason to use unhindered. These judgements make affection in a household, concord in a city, peace among nations; they make a man grateful towards God, confident in all places, for he looks on outward things as alien to him and as worth nothing. But though we are capable of writing and reading these sentiments, though we can praise them as we read, yet they do not bring conviction to us, nor anything like it. Wherefore the proverb about the Lacedaemonians,

Lions at home, foxes at Ephesus,

[Author unknown]

will fit us too. In the lecture-room we are lions, and foxes in the world outside!

CHAPTER VI

TO THOSE WHO ARE DISTRESSED AT BEING PITIED

'I AM vexed', he says, 'at being pitied.'

Is it your doing that you are pitied, or the doing of those who pity you? Or again, does it rest with you to stop their pity?

'Yes, if I show them that I do not deserve their pity.'

But is it in your power, or is it not, not to deserve pity?

'I think that it is in my power.'

But these men do not pity you for what would deserve pity, if anything did—I mean for your errors—but for poverty and lack of office and diseases and death and other things of this sort. Are you, then, prepared to persuade the multitude that none of these things, after all, is evil, but that it is possible for a man who is poor, and without office or honour, to be happy, or do you try to show off to them as a man of wealth and office? The second course stamps you as a braggart without taste or worth. And consider by what means you would achieve your pretence: you will have to borrow some wretched slaves and possess a few pieces of plate, and show them many times over, if you can, and try not to let men know that they are the same; and you must display gay apparel and other splendours and show yourself off as one who is honoured by eminent persons and must try to dine at their table, or at least be thought to do so; and you must use base arts on your person, to make yourself seem handsomer and better made than you really are: these are the contrivances you must adopt, if you wish to take the second way of avoiding pity.

But the first way is a long, nay an endless, one—to attempt the very task which Zeus could not accomplish—to convince all men of what is good and what is evil. Is this given to you? No! This only is given you—to convince yourself: you have not yet done that: and yet you are already attempting—are you?—to convince others. Why! Who has been your companion so long as you have been yourself, and who can exercise such persuasion on you as you can on yourself, and who is more kindly and friendly disposed to you than you are? How is it, then, that you have not yet persuaded yourself to learn? Are not your thoughts turned upside down? Have you set your mind on this, and not on learning how to be quit of pain and trouble and humiliation, and so to be free? Have you not heard, then, that there is but one way which leads to this—to give up all that lies beyond the will, to abandon it and confess that it is not yours?

To what class of things does another man's opinion about you belong?

'To what is outside the will.'

Then it concerns you not at all?

'Not at all.'

While, then, you still allow yourself to be vexed and troubled at men's opinion, do you imagine that you have attained conviction as to what is good and evil?

Will you not, then, let other men alone and become your own master and pupil? 'Other men shall see for themselves whether it is to their advantage to be in an unnatural state and live their lives so, but no man is nearer me than I am myself. Why is it, then, that though I have heard the arguments of philosophers and assent to them, they have not lightened my burden? Am I so wanting in ability? Why, in all the other things I chose to undertake, I was not found to be duller than most. I was quick at learning letters and wrestling and geometry and the analysis of syllogisms. Is it, then, that reason has failed to convince me? Why, there is nothing which I have so stamped with my approval and choice from the first—and even now these principles are the subject of my reading, I hear and write of nothing else: up till to-day we have found no argument to prevail against this. What then do I lack? Is it that the contrary judgements have not been removed from my mind? Is it that my own convictions are untrained and unaccustomed to confront facts, like arms put away in a cupboard and grown rusty, that cannot be fitted to my body? Yes, of course! In wrestling or writing or reading I am not content with merely learning; I twist the arguments put before me to and fro and construct new ones, and I deal with variable premisses in like manner. But when I have to deal with those necessary principles, which enable a man, if he grounds himself on them, to escape pain, fear, passion, hindrance—to be free, I do not exercise myself in them nor devote to them the practice that is proper for them. And then, am I concerned by what the multitude will say of me, and whether in their eyes I shall appear a happy or important personage?'

Miserable man, will you not see what opinion you pronounce on yourself? How do you appear to yourself? What manner of man in thought, in will to get and will to avoid: what manner of man in impulse, preparation, design, and the other activities of man? Yet you are concerned whether other men pity you?

'Yes, but they pity me when I do not deserve it.'

Is this what pains you? and is the man who is pained to be pitied?

'Yes.'

Then you are not pitied without deserving it after all. By the very feelings you entertain in regard to pity you make yourself worthy of pity. What does Antisthenes say? Did you never hear? 'It is the part of a king, Cyrus, to do well and be ill-spoken of.' My head is sound and all think that I have a headache. What do I care? I am free from fever, and men sympathize with me as though I had fever: 'Unhappy man, this long time you have had fever without ceasing.' I put on a gloomy face and assent: 'It is quite true I have been ill for a long time.' 'What is to happen then?' 'What God wills': and as I say it I laugh in my sleeve at those who pity me.

What prevents me, then, from doing the same here too? I am poor, but I hold a right judgement on poverty: what do I care then, whether they pity me for poverty? I am not in office and others are; but I hold the right opinion as to being in office and out of it. Those who pity me shall take their own views: I have neither hunger nor thirst nor cold, but their own hunger or thirst makes them imagine the same of me. What am I to do for them then? I go about proclaiming and saying, 'Sirs, be not deluded, all is well with me, I take no heed of poverty, or want of office, or, in a word, of anything at all except right judgements: these I hold free from hindrance, I have paid regard to nothing besides.' Yet what nonsense am I talking? How do I hold right judgements any longer if I am not content with being what I am, and am excited over other men's opinion of me?

'But others will get more than I do, and will be preferred to me.'

Well, what is more reasonable than that those who have spent their pains on any object should have the advantage in that on which they have spent their pains? They have spent their pains on office, you on judgements, they on wealth, you on the way to deal with impressions. See whether they have the advantage of you in that on which you have spent pains and which they neglect: whether in assent they keep more to natural standards, whether they are more successful in getting what they will to get, and in avoiding what they will to avoid, whether in design, in purpose, in impulse they aim better than you, whether they do what is fitting for them as men, as sons, and as parents, and in each relation that you name in turn. But if they hold office and you do not, will you not tell yourself the truth—that you do nothing to gain office, and they do everything, and it is most unreasonable that one who pays attention to a thing should have less success in it than one who does not?

'Nay, but I pay regard to right judgements and therefore it is more reasonable that I should rule.'

Yes, in judgements, for you have devoted yourself to them: but you must give place to others in that to which they have devoted themselves. You might as well claim to be a better shot with the bow than regular bowmen because you have right judgements, or to be better at smith's work than the professional smith. Give up your devotion to judgements then and busy yourself with the objects you wish to obtain, and then complain if you do not succeed, for you have a right to complain. But, as it is, you say you are bent on other things, and attending to other things, and the proverb of the people is a good one: 'One business has nothing in common with another.' One man rises at dawn and tries to find whom he can salute as he leaves home, or to whom he can make a pleasant speech, or send a gift, how he can please the dancer, how he can deal maliciously with one man to gratify another. When he prays, his prayers are for this object; when he sacrifices, his sacrifice is for this; the prayer of Pythagoras—

That sleep fall not upon his tender eyes—

[Ascribed to Pythagoras]

he has turned to this end. 'How went I wrong?' Was it in matters of flattery? 'What wrought I?' Have I acted as a free man and a gentleman? And if he finds himself acting so he blames and accuses himself and says, 'Whatever should you say this for? Might you not have told a lie? Even philosophers say, "There is nothing to hinder one's telling a lie."'

But if you have really given your mind to nothing but how to deal properly with impressions, then as soon as you get up in the morning you must consider, 'What do I lack to secure freedom from passion? What do I lack to be unperturbed? What am I? Am I a mere body, or property, or reputation?'

None of these.

What then?

A rational creature.

What then are the demands upon me?

Reflect upon your actions. 'Where have I gone wrong' in regard to peace of mind? 'What have I done' unfriendly, or unsociable, or heartless? What did I fail to accomplish in this regard that I ought to have done?

Seeing then that there is this great difference in men's desires and acts and prayers, do you still wish to be equal with them in matters to which they have given their minds and you have not? And, that being so, are you surprised and annoyed if they pity you? They are not annoyed if you pity them. Why? Because they are convinced that their lot is a good one, and you are not convinced. That is why you are not content with your portion, but hanker after theirs, and they are content with their portion and do not hanker after yours. For, if you were really convinced that you are right in regard to what is good and that they are far away from the truth, you would never have taken any account of what they say of you.

CHAPTER VII

ON FREEDOM FROM FEAR

WHAT makes the Emperor an object of fear?

The guards, one says, with their swords, and the chamberlains and those who close the door against those who enter.

Why is it then that, if you bring a child to him when his guards are with him, the child is not afraid? Is it because the child is not aware of them? Now if a man is aware of the guards and their swords, but comes for that very purpose, because his misfortunes make him wish to die and he is anxious to die easily by some one else's hand, does he fear the guards?

'No, for he wishes for the very thing which makes men fear them.'

If then a man whose will is not set on dying or living, but who is content with what is given him, comes before the Tyrant, what prevents him from coming without fear?

'Nothing.'

Now suppose a man is of the same mind in regard to property as this man in regard to his body: suppose he feels the same about wife and children: suppose, in a word, he is so distracted and desperate that he regards it as indifferent whether he has these things or not: just as children playing with potsherds are anxious about the game, but do not care for the potsherds in themselves, so he has not set his heart on material things, but accepts the game cheerfully, and enjoys handling them—how can any tyrant, how can any guards or swords inspire fear in such a one?

Yet if madness can produce this attitude of mind, if even habit can produce it in the Galilaeans, [5] can reason and demonstration teach no one that God has made all things in the world, and the world itself as a whole to have its own end without hindrance, but its individual parts to subserve the whole? Now all other things are without the capacity of understanding His governance, but the rational creature has faculties that enable him to reflect on all these things, to realize that he is a part, and what part he is, and that it is well for the parts to give way to the whole. And further, being by nature noble and generous and free, he sees that he has some of the things about him unhindered and in his own control, and some again subject to hindrance and dependent on others, the acts of his will unhindered, and things beyond his will subject to hindrance. And therefore if he makes up his mind that his good and his interest lie in the former alone, in things that are unhindered and depend upon himself, he will be free, tranquil, happy, unharmed, high-minded, reverent, giving thanks for everything to God, on no occasion blaming or accusing any one for what happens; but if he finds his good in things outside and beyond his will, he is bound to be hindered and hampered, and to be the slave of those who have authority over those things on which his admiration and his fear are centred, he is bound to be irreverent because he thinks that God is injuring him, and unfair, always seeking to win for himself more than his share; he is bound to be of a mean and paltry spirit.

If a man understands this, there is nothing to prevent him from living with an easy and obedient spirit, content with his past lot and awaiting with a gentle spirit all that may yet befall him.

'Would you give me poverty?' Give it me and you shall learn what poverty is when a good actor plays the part. 'Would you give me office?' Give it me, and troubles with it. 'Exile?' Wherever I go, it will be well with me: for even here it was not the place that made me well off, but my judgements, and these I shall carry away with me, for no one can rob me of them; these alone are my own and cannot be taken away, with these I am content wherever I am and whatever I do. 'But now the time is come to die.' What do you mean by 'die'? Do not use fine words, but state the facts as they are. 'Now is the time for your material part to be restored to the elements of which it was composed.' What is there dreadful in that? What loss to the universe will this mean, what strange or irrational event? Is this a thing to make one fear the tyrant? Is this what makes the swords of the guards seem long and sharp? Let others look to that; I have considered the whole matter, and no one has authority over me. God has set me free, I have learnt to understand His commands, no one can make a slave of me any more, my judges and he who claims my freedom are as they should be.

'Am I not master of your body?'

What does that concern *me?*

'Am I not master of your property?'

Well, how does that concern *me?*

'Am I not master of exile and imprisonment?'

Again, I resign all, yes, and my body itself for you to deal with, when you will. Only try your authority and you will learn how far it extends. What then can I fear any more? The chamberlains? What should I fear their doing? Fear their shutting me out? If they find me wanting to enter, let them shut me out!

'Why then do you come to the king's door?'

Because I think it is fitting for me to join in the game while it lasts.

'How then do you escape being shut out?'

If I am not received, it is not my will to enter; my will is always to prefer what comes to pass, for I consider what God wills better than what I will. I will attach myself to Him as His minister and servant, my impulses and my wishes are one with His, in a word my will is His will. There can be no exclusion for me, but only for those who try to press in.

Why then do I not press in?

Because I know that nothing good is given within to those who have entered. But when I hear a man called happy because he is honoured by Caesar I say, 'What is his portion?' 'A province or a procuratorship.' Does he also get a judgement, such as a governor should have? Does he get the skill to use a procuratorship? Why should I push my way in any more? Some one flings a shower of figs and nuts: the children try to seize them, and fight with one another for them; grown men do not, for they count it a small matter. If one fling potsherds even children do not try to catch them. Governorships are being given to this man and that: the children shall see to them! A praetorship, a consulship: let the children scramble for them: let them be shut out and beaten, let them kiss the hands of the giver and his slaves; for me they are figs and nuts. But what if a fig chance to fall into my lap when he is throwing? Take and eat it, for one may value a fig so far. But if I stoop for it and upset my neighbour or am upset by him, if I flatter those who enter, the fig is not worth while, nor is any other of the good things which the philosophers have persuaded me not to believe to be good.

Show me the swords of the guards.

'See how large and how sharp they are.'

Well, what do these large, sharp swords do?

'They kill.'

What does fever do?

'The same.'

What does a tile do?

'The same.'

Would you have me then stand in awe of all these things, and pay them reverence, and go about as the slave of all?

God forbid! No, if I have once learnt that what is born must needs also be destroyed in order that the world may not stand still or be hindered, it makes no difference to me whether a fever is to destroy it or a falling tile or a soldier, but if I must compare them I know that the soldier will do the thing quicker and with less pain. Seeing then that I neither fear anything that he can do to me nor desire anything that he can provide, why do I stand in awe and amazement before him any more? Why do I fear the guards? Why do I rejoice if he speaks to me in a friendly way and gives me a welcome? Why do I tell other people how he talked to me? Is he a Socrates or a Diogenes, that his praise of me should be a proof of what I am? Do I admire his character? No, it is to keep up the game that I come to him and serve him, so long as he commands me to do nothing stupid or unseemly. But if he says to me, 'Go and fetch Leon of Salamis', I say to him, 'Look for some one else, I will play no longer.'

'Away with him.'

I follow; it is in the game.

'But you lose your neck.'

Well! does the Emperor himself, and you who obey him, keep his neck for ever?

'But you will be flung abroad unburied.'

I shall be, if I and the dead body are one, but if I am not the same as the dead body, state the facts with more discrimination, and do not try to frighten me. These are things to frighten children and fools. But if a man has once entered a philosopher's lecture-room and does not know what his true self is, he deserves to fear and to flatter what he flattered afterwards: I mean, if he has not yet learnt that he is not flesh or bones or sinews, but the faculty which uses them, and which also governs the impressions and understands them.

'Yes, but these arguments make men despise the laws.'

Nay, these arguments of all others make those who adopt them obedient to the laws. Law is not what any fool can do. Yet see how these arguments make us behave rightly even towards our critics, since they teach us to claim nothing against them, in which they can surpass us. They teach us to give way in regard to our poor body, to give way in regard to property, children, parents, brothers, to give up everything, resign everything: only our judgements they reserve, and these Zeus willed should be each man's special property. How can you call this lawlessness, how can you call it stupidity? I give way to you in that wherein you are better and stronger than I: where, on the other hand, I am the better man, it is for you to give way to me, for I have made this my concern, and you have not. You make it your concern, how to live in a palace, how slaves and freedmen are to serve you, how you are to wear conspicuous raiment, how you are to have a multitude of huntsmen, minstrels, players. Do I lay claim to any of these? But you, for your part, have you concerned yourself with judgements? Have you concerned yourself with your own rational self? Do you know what are its constituents, what is its principle of union, how it is articulated, what are its faculties and of what nature? Why are you vexed then, if another who has made these things his study has the advantage of you here?

'But these are the greatest matters of all.'

Who, I ask, prevents you from busying yourself with these and devoting your attention to these? Who has a larger equipment of books, of leisure, of masters who will do you good? Only incline your mind to these things, bestow a little time, if no more, on your own Governing Principle, consider what this possession is and whence it has come to you, this faculty which uses all the rest, which proves all the rest, selecting and rejecting. So long as you busy yourself with external things, no one will succeed with them so well as you, but this faculty of reason will be, what your own choice makes it, mouldy and neglected.

CHAPTER VIII

TO THOSE WHO HASTILY ASSUME THE CHARACTER OF PHILOSOPHERS

NEVER bestow praise or blame on any one for qualities which are indifferent, nor credit them with skill or want of skill; then you will escape at once from recklessness and malice. 'This man washes hastily.' Does he do evil then? Not at all. What is it he does then? He washes hastily. Do you mean that everything is well done? By no means: but acts based on right judgements are done well and those based on bad judgements are done badly. Until you have learnt from what judgement each of a man's acts proceeds, do not praise or blame him. But a judgement is not easily determined by externals. 'This man is a carpenter.' Why? 'He uses an adze.' What has that to do with it? 'This man is a musician, for he sings.' What does that matter? 'This man is a philosopher.' Why? 'He wears a cloak and long hair.' But what do mountebanks wear? Therefore, if a man sees one of them misbehaving, he says at once, 'Look what the philosopher is doing.' But his misconduct should rather have led him to say that he was no philosopher. For, if this is the primary conception and profession of a philosopher, to wear a cloak and long hair, they would be right: but if it is rather this—to be free from error—why do they not deprive him of the name 'philosopher' because he does not fulfil the philosopher's profession? For this is what happens in other arts. When one sees a man planing badly, one does not say, 'What is the good of the carpenter's art, see what bad work carpenters do', but one says quite the contrary, 'This man is not a carpenter, for he planes badly.' In like manner if one hears a man singing badly, one does not say, 'See how badly musicians sing', but rather, 'This man is no musician.' It is only in regard to philosophy that men behave so: when they see any one acting contrary to the philosopher's profession, instead of refusing him the name, they assume that he is a philosopher, and then finding from the facts that he is misbehaving, they infer that there is no use in being a philosopher. What is the reason for this? The reason is that we pay regard to the primary notion of the carpenter, and to that of the musician, and to that of other craftsmen in like manner, but pay no regard to the notion of the philosopher, but as it is indistinct and inarticulate in our minds we judge it by externals only. Can you name any other art that is acquired by dress and hair, and is destitute of principles and subject-matter and end?

What then is the subject-matter of the philosopher? Is it a cloak?

No, it is reason.

What is his end? Is it to wear a cloak?

No, but to keep his reason right.

What are his principles? Are they concerned with how to grow a long beard or thick hair?

No, but rather, as Zeno says, to understand the elements of reason, the true nature of each, and how they are duly related to one another, and all that is consequential on this. Will you not, then, first see whether he fulfils his profession by behaving unseemly, and only then, if it be so, accuse his calling? As it is, when you think that he is behaving ill, when your own conduct is discreet, you say, 'Look at the philosopher', as though it were fitting to call the man who acts so a philosopher, and again, 'There's your philosopher!' But you do not say, 'Look at the carpenter', or 'Look at the musician', when you discover one of that class in adultery or see him eating greedily. So true it is that you realize the philosopher's profession to a certain extent, but you fall away from it and are confounded by sheer want of practice.

But even those who are called philosophers use vulgar means to pursue their calling: they just put on a cloak and let their beard grow and say, 'I am a philosopher.' But no one if he merely buys a harp and a plectrum will say, 'I am a musician', nor if he puts on a smith's cap and apron will say, 'I am a smith': no doubt they fit the dress to the art, but they take their name from the art and not from the dress. For this reason Euphrates was right in saying, 'For a long time I tried not to be known for a philosopher and this was useful to me. For, in the first place, I knew that what I did rightly was done for my own sake and not for the spectators: it was for myself that I ate rightly and was modest in my aspect and my gait: all was for myself and God. Secondly, as the performance was mine only, so also was the risk: if I did anything shameful or unseemly the cause of philosophy was not endangered, nor did I injure the public by going wrong as a philosopher. For this reason those who did not know my design wondered how it was that, though I was familiar and conversant with all philosophers, I was not a philosopher myself. What harm is there in the philosopher being discovered by my acts, and not by outward signs?'

See how I eat, how I drink, how I sleep, how I bear and forbear, how I work for others, how I exercise the will to get and the will to avoid, how I observe my relationships, natural and acquired, without confusion and without hindrance. Judge me by this, if you can. But if you are so deaf and blind, that you do not consider Hephaestus a good smith unless you see him with his smith's cap on his head, what harm is there in being unrecognized by so foolish a judge?

So it was that most men did not recognize Socrates for a philosopher, and they came to him and asked him to introduce them to philosophers. Well, was he annoyed with them, as we should be? Did he say, 'Do not you think me a philosopher?' No, he took them and introduced them, and was content with this one thing, that he was a philosopher, and was glad that he was not vexed at being not taken for one: for he remembered his proper business.

What is the business of a good and true man? To have many pupils?

Certainly not: those who have set their heart on that shall look to that. Is it then to take difficult principles and define them precisely?

Others there will be who will look to this.

Where then was it that Socrates asserted himself and wished to assert himself?

In the region of injury and benefit. 'If any one', said he, 'can injure me, I am of no good; if I wait for some one to benefit me, I am naught. If I will, and my will is not done, I am miserable.' This was the great field of conflict to which he challenged every man, and in which I think he would have given way to none. But how, think you? Was it by proclaiming aloud, 'This is the man I am'? Never! but by being the man he was. For, again, it is a fool's and a braggart's part to say, 'I am free from passion and tumult. Men, I would have you know, that, while you are in turmoil and disturbance about worthless matters, I alone am relieved from all perturbation.' What, are you not content to be free from pain, without proclaiming, 'Come, all ye who suffer from gout, headache, fever, come ye lame and blind and behold how I am untouched by any sickness'? That is a vain and vulgar boast, unless, like Asclepius, you can at once show them by what treatment they too can be relieved of disease, and for this purpose produce your own good health as an example.

Such is the character of the Cynic whom Zeus has deemed worthy of crown and sceptre. He says, 'Men, you are looking for happiness and peace not where it is but where it is not, and, that you may see this, behold I have been sent to you by God as an example, having neither property nor house nor wife nor children—no, not even a bed or a tunic or a piece of furniture. See how healthy I am. Try me, and if you see that I am at peace in my mind, hear my remedies and the treatment which cured me.' This indeed is a humane and noble saying. But notice whose work it is: the work of Zeus or whomsoever He thinks worthy of this service—never to lay bare before the multitude any weakness whereby he should make of none effect the witness which he bears to virtue, and bears against outward things.

> *His noble face ne'er paled, nor from his cheeks*
> *Wiped he a tear.*
>
> [Homer, *Odyssey,* XI. 529]

Not only so, he must not long for anything or hanker after anything—human being or place or way of life—as children hanker after sweet grapes or holidays: he must be adorned with self-respect on every side, as others find their adornment in walls and doors and door-keepers.

Instead of that your would-be philosophers just take a start towards philosophy, and, like dyspeptics rushing to some dainty food, of which they are bound soon to grow sick, they claim at once the sceptre and the kingdom. He lets his hair grow, assumes a cloak, bares his shoulder for all to see, fights with those that meet him, and, if he sees any one in a fine cloak, quarrels with him. Man, discipline yourself first: watch your own impulse, to see that it is not like the sickly craving of a woman with child. Study first not to let men know what you are: keep your philosophy to yourself for a little. That is how fruit is produced. The seed must needs be buried first, and be hidden, and increase by slow degrees, that it may come to fullness. But if it bear the ear before it grows the stalk, it is like a plant from the garden of Adonis and comes to no good. That is the sort of plant you are: you have blossomed sooner than you ought, and will wither away when the storm comes.

Look what farmers say about seeds, when the hot weather comes before its time. They are all anxiety for fear that the seeds should grow insolent and then a single frost seize them and expose their weakness. You, too, man, must beware: you have grown insolent and have leapt to an opinion before the time: you think yourself a somebody, fool that you are among fools; you will be frost-bitten, nay you are frost-bitten already down at the root, though above you still blossom for a little and therefore think you are still alive and flourishing. Leave us at least to ripen in the natural course. Why do you expose us to the air, why do you force us? We cannot bear the air yet. Let the root grow, and then produce the stem, first one joint, then the second, then the third: then in that way the fruit will force its way naturally, whether I will or no.

For who that has conceived and travailed with such great judgements does not become aware of his own gifts and hasten to act in accordance with them? Why, a bull is not ignorant of his own nature and endowment when he catches sight of a wild beast, nor does he wait for some one to encourage him; and so with a dog, when he sees a wild animal. If then I have the equipment of a good man, am I to wait for you to equip me to do my proper work? But as yet I have not the equipment, believe me. Why then would you make me wither away before the time, just as you have withered away yourself?

CHAPTER IX

TO ONE WHO WAS MODEST AND HAS BECOME SHAMELESS

WHEN you see another man in office, set against his office the fact that you have no need of office: when you see another rich, look what you have instead. If you have nothing instead, you are miserable, but if you have this—that you have no need of wealth—know that you are better off and have something much more valuable. Another has a beautiful wife, you have freedom from desire for a beautiful wife. Do these seem to you small matters? Nay, what a price the rich themselves, and those who hold office, and who live with beautiful wives, would give to despise wealth and office and the very women whom they love and win! Do you not know what the thirst of a man in a fever is like, how different from the thirst of a man in health? The healthy man drinks and his thirst is gone: the other is delighted for a moment and then grows giddy, the water turns to gall, and he vomits and has colic, and is more exceeding thirsty. Such is the condition of the man who is haunted by desire in wealth or in office, and in wedlock with a lovely woman: jealousy clings to him, fear of loss, shameful words, shameful thoughts, unseemly deeds.

'Nay, but what do I lose?' he says.

Man, you were self-respecting and are so no more; have you lost nothing? Instead of Chrysippus and Zeno you read Aristides and Evenus; have you lost nothing? Instead of Socrates and Diogenes you admire the man who can cajole and corrupt most women. You want to be handsome and you make yourself up as what you are not; you want to show off glittering clothes, that you may attract women's eyes, and you count yourself lucky if you light on some precious cosmetic. Before, you thought of none of these things; your only concern was to find seemly discourse, a man of worth, a noble thought; and therefore you slept like a man, you walked like a man, you dressed like a man, your conversation was what a good man's should be. Can you say then, 'I have lost nothing'? Do you mean that men lose nothing but mere money? Is there no loss of self-respect, no loss of decency? Does the loss of these count for nothing? To you perhaps the loss of these qualities seems as nothing: there was a time when you counted this the only loss and the only harm, and when your one anxiety was that no one should dislodge you from these views and these acts.

And lo! you have been dislodged from them, but by none other than yourself. Fight against yourself, deliver yourself, that you may be modest, self-respecting, free. If any one ever told you that some one was compelling me to be a profligate, to dress like a profligate, to scent myself, would you not go and murder the man who so abused me? Will you not help yourself then? And how much easier this help is to give! There is no need to kill or to imprison or to assault any one, no need to come out into the market-place: you have only to talk to yourself, to the man who is most likely to be persuaded, and whom no one can persuade better than yourself. Therefore, first realize what is happening to you, and having done so, do not be faint-hearted or behave as men of a mean spirit do, who when once they have given in surrender completely and are swept away, so to speak, by the stream: no, learn a lesson from the trainers. The boy has fallen, suppose. 'Get up', says the trainer, 'and wrestle again, until you are made strong.' Let this be your attitude; for know that nothing is more amenable than the mind of man. You have but to will a thing and it is done, and all is right; on the other hand you have but to relax your effort and all is lost. For destruction and deliverance lie within you.

'What good do I get then?'

What greater good do you look for than this? You were shameless and shall be self-respecting, you were undisciplined and shall be disciplined, untrustworthy and you shall be trusted, dissolute and you shall be self-controlled. If you look for greater things than these, go on doing as you do now: not even a god can save you.

CHAPTER X

WHAT THINGS WE SHOULD DESPISE, AND WHAT WE SHOULD DEEM IMPORTANT

ALL men's difficulties and perplexities are concerned with external things. 'What am I to do?' 'How is it to be done?' 'How is it to turn out?' 'I fear this or that may befall me.' All these phrases are used by persons occupied with matters outside their will. For who says, 'How am I to refuse assent to the false?' 'How am I to refuse to swerve from the true?' If a man is so gifted by nature as to be anxious about these things, I will remind him: 'Why are you anxious? It rests with you: be not troubled. Be not over-hasty in assent, before you have applied the rule of nature.'

Again, if he is anxious about his will to get, lest it should fail of its object and miss the mark, and about his will to avoid, lest it should fall into what it avoids, first of all I will salute him, because he has got rid of the excitements and fears of other men, and has turned his thoughts to his own business where his true self lies. Then I shall say to him: 'If you would not fail to get what you will, nor fall into what you will to avoid, do not will to get what is not your own, nor to avoid what is not in your control: otherwise you are bound to fail and to fall into disaster. Where is the difficulty if you do as I say? What room is there for phrases like, "How am I to get it?" "How is it to turn out?" "I fear this or that may befall me."'

Is not the issue of the future outside our will?

'Yes.'

And the essence of good and evil is in the region of the will?

'Yes.'

Is it in your power then to make a natural use of every event that happens? Can any one hinder you from that?

'No one.'

Say no more then, 'What is to happen?' For whatever happens, you will turn it to good purpose, and the issue will be your good fortune. What would Heracles have been if he had said, 'How am I to prevent a big lion from appearing, or a big boar, or brutal men?' What care you, I say? If a big boar appears, you will have a greater struggle to engage in; if evil men appear, you will free the world from evil men.

'But if I die thus?'

You will die a good man, fulfilling a noble action. For since you must die in any case, you must be found doing something—whatever it be—

farming or digging or trading or holding the counsulship or suffering indigestion or diarrhoea. What then would you have death find you doing? For my part I would be found busy with some humane task, whatever it be—something noble, beneficent, advancing the common weal. And if I cannot be found doing great things like these, I would do what none can hinder, what is given me to do, setting myself right, bringing to perfection the faculty that deals with impressions, working to achieve freedom from passion, rendering what is due to each relation in life; nay, if I am so fortunate, attaining to the third sphere of activity,[6] that concerned with certainty of judgements.

If death finds me thus occupied, I am content if I can lift up my hands to God and say, 'I have not neglected the faculties which I received from Thee, to enable me to understand Thy governance and follow it, I have not dishonoured Thee so far as in me lay. See how I have dealt with my senses, see how I have dealt with my primary notions. Did I ever complain of Thee, did I ever show discontent with anything that happened to any one, or wish it to happen otherwise, did I offend in my relations towards others? In that Thou didst beget me I am grateful for Thy gifts: in so far as I have used what Thou gavest me I am satisfied. Take Thy gifts back again and place them where Thou wilt: for they were all Thine, Thou hast given them to me.' Are you not content to leave the world in this state of mind? Nay, what life is better or more seemly than his who is so minded, and what end can be more happy?

But to achieve this, you must put up with great troubles and great losses. You cannot have this and wish to get a consulship, you cannot have this and set your heart on owning lands, you cannot take thought for yourself and for wretched slaves at the same time. No, if you wish for what is not your own, you lose what is yours. This is in the nature of things: nothing is done but at a price. And what need for wonder? If you wish to become consul, you must keep late hours, run to and fro, kiss people's hands, lie perishing at other men's doors, say and do many things unfit for a free man, send gifts to many, and presents every day to some. And what do you get for it? Twelve bundles of rods,[7] the privilege of sitting three or four times on the tribunal and of giving games in the Circus, and doles in baskets. If it be not so, let any one show me what there is besides. Will you then spend nothing, and use no effort to secure release from passion and perturbation, that sleeping you may sleep and waking you may wake, that you may fear nothing and be anxious for nothing? But if while you are thus engaged you have losses or spend money amiss, or if another gets what you ought to have got, are you going to be vexed all at once at what happens? Will you not weigh what the exchange is and how precious your gain, instead of wishing to obtain this great prize for nothing? Nay, how can you? 'One business interferes with another.'

You cannot combine attention to outward possessions with attention to your own Governing Principle. If you want outward things, let your reason go, or you will have neither the one nor the other, being pulled both ways. If you wish for reason, you must let outward things go. The oil will be spilt, my poor furniture will perish, but I shall be free from passion. Say a fire shall arise when I am away and my books perish, yet I shall deal with my impressions in accord with nature.

'But I shall have nothing to eat.'

If I am so miserable, death is my harbour. Death: this is the harbour, this the refuge from all things, therefore nothing in life is difficult. When you wish, you leave, and no smoke annoys you. Why then are you anxious, why keep late hours? Why do you not reckon up at once where your good and your evil lie, and say, 'Both are in my power: no one can deprive me of my good, and no one can plunge me in evil against my will. Why then do I not snore at my ease? I am secure in what is mine: what is not mine will be the concern of any one who gets it as a gift from Him who has authority to give it. Who am I to will that what is not mine should be thus or thus? Is it given to me to choose? Has any one set me to administer it? I am content with the things over which I have authority. These I must make as beautiful as possible; the rest must be as their master wills.'

If a man has this before his eyes he is no longer wakeful, 'hither and thither tossed'. [Homer, *Iliad,* XXIV. 5] What would he have, or what does he long for? Does he long for Patroclus or Antilochus or Menelaus? When did he think any of his friends was immortal? When had he not before his eyes the fact that to-morrow or the day after he or his friend must die?

'Yes,' he says, 'but I thought he would outlive me and enrich my son.'

Yes, for you were a fool, and set your thoughts on uncertainties. Why not then accuse yourself, instead of sitting crying like young girls?

'Nay, but he set food for me to eat.'

Yes, fool, for he was alive: now he cannot. But Automedon will set meat for you, and if he dies you will find another. If the pot in which your meat was boiling is broken, must you needs die of hunger, because you have lost the pot you are used to? Do not you send and buy another?

'Nay,' he says,

'No worse ill could befall me.'

[Homer, *Iliad,* XIX. 321]

What! Is this what you call ill? And yet you forbear to remove it and blame your mother for not warning you, that you might spend your days lamenting ever since. What think you? Did not Homer compose these lines on purpose that we might see that there is nothing to prevent the noblest, the strongest, the richest, the most handsome, from being most wretched and most miserable when they have not the judgements they should have? [8]

CHAPTER XI

ON CLEANLINESS

SOME men raise the question whether the social faculty is a necessary element in man's nature: nevertheless even they, I think, would not question that cleanliness at any rate is essential to it, and that this, if anything, divides him from the lower animals. So when we see one of the other animals cleaning itself, we are wont to say in our surprise, 'He does it like a man.' And again, if some one finds fault with an animal for being dirty we are wont to say at once, as if in defence, 'Of course he is not a man.' So true is it that we think the quality to be distinctive of man, deriving it first from the gods. For since the gods are by nature pure and unalloyed, just in so far as men have approached them by virtue of reason, they have a tendency to purity and cleanliness. But since it is impossible for their nature to be entirely pure, being composed of such stuff as it is, the reason which they have received endeavours, so far as in it lies, to make this stuff clean.

The primary and fundamental purity is that of the soul, and so with impurity. You cannot find the same impurity in a soul as in a body: the soul's impurity you will find to be just this—that which renders it unclean for its own functions; and the functions of a soul are: impulse to act and not to act, will to get and will to avoid, preparation, design, assent. What is it then which renders the soul foul and unclean in these functions? It is nothing but its evil judgements. And so the soul's impurity consists in bad judgements, and purification consists in producing in it right judgements, and the pure soul is one which has right judgements, for this alone is proof against confusion and pollution in its functions.

And one ought to endeavour, as far as may be, to achieve a similar cleanliness in one's body too. Man's temperament is such that there must needs be mucous discharge: for this reason nature made hands, and the nostrils themselves like channels to cleanse his humours. If he swallows them I say that he does not act as a man should. It was impossible for men's feet not to be made muddy and dirty when they pass through mud and dirt; for this reason nature provided water and hands to wash with. It was impossible that some impurity should not stick to the teeth from eating. Therefore we are bidden to wash our teeth. Why? That you may be a man and not a beast or a pig. It was impossible that sweat and the pressure of our clothes should not leave some defilement clinging to the body, and needing to be cleansed. Therefore we have water, olive-oil, hands, towel, strigils, soap, and on occasion every other sort of apparatus, to make the body clean.

'Not for me', you say.

What! The smith will clean his iron tool of rust, and will have instruments made for the purpose, and even you will wash your plate when you are going to eat, unless you are absolutely foul and dirty, and yet you will not wash nor make clean your poor body? 'Why should I?' says he. I will tell you again: first, that you may act like a man, next, that you may not annoy those you meet. You are doing something very like it even here, though you are not aware of it. You think you deserve to have a scent of your own. Very well, deserve it: but do you think those who sit by you deserve it too, and those who recline by you, and those who kiss you? Go away then into a wilderness, where you deserve to go, and live by yourself, and have your smell to yourself, for it is right that you should enjoy your uncleanness by yourself. But if you are in a city, what sort of man are you making yourself, to behave so thoughtlessly and inconsiderately? If nature had trusted a horse to your care, would you have left it uncared for? Imagine that your body has been committed to you as a horse: wash it, rub it down well, make it such that no one will shun it or turn from it. But who does not turn from a man who is dirty, odorous, foul-complexioned, more than from one who is bespattered with muck? The smell of the latter is external and accidental, that of the former comes from want of tendance; it is from within, and shows a sort of inward rottenness.

'But Socrates rarely washed.'

Why, his body was clean and bright, nay, it was so gracious and agreeable that the handsomest and noblest were in love with him, and desired to recline by him rather than by those who were perfect in beauty. He might have never washed or bathed, if he had liked: I tell you his ablutions, if rare, were powerful. If you will not wash in hot water, wash in cold.

But Aristophanes says:

I mean the pallid folk, that shoeless go.

[Aristophanes, *Clouds,* 103]

True, but he also says he trod the air and stole clothes from the Gymnasium. The fact is, that all who have written about Socrates bear witness to just the opposite: he was not only pleasant to hear, but pleasant to look upon. They write the same again about Diogenes.

You must not scare away the masses from philosophy by your bodily appearance, but show yourself cheerful and unruffled in the body as in other things. 'Men, look at me, I have nothing, I need nothing; without house, without city, an exile, if it so chance, and without a hearth, behold how I live a life more tranquil and happy than all the noble and the rich: but you see also that my poor body is not disfigured by my hard living!' But if a man says this to me, and wears the face and figure of one condemned, no god will ever persuade me to come near philosophy, if that is the sort of men she makes. Far be it from me: though it were to make me wise, I would not.

By the gods, when the young man feels the first stirrings of philosophy I would rather he came to me with his hair sleek than dishevelled and dirty: for that shows a sort of reflection of the beautiful, and a longing for the comely, and where he imagines these to be, there he spends his effort. It only remains then to point him the way and say, 'Young man, you are in search of the beautiful, and you do well. Know then, that it is to be found where your reason is. Seek for it in the region of impulses to act and not to act, in the region of the will to get and the will to avoid. This is your distinctive possession, your body is born to be but clay. Why do you toil for it in vain? Time, if nothing else, will teach you that it is nothing.' But if he comes to me befouled, dirty, with a beard trailing to his knees, what can I say to him, what similitude can I use to attract him? To what is he devoted that has any likeness to the beautiful, that I may change his direction and say, 'The beautiful is not here, but here'? Would you have me say to him, 'The beautiful is to be found not in filthiness but in reason'? Does he want the beautiful? Does he show any sign of it? Go and reason with a pig, that he wallow no more in the mire! That was why Xenocrates' discourses laid hold on Polemo, for he was a young man of taste; he had come with glimmerings of devotion to the beautiful, though he sought it elsewhere.

Why, nature did not make even those lower animals dirty who associate with men. Does a horse or a well-bred dog wallow in mire? No, it is only the pig, and greasy geese, and worms and spiders, creatures the furthest removed from human society. Do you then, being a man, choose to be a wretched worm or spider, lower even than the animals that associate with men? Will you never wash, be it how you will? Will you not cleanse yourself? Will you not come clean among us that you may give pleasure to your companions? What! do you enter our temples, where custom forbids spitting or wiping the nose, in this condition, a man of filth and drivel?

'What?' you ask. 'Do you call on us to adorn ourselves?'

Far from it, if it be not with our natural adornment of reason, judgements, activities, and the body only so far as to be cleanly and give no offence. If you hear that you must not wear scarlet, must you needs go off and spread filth on your cloak, or tear it in half?

'But how am I to have a beautiful cloak?'

Man, you have water, wash it. Here is a young man worthy to be loved, here is an old man worthy to love and to be loved, one to whom a man is to hand over his son to be instructed: daughters and young men will come to him, if it so chance, and for what? That he may discourse to them on a dunghill? God forbid. All eccentricity springs from some human source, but this comes near to being inhuman altogether.

CHAPTER XII

ON ATTENTION

When you relax your attention for a little, do not imagine that you will recover it wherever you wish, but bear this well in mind, that your error of to-day must of necessity put you in a worse position for other occasions. For in the first place—and this is the most serious thing—a habit of inattention is formed, and next a habit of deferring attention: and you get into the way of putting off from one time to another the tranquil and becoming life, the state and behaviour which nature prescribes. Now if such postponement of attention is profitable, it would be still more profitable to abandon it altogether: but if it is not profitable, why do you not keep up your attention continuously?

'I want to play to-day.'

What prevents you, if you attend?

'I want to sing.'

What prevents you, if you attend? Is any part of life excluded, on which attention has no bearing, any that you will make worse by attention, and better by inattention? Nay, is there anything in life generally which is done better by those who do not attend? Does the carpenter by inattention do his work better? Does the helmsman by inattention steer more safely? and is any of the minor duties of life fulfilled better by inattention? Do you not realize, that when once you have let your mind go wandering, you lose the power to recall it, to bring it to bear on what is seemly, self-respecting, and modest: you do anything that occurs to you and follow your inclinations?

To what then must I attend? First to those universal principles I have spoken of: these you must keep at command, and without them neither sleep nor rise, drink nor eat nor deal with men: the principle that no one can control another's will, and that the will alone is the sphere of good and evil. No one then has power to procure me good or to involve me in evil, but I myself alone have authority over myself in these matters. So, when I have made these secure, what need have I to be disturbed about outward things? What need have I to fear tyrant, or disease, or poverty, or disaster?

'But I do not please So-and-so.'

Well, is he my doing? Is he my judgement?

'No.'

What concern is it of mine then?

'Nay, but he is highly thought of.'

That will be for him to consider, and for those who think much of him: I have One Whom I must please, One to Whom I must submit myself and obey—God and those who come next to God. He commended me to myself, and made my will subject to me alone, and gave me rules for the right use of it; and if I follow these in syllogisms I pay no heed to any one who contradicts me, if I follow them in dealing with variable premisses I pay regard to no one. Why then am I annoyed by those who criticize me in greater matters? What is the reason for this perturbation? It is none other than that I have had no training in this sphere. For every science is entitled to despise ignorance and the ignorant, and this is true of arts as well as of sciences. Take any shoemaker, any carpenter you like, and you find he laughs the multitude to scorn when his own craft is in question.

First then we must have these principles ready to our hand. Without them we must do nothing. We must set our mind on this object: pursue nothing that is outside us, nothing that is not our own, even as He that is mighty has ordained: pursuing what lies within our will, and all else only so far as it is given us to do so. Further, we must remember who we are, and by what name we are called, and must try to direct our acts to fit each situation and its possibilities.

We must consider what is the time for singing, what the time for play, and in whose presence: what will be unsuited to the occasion; whether our companions are to despise us, or we to despise ourselves: when to jest, and whom to mock at: and on what occasion to be conciliatory and to whom: in a word, how one ought to maintain one's character in society. Wherever you swerve from any of these principles, you suffer loss at once; not loss from without, but issuing from the very act itself.

What then? Is it possible to escape error altogether? No, it is impossible: but it is possible to set one's mind continuously on avoiding error. For it is well worth while to persist in this endeavour, if in the end we escape a few errors, and no more. As it is, you say, 'I will fix my attention to-morrow': which means, let me tell you, 'To-day I will be shameless, inopportune, abject: others shall have power to vex me: to-day I will harbour anger and envy.' Look what evils you allow yourself. Nay, if it is well to fix my attention to-morrow, how much better to do so to-day! If it is profitable to-morrow, much more so is it to-day: that you may be able to do the same to-morrow, and not put off again to the day after.

CHAPTER XIII

TO THOSE WHO LIGHTLY COMMUNICATE THEIR SECRETS

WHEN a man seems to have talked frankly to us about his own affairs, how we are drawn to communicate our own secrets to him and think this is frankness! First because it seems unfair to have heard our neighbour's affairs and yet not give him a share of our own in turn: next because we think we shall not give the impression of being frank if we are silent about our own affairs. In fact we often find men in the habit of saying, 'I've told you all my affairs, won't you tell me any of yours? How it that?' Besides we think we may safely confide in one who has already confided his affairs to us: for we have a sort of feeling that he would never talk of our affairs for fear that we should talk of his. This is exactly the way in which reckless persons are caught by soldiers in Rome. A soldier sits by you in civilian dress, and begins to speak ill of the Emperor: then, as you have, so to speak, taken security from him for his good faith in the fact that he began the abuse, you are led to speak your own mind and so are arrested and imprisoned. The same sort of thing happens to us in ordinary life. Still, though he has confided his affairs to me with security, am I to do the same to the first man I meet? No, I hear and hold my tongue, if I am that sort of man, but he goes off and tells every one. Then, if I hear what he has done, if I am like him, I go and tell his secrets, because I want to have my revenge, and so I bring confusion to others and myself. But if I bear in mind, that one man does not harm another, but that it is his own acts which help or harm a man, I achieve this conquest—that I abstain from doing the same as he did, but still my own babbling has put me in the position I am in.

'Yes,' you say; 'but it is unfair to hear your neighbour's secrets, and give him no share of your own in return.'

Man, did I invite your confidences? Did you tell me your secrets on conditions, that you might hear mine in return? If you are a babbler and think every one you meet is a friend, do you want me to be like yourself? What! if you have done well to confide in me, but it is not possible to confide in you and do well, do you still want me to unbosom myself? That is just as though I had a sound cask and you an unsound one, and you came and handed over your wine to me to put it into my cask, and then were vexed that I did not trust my wine to you, because your cask had a hole in it.

What becomes of your equality now? You trusted to one who is trustworthy, self-respecting, who believes that good and harm depend on his own activities and on nothing outside: would you have me confide in you, you who have made light of your own will and want to get pelf or office or advancement at court, even at the cost of slaying your children like Medea? Where is the equality in that?

No, show yourself to me as one who is trustworthy, self-respecting, safe, show that your judgements are those of a friend, show that your vessel is not unsound, and then you will see that I will not wait for you to confide your affairs to me, but will come to you myself and ask you to hear mine. For who is there that will not use a goodly vessel, who that despises a loyal and faithful counsellor, who that will not gladly welcome one who is ready to share the burden of his distresses and to relieve him by the very fact of sharing in them?

'Yes; but I trust you, and you do not trust me.'

In the first place you do not trust me; you are only garrulous and therefore cannot keep anything back. For if what you say is true, trust your secrets to me and no one else: instead of which, whenever you see any one at leisure, you sit down by him and say, 'My brother, you are the dearest friend I have; I beg you to listen to my story'. And you do this to those you have not known even for a short while. If you really trust me, you trust me, of course, because I am trustworthy and self-respecting, not because I told you my secrets. Let me too then be allowed to think as you do. Prove to me that if a man tells his secrets to another, he is therefore trustworthy and self-respecting. If that were so, I should have gone about the world telling every man my affairs, if that were going to make me trustworthy and self-respecting. It is not really so. No, to be trustworthy a man needs judgements beyond the ordinary. If you see that a man is devoted to things outside his own will and has made his will subject to these, be sure that he has countless persons who hinder and constrain him. He has no need of a pitch-plaster or a rack to make him reveal what he knows, but the nod of a pretty maid, if it so chance, will shake his principles, a kindness from one of Caesar's officers, a lust for office or inheritance, and countless other motives such as these. You must therefore remember generally, that confidences require trust and trustworthy principles: and where can you easily find these nowadays? Let me be shown a man who is so minded as to say, 'I have no concern except with what is my own, with what is beyond hindrance and by nature free. This is the true good, and it is mine: all else I leave to the Giver of events to decide, and raise no question.'

FRAGMENTS[1]

I

FROM ARRIAN THE PUPIL OF EPICTETUS. TO ONE DISCOURSING ON SUBSTANCE

WHAT matters it whether the world is composed of atoms or of infinite parts or of fire and earth? Is it not enough to know the true nature of good and evil, and the limits of the will to get and the will to avoid, and again of impulses for action and against it, and using these as rules so to order our life, and dismiss those things that are beyond us. It may be that the human mind cannot comprehend them, and even if one should assume that it can, of what use is it to comprehend them? Should we not say that those who lay down that these things are necessary for the philosopher trouble themselves in vain? Is then the command at Delphi also superfluous: 'Know thyself'?

'No,' he replies.

What then is its meaning? If one ordered a chorus-singer to know himself, would he not attend to the order by paying heed to his fellows in the chorus so as to sing in harmony with them?

'Yes.'

And the same with a sailor and a soldier. Do you think then that man is a creature made to live by himself or for society?

'For society.'

By whom?

'By Nature.'

What Nature is and how it administers the universe and whether it is or no—these are matters it is not necessary to trouble ourselves with. Stob. *Flor.* 80. 14; *Ecl.* ii. 1. 18[a].

2

FROM ARRIAN

He who is discontented with what he has and with what is given him by fortune is an ignoramus in life, and he who bears it in a noble spirit and makes reasonable use of it deserves to be considered a good man. *Flor.* 108. 65.

3

FROM THE SAME

All things obey and serve the Universe[2]—earth and sea and sun and the other stars and the plants and animals of the earth; and our body too obeys it, enjoying sickness or health, and passing through youth and old age and other changes when the Universe wills. Is it not reasonable then that what is in our power, that is our judgement, should not be the only thing to strive against it? For the Universe is strong and superior to us and has provided for us better than we can, ordering our goings along with all things. And, besides, to act against it is to side with unreason, and brings nothing with it but vain struggle, involving us in miseries and pains. *Flor.* 108. 66.

4

RUFUS: FROM THE SAYINGS OF EPICTETUS ON FRIENDSHIP

God has divided all things into those that He put in our power, and those that are not in our power. He put in our power that which is noblest and highest, that which in fact constitutes His own happiness, the power to deal with impressions. For this faculty when rightly exercised is freedom, peace, courage, steadfastness, and this too is justice and law and self-control and all virtue. All else He put beyond our power. We ought then to will what God wills and, adopting His division, hold fast by all means to what is in our power and leave what is not in our power to the world's order, and gladly resign to it children, or country, or body, or anything else it may ask of us. *Ecl.* ii. 7. 30.

5

RUFUS: FROM EPICTETUS ON FRIENDSHIP

Which of us does not admire that saying of Lycurgus the Lacedaemonian? For when one of his young fellow citizens had blinded him in one eye and was handed over to Lycurgus by the people to be punished as he chose, he did not punish him but educated him and made a good man of him, and brought him before the Lacedaemonians in the theatre, and when they wondered he said, 'This man, when you gave him me, was insolent and violent; I give him back to you a free and reasonable citizen'. *Flor.* 19. 13.

6

FROM THE SAME

But this above all things is the function of Nature, to associate in close harmony the impulse that springs from the impression of what is fitting and that which springs from the impression of what is serviceable. *Flor.* 20. 60.

7

FROM THE SAME

It is a sure work of folly and want of breeding to think that we shall be contemptible if we do not take every means to injure the first enemies we meet; for we say that a man is perceived to be contemptible by his incapacity of doing harm, whereas really it is much more by his incapacity to do good. *Flor.* 20. 61.

8

RUFUS: FROM EPICTETUS ON FRIENDSHIP

Such was and is and shall be the nature of the universe, and it is impossible that what happens should be other than it is. And this process of revolution and change is shared not only by mankind and the other living creatures upon earth, but also by things divine; yes, and even by the four elements themselves, which turn and change upwards and downwards, earth turning into water and water into air, and this again into ether; and similarly the elements change from above downwards. If a man endeavours to adjust his mind to this and to persuade himself to accept necessity with a good will, he will live out his life very reasonably and harmoniously. *Flor.* 108. 60.

9

FROM THE SAME

A philosopher famous in the Stoic school . . . brought out of his satchel the fifth book of Epictetus the philosopher's *Discourses*, which were arranged by Arrian, and no doubt are in agreement with the writings of Zeno and Chrysippus. In this book, written of course in Greek, we read this sentence: 'Impressions (which philosophers call φαντασίαι), by which man's mind is struck at first sight of anything that reaches his intellect, are not under his will or control, but thrust themselves on the recognition of men by a certain force of their own; but the assents (which they call συγκαταθέσεις) by which these impressions are recognized are voluntary and depend on man's control. Therefore when some fearful sound of thunder or a falling house or sudden news of some danger or other, or something else of this sort happens, even the wise man is bound to be moved for a while and shrink and grow pale, not from anticipation of any evil, but from rapid and unconsidered movements forestalling the action of the rational mind. Presently, however, the wise man does not assent to such impressions (that is, these appearances which

are not punished, but are strong and rich, is acting just as absurdly as if, when they had lost their eyes, he said that they had not been punished, because their nails were sound. For my part I hold that there is a much greater difference between virtue and vice than between eyes and nails. *Ecl.* i. 3. 50.

14

FROM THE MEMORABILIA OF EPICTETUS

. . . bringing forward the peevish philosophers, who hold that pleasure is not natural, but accompanies things which are natural—justice, self-control, freedom. Why then does the soul take a calm delight, as Epicurus says, in the lesser goods, those of the body, and does not take pleasure in her own good things, which are the greatest? I tell you that nature has given me a sense of self-respect, and I often blush when I think I am saying something shameful. It is this emotion which prevents me from regarding pleasure as a good thing and as the end of life. *Flor.* 6. 50.

15

FROM THE SAME

In Rome women make a study of Plato's *Republic*, because he enacts community of wives; for they only attend to the man's words and not to his spirit, not noticing that he does not first enact the marriage of one man and one woman and then wish wives to be common, but removes the first kind of marriage and introduces another kind in its place. And in general men are fond of finding justifications for their own faults; for philosophy says that one ought not even *to hold out one's finger at random*. *Flor.* 6. 58.

16

FROM THE MEMORABILIA OF EPICTETUS

You must know that it is not easy for a man to arrive at a judgement, unless he should state and hear the same principles every day and apply them all the time to his life. *Flor.* 29. 84.

17

FROM EPICTETUS

When we are invited to a drinking-party we enjoy what is before us, and if one should bid his entertainer to serve him fish or cakes one would be thought eccentric. Yet in the world we ask the gods for what they do not give us, and that although there are many gifts which they have given us. *Flor.* 4. 92.

18

FROM THE SAME

Fine fellows, he said, are they who pride themselves on those things which are beyond our control. 'I am better than you,' says one, 'for I have abundance of lands, and you are prostrate with hunger.' Another says, 'I am a consular'; another, 'I am a procurator'; another, 'I have curly hair'. A horse does not say to a horse, 'I am better than you, for I have plenty of fodder and plenty of barley, and I have bridles of gold and saddles of inlaid work', but 'for I am swifter than you'. And every creature is better or worse according as its own virtue or vice makes it so. Is man then the only creature that has no virtue of his own, that we should have to look at his hair and his clothes and his ancestors? *Flor.* 4. 93.

19

Sick men are angry with their physician when he gives them no advice, and think that he has given them up. Why should one not adopt the same attitude to the philosopher and conclude that he has given up hope of one's wisdom, if he tells one nothing that is of use? *Flor.* 4. 94.

20

FROM EPICTETUS

Those whose bodies are in good condition can endure heat and cold; so those whose souls are in good condition can bear anger and pain and exultation and other emotions. *Flor.* 4. 95.

21

FROM THE SAME

It is right to praise Agrippinus for this reason, that having shown himself a man of the highest worth, he never praised himself, but blushed if any one else praised him. His character was such that when any distress befell him he wrote a eulogy of it; if fever was his portion he praised fever; if disrepute, he praised disrepute; and if exile, he praised exile. And one day, when he was about to breakfast, a messenger interrupted him to say that Nero ordered him into exile. 'Well then,' said he, 'we will breakfast at Aricia.' *Flor.* 7. 17.

22

FROM AGRIPPINUS

Agrippinus, when governor, tried to convince those whom he sentenced that it was proper for them to be sentenced. 'It is not as their enemy', he said, 'or as a robber that I give sentence against them, but as their guardian and kinsman, just as the physician encourages the man on whom he is operating and persuades him to submit his body.' *Flor.* 48. 44.

23

FROM EPICTETUS

Wondrous is Nature, and 'fond of her creatures', as Xenophon says. At any rate, we love and tend the body, the least agreeable and most vile of all things! For if we had to tend our neighbour's body for ten days only we could not bear it. Consider what it would be to get up in the morning and clean some one else's teeth, and then to perform some other necessary office for him. Truly it is wondrous that we should love that for which we do such mean services day by day. I stuff this bag; then I empty it; what could be more tiresome? But I am bound to serve God. That is why I stay here and put up with washing this miserable body of mine, and giving it fodder and shelter; and when I was younger, it laid other commands on me as well, and yet I bore with it. Why then, when Nature, who gave you your body, takes it away, can you not bear it? 'I love it,' he says. Well, but is it not Nature, as I said just now, that has given you this very love of it? And yet Nature too says, 'Let it go now, and trouble no more'. *Flor.* 121. 29.

24

FROM THE SAME

If a man dies young he accuses the gods, and an old man sometimes accuses them because he still is put to trouble when the time for rest has fully come, and yet, when death comes near, he is fain to live and sends to his doctor and bids him spare no pains or effort. Wondrous, he said, are men, for they are unwilling to live or to die. *Flor.* 121. 30.

25

FROM THE SAME

When you attack a man with threats and show of violence, remember to warn yourself that you are not a wild beast; then you will do nothing savage, and will live your life through without having to repent or be called to account. *Flor.* 20. 67.

26

You are a little soul, carrying a corpse, as Epictetus used to say. M. Aurelius, iv. 41.

27

Epictetus said that we must discover the art of assent, and use careful attention in the sphere of the will; our impulses must be 'with qualification', and social and according to desert: we must abstain altogether from the will to get, and not attempt to avoid any of those things that are not in our power. M. Aurelius, xi. 37.

28

It is no ordinary matter that is at stake, he said; the question is between sanity and madness. M. Aurelius, xi. 38.

29[3]

Always take thought for nothing so much as what is safe; silence is safer than speech; refrain from saying what shall be void of sense and open to blame. *Flor.* 35. 10.

30

We must not fasten our ship to one small anchor nor our life to one hope. *Flor.* 110. 22.

31

We must not stretch our hopes too wide, any more than our stride. *Flor.* 110. 23.

32

It is more needful to heal soul than body; for death is better than living ill. *Flor.* 121. 27.

33

The rarest pleasures give most delight. *Flor.* 6. 59.

34

If a man should go beyond the mean, the most joyous things would turn to utter joylessness. *Flor.* 6. 60.

35

No one is free that is not his own master. *Flor*. 6. 59.

36

Truth is a thing immortal and eternal; it gives us not a beauty that fades with time; nor does it take away the confident speech that is based on justice, but confirms things just and lawful, distinguishing things unjust from them and showing their falsehood. Antonius, i. 21.

THE MANUAL OF EPICTETUS[1]

I

OF ALL existing things some are in our power, and others are not in our power. In our power are thought, impulse, will to get and will to avoid, and, in a word, everything which is our own doing. Things not in our power include the body, property, reputation, office, and, in a word, everything which is not our own doing. Things in our power are by nature free, unhindered, untrammelled; things not in our power are weak, servile, subject to hindrance, dependent on others. Remember then that if you imagine that what is naturally slavish is free, and what is naturally another's is your own, you will be hampered, you will mourn, you will be put to confusion, you will blame gods and men; but if you think that only your own belongs to you, and that what is another's is indeed another's, no one will ever put compulsion or hindrance on you, you will blame none, you will accuse none, you will do nothing against your will, no one will harm you, you will have no enemy, for no harm can touch you.

Aiming then at these high matters, you must remember that to attain them requires more than ordinary effort; you will have to give up some things entirely, and put off others for the moment. And if you would have these also—office and wealth—it may be that you will fail to get them, just because your desire is set on the former, and you will certainly fail to attain those things which alone bring freedom and happiness.

Make it your study then to confront every harsh impression with the words, 'You are but an impression, and not at all what you seem to be'. Then test it by those rules that you possess; and first by this—the chief test of all—'Is it concerned with what is in our power or with what is not in our power?' And if it is concerned with what is not in our power, be ready with the answer that it is nothing to you.

2

Remember that the will to get promises attainment of what you will, and the will to avoid promises escape from what you avoid; and he who fails to get what he wills is unfortunate, and he who does not escape what he wills to avoid is miserable. If then you try to avoid only what is unnatural in the region within your control, you will escape from all that you avoid; but if you try to avoid disease or death or poverty you will be miserable.

Therefore let your will to avoid have no concern with what is not in man's power; direct it only to things in man's power that are contrary to nature. But for the moment you must utterly remove the will to get; for if you will to get something not in man's power you are bound to be unfortunate; while none of the things in man's power that you could honourably will to get is yet within your reach. Impulse to act and not to act, these are your concern; yet exercise them gently and without strain, and provisionally.

3

When anything, from the meanest thing upwards, is attractive or serviceable or an object of affection, remember always to say to yourself, 'What is its nature?' If you are fond of a jug, say you are fond of a jug; then you will not be disturbed if it be broken. If you kiss your child or your wife, say to yourself that you are kissing a human being, for then if death strikes it you will not be disturbed.

4

When you are about to take something in hand, remind yourself what manner of thing it is. If you are going to bathe put before your mind what happens in the bath—water pouring over some, others being jostled, some reviling, others stealing; and you will set to work more securely if you say to yourself at once: 'I want to bathe, and I want to keep my will in harmony with nature,' and so in each thing you do; for in this way, if anything turns up to hinder you in your bathing, you will be ready to say, 'I did not want only to bathe, but to keep my will in harmony with nature, and I shall not so keep it, if I lose my temper at what happens'.

5

What disturbs men's minds is not events but their judgements on events. For instance, death is nothing dreadful, or else Socrates would have thought it so. No, the only dreadful thing about it is men's judgement that it is dreadful. And so when we are hindered, or disturbed, or distressed, let us never lay the blame on others, but on ourselves, that is, on our own judgements. To accuse others for one's own misfortunes is a sign of want of education; to accuse oneself shows that one's education has begun; to accuse neither oneself nor others shows that one's education is complete.

6

Be not elated at an excellence which is not your own. If the horse in his pride were to say, 'I am handsome', we could bear with it. But when you say with pride, 'I have a handsome horse', know that the good horse is the ground of your pride. You ask then what you can call your own. The answer is—the way you deal with your impressions. Therefore when you deal with your impressions in accord with nature, then you may be proud indeed, for your pride will be in a good which is your own.

7

When you are on a voyage, and your ship is at anchorage, and you disembark to get fresh water, you may pick up a small shellfish or a truffle by the way, but you must keep your attention fixed on the ship, and keep looking towards it constantly, to see if the Helmsman calls you; and if he does, you have to leave everything, or be bundled on board with your legs tied like a sheep. So it is in life. If you have a dear wife or child given you, they are like the shellfish or the truffle, they are very well in their way. Only, if the Helmsman call, run back to your ship, leave all else, and do not look behind you. And if you are old, never go far from the ship, so that when you are called you may not fail to appear.

8

Ask not that events should happen as you will, but let your will be that events should happen as they do, and you shall have peace.

9

Sickness is a hindrance to the body, but not to the will, unless the will consent. Lameness is a hindrance to the leg, but not to the will. Say this to yourself at each event that happens, for you shall find that though it hinders something else it will not hinder you.

10

When anything happens to you, always remember to turn to yourself and ask what faculty you have to deal with it. If you see a beautiful boy or a beautiful woman, you will find continence the faculty to exercise there; if trouble is laid on you, you will find endurance; if ribaldry, you will find patience. And if you train yourself in this habit your impressions will not carry you away.

11

Never say of anything, 'I lost it', but say, 'I gave it back'. Has your child died? It was given back. Has your wife died? She was given back. Has your estate been taken from you? Was not this also given back? But you say, 'He who took it from me is wicked'. What does it matter to you through whom the Giver asked it back? As long as He gives it you, take care of it, but not as your own; treat it as passers-by treat an inn.

12

If you wish to make progress, abandon reasonings of this sort: 'If I neglect my affairs I shall have nothing to live on'; 'If I do not punish my son, he will be wicked.' For it is better to die of hunger, so that you be free from pain and free from fear, than to live in plenty and be troubled in mind. It is better for your son to be wicked than for you to be miserable.[2] Wherefore begin with little things. Is your drop of oil spilt? Is your sup of wine stolen? Say to yourself, 'This is the price paid for freedom from passion, this is the price of a quiet mind.' Nothing can be had without a price. When you call your slave-boy, reflect that he may not be able to hear you, and if he hears you, he may not be able to do anything you want. But he is not so well off that it rests with him to give you peace of mind.

13

If you wish to make progress, you must be content in external matters to seem a fool and a simpleton; do not wish men to think you know anything, and if any should think you to be somebody, distrust yourself. For know that it is not easy to keep your will in accord with nature and at the same time keep outward things; if you attend to one you must needs neglect the other.

14

It is silly to want your children and your wife and your friends to live for ever, for that means that you want what is not in your control to be in your control, and what is not your own to be yours. In the same way if you want your servant to make no mistakes, you are a fool, for you want vice not to be vice but something different. But if you want not to be disappointed in your will to get, you can attain to that.

Exercise yourself then in what lies in your power. Each man's master is the man who has authority over what he wishes or does not wish, to secure the one or to take away the other. Let him then who wishes to be free not wish for anything or avoid anything that depends on others; or else he is bound to be a slave.

15

Remember that you must behave in life as you would at a banquet. A dish is handed round and comes to you; put out your hand and take it politely. It passes you; do not stop it. It has not reached you; do not be impatient to get it, but wait till your turn comes. Bear yourself thus towards children, wife, office, wealth, and one day you will be worthy to banquet with the gods. But if when they are set before you, you do not take them but despise them, then you shall not only share the gods' banquet, but shall share their rule. For by so doing Diogenes and Heraclitus and men like them were called divine and deserved the name.

16

When you see a man shedding tears in sorrow for a child abroad or dead, or for loss of property, beware that you are not carried away by the impression that it is outward ills that make him miserable. Keep this thought by you: 'What distresses him is not the event, for that does not distress another, but his judgement on the event.' Therefore do not hesitate to sympathize with him so far as words go, and if it so chance, even to groan with him; but take heed that you do not also groan in your inner being.

17

Remember that you are an actor in a play, and the Playwright chooses the manner of it: if he wants it short, it is short; if long, it is long. If he wants you to act a poor man you must act the part with all your powers; and so if your part be a cripple or a magistrate or a plain man. For your business is to act the character that is given you and act it well; the choice of the cast is Another's.

18

When a raven croaks with evil omen, let not the impression carry you away, but straightway distinguish in your own mind and say, 'These portents mean nothing to me; but only to my bit of a body or my bit of property or name, or my children or my wife. But for me all omens are favourable if I will, for, whatever the issue may be, it is in my power to get benefit therefrom.'

19

You can be invincible, if you never enter on a contest where victory is not in your power. Beware then that when you see a man raised to honour or great power or high repute you do not let your impression carry you away. For if the reality of good lies in what is in our power, there is no room for envy or jealousy. And you will not wish to be praetor, or prefect or consul, but to be free; and there is but one way to freedom—to despise what is not in our power.

20

Remember that foul words or blows in themselves are no outrage, but your judgement that they are so. So when any one makes you angry, know that it is your own thought that has angered you. Wherefore make it your first endeavour not to let your impressions carry you away. For if once you gain time and delay, you will find it easier to control yourself.

21

Keep before your eyes from day to day death and exile and all things that seem terrible, but death most of all, and then you will never set your thoughts on what is low and will never desire anything beyond measure.

22

If you set your desire on philosophy you must at once prepare to meet with ridicule and the jeers of many who will say, 'Here he is again, turned philosopher. Where has he got these proud looks?' Nay, put on no proud looks, but hold fast to what seems best to you, in confidence that God has set you at this post. And remember that if you abide where you are, those who first laugh at you will one day admire you, and that if you give way to them, you will get doubly laughed at.

23

If it ever happen to you to be diverted to things outside, so that you desire to please another, know that you have lost your life's plan. Be content then always to be a philosopher; if you wish to be regarded as one too, show yourself that you are one and you will be able to achieve it.

24

Let not reflections such as these afflict you: 'I shall live without honour, and never be of any account'; for if lack of honour is an evil, no one but yourself can involve you in evil any more than in shame. Is it your business to get office or to be invited to an entertainment?

Certainly not.

Where then is the dishonour you talk of? How can you be 'of no account anywhere', when you ought to count for something in those matters only which are in your power, where you may achieve the highest worth?

'But my friends,' you say, 'will lack assistance.'

What do you mean by 'lack assistance'? They will not have cash from you and you will not make them Roman citizens. Who told you that to do these things is in our power, and not dependent upon others? Who can give to another what is not his to give?

'Get them then,' says he, 'that we may have them.'

If I can get them and keep my self-respect, honour, magnanimity, show the way and I will get them. But if you call on me to lose the good things that are mine, in order that you may win things that are not good, look how unfair and thoughtless you are. And which do you really prefer? Money, or a faithful, modest friend? Therefore help me rather to keep these qualities, and do not expect from me actions which will make me lose them.

'But my country,' says he, 'will lack assistance, so far as lies in me.'

Once more I ask, What assistance do you mean? It will not owe colonnades or baths to you. What of that? It does not owe shoes to the blacksmith or arms to the shoemaker; it is sufficient if each man fulfils his own function. Would you do it no good if you secured to it another faithful and modest citizen?

'Yes.'

Well, then, you would not be useless to it.

'What place then shall I have in the city?'

Whatever place you can hold while you keep your character for honour and self-respect. But if you are going to lose these qualities in trying to benefit your city, what benefit, I ask, would you have done her when you attain to the perfection of being lost to shame and honour?

25

Has some one had precedence of you at an entertainment or a levée or been called in before you to give advice? If these things are good you ought to be glad that he got them; if they are evil, do not be angry that you did not get them yourself. Remember that if you want to get what is not in your power, you cannot earn the same reward as others unless you act as they do. How is it possible for one who does not haunt the great man's door to have equal shares with one who does, or one who does not go in his train equality with one who does; or one who does not praise him with one who does? You will be unjust then and insatiable if you wish to get these privileges for nothing, without paying their price. What is the price of a lettuce? An obol perhaps. If then a man pays his obol and gets his lettuces, and you do not pay and do not get them, do not think you are defrauded. For as he has the lettuces so you have the obol you did not give. The same principle holds good too in conduct. You were not invited to some one's entertainment? Because you did not give the host the price for which he sells his dinner. He sells it for compliments, he sells it for attentions. Pay him the price then, if it is to your profit. But if you wish to get the one and yet not give up the other, nothing can satisfy you in your folly.

What! you say, you have nothing instead of the dinner?

Nay, you have this, you have not praised the man you did not want to praise, you have not had to bear with the insults of his doorstep.

26

It is in our power to discover the will of Nature from those matters on which we have no difference of opinion. For instance, when another man's slave has broken the wine-cup we are very ready to say at once, 'Such things must happen'. Know then that when your own cup is broken, you ought to behave in the same way as when your neighbour's was broken. Apply the same principle to higher matters. Is another's child or wife dead? Not one of us but would say, 'Such is the lot of man'; but when one's own dies, straightway one cries, 'Alas! miserable am I'. But we ought to remember what our feelings are when we hear it of another.

27

As a mark is not set up for men to miss it, so there is nothing intrinsically evil in the world.

28

If any one trusted your body to the first man he met, you would be indignant, but yet you trust your mind to the chance comer, and allow it to be disturbed and confounded if he revile you; are you not ashamed to do so?

29[3]

In everything you do consider what comes first and what follows, and so approach it. Otherwise you will come to it with a good heart at first because you have not reflected on any of the consequences, and afterwards, when difficulties have appeared, you will desist to your shame. Do you wish to win at Olympia? So do I, by the gods, for it is a fine thing. But consider the first steps to it, and the consequences, and so lay your hand to the work. You must submit to discipline, eat to order, touch no sweets, train under compulsion, at a fixed hour, in heat and cold, drink no cold water, nor wine, except by order; you must hand yourself over completely to your trainer as you would to a physician, and then when the contest comes you must risk getting hacked, and sometimes dislocate your hand, twist your ankle, swallow plenty of sand, sometimes get a flogging, and with all this suffer defeat. When you have considered all this well, then enter on the athlete's course, if you still wish it. If you act without thought you will be behaving like children, who one day play at wrestlers, another day at gladiators, now sound the trumpet, and next strut the stage. Like them you will be now an athlete, now a gladiator, then orator, then philosopher, but nothing with all your soul. Like an ape, you imitate every sight you see, and one thing after another takes your fancy. When you undertake a thing you do it casually and half-heartedly, instead of considering it and looking at it all round. In the same way some people, when they see a philosopher and hear a man speaking like Euphrates (and indeed who can speak as he can?), wish to be philosophers themselves.

Man, consider first what it is you are undertaking; then look at your own powers and see if you can bear it. Do you want to compete in the pentathlon or in wrestling? Look to your arms, your thighs, see what your loins are like. For different men are born for different tasks. Do you suppose that if you do this you can live as you do now—eat and drink as you do now, indulge desire and discontent just as before? Nay, you must sit up late, work hard, abandon your own people, be looked down on by a mere slave, be ridiculed by those who meet you, get the worst of it in everything—in honour, in office, in justice, in every possible thing. This is what you have to consider: whether you are willing to pay this price for peace of mind, freedom, tranquillity. If not, do not come near; do not be, like the children, first a philosopher, then a tax-collector, then an orator, then one of Caesar's procurators. These callings do not agree. You must be one man, good or bad; you must develop either your Governing Principle, or your outward endowments; you must study either your inner man, or outward things—in a word, you must choose between the position of a philosopher and that of a mere outsider.

30

Appropriate acts are in general measured by the relations they are concerned with. 'He is your father.' This means you are called on to take care of him, give way to him in all things, bear with him if he reviles or strikes you.

'But he is a bad father.'

Well, have you any natural claim to a good father? No, only to a father.

'My brother wrongs me.'

Be careful then to maintain the relation you hold to him, and do not consider what he does, but what you must do if your purpose is to keep in accord with nature. For no one shall harm you, without your consent; you will only be harmed, when you think you are harmed. You will only discover what is proper to expect from neighbour, citizen, or praetor, if you get into the habit of looking at the relations implied by each.

31

For piety towards the gods know that the most important thing is this: to have right opinions about them—that they exist, and that they govern the universe well and justly—and to have set yourself to obey them, and to give way to all that happens, following events with a free will, in the belief that they are fulfilled by the highest mind. For thus you will never blame the gods, nor accuse them of neglecting you. But this you cannot achieve, unless you apply your conception of good and evil to those things only which are in our power, and not to those which are out of our power. For if you apply your notion of good or evil to the latter, then, as soon as you fail to get what you will to get or fail to avoid what you will to avoid, you will be bound to blame and hate those you hold responsible. For every living creature has a natural tendency to avoid and shun what seems harmful and all that causes it, and to pursue and admire what is helpful and all that causes it. It is not possible then for one who thinks he is harmed to take pleasure in what he thinks is the author of the harm, any more than to take pleasure in the harm itself. That is why a father is reviled by his son, when he does not give his son a share of what the son regards as good things; thus Polynices and Eteocles were set at enmity with one another by thinking that a king's throne was a good thing. That is why the farmer, and the sailor, and the merchant, and those who lose wife or children revile the gods. For men's religion is bound up with their interest. Therefore he who makes it his concern rightly to direct his will to get and his will to avoid, is thereby making piety his concern. But it is proper on each occasion to make libation and sacrifice and to offer first-fruits according to the custom of our fathers, with purity and not in slovenly or careless fashion, without meanness and without extravagance.

32

When you make use of prophecy remember that while you know not what the issue will be, but are come to learn it from the prophet, you do know before you come what manner of thing it is, if you are really a philosopher. For if the event is not in our control, it cannot be either good or evil. Therefore do not bring with you to the prophet the will to get or the will to avoid, and do not approach him with trembling, but with your mind made up, that the whole issue is indifferent and does not affect you and that, whatever it be, it will be in your power to make good use of it, and no one shall hinder this. With confidence then approach the gods as counsellors, and further, when the counsel is given you, remember whose counsel it is, and whom you will be disregarding if you disobey. And consult the oracle, as Socrates thought men should, only when the whole question turns upon the issue of events, and neither reason nor any art of man provides opportunities for discovering what lies before you. Therefore, when it is your duty to risk your life with friend or country, do not ask the oracle whether you should risk your life. For if the prophet warns you that the sacrifice is unfavourable, though it is plain that this means death or exile or injury to some part of your body, yet reason requires that even at this cost you must stand by your friend and share your country's danger. Wherefore pay heed to the greater prophet, Pythian Apollo, who cast out of his temple the man who did not help his friend when he was being killed.[4]

33

Lay down for yourself from the first a definite stamp and style of conduct, which you will maintain when you are alone and also in the society of men. Be silent for the most part, or, if you speak, say only what is necessary and in a few words. Talk, but rarely, if occasion calls you, but do not talk of ordinary things—of gladiators, or horse-races, or athletes, or of meats or drinks—these are topics that arise everywhere—but above all do not talk about men in blame or compliment or comparison. If you can, turn the conversation of your company by your talk to some fitting subject; but if you should chance to be isolated among strangers, be silent. Do not laugh much, nor at many things, nor without restraint.

Refuse to take oaths, altogether if that be possible, but if not, as far as circumstances allow.

Refuse the entertainments of strangers and the vulgar.[5] But if occasion arise to accept them, then strain every nerve to avoid lapsing into the state of the vulgar. For know that, if your comrade have a stain on him, he that associates with him must needs share the stain, even though he be clean in himself.

For your body take just so much as your bare need requires, such as food, drink, clothing, house, servants, but cut down all that tends to luxury and outward show.

Avoid impurity to the utmost of your power before marriage, and if you indulge your passion, let it be done lawfully. But do not be offensive or censorious to those who indulge it, and do not be always bringing up your own chastity. If some one tells you that so and so speaks ill of you, do not defend yourself against what he says, but answer, 'He did not know my other faults, or he would not have mentioned these alone.'

It is not necessary for the most part to go to the games; but if you should have occasion to go, show that your first concern is for yourself; that is, wish that only to happen which does happen, and him only to win who does win, for so you will suffer no hindrance. But refrain entirely from applause, or ridicule, or prolonged excitement. And when you go away do not talk much of what happened there, except so far as it tends to your improvement. For to talk about it implies that the spectacle excited your wonder.

Do not go lightly or casually to hear lectures; but if you do go, maintain your gravity and dignity and do not make yourself offensive. When you are going to meet any one, and particularly some man of reputed eminence, set before your mind the thought, 'What would Socrates or Zeno have done?' and you will not fail to make proper use of the occasion.

When you go to visit some great man, prepare your mind by thinking that you will not find him in, that you will be shut out, that the doors will be slammed in your face, that he will pay no heed to you. And if in spite of all this you find it fitting for you to go, go and bear what happens and never say to yourself, 'It was not worth all this'; for that shows a vulgar mind and one at odds with outward things.

In your conversation avoid frequent and disproportionate mention of your own doings or adventures; for other people do not take the same pleasure in hearing what has happened to you as you take in recounting your adventures.

Avoid raising men's laughter; for it is a habit that easily slips into vulgarity, and it may well suffice to lessen your neighbour's respect.

It is dangerous too to lapse into foul language; when anything of the kind occurs, rebuke the offender, if the occasion allow, and if not, make it plain to him by your silence, or a blush or a frown, that you are angry at his words.

34

When you imagine some pleasure, beware that it does not carry you away, like other imaginations. Wait a while, and give yourself pause. Next remember two things: how long you will enjoy the pleasure, and also how long you will afterwards repent and revile yourself. And set on the other side the joy and self-satisfaction you will feel if you refrain. And if the moment seems come to realize it, take heed that you be not overcome by the winning sweetness and attraction of it; set in the other scale the thought how much better is the consciousness of having vanquished it.

35

When you do a thing because you have determined that it ought to be done, never avoid being seen doing it, even if the opinion of the multitude is going to condemn you. For if your action is wrong, then avoid doing it altogether, but if it is right, why do you fear those who will rebuke you wrongly?

36

The phrases, 'It is day' and 'It is night', mean a great deal if taken separately, but have no meaning if combined. In the same way, to choose the larger portion at a banquet may be worth while for your body, but if you want to maintain social decencies it is worthless. Therefore, when you are at meat with another, remember not only to consider the value of what is set before you for the body, but also to maintain your self-respect before your host.

37

If you try to act a part beyond your powers, you not only disgrace yourself in it, but you neglect the part which you could have filled with success.

38

As in walking you take care not to tread on a nail or to twist your foot, so take care that you do not harm your Governing Principle. And if we guard this in everything we do, we shall set to work more securely.

39

Every man's body is a measure for his property, as the foot is the measure for his shoe. If you stick to this limit, you will keep the right measure; if you go beyond it, you are bound to be carried away down a precipice in the end; just as with the shoe, if you once go beyond the foot, your shoe puts on gilding, and soon purple and embroidery. For when once you go beyond the measure there is no limit.

40

Women from fourteen years upwards are called 'madam' by men. Wherefore, when they see that the only advantage they have got is to be marriageable, they begin to make themselves smart and to set all their hopes on this. We must take pains then to make them understand that they are really honoured for nothing but a modest and decorous life.

41

It is a sign of a dull mind to dwell upon the cares of the body, to prolong exercise, eating, drinking, and other bodily functions. These things are to be done by the way; all your attention must be given to the mind.

42

When a man speaks evil or does evil to you, remember that he does or says it because he thinks it is fitting for him. It is not possible for him to follow what seems good to you, but only what seems good to him, so that, if his opinion is wrong, he suffers, in that he is the victim of deception. In the same way, if a composite judgement which is true is thought to be false, it is not the judgement that suffers, but the man who is deluded about it. If you act on this principle you will be gentle to him who reviles you, saying to yourself on each occasion, 'He thought it right.'

43

Everything has two handles, one by which you can carry it, the other by which you cannot. If your brother wrongs you, do not take it by that handle, the handle of his wrong, for you cannot carry it by that, but rather by the other handle—that he is a brother, brought up with you, and then you will take it by the handle that you can carry by.

44

It is illogical to reason thus, 'I am richer than you, therefore I am superior to you', 'I am more eloquent than you, therefore I am superior to you.' It is more logical to reason, 'I am richer than you, therefore my property is superior to yours', 'I am more eloquent than you, therefore my speech is superior to yours.' You are something more than property or speech.

45

If a man wash quickly, do not say that he washes badly, but that he washes quickly. If a man drink much wine, do not say that he drinks badly, but that he drinks much. For till you have decided what judgement prompts him, how do you know that he acts badly? If you do as I say, you will assent to your apprehensive impressions and to none other.

46

On no occasion call yourself a philosopher, nor talk at large of your principles among the multitude, but act on your principles. For instance, at a banquet do not say how one ought to eat, but eat as you ought. Remember that Socrates had so completely got rid of the thought of display that when men came and wanted an introduction to philosophers he took them to be introduced; so patient of neglect was he. And if a discussion arise among the multitude on some principle, keep silent for the most part; for you are in great danger of blurting out some undigested thought. And when some one says to you, 'You know nothing', and you do not let it provoke you, then know that you are really on the right road. For sheep do not bring grass to their shepherds and show them how much they have eaten, but they digest their fodder and then produce it in the form of wool and milk. Do the same yourself; instead of displaying your principles to the multitude, show them the results of the principles you have digested.

47

When you have adopted the simple life, do not pride yourself upon it, and if you are a water-drinker do not say on every occasion, 'I am a water-drinker.' And if you ever want to train laboriously, keep it to yourself and do not make a show of it. Do not embrace statues. If you are very thirsty take a good draught of cold water, and rinse you mouth and tell no one.

48

The ignorant man's position and character is this: he never looks to himself for benefit or harm, but to the world outside him. The philosopher's position and character is that he always look to himself for benefit and harm.

The signs of one who is making progress are: he blames none, praises none, complains of none, accuses none, never speaks of himself as if he were somebody, or as if he knew anything. And if any one compliments him he laughs in himself at his compliment; and if one blames him, he makes no defence. He goes about like a convalescent, careful not to disturb his constitution on its road to recovery, until it has got firm hold. He has got rid of the will to get, and his will to avoid is directed no longer to what is beyond our power but only to what is in our power and contrary to nature. In all things he exercises his will without strain. If men regard him as foolish or ignorant he pays no heed. In one word, he keeps watch and guard on himself as his own enemy, lying in wait for him.

49

When a man prides himself on being able to understand and interpret the books of Chrysippus, say to yourself, 'If Chrysippus had not written obscurely this man would have had nothing on which to pride himself.'

What is my object? To understand Nature and follow her. I look then for some one who interprets her, and having heard that Chrysippus does I come to him. But I do not understand his writings, so I seek an interpreter. So far there is nothing to be proud of. But when I have found the interpreter it remains for me to act on his precepts; that and that alone is a thing to be proud of. But if I admire the mere power of exposition, it comes to this—that I am turned into a grammarian instead of a philosopher, except that I interpret Chrysippus in place of Homer. Therefore, when some one says to me, 'Read me Chrysippus', when I cannot point to actions which are in harmony and correspondence with his teaching, I am rather inclined to blush.

50

Whatever principles you put before you, hold fast to them as laws which it will be impious to transgress. But pay no heed to what any one says of you; for this is something beyond your own control.

51

How long will you wait to think yourself worthy of the highest and transgress in nothing the clear pronouncement of reason? You have received the precepts which you ought to accept, and you have accepted them. Why then do you still wait for a master, that you may delay the amendment of yourself till he comes? You are a youth no longer, you are now a full-grown man. If now you are careless and indolent and are always putting off, fixing one day after another as the limit when you mean to begin attending to yourself, then, living or dying, you will make no progress but will continue unawares in ignorance. Therefore make up your mind before it is too late to live as one who is mature and proficient, and let all that seems best to you be a law that you cannot transgress. And if you encounter anything troublesome or pleasant or glorious or inglorious, remember that the hour of struggle is come, the Olympic contest is here and you may put off no longer, and that one day and one action determines whether the progress you have achieved is lost or maintained.

This was how Socrates attained perfection, paying heed to nothing but reason, in all that he encountered. And if you are not yet Socrates, yet ought you to live as one who would wish to be a Socrates.

52

The first and most necessary department of philosophy deals with the application of principles; for instance, 'not to lie'. The second deals with demonstrations; for instance, 'How comes it that one ought not to lie?' The third is concerned with establishing and analysing these processes; for instance, 'How comes it that this is a demonstration? What is demonstration, what is consequence, what is contradiction, what is true, what is false?' It follows then that the third department is necessary because of the second, and the second because of the first. The first is the most necessary part, and that in which we must rest. But we reverse the order: we occupy ourselves with the third, and make that our whole concern, and the first we completely neglect. Wherefore we lie, but are ready enough with the demonstration that lying is wrong.

53

On every occasion we must have these thoughts at hand,

> 'Lead me, O Zeus, and lead me, Destiny,
> Whither ordainèd is by your decree.
> I'll follow, doubting not, or if with will
> Recreant I falter, I shall follow still.'

[Cleanthes]

> 'Who rightly with necessity complies
> In things divine we count him skilled and wise.'

[Euripides, Fragment 965]

'Well, Crito, if this be the gods' will, so be it.'

[Plato, *Crito*, 43d]

'Anytus and Meletus have power to put me to death,
but not to harm me.'

[Plato, *Apology*, 30c]

NOTES

The *Discourses.*

Book I.

[1] This technical Stoic word, as Matheson points out, includes 'the power of presenting an image to the mind's eye' and 'the image so presented'. It is almost the equivalent of 'the data of consciousness'.

[2] These words frequently recur in Epictetus.

[3] Primary notions. 'They are certain general terms used commonly by men (such as good, happiness, justice), and their proper application not being reasoned out by the individual before he uses them, they are in a sense anticipations of reasoned knowledge.' (Matheson)

[4] The Greek says, 'to hold the pot'.

[5] The interruption here of one of the listeners is perfectly typical of the informal character of the *Discourses.*

[6] This is a technical Stoic term.

[7] This is a summary of the three spheres of man's activity, according to the Stoics: (a) The will to get and will to avoid; (b) impulse positive and negative; (c) assent. (Matheson)

[8] 'A premiss is said to "vary" when it becomes untrue at some subsequent time.' (Matheson)

[9] 'τὸ βάραθρον. The ravine at Athens into which the corpses of criminals were thrown: hence used metaphorically of the extreme of misery or degradation.' (Matheson)

[10] Epictetus uses Zeus 'interchangeably with "God" and "the divine", to express the Divine Spirit of the universe.' (Matheson)

[11] Sometimes this is rendered literally by the word 'daemon' and it connoted to the Stoic the higher element within man, his reason.

[12] This is 'the governing principle of the soul, and as the highest aspect of the soul is rational, it is often equivalent to διάνοια and λογισμός, but must not be regarded as purely intellectual: it is the soul as feeling and willing, as well as thinking.' (Matheson)

[13] Cf. above, note 3.

[14] 'Epictetus, lecturing at Nicopolis in Epirus, speaks of sending his pupil to Rome to spy out the land, to see how things are going in the capital under Domitian, who had expelled all philosophers.' (Matheson)

[15] Medea.

Book II.

[1] These were used by beaters in hunting.

[2] This refers to the ceremony of manumission. Epictetus may mention this so frequently because he himself was a freedman.

[3] It is not certain whether in this sentence and the next Epictetus is thinking of Jews or of Christians, who at this time were often confused with them.' (Matheson)

[4] 'Three campaigns in the cavalry or six in the infantry were the period laid down in the so-called Municipal Law of Caesar as a qualification for a seat in a municipal Senate.' (Matheson)

[5] The ancient cure for insanity.

[6] I.e., from the Marcian aqueduct at Rome.

[7] Cf. Book I, note 7.

[8] 'The best-known instance of this sophism is "Epimenides says the Cretans are always liars, but he is himself a Cretan. Does he lie or tell the truth?" ' (Matheson)

[9] Cf. Book II, chap. XIX.

[10] The text is corrupt here.

[11] Cf. Book II, note 8.

[12] 'According to the Stoics the "spirit" of vision connected the central mind with the pupil of the eye and similarly with other senses.' (Matheson)

[13] Cf. Epicurus, fragment 30.

Book III.

[1] 'The *pancratium* consisted of boxing and wrestling, and was supposed to test all a man's powers. The *pentathlon* included running, jumping, quoit-throwing, spear-throwing, and wrestling.' (Matheson)

[2] 'Young men of 18-20, under military training.' (Matheson)

[3] Cf. Book I, note 7.

[4] 'Such special commissioners, sent to set in order the affairs of the "free cities", date from Trajan's reign.' (Matheson)

[5] These men are otherwise unknown. Matheson suggests that they were freedmen who had risen to high position.

[6] A technical Stoic term.

[7] I.e., a representative of the town at Rome.

[8] A very valuable material.

[9] A reference to the Stoic doctrine, ultimately derived from Heraclitus, that the universe was periodically consumed by fire.

[10] 'Trajan after his conquest of Dacia.' (Matheson)

[11] 'It is the drivel of the sickly novice in philosophy.' (Matheson)

[12] Cf. the *Manual,* chap. 29.

[13] Probably a slave.

[14] 'The Cynic whom Epictetus describes is the ideal Stoic teacher, who is distinguished from the ordinary Stoic by a more austere and isolated life.' (Matheson)

[15] 'Used to get a smooth skin.' (Matheson)

[16] Cf. Xenophon, *Memorabilia, init.*

[17] 'Probably refers to the story that Nicocreon ordered Anaxarchus' tongue to be cut out, whereupon he bit it off himself and spat it in Nicocreon's face. Cf. Diogenes Laertius, IX. 59.' (Matheson)

[18] 'A saying attributed to Solon, Anaxagoras, and Xenophon.' (Matheson)

[19] The name of a slave.

Book IV.

[1] 'The gold ring given to a freedman would open to him an official career as a knight.' (Matheson)

[2] Cf. Book II, note 4.

[3] One of the prerogatives of a consul.

[4] Cf. Diogenes Laertius, VI. 29.

[5] The only certain reference to the Christians in Epictetus.

[6] Cf. Book I, note 7.

[7] Cf. above, note 3.

[8] With this passage, cf. the criticism of Homer by Plato, in the *Republic,* Books II and III.

Fragments.

[1] 'Most of these fragments come from two selections from Greek writers, made by Stobaeus, John of Stobi in Macedonia (sixth century A.D.). Those marked *Ecl.* are from his *Eclogues,* and those marked *Flor.* from his *Anthology.* Fragments 9 and 10 are from the *Noctes Atticae* of Aulus Gellius, a Latin grammarian of the second century A.D.; 26, 27, 28 from the *Meditations* of the Emperor Marcus Aurelius Antoninus; 10a from the *Against the Heathen* of Arnobius, an African Latin writer (*ca.* A.D. 300); 36 from Antonius Melissa ('The Bee'), a Greek monk of uncertain date. The reference to Musonius Rufus in the headings of 4-8 is not clear; the natural meaning would be that they are sayings of Rufus, incorporated by Epictetus in his discourses on Friendship.' (Matheson)

[2] 'The ordered universe, which is sometimes identified with its Creator, God.' (Matheson)

[3] The genuineness of the remaining fragments has been suspected.

The Manual.

[1] This 'hand-book' of Epictetus' principles was probably compiled by Arrian, and contains an excellent summary of the master's thought.

[2] Matheson's translation of παῖδα as 'son' here and at the beginning of chapter 12 can hardly be correct. Throughout the whole section it should be rendered as 'slave-boy'. The reading 'son' imposes unnecessarily upon Stoicism a brutality and lack of normal human sympathy and affection which it can ill afford to carry.

[3] Cf. Book III, chap. 15.

[4] 'Aelian, *Var. Hist.,* tells how three men sent to Delphi had an encounter with robbers. One ran away, another accidentally killed the third in trying to defend him. The Oracle would have nothing to say to the runaway, and absolved the homicide.' (Matheson)

[5] I.e., those untrained in philosophy.

THE MEDITATIONS
OF
MARCUS AURELIUS ANTONINUS

THE MEDITATIONS OF MARCUS AURELIUS ANTONINUS

BOOK I

From my grandfather Verus I learned good morals and the government of my temper.

2. From the reputation and remembrance of my father,[1] modesty and a manly character.

3. From my mother,[2] piety and beneficence, and abstinence, not only from evil deeds, but even from evil thoughts; and further, simplicity in my way of living, far removed from the habits of the rich.

4. From my great-grandfather,[3] not to have frequented public schools, and to have had good teachers at home, and to know that on such things a man should spend liberally.

5. From my governor, to be neither of the green nor of the blue party at the games in the Circus, nor a partizan either of the Parmularius or the Scutarius at the gladiators' fights; from him too I learned endurance of labour, and to want little, and to work with my own hands, and not to meddle with other people's affairs, and not to be ready to listen to slander.

6. From Diognetus, not to busy myself about trifling things, and not to give credit to what was said by miracle-workers and jugglers about incantations and the driving away of daemons and such things; and not to breed quails for fighting, nor to give myself up passionately to such things; and to endure freedom of speech; and to have become intimate with philosophy; and to have been a hearer, first of Bacchius, then of Tandasis and Marcianus; and to have written dialogues in my youth; and to have desired a plank bed and skin, and whatever else of the kind belongs to the Grecian discipline.

7. From Rusticus I received the impression that my character required improvement and discipline; and from him I learned not to be led astray to sophistic emulation, nor to writing on speculative matters, nor to delivering little hortatory orations, nor to showing myself off as a man who practises much discipline, or does benevolent acts in order to make a display; and to abstain from rhetoric, and poetry, and fine

writing; and not to walk about in the house in my outdoor dress, nor to do other things of the kind; and to write my letters with simplicity, like the letter which Rusticus wrote from Sinuessa to my mother; and with respect to those who have offended me by words, or done me wrong, to be easily disposed to be pacified and reconciled, as soon as they have shown a readiness to be reconciled; and to read carefully, and not to be satisfied with a superficial understanding of a book; nor hastily to give my assent to those who talk overmuch; and I am indebted to him for being acquainted with the discourses of Epictetus, which he communicated to me out of his own collection.

8. From Apollonius I learned freedom of will and undeviating steadiness of purpose; and to look to nothing else, not even for a moment, except to reason; and to be always the same, in sharp pains, on the occasion of the loss of a child, and in long illness; and to see clearly in a living example that the same man can be both most resolute and yielding, and not peevish in giving his instruction; and to have had before my eyes a man who clearly considered his experience and his skill in expounding philosophical principles as the smallest of his merits; and from him I learned how to receive from friends what are esteemed favours, without being either humbled by them or letting them pass unnoticed.

9. From Sextus, a benevolent disposition, and the example of a family governed in a fatherly manner, and the idea of living conformably to nature; and gravity without affectation, and to look carefully after the interests of friends, and to tolerate ignorant persons, and those who form opinions without consideration: he had the power of readily accommodating himself to all, so that intercourse with him was more agreeable than any flattery; and at the same time he was most highly venerated by those who associated with him: and he had the faculty both of discovering and ordering, in an intelligent and methodical way, the principles necessary for life; and he never showed anger or any other passion, but was entirely free from passion, and also most affectionate; and he could express approbation without noisy display, and he possessed much knowledge without ostentation.

10. From Alexander the grammarian, to refrain from fault-finding, and not in a reproachful way to chide those who uttered any barbarous or solecistic or strange-sounding expression; but dexterously to introduce the very expression which ought to have been used, and in the way of answer or giving confirmation, or joining in an inquiry about the thing itself, not about the word, or by some other fit suggestion.

11. From Fronto I learned to observe what envy, and duplicity, and hypocrisy are in a tyrant, and that generally those among us who are called Patricians are rather deficient in paternal affection.

12. From Alexander the Platonic, not frequently nor without necessity to say to any one, or to write in a letter, that I have no leisure; nor continually to excuse the neglect of duties required by our relation to those with whom we live, by alleging urgent occupations.

13. From Catulus, not to be indifferent when a friend finds fault, even if he should find fault without reason, but to try to restore him to his usual disposition; and to be ready to speak well of teachers, as it is reported of Domitius and Athenodotus; and to love my children truly.

14. From my brother Severus, to love my kin, and to love truth, and to love justice; and through him I learned to know Thrasea, Helvidius, Cato, Dion, Brutus; and from him I received the idea of a polity in which there is the same law for all, a polity administered with regard to equal rights and equal freedom of speech, and the idea of a kingly government which respects most of all the freedom of the governed; I learned from him also consistency and undeviating steadiness in my regard for philosophy; and a disposition to do good, and to give to others readily, and to cherish good hopes, and to believe that I am loved by my friends; and in him I observed no concealment of his opinions with respect to those whom he condemned, and that his friends had no need to conjecture what he wished or did not wish, but it was quite plain.

15. From Maximus I learned self-government, and not to be led aside by anything; and cheerfulness in all circumstances, as well as in illness; and a just admixture in the moral character of sweetness and dignity, and to do what was set before me without complaining. I observed that everybody believed that he thought as he spoke, and that in all that he did he never had any bad intention; and he never showed amazement and surprise, and was never in a hurry, and never put off doing a thing, nor was perplexed nor dejected, nor did he ever laugh to disguise his vexation, nor, on the other hand, was he ever passionate or suspicious. He was accustomed to do acts of beneficence, and was ready to forgive, and was free from all falsehood; and he presented the appearance of a man who could not be diverted from right rather than of a man who had been improved. I observed, too, that no man could ever think that he was despised by Maximus, or ever venture to think himself a better man. He had also the art of being humorous in an agreeable way.

16. In my father [4] I observed mildness of temper, and unchangeable resolution in the things which he had determined after due deliberation; and no vainglory in those things which men call honours; and a love of labour and perseverance; and a readiness to listen to those who had anything to propose for the common weal; and undeviating firmness in giving to every man according to his deserts; and a knowledge derived

from experience of the occasions for vigorous action and for remission. And I observed that he had overcome all passion for boys; and he considered himself no more than any other citizen; and he released his friends from all obligation to sup with him or to attend him of necessity when he went abroad, and those who had failed to accompany him, by reason of any urgent circumstances, always found him the same. I observed too his habit of careful inquiry in all matters of deliberation, and his persistency, and that he never stopped his investigation through being satisfied with appearances which first present themselves; and that his disposition was to keep his friends, and not to be soon tired of them, nor yet to be extravagant in his affection; and to be satisfied on all occasions, and cheerful; and to foresee things a long way off, and to provide for the smallest without display; and to check immediately popular applause and all flattery; and to be ever watchful over the things which were necessary for the administration of the empire, and to be a good manager of the expenditure, and patiently to endure the blame which he got for such conduct; and he was neither superstitious with respect to the gods, nor did he court men by gifts or by trying to please them, or by flattering the populace; but he showed sobriety in all things and firmness, and never any mean thoughts or action, nor love of novelty. And the things which conduce in any way to the commodity of life, and of which fortune gives an abundant supply, he used without arrogance and without excusing himself; so that when he had them, he enjoyed them without affectation, and when he had them not, he did not want them. No one could ever say of him that he was either a sophist or a home-bred flippant slave or a pedant; but every one acknowledged him to be a man ripe, perfect, above flattery, able to manage his own and other men's affairs. Besides this, he honoured those who were true philosophers, and he did not reproach those who pretended to be philosophers, nor yet was he easily led by them. He was also easy in conversation, and he made himself agreeable without any offensive affectation. He took a reasonable care of his body's health, not as one who was greatly attached to life, nor out of regard to personal appearance, nor yet in a careless way, but so that, through his own attention, he very seldom stood in need of the physician's art or of medicine or external applications. He was most ready to give way without envy to those who possessed any particular faculty, such as that of eloquence or knowledge of the law or of morals, or of anything else; and he gave them his help, that each might enjoy reputation according to his deserts; and he always acted conformably to the institutions of his country, without showing any affectation of doing so. Further, he was not fond of change nor unsteady, but he loved to stay in the same places, and to employ himself about the same things; and after his paroxysms of headache he came immediately fresh and vigorous to his usual occupations. His secrets were not many, but very few and very rare, and these only about public matters; and he showed prudence and economy in the exhibition of the public spectacles and the construction of public buildings, his donations to the people, and in such things, for he was a man who looked to what ought to be done, not to the reputation which is got by a man's acts. He did not take the bath at unseasonable hours; he was not fond of building houses, nor curious about what he ate, nor about the texture and colour of his clothes, nor about the beauty of his slaves. His dress came from Lorium, his villa on the coast, and from Lanuvium generally. We know how he behaved to the toll-collector at Tusculum who asked his pardon; and such was all his behaviour. There was in him nothing harsh, nor implacable, nor violent, nor, as one may say, anything carried to the sweating point; but he examined all things severally, as if he had abundance of time, and without confusion, in an orderly way, vigorously and consistently. And that might be applied to him which is recorded of Socrates,[5] that he was able both to abstain from, and to enjoy, those things which many are too weak to abstain from, and cannot enjoy without excess. But to be strong enough both to bear the one and to be sober in the other is the mark of a man who has a perfect and invincible soul, such as he showed in the illness of Maximus.

17. To the gods I am indebted for having good grandfathers, good parents, a good sister, good teachers, good associates, good kinsmen and friends, nearly everything good. Further, I owe it to the gods that I was not hurried into any offence against any of them, though I had a disposition which, if opportunity had offered, might have led me to do something of this kind; but, through their favour, there never was such a concurrence of circumstances as put me to the trial. Further, I am thankful to the gods that I was not longer brought up with my grandfather's concubine, and that I preserved the flower of my youth, and that I did not make proof of my virility before the proper season, but even deferred the time; that I was subjected to a ruler and a father who was able to take away all pride from me, and to bring me to the knowledge that it is possible for a man to live in a palace without wanting either guards or embroidered dresses, or torches and statues, and suchlike show; but that it is in such a man's power to bring himself very near to the fashion of a private person, without being for this reason either meaner in thought, or more remiss in action, with respect to the things which must be done for the public interest in a manner that befits a ruler. I thank the gods for giving me such a brother,[6] who was able by his moral character to rouse me to vigilance over myself, and who, at the same time, pleased me by his respect and

affection; that my children have not been stupid nor deformed in body; that I did not make more proficiency in rhetoric, poetry, and the other studies, in which I should perhaps have been completely engaged, if I had seen that I was making progress in them; that I made haste to place those who brought me up in the station of honour, which they seemed to desire, without putting them off with hope of my doing it some time after, because they were then still young; that I knew Apollonius, Rusticus, Maximus; that I received clear and frequent impressions about living according to nature, and what kind of a life that is, so that, so far as depended on the gods, and their gifts, and help, and inspirations, nothing hindered me from forthwith living according to nature, though I still fall short of it through my own fault, and through not observing the admonitions of the gods, and, I may almost say, their direct instructions; that my body has held out so long in such a kind of life; that I never touched either Benedicta or Theodotus, and that, after having fallen into amatory passions, I was cured; and, though I was often out of humour with Rusticus, I never did anything of which I had occasion to repent; that, though it was my mother's fate to die young, she spent the last years of her life with me; that, whenever I wished to help any man in his need, or on any other occasion, I was never told that I had not the means of doing it; and that to myself the same necessity never happened, to receive anything from another; that I have such a wife, so obedient, and so affectionate, and so simple; that I had abundance of good masters for my children; and that remedies have been shown to me by dreams, both others, and against bloodspitting and giddiness[7] . . . .; and that, when I had an inclination to philosophy, I did not fall into the hands of any sophist, and that I did not waste my time on writers of histories, or in the resolution of syllogisms, or occupy myself about the investigation of appearances in the heavens; for all these things require the help of the gods and fortune.

Among the Quadi at the Granua.[8]

BOOK II

Begin the morning by saying to thyself, I shall meet with the busy-body, the ungrateful, arrogant, deceitful, envious, unsocial. All these things happen to them by reason of their ignorance of what is good and evil. But I who have seen the nature of the good that it is beautiful, and of the bad that it is ugly, and the nature of him who does wrong, that it is akin to me, not only of the same blood or seed, but that it participates in the same intelligence and the same portion of the divinity, I can neither be injured by any of them, for no one can fix on me what is ugly, nor can I be angry with my kinsman, nor hate him. For we are made for co-operation, like feet, like hands, like eyelids, like the rows of the upper and lower teeth.[1] To act against one another then is contrary to nature; and it is acting against one another to be vexed and to turn away.

2. Whatever this is that I am, it is a little flesh and breath, and the ruling part. Throw away thy books; no longer distract thyself: it is not allowed; but as if thou wast now dying, despise the flesh; it is blood and bones and a network, a contexture of nerves, veins, and arteries. See the breath also, what kind of a thing it is, air, and not always the same, but every moment sent out and again sucked in. The third then is the ruling part: consider thus: Thou art an old man; no longer let this be a slave, no longer be pulled by the strings like a puppet to unsocial movements, no longer be either dissatisfied with thy present lot, or shrink from the future.

3. All that is from the gods is full of Providence. That which is from fortune is not separated from nature or without an interweaving and involution with the things which are ordered by Providence. From thence all things flow; and there is besides necessity, and that which is for the advantage of the whole universe, of which thou art a part. But that is good for every part of nature which the nature of the whole brings, and what serves to maintain this nature. Now the universe is preserved, as by the changes of the elements so by the changes of things compounded of the elements. Let these principles be enough for thee, let them always be fixed opinions. But cast away the thirst after books, that thou mayest not die murmuring, but cheerfully, truly, and from thy heart thankful to the gods.

4. Remember how long thou hast been putting off these things, and how often thou hast received an opportunity from the gods, and yet dost not use it. Thou must now at last perceive of what universe thou

art a part, and of what administrator of the universe thy existence is an efflux, and that a limit of time is fixed for thee, which if thou dost not use for clearing away the clouds from thy mind, it will go and thou wilt go, and it will never return.

5. Every moment think steadily as a Roman and a man to do what thou hast in hand with perfect and simple dignity, and feeling of affection, and freedom, and justice; and to give thyself relief from all other thoughts. And thou wilt give thyself relief, if thou doest every act of thy life as if it were the last, laying aside all carelessness and passionate aversion from the commands of reason, and all hypocrisy, and self-love, and discontent with the portion which has been given to thee. Thou seest how few the things are, the which if a man lays hold of, he is able to live a life which flows in quiet, and is like the existence of the gods; for the gods on their part will require nothing more from him who observes these things.

6. Do wrong to thyself, do wrong to thyself, my soul; but thou wilt no longer have the opportunity of honouring thyself. Every man's life is sufficient. But thine is nearly finished, though thy soul reverences not itself, but places thy felicity in the souls of others.

7. Do the things external which fall upon thee distract thee? Give thyself time to learn something new and good, and cease to be whirled around. But then thou must also avoid being carried about the other way. For those too are triflers who have wearied themselves in life by their activity, and yet have no object to which to direct every movement, and, in a word, all their thoughts.

8. Through not observing what is in the mind of another a man has seldom been seen to be unhappy; but those who do not observe the movements of their own minds must of necessity be unhappy.

9. This thou must always bear in mind, what is the nature of the whole, and what is my nature, and how this is related to that, and what kind of a part it is of what kind of a whole; and that there is no one who hinders thee from always doing and saying the things which are according to the nature of which thou art a part.

10. Theophrastus, in his comparison of bad acts—such a comparison as one would make in accordance with the common notions of mankind—says, like a true philosopher, that the offences which are committed through desire are more blameable than those which are committed through anger. For he who is excited by anger seems to turn away from reason with a certain pain and unconscious contraction; but he who offends through desire, being overpowered by pleasure, seems to be in a manner more intemperate and more womanish in his offences. Rightly then, and in a way worthy of philosophy, he said that the offence which is committed with pleasure is more blameable than that which is com-

mitted with pain; and on the whole the one is more like a person who has been first wronged and through pain is compelled to be angry; but the other is moved by his own impulse to do wrong, being carried towards doing something by desire.

11. Since it is possible that thou mayest depart from life this very moment, regulate every act and thought accordingly. But to go away from among men, if there are gods, is not a thing to be afraid of, for the gods will not involve thee in evil; but if indeed they do not exist, or if they have no concern about human affairs, what is it to me to live in a universe devoid of gods or devoid of Providence? But in truth they do exist, and they do care for human things, and they have put all the means in man's power to enable him not to fall into real evils. And as to the rest, if there was anything evil, they would have provided for this also, that it should be altogether in a man's power not to fall into it. Now that which does not make a man worse, how can it make a man's life worse? But neither through ignorance, nor having the knowledge, but not the power to guard against or correct these things, is it possible that the nature of the universe has overlooked them; nor is it possible that it has made so great a mistake, either through want of power or want of skill, that good and evil should happen indiscriminately to the good and the bad. But death certainly, and life, honour and dishonour, pain and pleasure, all these things equally happen to good men and bad, being things which make us neither better nor worse. Therefore they are neither good nor evil.

12. How quickly all things disappear, in the universe the bodies themselves, but in time the remembrance of them; what is the nature of all sensible things, and particularly those which attract with the bait of pleasure or terrify by pain, or are noised abroad by vapoury fame; how worthless, and contemptible, and sordid, and perishable, and dead they are—all this it is the part of the intellectual faculty to observe. To observe too who these are whose opinions and voices give reputation; what death is, and the fact that, if a man looks at it in itself, and by the abstractive power of reflection resolves into their parts all the things which present themselves to the imagination in it, he will then consider it to be nothing else than an operation of nature; and if any one is afraid of an operation of nature, he is a child. This, however, is not only an operation of nature, but it is also a thing which conduces to the purposes of nature. To observe too how man comes near to the deity, and by what part of him, and when this part of man is so disposed.

13. Nothing is more wretched than a man who traverses everything in a round, and pries into the things beneath the earth, as the poet[2] says, and seeks by conjecture what is in the minds of his neighbours, without perceiving that it is sufficient to attend to the daemon[3] within

him, and to reverence it sincerely. And reverence of the daemon consists in keeping it pure from passion and thoughtlessness, and dissatisfaction with what comes from gods and men. For the things from the gods merit veneration for their excellence; and the things from men should be dear to us by reason of kinship; and sometimes even, in a manner, they move our pity by reason of men's ignorance of good and bad; this defect being not less than that which deprives us of the power of distinguishing things that are white and black.

14. Though thou shouldst be going to live three thousand years, and as many times ten thousand years, still remember that no man loses any other life than this which he now lives, nor lives any other than this which he now loses. The longest and shortest are thus brought to the same. For the present is the same to all, though that which perishes is not the same; and so that which is lost appears to be a mere moment. For a man cannot lose either the past or the future: for what a man has not, how can any one take this from him? These two things then thou must bear in mind; the one, that all things from eternity are of like forms and come round in a circle, and that it makes no difference whether a man shall see the same things during a hundred years or two hundred, or an infinite time; and the second, that the longest liver and he who will die soonest lose just the same. For the present is the only thing of which a man can be deprived, if it is true that this is the only thing which he has, and that a man cannot lose a thing if he has it not.

15. Remember that all is opinion. For what was said by the Cynic Monimus is manifest: and manifest too is the use of what was said, if a man receives what may be got out of it as far as it is true.

16. The soul of man does violence to itself, first of all, when it becomes an abscess and, as it were, a tumour on the universe, so far as it can. For to be vexed at anything which happens is a separation of ourselves from nature, in some part of which the natures of all other things are contained. In the next place, the soul does violence to itself when it turns away from any man, or even moves towards him with the intention of injuring, such as are the souls of those who are angry. In the third place, the soul does violence to itself when it is overpowered by pleasure or by pain. Fourthly, when it plays a part, and does or says anything insincerely and untruly. Fifthly, when it allows any act of its own and any movement to be without an aim, and does anything thoughtlessly and without considering what it is, it being right that even the smallest things be done with reference to an end; and the end of rational animals is to follow the reason and the law of the most ancient city and polity.

17. Of human life the time is a point, and the substance is in a flux, and the perception dull, and the composition of the whole body subject

to putrefaction, and the soul a whirl, and fortune hard to divine, and fame a thing devoid of judgement. And, to say all in a word, everything which belongs to the body is a stream, and what belongs to the soul is a dream and vapour, and life is a warfare and a stranger's sojourn, and after-fame is oblivion. What then is that which is able to conduct a man? One thing and only one, philosophy. But this consists in keeping the daemon within a man free from violence and unharmed, superior to pains and pleasures, doing nothing without a purpose, nor yet falsely and with hypocrisy, not feeling the need of another man's doing or not doing anything; and besides, accepting all that happens, and all that is allotted, as coming from thence, wherever it is, from whence he himself came; and, finally, waiting for death with a cheerful mind, as being nothing else than a dissolution of the elements of which every living being is compounded. But if there is no harm to the elements themselves in each continually changing into another, why should a man have any apprehension about the change and dissolution of all the elements? For it is according to nature, and nothing is evil which is according to nature.

This in Carnuntum.[4]

BOOK III

We ought to consider not only that our life is daily wasting away and a smaller part of it is left, but another thing also must be taken into the account, that if a man should live longer, it is quite uncertain whether the understanding will still continue sufficient for the comprehension of things, and retain the power of contemplation which strives to acquire the knowledge of the divine and the human. For if he shall begin to fall into dotage, perspiration and nutrition and imagination and appetite, and whatever else there is of the kind, will not fail; but the power of making use of ourselves, and filling up the measure of our duty, and clearly separating all appearances, and considering whether a man should now depart from life, and whatever else of the kind absolutely requires a disciplined reason, all this is already extinguished. We must make haste then, not only because we are daily nearer to death, but also because the conception of things and the understanding of them cease first.

2. We ought to observe also that even the things which follow after the things which are produced according to nature contain something pleasing and attractive. For instance, when bread is baked some parts are split at the surface, and these parts which thus open, and have a certain fashion contrary to the purpose of the baker's art, are beautiful in a manner, and in a peculiar way excite a desire for eating. And again, figs, when they are quite ripe, gape open; and in the ripe olives the very circumstance of their being near to rottenness adds a peculiar beauty to the fruit. And the ears of corn bending down, and the lion's eyebrows, and the foam which flows from the mouth of wild boars, and many other things—though they are far from being beautiful, if a man should examine them severally—still, because they are consequent upon the things which are formed by nature, help to adorn them, and they please the mind; so that if a man should have a feeling and deeper insight with respect to the things which are produced in the universe, there is hardly one of those which follow by way of consequence which will not seem to him to be in a manner disposed so as to give pleasure. And so he will see even the real gaping jaws of wild beasts with no less pleasure than those which painters and sculptors show by imitation; and in an old woman and an old man he will be able to see a certain maturity and comeliness; and the attractive loveliness of young persons he will be able to look on with chaste eyes; and many such things will present

themselves, not pleasing to every man, but to him only who has become truly familiar with nature and her works.

3. Hippocrates after curing many diseases himself fell sick and died. The Chaldaei foretold the deaths of many, and then fate caught them too. Alexander, and Pompeius, and Caius Caesar, after so often completely destroying whole cities, and in battle cutting to pieces many ten thousands of cavalry and infantry, themselves too at last departed from life. Heraclitus, after so many speculations on the conflagration of the universe, was filled with water internally and died smeared all over with mud. And lice destroyed Democritus; and other lice killed Socrates. What means all this? Thou hast embarked, thou hast made the voyage, thou art come to shore; get out. If indeed to another life, there is no want of gods, not even there. But if to a state without sensation, thou wilt cease to be held by pains and pleasures, and to be a slave to the vessel, which is as much inferior as that which serves it is superior: for the one is intelligence and deity; the other is earth and corruption.

4. Do not waste the remainder of thy life in thoughts about others, when thou dost not refer thy thoughts to some object of common utility. For thou losest the opportunity of doing something else when thou hast such thoughts as these, What is such a person doing, and why, and what is he saying, and what is he thinking of, and what is he contriving, and whatever else of the kind makes us wander away from the observation of our own ruling power. We ought then to check in the series of our thoughts everything that is without a purpose and useless, but most of all the overcurious feeling and the malignant; and a man should use himself to think of those things only about which if one should suddenly ask, What hast thou now in thy thoughts? With perfect openness thou mightest, immediately answer, This or That; so that from thy words it should be plain that everything in thee is simple and benevolent, and such as befits a social animal, and one that cares not for thoughts about pleasure or sensual enjoyments at all, nor has any rivalry or envy and suspicion, or anything else for which thou wouldst blush if thou shouldst say that thou hadst it in thy mind. For the man who is such and no longer delays being among the number of the best, is like a priest and minister of the gods, using too the deity which is planted within him, which makes the man uncontaminated by pleasure, unharmed by any pain, untouched by any insult, feeling no wrong, a fighter in the noblest fight, one who cannot be overpowered by any passion, dyed deep with justice, accepting with all his soul everything which happens and is assigned to him as his portion; and not often, nor yet without great necessity and for the general interest, imagining what another says, or does, or thinks. For it is only what belongs to himself that he makes the matter for his activity; and he constantly thinks of

that which is allotted to himself out of the sum total of things, and he makes his own acts fair, and he is persuaded that his own portion is good. For the lot which is assigned to each man is carried along with him and carries him along with it. And he remembers also that every rational animal is his kinsman, and that to care for all men is according to man's nature; and a man should hold on to the opinion not of all, but of those only who confessedly live according to nature. But as to those who live not so, he always bears in mind what kind of men they are both at home and from home, both by night and by day, and what they are, and with what men they live an impure life. Accordingly, he does not value at all the praise which comes from such men, since they are not even satisfied with themselves.

5. Labour not unwillingly, nor without regard to the common interest, nor without due consideration, nor with distraction; nor let studied ornament set off thy thoughts, and be not either a man of many words, or busy about too many things. And further, let the deity which is in thee be the guardian of a living being, manly and of ripe age, and engaged in matter political, and a Roman, and a ruler, who has taken his post like a man waiting for the signal which summons him from life, and ready to go, having need neither of oath nor of any man's testimony. Be cheerful also, and seek not external help nor the tranquillity which others give. A man then must stand erect, not be kept erect by others.

6. If thou findest in human life anything better than justice, truth, temperance, fortitude, and, in a word, anything better than thy own mind's self-satisfaction in the things which it enables thee to do according to right reason, and in the condition that is assigned to thee without thy own choice; if, I say, thou seest anything better than this, turn to it with all thy soul, and enjoy that which thou hast found to be the best. But if nothing appears to be better than the deity which is planted in thee, which has subjected to itself all thy appetites, and carefully examines all the impressions, and, as Socrates said, has detached itself from the persuasions of sense, and has submitted itself to the gods, and cares for mankind; if thou findest everything else smaller and of less value than this, give place to nothing else, for if thou dost once diverge and incline to it, thou wilt no longer without distraction be able to give the preference to that good thing which is thy proper possession and thy own; for it is not right that anything of any other kind, such as praise from the many, or power, or enjoyment of pleasure, should come into competition with that which is rationally and politically or practically good. All these things, even though they may seem to adapt themselves to the better things in a small degree, obtain the superiority all at once, and carry us away. But do thou, I say, simply and freely choose the better, and hold to it.—But that which is useful is the better.—Well

then, if it is useful to thee as a rational being, keep to it; but if it is only useful to thee as an animal, say so, and maintain thy judgement without arrogance: only take care that thou makest the inquiry by a sure method.

7. Never value anything as profitable to thyself which shall compel thee to break thy promise, to lose thy self-respect, to hate any man, to suspect, to curse, to act the hypocrite, to desire anything which needs walls and curtains: for he who has preferred to everything else his own intelligence and daemon and the worship of its excellence, acts no tragic part, does not groan, will not need either solitude or much company; and, what is chief of all, he will live without either pursuing or flying from death; but whether for a longer or a shorter time he shall have the soul inclosed in the body, he cares not at all: for even if he must depart immediately, he will go as readily as if he were going to do anything else which can be done with decency and order; taking care of this only all through life, that his thoughts turn not away from anything which belongs to an intelligent animal and a member of a civil community.

8. In the mind of one who is chastened and purified thou wilt find no corrupt matter, nor impurity, nor any sore skinned over. Nor is his life incomplete when fate overtakes him, as one may say of an actor who leaves the stage before ending and finishing the play. Besides, there is in him nothing servile, nor affected, nor too closely bound to other things, nor yet detached from other things, nothing worthy of blame, nothing which seeks a hiding-place.

9. Reverence the faculty which produces opinion. On this faculty it entirely depends whether there shall exist in thy ruling part any opinion inconsistent with nature and the constitution of the rational animal. And this faculty promises freedom from hasty judgement, and friendship towards men, and obedience to the gods.

10. Throwing away then all things, hold to these only which are few; and besides bear in mind that every man lives only this present time, which is an indivisible point, and that all the rest of his life is either past or it is uncertain. Short then is the time which every man lives, and small the nook of the earth where he lives; and short too the longest posthumous fame, and even this only continued by a succession of poor human beings, who will very soon die, and who know not even themselves, much less him who died long ago.

11. To the aids which have been mentioned let this one still be added: —Make for thyself a definition or description of the thing which is presented to thee, so as to see distinctly what kind of a thing it is in its substance, in its nudity, in its complete entirety, and tell thyself its proper name, and the names of the things of which it has been compounded, and into which it will be resolved. For nothing is so produc-

tive of elevation of mind as to be able to examine methodically and truly every object which is presented to thee in life, and always to look at things so as to see at the same time what kind of universe this is, and what kind of use everything performs in it, and what value everything has with reference to the whole, and what with reference to man, who is a citizen of the highest city, of which all other cities are like families; what each thing is, and of what it is composed, and how long it is the nature of this thing to endure which now makes an impression on me, and what virtue I have need of with respect to it, such as gentleness, manliness, truth, fidelity, simplicity, contentment, and the rest. Wherefore, on every occasion a man should say: this comes from God; and this is according to the apportionment and spinning of the thread of destiny, and such-like coincidence and chance; and this is from one of the same stock, and a kinsman and partner, one who knows not however what is according to his nature. But I know; for this reason I behave towards him according to the natural law of fellowship with benevolence and justice. At the same time however in things indifferent I attempt to ascertain the value of each.

12. If thou workest at that which is before thee, following right reason seriously, vigorously, calmly, without allowing anything else to distract thee, but keeping thy divine part pure, as if thou shouldst be bound to give it back immediately; if thou holdest to this, expecting nothing, fearing nothing, but satisfied with thy present activity according to nature, and with heroic truth in every word and sound which thou utterest, thou wilt live happy. And there is no man who is able to prevent this.

13. As physicians have always their instruments and knives ready for cases which suddenly require their skill, so do thou have principles ready for the understanding of things divine and human, and for doing everything, even the smallest, with a recollection of the bond which unites the divine and human to one another. For neither wilt thou do anything well which pertains to man without at the same time having a reference to things divine; nor the contrary.

14. No longer wander at hazard; for neither wilt thou read thy own memoirs, nor the acts of the ancient Romans and Hellenes, and the selections from books which thou wast reserving for thy old age. Hasten then to the end which thou hast before thee, and, throwing away idle hopes, come to thy own aid, if thou carest at all for thyself, while it is in thy power.

15. They know not how many things are signified by the words stealing, sowing, buying, keeping quiet, seeing what ought to be done; for this is not effected by the eyes, but by another kind of vision.

16. Body, soul, intelligence: to the body belong sensations, to the

soul appetites, to the intelligence principles. To receive the impressions of forms by means of appearances belongs even to animals; to be pulled by the strings of desire belongs both to wild beasts and to men who have made themselves into women, and to a Phalaris and a Nero: and to have the intelligence that guides to the things which appear suitable belongs also to those who do not believe in the gods, and who betray their country, and do their impure deeds when they have shut the doors. If then everything else is common to all that I have mentioned, there remains that which is peculiar to the good man, to be pleased and content with what happens, and with the thread which is spun for him; and not to defile the divinity which is planted in his breast, nor disturb it by a crowd of images, but to preserve it tranquil, following it obediently as a god, neither saying anything contrary to the truth, nor doing anything contrary to justice. And if all men refuse to believe that he lives a simple, modest, and contented life, he is neither angry with any of them, nor does he deviate from the way which leads to the end of life, to which a man ought to come pure, tranquil, ready to depart, and without any compulsion perfectly reconciled to his lot.

BOOK IV

THAT which rules within, when it is according to nature, is so affected with respect to the events which happen, that it always easily adapts itself to that which is possible and is presented to it. For it requires no definite material, but it moves towards its purpose, under certain conditions however; and it makes a material for itself out of that which opposes it, as fire lays hold of what falls into it, by which a small light would have been extinguished: but when the fire is strong, it soon appropriates to itself the matter which is heaped on it, and consumes it, and rises higher by means of this very material.

2. Let no act be done without a purpose, nor otherwise than according to the perfect principles of art.

3. Men seek retreats for themselves, houses in the country, sea-shores, and mountains; and thou too art wont to desire such things very much. But this is altogether a mark of the most common sort of men, for it is in thy power whenever thou shalt choose to retire into thyself. For nowhere either with more quiet or more freedom from trouble does a man retire than into his own soul, particularly when he has within him such thoughts that by looking into them he is immediately in perfect tranquillity; and I affirm that tranquillity is nothing else than the good ordering of the mind. Constantly then give to thyself this retreat, and renew thyself; and let thy principles be brief and fundamental, which, as soon as thou shalt recur to them, will be sufficient to cleanse the soul completely, and to send thee back free from all discontent with the things to which thou returnest. For with what art thou discontented? With the badness of men? Recall to thy mind this conclusion, that rational animals exist for one another, and that to endure is a part of justice, and that men do wrong involuntarily; and consider how many already, after mutual enmity, suspicion, hatred, and fighting, have been stretched dead, reduced to ashes; and be quiet at last.—But perhaps thou art dissatisfied with that which is assigned to thee out of the universe.—Recall to thy recollection this alternative; either there is providence or atoms, fortuitous concurrence of things; or remember the arguments by which it has been proved that the world is a kind of political community, and be quiet at last.—But perhaps corporeal things will still fasten upon thee.—Consider then further that the mind mingles not with the breath, whether moving gently or violently, when it has once drawn itself apart and discovered its own power, and think also of all that thou hast heard and assented to about pain and pleasure, and be quiet at last.—But

perhaps the desire of the thing called fame will torment thee.—See how soon everything is forgotten, and look at the chaos of infinite time on each side of the present, and the emptiness of applause, and the changeableness and want of judgement in those who pretend to give praise, and the narrowness of the space within which it is circumscribed, and be quiet at last. For the whole earth is a point, and how small a nook in it is this thy dwelling, and how few are there in it, and what kind of people are they who will praise thee.

This then remains: Remember to retire into this little territory of thy own, and above all do not distract or strain thyself, but be free, and look at things as a man, as a human being, as a citizen, as a mortal. But among the things readiest to thy hand to which thou shalt turn, let there be these, which are two. One is that things do not touch the soul, for they are external and remain immovable; but our perturbations come only from the opinion which is within. The other is that all these things, which thou seest, change immediately and will no longer be; and constantly bear in mind how many of these changes thou hast already witnessed. The universe is transformation: life is opinion.

4. If our intellectual part is common, the reason also, in respect of which we are rational beings, is common: if this is so, common also is the reason which commands us what to do, and what not to do; if this is so, there is a common law also; if this is so, we are fellow-citizens; if this is so, we are members of some political community; if this is so, the world is in a manner a state. For of what other common political community will any one say that the whole human race are members? And from thence, from this common political community comes also our very intellectual faculty and reasoning faculty and our capacity for law; or whence do they come? For as my earthly part is a portion given to me from certain earth, and that which is watery from another element, and that which is hot and fiery from some peculiar source (for nothing comes out of that which is nothing, as nothing also returns to non-existence), so also the intellectual part comes from some source.

5. Death is such as generation is, a mystery of nature; a composition out of the same elements, and a decomposition into the same; and altogether not a thing of which any man should be ashamed, for it is not contrary to the nature of a reasonable animal, and not contrary to the reason of our constitution.

6. It is natural that these things should be done by such persons, it is a matter of necessity; and if a man will not have it so, he will not allow the fig-tree to have juice. But by all means bear this in mind, that within a very short time both thou and he will be dead; and soon not even your names will be left behind.

7. Take away thy opinion, and then there is taken away the com-

plaint, 'I have been harmed.' Take away the complaint, 'I have been harmed,' and the harm is taken away.

8. That which does not make a man worse than he was, also does not make his life worse, nor does it harm him either from without or from within.

9. The nature of that which is universally useful has been compelled to do this.

10. Consider that everything which happens, happens justly, and if thou observest carefully, thou wilt find it to be so. I do not say only with respect to the continuity of the series of things, but with respect to what is just, and as if it were done by one who assigns to each thing its value. Observe then as thou hast begun; and whatever thou doest, do it in conjunction with this, the being good, and in the sense in which a man is properly understood to be good. Keep to this in every action.

11. Do not have such an opinion of things as he has who does thee wrong, or such as he wishes thee to have, but look at them as they are in truth.

12. A man should always have these two rules in readiness; the one, to do only whatever the reason of the ruling and legislating faculty may suggest for the use of men; the other, to change thy opinion, if there is any one at hand who sets thee right and moves thee from any opinion. But this change of opinion must proceed only from a certain persuasion, as of what is just or of common advantage, and the like, not because it appears pleasant or brings reputation.

13. Hast thou reason? I have.—Why then dost not thou use it? For if this does its own work, what else dost thou wish?

14. Thou hast existed as a part. Thou shalt disappear in that which produced thee; but rather thou shalt be received back into its seminal principle by transmutation.

15. Many grains of frankincense on the same altar: one falls before, another falls after; but it makes no difference.

16. Within ten days thou wilt seem a god to those to whom thou art now a beast and an ape, if thou wilt return to thy principles and the worship of reason.

17. Do not act as if thou wert going to live ten thousand years. Death hangs over thee. While thou livest, while it is in thy power, be good.

18. How much trouble he avoids who does not look to see what his neighbour says or does or thinks, but only to what he does himself, that it may be just and pure; or as Agathon says, look not round at the depraved morals of others, but run straight along the line without deviating from it.

19. He who has a vehement desire for posthumous fame does not consider that every one of those who remember him will himself also

die very soon; then again also they who have succeeded them, until the whole remembrance shall have been extinguished as it is transmitted through men who foolishly admire and perish. But suppose that those who will remember are even immortal, and that the remembrance will be immortal, what then is this to thee? And I say not what is it to the dead, but what is it to the living? What is praise except indeed so far as it has a certain utility? For thou now rejectest unseasonably the gift of nature, clinging to something else . . .[1]

20. Everything which is in any way beautiful is beautiful in itself, and terminates in itself, not having praise as part of itself. Neither worse then nor better is a thing made by being praised. I affirm this also of the things which are called beautiful by the vulgar, for example, material things and works of art. That which is really beautiful has no need of anything; not more than law, not more than truth, not more than benevolence or modesty. Which of these things is beautiful because it is praised, or spoiled by being blamed? Is such a thing as an emerald made worse than it was, if it is not praised? Or gold, ivory, purple, a lyre, a little knife, a flower, a shrub?

21. If souls continue to exist, how does the air contain them from eternity?—But how does the earth contain the bodies of those who have been buried from time so remote? For as here the mutation of these bodies after a certain continuance, whatever it may be, and their dissolution make room for other dead bodies; so the souls which are removed into the air after subsisting for some time are transmuted and diffused, and assume a fiery nature by being received into the seminal intelligence of the universe, and in this way make room for the fresh souls which come to dwell there. And this is the answer which a man might give on the hypothesis of souls continuing to exist. But we must not only think of the number of bodies which are thus buried, but also of the number of animals which are daily eaten by us and the other animals. For what a number is consumed, and thus in a manner buried in the bodies of those who feed on them! And nevertheless this earth receives them by reason of the changes of these bodies into blood, and the transformations into the aërial or the fiery element.

What is the investigation into the truth in this matter? The division into that which is material and that which is the cause of form, the formal.

22. Do not be whirled about, but in every movement have respect to justice, and on the occasion of every impression maintain the faculty of comprehension or understanding.

23. Everything harmonizes with me, which is harmonious to thee, O Universe. Nothing for me is too early nor too late, which is in due time for thee. Everything is fruit to me which thy seasons bring, O

Nature: from thee are all things, in thee are all things, to thee all things return. The poet says, Dear city of Cecrops; and wilt not thou say, Dear city of Zeus?

24. Occupy thyself with few things, says the philosopher, if thou wouldst be tranquil.—But consider if it would not be better to say, Do what is necessary, and whatever the reason of the animal which is naturally social requires, and as it requires. For this brings not only the tranquillity which comes from doing well, but also that which comes from doing few things. For the greatest part of what we say and do being unnecessary, if a man takes this away, he will have more leisure and less uneasiness. Accordingly on every occasion a man should ask himself, Is this one of the unnecessary things? Now a man should take away not only unnecessary acts, but also, unnecessary thoughts, for thus superfluous acts will not follow after.

25. Try how the life of the good man suits thee, the life of him who is satisfied with his portion out of the whole, and satisfied with his own just acts and benevolent disposition.

26. Hast thou seen those things? Look also at these. Do not disturb thyself. Make thyself all simplicity. Does any one do wrong? It is to himself that he does the wrong. Has anything happened to thee? Well; out of the universe from the beginning everything which happens has been apportioned and spun out to thee. In a word, thy life is short. Thou must turn to profit the present by the aid of reason and justice. Be sober in thy relaxation.

27. Either it is a well-arranged universe or a chaos huddled together, but still a universe. But can a certain order subsist in thee, and disorder in the All? And this too when all things are so separated and diffused and sympathetic.

28. A black character, a womanish character, a stubborn character, bestial, childish, animal, stupid, counterfeit, scurrilous, fraudulent, tyrannical.

29. If he is a stranger to the universe who does not know what is in it, no less is he a stranger who does not know what is going on in it. He is a runaway, who flies from social reason; he is blind, who shuts the eyes of the understanding; he is poor, who has need of another, and has not from himself all things which are useful for life. He is an abscess on the universe who withdraws and separates himself from the reason of our common nature through being displeased with the things which happen, for the same nature produces this, and has produced thee too: he is a piece rent asunder from the state, who tears his own soul from that of reasonable animals, which is one.

30. The one is a philosopher without a tunic, and the other without a book: here is another half naked: Bread I have not, he says, and I

abide by reason.—And I do not get the means of living out of my learning, and I abide by my reason.

31. Love the art, poor as it may be, which thou hast learned, and be content with it; and pass through the rest of life like one who has intrusted to the gods with his whole soul all that he has, making thyself neither the tyrant nor the slave of any man.

32. Consider, for example, the times of Vespasian. Thou wilt see all these things, people marrying, bringing up children, sick, dying, warring, feasting, trafficking, cultivating the ground, flattering, obstinately arrogant, suspecting, plotting, wishing for some to die, grumbling about the present, loving, heaping up treasure, desiring counsulship, kingly power. Well then, that life of these people no longer exists at all. Again, remove to the times of Trajan. Again, all is the same. Their life too is gone. In like manner view also the other epochs of time and of whole nations, and see how many after great efforts soon fell and were resolved into the elements. But chiefly thou shouldst think of those whom thou hast thyself known distracting themselves about idle things, neglecting to do what was in accordance with their proper constitution, and to hold firmly to this and to be content with it. And herein it is necessary to remember that the attention given to everything has its proper value and proportion. For thus thou wilt not be dissatisfied, if thou appliest thyself to smaller matters no further than is fit.

33. The words which were formerly familiar are now antiquated: so also the names of those who were famed of old, are now in a manner antiquated, Camillus, Caeso, Volesus, Leonnatus, and a little after also Scipio and Cato, then Augustus, then also Hadrian and Antoninus. For all things soon pass away and become a mere tale, and complete oblivion soon buries them. And I say this of those who have shone in a wondrous way. For the rest, as soon as they have breathed out their breath, they are gone, and no man speaks of them. And, to conclude the matter, what is even an eternal remembrance? A mere nothing. What then is that about which we ought to employ our serious pains? This one thing, thoughts just, and acts social, and words which never lie, and a disposition which gladly accepts all that happens, as necessary, as usual, as flowing from a principle and source of the same kind.

34. Willingly give thyself up to Clotho, one of the Fates, allowing her to spin thy thread into whatever things she pleases.

35. Everything is only for a day, both that which remembers and that which is remembered.

36. Observe constantly that all things take place by change, and accustom thyself to consider that the nature of the Universe loves nothing so much as to change the things which are and to make new things like them. For everything that exists is in a manner the seed of that

which will be. But thou art thinking only of seeds which are cast into the earth or into a womb: but this is a very vulgar notion.

37. Thou wilt soon die, and thou art not yet simple, not free from perturbations, nor without suspicion of being hurt by external things, nor kindly disposed towards all; nor dost thou yet place wisdom only in acting justly.

38. Examine men's ruling principles, even those of the wise, what kind of things they avoid, and what kind they pursue.

39. What is evil to thee does not subsist in the ruling principle of another; nor yet in any turning and mutation of thy corporeal covering. Where is it then? It is in that part of thee in which subsists the power of forming opinions about evils. Let this power then not form such opinions, and all is well. And if that which is nearest to it, the poor body, is cut, burnt, filled with matter and rottenness, nevertheless let the part which forms opinions about these things be quiet, that is, let it judge that nothing is either bad or good which can happen equally to the bad man and the good. For that which happens equally to him who lives contrary to nature and to him who lives according to nature, is neither according to nature nor contrary to nature.

40. Constantly regard the universe as one living being, having one substance and one soul; and observe how all things have reference to one perception, the perception of this one living being; and how all things act with one movement; and how all things are the co-operating causes of all things which exist; observe too the continuous spinning of the thread and the contexture of the web.

41. Thou art a little soul bearing about a corpse, as Epictetus used to say.

42. It is no evil for things to undergo change, and no good for things to subsist in consequence of change.

43. Time is like a river made up of the events which happen, and a violent stream; for as soon as a thing has been seen, it is carried away, and another comes in its place, and this will be carried away too.

44. Everything which happens is as familiar and well known as the rose in spring and the fruit in summer; for such is disease, and death, and calumny, and treachery, and whatever else delights fools or vexes them.

45. In the series of things those which follow are always aptly fitted to those which have gone before; for this series is not like a mere enumeration of disjointed things, which has only a necessary sequence, but it is a rational connection: and as all existing things are arranged together harmoniously, so the things which come into existence exhibit no mere succession, but a certain wonderful relationship.

46. Always remember the saying of Heraclitus, that the death of

earth is to become water, and the death of water is to become air, and the death of air is to become fire, and reversely. And think too of him who forgets whither the way leads, and that men quarrel with that with which they are most constantly in communion, the reason which governs the universe; and the things which they daily meet with seem to them strange: and consider that we ought not to act and speak as if we were asleep, for even in sleep we seem to act and speak; and that we ought not, like children who learn from their parents, simply to act and speak as we have been taught.

47. If any god told thee that thou shalt die to-morrow, or certainly on the day after to-morrow, thou wouldst not care much whether it was on the third day or on the morrow, unless thou wast in the highest degree mean-spirited—for how small is the difference?—so think it no great thing to die after as many years as thou canst name rather than to-morrow.

48. Think continually how many physicians are dead after often contracting their eyebrows over the sick; and how many astrologers after predicting with great pretensions the deaths of others; and how many philosophers after endless discourses on death or immortality; how many heroes after killing thousands; and how many tyrants who have used their power over men's lives with terrible insolence as if they were immortal; and how many cities are entirely dead, so to speak, Helice and Pompeii and Herculaneum, and others innumerable. Add to the reckoning all whom thou hast known, one after another. One man after burying another has been laid out dead, and another buries him: and all this in a short time. To conclude, always observe how ephemeral and worthless human things are, and what was yesterday a little mucus to-morrow will be a mummy or ashes. Pass then through this little space of time conformably to nature, and end thy journey in content, just as an olive falls off when it is ripe, blessing nature who produced it, and thanking the tree on which it grew.

49. Be like the promontory against which the waves continually break, but it stands firm and tames the fury of the water around it.

Unhappy am I, because this has happened to me.—Not so, but happy am I, though this has happened to me, because I continue free from pain, neither crushed by the present nor fearing the future. For such a thing as this might have happened to every man; but every man would not have continued free from pain on such an occasion. Why then is that rather a misfortune than this a good fortune? And dost thou in all cases call that a man's misfortune, which is not a deviation from man's nature? And does a thing seem to thee to be a deviation from man's nature, when it is not contrary to the will of man's nature? Well, thou knowest the will of nature. Will then this which has happened prevent thee from being just, magnanimous, temperate, prudent, secure against inconsiderate opinions and falsehood; will it prevent thee from having modesty, freedom, and everything else, by the presence of which man's nature obtains all that is its own? Remember too on every occasion which leads thee to vexation to apply this principle: not that this is a misfortune, but that to bear it nobly is good fortune.

50. It is a vulgar, but still a useful help towards contempt of death, to pass in review those who have tenaciously stuck to life. What more then have they gained than those who have died early? Certainly they lie in their tombs somewhere at last, Cadicianus, Fabius, Julianus, Lepidus, or any one else like them, who have carried out many to be buried, and then were carried out themselves. Altogether the interval is small between birth and death; and consider with how much trouble, and in company with what sort of people and in what a feeble body this interval is laboriously passed. Do not then consider life a thing of any value. For look to the immensity of time behind thee, and to the time which is before thee, another boundless space. In this infinity then what is the difference between him who lives three days and him who lives three generations?[2]

51. Always run to the short way; and the short way is the natural: accordingly say and do everything in conformity with the soundest reason. For such a purpose frees a man from trouble, and warfare, and all artifice and ostentatious display.

BOOK V

In the morning when thou risest unwillingly, let this thought be present—I am rising to the work of a human being. Why then am I dissatisfied if I am going to do the things for which I exist and for which I was brought into the world? Or have I been made for this, to lie in the bed-clothes and keep myself warm?—But this is more pleasant.—Dost thou exist then to take thy pleasure, and not at all for action or exertion? Dost thou not see the little plants, the little birds, the ants, the spiders, the bees working together to put in order their several parts of the universe? And art thou unwilling to do the work of a human being, and dost thou not make haste to do that which is according to thy nature?—But it is necessary to take rest also.—It is necessary: however nature has fixed bounds to this too: she has fixed bounds both to eating and drinking, and yet thou goest beyond these bounds, beyond what is sufficient; yet in thy acts it is not so, but thou stoppest short of what thou canst do. So thou lovest not thyself, for if thou didst, thou wouldst love thy nature and her will. But those who love their several arts exhaust themselves in working at them unwashed and without food; but thou valuest thy own nature less than the turner values the turning art, or the dancer the dancing art, or the lover of money values his money, or the vainglorious man his little glory. And such men, when they have a violent affection to a thing, choose neither to eat nor to sleep rather than to perfect the things which they care for. But are the acts which concern society more vile in thy eyes and less worthy of thy labour?

2. How easy it is to repel and to wipe away every impression which is troublesome or unsuitable, and immediately to be in all tranquillity.

3. Judge every word and deed which are according to nature to be fit for thee; and be not diverted by the blame which follows from any people nor by their words, but if a thing is good to be done or said, do not consider it unworthy of thee. For those persons have their peculiar leading principle and follow their peculiar movement; which things do not thou regard, but go straight on, following thy own nature and the common nature; and the way of both is one.

4. I go through the things which happen according to nature until I shall fall and rest, breathing out my breath into that element out of which I daily draw it in, and falling upon that earth out of which my father collected the seed, and my mother the blood, and my nurse the milk; out of which during so many years I have been supplied with food

and drink; which bears me when I tread on it and abuse it for so many purposes.

5. Thou sayest, Men cannot admire the sharpness of thy wits.—Be it so: but there are many other things of which thou canst not say, I am not formed for them by nature. Show those qualities then which are altogether in thy power, sincerity, gravity, endurance of labour, aversion to pleasure, contentment with thy portion and with few things, benevolence, frankness, no love of superfluity, freedom from trifling magnanimity. Dost thou not see how many qualities thou art immediately able to exhibit, in which there is no excuse of natural incapacity and unfitness, and yet thou still remainest voluntarily below the mark? Or art thou compelled through being defectively furnished by nature to murmur, and to be stingy, and to flatter, and to find fault with thy poor body, and to try to please men, and to make great display, and to be so restless in thy mind? No, by the gods: but thou mightest have been delivered from these things long ago. Only if in truth thou canst be charged with being rather slow and dull of comprehension, thou must exert thyself about this also, not neglecting it nor yet taking pleasure in thy dulness.

6. One man, when he has done a service to another, is ready to set it down to his account as a favour conferred. Another is not ready to do this, but still in his own mind he thinks of the man as his debtor, and he knows what he has done. A third in a manner does not even know what he has done, but he is like a vine which has produced grapes, and seeks for nothing more after it has once produced its proper fruit. As a horse when he has run, a dog when he has tracked the game, a bee when it has made the honey, so a man when he has done a good act, does not call out for others to come and see, but he goes on to another act, as a vine goes on to produce again the grapes in season.—Must a man then be one of these, who in a manner act thus without observing it? —Yes.—But this very thing is necessary, the observation of what a man is doing: for, it may be said, it is characteristic of the social animal to perceive that he is working in a social manner, and indeed to wish that his social partner also should perceive it.—It is true what thou sayest, but thou dost not rightly understand what is now said: and for this reason thou wilt become one of those of whom I spoke before, for even they are misled by a certain show of reason. But if thou wilt choose to understand the meaning of what is said, do not fear that for this reason thou wilt omit any social act.

7. A prayer of the Athenians: Rain, rain, O dear Zeus, down on the ploughed fields of the Athenians and on the plains.—In truth we ought not to pray at all, or we ought to pray in this simple and noble fashion.

8. Just as we must understand when it is said, That Aesculapius

prescribed to this man horse-exercise, or bathing in cold water or going without shoes; so we must understand it when it is said, That the nature of the universe prescribed to this man disease or mutilation or loss or anything else of the kind. For in the first case Prescribed means something like this: he prescribed this for this man as a thing adapted to procure health; and in the second case it means: That which happens to (or, suits) every man is fixed in a manner for him suitably to his destiny. For this is what we mean when we say that things are suitable to us, as the workmen say of squared stones in walls or the pyramids, that they are suitable, when they fit them to one another in some kind of connexion. For there is altogether one fitness, harmony. And as the universe is made up out of all bodies to be such a body as it is, so out of all existing causes necessity (destiny) is made up to be such a cause as it is. And even those who are completely ignorant understand what I mean, for they say, It (necessity, destiny) brought this to such a person.—This then was brought and this was prescribed to him. Let us then receive these things, as well as those which Aesculapius prescribes. Many as a matter of course even among his prescriptions are disagreeable, but we accept them in the hope of health. Let the perfecting and accomplishment of the things, which the common nature judges to be good, be judged by thee to be of the same kind as thy health. And so accept everything which happens, even if it seem disagreeable, because it leads to this, to the health of the universe and to the prosperity and felicity of Zeus (the universe). For he would not have brought on any man what he has brought, if it were not useful for the whole. Neither does the nature of anything, whatever it may be, cause anything which is not suitable to that which is directed by it. For two reasons then it is right to be content with that which happens to thee; the one, because it was done for thee and prescribed for thee, and in a manner had reference to thee, originally from the most ancient causes spun with thy destiny; and the other, because even that which comes severally to every man is to the power which administers the universe a cause of felicity and perfection, nay even of its very continuance. For the integrity of the whole is mutilated, if thou cuttest off anything whatever from the conjunction and the continuity either of the parts or of the causes. And thou dost cut off, as far as it is in thy power, when thou art dissatisfied, and in a manner triest to put anything out of the way.

9. Be not disgusted, nor discouraged, nor dissatisfied, if thou dost not succeed in doing everything according to right principles; but when thou hast failed, return back again, and be content if the greater part of what thou doest is consistent with man's nature, and love this to which thou returnest; and do not return to philosophy as if she were a master, but act like those who have sore eyes and apply a bit of sponge

and egg, or as another applies a plaster, or drenching with water. For thus thou wilt not fail to obey reason, and thou wilt repose in it. And remember that philosophy requires only the things which thy nature requires; but thou wouldst have something else which is not according to nature.—It may be objected, Why what is more agreeable than this which I am doing?—But is not this the very reason why pleasure deceives us? And consider if magnanimity, freedom, simplicity, equanimity, piety, are not more agreeable. For what is more agreeable than wisdom itself, when thou thinkest of the security and the happy course of all things which depend on the faculty of understanding and knowledge?

10. Things are in such a kind of envelopment that they have seemed to philosophers, not a few nor those common philosophers, altogether unintelligible; nay even to the Stoics themselves they seem difficult to understand. And all our assent is changeable; for where is the man who never changes? Carry thy thoughts then to the objects themselves, and consider how short-lived they are and worthless, and that they may be in the possession of a filthy wretch or a whore or a robber. Then turn to the morals of those who live with thee, and it is hardly possible to endure even the most agreeable of them, to say nothing of a man being hardly able to endure himself. In such darkness then and dirt and in so constant a flux both of substance and of time, and of motion and of things moved, what there is worth being highly prized or even an object of serious pursuit, I cannot imagine. But on the contrary it is a man's duty to comfort himself, and to wait for the natural dissolution and not to be vexed at the delay, but to rest in these principles only: the one, that nothing will happen to me which is not conformable to the nature of the universe; and the other, that it is in my power never to act contrary to my god and daemon: for there is no man who will compel me to this.

11. About what am I now employing my own soul? On every occasion I must ask myself this question, and inquire, what have I now in this part of me which they call the ruling principle? And whose soul have I now? That of a child, or of a young man, or of a feeble woman, or of a tyrant, or of a domestic animal, or of a wild beast?

12. What kind of things those are which appear good to the many, we may learn even from this. For if any man should conceive certain things as being really good, such as prudence, temperance, justice, fortitude, he would not after having first conceived these endure to listen to anything which should not be in harmony with what is really good. But if a man has first conceived as good the things which appear to the many to be good, he will listen and readily receive as very applicable that which was said by the comic writer. Thus even the many perceive the difference. For were it not so, this saying would not offend and

would not be rejected in the first case, while we receive it when it is said of wealth, and of the means which further luxury and fame, as said fitly and wittily. Go on then and ask if we should value and think those things to be good, to which after their first conception in the mind the words of the comic writer might be aptly applied—that he who has them, through pure abundance has not a place to ease himself in.[1]

13. I am composed of the formal and the material; and neither of them will perish into non-existence, as neither of them came into existence out of non-existence. Every part of me then will be reduced by change into some part of the universe, and that again will change into another part of the universe, and so on for ever. And by consequence of such a change I too exist, and those who begot me, and so on for ever in the other direction. For nothing hinders us from saying so, even if the universe is administered according to definite periods of revolution.

14. Reason and the reasoning art (philosophy) are powers which are sufficient for themselves and for their own works. They move then from a first principle which is their own, and they make their way to the end which is proposed to them; and this is the reason why such acts are named *catorthôseis* or right acts, which word signifies that they proceed by the right road.

15. None of these things ought to be called a man's, which do not belong to a man, as man. They are not required of a man, nor does man's nature promise them, nor are they the means of man's nature attaining its end. Neither then does the end of man lie in these things, nor yet that which aids to the accomplishment of this end, and that which aids towards this end is that which is good. Besides, if any of these things did belong to man, it would not be right for a man to despise them and to set himself against them; nor would a man be worthy of praise who showed that he did not want these things, nor would he who stinted himself in any of them be good, if indeed these things were good. But now the more of these things a man deprives himself of, or of other things like them, or even when he is deprived of any of them, the more patiently he endures the loss, just in the same degree he is a better man.

16. Such as are thy habitual thoughts, such also will be the character of thy mind; for the soul is dyed by the thoughts. Dye it then with a continuous series of such thoughts as these: for instance, that where a man can live, there he can also live well. But he must live in a palace;—well then, he can also live well in a palace. And again, consider that for whatever purpose each thing has been constituted, for this it has been constituted, and towards this it is carried, and its end is in that towards which it is carried; and where the end is, there also is the advantage and the good of each thing. Now the good for the reasonable animal is

society; for that we are made for society has been shown above.[2] Is it not plain that the inferior exist for the sake of the superior? But the things which have life are superior to those which have not life, and of those which have life the superior are those which have reason.

17. To seek what is impossible is madness: and it is impossible that the bad should not do something of this kind.

18. Nothing happens to any man which he is not formed by nature to bear. The same things happen to another, and either because he does not see that they have happened or because he would show a great spirit he is firm and remains unharmed. It is a shame then that ignorance and conceit should be stronger than wisdom.

19. Things themselves touch not the soul, not in the least degree; nor have they admission to the soul, nor can they turn or move the soul: but the soul turns and moves itself alone, and whatever judgements it may think proper to make, such it makes for itself the things which present themselves to it.

20. In one respect man is the nearest thing to me, so far as I must do good to men and endure them. But so far as some men make themselves obstacles to my proper acts, man becomes to me one of the things which are indifferent, no less than the sun or wind or a wild beast. Now it is true that these may impede my action, but they are no impediments to my affects and disposition, which have the power of acting conditionally and changing: for the mind converts and changes every hindrance to its activity into an aid; and so that which is a hindrance is made a furtherance to an act; and that which is an obstacle on the road helps us on this road.

21. Reverence that which is best in the universe; and this is that which makes use of all things and directs all things. And in like manner also reverence that which is best in thyself; and this is of the same kind as that. For in thyself also, that which makes use of everything else, is this, and thy life is directed by this.

22. That which does no harm to the state, does no harm to the citizen. In the case of every appearance of harm apply this rule: if the state is not harmed by this, neither am I harmed. But if the state is harmed, thou must not be angry with him who does harm to the state. Show him where his error is.

23. Often think of the rapidity with which things pass by and disappear, both the things which are and the things which are produced. For substance is like a river in a continual flow, and the activities of things are in constant change, and the causes work in infinite varieties; and there is hardly anything which stands still. And consider this which is near to thee, this boundless abyss of the past and of the future in which all things disappear. How then is he not a fool who is puffed

up with such things or plagued about them and makes himself miserable? for they vex him only for a time, and a short time.

24. Think of the universal substance, of which thou hast a very small portion; and of universal time, of which a short and indivisible interval has been assigned to thee; and of that which is fixed by destiny, and how small a part of it thou art.

25. Does another do me wrong? Let him look to it. He has his own disposition, his own activity. I now have what the universal nature wills me to have; and I do what my nature now wills me to do.

26. Let the part of thy soul which leads and governs be undisturbed by the movements in the flesh, whether of pleasure or of pain; and let it not unite with them, but let it circumscribe itself and limit those affects to their parts. But when these affects rise up to the mind by virtue of that other sympathy that naturally exists in a body which is all one, then thou must not strive to resist the sensation, for it is natural: but let not the ruling part of itself add to the sensation the opinion that it is either good or bad.

27. Live with the gods. And he does live with the gods who constantly shows to them that his own soul is satisfied with that which is assigned to him, and that it does all that the daemon wishes, which Zeus hath given to every man for his guardian and guide, a portion of himself. And this is every man's understanding and reason.

28. Art thou angry with him whose arm-pits stink? Art thou angry with him whose mouth smells foul? What good will this danger do thee? He has such a mouth, he has such arm-pits: it is necessary that such an emanation must come from such things—but the man has reason, it will be said, and he is able, if he takes pains, to discover wherein he offends —I wish thee well of thy discovery. Well then, and thou hast reason: by thy rational faculty stir up his rational faculty; show him his error, admonish him. For if he listens, thou wilt cure him, and there is no need of anger. Neither tragic actor nor whore.[3]

29. As thou intendest to live when thou art gone out, . . . so it is in thy power to live here. But if men do not permit thee, then get away out of life, yet so as if thou wert suffering no harm. The house is smoky, and I quit it.[4] Why dost thou think that this is any trouble? But so long as nothing of the kind drives me out, I remain, am free, and no man shall hinder me from doing what I choose; and I choose to do what is according to the nature of the rational and social animal.

30. The intelligence of the universe is social. Accordingly it has made the inferior things for the sake of the superior, and it has fitted the superior to one another. Thou seest how it has subordinated, co-ordinated and assigned to everything its proper portion, and has brought together into concord with one another the things which are the best.

31. How hast thou behaved hitherto to the gods, thy parents, brethren, children, teachers, to those who looked after thy infancy, to thy friends, kinsfolk, to thy slaves? Consider if thou hast hitherto behaved to all in such a way that this may be said of thee:

Never has wronged a man in deed or word.[5]

And call to recollection both how many things thou hast passed through, and how many things thou hast been able to endure: and that the history of thy life is now complete and thy service is ended: and how many beautiful things thou hast seen: and how many pleasures and pains thou hast despised; and how many things called honourable thou hast spurned; and to how many ill-minded folks thou hast shown a kind disposition.

32. Why do unskilled and ignorant souls disturb him who has skill and knowledge? What soul then has skill and knowledge? That which knows beginning and end, and knows the reason which pervades all substance and through all time by fixed periods (revolutions) administers the universe.

33. Soon, very soon, thou wilt be ashes, or a skeleton, and either a name or not even a name; but name is sound and echo. And the things which are much valued in life are empty and rotten and trifling, and like little dogs biting one another, and little children quarrelling, laughing, and then straightway weeping. But fidelity and modesty and justice and truth are fled

Up to Olympus from the wide-spread earth.[6]

What then is there which still detains thee here? If the objects of sense are easily changed and never stand still, and the organs of perception are dull and easily receive false impressions; and the poor soul itself is an exhalation from blood. But to have good repute amidst such a world as this is an empty thing. Why then dost thou not wait in tranquillity for thy end, whether it is extinction or removal to another state? And until that time comes, what is sufficient? Why, what else than to venerate the gods and bless them, and to do good to men, and to practise tolerance and self-restraint; [7] but as to everything which is beyond the limits of the poor flesh and breath, to remember that this is neither thine nor in thy power.

34. Thou canst pass thy life in an equable flow of happiness, if thou canst go by the right way, and think and act in the right way. These two things are common both to the soul of God and to the soul of man, and to the soul of every rational being, not to be hindered by another; and to hold good to consist in the disposition to justice and the practice of it, and in this to let thy desire find its termination.

35. If this is neither my own badness, nor an effect of my own badness, and the common weal is not injured, why am I troubled about it? And what is the harm to the common weal?

36. Do not be carried along inconsiderately by the appearance of things, but give help to all according to thy ability and their fitness; and if they should have sustained loss in matters which are indifferent, do not imagine this to be a damage. For it is a bad habit. But as the old man, when he went away, asked back his foster-child's top, remembering that it was a top, so do thou in this case also.

When thou art calling out on the Rostra, hast thou forgotten, man, what these things are?—Yes; but they are objects of great concern to these people—wilt thou too then be made a fool for these things?—I was once a fortunate man, but I lost it, I know not how.—But fortunate means that a man has assigned to himself a good fortune: and a good fortune is good disposition of the soul, good emotions, good actions.[8]

BOOK VI

THE substance of the universe is obedient and compliant; and the reason which governs it has in itself no cause for doing evil, for it has no malice, nor does it do evil to anything, nor is anything harmed by it. But all things are made and perfected according to this reason.

2. Let it make no difference to thee whether thou art cold or warm, if thou art doing thy duty; and whether thou art drowsy or satisfied with sleep; and whether ill-spoken of or praised; and whether dying or doing something else. For it is one of the acts of life, this act by which we die: it is sufficient then in this act also to do well what we have in hand.

3. Look within. Let neither the peculiar quality of anything nor its value escape thee.

4. All existing things soon change, and they will either be reduced to vapour, if indeed all substance is one, or they will be dispersed.

5. The reason which governs knows what its own disposition is, and what it does, and on what material it works.

6. The best way of avenging thyself is not to become like the wrong doer.

7. Take pleasure in one thing and rest in it, in passing from one social act to another social act, thinking of God.

8. The ruling principle is that which rouses and turns itself, and while it makes itself such as it is and such as it wills to be, it also makes everything which happens appear to itself to be such as it wills.

9. In conformity to the nature of the universe every single thing is accomplished, for certainly it is not in conformity to any other nature that each thing is accomplished, either a nature which externally comprehends this, or a nature which is comprehended within this nature, or a nature external and independent of this.

10. The universe is either a confusion, and a mutual involution of things, and a dispersion; or it is unity and order and providence. If then it is the former, why do I desire to tarry in a fortuitous combination of things and such a disorder? And why do I care about anything else than how I shall at last become earth? And why am I disturbed, for the dispersion of my elements will happen whatever I do. But if the other supposition is true, I venerate, and I am firm, and I trust in him who governs.

11. When thou hast been compelled by circumstances to be disturbed in a manner, quickly return to thyself and do not continue out

of tune longer than the compulsion lasts; for thou wilt have more mastery over the harmony by continually recurring to it.

12. If thou hadst a step-mother and a mother at the same time, thou wouldst be dutiful to thy step-mother, but still thou wouldst constantly return to thy mother. Let the court and philosophy now be to thee step-mother and mother: return to philosophy frequently and repose in her, through whom what thou meetest with in the court appears to thee tolerable, and thou appearest tolerable in the court.

13. When we have meat before us and such eatables, we receive the impression, that this is the dead body of a fish, and this is the dead body of a bird or of a pig; and again, that this Falernian is only a little grape juice, and this purple robe some sheep's wool dyed with the blood of a shell-fish: such then are these impressions, and they reach the things themselves and penetrate them, and so we see what kind of things they are. Just in the same way ought we to act all through life, and where there are things which appear most worthy of our approbation, we ought to lay them bare and look at their worthlessness and strip them of all the words by which they are exalted. For outward show is a wonderful perverter of the reason, and when thou art most sure that thou art employed about things worth thy pains, it is then that it cheats thee most. Consider then what Crates says of Xenocrates himself.

14. Most of the things which the multitude admire are referred to objects of the most general kind, those which are held together by cohesion or natural organization, such as stones, wood, fig-trees, vines, olives. But those which are admired by men who are a little more reasonable are referred to the things which are held together by a living principle, as flocks, herds. Those which are admired by men who are still more instructed are the things which are held together by a rational soul, not however a universal soul, but rational so far as it is a soul skilled in some art, or expert in some other way, or simply rational so far as it possesses a number of slaves. But he who values a rational soul, a soul universal and fitted for political life, regards nothing else except this; and above all things he keeps his soul in a condition and in an activity conformable to reason and social life, and he co-operates to this end with those who are of the same kind as himself.

15. Some things are hurrying into existence, and others are hurrying out of it; and of that which is coming into existence part is already extinguished. Motions and changes are continually renewing the world, just as the uninterrupted course of time is always renewing the infinite duration of ages. In this flowing stream then, on which there is no abiding, what is there of the things which hurry by on which a man would set a high price? It would be just as if a man should fall in love with one of the sparrows which fly by, but it has already passed out of

sight. Something of this kind is the very life of every man, like the exhalation of the blood and the respiration of the air. For such as it is to have once drawn in the air and to have given it back, which we do every moment, just the same is it with the whole respiratory power, which thou didst receive at thy birth yesterday and the day before, to give it back to the element from which thou didst first draw it.

16. Neither is transpiration, as in plants, a thing to be valued, nor respiration, as in domesticated animals and wild beasts, nor the receiving of impressions by the appearances of things, nor being moved by desires as puppets by strings, nor assembling in herds, nor being nourished by food; for this is just like the act of separating and parting with the useless part of our food. What then is worth being valued? To be received with clapping of hands? No. Neither must we value the clapping of tongues, for the praise which comes from the many is a clapping of tongues. Suppose then that thou hast given up this worthless thing called fame, what remains that is worth valuing? This in my opinion, to move thyself and to restrain thyself in conformity to thy proper constitution, to which end both all employments and arts lead. For every art aims at this, that the thing which has been made should be adapted to the work for which it has been made; and both the vine-planter who looks after the vine, and the horse-breaker, and he who trains the dog, seek this end. But the education and the teaching of youth aim at something. In this then is the value of the education and the teaching. And if this is well, thou wilt not seek anything else. Wilt thou not cease to value many other things too? Then thou wilt be neither free, nor sufficient for thy own happiness, nor without passion. For of necessity thou must be envious, jealous, and suspicious of those who can take away those things, and plot against those who have that which is valued by thee. Of necessity a man must be altogether in a state of perturbation who wants any of these things; and besides, he must often find fault with the gods. But to reverence and honour thy own mind will make thee content with thyself, and in harmony with society, and in agreement with the gods, that is, praising all that they give and have ordered.

17. Above, below, all around are the movements of the elements. But the motion of virtue is in none of these: it is something more divine, and advancing by a way hardly observed it goes happily on its road.

18. How strangely men act. They will not praise those who are living at the same time and living with themselves; but to be themselves praised by posterity, by those whom they have never seen or ever will see, this they set much value on. But this is very much the same as if thou shouldst be grieved because those who have lived before thee did not praise thee.

19. If a thing is difficult to be accomplished by thyself, do not think

that it is impossible for man: but if anything is possible for man and conformable to his nature, think that this can be attained by thyself too.

20. In the gymnastic exercises suppose that a man has torn thee with his nails, and by dashing against thy head has inflicted a wound. Well, we neither show any signs of vexation, nor are we offended, nor do we suspect him afterwards as a treacherous fellow; and yet we are on our guard against him, not however as an enemy, nor yet with suspicion, but we quietly get out of his way. Something like this let thy behaviour be in all the other parts of life; let us overlook many things in those who are like antagonists in the gymnasium. For it is in our power, as I said, to get out of the way, and to have no suspicion nor hatred.

21. If any man is able to convince me and show me that I do not think or act right, I will gladly change; for I seek the truth by which no man was ever injured. But he is injured who abides in his error and ignorance.

22. I do my duty: other things trouble me not; for they are either things without life, or things without reason, or things that have rambled and know not the way.

23. As to the animals which have no reason and generally all things and objects, do thou, since thou hast reason and they have none, make use of them with a generous and liberal spirit. But towards human beings, as they have reason, behave in a social spirit. And on all occasions call on the gods, and do not perplex thyself about the length of time in which thou shalt do this; for even three hours so spent are sufficient.

24. Alexander the Macedonian and his groom by death were brought to the same state; for either they were received among the same seminal principles of the universe, or they were alike dispersed among the atoms.

25. Consider how many things in the same indivisible time take place in each of us, things which concern the body and things which concern the soul: and so thou wilt not wonder if many more things, or rather all things which come into existence in that which is the one and all, which we call Cosmos, exist in it at the same time.

26. If any man should propose to thee the question, how the name Antoninus is written, wouldst thou with a straining of the voice utter each letter? What then if they grow angry, wilt thou be angry too? Wilt thou not go on with composure and number every letter? Just so then in this life also remember that every duty is made up of certain parts. These it is thy duty to observe and without being disturbed or showing anger towards those who are angry with thee to go on thy way and finish that which is set before thee.

27. How cruel it is not to allow men to strive after the things which

appear to them to be suitable to their nature and profitable! And yet in a manner thou dost not allow them to do this, when thou art vexed because they do wrong. For they are certainly moved towards things because they suppose them to be suitable to their nature and profitable to them.—But it is not so.—Teach them then, and show them without being angry.

28. Death is a cessation of the impressions through the senses, and of the pulling of the strings which move the appetites, and of the discursive movements of the thoughts, and of the service to the flesh.

29. It is a shame for the soul to be first to give way in this life, when thy body does not give way.

30. Take care that thou art not made into a Caesar, that thou art not dyed with this dye; for such things happen. Keep thyself then simple, good, pure, serious, free from affectation, a friend of justice, a worshipper of the gods, kind, affectionate, strenuous in all proper acts. Strive to continue to be such as philosophy wished to make thee. Reverence the gods, and help men. Short is life. There is only one fruit of this terrene life, a pious disposition and social acts. Do everything as a disciple of Antoninus. Remember his constancy in every act which was conformable to reason, and his evenness in all things, and his piety, and the serenity of his countenance, and his sweetness, and his disregard of empty fame, and his efforts to understand things; and how he would never let anything pass without having first most carefully examined it and clearly understood it; and how he bore with those who blamed him unjustly without blaming them in return; how he did nothing in a hurry; and how he listened not to calumnies, and how exact an examiner of manners and actions he was; and not given to reproach people, nor timid, nor suspicious, nor a sophist; and with how little he was satisfied, such as lodging, bed, dress, food, servants; and how laborious and patient; and how he was able on account of his sparing diet to hold out to the evening, not even requiring to relieve himself by any evacuations except at the usual hour; and his firmness and uniformity in his friendships; and how he tolerated freedom of speech in those who opposed his opinions; and the pleasure that he had when any man showed him anything better; and how religious he was without superstition. Imitate all this that thou mayest have as good a conscience, when thy last hour comes, as he had.

31. Return to thy sober senses and call thyself back; and when thou hast roused thyself from sleep and hast perceived that they were only dreams which troubled thee, now in thy waking hours look at these (the things about thee) as thou didst look at those (the dreams).

32. I consist of a little body and a soul. Now to this little body all things are indifferent, for it is not able to perceive differences. But to

the understanding those things only are indifferent, which are not the works of its own activity. But whatever things are the works of its own activity, all these are in its power. And of these however only those which are done with reference to the present; for as to the future and the past activities of the mind, even these are for the present indifferent.

33. Neither the labour which the hand does nor that of the foot is contrary to nature, so long as the foot does the foot's work and the hand the hand's. So then neither to a man as a man is his labour contrary to nature, so long as it does the things of a man. But if the labour is not contrary to his nature, neither is it an evil to him.

34. How many pleasures have been enjoyed by robbers, patricides, tyrants.

35. Dost thou not see how the handicraftsmen accommodate themselves up to a certain point to those who are not skilled in their craft—nevertheless they cling to the reason (the principles) of their art and do not endure to depart from it? Is it not strange if the architect and the physician shall have more respect to the reason (the principles) of their own arts than man to his own reason, which is common to him and the gods?

36. Asia, Europe are corners of the universe: all the sea a drop in the universe; Athos a little clod of the universe: all the present time is a point in eternity. All things are little, changeable, perishable. All things come from thence, from that universal ruling power either directly proceeding or by way of sequence. And accordingly the lion's gaping jaws, and that which is poisonous, and every harmful thing, as a thorn, as mud, are after-products of the grand and beautiful. Do not then imagine that they are of another kind from that which thou dost venerate, but form a just opinion of the source of all.

37. He who has seen present things has seen all, both everything which has taken place from all eternity and everything which will be for time without end; for all things are of one kin and of one form.

38. Frequently consider the connexion of all things in the universe and their relation to one another. For in a manner all things are implicated with one another, and all in this way are friendly to one another; for one thing comes in order after another, and this is by virtue of the active movement and mutual conspiration and the unity of the substance.

39. Adapt thyself to the things with which thy lot has been cast: and the men among whom thou hast received thy portion, love them, but do it truly, sincerely.

40. Every instrument, tool, vessel, if it does that for which it has been made, is well, and yet he who made it is not there. But in the things which are held together by nature there is within and there

abides in them the power which made them; wherefore the more is it fit to reverence this power, and to think, that, if thou dost live and act according to its will, everything in thee is in conformity to intelligence. And thus also in the universe the things which belong to it are in conformity to intelligence.

41. Whatever of the things which are not within thy power thou shalt suppose to be good for thee or evil, it must of necessity be that, if such a bad thing befall thee or the loss of such a good thing, thou wilt blame the gods, and hate men too, those who are the cause of the misfortune or the loss, or those who are suspected of being likely to be the cause; and indeed we do much injustice, because we make a difference between these things. But if we judge only those things which are in our power to be good or bad, there remains no reason either for finding fault with God or standing in a hostile attitude to man.

42. We are all working together to one end, some with knowledge and design, and others without knowing what they do; as men also when they are asleep, of whom it is Heraclitus, I think, who says that they are labourers and co-operators in the things which take place in the universe. But men co-operate after different fashions: and even those co-operate abundantly, who find fault with what happens and those who try to oppose it and to hinder it; for the universe had need even of such men as these. It remains then for thee to understand among what kind of workmen thou placest thyself; for he who rules all things will certainly make a right use of thee, and he will receive thee among some part of the co-operators and of those whose labours conduce to one end. But be not thou such a part as the mean and ridiculous verse in the play, which Chrysippus speaks of.[1]

43. Does the sun undertake to do the work of the rain, or Aesculapius the work of the Fruit-bearer (the earth)? And how is it with respect to each of the stars, are they not different and yet they work together to the same end?

44. If the gods have determined about me and about the things which must happen to me, they have determined well, for it is not easy even to imagine a deity without forethought; and as to doing me harm, why should they have any desire towards that? For what advantage would result to them from this or to the whole, which is the special object of their providence? But if they have not determined about me individually, they have certainly determined about the whole at least, and the things which happen by way of sequence in this general arrangement I ought to accept with pleasure and to be content with them. But if they determine about nothing—which it is wicked to believe, or if we do believe it, let us neither sacrifice nor pray nor swear by them nor do anything else which we do as if the gods were present and lived with

us--but if however the gods determine about none of the things which concern us, I am able to determine about myself, and I can inquire about that which is useful; and that is useful to every man which is conformable to his own constitution and nature. But my nature is rational and social; and my city and country, so far as I am Antoninus, is Rome, but so far as I am a man, it is the world. The things then which are useful to these cities are alone useful to me.

45. Whatever happens to every man, this is for the interest of the universal: this might be sufficient. But further thou wilt observe this also as a general truth, if thou dost observe, that whatever is profitable to any man is profitable also to other men. But let the word profitable be taken here in the common sense as said of things of the middle kind, neither good nor bad.

46. As it happens to thee in the amphitheatre and such places, that the continual sight of the same things and the uniformity make the spectacle wearisome, so it is in the whole of life; for all things above, below, are the same and from the same. How long then?

47. Think continually that all kinds of men and of all kinds of pursuits and of all nations are dead, so that thy thoughts come down even to Philistion and Phoebus and Origanion. Now turn thy thoughts to the other kinds of men. To that place then we must remove, where there are so many great orators, and so many noble philosophers, Heraclitus, Pythagoras, Socrates; so many heroes of former days, and so many generals after them, and tyrants; besides these, Eudoxus, Hipparchus, Archimedes, and other men of acute natural talents, great minds, lovers of labour, versatile, confident, mockers even of the perishable and ephemeral life of man, as Menippus and such as are like him. As to all these consider that they have long been in the dust. What harm then is this to them; and what to those whose names are altogether unknown? One thing here is worth a great deal, to pass thy life in truth and justice, with a benevolent disposition even to liars and unjust men.

48. When thou wishest to delight thyself, think of the virtues of those who live with thee; for instance, the activity of one, and the modesty of another, and the liberality of a third, and some other good quality of a fourth. For nothing delights so much as the examples of the virtues, when they are exhibited in the morals of those who live with us and present themselves in abundance, as far as is possible. Wherefore we must keep them before us.

49. Thou art not dissatisfied, I suppose, because thou weighest only so many litrae and not three hundred. Be not dissatisfied then that thou must live only so many years and not more; for as thou art satisfied with the amount of substance which has been assigned to thee, so be content with the time.

50. Let us try to persuade them (men). But act even against their will, when the principles of justice lead that way. If however any man by using force stands in thy way, betake thyself to contentment and tranquillity, and at the same time employ the hindrance towards the exercise of some other virtue; and remember that thy attempt was with a reservation, that thou didst not desire to do impossibilities. What then didst thou desire?—Some such effort as this.—But thou attainest thy object, if the things to which thou wast moved are accomplished.

51. He who loves fame considers another man's activity to be his own good; and he who loves pleasure, his own sensations; but he who has understanding, considers his own acts to be his own good.

52. It is in our power to have no opinion about a thing, and not to be disturbed in our soul; for things themselves have no natural power to form our judgements.

53. Accustom thyself to attend carefully to what is said by another, and as much as it is possible, be in the speaker's mind.

54. That which is not good for the swarm, neither is it good for the bee.

55. If sailors abused the helmsman or the sick the doctor, would they listen to anybody else; or how could the helmsman secure the safety of those in the ship or the doctor the health of those whom he attends?

56. How many together with whom I came into the world are already gone out of it.

57. To the jaundiced honey tastes bitter, and to those bitten by mad dogs water causes fear; and to little children the ball is a fine thing. Why then am I angry? Dost thou think that a false opinion has less power than the bile in the jaundiced or the poison in him who is bitten by a mad dog?

58. No man will hinder thee from living according to the reason of thy own nature: nothing will happen to thee contrary to the reason of the universal nature.

59. What kind of people are those whom men wish to please, and for what objects, and by what kind of acts? How soon will time cover all things, and how many it has covered already.

BOOK VII

WHAT is badness? It is that which thou hast often seen. And on the occasion of everything which happens keep this in mind, that it is that which thou hast often seen. Everywhere up and down thou wilt find the same things, with which the old histories are filled, those of the middle ages and those of our own day; with which cities and houses are filled now. There is nothing new: all things are both familiar and short-lived.

2. How can our principles become dead, unless the impressions (thoughts) which correspond to them are extinguished? But it is in thy power continuously to fan these thoughts into a flame. I can have that opinion about anything, which I ought to have. If I can, why am I disturbed? The things which are external to my mind have no relation at all to my mind.—Let this be the state of thy affects, and thou standest erect. To recover thy life is in thy power. Look at things again as thou didst use to look at them; for in this consists the recovery of thy life.

3. The idle business of show, plays on the stage, flocks of sheep, herds, exercises with spears, a bone cast to little dogs, a bit of bread into fish-ponds, labourings of ants and burden-carrying, runnings about of frightened little mice, puppets pulled by strings—all alike. It is thy duty then in the midst of such things to show good humour and not a proud air; to understand however that every man is worth just so much as the things are worth about which he busies himself.

4. In discourse thou must attend to what is said, and in every movement thou must observe what is doing. And in the one thou shouldst see immediately to what end it refers, but in the other watch carefully what is the thing signified.

5. Is my understanding sufficient for this or not? If it is sufficient, I use it for the work as an instrument given by the universal nature. But if it is not sufficient, then either I retire from the work and give way to him who is able to do it better, unless there be some reason why I ought not to do so; or I do it as well as I can, taking to help me the man who with the aid of my ruling principle can do what is now fit and useful for the general good. For whatsoever either by myself or with another I can do, ought to be directed to this only, to that which is useful and well suited to society.

6. How many after being celebrated by fame have been given up to

oblivion; and how many who have celebrated the fame of others have long been dead.

7. Be not ashamed to be helped; for it is thy business to do thy duty like a soldier in the assault on a town. How then, if being lame thou canst not mount up on the battlements alone, but with the help of another it is possible?

8. Let not future things disturb thee, for thou wilt come to them, if it shall be necessary, having with thee the same reason which now thou usest for present things.

9. All things are implicated with one another, and the bond is holy; and there is hardly anything unconnected with any other thing. For things have been co-ordinated, and they combine to form the same universe (order). For there is one universe made up of all things, and one God who pervades all things, and one substance, and one law, one common reason in all intelligent animals, and one truth; if indeed there is also one perfection for all animals which are of the same stock and participate in the same reason.

10. Everything material soon disappears in the substance of the whole; and everything formal (causal) is very soon taken back into the universal reason; and the memory of everything is very soon overwhelmed in time.

11. To the rational animal the same act is according to nature and according to reason.

12. Be thou erect, or be made erect.

13. Just as it is with the members in those bodies which are united in one, so it is with rational beings which exist separate, for they have been constituted for one co-operation. And the perception of this will be more apparent to thee, if thou often sayest to thyself that I am a member (μέλος) of the system of rational beings. But if (using the letter *r*) thou sayest that thou art a part (μέρος), thou dost not yet love men from thy heart; beneficence does not yet delight thee for its own sake; thou still doest it barely as a thing of propriety, and not yet as doing good to thyself.

14. Let there fall externally what will on the parts which can feel the effects of this fall. For those parts which have felt will complain, if they choose. But I, unless I think that what has happened is an evil, am not injured. And it is in my power not to think so.

15. Whatever any one does or says, I must be good, just as if the gold, or the emerald, or the purple were always saying this, Whatever any one does or says, I must be emerald and keep my colour.

16. The ruling faculty does not disturb itself; I mean, does not frighten itself or cause itself pain. But if any one else can frighten or pain it, let him do so. For the faculty itself will not by its own opinion

turn itself into such ways. Let the body itself take care, if it can, that it suffer nothing, and let it speak, if it suffers. But the soul itself, that which is subject to fear, to pain, which has completely the power of forming an opinion about these things, will suffer nothing, for it will never deviate into such a judgement. The leading principle in itself wants nothing, unless it makes a want for itself; and therefore it is both free from perturbation and unimpeded, if it does not disturb and impede itself.

17. Eudaemonia (happiness) is a good daemon, or a good thing. What then art thou doing here, O imagination? Go away, I entreat thee by the gods, as thou didst come, for I want thee not. But thou art come according to thy old fashion. I am not angry with thee: only go away.

18. Is any man afraid of change? Why what can take place without change? What then is more pleasing or more suitable to the universal nature? And canst thou take a bath unless the wood undergoes a change? And canst thou be nourished, unless the food undergoes a change? And can anything else that is useful be accomplished without change? Dost thou not see then that for thyself also to change is just the same, and equally necessary for the universal nature?

19. Through the universal substance as through a furious torrent all bodies are carried, being by their nature united with and co-operating with the whole, as the parts of our body with one another. How many a Chrysippus, how many a Socrates, how many an Epictetus has time already swallowed up? And let the same thought occur to thee with reference to every man and thing.

20. One thing only troubles me, lest I should do something which the constitution of man does not allow, or in the way which it does not allow, or what it does not allow now.

21. Near is thy forgetfulness of all things; and near the forgetfulness of thee by all.

22. It is peculiar to man to love even those who do wrong. And this happens, if when they do wrong it occurs to thee that they are kinsmen, and that they do wrong through ignorance and unintentionally, and that soon both of you will die; and above all, that the wrong-doer has done thee no harm, for he has not made thy ruling faculty worse than it was before.

23. The universal nature out of the universal substance, as if it were wax, now moulds a horse, and when it has broken this up, it uses the material for a tree, then for a man, then for something else; and each of these things subsists for a very short time. But it is no hardship for the vessel to be broken up, just as there was none in its being fastened together.

24. A scowling look is altogether unnatural; when it is often assumed, the result is that all comeliness dies away, and at last is so completely extinguished that it cannot be again lighted up at all. Try to conclude from this very fact that it is contrary to reason. For if even the perception of doing wrong shall depart, what reason is there for living any longer?

25. Nature which governs the whole will soon change all things which thou seest, and out of their substance will make other things, and again other things from the substance of them, in order that the world may be ever new.

26. When a man has done thee any wrong, immediately consider with what opinion about good or evil he has done wrong. For when thou hast seen this, thou wilt pity him, and wilt neither wonder nor be angry. For either thou thyself thinkest the same thing to be good that he does or another thing of the same kind. It is thy duty then to pardon him. But if thou dost not think such things to be good or evil, thou wilt more readily be well disposed to him who is in error.

27. Think not so much of what thou hast not as of what thou hast: but of the things which thou hast select the best, and then reflect how eagerly they would have been sought, if thou hadst them not. At the same time however take care that thou dost not through being so pleased with them accustom thyself to overvalue them, so as to be disturbed if ever thou shouldst not have them.

28. Retire into thyself. The rational principle which rules has this nature, that it is content with itself when it does what is just, and so secures tranquillity.

29. Wipe out the imagination. Stop the pulling of the strings. Confine thyself to the present. Understand well what happens either to thee or to another. Divide and distribute every object into the causal (formal) and the material. Think of thy last hour. Let the wrong which is done by a man stay there where the wrong was done.

30. Direct thy attention to what is said. Let thy understanding enter into the things that are doing and the things which do them.

31. Adorn thyself with simplicity and modesty and with indifference towards the things which lie between virtue and vice. Love mankind. Follow God. The poet says that Law rules all.—And it is enough to remember that Law rules all.[1]

32. About death: Whether it is a dispersion, or a resolution into atoms, or annihilation, it is either extinction or change.

33. About pain: The pain which is intolerable carries us off; but that which lasts a long time is tolerable; and the mind maintains its own tranquillity by retiring into itself, and the ruling faculty is not made

worse. But the parts which are harmed by pain, let them, if they can, give their opinion about it.

34. About fame: Look at the minds of those who seek fame, observe what they are, and what kind of things they avoid, and what kind of things they pursue. And consider that as the heaps of sand piled on one another hide the former sands, so in life the events which go before are soon covered by those which come after.

35. From Plato: The man who has an elevated mind and takes a view of all time and of all substance, dost thou suppose it possible for him to think that human life is anything great? it is not possible, he said.—Such a man then will think that death also is no evil.—Certainly not.[2]

36. From Antisthenes: It is royal to do good and to be abused.

37. It is a base thing for the countenance to be obedient and to regulate and compose itself as the mind commands, and for the mind not to be regulated and composed by itself.

38. It is not right to vex ourselves at things,
For they care nought about it.[3]

39. To the immortal gods and us give joy.

40. Life must be reaped like the ripe ears of corn:
One man is born; another dies.[4]

41. If gods care not for me and for my children,
There is a reason for it.[5]

42. For the good is with me, and the just.[6]

43. No joining others in their wailing, no violent emotion.

44. From Plato: But I would make this man a sufficient answer, which is this: Thou sayest not well, if thou thinkest that a man who is good for anything at all ought to compute the hazard of life or death, and should not rather look to this only in all that he does, whether he is doing what is just or unjust, and the works of a good or a bad man.[7]

45. For thus it is, men of Athens, in truth: wherever a man has placed himself thinking it the best place for him, or has been placed by a commander, there in my opinion he ought to stay and to abide the hazard, taking nothing into the reckoning, either death or anything else, before the baseness of deserting his post.[8]

46. But, my good friend, reflect whether that which is noble and good is not something different from saving and being saved; for as to a man living such or such a time, at least one who is really a man, consider if this is not a thing to be dismissed from the thoughts: and there must be no love of life: but as to these matters a man must intrust them to the deity and believe what the women say, that no man

can escape his destiny, the next inquiry being how he may best live the time that he has to live.[9]

47. Look round at the courses of the stars, as if thou wert going along with them; and constantly consider the changes of the elements into one another; for such thoughts purge away the filth of the terrene life.

48. This is a fine saying of Plato: That he who is discoursing about men should look also at earthly things as if he viewed them from some higher place; should look at them in their assemblies, armies, agricultural labours, marriages, treaties, births, deaths, noise of the courts of justice, desert places, various nations of barbarians, feasts, lamentations, markets, a mixture of all things and an orderly combination of contraries.[10]

49. Consider the past; such great changes of political supremacies. Thou mayest foresee also the things which will be. For they will certainly be of like form, and it is not possible that they should deviate from the order of the things which take place now: accordingly to have contemplated human life for forty years is the same as to have contemplated it for ten thousand years. For what more wilt thou see?

50. That which has grown from the earth to the earth,
But that which has sprung from heavenly seed,
Back to the heavenly realms returns.[11]

This is either a dissolution of the mutual involution of the atoms, or a similar dispersion of the unsentient elements.

51. With food and drinks and cunning magic arts
Turning the channel's course to 'scape from death.[12]
The breeze which heaven has sent
We must endure, and toil without complaining.[13]

52. Another may be more expert in casting his opponent; but he is not more social, nor more modest, nor better disciplined to meet all that happens, nor more considerate with respect to the faults of his neighbours.

53. Where any work can be done conformably to the reason which is common to gods and men, there we have nothing to fear: for where we are able to get profit by means of the activity which is successful and proceeds according to our constitution, there no harm is to be suspected.

54. Everywhere and at all times it is in thy power piously to acquiesce in thy present condition, and to behave justly to those who are about thee, and to exert thy skill upon thy present thoughts, that nothing shall steal into them without being well examined.

55. Do not look around thee to discover other men's ruling principles, but look straight to this, to what nature leads thee, both the universal

nature through the things which happen to thee, and thy own nature through the acts which must be done by thee. But every being ought to do that which is according to its constitution; and all other things have been constituted for the sake of rational beings, just as among irrational things the inferior for the sake of the superior, but the rational for the sake of one another.

The prime principle then in man's constitution is the social. And the second is not to yield to the persuasions of the body, for it is the peculiar office of the rational and intelligent motion to circumscribe itself, and never to be overpowered either by the motion of the senses or of the appetites, for both are animal; but the intelligent motion claims superiority and does not permit itself to be overpowered by the others. And with good reason, for it is formed by nature to use all of them. The third thing in the rational constitution is freedom from error and from deception. Let then the ruling principle holding fast to these things go straight on, and it has what is its own.

56. Consider thyself to be dead, and to have completed thy life up to the present time; and live according to nature the remainder which is allowed thee.

57. Love that only which happens to thee and is spun with the thread of thy destiny. For what is more suitable?

58. In everything which happens keep before thy eyes those to whom the same things happened, and how they were vexed, and treated them as strange things, and found fault with them: and now where are they? Nowhere. Why then dost thou too choose to act in the same way? And why dost thou not leave these agitations which are foreign to nature, to those who cause them and those who are moved by them? And why art thou not altogether intent upon the right way of making use of the things which happen to thee? For then thou wilt use them well, and they will be a material for thee to work on. Only attend to thyself, and resolve to be a good man in every act which thou doest: and remember . . .[14]

59. Look within. Within is the fountain of good, and it will ever bubble up, if thou wilt ever dig.

60. The body ought to be compact, and to show no irregularity either in motion or attitude. For what the mind shows in the face by maintaining in it the expression of intelligence and propriety, that ought to be required also in the whole body. But all of these things should be observed without affectation.

61. The art of life is more like the wrestler's art than the dancer's, in respect of this, that it should stand ready and firm to meet onsets which are sudden and unexpected.

62. Constantly observe who those are whose approbation thou wish-

est to have, and what ruling principles they possess. For then thou wilt neither blame those who offend involuntarily, nor wilt thou want their approbation, if thou lookest to the sources of their opinions and appetites.

63. Every soul, the philosopher says, is involuntarily deprived of truth; consequently in the same way it is deprived of justice and temperance and benevolence and everything of the kind. It is most necessary to bear this constantly in mind, for thus thou wilt be more gentle towards all.

64. In every pain let this thought be present, that there is no dishonour in it, nor does it make the governing intelligence worse, for it does not damage the intelligence either so far as the intelligence is rational or so far as it is social. Indeed in the case of most pains let this remark of Epicurus aid thee, that pain is neither intolerable nor everlasting, if thou bearest in mind that it has its limits, and if thou addest nothing to it in imagination: and remember this too, that we do not perceive that many things which are disagreeable to us are the same as pain, such as excessive drowsiness, and the being scorched by heat, and the having no appetite. When then thou art discontented about any of these things, say to thyself, that thou art yielding to pain.

65. Take care not to feel towards the inhuman, as they feel towards men.

66. How do we know if Telauges was not superior in character to Socrates? For it is not enough that Socrates died a more noble death, and disputed more skilfully with the sophists, and passed the night in the cold with more endurance, and that when he was bid to arrest Leon of Salamis, he considered it more noble to refuse, and that he walked in a swaggering way in the streets [15]—though as to this fact one may have great doubts if it was true. But we ought to inquire, what kind of a soul it was that Socrates possessed, and if he was able to be content with being just towards men and pious towards the gods, neither idly vexed on account of men's villainy, nor yet making himself a slave to any man's ignorance, nor receiving as strange anything that fell to his share out of the universal, nor enduring it as intolerable, nor allowing his understanding to sympathise with the affects of the miserable flesh.

67. Nature has not so mingled the intelligence with the composition of the body, as not to have allowed thee the power of circumscribing thyself and of bringing under subjection to thyself all that is thy own; for it is very possible to be a divine man and to be recognised as such by no one. Always bear this in mind; and another thing too, that very little indeed is necessary for living a happy life. And because thou hast despaired of becoming a dialectician and skilled in the knowledge of

nature, do not for this reason renounce the hope of being both free and modest and social and obedient to God.

68. It is in thy power to live free from all compulsion in the greatest tranquillity of mind, even if all the world cry out against thee as much as they choose, and even if wild beasts tear in pieces the members of this kneaded matter which has grown around thee. For what hinders the mind in the midst of all this from maintaining itself in tranquillity and in a just judgement of all surrounding things and in a ready use of the objects which are presented to it, so that the judgement may say to the thing which falls under its observation: This thou art in substance (reality), though in men's opinion thou mayest appear to be of a different kind; and the use shall say to that which falls under the hand: Thou art the thing that I was seeking; for to me that which presents itself is always a material for virtue both rational and political, and in a word, for the exercise of art, which belongs to man or God. For everything which happens has a relationship either to God or man, and is neither new nor difficult to handle, but usual and apt matter to work on.

69. The perfection of moral character consists in this, in passing every day as the last, and in being neither violently excited nor torpid nor playing the hypocrite.

70. The gods who are immortal are not vexed because during so long a time they must tolerate continually men such as they are and so many of them bad; and besides this, they also take care of them in all ways. But thou, who art destined to end so soon, art thou wearied of enduring the bad, and this too when thou art one of them?

71. It is a ridiculous thing for a man not to fly from his own badness, which is indeed possible, but to fly from other men's badness, which is impossible.

72. Whatever the rational and political (social) faculty finds to be neither intelligent nor social, it properly judges to be inferior to itself.

73. When thou hast done a good act and another has received it, why dost thou look for a third thing besides these, as fools do, either to have the reputation of having done a good act or to obtain a return?

74. No man is tired of receiving what is useful. But it is useful to act according to nature. Do not then be tired of receiving what is useful by doing it to others.

75. The nature of the All moved to make the universe. But now either everything that takes place comes by way of consequence or continuity; or even the chief things towards which the ruling power of the universe directs its own movement are governed by no rational principle. If this is remembered it will make thee more tranquil in many things.

BOOK VIII

THIS reflection also tends to the removal of the desire of empty fame, that it is no longer in thy power to have lived the whole of thy life, or at least thy life from thy youth upwards, like a philosopher; but both to many others and to thyself it is plain that thou art far from philosophy. Thou hast fallen into disorder then, so that it is no longer easy for thee to get the reputation of a philosopher; and thy plan of life also opposes it. If then thou hast truly seen where the matter lies, throw away the thought, How thou shalt seem to others, and be content if thou shalt live the rest of thy life in such wise as thy nature wills. Observe then what it wills, and let nothing else distract thee; for thou hast had experience of many wanderings without having found happiness anywhere, not in syllogisms, nor in wealth, nor in reputation, nor in enjoyment, nor anywhere. Where is it then? In doing what man's nature requires. How then shall a man do this? If he has principles from which come his affects and his acts. What principles? Those which relate to good and bad: the belief that there is nothing good for man, which does not make him just, temperate, manly, free; and that there is nothing bad, which does not do the contrary to what has been mentioned.

2. On the occasion of every act ask thyself, How is this with respect to me? Shall I repent of it? A little time and I am dead, and all is gone. What more do I seek, if what I am now doing is the work of an intelligent living being, and a social being, and one who is under the same law with God?

3. Alexander and Gaius [1] and Pompeius, what are they in comparison with Diogenes and Heraclitus and Socrates? For they were acquainted with things, and their causes (forms), and their matter, and the ruling principles of these men were the same.[2] But as to the others, how many things had they to care for, and to how many things were they slaves.

4. Consider that men will do the same things nevertheless, even though thou shouldst burst.

5. This is the chief thing: Be not perturbed, for all things are according to the nature of the universal; and in a little time thou wilt be nobody and nowhere, like Hadrian and Augustus. In the next place having fixed thy eyes steadily on thy business look at it, and at the same time remembering that it is thy duty to be a good man, and what man's nature demands, do that without turning aside; and speak

as it seems to thee most just, only let it be with a good disposition and with modesty and without hypocrisy.

6. The nature of the universal has this work to do, to remove to that place the things which are in this, to change them, to take them away hence, and to carry them there. All things are change, yet we need not fear anything new. All things are familiar to us; but the distribution of them still remains the same.

7. Every nature is contented with itself when it goes on its way well; and a rational nature goes on its way well, when in its thoughts it assents to nothing false or uncertain, and when it directs its movements to social acts only, and when it confines its desires and aversions to the things which are in its power, and when it is satisfied with everything that is assigned to it by the common nature. For of this common nature every particular nature is a part, as the nature of the leaf is a part of the nature of the plant; except that in the plant the nature of the leaf is part of a nature which has not perception or reason, and is subject to be impeded; but the nature of man is part of a nature which is not subject to impediments, and is intelligent and just, since it gives to everything in equal portions and according to its worth, times, substance, cause (form), activity, and incident. But examine, not to discover that any one thing compared with any other single thing is equal in all respects, but by taking all the parts together of one thing and comparing them with all the parts together of another.

8. Thou hast not leisure or ability to read. But thou hast leisure or ability to check arrogance: thou hast leisure to be superior to pleasure and pain: thou hast leisure to be superior to love of fame, and not to be vexed at stupid and ungrateful people, nay even to care for them.

9. Let no man any longer hear thee finding fault with the court life or with thy own.

10. Repentance is a kind of self-reproof for having neglected something useful; but that which is good must be something useful, and the perfect good man should look after it. But no such man would ever repent of having refused any sensual pleasure. Pleasure then is neither good nor useful.

11. This thing, what is it in itself, in its own constitution? What is its substance and material? And what its causal nature (or form)? And what is it doing in the world? And how long does it subsist?

12. When thou risest from sleep with reluctance, remember that it is according to thy constitution and according to human nature to perform social acts, but sleeping is common also to irrational animals. But that which is according to each individual's nature is also more peculiarly its own, and more suitable to its nature, and indeed also more agreeable.

13. Constantly and, if it be possible, on the occasion of every impression on the soul, apply to it the principles of Physic, of Ethic, and of Dialectic.

14. Whatever man thou meetest with, immediately say to thyself: What opinions has this man about good and bad? For if with respect to pleasure and pain and the causes of each, and with respect to fame and ignominy, death and life, he has such and such opinions, it will seem nothing wonderful or strange to me, if he does such and such things; and I shall bear in mind that he is compelled to do so.

15. Remember that as it is a shame to be surprised if the fig-tree produces figs, so it is to be surprised if the world produces such and such things of which it is productive; and for the physician and the helmsman it is a shame to be surprised, if a man has a fever, or if the wind is unfavourable.

16. Remember that to change thy opinion and to follow him who corrects thy error is as consistent with freedom as it is to persist in thy error. For it is thy own, the activity which is exerted according to thy own movement and judgement, and indeed according to thy own understanding too.

17. If a thing is in thy own power, why dost thou do it? But if it is in the power of another, whom dost thou blame? The atoms (chance) or the gods? Both are foolish. Thou must blame nobody. For if thou canst, correct that which is the cause; but if thou canst not do this, correct at least the thing itself; but if thou canst not do even this, of what use is it to thee to find fault? For nothing should be done without a purpose.

18. That which has died falls not out of the universe. If it stays here, it also changes here, and is dissolved into its proper parts, which are elements of the universe and of thyself. And these too change, and they murmur not.

19. Everything exists for some end, a horse, a vine. Why dost thou wonder? Even the sun will say, I am for some purpose, and the rest of the gods will say the same. For what purpose then art thou? to enjoy pleasure? See if common sense allows this.

20. Nature has had regard in everything no less to the end than to the beginning and the continuance, just like the man who throws up a ball. What good is it then for the ball to be thrown up, or harm for it to come down, or even to have fallen? And what good is it to the bubble while it holds together, or what harm when it is burst? The same may be said of a light also.

21. Turn it (the body) inside out, and see what kind of thing it is; and when it has grown old, what kind of thing it becomes, and when it is diseased.

Short-lived are both the praiser and the praised, and the rememberer and the remembered: and all this in a nook of this part of the world; and not even here do all agree, no, not any one with himself: and the whole earth too is a point.

22. Attend to the matter which is before thee, whether it is an opinion or an act or a word.

Thou sufferest this justly: for thou choosest rather to become good to-morrow than to be good to-day.

23. Am I doing anything? I do it with reference to the good of mankind. Does anything happen to me? I receive it and refer it to the gods, and the source of all things, from which all that happens is derived.

24. Such as bathing appears to thee—oil, sweat, dirt, filthy water, all things disgusting—so is every part of life and everything.

25. Lucilla saw Verus die, and then Lucilla died. Secunda saw Maximus die, and then Secunda died. Epitynchanus saw Diotimus die, and then Epitynchanus died. Antoninus saw Faustina die, and then Antoninus died. Such is everything. Celer saw Hadrian die, and then Celer died. And those sharp-witted men, either seers or men inflated with pride, where are they? For instance the sharp-witted men, Charax and Demetrius the Platonist and Eudaemon, and any one else like them. All ephemeral, dead long ago. Some indeed have not been remembered even for a short time, and others have become the heroes of fables, and again others have disappeared even from fables. Remember this then, that this little compound, thyself, must either be dissolved, or thy poor breath must be extinguished, or be removed and placed elsewhere.

26. It is satisfaction to a man to do the proper works of a man. Now it is a proper work of a man to be benevolent to his own kind, to despise the movements of the senses, to form a just judgement of plausible appearances, and to take a survey of the nature of the universe and of the things which happen in it.

27. There are three relations between thee and other things: the one to the body which surrounds thee; the second to the divine cause from which all things come to all; and the third to those who live with thee.

28. Pain is either an evil to the body—then let the body say what it thinks of it—or to the soul; but it is in the power of the soul to maintain its own serenity and tranquillity, and not to think that pain is an evil. For every judgement and movement and desire and aversion is within, and no evil ascends so high.

29. Wipe out thy imaginations by often saying to thyself: now it is in my power to let no badness be in this soul, nor desire nor any perturbation at all; but looking at all things I see what is their nature, and I use each according to its value.—Remember this power which thou hast from nature.

30. Speak both in the senate and to every man, whoever he may be, appropriately, not with any affectation: use plain discourse.

31. Augustus' court, wife, daughter, descendants, ancestors, sister, Agrippa, kinsmen, intimates, friends, Areius, Maecenas, physicians and sacrificing priests—the whole court is dead. Then turn to the rest, not considering the death of a single man, but of a whole race, as of the Pompeii; and that which is inscribed on the tombs—The last of his race. Then consider what trouble those before them have had that they might leave a successor; and then, that of necessity some one must be the last. Again here consider the death of a whole race.

32. It is thy duty to order thy life well in every single act; and if every act does its duty, as far as is possible, be content; and no one is able to hinder thee so that each act shall not do its duty.—But something external will stand in the way.—Nothing will stand in the way of thy acting justly and soberly and considerately.—But perhaps some other active power will be hindered.—Well, but by acquiescing in the hindrance and by being content to transfer thy efforts to that which is allowed, another opportunity of action is immediately put before thee in place of that which was hindered, and one which will adapt itself to this ordering of which we are speaking.

33. Receive wealth or prosperity without arrogance; and be ready to let it go.

34. If thou didst ever see a hand cut off, or a foot, or a head, lying anywhere apart from the rest of the body, such does a man make himself, as far as he can, who is not content with what happens, and separates himself from others, or does anything unsocial. Suppose that thou hast detached thyself from the natural unity—for thou wast made by nature a part, but now thou hast cut thyself off—yet here there is this beautiful provision, that it is in thy power again to unite thyself. God has allowed this to no other part, after it has been separated and cut asunder, to come together again. But consider the kindness by which he has distinguished man, for he has put it in his power not to be separated at all from the universal; and when he has been separated, he has allowed him to return and to be united and to resume his place as a part.

35. As the nature of the universal has given to every rational being all the other powers that it has, so we have received from it this power also. For as the universal nature converts and fixes in its predestined place everything which stands in the way and opposes it, and makes such things a part of itself, so also the rational animal is able to make every hindrance its own material, and to use it for such purposes as it may have designed.

36. Do not disturb thyself by thinking of the whole of thy life. Let

not thy thoughts at once embrace all the various troubles which thou mayest expect to befall thee: but on every occasion ask thyself, What is there in this which is intolerable and past bearing? For thou wilt be ashamed to confess. In the next place remember that neither the future nor the past pains thee, but only the present. But this is reduced to a very little, if thou only circumscribest it, and chidest thy mind, if it is unable to hold out against even this.

37. Does Panthea or Pergamus now sit by the tomb of Verus? Does Chaurias or Diotimus sit by the tomb of Hadrian? That would be ridiculous. Well, suppose they did sit there, would the dead be conscious of it? And if the dead were conscious, would they be pleased? And if they were pleased, would that make them immortal? Was it not in the order of destiny that these persons too should first become old women and old men and then die? What then would those do after these were dead? All this is foul smell and blood in a bag.

38. If thou canst see sharp, look and judge wisely, says the philosopher.

39. In the constitution of the rational animal I see no virtue which is opposed to justice; but I see a virtue which is opposed to love of pleasure, and that is temperance.

40. If thou takest away thy opinion about that which appears to give thee pain, thou thyself standest in perfect security.—Who is this self?—The reason.—But I am not reason.—Be it so. Let then the reason itself not trouble itself. But if any other part of thee suffers, let it have its own opinion about itself.

41. Hindrance to the perceptions of sense is an evil to the animal nature. Hindrance to the movements (desires) is equally an evil to the animal nature. And something else also is equally an impediment and an evil to the constitution of plants. So then that which is a hindrance to the intelligence is an evil to the intelligent nature. Apply all these things then to thyself. Does pain or sensuous pleasure affect thee? The senses will look to that.—Has any obstacle opposed thee in thy efforts towards an object? if indeed thou wast making this effort absolutely (unconditionally, or without any reservation), certainly this obstacle is an evil to thee considered as a rational animal. But if thou takest into consideration the usual course of things, thou hast not yet been injured nor even impeded. The things however which are proper to the understanding no other man is used to impede, for neither fire, nor iron, nor tyrant, nor abuse, touches it in any way. When it has been made a sphere, it continues a sphere.

42. It is not fit that I should give myself pain, for I have never intentionally given pain even to another.

43. Different things delight different people. But it is my delight to

keep the ruling faculty sound without turning away either from any man or from any of the things which happen to men, but looking at and receiving all with welcome eyes and using everything according to its value.

44. See that thou secure this present time to thyself: for those who rather pursue posthumous fame do not consider that the men of after time will be exactly such as these whom they cannot bear now; and both are mortal. And what is it in any way to thee if these men of after time utter this or that sound, or have this or that opinion about thee?

45. Take me and cast me where thou wilt; for there I shall keep my divine part tranquil, that is, content, if it can feel and act conformably to its proper constitution. Is this change of place sufficient reason why my soul should be unhappy and worse than it was, depressed, expanded, shrinking, affrighted? And what wilt thou find which is sufficient reason for this?

46. Nothing can happen to any man which is not a human accident, nor to an ox which is not according to the nature of an ox, nor to a vine which is not according to the nature of a vine, nor to a stone which is not proper to a stone. If then there happens to each thing both what is usual and natural, why shouldst thou complain? For the common nature brings nothing which may not be borne by thee.

47. If thou art pained by any external thing, it is not this thing that disturbs thee, but thy own judgement about it. And it is in thy power to wipe out this judgement now. But if anything in thy own disposition gives thee pain, who hinders thee from correcting thy opinion? And even if thou art pained because thou art not doing some particular thing which seems to thee to be right, why dost thou not rather act than complain?—But some insuperable obstacle is in the way?—Do not be grieved then, for the cause of its not being done depends not on thee.—But it is not worth while to live, if this cannot be done.—Take thy departure then from life contentedly, just as he dies who is in full activity, and well pleased too with the things which are obstacles.

48. Remember that the ruling faculty is invincible, when self-collected it is satisfied with itself, if it does nothing which it does not choose to do, even if it resist from mere obstinacy. What then will it be when it forms a judgement about anything aided by reason and deliberately? Therefore the mind which is free from passions is a citadel, for man has nothing more secure to which he can fly for refuge and for the future be inexpugnable. He then who has not seen this is an ignorant man; but he who has seen it and does not fly to this refuge is unhappy.

49. Say nothing more to thyself than what the first appearances report. Suppose that it has been reported to thee that a certain person

speaks ill of thee. This has been reported; but that thou hast been injured, that has not been reported. I see that my child is sick. I do see; but that he is in danger, I do not see. Thus then always abide by the first appearances, and add nothing thyself from within, and then nothing happens to thee. Or rather add something, like a man who knows everything that happens in the world.

50. A cucumber is bitter.—Throw it away.—There are briars in the road.—Turn aside from them.—This is enough. Do not add, And why were such things made in the world? For thou wilt be ridiculed by a man who is acquainted with nature, as thou wouldst be ridiculed by a carpenter and shoemaker if thou didst find fault because thou seest in their workshop shavings and cuttings from the things which they make. And yet they have places into which they can throw these shavings and cuttings, and the universal nature has no external space; but the wondrous part of her art is that though she has circumscribed herself, everything within her which appears to decay and to grow old and to be useless she changes into herself, and again makes other new things from these very same, so that she requires neither substance from without nor wants a place into which she may cast that which decays. She is content then with her own space, and her own matter and her own art.

51. Neither in thy actions be sluggish nor in thy conversation without method, nor wandering in thy thoughts, nor let there be in thy soul inward contention nor external effusion, nor in life be so busy as to have no leisure.

Suppose that men kill thee, cut thee in pieces, curse thee. What then can these things do to prevent thy mind from remaining pure, wise, sober, just? For instance, if a man should stand by a limpid pure spring, and curse it, the spring never ceases sending up potable water; and if he should cast clay into it or filth, it will speedily disperse them and wash them out, and will not be at all polluted. How then shalt thou possess a perpetual fountain and not a mere well? By forming thyself hourly to freedom conjoined with contentment, simplicity and modesty.

52. He who does not know what the world is, does not know where he is. And he who does not know for what purpose the world exists, does not know who he is, nor what the world is. But he who has failed in any one of these things could not even say for what purpose he exists himself. What then dost thou think of him who avoids or seeks the praise of those who applaud, of men who know not either where they are or who they are?

53. Dost thou wish to be praised by a man who curses himself thrice every hour? Wouldst thou wish to please a man who does not please himself? Does a man please himself who repents of nearly everything that he does?

54. No longer let thy breathing only act in concert with the air which surrounds thee, but let thy intelligence also now be in harmony with the intelligence which embraces all things. For the intelligent power is no less diffused in all parts and pervades all things for him who is willing to draw it to him than the aërial power for him who is able to respire it.

55. Generally, wickedness does no harm at all to the universe; and particularly, the wickedness of one man does no harm to another. It is only harmful to him who has it in his power to be released from it, as soon as he shall choose.

56. To my own free will the free will of my neighbour is just as indifferent as his poor breath and flesh. For though we are made especially for the sake of one another, still the ruling power of each of us has its own office, for otherwise my neighbour's wickedness would be my harm, which God has not willed in order that my unhappiness may not depend on another.

57. The sun appears to be poured down, and in all directions indeed it is diffused, yet it is not effused. For this diffusion is extension: Accordingly its rays are called Extensions [ἀκτῖνες] because they are extended [ἀπὸ τοῦ ἐκτείνεσθαι].[3] But one may judge what kind of a thing a ray is, if he looks at the sun's light passing through a narrow opening into a darkened room, for it is extended in a right line, and as it were is divided when it meets with any solid body which stands in the way and intercepts the air beyond; but there the light remains fixed and does not glide or fall off. Such then ought to be the out-pouring and diffusion of the understanding, and it should in no way be an effusion, but an extension, and it should make no violent or impetuous collision with the obstacles which are in its way; nor yet fall down, but be fixed and enlighten that which receives it. For a body will deprive itself of the illumination, if it does not admit it.

58. He who fears death either fears the loss of sensation or a different kind of sensation. But if thou shalt have no sensation, neither wilt thou feel any harm; and if thou shalt acquire another kind of sensation, thou wilt be a different kind of living being and thou wilt not cease to live.

59. Men exist for the sake of one another. Teach them then or bear with them.

60. In one way an arrow moves, in another way the mind. The mind indeed, both when it exercises caution and when it is employed about inquiry, moves straight onward not the less, and to its object.

61. Enter into every man's ruling faculty; and also let every other man enter into thine.

BOOK IX

He who acts unjustly acts impiously. For since the universal nature has made rational animals for the sake of one another to help one another according to their deserts, but in no way to injure one another, he who transgresses her will, is clearly guilty of impiety towards the highest divinity. And he too who lies is guilty of impiety to the same divinity; for the universal nature is the nature of things that are; and things that are have a relation to all things that come into existence. And further, this universal nature is named truth, and is the prime cause of all things that are true. He then who lies intentionally is guilty of impiety inasmuch as he acts unjustly by deceiving; and he also who lies unintentionally, inasmuch as he is at variance with the universal nature, and inasmuch as he disturbs the order by fighting against the nature of the world; for he fights against it, who is moved of himself to that which is contrary to truth, for he had received powers from nature through the neglect of which he is not able now to distinguish falsehood from truth. And indeed he who pursues pleasure as good, and avoids pain as evil, is guilty of impiety. For of necessity such a man must often find fault with the universal nature, alleging that it assigns things to the bad and the good contrary to their deserts, because frequently the bad are in the enjoyment of pleasure and possess the things which procure pleasure, but the good have pain for their share and the things which cause pain. And further, he who is afraid of pain will sometimes also be afraid of some of the things which will happen in the world, and even this is impiety. And he who pursues pleasure will not abstain from injustice, and this is plainly impiety. Now with respect to the things towards which the universal nature is equally affected—for it would not have made both, unless it was equally affected towards both—towards these they who wish to follow nature should be of the same mind with it, and equally affected. With respect to pain, then, and pleasure, or death and life, or honour and dishonour, which the universal nature employs equally, whoever is not equally affected is manifestly acting impiously. And I say that the universal nature employs them equally, instead of saying that they happen alike to those who are produced in continuous series and to those who come after them by virtue of a certain original movement of Providence, according to which it moved from a certain beginning to this ordering of things, having conceived certain principles of the things which were to be, and having determined powers productive of beings and of changes and of such like successions.

2. It would be a man's happiest lot to depart from mankind without having had any taste of lying and hypocrisy and luxury and pride. However to breathe out one's life when a man has had enough of these things is the next best voyage, as the saying is. Hast thou determined to abide with vice, and has not experience yet induced thee to fly from this pestilence? For the destruction of the understanding is a pestilence, much more indeed than any such corruption and change of this atmosphere which surrounds us. For this corruption is a pestilence of animals so far as they are animals; but the other is a pestilence of men so far as they are men.

3. Do not despise death, but be well content with it, since this too is one of those things which nature wills. For such as it is to be young and to grow old, and to increase and to reach maturity, and to have teeth and beard and grey hairs, and to beget, and to be pregnant and to bring forth, and all the other natural operations which the seasons of thy life bring, such also is dissolution. This, then, is consistent with the character of a reflecting man, to be neither careless nor impatient nor contemptuous with respect to death, but to wait for it as one of the operations of nature. As thou now waitest for the time when the child shall come out of thy wife's womb, so be ready for the time when thy soul shall fall out of this envelope. But if thou requirest also a vulgar kind of comfort which shall reach thy heart, thou wilt be made best reconciled to death by observing the objects from which thou art going to be removed, and the morals of those with whom thy soul will no longer be mingled. For it is no way right to be offended with men, but it is thy duty to care for them and to bear with them gently; and yet to remember that thy departure will be not from men who have the same principles as thyself. For this is the only thing, if there be any, which could draw us the contrary way and attach us to life, to be permitted to live with those who have the same principles as ourselves. But now thou seest how great is the trouble arising from the discordance of those who live together, so that thou mayest say, Come quick, O death, lest perchance I, too, should forget myself.

4. He who does wrong does wrong against himself. He who acts unjustly acts unjustly to himself, because he makes himself bad.

5. He often acts unjustly who does not do a certain thing; not only he who does a certain thing.

6. Thy present opinion founded on understanding, and thy present conduct directed to social good, and thy present disposition of contentment with everything which happens—that is enough.

7. Wipe out imagination: check desire: extinguish appetite: keep the ruling faculty in its own power.

8. Among the animals which have not reason one life is distributed;

but among reasonable animals one intelligent soul is distributed: just as there is one earth of all things which are of an earthy nature, and we see by one light, and breathe one air, all of us that have the faculty of vision and all that have life.

9. All things which participate in anything which is common to them all move towards that which is of the same kind with themselves. Everything which is earthy turns towards the earth, everything which is liquid flows together, and everything which is of an aërial kind does the same, so that they require something to keep them asunder, and the application of force. Fire indeed moves upwards on account of the elemental fire, but it is so ready to be kindled together with all the fire which is here, that even every substance which is somewhat dry, is easily ignited, because there is less mingled with it of that which is a hindrance to ignition. Accordingly then everything also which participates in the common intelligent nature moves in like manner towards that which is of the same kind with itself, or moves even more. For so much as it is superior in comparison with all other things, in the same degree also is it more ready to mingle with and to be fused with that which is akin to it. Accordingly among animals devoid of reason we find swarms of bees, and herds of cattle, and the nurture of young birds, and in a manner, loves; for even in animals there are souls, and that power which brings them together is seen to exert itself in the superior degree, and in such a way as never has been observed in plants nor in stones nor in trees. But in rational animals there are political communities and friendships, and families and meetings of people; and in wars, treaties and armistices. But in the things which are still superior, even though they are separated from one another, unity in a manner exists, as in the stars. Thus the ascent to the higher degree is able to produce a sympathy even in things which are separated. See, then, what now takes place. For only intelligent animals have now forgotten this mutual desire and inclination, and in them alone the property of flowing together is not seen. But still though men strive to avoid this union, they are caught and held by it, for their nature is too strong for them; and thou wilt see what I say, if thou only observest. Sooner, then, will one find anything earthy which comes in contact with no earthy thing than a man altogether separated from other men.

10. Both man and God and the universe produce fruit; at the proper seasons each produces it. But if usage has especially fixed these terms to the vine and like things, this is nothing. Reason produces fruit both for all and for itself, and there are produced from it other things of the same kind as reason itself.

11. If thou art able, correct by teaching those who do wrong; but if thou canst not, remember that indulgence is given to thee for this pur-

pose. And the gods, too, are indulgent to such persons; and for some purposes they even help them to get health, wealth, reputation; so kind they are. And it is in thy power also; or say, who hinders thee?

12. Labour not as one who is wretched, nor yet as one who would be pitied or admired: but direct thy will to one thing only, to put thyself in motion and to check thyself, as the social reason requires.

13. To-day I have got out of all trouble, or rather I have cast out all trouble, for it was not outside, but within and in my opinions.

14. All things are the same, familiar in experience, and ephemeral in time, and worthless in the matter. Everything now is just as it was in the time of those whom we have buried.

15. Things stand outside of us, themselves by themselves, neither knowing aught of themselves, nor expressing any judgement. What is it, then, which does judge about them? The ruling faculty.

16. Not in passivity, but in activity lie the evil and the good of the rational social animal, just as his virtue and his vice lie not in passivity, but in activity.

17. For the stone which has been thrown up it is no evil to come down, nor indeed any good to have been carried up.

18. Penetrate inwards into men's leading principles, and thou wilt see what judges thou art afraid of, and what kind of judges they are of themselves.

19. All things are changing: and thou thyself art in continuous mutation and in a manner in continuous destruction, and the whole universe too.

20. It is thy duty to leave another man's wrongful act there where it is.

21. Termination of activity, cessation from movement and opinion, and in a sense their death, is no evil. Turn thy thoughts now to the consideration of thy life, thy life as a child, as a youth, thy manhood, thy old age, for in these also every change was a death. Is this anything to fear? Turn thy thoughts now to thy life under thy grandfather, then to thy life under thy mother, then to thy life under thy father; and as thou findest many other differences and changes and terminations, ask thyself, Is this anything to fear? In like manner, then, neither are the termination and cessation and change of thy whole life a thing to be afraid of.

22. Hasten to examine thy own ruling faculty and that of the universe and that of thy neighbour: thy own that thou mayest make it just: and that of the universe, that thou mayest remember of what thou art a part; and that of thy neighbour, that thou mayest know whether he has acted ignorantly or with knowledge, and that thou mayest also consider that his ruling faculty is akin to thine.

23. As thou thyself art a component part of a social system, so let every act of thine be a component part of social life. Whatever act of thine then has no reference either immediately or remotely to a social end, this tears asunder thy life, and does not allow it to be one, and it is of the nature of a mutiny, just as when in a popular assembly a man acting by himself stands apart from the general agreement.

24. Quarrels of little children and their sports, and poor spirits carrying about dead bodies, such is everything; and so what is exhibited in the representation of the mansions of the dead strikes our eyes more clearly.

25. Examine into the quality of the form of an object, and detach it altogether from its material part, and then contemplate it; then determine the time, the longest which a thing of this peculiar form is naturally made to endure.

26. Thou hast endured infinite troubles through not being contented with thy ruling faculty, when it does the things which it is constituted by nature to do. But enough of this.

27. When another blames thee or hates thee, or when men say about thee anything injurious, approach their poor souls, penetrate within, and see what kind of men they are. Thou wilt discover that there is no reason to take any trouble that these men may have this or that opinion about thee. However thou must be well disposed towards them, for by nature they are friends. And the gods too aid them in all ways, by dreams, by signs, towards the attainment of those things on which they set a value.

28. The periodic movements of the universe are the same, up and down from age to age. And either the universal intelligence puts itself in motion for every separate effect, and if this is so, be thou content with that which is the result of its activity; or it puts itself in motion once, and everything else comes by way of sequence in a manner; or indivisible elements are the origin of all things.—In a word, if there is a god, all is well; and if chance rules, do not thou also be governed by it.

Soon will the earth cover us all: then the earth, too, will change, and the things also which result from change will continue to change for ever, and these again for ever. For if a man reflects on the changes and transformations which follow one another like wave after wave and their rapidity, he will despise everything which is perishable.

29. The universal cause is like a winter torrent: it carries everything along with it. But how worthless are all these poor people who are engaged in matters political, and, as they suppose, are playing the philosopher! All drivellers. Well then, man: do what nature now requires. Set thyself in motion, if it is in thy power, and do not look about thee to see if any one will observe it; nor yet expect Plato's *Republic:* but be con-

tent if the smallest thing goes on well, and consider such an event to be no small matter. For who can change men's opinions? And without a change of opinions what else is there than the slavery of men who groan while they pretend to obey? Come now and tell me of Alexander and Philip and Demetrius of Phalerum. They themselves shall judge whether they discovered what the common nature required, and trained themselves accordingly. But if they acted like tragedy heroes, no one has condemned me to imitate them. Simple and modest is the work of philosophy. Draw me not aside to indolence and pride.

30. Look down from above on the countless herds of men and their countless solemnities, and the infinitely varied voyagings in storms and calms, and the differences among those who are born, who live together, and die. And consider, too, the life lived by others in olden time, and the life of those who will live after thee, and the life now lived among barbarous nations, and how many know not even thy name, and how many will soon forget it, and how they who perhaps now are praising thee will very soon blame thee, and that neither a posthumous name is of any value, nor reputation, nor anything else.

31. Let there be freedom from perturbations with respect to the things which come from the external cause; and let there be justice in the things done by virtue of the internal cause, that is, let there be movement and action terminating in this, in social acts, for this is according to thy nature.

32. Thou canst remove out of the way many useless things among those which disturb thee, for they lie entirely in thy opinion; and thou wilt then gain for thyself ample space by comprehending the whole universe in thy mind, and by contemplating the eternity of time, and observing the rapid change of every several thing, how short is the time from birth to dissolution, and the illimitable time before birth as well as the equally boundless time after dissolution.

33. All that thou seest will quickly perish, and those who have been spectators of its dissolution will very soon perish too. And he who dies at the extremest old age will be brought into the same condition with him who died prematurely.

34. What are these men's leading principles, and about what kind of things are they busy, and for what kind of reasons do they love and honour? Imagine that thou seest their poor souls laid bare. When they think that they do harm by their blame or good by their praise, what an idea!

35. Loss is nothing else than change. But the universal nature delights in change, and in obedience to her all things are now done well, and from eternity have been done in like form, and will be such to time without end. What, then, dost thou say? That all things have

been and all things always will be bad, and that no power has ever been found in so many gods to rectify these things, but the world has been condemned to be bound in never ceasing evil?

36. The rottenness of the matter which is the foundation of everything! Water, dust, bones, filth: or again, marble rocks, the callosities of the earth; and gold and silver, the sediments; and garments, only bits of hair; and purple dye, blood; and everything else is of the same kind. And that which is of the nature of breath is also another thing of the same kind, changing from this to that.

37. Enough of this wretched life and murmuring and apish tricks. Why art thou disturbed? What is there new in this? What unsettles thee? Is it the form of the thing? Look at it. Or is it the matter? Look at it. But besides these there is nothing. Towards the gods, then, now become at last more simple and better. It is the same whether we examine these things for a hundred years or three.

38. If any man has done wrong, the harm is his own. But perhaps he has not done wrong.

39. Either all things proceed from one intelligent source and come together as in one body, and the part ought not to find fault with what is done for the benefit of the whole; or there are only atoms, and nothing else than mixture and dispersion. Why, then, art thou disturbed? Say to the ruling faculty, Art thou dead, art thou corrupted, art thou playing the hypocrite, art thou become a beast, dost thou herd and feed with the rest?

40. Either the gods have no power or they have power. If, then, they have no power, why dost thou pray to them? But if they have power, why dost thou not pray for them to give thee the faculty of not fearing any of the things which thou fearest, or of not desiring any of the things which thou desirest, or not being pained at anything, rather than pray that any of these things should not happen or happen? for certainly if they can co-operate with men, they can co-operate for these purposes. But perhaps thou wilt say, the gods have placed them in thy power. Well, then, is it not better to use what is in thy power like a free man than to desire in a slavish and abject way what is not in thy power? And who has told thee that the gods do not aid us even in the things which are in our power? Begin, then, to pray for such things, and thou wilt see. One man prays thus: How shall I be able to lie with that woman? Do thou pray thus: How shall I not desire to lie with her? Another prays thus: How shall I be released from this? Another prays: How shall I not desire to be released? Another thus: How shall I not lose my little son? Thou thus: How shall I not be afraid to lose him? In fine, turn thy prayers this way, and see what comes.

41. Epicurus says, In my sickness my conversation was not about

my bodily sufferings, nor, says he, did I talk on such subjects to those who visited me; but I continued to discourse on the nature of things as before, keeping to this main point, how the mind, while participating in such movements as go on in the poor flesh, shall be free from perturbations and maintain its proper good. Nor did I, he says, give the physicians an opportunity of putting on solemn looks, as if they were doing something great, but my life went on well and happily. Do, then, the same that he did both in sickness, if thou art sick, and in any other circumstances; for never to desert philosophy in any events that may befall us, nor to hold trifling talk either with an ignorant man or with one unacquainted with nature, is a principle of all schools of philosophy; but to be intent only on that which thou art now doing and on the instrument by which thou doest it.

42. When thou art offended with any man's shameless conduct, immediately ask thyself, Is it possible, then, that shameless men should not be in the world? It is not possible. Do not, then, require what is impossible. For this man also is one of those shameless men who must of necessity be in the world. Let the same considerations be present to thy mind in the case of the knave, and the faithless man, and of every man who does wrong in any way. For at the same time that thou dost remind thyself that it is impossible that such kind of men should not exist, thou wilt become more kindly disposed towards every one individually. It is useful to perceive this, too, immediately when the occasion arises, what virtue nature has given to man to oppose to every wrongful act. For she has given to man, as an antidote against the stupid man, mildness, and against another kind of man some other power. And in all cases it is possible for thee to correct by teaching the man who is gone astray; for every man who errs misses his object and is gone astray. Besides wherein hast thou been injured? For thou wilt find that no one among those against whom thou art irritated has done anything by which thy mind could be made worse; but that which is evil to thee and harmful has its foundation only in the mind. And what harm is done or what is there strange, if the man who has not been instructed does the acts of an uninstructed man? Consider whether thou shouldst not rather blame thyself, because thou didst not expect such a man to err in such a way. For thou hadst means given thee by thy reason to suppose that it was likely that he would commit this error, and yet thou hast forgotten and art amazed that he has erred. But most of all when thou blamest a man as faithless or ungrateful, turn to thyself. For the fault is manifestly thy own, whether thou didst trust that a man who had such a disposition would keep his promise, or when conferring thy kindness thou didst not confer it absolutely, nor yet in such way as to have received from thy very act

all the profit. For what more dost thou want when thou hast done a man a service? Art thou not content that thou hast done something conformable to thy nature, and dost thou seek to be paid for it? Just as if the eye demanded a recompense for seeing, or the feet for walking. For as these members are formed for a particular purpose, and by working according to their several constitutions obtain what is their own; so also as man is formed by nature to acts of benevolence, when he has done anything benevolent or in any other way conducive to the common interest, he has acted conformably to his constitution, and he gets what is his own.

BOOK X

WILT thou, then, my soul, never be good and simple and one and naked, more manifest than the body which surrounds thee? Wilt thou never enjoy an affectionate and contented disposition? Wilt thou never be full and without a want of any kind, longing for nothing more, nor desiring anything, either animate or inanimate, for the enjoyment of pleasures? Nor yet desiring time wherein thou shalt have longer enjoyment, or place, or pleasant climate, or society of men with whom thou mayest live in harmony? But wilt thou be satisfied with thy present condition, and pleased with all that is about thee, and wilt thou convince thyself that thou hast everything and that it comes from the gods, that everything is well for thee, and will be well whatever shall please them, and whatever they shall give for the conservation of the perfect living being, the good and just and beautiful, which generates and holds together all things, and contains and embraces all things which are dissolved for the production of other like things? Wilt thou never be such that thou shalt so dwell in community with gods and men as neither to find fault with them at all, nor to be condemned by them?

2. Observe what thy nature requires, so far as thou art governed by nature only: then do it and accept it, if thy nature, so far as thou art a living being, shall not be made worse by it. And next thou must observe what thy nature requires so far as thou art a living being. And all this thou mayest allow thyself, if thy nature, so far as thou art a rational animal, shall not be made worse by it. But the rational animal is consequently also a political (social) animal. Use these rules, then, and trouble thyself about nothing else.

3. Everything which happens either happens in such wise as thou art formed by nature to bear it, or as thou art not formed by nature to bear it. If, then, it happens to thee in such way as thou art formed by nature to bear it, do not complain, but bear it as thou art formed by nature to bear it. But if it happens in such wise as thou art not formed by nature to bear it, do not complain, for it will perish after it has consumed thee. Remember, however, that thou art formed by nature to bear everything, with respect to which it depends on thy own opinion to make it endurable and tolerable, by thinking that it is either thy interest or thy duty to do this.

4. If a man is mistaken, instruct him kindly and show him his error. But if thou art not able, blame thyself, or blame not even thyself.

5. Whatever may happen to thee, it was prepared for thee from all eternity; and the implication of causes was from eternity spinning the thread of thy being, and of that which is incident to it.

6. Whether the universe is a concourse of atoms, or nature is a system, let this first be established, that I am a part of the whole which is governed by nature; next, I am in a manner intimately related to the parts which are of the same kind with myself. For remembering this, inasmuch as I am a part, I shall be discontented with none of the things which are assigned to me out of the whole; for nothing is injurious to the part, if it is for the advantage of the whole. For the whole contains nothing which is not for its advantage; and all natures indeed have this common principle, but the nature of the universe has this principle besides, that it cannot be compelled even by any external cause to generate anything harmful to itself. By remembering, then, that I am a part of such a whole, I shall be content with everything that happens. And inasmuch as I am in a manner intimately related to the parts which are of the same kind with myself, I shall do nothing unsocial, but I shall rather direct myself to the things which are of the same kind with myself, and I shall turn all my efforts to the common interest, and divert them from the contrary. Now, if these things are done so, life must flow on happily, just as thou mayest observe that the life of a citizen is happy, who continues a course of action which is advantageous to his fellow-citizens, and is content with whatever the state may assign to him.

7. The parts of the whole, everything, I mean, which is naturally comprehended in the universe, must of necessity perish; but let this be understood in this sense, that they must undergo change. But if this is naturally both an evil and a necessity for the parts, the whole would not continue to exist in a good condition, the parts being subject to change and constituted so as to perish in various ways. For whether did nature herself design to do evil to the things which are parts of herself, and to make them subject to evil and of necessity fall into evil, or have such results happened without her knowing it? Both these suppositions, indeed, are incredible. But if a man should even drop the term Nature (as an efficient power), and should speak of these things as natural, even then it would be ridiculous to affirm at the same time that the parts of the whole are in their nature subject to change, and at the same time to be surprised or vexed as if something were happening contrary to nature, particularly as the dissolution of things is into those things of which each thing is composed. For there is either a dispersion of the elements out of which everything has been compounded, or a change from the solid to the earthy and from the airy to the aërial, so that these parts are taken back into the universal reason, whether

this at certain periods is consumed by fire or renewed by eternal changes. And do not imagine that the solid and the airy part belong to thee from the time of generation. For all this received its accretion only yesterday and the day before, as one may say, from the food and the air which is inspired. This, then, which has received the accretion, changes, not that which thy mother brought forth. But suppose that this which thy mother brought forth implicates thee very much with that other part, which has the peculiar quality of change, this is nothing in fact in the way of objection to what is said.[1]

8. When thou hast assumed these names, good, modest, true, rational, a man of equanimity, and magnanimous, take care that thou dost not change these names; and if thou shouldst lose them, quickly return to them. And remember that the term Rational was intended to signify a discriminating attention to every several thing and freedom from negligence; and that Equanimity is the voluntary acceptance of the things which are assigned to thee by the common nature; and that Magnanimity is the elevation of the intelligent part above the pleasurable or painful sensations of the flesh, and above that poor thing called fame, and death, and all such things. If, then, thou maintainest thyself in the possession of these names, without desiring to be called by these names by others, thou wilt be another person and wilt enter on another life. For to continue to be such as thou hast hitherto been, and to be torn in pieces and defiled in such a life, is the character of a very stupid man and one overfond of his life, and like those half-devoured fighters with wild beasts, who though covered with wounds and gore, still intreat to be kept to the following day, though they will be exposed in the same state to the same claws and bites. Therefore fix thyself in the possession of these few names: and if thou art able to abide in them, abide as if thou wast removed to certain islands of the Happy. But if thou shalt perceive that thou fallest out of them and dost not maintain thy hold, go courageously into some nook where thou shalt maintain them, or even depart at once from life, not in passion, but with simplicity and freedom and modesty, after doing this one laudable thing at least in thy life, to have gone out of it thus. In order, however, to the remembrance of these names, it will greatly help thee, if thou rememberest the gods, and that they wish not to be flattered, but wish all reasonable beings to be made like themselves; and if thou rememberest that what does the work of a fig-tree is a fig-tree, and that what does the work of a dog is a dog, and that what does the work of a bee is a bee, and that what does the work of a man is a man.

9. Mimi,[2] war, astonishment, torpor, slavery, will daily wipe out those holy principles of thine. How many things without studying nature dost thou imagine, and how many dost thou neglect? But it is thy duty

so to look on and so to do everything, that at the same time the power of dealing with circumstances is perfected, and the contemplative faculty is exercised, and the confidence which comes from the knowledge of each several thing is maintained without showing it, but yet not concealed. For when wilt thou enjoy simplicity, when gravity, and when the knowledge of every several thing, both what it is in substance, and what place it has in the universe, and how long it is formed to exist and of what things it is compounded, and to whom it can belong, and who are able both to give it and take it away?

10. A spider is proud when it has caught a fly, and another when he has caught a poor hare, and another when he has taken a little fish in a net, and another when he has taken wild boars, and another when he has taken bears, and another when he has taken Sarmatians. Are not these robbers, if thou examinest their opinions?

11. Acquire the contemplative way of seeing how all things change into one another, and constantly attend to it, and exercise thyself about this part of philosophy. For nothing is so much adapted to produce magnanimity. Such a man has put off the body, and as he sees that he must, no one knows how soon, go away from among men and leave everything here, he gives himself up entirely to just doing in all his actions, and in everything else that happens he resigns himself to the universal nature. But as to what any man shall say or think about him or do against him, he never even thinks of it, being himself contented with these two things, with acting justly in what he now does, and being satisfied with what is now assigned to him; and he lays aside all distracting and busy pursuits, and desires nothing else than to accomplish the straight course through the law, and by accomplishing the straight course to follow God.

12. What need is there of suspicious fear, since it is in thy power to inquire what ought to be done? And if thou seest clear, go by this way content, without turning back: but if thou dost not see clear, stop and take the best advisers. But if any other things oppose thee, go on according to thy powers with due consideration, keeping to that which appears to be just. For it is best to reach this object, and if thou dost fail, let thy failure be in attempting this. He who follows reason in all things is both tranquil and active at the same time, and also cheerful and collected.

13. Inquire of thyself as soon as thou wakest from sleep, whether it will make any difference to thee, if another does what is just and right. It will make no difference.

Thou hast not forgotten, I suppose, that those who assume arrogant airs in bestowing their praise or blame on others, are such as they are at bed and at board, and thou hast not forgotten what they do, and what they avoid and what they pursue, and how they steal and how they rob, not with hands and feet, but with their most valuable part, by means of which there is produced, when a man chooses, fidelity, modesty, truth, law, a good daemon (happiness)?

14. To her who gives and takes back all, to nature, the man who is instructed and modest says, Give what thou wilt; take back what thou wilt. And he says this not proudly, but obediently and well pleased with her.

15. Short is the little which remains to thee of life. Live as on a mountain. For it makes no difference whether a man lives there or here, if he lives everywhere in the world as in a state (political community). Let men see, let them know a real man who lives according to nature. If they cannot endure him, let them kill him. For that is better than to live thus as men do.

16. No longer talk at all about the kind of man that a good man ought to be, but be such.

17. Constantly contemplate the whole of time and the whole of substance, and consider that all individual things as to substance are a grain of a fig, and as to time, the turning of a gimlet.

18. Look at everything that exists, and observe that it is already in dissolution and in change, and as it were putrefaction or dispersion, or that everything is so constituted by nature as to die.

19. Consider what men are when they are eating, sleeping, generating, easing themselves and so forth. Then what kind of men they are when they are imperious and arrogant, or angry and scolding from their elevated place. But a short time ago to how many they were slaves and for what things; and after a little time consider in what a condition they will be.

20. That is for the good of each thing, which the universal nature brings to each. And it is for its good at the time when nature brings it.

21. 'The earth loves the shower;' and 'the solemn aether loves:'[3] and the universe loves to make whatever is about to be. I say then to the universe, that I love as thou lovest. And is not this too said, that 'this or that loves (is wont) to be produced'?

22. Either thou livest here and hast already accustomed thyself to it, or thou art going away, and this was thy own will; or thou art dying and hast discharged thy duty. But besides these things there is nothing. Be of good cheer, then.

23. Let this always be plain to thee, that this piece of land is like any other; and that all things here are the same with things on the top of a mountain, or on the sea-shore, or wherever thou choosest to be. For thou wilt find just what Plato says, Dwelling within the walls of a city as in a shepherd's fold on a mountain.[4]

24. What is my ruling faculty now to me? And of what nature am I now making it? And for what purpose am I now using it? Is it void of understanding? Is it loosed and rent asunder from social life? Is it melted into and mixed with the poor flesh so as to move together with it?

25. He who flies from his master is a runaway; but the law is master, and he who breaks the law is a runaway. And he also who is grieved or angry or afraid, is dissatisfied because something has been or is or shall be of the things which are appointed by him who rules all things, and he is Law, and assigns to every man what is fit. He then who fears or is grieved or is angry is a runaway.

26. A man deposits seed in a womb and goes away, and then another cause takes it, and labours on it and makes a child. What a thing from such a material! Again, the child passes food down through the throat, and then another cause takes it and makes perception and motion, and in fine life and strength and other things; how many and how strange! Observe then the things which are produced in such a hidden way, and see the power just as we see the power which carries things downwards and upwards, not with the eyes, but still no less plainly.

27. Constantly consider how all things such as they now are, in time past also were; and consider that they will be the same again. And place before thy eyes entire dramas and stages of the same form, whatever thou hast learned from thy experience or from older history; for example, the whole court of Hadrian, and the whole court of Antoninus, and the whole court of Philip, Alexander, Croesus; for all those were such dramas as we see now, only with different actors.

28. Imagine every man who is grieved at anything or discontented to be like a pig which is sacrificed and kicks and screams.

Like this pig also is he who on his bed in silence laments the bonds in which we are held. And consider that only to the rational animal is it given to follow voluntarily what happens; but simply to follow is a necessity imposed on all.

29. Severally on the occasion of everything that thou doest, pause and ask thyself, if death is a dreadful thing because it deprives thee of this.

30. When thou art offended at any man's fault, forthwith turn to thyself and reflect in what like manner thou dost err thyself; for example, in thinking that money is a good thing, or pleasure, or a bit of reputation, and the like. For by attending to this thou wilt quickly forget thy anger, if this consideration also is added, that the man is compelled: for what else could he do? or, if thou art able, take away from him the compulsion.

31. When thou hast seen Satyron the Socratic, think of either Eutyches or Hymen, and when thou hast seen Euphrates, think of

Eutychion or Silvanus, and when thou hast seen Alciphron think of Tropaeophorus, and when thou hast seen Xenophon think of Crito or Severus, and when thou hast looked on thyself, think of any other Caesar, and in the case of every one do in like manner. Then let this thought be in thy mind, Where then are those men? Nowhere, or nobody knows where. For thus continuously thou wilt look at human things as smoke and nothing at all; especially if thou reflectest at the same time that what has once changed will never exist again in the infinite duration of time. But thou, in what a brief space of time is thy existence? And why art thou not content to pass through this short time in an orderly way? What matter and opportunity for thy activity art thou avoiding? For what else are all these things, except exercises for the reason, when it has viewed carefully and by examination into their nature the things which happen in life? Persevere then until thou shalt have made these things thy own, as the stomach which is strengthened makes all things its own, as the blazing fire makes flame and brightness out of everything that is thrown into it.

32. Let it not be in any man's power to say truly of thee that thou art not simple or that thou art not good; but let him be a liar whoever shall think anything of this kind about thee; and this is altogether in thy power. For who is he that shall hinder thee from being good and simple? Do thou only determine to live no longer, unless thou shalt be such. For neither does reason allow thee to live, if thou art not such.

33. What is that which as to this material (our life) can be done or said in the way most conformable to reason. For whatever this may be, it is in thy power to do it or to say it, and do not make excuses that thou art hindered. Thou wilt not cease to lament till thy mind is in such a condition that, what luxury is to those who enjoy pleasure, such shall be to thee, in the matter which is subjected and presented to thee, the doing of the things which are conformable to man's constitution; for a man ought to consider as an enjoyment everything which it is in his power to do according to his own nature. And it is in his power everywhere. Now, it is not given to a cylinder to move everywhere by its own motion, nor yet to water nor to fire, nor to anything else which is governed by nature or an irrational soul, for the things which check them and stand in the way are many. But intelligence and reason are able to go through everything that opposes them, and in such manner as they are formed by nature and as they choose. Place before thy eyes this facility with which the reason will be carried through all things, as fire upwards, as a stone downwards, as a cylinder down an inclined surface, and seek for nothing further. For all other obstacles either affect the body only which is a dead thing; or, except through opinion and the yielding of the reason itself, they do not crush nor do any harm

of any kind; for if they did, he who felt it would immediately become bad. Now, in the case of all things which have a certain constitution, whatever harm may happen to any of them, that which is so affected becomes consequently worse; but in the like case, a man becomes both better, if one may say so, and more worthy of praise by making a right use of these accidents. And finally remember that nothing harms him who is really a citizen, which does not harm the state; nor yet does anything harm the state, which does not harm law (order); and of these things which are called misfortunes not one harms law. What then does not harm law does not harm either state or citizen.

34. To him who is penetrated by true principles even the briefest precept is sufficient, and any common precept, to remind him that he should be free from grief and fear. For example—

> Leaves, some the wind scatters on the ground—
> So is the race of men.[5]

Leaves, also, are thy children; and leaves, too, are they who cry out as if they were worthy of credit and bestow their praise, or on the contrary curse, or secretly blame and sneer; and leaves, in like manner, are those who shall receive and transmit a man's fame to after-times. For all such things as these 'are produced in the season of spring,' as the poet says; then the wind casts them down; then the forest produces other leaves in their places. But a brief existence is common to all things, and yet thou avoidest and pursuest all things as if they would be eternal. A little time, and thou shalt close thy eyes; and him who has attended thee to thy grave another soon will lament.

35. The healthy eye ought to see all visible things and not to say, I wish for green things; for this is the condition of a diseased eye. And the healthy hearing and smelling ought to be ready to perceive all that can be heard and smelled. And the healthy stomach ought to be with respect to all food just as the mill with respect to all things which it is formed to grind. And accordingly the healthy understanding ought to be prepared for everything which happens; but that which says, Let my dear children live, and let all men praise whatever I may do, is an eye which seeks for green things, or teeth which seek for soft things.

36. There is no man so fortunate that there shall not be by him when he is dying some who are pleased with what is going to happen. Suppose that he was a good and wise man, will there not be at last some one to say to himself, Let us at last breathe freely being relieved from this schoolmaster? It is true that he was harsh to none of us, but I perceived that he tacitly condemns us.—This is what is said of a good man. But in our own case how many other things are there for which there are many who wish to get rid of us. Thou wilt consider this then when thou

art dying, and thou wilt depart more contentedly by reflecting thus: I am going away from such a life, in which even my associates in behalf of whom I have striven so much, prayed, and cared, themselves wish me to depart, hoping perchance to get some little advantage by it. Why then should a man cling to a longer stay here? Do not however for this reason go away less kindly disposed to them, but preserving thy own character, and friendly and benevolent and mild, and on the other hand not as if thou wast torn away; but as when a man dies a quiet death, the poor soul is easily separated from the body, such also ought thy departure from men to be, for nature united thee to them and associated thee. But does she now dissolve the union? Well, I am separated as from kinsmen, not however dragged resisting, but without compulsion; for this too is one of the things according to nature.

37. Accustom thyself as much as possible on the occasion of anything being done by any person to inquire with thyself, For what object is this man doing this? But begin with thyself, and examine thyself first.

38. Remember that this which pulls the strings is the thing which is hidden within: this is the power of persuasion, this is life, this, if one may so say, is man. In contemplating thyself never include the vessel which surrounds thee and these instruments which are attached about it. For they are like to an axe, differing only in this that they grow to the body. For indeed there is no more use in these parts without the cause which moves and checks them than in the weaver's shuttle, and the writer's pen and the driver's whip.

BOOK XI

THESE are the properties of the rational soul: it sees itself, analyses itself, and makes itself such as it chooses; the fruit which it bears itself enjoys—for the fruits of plants and that in animals which corresponds to fruits others enjoy—it obtains its own end, wherever the limit of life may be fixed. Not as in a dance and in a play and in such like things, where the whole action is incomplete, if anything cuts it short; but in every part and wherever it may be stopped, it makes what has been set before it full and complete, so that it can say, I have what is my own. And further it traverses the whole universe, and the surrounding vacuum, and surveys its form, and it extends itself into the infinity of time, and embraces and comprehends the periodical renovation of all things, and it comprehends that those who come after us will see nothing new, nor have those before us seen anything more, but in a manner he who is forty years old, if he has any understanding at all, has seen by virtue of the uniformity that prevails all things which have been and all that will be. This too is a property of the rational soul, love of one's neighbour, and truth and modesty, and to value nothing more than itself, which is also the property of Law. Thus then right reason differs not at all from the reason of justice.

2. Thou wilt set little value on pleasing song and dancing and the pancratium, if thou wilt distribute the melody of the voice into its several sounds, and ask thyself as to each, if thou art mastered by this; for thou wilt be prevented by shame from confessing it: and in the matter of dancing, if at each movement and attitude thou wilt do the same; and the like also in the matter of the pancratium. In all things, then, except virtue and the acts of virtue, remember to apply thyself to their several parts, and by this division to come to value them little: and apply this rule also to thy whole life.

3. What a soul that is which is ready, if at any moment it must be separated from the body, and ready either to be extinguished or dispersed or continue to exist; but so that this readiness comes from a man's own judgement, not from mere obstinacy, as with the Christians,[1] but considerately and with dignity and in a way to persuade another, without tragic show.

4. Have I done something for the general interest? Well then I have had my reward. Let this always be present to thy mind, and never stop doing such good.

5. What is thy art? To be good. And how is this accomplished well

except by general principles, some about the nature of the universe, and others about the proper constitution of man?

6. At first tragedies were brought on the stage as means of reminding men of the things which happen to them, and that it is according to nature for things to happen so, and that, if you are delighted with what is shown on the stage, you should not be troubled with that which takes place on the larger stage. For you see that these things must be accomplished thus, and that even they bear them who cry out 'O Cithaeron.'[2] And, indeed, some things are said well by the dramatic writers, of which kind is the following especially:—

> Me and my children if the gods neglect,
> This has its reason too.[3]

And again—

> We must not chafe and fret at that which happens.[4]

And—

> Life's harvest reap like the wheat's fruitful ear.[5]

And other things of the same kind.

After tragedy the old comedy was introduced, which had a magisterial freedom of speech, and by its very plainness of speaking was useful in reminding men to beware of insolence; and for this purpose too Diogenes used to take from these writers.

But as to the middle comedy which came next, observe what it was, and again, for what object the new comedy was introduced, which gradually sunk down into a mere mimic artifice. That some good things are said even by these writers, everybody knows: but the whole plan of such poetry and dramaturgy, to what end does it look!

7. How plain does it appear that there is not another condition of life so well suited for philosophising as this in which thou now happenest to be.

8. A branch cut off from the adjacent branch must of necessity be cut off from the whole tree also. So too a man when he is separated from another man has fallen off from the whole social community. Now as to a branch, another cuts it off, but a man by his own act separates himself from his neighbour when he hates him and turns away from him, and he does not know that he has at the same time cut himself off from the whole social system. Yet he has this privilege certainly from Zeus who framed society, for it is in our power to grow again to that which is near to us, and again to become a part which helps to make up the whole. However, if it often happens, this kind of separation, it makes it difficult for that which detaches itself to be brought to unity and to be

restored to its former condition. Finally, the branch, which from the first grew together with the tree, and has continued to have one life with it, is not like that which after being cut off is then ingrafted, for this is something like what the gardeners mean when they say that it grows with the rest of the tree, but that it has not the same mind with it.

9. As those who try to stand in thy way when thou art proceeding according to right reason, will not be able to turn thee aside from thy proper action, so neither let them drive thee from thy benevolent feelings towards them, but be on thy guard equally in both matters, not only in the matter of steady judgement and action, but also in the matter of gentleness towards those who try to hinder or otherwise trouble thee. For this also is a weakness, to be vexed at them, as well as to be diverted from thy course of action and to give way through fear; for both are equally deserters from their post, the man who does it through fear, and the man who is alienated from him who is by nature a kinsman and a friend.

10. There is no nature which is inferior to art, for the arts imitate the nature of things. But if this is so, that nature which is the most perfect and the most comprehensive of all natures, cannot fall short of the skill of art. Now all arts do the inferior things for the sake of the superior; therefore the universal nature does so too. And, indeed, hence is the origin of justice, and in justice the other virtues have their foundation: for justice will not be observed, if we either care for middle things (things indifferent), or are easily deceived and careless and changeable.

11. If the things do not come to thee, the pursuits and avoidances of which disturb thee, still in a manner thou goest to them. Let then thy judgement about them be at rest, and they will remain quiet, and thou wilt not be seen either pursuing or avoiding.

12. The spherical form of the soul maintains its figure, when it is neither extended towards any object, nor contracted inwards, nor dispersed nor sinks down, but is illuminated by light, by which it sees the truth, the truth of all things and the truth that is in itself.

13. Suppose any man shall despise me. Let him look to that himself. But I will look to this, that I be not discovered doing or saying anything deserving of contempt. Shall any man hate me? Let him look to it. But I will be mild and benevolent towards every man, and ready to show even him his mistake, not reproachfully, nor yet as making a display of my endurance, but nobly and honestly, like the great Phocion, unless indeed he only assumed it. For the interior parts ought to be such, and a man ought to be seen by the gods neither dissatisfied with anything nor complaining. For what evil is it to thee, if thou art now doing what is agreeable to thy own nature, and art satisfied with that which at this

moment is suitable to the nature of the universe, since thou art a human being placed at thy post in order that what is for the common advantage may be done in some way?

14. Men despise one another and flatter one another; and men wish to raise themselves above one another, and crouch before one another.

15. How unsound and insincere is he who says, I have determined to deal with thee in a fair way.—What art thou doing, man? There is no occasion to give this notice. It will soon show itself by acts. The voice ought to be plainly written on the forehead. Such as a man's character is, he immediately shows it in his eyes, just as he who is beloved forthwith reads everything in the eyes of lovers. The man who is honest and good ought to be exactly like a man who smells strong, so that the bystander as soon as he comes near him must smell whether he choose or not. But the affectation of simplicity is like a crooked stick. Nothing is more disgraceful than a wolfish friendship (false friendship). Avoid this most of all. The good and simple and benevolent show all these things in the eyes, and there is no mistaking.

16. As to living in the best way, this power is in the soul, if it be indifferent to things which are indifferent. And it will be indifferent, if it looks on each of these things separately and all together, and if it remembers that not one of them produces in us an opinion about itself, nor comes to us; but these things remain immovable, and it is we ourselves who produce the judgements about them, and, as we may say, write them in ourselves, it being in our power not to write them, and it being in our power, if perchance these judgements have imperceptibly got admission to our minds, to wipe them out; and if we remember also that such attention will only be for a short time, and then life will be at an end. Besides, what trouble is there at all in doing this? For if these things are according to nature, rejoice in them, and they will be easy to thee: but if contrary to nature, seek what is conformable to thy own nature, and strive towards this, even if it bring no reputation; for every man is allowed to seek his own good.

17. Consider whence each thing is come, and of what it consists, and into what it changes, and what kind of a thing it will be when it has changed, and that it will sustain no harm.

18. If any have offended against thee, consider first: What is my relation to men, and that we are made for one another; and in another respect, I was made to be set over them, as a ram over the flock or a bull over the herd. But examine the matter from first principles, from this: If all things are not mere atoms, it is nature which orders all things: if this is so, the inferior things exist for the sake of the superior, and these for the sake of one another.

Second, consider what kind of men they are at table, in bed, and so forth: and particularly, under what compulsions in respect of opinions they are; and as to their acts, consider with what pride they do what they do.

Third, that if men do rightly what they do, we ought not to be displeased; but if they do not right, it is plain that they do so involuntarily and in ignorance. For as every soul is unwillingly deprived of the truth, so also is it unwillingly deprived of the power of behaving to each man according to his deserts. Accordingly men are pained when they are called unjust, ungrateful, and greedy, and in a word wrong-doers to their neighbours.

Fourth, consider that thou also doest many things wrong, and that thou art a man like others; and even if thou dost abstain from certain faults, still thou hast the disposition to commit them, though either through cowardice, or concern about reputation, or some such mean motive, thou dost abstain from such faults.

Fifth, consider that thou dost not even understand whether men are doing wrong or not, for many things are done with a certain reference to circumstances. And in short, a man must learn a great deal to enable him to pass a correct judgement on another man's acts.

Sixth, consider when thou art much vexed or grieved, that man's life is only a moment, and after a short time we are all laid out dead.

Seventh, that it is not men's acts which disturb us, for those acts have their foundation in men's ruling principles, but it is our own opinions which disturb us. Take away these opinions then, and resolve to dismiss thy judgement about an act as if it were something grievous, and thy anger is gone. How then shall I take away these opinions? By reflecting that no wrongful act of another brings shame on thee: for unless that which is shameful is alone bad, thou also must of necessity do many things wrong, and become a robber and everything else.

Eighth, consider how much more pain is brought on us by the anger and vexation caused by such acts than by the acts themselves, at which we are angry and vexed.

Ninth, consider that a good disposition is invincible, if it be genuine, and not an affected smile and acting a part. For what will the most violent man do to thee, if thou continuest to be of a kind disposition towards him, and if, as opportunity offers, thou gently admonishest him and calmly correctest his errors at the very time when he is trying to do thee harm, saying, Not so, my child: we are constituted by nature for something else: I shall certainly not be injured, but thou art injuring thyself, my child.—And show him with gentle tact and by general principles that this is so, and that even bees do not do as he does, nor any animals which are formed by nature to be gregarious. And thou must do this neither with any double meaning nor in the way of reproach, but affectionately and without any rancour in thy soul; and not as if thou wert lecturing him, nor yet that any bystander may admire, but either when he is alone, and if others are present . . .[6]

Remember these nine rules, as if thou hadst received them as a gift from the Muses, and begin at last to be a man while thou livest. But thou must equally avoid flattering men and being vexed at them, for both are unsocial and lead to harm. And let this truth be present to thee in the excitement of anger, that to be moved by passion is not manly, but that mildness and gentleness, as they are more agreeable to human nature, so also are they more manly; and he who possesses these qualities possesses strength, nerves and courage, and not the man who is subject to fits of passion and discontent. For in the same degree in which a man's mind is nearer to freedom from all passion, in the same degree also is it nearer to strength: and as the sense of pain is a characteristic of weakness, so also is anger. For he who yields to pain and he who yields to anger, both are wounded and both submit.

But if thou wilt, receive also a tenth present from the leader of the Muses (Apollo), and it is this—that to expect bad men not to do wrong is madness, for he who expects this desires an impossibility. But to allow men to behave so to others, and to expect them not to do thee any wrong, is irrational and tyrannical.

19. There are four principal aberrations of the superior faculty against which thou shouldst be constantly on thy guard, and when thou hast detected them, thou shouldst wipe them out and say on each occasion thus: this thought is not necessary: this tends to destroy social union: this which thou art going to say comes not from the real thoughts; for thou shouldst consider it among the most absurd of things for a man not to speak from his real thoughts. But the fourth is when thou shalt reproach thyself for anything, for this is an evidence of the diviner part within thee being overpowered and yielding to the less honourable and to the perishable part, the body, and to its gross pleasures.

20. Thy aërial part and all the fiery parts which are mingled in thee, though by nature they have an upward tendency, still in obedience to the disposition of the universe they are overpowered here in the compound mass (the body). And also the whole of the earthy part in thee and the watery, though their tendency is downward, still are raised up and occupy a position which is not their natural one. In this manner then the elemental parts obey the universal, for when they have been fixed in any place perforce they remain there until again the universal shall sound the signal for dissolution. Is it not then strange that thy intelligent part only should be disobedient and discontented with its own place? And yet no force is imposed on it, but only those things

which are conformable to its nature: still it does not submit, but is carried in the opposite direction. For the movement towards injustice and intemperance and to anger and grief and fear is nothing else than the act of one who deviates from nature. And also when the ruling faculty is discontented with anything that happens, then too it deserts its post: for it is constituted for piety and reverence towards the gods no less than for justice. For these qualities also are comprehended under the generic term of contentment with the constitution of things, and indeed they are prior to acts of justice.

21. He who has not one and always the same object in life, cannot be one and the same all through his life. But what I have said is not enough, unless this also is added, what this object ought to be. For as there is not the same opinion about all the things which in some way or other are considered by the majority to be good, but only about some certain things, that is, things which concern the common interest; so also ought we to propose to ourselves an object which shall be of a common kind (social) and political. For he who directs all his own efforts to this object, will make all his acts alike, and thus will always be the same.

22. Think of the country mouse and of the town mouse, and of the alarm and trepidation of the town mouse.[7]

23. Socrates used to call the opinions of the many by the name of Lamiae, bugbears to frighten children.

24. The Lacedaemonians at their public spectacles used to set seats in the shade for strangers, but themselves sat down anywhere.

25. Socrates excused himself to Perdiccas [8] for not going to him, saying, It is because I would not perish by the worst of all ends, that is, I would not receive a favour and then be unable to return it.

26. In the writings of the Ephesians [9] there was this precept, constantly to think of some one of the men of former times who practised virtue.

27. The Pythagoreans bid us in the morning look to the heavens that we may be reminded of those bodies which continually do the same things and in the same manner perform their work, and also be reminded of their purity and nudity. For there is no veil over a star.

28. Consider what a man Socrates was when he dressed himself in a skin, after Xanthippe had taken his cloak and gone out, and what Socrates said to his friends who were ashamed of him and drew back from him when they saw him dressed thus.

29. Neither in writing nor in reading wilt thou be able to lay down rules for others before thou shalt have first learned to obey rules thyself. Much more is this so in life.

30. A slave thou art: free speech is not for thee.

31. ——And my heart laughed within.[10]

32. And virtue they will curse, speaking harsh words.[11]

33. To look for the fig in winter is a madman's act: such is he who looks for his child when it is no longer allowed.[12]

34. When a man kisses his child, said Epictetus, he should whisper to himself, 'To-morrow perchance thou wilt die.'—But those are words of bad omen.—'No word is a word of bad omen,' said Epictetus, 'which expresses any work of nature; or if it is so, it is also a word of bad omen to speak of the ears of corn being reaped.'[13]

35. The unripe grape, the ripe bunch, the dried grape, all are changes, not into nothing, but into something which exists not yet.[14]

36. No man can rob us of our free will.[15]

37. Epictetus also said, A man must discover an art (or rules) with respect to giving his assent; and in respect to his movements he must be careful that they be made with regard to circumstances, that they be consistent with social interests, that they have regard to the value of the object; and as to sensual desire, he should altogether keep away from it; and as to avoidance (aversion) he should not show it with respect to any of the things which are not in our power.

38. The dispute then, he said, is not about any common matter, but about being mad or not.

39. Socrates used to say, What do you want? Souls of rational men or irrational?—Souls of rational men.—Of what rational men? Sound or unsound?—Sound.—Why then do you not seek for them?—Because we have them.—Why then do you fight and quarrel?

BOOK XII

All those things at which thou wishest to arrive by a circuitous road, thou canst have now, if thou dost not refuse them to thyself. And this means, if thou wilt take no notice of all the past, and trust the future to providence, and direct the present only conformably to piety and justice. Conformably to piety, that thou mayest be content with the lot which is assigned to thee, for nature designed it for thee and thee for it. Conformably to justice, that thou mayest always speak the truth freely and without disguise, and do the things which are agreeable to law and according to the worth of each. And let neither another man's wickedness hinder thee, nor opinion nor voice, nor yet the sensations of the poor flesh which has grown about thee; for the passive part will look to this. If then, whatever the time may be when thou shalt be near to thy departure, neglecting everything else thou shalt respect only thy ruling faculty and the divinity within thee, and if thou shalt be afraid not because thou must some time cease to live, but if thou shalt fear never to have begun to live according to nature—then thou wilt be a man worthy of the universe which has produced thee, and thou wilt cease to be a stranger in thy native land, and to wonder at things which happen daily as if they were something unexpected, and to be dependent on this or that.

2. God sees the minds (ruling principles) of all men bared of the material vesture and rind and impurities. For with his intellectual part alone he touches the intelligence only which has flowed and been derived from himself into these bodies. And if thou also usest thyself to do this, thou wilt rid thyself of thy much trouble. For he who regards not the poor flesh which envelops him, surely will not trouble himself by looking after raiment and dwelling and fame and such like externals and show.

3. The things are three of which thou art composed, a little body, a little breath (life), intelligence. Of these the first two are thine, so far as it is thy duty to take care of them; but the third alone is properly thine. Therefore if thou shalt separate from thyself, that is, from thy understanding, whatever others do or say, and whatever thou hast done or said thyself, and whatever future things trouble thee because they may happen, and whatever in the body which envelops thee or in the breath (life), which is by nature associated with the body, is attached to thee independent of thy will, and whatever the external circumfluent vortex whirls round, so that the intellectual power exempt from the things of

fate can live pure and free by itself, doing what is just and accepting what happens and saying the truth: if thou wilt separate, I say, from this ruling faculty the things which are attached to it by the impressions of sense, and the things of time to come and of time that is past, and wilt make thyself like Empedocles' sphere,

All round, and in its joyous rest reposing;

and if thou shalt strive to live only what is really thy life, that is, the present—then thou wilt be able to pass that portion of life which remains for thee up to the time of thy death, free from perturbations, nobly, and obedient to thy own daemon (to the god that is within thee).

4. I have often wondered how it is that every man loves himself more than all the rest of men, but yet sets less value on his own opinion of himself than on the opinion of others. If then a god or a wise teacher should present himself to a man and bid him to think of nothing and to design nothing which he would not express as soon as he conceived it, he could not endure it even for a single day. So much more respect have we to what our neighbours shall think of us than to what we shall think of ourselves.

5. How can it be that the gods after having arranged all things well and benevolently for mankind, have overlooked this alone, that some men and very good men, and men who, as we may say, have had most communion with the divinity, and through pious acts and religious observances have been most intimate with the divinity, when they have once died should never exist again, but should be completely extinguished?

But if this is so, be assured that if it ought to have been otherwise, the gods would have done it. For if it were just, it would also be possible; and if it were according to nature, nature would have had it so. But because it is not so, if in fact it is not so, be thou convinced that it ought not to have been so:—for thou seest even of thyself that in this inquiry thou art disputing with the deity; and we should not thus dispute with the gods, unless they were most excellent and most just;—but if this is so, they would not have allowed anything in the ordering of the universe to be neglected unjustly and irrationally.

6. Practise thyself even in the things which thou despairest of accomplishing. For even the left hand, which is ineffectual for all other things for want of practice, holds the bridle more vigorously than the right hand; for it has been practised in this.

7. Consider in what condition both in body and soul a man should be when he is overtaken by death; and consider the shortness of life, the boundless abyss of time past and future, the feebleness of all matter.

8. Contemplate the formative principles (forms) of things bare of

their coverings; the purposes of actions; consider what pain is, what pleasure is, and death, and fame; who is to himself the cause of his uneasiness; how no man is hindered by another; that everything is opinion.

9. In the application of thy principles thou must be like the pancratiast, not like the gladiator; for the gladiator lets fall the sword which he uses and is killed; but the other always has his hand, and needs to do nothing else than use it.

10. See what things are in themselves, dividing them into matter, form and purpose.

11. What a power man has to do nothing except what God will approve, and to accept all that God may give him.

12. With respect to that which happens conformably to nature, we ought to blame neither gods, for they do nothing wrong either voluntarily or involuntarily, nor men, for they do nothing wrong except involuntarily. Consequently we should blame nobody.

13. How ridiculous and what a stranger he is who is surprised at anything which happens in life.

14. Either there is a fatal necessity and invincible order, or a kind Providence, or a confusion without a purpose and without a director (IV. 27). If then there is an invincible necessity, why dost thou resist? But if there is a Providence which allows itself to be propitiated, make thyself worthy of the help of the divinity. But if there is a confusion without a governor, be content that in such a tempest thou hast in thyself a certain ruling intelligence. And even if the tempest carry thee away, let it carry away the poor flesh, the poor breath, everything else; for the intelligence at least it will not carry away.

15. Does the light of the lamp shine without losing its splendour until it is extinguished; and shall the truth which is in thee and justice and temperance be extinguished before thy death?

16. When a man has presented the appearance of having done wrong, say, How then do I know if this is a wrongful act? And even if he has done wrong, how do I know that he has not condemned himself? and so this is like tearing his own face. Consider that he, who would not have the bad man do wrong, is like the man who would not have the fig-tree to bear juice in the figs and infants to cry and the horse to neigh, and whatever else must of necessity be. For what must a man do who has such a character? If then thou art irritable, cure this man's disposition.

17. If it is not right, do not do it: if it is not true, do not say it. For let thy efforts be—[1]

18. In everything always observe what the thing is which produces for thee an appearance, and resolve it by dividing it into the formal, the material, the purpose, and the time within which it must end.

19. Perceive at last that thou hast in thee something better and more divine than the things which cause the various affects, and as it were pull thee by the strings. What is there now in my mind? Is it fear, or suspicion, or desire, or anything of the kind?

20. First, do nothing inconsiderately, nor without a purpose. Second, make thy acts refer to nothing else than to a social end.

21. Consider that before long thou wilt be nobody and nowhere, nor will any of the things exist which thou now seest, nor any of those who are now living. For all things are formed by nature to change and be turned and to perish in order that other things in continuous succession may exist.

22. Consider that everything is opinion, and opinion is in thy power. Take away then, when thou choosest, thy opinion, and like a mariner, who has doubled the promontory, thou wilt find calm, everything stable, and a waveless bay.

23. Any one activity whatever it may be, when it has ceased at its proper time, suffers no evil because it has ceased; nor he who has done this act, does he suffer any evil for this reason that the act has ceased. In like manner then the whole which consists of all the acts, which is our life, if it cease at its proper time, suffers no evil for this reason that it has ceased; nor he who has terminated this series at the proper time, has he been ill dealt with. But the proper time and the limit nature fixes, sometimes as in old age the peculiar nature of man, but always the universal nature, by the change of whose parts the whole universe continues ever young and perfect. And everything which is useful to the universal is always good and in season. Therefore the termination of life for every man is no evil, because neither is it shameful, since it is both independent of the will and not opposed to the general interest, but it is good, since it is seasonable and profitable to and congruent with the universal. For thus too he is moved by the deity who is moved in the same manner with the deity and moved towards the same things in his mind.

24. These three principles thou must have in readiness. In the things which thou doest do nothing either inconsiderately or otherwise than as justice herself would act; but with respect to what may happen to thee from without, consider that it happens either by chance or according to Providence, and thou must neither blame chance nor accuse Providence. Second, consider what every being is from the seed to the time of its receiving a soul, and from the reception of a soul to the giving back of the same, and of what things every being is compounded and into what things it is resolved. Third, if thou shouldst suddenly be raised up above the earth, and shouldst look down on human things, and observe the variety of them how great it is, and at the same time also shouldst see

at a glance how great is the number of beings who dwell all around in the air and the aether, consider that as often as thou shouldst be raised up, thou wouldst see the same things, sameness of form and shortness of duration. Are these things to be proud of?

25. Cast away opinion: thou art saved. Who then hinders thee from casting it away?

26. When thou art troubled about anything, thou hast forgotten this, that all things happen according to the universal nature; and forgotten this, that a man's wrongful act is nothing to thee; and further thou hast forgotten this, that everything which happens, always happened so and will happen so, and now happens so everywhere; forgotten this too, how close is the kinship between a man and the whole human race, for it is a community, not of a little blood or seed, but of intelligence. And thou hast forgotten this too, that every man's intelligence is a god, and is an efflux of the deity; and forgotten this, that nothing is a man's own, but that his child and his body and his very soul came from the deity; forgotten this, that everything is opinion; and lastly thou hast forgotten that every man lives the present time only, and loses only this.

27. Constantly bring to thy recollection those who have complained greatly about anything, those who have been most conspicuous by the greatest fame or misfortunes or enmities or fortunes of any kind: then think where are they all now? Smoke and ash and a tale, or not even a tale. And let there be present to thy mind also everything of this sort, how Fabius Catullinus lived in the country, and Lucius Lupus in his gardens, and Stertinius at Baiae, and Tiberius at Capreae and Velius Rufus (or Rufus at Velia); and in fine think of the eager pursuit of anything conjoined with pride; and how worthless everything is after which men violently strain; and how much more philosophical it is for a man in the opportunities presented to him to show himself just, temperate, obedient to the gods, and to do this with all simplicity: for the pride which is proud of its want of pride is the most intolerable of all.

28. To those who ask, Where hast thou seen the gods or how dost thou comprehend that they exist and so worshipest them, I answer, in the first place, they may be seen even with the eyes;[2] in the second place neither have I seen even my own soul and yet I honour it. Thus then with respect to the gods, from what I constantly experience of their power, from this I comprehend that they exist and I venerate them.

29. The safety of life is this, to examine everything all through, what it is itself. what is its material, what the formal part; with all thy soul to do justice and to say the truth. What remains except to enjoy life by joining one good thing to another so as not to leave even the smallest intervals between?

30. There is one light of the sun, though it is interrupted by walls,

mountains, and other things infinite. There is one common substance, though it is distributed among countless bodies which have their several qualities. There is one soul, though it is distributed among infinite natures and individual circumscriptions (or individuals). There is one intelligent soul, though it seems to be divided. Now in the things which have been mentioned all the other parts, such as those which are air and matter, are without sensation and have no fellowship: and yet even these parts the intelligent principle holds together and the gravitation towards the same. But intellect in a peculiar manner tends to that which is of the same kin, and combines with it, and the feeling for communion is not interrupted.

31. What dost thou wish? To continue to exist? Well, dost thou wish to have sensation? Movement? Growth? And then again to cease to grow? To use thy speech? To think? What is there of all these things which seems to thee worth desiring? But if it is easy to set little value on all these things, turn to that which remains, which is to follow reason and God. But it is inconsistent with honouring reason and God to be troubled because by death a man will be deprived of the other things.

32. How small a part of the boundless and unfathomable time is assigned to every man? For it is very soon swallowed up in the eternal. And how small a part of the whole substance? And how small a part of the universal soul? And on what a small clod of the whole earth thou creepest? Reflecting on all this consider nothing to be great, except to act as thy nature leads thee, and to endure that which the common nature brings.

33. How does the ruling faculty make use of itself? For all lies in this. But everything else, whether it is in the power of thy will or not, is only lifeless ashes and smoke.

34. This reflection is most adapted to move us to contempt of death, that even those who think pleasure to be a good and pain an evil still have despised it.

35. The man to whom that only is good which comes in due season, and to whom it is the same thing whether he has done more or fewer acts conformable to right reason, and to whom it makes no difference whether he contemplates the world for a longer or a shorter time—for this man neither is death a terrible thing.

36. Man, thou hast been a citizen in this great state (the world): what difference does it make to thee whether for five years (or three)? For that which is conformable to the laws is just for all. Where is the hardship then, if no tyrant nor yet an unjust judge sends thee away from the state, but nature who brought thee into it? The same as if a praetor who has employed an actor dismisses him from the stage.—'But I have not finished the five acts, but only three of them.'—Thou sayest well,

but in life the three acts are the whole drama; for what shall be a complete drama is determined by him who was once the cause of its composition, and now of its dissolution: but thou art the cause of neither. Depart then satisfied, for he also who releases thee is satisfied.

NOTES

Book I.

[1] His real father's name was Annius Verus.
[2] Domitia Calvilla, also called Lucilla.
[3] 'Perhaps his mother's grandfather, Catilius Severus.' (Long)
[4] His adoptive father, the Emperor Antoninus Pius.
[5] Cf. Xenophon, *Memorabilia,* I. 3. 15.
[6] Presumably his brother by adoption, L. Verus.
[7] The text is corrupt here.
[8] The Quadi, against whom M. Aurelius campaigned successfully in A.D. 174, lived in the south-east of Germany.

Book II.

[1] Cf. Xenophon, *Memorabilia,* II. 3. 18.
[2] Cf. Plato, *Theaetetus,* 173e.
[3] Cf. Epictetus, Book I, note 11.
[4] A town in Pannonia, the Roman province lying to the north of modern Dalmatia.

Book IV.

[1] The text is doubtful here.
[2] The reference is probably to Homer's Nestor.

Book V.

[1] Cf. Menander, Fragment 530 (Kock).
[2] Cf. Book II, section 1.
[3] The text is corrupt here.
[4] Cf. Epictetus, Book I, chap. 25.
[5] Homer, *Odyssey,* IV. 690.
[6] Hesiod, *Works and Days,* 197.
[7] The Stoic precept, 'Bear and Forebear'.
[8] The text of this section is very corrupt.

Book VI.

[1] Cf. Plutarch, *adversus Stoicos,* 13-14.

Book VII.

[1] The text here is very corrupt.
[2] *Republic,* 486a.
[3] Euripides, *Bellerophon,* Fragment 289.
[4] Euripides, *Hypsipyle,* Fragment 757.
[5] Euripides, *Antiope,* Fragment 207.
[6] Euripides, Fragment 910. Cf. Aristophanes, *Acharnians,* 661.

[7] *Apology,* 28b.
[8] *Apology,* 28e.
[9] Plato, *Gorgias,* 512d-e.
[10] This is apparently not in the Platonic corpus.
[11] Euripides, *Chrysippus,* Fragment 836.
[12] Euripides, *Suppliants,* 1110.
[13] Author unknown.
[14] The text here is corrupt.
[15] Cf. Aristophanes, *Clouds,* 363.

Book VIII.
[1] I.e., Julius Caesar.
[2] The text is uncertain here.
[3] The etymology is incorrect.

Book X.
[1] The text may be corrupt here.
[2] A kind of Roman stage play.
[3] Euripides, Fragment 890.
[4] Cf. *Theaetetus* 174d.
[5] Homer, *Iliad,* VI. 147.

Book XI.
[1] Haines in his translation of the *Meditations* in the Loeb Classical Library argues that this reference to the Christians is a gloss.
[2] Sophocles, *Oedipus the King,* 1391.
[3] Euripides, *Antiope,* Fragment 207.
[4] Euripides, *Bellerophon,* Fragment 289.
[5] Euripides, *Hypsipyle,* Fragment 757.
[6] The text is defective here.
[7] Cf. Horace, *Sermones,* II. 6.
[8] Other authorities say this was Archelaus, the son of Perdiccas.
[9] It is possible that 'Epicureans' should be substituted for 'Ephesians'.
[10] Homer, *Odyssey,* IX. 413.
[11] Hesiod, *Works and Days,* 185.
[12] Epictetus, III. 24. 87.
[13] These quotations come from Epictetus, III. 24. 88.
[14] Epictetus, III. 24. 91.
[15] Epictetus, III. 24. 105.

Book XII.
[1] The text is apparently defective here.
[2] This probably refers to the belief held by the Stoics that the celestial bodies were divine.

APPENDIX

CLEANTHES' *HYMN TO ZEUS*

O God most glorious, called by many a name,
Nature's great King, through endless years the same;
Omnipotence, who by thy just decree
Controllest all, hail, Zeus, for unto thee
Behoves thy creatures in all lands to call.
We are thy children, we alone, of all
On earth's broad ways that wander to and fro,
Bearing thine image wheresoe'er we go.
Wherefore with songs of praise thy power I will forth show.
Lo! yonder Heaven, that round the earth is wheeled,
Follows thy guidance, still to thee doth yield
Glad homage; thine unconquerable hand
Such flaming minister, the levin brand,
Wieldeth, a sword two-edged, whose deathless might
Pulsates through all that Nature brings to light;
Vehicle of the universal Word, that flows
Through all, and in the light celestial glows
Of stars both great and small. A King of Kings
Through ceaseless ages, God, whose purpose brings
To birth, whate'er on land or in the sea
Is wrought, or in high heaven's immensity;
Save what the sinner works infatuate.
Nay, but thou knowest to make crooked straight:
Chaos to thee is order: in thine eyes
The unloved is lovely, who didst harmonize
Things evil with things good, that there should be
One Word through all things everlastingly.
One Word—whose voice alas! the wicked spurn;
Insatiate for the good their spirits yearn:
Yet seeing see not, neither hearing hear
God's universal law, which those revere,
By reason guided, happiness who win.
The rest, unreasoning, diverse shapes of sin
Self-prompted follow: for an idle name
Vainly they wrestle in the lists of fame:
Others inordinately riches woo,
Or dissolute, the joys of flesh pursue.
Now here, now there they wander, fruitless still,
For ever seeking good and finding ill.
Zeus the all-bountiful, whom darkness shrouds,
Whose lightning lightens in the thunder-clouds;
Thy children save from error's deadly sway:

Turn thou the darkness from their souls away:
Vouchsafe that unto knowledge they attain;
For thou by knowledge art made strong to reign
O'er all, and all things rulest righteously.
So by thee honoured, we will honour thee,
Praising thy works continually with songs,
As mortals should; nor higher meed belongs
E'en to the gods, than justly to adore
The universal law for evermore.

AN ESSAY ON MARCUS AURELIUS

BY

MATTHEW ARNOLD

Mr. Mill says, in his book on Liberty, that "Christian morality is in great part merely a protest against paganism; its ideal is negative rather than positive, passive rather than active." He says that, in certain most important respects, "it falls far below the best morality of the ancients." Now, the object of systems of morality is to take possession of human life, to save it from being abandoned to passion or allowed to drift at hazard, to give it happiness by establishing it in the practice of virtue; and this object they seek to attain by prescribing to human life fixed principles of action, fixed rules of conduct. In its uninspired as well as in its inspired moments, in its days of languor and gloom as well as in its days of sunshine and energy, human life has thus always a clue to follow, and may always be making way towards its goal. Christian morality has not failed to supply to human life aids of this sort. It has supplied them far more abundantly than many of its critics imagine. The most exquisite document after those of the New Testament, of all the documents the Christian spirit has ever inspired,—the *Imitation,*—by no means contains the whole of Christian morality; nay, the disparagers of this morality would think themselves sure of triumphing if one agreed to look for it in the *Imitation* only. But even the *Imitation* is full of passages like these: "Vita sine proposito languida et vaga est;"—"Omni die renovare debemus propositum nostrum, dicentes: nunc hodiè perfectè incipiamus, quia nihil est quod hactenus fecimus;"—"Secundum propositum nostrum est cursus profectûs nostri;"—"Raro etiam unum vitium perfectè vincimus, et ad *quotidianum* profectum non accendimur;" "Semper aliquid certi proponendum est;"—"Tibi ipsi violentiam frequenter fac:" (*A life without a purpose is a languid, drifting thing;—Every day we ought to renew our purpose, saying to ourselves: This day let us make a sound beginning, for what we have hitherto done is naught;—Our improvement is in proportion to our purpose;—We hardly ever manage to get completely rid even of one fault, and do not set our hearts on* daily *improvement;—Always place a definite purpose before thee;—Get the habit of mastering thine inclination.*) These are moral precepts, and moral precepts of the best kind. As rules to hold possession of our conduct, and to keep us in the right course through outward troubles and inward perplexity, they are equal to the best ever furnished by the great masters of morals—Epictetus or Marcus Aurelius.

But moral rules, apprehended as ideas first, and then rigorously followed as laws, are, and must be, for the sage only. The mass of mankind have neither force of intellect enough to apprehend them clearly as ideas, nor force of character enough to follow them strictly as laws. The mass of mankind can be carried along a course full of hardship for the natural man, can be borne over the thousand impediments of the narrow way, only by the tide of a joyful and bounding emotion. It is impossible to rise from reading Epictetus or Marcus Aurelius without a sense of constraint and melancholy, without feeling that the burden laid upon man is well-nigh greater than he can bear. Honour to the sages who have felt this, and yet have borne it! Yet, even for the sage, this sense of labour and sorrow in his march towards the goal constitutes a relative inferiority; the noblest souls of whatever creed, the pagan Empedocles as well as the Christian Paul, have insisted on the necessity of an inspiration, a joyful emotion, to make moral action perfect; an obscure indication of this necessity is the one drop of truth in the ocean of verbiage with which the controversy on justification by faith has flooded the world. But, for the ordinary man, this sense of labour and sorrow constitutes an absolute disqualification; it paralyses him; under the weight of it, he cannot make way towards the goal at all. The paramount virtue of religion is, that it has *lighted up* morality; that it has supplied the emotion and inspiration needful for carrying the sage along the narrow way perfectly, for carrying the ordinary man along it at all. Even the religions with most dross in them have had something of this virtue; but the Christian religion manifests it with unexampled splendour. "Lead me, Zeus and Destiny!" says the prayer of Epictetus, "withersoever I am appointed to go; I will follow without wavering; even though I turn coward and shrink, I shall have to follow all the same." The fortitude of that is for the strong, for the few; even for them the spiritual atmosphere with which it surrounds them is bleak and gray. But, "Let thy loving spirit lead me forth into the land of righteousness;"—"The Lord shall be unto thee an everlasting light, and thy God thy glory;"—"Unto you that fear my name shall the sun of righteousness arise with healing in his wings," says the Old Testament; "Born, not of blood, nor of the will of the flesh, nor of the will of man, but of God;"—"Except a man be born again, he cannot see the kingdom of God;"—"Whatsoever is born of God, overcometh the world," says the New. The ray of sunshine is there, the glow of a divine warmth;—the austerity of the sage melts away under it, the paralysis of the weak is healed; he who is vivified by it renews his strength; "all things are possible to him;" "he is a new creature."

Epictetus says: "Every matter has two handles, one of which will bear taking hold of, the other not. If thy brother sin against thee, lay not hold of the matter by this, that he sins against thee; for by this handle the matter will not bear taking hold of. But rather lay hold of it by this, that he is thy brother, thy born mate; and thou wilt take hold of it by what will bear handling." Jesus, being asked whether a man is bound to forgive his brother as often as seven times, answers:

"I say not unto thee, until seven times, but until seventy times seven." Epictetus here suggests to the reason grounds for forgiveness of injuries which Jesus does not; but it is vain to say that Epictetus is on that account a better moralist than Jesus, if the warmth, the emotion, of Jesus's answer fires his hearer to the practice of forgiveness of injuries, while the thought in Epictetus's leaves him cold. So with Christian morality in general: its distinction is not that it propounds the maxim, "Thou shalt love God and thy neighbour," with more development, closer reasoning, truer sincerity, than other moral systems; it is that it propounds this maxim with an inspiration which wonderfully catches the hearer and makes him act upon it. It is because Mr. Mill has attained to the perception of truths of this nature, that he is,—instead of being, like the school from which he proceeds, doomed to sterility,—a writer of distinguished mark and influence, a writer deserving all attention and respect; it is (I must be pardoned for saying) because he is not sufficiently leavened with them, that he falls just short of being a great writer.

That which gives to the moral writings of the Emperor Marcus Aurelius their peculiar character and charm, is their being suffused and softened by something of this very sentiment whence Christian morality draws its best power. Mr. Long has recently published in a convenient form a translation of these writings, and has thus enabled English readers to judge Marcus Aurelius for themselves; he has rendered his countrymen a real service by so doing. Mr. Long's reputation as a scholar is a sufficient guarantee of the general fidelity and accuracy of his translation; on these matters, besides, I am hardly entitled to speak, and my praise is of no value. But that for which I and the rest of the unlearned may venture to praise Mr. Long is this; that he treats Marcus Aurelius's writings, as he treats all the other remains of Greek and Roman antiquity which he touches, not as a dead and dry matter of learning, but as documents with a side of modern applicability and living interest, and valuable mainly so far as this side in them can be made clear; that as in his notes on Plutarch's *Roman Lives* he deals with the modern epoch of Caesar and Cicero, not as food for schoolboys, but as food for men, and men engaged in the current of contemporary life and action, so in his remarks and essays on Marcus Aurelius he treats this truly modern striver and thinker not as a Classical Dictionary hero, but as a present source from which to draw "example of life, and instruction of manners." Why may not a son of Dr. Arnold say, what might naturally here be said by any other critic, that in this lively and fruitful way of considering the men and affairs of ancient Greece and Rome, Mr. Long resembles Dr. Arnold?

One or two little complaints, however, I have against Mr. Long, and I will get them off my mind at once. In the first place, why could he not have found gentler and juster terms to describe the translation of his predecessor, Jeremy Collier,—the redoubtable enemy of stage plays,—than these: "a most coarse and vulgar copy of the original?" As a matter of taste, a translator should deal leniently with his predecessor; but putting that out of the question, Mr. Long's language is a great deal too hard. Most English people who knew Marcus Aurelius before Mr. Long appeared as his introducer, knew him through Jeremy Collier. And the acquaintance of a man like Marcus Aurelius is such an imperishable benefit, that one can never lose a peculiar sense of obligation towards the man who confers it. Apart from this claim upon one's tenderness, however, Jeremy Collier's version deserves respect for its genuine spirit and vigour, the spirit and vigour of the age of Dryden. Jeremy Collier too, like Mr. Long, regarded in Marcus Aurelius the living moralist, and not the dead classic; and his warmth of feeling gave to his style an impetuosity and rhythm which from Mr. Long's style (I do not blame it on that account) are absent. Let us place the two side by side. The impressive opening of Marcus Aurelius's fifth book, Mr. Long translates thus:—

"In the morning when thou risest unwillingly, let this thought be present: I am rising to the work of a human being. Why then am I dissatisfied if I am going to do the things for which I exist and for which I was brought into the world? Or have I been made for this, to lie in the bedclothes and keep myself warm?—But this is more pleasant.—Dost thou exist then to take thy pleasure, and not at all for action or exertion?"

Jeremy Collier has:—

"When you find an unwillingness to rise early in the morning, make this short speech to yourself: 'I am getting up now to do the business of a man; and am I out of humour for going about that which I was made for, and for the sake of which I was sent into the world? Was I then designed for nothing but to doze and batten beneath the counterpane? I thought action had been the end of your being.' "

In another striking passage, again, Mr. Long has:—

"No longer wonder at hazard; for neither wilt thou read thy own memoirs, nor the acts of the ancient Romans and Hellenes, and the selections from books which thou wast reserving for thy old age. Hasten then to the end which thou hast before thee, and, throwing away idle hopes, come to thine own aid, if thou carest at all for thyself, while it is in thy power."

Here his despised predecessor has:—

"Don't go too far in your books and overgrasp yourself. Alas, you have no time left to peruse your diary, to read over the Greek and Roman history: come, don't flatter and deceive yourself; look to the main chance, to the end and design of reading, and mind life more than notion: I say, if you have a kindness for your person, drive at the practice and help yourself, for that is in your own power."

It seems to me that here for style and force Jeremy Collier can (to say the least) perfectly stand comparison with Mr. Long. Jeremy Collier's real defect as a translator is not his coarseness and vulgarity, but his imperfect acquaintance with Greek; this is a serious defect, a fatal one; it rendered a translation like Mr. Long's necessary. Jeremy Collier's work will now be forgotten, and Mr. Long stands master of the field; but he may be content, at any rate, to leave his predecessor's grave unharmed, even if he will not throw upon it, in passing, a handful of kindly earth.

Another complaint I have against Mr. Long is, that he is not quite idiomatic and simple enough. It is a little formal, at least, if not pedantic, to say *Ethic* and *Dialectic,* instead of *Ethics* and *Dialectics,* and to say "*Hellenes* and Romans" instead of "*Greeks* and Romans." And why, too,—the name of Antoninus being preoccupied by Antoninus Pius, —will Mr. Long call his author Marcus *Antoninus* instead of Marcus *Aurelius?* Small as these matters appear, they are important when one has to deal with the general public, and not with a small circle of scholars; and it is the general public that the translator of a short masterpiece on morals, such as is the book of Marcus Aurelius, should have in view; his aim should be to make Marcus Aurelius's work as popular as the *Imitation,* and Marcus Aurelius's name as familiar as Socrates's. In rendering or naming him, therefore, punctilious accuracy of phrase is not so much to be sought as accessibility and currency; everything which may best enable the Emperor and his precepts *volitare per ora virûm.* It is essential to render him in language perfectly plain and unprofessional, and to call him by the name by which he is best and most distinctly known. The translators of the Bible talk of *pence* and not *denarii,* and the admirers of Voltaire do not celebrate him under the name of Arouet.

But, after these trifling complaints are made, one must end, as one began, in unfeigned gratitude to Mr. Long for his excellent and substantial reproduction in English of an invaluable work. In general the substantiality, soundness, and precision of Mr. Long's rendering are (I will venture, after all, to give my opinion about them) as conspicuous as the living spirit with which he treats antiquity; and these qualities are particularly desirable in the translator of a work like that of Marcus Aurelius, of which the language is often corrupt, almost always hard and obscure. Any one who wants to appreciate Mr. Long's merits as a translator may read, in the original and in Mr. Long's translation, the seventh chapter of the tenth book; he will see how, through all the dubiousness and involved manner of the Greek, Mr. Long has firmly seized upon the clear thought which is certainly at the bottom of that troubled wording, and, in distinctly rendering this thought, has at the same time thrown round its expression a characteristic shade of painfulness and difficulty which just suits it. And Marcus Aurelius's book is one which, when it is rendered so accurately as Mr. Long renders it, even those who know Greek tolerably well may choose to read rather in the translation than in the original. For not only are the contents here incomparably more valuable than the external form, but this form, the Greek of a Roman, is not exactly one of those styles which have a physiognomy, which are an essential part of their author, which stamp an indelible impression of him on the reader's mind. An old Lyons commentator finds, indeed, in Marcus Aurelius's Greek, something characteristic, something specially firm and imperial; but I think an ordinary mortal will hardly find this: he will find crabbed Greek, without any great charm of distinct physiognomy. The Greek of Thucydides and Plato has this charm, and he who reads them in a translation, however accurate, loses it, and loses much in losing it; but the Greek of Marcus Aurelius, like the Greek of the New Testament, and even more than the Greek of the New Testament, is wanting in it. If one could be assured that the English Testament were made perfectly accurate, one might be almost content never to open a Greek Testament again; and, Mr. Long's version of Marcus Aurelius being what it is, an Englishman who reads to live, and does not live to read, may henceforth let the Greek original repose upon its shelf.

The man whose thoughts Mr. Long has thus faithfully reproduced, is perhaps the most beautiful figure in history. He is one of those consoling and hope-inspiring marks, which stand for ever to remind our weak and easily discouraged race how high human goodness and perseverance have once been carried, and may be carried again. The interest of mankind is peculiarly attracted by examples of signal goodness in high places; for that testimony to the worth of goodness is the most striking which is borne by those to whom all the means of pleasure and self-indulgence lay open, by those who had at their command the kingdoms of the world and the glory of them. Marcus Aurelius was the ruler of the grandest of empires; and he was one of the best of men. Besides him, history presents one or two sovereigns eminent for their goodness, such as Saint Louis or Alfred. But Marcus Aurelius has, for us moderns, this great superiority in interest over Saint Louis or Alfred, that he lived and acted in a state of society modern by its essential characteristics, in an epoch akin to our own, in a brilliant centre of civilisation. Trajan talks of "our enlightened age" just as glibly as the *Times* talks of it. Marcus Aurelius thus becomes for us a man like ourselves, a man in all things tempted as we are. Saint Louis inhabits an atmosphere of mediaeval Catholicism, which the man of the nineteenth century may admire, indeed, may even passionately wish to inhabit, but which, strive as he will, he cannot really inhabit. Alfred belongs to a state of society (I say it with all deference to the *Saturday Review* critic who keeps such jealous watch over the honour of our Saxon ancestors) half barbarous. Neither Alfred nor Saint Louis can be morally and intellectually as near to us as Marcus Aurelius.

The record of the outward life of this admirable man has in it little of striking incident. He was born at Rome on the 26th of April, in the year 121 of the Christian era. He was nephew and son-in-law to his predecessor on the throne, Antoninus Pius. When Antoninus died, he was forty years old, but from the time of his earliest manhood he had assisted in administering public affairs. Then, after his uncle's death in 161, for nineteen years he reigned as emperor. The barbarians were pressing on the Roman frontier, and a great part of Marcus Aurelius's nineteen years of reign was passed in campaigning. His absences from Rome were numerous and long. We hear of him in Asia Minor, Syria, Egypt, Greece; but, above all, in the countries on the Danube, where the war with the barbarians was going on,—in Austria, Moravia, Hungary. In these countries much of his *Journal* seems to have been written; parts of it are dated from them; and there, a few weeks before his fifty-ninth birthday, he fell sick and died. The record of him on which his fame chiefly rests is the record of his inward life,—his *Journal*, or *Commentaries*, or *Meditations*, or *Thoughts*, for by all these names has the work been called. Perhaps the most interesting of the records of his outward life is that which the first book of his work supplies, where he gives an account of his education, recites the names of those to whom he is indebted for it, and enumerates his obligations to each of them. It is a refreshing and consoling picture, a priceless treasure for those, who, sick of the "wild and dreamlike trade of blood and guile," which seems to be nearly the whole of what history has to offer to our view, seek eagerly for that substratum of right thinking and well-doing which in all ages must surely have somewhere existed, for without it the continued life of humanity would have been impossible. "From my mother I learnt piety and beneficence, and abstinence not only from evil deeds but even from evil thoughts; and further, simplicity in my way of living, far removed from the habits of the rich." Let us remember that, the next time we are reading the sixth satire of Juvenal. "From my tutor I learnt" (hear it, ye tutors of princes!) "endurance of labour, and to want little, and to work with my own hands, and not to meddle with other people's affairs, and not to be ready to listen to slander." The vices and foibles of the Greek sophist or rhetorician—the *Graeculus esuriens*—are in everybody's mind; but he who reads Marcus Aurelius's account of his Greek teachers and masters, will understand how it is that, in spite of the vices and foibles of individual *Graeculi,* the education of the human race owes to Greece a debt which can never be overrated. The vague and colourless praise of history leaves on the mind hardly any impression of Antoninus Pius: it is only from the private memoranda of his nephew that we learn what a disciplined, hard-working, gentle, wise, virtuous man he was; a man who, perhaps, interests mankind less than his immortal nephew only because he has left in writing no record of his inner life,—*caret quia vate sacro.*

Of the outward life and circumstances of Marcus Aurelius, beyond these notices which he has himself supplied, there are few of much interest and importance. There is the fine anecdote of his speech when he heard of the assassination of the revolted Avidius Cassius, against whom he was marching; *he was sorry,* he said, *to be deprived of the pleasure of pardoning him.* And there are one or two more anecdotes of him which show the same spirit. But the great record for the outward life of a man who has left such a record of his lofty inward aspirations as that which Marcus Aurelius has left, is the clear consenting voice of all his contemporaries,—high and low, friend and enemy, pagan and Christian,—in praise of his sincerity, justice, and goodness. The world's charity does not err on the side of excess, and here was a man occupying the most conspicuous station in the world, and professing the highest possible standard of conduct;—yet the world was obliged to declare that he walked worthily of his profession. Long after his death, his bust was to be seen in the houses of private men through the wide Roman empire. It may be the vulgar part of human nature which busies itself with the semblance and doings of living sovereigns, it is its nobler part which busies itself with those of the dead; these busts of Marcus Aurelius, in the homes of Gaul, Britain, and Italy, bear witness, not to the inmates' frivolous curiosity about princes and palaces, but to their reverential memory of the passage of a great man upon the earth.

Two things, however, before one turns from the outward to the inward life of Marcus Aurelius, force themselves upon one's notice, and demand a word of comment; he persecuted the Christians, and he had for his son the vicious and brutal Commodus. The persecution at Lyons, in which Attalus and Pothinus suffered, the persecution at Smyrna, in which Polycarp suffered, took place in his reign. Of his humanity, of his tolerance, of his horror of cruelty and violence, of his wish to refrain from severe measures against the Christians, of his anxiety to temper the severity of these measures when they appeared to him indispensable, there is no doubt: but, on the one hand, it is certain that the letter, attributed to him, directing that no Christian should be punished for being a Christian, is spurious; it is almost certain that his alleged answer to the authorities of Lyons, in which he directs that Christians persisting in their profession shall be dealt with according to law, is genuine. Mr. Long seems inclined to try and throw doubt over the persecution at Lyons, by pointing out that the letter of the Lyons Christians relating it, alleges it to have been attended by miraculous and incredible incidents. "A man," he says, "can only act consistently by accepting all this letter or rejecting it all, and we cannot blame him for either." But it is contrary to all experience to say that because a fact is related with incorrect additions and embellishments, therefore it probably never happened at all; or that it is not, in general, easy for an impartial mind to distinguish between the fact and the embellishments. I cannot doubt that the Lyons persecution took place, and that the punishment of Christians for being Christians was sanctioned by Marcus Aurelius. But then I must add that nine modern readers out of ten, when they read this, will, I believe, have a perfectly false notion of what the moral action of Marcus Aurelius, in sanctioning that punishment, really was. They imagine Trajan, or Antoninus Pius, or Marcus Aurelius, fresh from the perusal of the Gospel, fully aware of the spirit and holiness of the Christian saints, ordering their extermination because he loved darkness rather than light. Far from this, the Christianity which these emperors aimed at repressing was, in their conception of it, something philosophically contemptible, politically subversive, and morally abominable. As men, they sincerely regarded it much as well-conditioned people, with us, regard Mormonism; as rulers, they regarded it much as Liberal statesmen, with us, regard the Jesuits. A kind of Mormonism, constituted as a vast secret society, with obscure aims of political and social subversion, was what Antoninus Pius and Marcus Aurelius believed themselves to be repressing when they punished Christians. The early Christian apologists again and again declare to us under what odious imputations the Christians lay, how general was the belief that these imputations were well-grounded, how sincere was the horror which the belief inspired. The multitude, convinced that the Christians were atheists who ate human flesh and thought incest no crime, displayed against them a fury so passionate as to embarrass and alarm their rulers. The severe expressions of Tacitus, *exitiabilis superstitio—odio humani generis convicti,* show how deeply the prejudices of the multitude imbued the educated class also. One asks oneself with astonishment how a doctrine so benign as that of Jesus Christ can have incurred misrepresentation so monstrous. The inner and moving cause of the misrepresentation lay, no doubt, in this, —that Christianity was a new spirit in the Roman world, destined to act in that world as its dissolvent; and it was inevitable that Christianity in the Roman world, like democracy in the modern world, like every new spirit with a similar mission assigned to it, should at its first appearance occasion an instinctive shrinking and repugnance in the world which it was to dissolve. The outer and palpable causes of the misrepresentation were, for the Roman public at large, the confounding of the Christians with the Jews, that isolated, fierce, and stubborn race, whose stubbornness, fierceness, and isolation, real as they were, the fancy of a civilised Roman yet further exaggerated; the atmosphere of mystery and novelty which surrounded the Christian rites; the very simplicity of Christian theism. For the Roman statesman, the cause of mistake lay in that character of secret assemblages which the meetings of the Christian community wore, under a State-system as jealous of unauthorised associations as is the State-system of modern France.

A Roman of Marcus Aurelius's time and position could not well see the Christians except through the mist of these prejudices. Seen through such a mist, the Christians appeared with a thousand faults not their own; but it has not been sufficiently remarked that faults really their own many of them assuredly appeared with besides, faults especially likely to strike such an observer as Marcus Aurelius, and to confirm him in the prejudices of his race, station, and rearing. We look back upon Christianity after it has proved what a future it bore within it, and for us the sole representatives of its early struggles are the pure and devoted spirits through whom it proved this; Marcus Aurelius saw it with its future yet unshown, and with the tares among its professed progeny not less conspicuous than the wheat. Who can doubt that among the professing Christians of the second century, as among the professing Christians of the nineteenth, there was plenty of folly, plenty of rabid nonsense, plenty of gross fanaticism? Who will even venture to affirm that, separated in great measure from the intellect and civilisation of the world for one or two centuries, Christianity, wonderful as have been its fruits, had the development perfectly worthy of its inestimable germ? Who will venture to affirm that, by the alliance of Christianity with the virtue and intelligence of men like the Antonines —of the best product of Greek and Roman civilisation, while Greek and Roman civilisation had yet life and power,—Christianity and the world, as well as the Antonines themselves, would not have been gainers? That alliance was not to be. The Antonines lived and died with an utter misconception of Christianity; Christianity grew up in the Catacombs, not on the Palatine. And Marcus Aurelius incurs no moral reproach by having authorised the punishment of the Christians; he does not thereby become in the least what we mean by a *persecutor*. One may concede that it was impossible for him to see Christianity as it really was;—as impossible as for even the moderate and sensible Fleury to see the Antonines as they really were;—one may concede that the point of view from which Christianity appeared something anti-civil and anti-social, which the State had the faculty to judge and the duty to suppress, was inevitably his. Still, however, it remains true that this sage, who made perfection his aim and reason his law, did Christianity an immense injustice and rested in an idea of State-attributes which was illusive. And this is, in truth, characteristic of Marcus Aurelius, that he is blameless, yet, in a certain sense, unfortunate; in his character, beautiful as it is, there is something melancholy, circumscribed, and ineffectual.

For of his having such a son as Commodus, too, one must say that he is not to be blamed on that account, but that he is unfortunate. Disposition and temperament are inexplicable things; there are natures on which the best education and example are thrown away; excellent fathers may have, without any fault of theirs, incurably vicious sons. It is to be remembered, also, that Commodus was left, at the perilous age of nineteen, master of the world; while his father, at that age, was but beginning a twenty years' apprenticeship to wisdom, labour, and self-command, under the sheltering teachership of his uncle Antoninus. Commodus was a prince apt to be led by favourites; and if the story is true which says that he left, all through his reign, the Christians untroubled, and ascribes this lenity to the influence of his mistress Marcia, it shows that he could be led to good as well as to evil. But for such a nature to be left at a critical age with absolute power, and wholly without good counsel and direction, was the more fatal. Still one cannot help wishing that the example of Marcus Aurelius could have availed more with his own only son. One cannot but think that with such virtue as his there should go, too, the ardour which removes mountains, and that the ardour which removes mountains might have even won Commodus. The word *ineffectual* again rises to one's mind; Marcus Aurelius saved his own soul by his righteousness, and he could do no more. Happy they who can do this! But still happier, who can do more! Yet, when one passes from his outward to his inward life, when one turns over the pages of his *Meditations*,—entries jotted down from day to day, amid the business of the city or the fatigues of the camp, for his own guidance and support, meant for no eye but his own, without the slightest attempt at style, with no care, even, for correct writing, not to be surpassed for naturalness and sincerity,—all disposition to carp and cavil dies away, and one is overpowered by the charm of a character of such purity, delicacy, and virtue. He fails neither in small things nor in great; he keeps watch over himself both that the great springs of action may be right in him, and that the minute details of action may be right also. How admirable in a hard-tasked ruler, and a ruler, too, with a passion for thinking and reading, is such a memorandum as the following:—

"Not frequently nor without necessity to say to any one, or to write in a letter, that I have no leisure; nor continually to excuse the neglect of duties required by our relation to those with whom we live, by alleging urgent occupation."

And, when that ruler is a Roman emperor, what an "idea" is this to be written down and meditated by him:—

"The idea of a polity in which there is the same law for all, a polity administered with regard to equal rights and equal freedom of speech, and the idea of a kingly government which respects most of all the freedom of the governed."

And, for all men who "drive at practice," what practical rules may not one accumulate out of these *Meditations*:—

"The greatest part of what we say or do being unnecessary, if a man takes this away, he will have more leisure and less uneasiness. Accordingly, on every occasion a man should ask himself: 'Is this one of the unnecessary things?' Now a man should take away not only unnecessary acts, but also unnecessary thoughts, for thus superfluous acts will not follow after."

And again:—

"We ought to check in the series of our thoughts everything that is without a purpose and useless, but most of all the over-curious feeling and the malignant; and a man should use himself to think of those things only about which if one should suddenly ask, 'What hast thou now in thy thoughts?' with perfect openness thou mightest immediately answer, 'This or That;' so that from thy words it should be plain that everything in thee is simple and benevolent, and such as befits a social animal, and one that cares not for thoughts about sensual enjoyments, or any rivalry or envy and suspicion, or anything else for which thou wouldst blush if thou shouldst say thou hadst it in thy mind."

So, with a stringent practicalness worthy of Franklin, he discourses on his favourite text, *Let nothing be done without a purpose*. But it is when he enters the region where Franklin cannot follow him, when he utters his thoughts on the ground-motives of human action, that he is most interesting; that he becomes the unique, the incomparable Marcus Aurelius. Christianity uses language very liable to be misunderstood when it seems to tell men to do good, not, certainly, from the vulgar motives of worldly interest, or vanity, or love of human praise, but "that their Father which seeth in secret may reward them openly." The motives of reward and punishment have come, from the misconception of language of this kind, to be strangely overpressed by many Christian moralists, to the deterioration and disfigurement of Christianity. Marcus Aurelius says, truly and nobly:—

"One man, when he has done a service to another, is ready to set it down to his account as a favour conferred. Another is not ready to do this, but still in his own mind he thinks of the man as his debtor, and he knows what he has done. A third in a manner does not even know what he has done, *but he is like a vine which has produced grapes, and seeks for nothing more after it has once produced its proper fruit.* As a horse when he has run, a dog when he has caught the game, a bee when it has made its honey, so a man when he has done a good act, does not call out for others to come and see, but he goes on to another act, as a vine goes on to produce again the grapes in season. Must a man, then, be one of these, who in a manner acts thus without observing it? Yes."

And again:—

"What more dost thou want when thou hast done a man a service? Art thou not content that thou hast done something conformable to thy nature, and dost thou seek to be paid for it, *just as if the eye demanded a recompense for seeing, or the feet for walking?"*

Christianity, in order to match morality of this strain, has to correct its apparent offers of external reward, and to say: *The kingdom of God is within you.*

I have said that it is by its accent of emotion that the morality of Marcus Aurelius acquires a special character, and reminds one of Christian morality. The sentences of Seneca are stimulating to the intellect; the sentences of Epictetus are fortifying to the character; the sentences of Marcus Aurelius find their way to the soul. I have said that religious emotion has the power to *light up* morality: the emotion of Marcus Aurelius does not quite light up his morality, but it suffuses it; it has not power to melt the clouds of effort and austerity quite away, but it shines through them and glorifies them; it is a spirit, not so much of gladness and elation, as of gentleness and sweetness; a delicate and tender sentiment, which is less than joy and more than resignation. He says that in his youth he learned from Maximus, one of his teachers, "cheerfulness in all circumstances as well as in illness; *and a just admixture in the moral character of sweetness and dignity:"* and it is this very admixture of sweetness with his dignity which makes him so beautiful a moralist. It enables him to carry even into his observation of nature, a delicate penetration, a sympathetic tenderness, worthy of Wordsworth;

the spirit of such a remark as the following has hardly a parallel, so far as my knowledge goes, in the whole range of Greek and Roman literature:—

"Figs, when they are quite ripe, gape open; and in the ripe olives the very circumstance of their being near to rottenness adds a peculiar beauty to the fruit. And the ears of corn bending down, and the lion's eyebrows, and the foam which flows from the mouth of wild boars, and many other things,—though they are far from being beautiful, in a certain sense,—still, because they come in the course of nature, have a beauty in them, and they please the mind; so that if a man should have a feeling and a deeper insight with respect to the things which are produced in the universe, there is hardly anything which comes in the course of nature which will not seem to him to be in a manner disposed so as to give pleasure."

But it is when his strain passes to directly moral subjects that his delicacy and sweetness lend to it the greatest charm. Let those who can feel the beauty of spiritual refinement read this, the reflection of an emperor who prized mental superiority highly:—

"Thou sayest, 'Men cannot admire the sharpness of thy wits.' Be it so; but there are many other things of which thou canst not say, 'I am not formed for them by nature.' Show those qualities, then, which are altogether in thy power,—sincerity, gravity, endurance of labour, aversion to pleasure, contentment with thy portion and with few things, benevolence, frankness, no love of superfluity, freedom from trifling, magnanimity. Dost thou not see how many qualities thou art at once able to exhibit, as to which there is no excuse of natural incapacity and unfitness, and yet thou still remainest voluntarily below the mark? Or art thou compelled, through being defectively furnished by nature, to murmur, and to be mean, and to flatter, and to find fault with thy poor body, and to try to please men, and to make great display, and to be so restless in thy mind? No, indeed; but thou mightest have been delivered from these things long ago. Only, if in truth thou canst be charged with being rather slow and dull of comprehension, thou must exert thyself about this also, not neglecting nor yet taking pleasure in thy dulness."

The same sweetness enables him to fix his mind, when he sees the isolation and moral death caused by sin, not on the cheerless thought of the misery of this condition, but on the inspiriting thought that man is blest with the power to escape from it:—

"Suppose that thou hast detached thyself from the natural unity,—for thou wast made by nature a part, but now thou hast cut thyself off,—yet here is this beautiful provision, that it is in thy power again to unite thyself. God has allowed this to no other part,—after it has been separated and cut asunder, to come together again. But consider the goodness with which he has privileged man; for he has put it in his power, when he has been separated, to return and to be united and to resume his place."

It enables him to control even the passion for retreat and solitude, so strong in a soul like his, to which the world could offer no abiding city:—

"Men seek retreat for themselves, houses in the country, seashores, and mountains; and thou, too, art wont to desire such things very much. But this is altogether a mark of the most common sort of men, for it is in thy power whenever thou shalt choose to retire into thyself. For nowhere either with more quiet or more freedom from trouble does a man retire than into his own soul, particularly when he has within him such thoughts that by looking into them he is immediately in perfect tranquillity. Constantly, then, give to thyself this retreat, and renew thyself; and let thy principles be brief and fundamental, which, as soon as thou shalt recur to them, will be sufficient to cleanse the soul completely, and to send thee back free from all discontent with the things to which thou returnest."

Against this feeling of discontent and weariness, so natural to the great for whom there seems nothing left to desire or to strive after, but so enfeebling to them, so deteriorating, Marcus Aurelius never ceased to struggle. With resolute thankfulness he kept in remembrance the blessings of his lot; the true blessings of it, not the false:—

"I have to thank Heaven that I was subjected to a ruler and a father (Antoninus Pius) who was able to take away all pride from me, and to bring me to the knowledge that it is possible for a man to live in a palace without either guards, or embroidered dresses, or any show of this kind; but that it is in such a man's power to bring himself very near to the fashion of a private person, without being for this reason either meaner in thought or more remiss in action with respect to the things which must be done for public interest. . . . I have to be thankful that my children have not been stupid nor deformed in body; that I did not make more proficiency in rhetoric, poetry, and the other studies, by which I should perhaps have been completely engrossed, if I had seen that I was making great progress in them; . . . that I knew Apollonius, Rusticus, Maximus; . . . that I received clear and frequent impressions about living according to nature, and what kind of a life that is, so that, so far as depended on Heaven, and its gifts, help, and inspiration, nothing hindered me from forthwith living according to nature, though I still fall short of it through my own fault, and through not observing the admonitions of Heaven, and, I may almost say, its direct instructions; that my body has held out so long in such a kind of life as mine; that though it was my mother's lot to die young, she spent the last years of her life with me; that whenever I wished to help any man in his need, I was never told that I had not the means of doing it; that, when I had an inclination to philosophy, I did not fall into the hands of a sophist."

And, as he dwelt with gratitude on these helps and blessings vouchsafed to him, his mind (so, at least, it seems to me) would sometimes revert with awe to the perils and temptations of the lonely height where he stood, to the lives of Tiberius, Caligula, Nero, Domitian, in their hideous blackness and ruin; and then he wrote down for himself such a warning entry as this, significant and terrible in its abruptness:—

"A black character, a womanish character, a stubborn character, bestial, childish, animal, stupid, counterfeit, scurrilous, fraudulent, tyrannical."

Or this:—

"About what am I now employing my soul? On every occasion I must ask myself this question, and enquire, What have I now in this part of me which they call the ruling principle, and whose soul have I now?—that of a child, or of a young man, or of a weak woman, or of a tyrant, or of one of the lower animals in the service of man, or of a wild beast?"

The character he wished to attain he knew well, and beautifully he has marked it, and marked, too, his sense of shortcoming:—

"When thou hast assumed these names,—good, modest, true, rational, equal-minded, magnanimous,—take care that thou dost not change these names; and, if thou shouldst lose them, quickly return to them. If thou maintainest thyself in possession of these names without desiring that others should call thee by them, thou wilt be another being, and wilt enter on another life. For to continue to be such as thou hast hitherto been, and to be torn in pieces and defiled in such a life, is the character of a very stupid man, and one overfond of his life, and like those half-devoured fighters with wild beasts, who though covered with wounds and gore still entreat to be kept to the following day, though they will be exposed in the same state to the same claws and bites. Therefore fix thyself in the possession of these few names: and if thou art able to abide in them, abide as if thou wast removed to the Happy Islands."

For all his sweetness and serenity, however, man's point of life "between two infinities" (of that expression Marcus Aurelius is the real owner) was to him anything but a Happy Island, and the performances on it he saw through no veils of illusion. Nothing is in general more gloomy and monotonous than declamations on the hollowness and transitoriness of human life and grandeur: but here, too, the great charm of Marcus Aurelius, his emotion, comes in to relieve the monotony and to break through the gloom; and even on this eternally used topic he is imaginative, fresh, and striking:—

"Consider, for example, the times of Vespasian. Thou wilt see all these things, people marrying, bringing up children, sick, dying, warring, feasting, trafficking, cultivating the ground, flattering, obstinately arrogant, suspecting, plotting, wishing for somebody to die, grumbling about the present, loving, heaping up treasure, desiring to be consuls or kings. Well then that life of these people no longer exists at all. Again, go to the times of Trajan. All is again the same. Their life too is gone. But chiefly thou shouldst think of those whom thou hast thyself known distracting themselves about idle things, neglecting to do what was in accordance with their proper constitution, and to hold firmly to this and to be content with it."

Again:—

"The things which are much valued in life are empty, and rotten, and trifling; and people are like little dogs, biting one another, and little children quarrelling, crying, and then straightway laughing. But fidelity, and modesty, and justice, and truth, are fled

'Up to Olympus from the wide-spread earth.'

What then is there which still detains thee here?"

And once more:—

"Look down from above on the countless herds of men, and their countless solemnities, and the infinitely varied voyagings in storms and calms, and the differences among those who are born, who live together, and die. And consider too the life lived by others in olden time, and the life now lived among barbarous nations, and how many know not even thy name, and how many will soon forget it, and how they who perhaps now are praising thee will very soon blame thee, and that neither a posthumous name is of any value, nor reputation, nor anything else."

He recognised, indeed, that (to use his own words) "the prime principle in man's constitution is the social;" and he laboured sincerely to make not only his acts towards his fellow-men, but his thoughts also, suitable to this conviction:—

"When thou wishest to delight thyself, think of the virtues of those who live with thee; for instance, the activity of one, and the modesty of another, and the liberality of a third, and some other good quality of a fourth."

Still, it is hard for a pure and thoughtful man to live in a state of rapture at the spectacle afforded to him by his fellow-creatures; above all it is hard, when such a man is placed as Marcus Aurelius was placed, and has had the meanness and perversity of his fellow-creatures thrust, in no common measure, upon his notice,—has had, time after time, to experience how "within ten days thou wilt seem a god to those to whom thou art now a beast and an ape." His true strain of thought as to his relations with his fellow-men is rather the following. He has been enumerating the higher consolations which may support a man at the approach of death, and he goes on:—

"But if thou requirest also a vulgar kind of comfort which shall reach thy heart, thou wilt be made best reconciled to death by observing the objects from which thou art going to be removed, and the morals of those with whom thy soul will no longer be mingled. For it is no way right to be offended with men, but it is thy duty to care for them and to bear with them gently; and yet to remember that thy departure will not be from men who have the same principles as thyself. For this is the only thing, if there be any, which could draw us the contrary way and attach us to life, to be permitted to live with those who have the same principles as ourselves. But now thou seest how great is the distress caused by the difference of those who live together, so that thou mayest say: 'Come quick, O death, lest perchance I too should forget myself.' "

O faithless and perverse generation! how long shall I be with you? how long shall I suffer you? Sometimes this strain rises even to passion:—

"Short is the little which remains to thee of life. Live as on a mountain. Let men see, let them know, a real man, who lives as he was meant to live. If they cannot endure him, let them kill him. For that is better than to live as men do."

It is remarkable how little of a merely local and temporary character, how little of those *scoriae* which a reader has to clear away before he gets to the precious ore, how little that even admits of doubt or question, the morality of Marcus Aurelius exhibits. Perhaps as to one point we must make an exception. Marcus Aurelius is fond of urging as a motive for man's cheerful acquiescence in whatever befalls him, that "whatever happens to every man *is for the interest of the universal*"; that the whole contains nothing *which is not for its advantage;* that everything which happens to a man is to be accepted, "even if it seems disagreeable, *because it leads to the health of the universe.*" And the whole course of the universe, he adds, has a providential reference to man's welfare: *"all other things have been made for the sake of rational beings."* Religion has in all ages freely used this language, and it is not religion which will object to Marcus Aurelius's use of it; but science can hardly accept as severely accurate this employment of terms *interest* and *advantage.* To a sound nature and a clear reason the proposition that things happen "for the interest of the universal," as men conceive of interest, may seem to have no meaning at all, and the proposition that "all things have been made for the sake of rational beings" may seem to be false. Yet even to this language, not irresistibly cogent when it is thus absolutely used, Marcus Aurelius gives a turn which makes it true and useful, when he says: "The ruling part of man can make a material for itself out of that which opposes it, as fire lays hold of what falls into it, and rises higher by means of this very material;"—when he says: "What else are all things except exercises for the reason? Persevere then until thou shalt have made all things thine own, as the stomach which is strengthened makes all things its own, as the blazing fire makes flame and brightness out of everything that is thrown into it;"—when he says: "Thou wilt not cease to be miserable till thy mind is in such a condition, that, what luxury is to those who enjoy pleasure, such shall be to thee, in every matter which presents itself, the doing of the things which are conformable to man's constitution; for a man ought to consider as an enjoyment everything which it is in his power to do according to his own nature,—and it is in his power everywhere." In this sense it is, indeed, most true that "all things have been made for the sake of rational beings;" that "all things work together for good."

In general, however, the action Marcus Aurelius prescribes is action which every sound nature must recognise as right, and the motives he assigns are motives which every clear reason must recognise as valid. And so he remains the especial friend and comforter of all clear-headed and scrupulous, yet pure-hearted and upward-striving men, in those ages most especially that walk by sight, not by faith, but yet have no open vision. He cannot give such souls, perhaps, all they yearn for, but he gives them much; and what he gives them, they can receive.

Yet no, it is not for what he thus gives them that such souls love him most! It is rather because of the emotion which lends to his voice so touching an accent, it is because he too yearns as they do for something unattained by him. What an affinity for Christianity had this persecutor of the Christians! The effusion of Christianity, its relieving tears, its happy self-sacrifice, were the very element, one feels, for which his soul longed; they were near him, they brushed him, he touched them, he passed them by. One feels, too, that the Marcus Aurelius one reads must still have remained, even had Christianity been fully known to him, in a great measure himself; he would have been no Justin;—but how would Christianity have affected him? In what measure would it have changed him? Granted that he might have found, like the *Alogi* of modern times, in the most beautiful of the Gospels, the Gospel which has leavened Christendom most powerfully, the Gospel of St. John, too much Greek metaphysics, too much *gnosis;* granted that this Gospel might have looked too like what he knew already to be a total surprise to him: what, then, would he have said to the Sermon on the Mount, to the twenty-sixth chapter of St. Matthew? What would have become of his notions of the *exitiabilis superstitio,* of the "obstinacy of the Christians"? Vain question! Yet the greatest charm of Marcus Aurelius is that he makes us ask it. We see him wise, just, self-governed, tender, thankful, blameless; yet, with all this, agitated, stretching out his arms for something beyond,—*tendentemque manus ripae ulterioris amore.*

SUBJECT INDEX TO *THE DISCOURSES OF EPICTETUS*

(The numbers refer to pages)

SUBJECT INDEX TO *THE MEDITATIONS OF MARCUS AURELIUS*

(The references are to books and sections)

GLOSSARY

ACADEMY: Name of Plato's school. Epictetus combatted the so-called Middle and New Academy, whose views coincided to some extent with those of the Sceptics.

ACHERON: A river of the underworld.

ACHERUSIA: A name for the underworld.

ACHILLES: Son of Peleus, hero of the *Iliad*.

ADMETUS' FATHER: Pheres, a king of Thessaly. He is used as a typical instance of a desire for long life. See *Alcestis* of Euripides.

ADONIS: A youth beloved by Aphrodite. He was worshipped in a festival in the spring.

AENEADAE: A name for the Romans as descendants from Aeneas, according to tradition.

AESCULAPIUS: See ASCLEPIUS.

AETNA: The famous volcano in Sicily.

AGATHON: A tragic poet of the fifth century B.C. See Plato's *Symposium*.

AGRIPPA: One of Augustus' most trusted ministers.

AGRIPPINUS, PACONIUS: A famous Stoic. Two years proconsul of Crete under Claudius.

ALCIBIADES: An Athenian statesman, pupil and friend of Socrates. See Plato, *Symposium*.

ALEXANDER: See PARIS.

ALEXANDER: Of Phrygia, a grammarian, who wrote a commentary on Homer.

ALEXANDER: A Platonist, Greek secretary to Marcus Aurelius.

AMPHIARAUS: Legendary king of Argos, persuaded by his wife Eriphyle, who had been bribed with a necklace by Polynices, to take part in the expedition against Thebes, though he foresaw that it meant his death.

ANAXAGORAS: A great Greek philosopher of the fifth century B.C. His signal contribution to thought was the introduction of the principle Nous (Mind) as in control of all things.

ANCUS MARCIUS: The fourth legendary king of Rome.

ANTIGONUS GONATAS: Lived *ca.* 320–240 B.C. King of Macedonia, friend and admirer of Zeno who founded the Stoic School.

ANTILOCHUS: Son of Nestor, and friend of Achilles.

ANTIPATER: Of Tarsus. A Stoic who taught Panaetius, the friend of the Scipios.

ANTISTHENES: Founder of the Cynic School (*ca.* 426–356 B.C.).

ANTONINUS PIUS: Emperor A.D. 138–161.

ANYTUS and MELETUS: Two of the accusers of Socrates at his trial. See Plato, *Apology*.
APOLLONIUS: A Pythagorean philosopher of Tyana in Cappadocia.
APOLLONIUS: Of Chalcis, a Stoic teacher of M. Aurelius.
APRULLA: Apparently a rich woman, to whom some legacy-hunter was enslaved.
ARCHEDEMUS: A Stoic of Tarsus, coupled with Antipater by Cicero and Epictetus.
ARCHIDAMUS: King of Sparta, 361–338 B.C.
ARCHIMEDES: The famous Syracusan mathematician and natural scientist of the third century B.C.
AREIUS: A philosopher who was intimate with Augustus.
ARGUS: The legendary hundred-eyed guardian of Io.
ARICIA: A country town, about twenty miles south of Rome.
ARISTIDES: Of Miletus, supposed author of licentious 'Milesian tales' of the Alexandrian period.
ARISTIPPUS: A Greek philosopher who founded the Cyrenaic School of Hedonism (*flor. ca.* 370 B.C.).
ASCLEPIUS: The god of healing. According to one account Alexander, on the death of Hephaestion, ordered the shrine of Asclepius at Ecbatana to be destroyed.
ATHENODOTUS: A disciple of Musonius Rufus and a teacher of Fronto.
ATHOS: A mountain on a peninsula which projects from Chalcidice in Macedonia.
AUTOMEDON: The charioteer of Achilles.
AVERNUS: A lake in Italy near the bay of Naples, supposed to be an entrance to the lower world.

BATO: Probably the name of a famous trainer, who lived in the reign of M. Aurelius.
BENEDICTA: An imperial concubine.
BISTONES: A people of Thrace.
BRUTUS: The famous Roman, leader of the conspiracy against Julius Caesar.

CADICIANUS: A man supposed to have been long-lived.
CAESO: An early Roman hero.
CALLICLES: A character in Plato's *Gorgias*, who advocates the free life of uncontrolled passions.
CAMILLUS: A famous hero of the early Roman Republic.
CARNEADES: A Greek sceptical philosopher who founded the New Academy in the second century B.C.
CASSIOPE: A port in Epirus.
CASSIUS: C. Cassius Longinus, a great jurist in the first century A.D., the founder of a legal school.
CATO: The Censor, a dominating political figure in Rome in the first half of the second century B.C., noted for his strict virtue.

CATO: Of Utica, the famous Roman Stoic, who committed suicide after Caesar's victory at Thapsus.
CATULUS: Cinna Catulus, a Stoic philosopher.
CECROPS: The traditional first king of Attica.
CELER: A Greek rhetorician, one of Hadrian's secretaries, who became one of the teachers of M. Aurelius.
CENTAURS: Legendary monsters whose bodies were half-man, half-horse.
CERBERUS: The monster dog who guards the entrance to the underworld.
CERES: The Roman name for Demeter.
CHAERONEA: A town in Boeotia where Philip of Macedon defeated the combined Athenian and Boeotian forces in 338 B.C.
CHALDAEA: A province of Babylonia, where the science of astronomy, coupled with astrology, early developed.
CHAURIAS: A favourite of Hadrian.
CHRYSANTAS: A Persian, who, when about to strike his enemy, obeyed Cyrus who suddenly ordered the retreat.
CHRYSIPPUS: The great Stoic teacher (280-207 B.C.).
CITHAERON: A mountain near Thebes.
CLEANTHES: A famous Stoic (*ca.* 300–220 B.C.) whose *Hymn to Zeus* is still extant.
CLOTHO: One of the Fates, the spinner of the thread.
CNOSSUS: The chief town of Crete, with a Roman colony.
COCYTUS: A river in the underworld.
CRATES: A Theban pupil of Diogenes the Cynic (*flor. ca.* 320 B.C.).
CRINIS: A Stoic philosopher who wrote on Dialectic.
CRITO: The friend of Socrates. See Plato's *Crito*.
CROESUS: King of Lydia, the typical rich man.
CUMAE: A town in Campania, supposedly the haunt of the earliest Sibyl.

DEMETER: Mentioned with Kore (= Persephone) and Pluto, as giver of grain to men.
DEMETRIUS: A distinguished Cynic teacher, often referred to by Seneca, his contemporary. Tacitus (*Ann.* XVI. 34) names him as one of those whose discourses Thrasea had attended.
DEMETRIUS: Of Phalerum, an orator, statesman, and philosopher in Athens at the close of the fourth century B.C.
DEMOCRITUS: Of Abdera. A Greek philosopher of the fifth century whose great contribution to Greek thought was the development of the atomic theory.
DEMOSTHENES: The greatest Athenian orator of the fourth century B.C.
DIODORUS: A philosopher of Alexandria under Ptolemy Soter, famous for his skill in Dialectic.
DIOGENES: Of Babylon, a pupil of Chrysippus, and successor of Zeno as head of the Stoic School; sent on an embassy from Athens to Rome in 155 B.C.

DIOGENES: The Cynic (*ca.* 412–323 B.C.), to Epictetus one of the great heroes of the world who have left an example for all time.
DIOGNETUS: Possibly a tutor of M. Aurelius.
DIOMEDE: A king of Thrace who owned man-eating horses.
DION: The Syracusan statesman, friend of Plato.
DION CHRYSOSTOM: Of Prusa in Bithynia, a contemporary of Epictetus; his orations are good specimens of the discourses of the Greek teachers or 'sophists' of that day.
DIONYSIUS: Of Halicarnassus. A Greek rhetorician and historian, active in Rome during the time of Augustus.
DIOSCURI: Castor and Pollux, gods whose special province was the protection of sailors.
DIOTIMUS: A freedman of Hadrian.
DIRCE: A famous clear-flowing river in Boeotia.
DOMITIAN: The last Flavian emperor (A.D. 81–96), in whose reign Epictetus with other philosophers was driven into exile.
DOMITIUS: An adoptive ancestor of M. Aurelius.

ECBATANA: The capital of the Median kingdom.
ELEUSIS: North-west of Athens, the home of the Mysteries of Demeter and Persephone.
EMPEDOCLES: A physical philosopher of the fifth century B.C. whose work in verse profoundly influenced Lucretius.
ENNIUS: A famous early Latin poet (239–169 B.C.), known as the 'father of Latin poetry', to whom many of the subsequent Roman writers are more or less indebted.
EPAMINONDAS: General and statesman, who raised Thebes to be the leading power in Greece (379–366 B.C.).
EPAPHRODITUS: Freedman and secretary of Nero, and master of Epictetus.
EPIRUS: A region north-west of Greece.
EPITYNCHANUS: Possibly an associate of Hadrian.
ETEOCLES and POLYNICES: The sons of Oedipus, whose quarrel over the government of Thebes led to the expedition of 'The Seven against Thebes'.
ETESIAN: Periodical winds from the north.
EUDOXUS: Of Cnidus, a famous geometer and astronomer of the fourth century B.C.
EUPHRATES: An eloquent Stoic contemporary of Epictetus.
EURUS: The south-east wind.
EURYSTHEUS: A legendary king of Tiryns, in whose service Heracles accomplished his labours.
EVENUS: A writer of elegiac poems (*ca.* 460–390 B.C.).

FABIUS: A man supposed to have been long-lived.
FALERNIAN: A famous native Italian wine.
FAUSTINA: Wife of Antoninus Pius.
FAVONIUS: The Latin name for Zephyr, the west wind.

FELICIO: A name used for the type of an influential slave.
FLORA: Roman goddess of spring.
FLORUS: Possibly L. Annaeus Florus, who wrote an epitome of Roman history; probably a contemporary of Epictetus.
FRONTO: M. Cornelius Fronto, a rhetorician, favourite of M. Aurelius. Some of his correspondence with the Emperor is still extant.

GADES: A town in Spain, the modern Cadiz.
GALBA: Roman emperor for six months after Nero's fall (A.D. 68–69).
GERYON: A triple-bodied monster slain by Heracles.
GETAE: Epictetus uses this name for the Dacian tribes on the Danube with whom the Romans were at war from Domitian to Trajan.
GETAS: A character in Menander's play, *Hated*.
GRATILLA: A noble Roman lady, exiled by Domitian.
GYARA: One of the smaller Cyclades, used as a place of banishment under the Empire.

HADRIAN: Emperor A.D. 117-138.
HAMMON: An Egyptian deity identified by the Greeks and Romans with Zeus and Jupiter. His famous temple was in the present oasis Siwah.
HELEN: Wife of Menelaus, the traditional cause of the Trojan War.
HELICE: A town in Achaea which was submerged by the sea.
HELICON: A group of mountains in Boeotia sacred to the Muses.
HELLANICUS: Of Lesbos, one of the earliest Greek historians (*ca.* 496–410 B.C.).
HELVIDIUS PRISCUS: Son-in-law of Thrasea Paetus, whose Stoic principles he shared; put to death by Vespasian.
HERACLES: The hero, son of Zeus and Alcmena. Epictetus considered him, in the same category with Socrates and Diogenes, as a great proponent of devoted human service.
HERACLITUS: A friend of Epictetus.
HERACLITUS: The great philosopher of Ephesus (fifth century B.C.) who believed that fire was the prime element in the universe and that everything was in a continual state of flux.
HERCULANEUM: A town near Pompeii, buried by the eruption of Vesuvius in A.D. 79.
HIPPARCHUS: A famous mathematician and astronomer of the second century B.C.
HIPPIAS: Of Elis, one of the most famous of the sophists, contemporary with Socrates.
HIPPOCRATES: Of Cos, the great physician (*ca.* 460–360 B.C.).
HOMOEOMERIA: Parts uniform with themselves and with the whole of which they are parts.
HYPERBOREANS: A people who were supposed to live in a land beyond the north wind.
HYRCANIA: A region on the shores of the Caspian.

IACCHUS: Another name for Bacchus.
IDA: The famous mountain in the Troad.
ISMARA: A town in Thrace.
ISOCRATES: One of the ten Greek orators, a contemporary of Demosthenes, and master of a fluent and finished style.
IXION: One of the stock sufferers in Hades, who was stretched upon a wheel.

JULIANUS: A man supposed to have been long-lived.

LAIUS: The father of Oedipus. When he consulted the oracle at Delphi, he was warned that his son would kill him if he begat one.
LAMIAE: Monsters who were supposed to eat human flesh.
LANUVIUM: A town on the Appian Way where Antoninus Pius was born.
LATERANUS, PLAUTIUS: Executed by Nero for complicity in the conspiracy of Piso in A.D. 65.
LEON: Of Salamis, whom Socrates was ordered by the Thirty Tyrants to arrest.
LEONNATUS: A general of Alexander the Great.
LEPIDUS: A man who was supposed to have been a lover of long life. Possibly the Triumvir.
LERNA: A district in Argolis where Heracles killed the Hydra.
LEUCIPPUS: The reputed founder of the atomic theory, subsequently developed by Democritus.
LIBER: Another name for Bacchus.
LUCILLA: Mother of M. Aurelius.
LYCEUM: A gymnasium north-east of Athens, a haunt of Socrates.
LYCURGUS: The Spartan lawgiver.
LYSIAS: An Attic orator of the fourth century B.C., famous for the charm of his plain style.

MAECENAS: A wealthy Roman, patron of letters, an intimate friend and adviser of Augustus.
MAGNESIA: A city of Lydia.
MASURIUS SABINUS: A Roman knight and jurisconsult under Augustus and Tiberius.
MATUTA: The goddess of the dawn.
MAVORS: Mars, the god of war.
MAXIMUS: Claudius Maximus, a Stoic philosopher, highly esteemed by Antoninus Pius.
MAXIMUS: Perhaps L. Appius Maximus Norbanus, who suppressed the rebellion of Saturninus in A.D. 88, and afterwards went with Trajan against the Parthians and died in Parthia.
MEDEA: Wife of Jason who took vengeance on her unfaithful husband by killing their children. See Euripides, *Medea*.
MELETUS: See ANYTUS.
MENIPPUS: Of Gadara, the well-known Cynic philosopher, who with Diogenes became one of the heroes of the sect.

MENOECEUS: Son of Creon, who, in the Greek legend, sacrificed himself to save Thebes.
METRODORUS: A well-known pupil and disciple of Epicurus.
MILO: The typical 'strong man' of antiquity (sixth century B.C.).
MINA: An Attic silver coin worth approximately sixteen to twenty dollars.
MOLOSSIA: A region in Epirus, famous for its hounds.
MONIMUS: A Cynic pupil of Diogenes.
MYRO: The name of a gladiator.

NASO: A hearer of Epictetus.
NERO: Emperor A.D. 54–68.
NESTOR: King of Pylos, the old and trusted councillor of the Greeks in the Trojan War.
NICOPOLIS: A town in Epirus, founded by Augustus in memory of the victory of Actium. There Epictetus lived and taught.

ODYSSEUS: The hero of the *Odyssey*. Often cited by the Stoics as exhibiting many favourite Stoic characteristics.
OEDIPUS: A legendary king of Thebes, the type of tragic suffering.
OPHELLIUS: A gladiator.
ORCUS: A name for the underworld.

PAN: A god of flocks and shepherds.
PANDION: Legendary king of Athens.
PANTHEA: The concubine of L. Verus.
PANTHOIDES: A Stoic, who wrote on Logic (early third century B.C.).
PARIS: Second son of Priam, who carried off Helen, and so caused the Trojan War.
PATROCLUS: The friend of Achilles who was slain by Hector.
PERGAMUS: A favourite of L. Verus.
PERRHAEBIANS: A powerful tribe of northern Greece; to go among them means to go into wild outlandish regions.
PHAETHON: Son of Helios. He was allowed by his father to drive the chariot of the sun, but was unable to control the horses and was destroyed by the lightning of Zeus.
PHALARIS: A tyrant in Sicily in the sixth century B.C., notorious for his great cruelty.
PHIDIAS: The sculptor who adorned the Parthenon at Athens (490–432 B.C.).
PHILIP: King of Macedon, father of Alexander the Great, who conquered the Greeks at the battle of Chaeronea in 338 B.C.
PHILODEMUS: An Epicurean, who taught in the Roman Republic in the last century before Christ.
PHILOSTORGUS: An example of a rich but degraded man.
PHOCION: A great Athenian general and statesman of the fourth century B.C.
POENI: The Carthaginians.

POLEMO: A young profligate converted to the philosophic life by Xenocrates; head of the Academy, *ca.* 314–273 B.C.
POLUS: A Sicilian sophist of the fifth century B.C.; a character in Plato's *Gorgias*.
POLYNICES: See ETEOCLES.
POMPEII: The famous city on the bay of Naples buried by the eruption of Vesuvius in A.D. 79.
PONTOS: The Black Sea, whose current flows always through the Propontis and the Hellespont.
POSIDONIUS: A famous Stoic philosopher in the second and first centuries B.C.
PRIAM: King of Troy during the Trojan War.
PROCRUSTES: See THESEUS.
PROTAGORAS: Of Abdera, one of the most distinguished sophists of the fifth century B.C., who lived for many years in Athens.
PYRIPHLEGETHON: A river in the underworld.
PYRRHONISTS: Followers of Pyrrho the Sceptic (fourth century B.C.), who denied the possibility of knowledge.
PYTHAGORAS: Of Samos, one of the earliest Greek philosophers according to tradition (*flor.* 540–510 B.C.). His school believed number to be ultimate in the universe.

QUADRATUS: C. Ummidius Quadratus was governor of Lusitania in A.D. 37 and of Syria *ca.* A.D. 50–60.

RUFUS, C. MUSONIUS: An Etruscan knight who lectured on Stoicism and was one of the teachers of Epictetus.
RUSTICUS: Q. Junius Rusticus, a Stoic adviser of M. Aurelius.

SAMOTHRACE: An island in the north Aegean.
SARDANAPALUS: King of Nineveh, a typical tyrant.
SARMATIANS: A Slavic people against whom M. Aurelius fought.
SARPEDON: A prince of Lycia, son of Zeus, ally of the Trojans in the Trojan War.
SATURNALIA: Festival of Saturn, December 17 and following days; one feature of it was that slaves were waited on by their masters.
SCAPTENSULA: A town in Thrace noted for its gold mines.
SCIRON: See THESEUS.
SECUNDA: Wife of Maximus.
SEVERUS: A philosopher, possibly the Peripatetic.
SEXTUS: Of Chaeronea, probably a grandson of Plutarch.
SEXTUS EMPIRICUS: A Sceptic philosopher of the second century B.C.
SOPHRON: An actor.
STERTINIUS: Possibly a rich physician of Naples.
STYMPHALIS: A lake in Arcadia.
SUMMANUS: A god of the night sky.
SURA: Possibly the Palfurius Sura of Juvenal IV. 53, an orator said to

have been expelled from the Senate by Vespasian; afterwards an informer under Domitian; he was condemned on Domitian's death.

SUSA: Capital of Elam, a favourite residence of the Persian kings.

TARTARUS: A name for the underworld.

TELAUGES: Son of Pythagoras.

TEUCRAN: Equivalent of Trojan.

THEODOTUS: A freedman of Hadrian.

THEOPHRASTUS: Pupil and successor of Aristotle in the Peripatetic School.

THEOPOMPUS: An historian and rhetorician, *ca.* 380–305 B.C.

THERMOPYLAE: The pass between Thessaly and Locris, defended against Xerxes by Leonidas and three hundred Lacedaemonians in 480 B.C.

THERSITES: The type of ugliness and insolence in the *Iliad*.

THESEUS: The legendary hero of Attica, who cleared the land of robbers, among them Sciron and Procrustes.

THRASEA PAETUS: A senator and great Stoic put to death in A.D. 66 under Nero.

THRASONIDES: A character in Menander's play, *Hated*.

THRASYMACHUS: The famous sophist of Chalcedon, often mentioned by Plato. See especially *Republic*, Book I.

TIBERIUS: Emperor A.D. 14–37.

TIMON: Of Phlius. A Sceptic who flourished in the early third century B.C.

TITYOS: A giant, one of the stock sufferers in Hades, whose liver was continually gnawed by vultures.

TRAJAN: Emperor A.D. 68–117.

TRIPTOLEMUS: The legendary founder of agriculture and civilised life.

TYNDARUS: Father of Clytemnestra, the wife of Agamemnon.

VERUS: L. Aurelius Verus, adopted brother of M. Aurelius.

VERUS: M. Annius Verus, the father of M. Aurelius.

VESPASIAN: Emperor A.D. 70–79.

VOLESUS: A hero of the early Roman Republic.

VOLTURNUS: The name of a southerly wind.

XANTHIPPE: The shrewish wife of Socrates.

XENOCRATES: Of Chalcedon, a Platonist and for twenty-five years head of the Academy (396–314 B.C.).

XENOPHON: An Athenian, a pupil of Socrates, of whose life and teaching he gave an account in his *Memorabilia* (*ca.* 440–350 B.C.).

ZENO: Of Citium in Cyprus, the founder of Stoicism.

ZEPHYR: The west wind.

MODERN LIBRARY GIANTS

A series of sturdily bound and handsomely printed, full-sized library editions of books formerly available only in expensive sets. These volumes contain from 600 to 1,400 pages each.

THE MODERN LIBRARY GIANTS REPRESENT A SELECTION OF THE WORLD'S GREATEST BOOKS

G76 ANDERSEN & GRIMM: *Tales*
G74 AUGUSTINE, ST.: *The City of God*
G58 AUSTEN, JANE: *Complete Novels*
G97 BALZAC, HONORÉ DE: *Lost Illusions*
G70 BLAKE, WILLIAM & DONNE, JOHN: *Complete Poetry*
G2 BOSWELL, JAMES: *Life of Samuel Johnson*
G95 BROCKWAY, WALLACE & WEINSTOCK, HERBERT: *The World of Opera*
G17 BROWNING, ROBERT: *Poems and Plays*
G14 BULFINCH: *Mythology* (ILLUSTRATED)
G35 BURY, J. B.: *A History of Greece*
G13 CARLYLE, THOMAS: *The French Revolution*
G28 CARROLL, LEWIS: *Complete Works*
G15 CERVANTES: *Don Quixote*
G33 COLLINS, WILKIE: *The Moonstone* and *The Woman in White*
G94 COOPER, JAMES FENIMORE: *The Leatherstocking Saga*
G27 DARWIN, CHARLES: *Origin of Species* and *The Descent of Man*
G43 DEWEY, JOHN: *Intelligence in the Modern World*
G70 DONNE, JOHN & BLAKE, WILLIAM: *Complete Poetry*
G36 DOSTOYEVSKY, FYODOR: *The Brothers Karamazov*
G60 DOSTOYEVSKY, FYODOR: *The Idiot*
G51 ELIOT, GEORGE: *Best-Known Novels*
G41 FARRELL, JAMES T.: *Studs Lonigan*
G82 FAULKNER, WILLIAM: *The Faulkner Reader*
G39 FREUD, SIGMUND: *The Basic Writings*
G6, G7, G8 GIBBON, EDWARD: *The Decline and Fall of the Roman Empire* (complete in three volumes)
G25 GILBERT & SULLIVAN: *Complete Plays*
G76 GRIMM & ANDERSEN: *Tales*
G37 HAWTHORNE, NATHANIEL: *Compl. Novels & Selected Tales*
G78 HOLMES, OLIVER WENDELL: *The Mind and Faith of Justice [Holmes*
G19 HOMER: *Complete Works*
G3 HUGO, VICTOR: *Les Miserables*
G18 IBSEN, HENRIK: *Eleven Plays*
G11 JAMES, HENRY: *Short Stories*
G52 JOYCE, JAMES: *Ulysses*
G4 KEATS & SHELLEY: *Complete Poems*
G24 LAMB, CHARLES: *The Complete Works and Letters*
G20 LINCOLN, ABRAHAM: *The Life and Writings of Abraham [Lincoln*
G84 MANN, THOMAS: *Stories of Three Decades*
G26 MARX, KARL: *Capital*
G57 MELVILLE, HERMAN: *Selected Writings*
G38 MURASAKA, LADY: *The Tale of Genji*
G30 MYERS, GUSTAVUS: *History of the Great American Fortunes*
G34 NIETZSCHE, FRIEDRICH: *The Philosophy of Nietzsche*
G88 O'HARA, JOHN: *49 Stories*
G55 O'NEILL, EUGENE: *Nine Plays*

G68 PAINE, TOM: *Selected Work*
G86 PASTERNAK, BORIS: *Doctor Zhivago*
G5 PLUTARCH: *Lives* (The Dryden Translation)
G40 POE, EDGAR ALLAN: *Complete Tales and Poems*
G29 PRESCOTT, WILLIAM H.: *The Conquest of Mexico* and *The Conquest of Peru*
G62 PUSHKIN: *Poems, Prose and Plays*
G65 RABELAIS: *Complete Works*
G12 SCOTT, SIR WALTER: *The Most Popular Novels* (Quentin Durward, Ivanhoe & Kenilworth)
G4 SHELLEY & KEATS: *Complete Poems*
G32 SMITH, ADAM: *The Wealth of Nations*
G61 SPAETH, SIGMUND: *A Guide to Great Orchestral Music*
G92 SPENGLER, OSWALD: *The Decline of the West* (one volume)
G91 SPENSER, EDMUND: *Selected Poetry*
G75 STEVENSON, ROBERT LOUIS: *Selected Writings*
G53 SUE, EUGENE: *The Wandering Jew*
G42 TENNYSON: *The Poems and Plays*
G23 TOLSTOY, LEO: *Anna Karenina*—tr. revised
G1 TOLSTOY, LEO: *War and Peace*
G49 TWAIN, MARK: *Tom Sawyer* and *Huckleberry Finn*
G50 WHITMAN, WALT: *Leaves of Grass*
G83 WILSON, EDMUND: *The Shock of Recognition*

MISCELLANEOUS

G77 *An Anthology of Famous American Stories*
G54 *An Anthology of Famous British Stories*
G67 *Anthology of Famous English and American Poetry*
G81 *An Encyclopedia of Modern American Humor*
G47 *The English Philosophers from Bacon to Mill*
G16 *The European Philosophers from Descartes to Nietzsche*
G31 *Famous Science-Fiction Stories*
G85 *Great Ages and Ideas of the Jewish People*
G89 *Great Classical Myths*
G72 *Great Tales of Terror and the Supernatural*
G9 *Great Voices of the Reformation*
G87 *Medieval Epics*
G48 *The Metropolitan Opera Guide*
G46 *A New Anthology of Modern Poetry*
G69 *One Hundred and One Years' Entertainment*
G93 *Parodies: An Anthology from Chaucer to Beerbohm and After*
G90 *Philosophies of Art and Beauty: Readings in Aesthetics from Plato to Heidegger*
G21 *Sixteen Famous American Plays*
G63 *Sixteen Famous British Plays*
G71 *Sixteen Famous European Plays*
G45 *Stoic and Epicurean Philosophers*
G22 *Thirty Famous One-Act Plays*
G66 *Three Famous Murder Novels, Before the Fact*, FRANCIS ILES, *Trent's Last Case*, E. C. BENTLEY, *The House of the Arrow*, A. E. W. MASON
G10 *Twelve Famous Plays of the Restoration and Eighteenth Century* (1660–1820): Dryden, Congreve, Wycherley, Gay, etc.
G56 *The Wisdom of Catholicism*
G59 *The Wisdom of China and India*
G79 *The Wisdom of Israel*